Y0-DYJ-700

CASPIAN SEA

ARMENIA

BLACK SEA

TURKEY

RUSSIA

UKRAINE

LATVIA

LITHUANIA

POLAND

RUMANIA

BULGARIA

FINLAND

SWEDEN

NORWAY

CZECHO SLOVAKIA

HUNGARY

AUSTRIA

YUGOSLAVIA

GREECE

DENMARK

GERMANY

ENGLAND

BELGIUM

FRANCE

ITALY

SICILY

IRELAND

SPAIN

PORTUGAL

EUROPE
OF TODAY

ATLANTIC OCEAN

EUROPE
after the
TREATY OF WESTPHALIA (1648)

SCALE OF MILES
0   100   200   300

- - - Boundary of the Empire
TERRITORY GAINED
France
Sweden
The Hohenzollerns
Bavaria
Districts that became
Independent

A SURVEY OF

European

Civilization

VOLUME II · SINCE 1660

GEOFFREY BRUUN
ASSISTANT PROFESSOR OF HISTORY
NEW YORK UNIVERSITY

UNDER THE EDITORIAL SUPERVISION OF
CARL L. BECKER
JOHN STAMBAUGH PROFESSOR OF HISTORY
CORNELL UNIVERSITY

HOUGHTON MIFFLIN COMPANY

BOSTON · NEW YORK · CHICAGO · DALLAS · ATLANTA · SAN FRANCISCO

The Riverside Press Cambridge

The Riverside Press

CAMBRIDGE   MASSACHUSETTS

PRINTED IN THE U S.A.

TO

JOHN AND GRACE MUSSER

*with admiration
and affection*

Editor's Introduction

TEACHING and learning are most effectively conjoined when an alert and informed teacher engages in informal discussion with a small group of alert and informed students. If the subject be history, the students will on their own initiative and with mounting enthusiasm (it is an ideal we are describing) spend much of their time in the library, where they will be provided with tables and the necessary books for an independent study of the subject. Once or twice a week the professor will meet his pupils. In so small a group he may dispense with lectures — those exercises in which students assemble, and amiably and passively sit while the professor, with great advantage to himself, clarifies his ideas by oral discourse. The students also will have an opportunity to clarify their ideas by oral discourse. Teaching and learning will then be conjoined, as they always must be to be any way effective: professor and pupils, each according to his talent, will be both teachers and learners. This ideal system is often realized in the graduate school — in the graduate seminary. Under such ideal conditions, there is obviously no occasion for a textbook.

In our undergraduate colleges, textbooks are nevertheless everywhere in use, and even the professors regard them as indispensable. There are two good reasons for this insistence on the use of textbooks. One is that many students are incapable of studying any subject on their own initiative, but, being docile, they will do what they are told to do, and the simplest thing to tell them to do is to read, on successive Mondays, Wednesdays, Fridays, successive chapters in a prescribed textbook. The second reason is that the facilities for studying history in the right way are commonly inadequate. If, some bright afternoon, all the students in philosophy, literature, and the social sciences should take it into their heads to invade the library in order to do what they are conventionally expected to do, there would scarcely be standing room for them, to say nothing about tables to work at; and the books and documents called for could be supplied by the distracted attendants to no more than a few of the first comers. The others would perforce turn away, sorrowing no doubt, with nothing for it but to review their lecture notes and read the prescribed chapter in the textbook. As it is, most of them save time and avoid mental anguish by not going to the library in the first place. It is not wholly their fault. There is a limit to the obstacles that anyone will cheerfully surmount in order to obtain access to books. Hence the textbook is an indispensable substitute for books.

Accepting conditions as they find them, Professors Ferguson and Bruun have prepared these two volumes. Frankly designed to be used as textbooks, they are provided with the customary "select bibliographies" for such further study as the requirements of the instructor, the inclination of the students, and the facilities of the average college library may make desirable or possible. Nevertheless, knowing from experience that the textbook is likely to be the principal source of information for most students, the authors have made their books something more than summary manuals of events. Taken together, the two volumes are sufficiently comprehensive to enable the students, with reasonable mastery of their contents, to obtain an intelligent grasp of the last fifteen centuries of European history. Besides presenting the essential facts with accuracy, they have correlated and interpreted the facts in such a way that the significant events, institutions, and ideas may be understood and not merely "got up" for examinations or tests. Above all they have endeavored to make the story readable, interesting in its own right, and relevant as an explanation of the influences that have made modern civilization what it is. In short, Professors Ferguson and Bruun have attempted to write books that have merit as books, and not merely as textbooks. They have aimed to serve the practical requirements of teaching history in colleges, and at the same time make the student realize that a knowledge of history is an essential part of a "liberal education."

The period covered by these two volumes is commonly divided into three periods — Medieval, Renaissance and Reformation, and Modern. All the conventional labels employed by historians for dividing the history of civilization into periods are largely arbitrary, at best unrevealing, at worst positively misleading. The reason is that, being themselves by-products of the history they profess to clarify, they are easily outmoded by the increase of knowledge. The term medieval, to take but one example, means in itself nothing except a period in between an earlier and a later period. Actually, it originated in a mythical notion of human history, and was retained to indicate a supposedly "dark age" intervening between the golden age of Greek and Roman civilization, and the recovery of classical knowledge brought about by the "renaissance." It therefore took on a derogatory connotation, which it still retains: in spite of all that devoted "medievalists" can urge to the contrary, "medieval" is still in common speech a synonym for ignorance and barbarism. Applied to the period between the fifth and the fourteenth centuries, the term means either nothing at all or else something that is not true.

Since textbooks must be adapted to established courses and to conventional practices, Professors Ferguson and Bruun have not thought it wise to dispense with the conventional divisions altogether. But they have made it clear that these conventional divisions are not to be taken too seriously. They have regarded their separate tasks as related parts of a common enterprise, which is to explain the evolution of "western" civilization from Roman times, and by dividing their books into "parts" which have some real relation to the successive aspects of this evolution, and in the brief introductions to the various parts, they have endeavored to correct the mistaken notions that are implied by the terms Medieval, Renaissance and Reformation, and Modern. In short, they have endeavored to make it clear that the history of Europe since the breakdown of the Western Roman Empire exhibits a continuous development without sharp breaks or dramatic dislocations.

CARL L. BECKER

Foreword

THE changes which have taken place in Europe in the last three hundred years, coupled with the expansion of European civilization overseas during the same period, make these centuries the most complicated and eventful in world history. The present volume presents the historical development of modern Europe in the form which seemed to the writer best suited to the needs of students entering college. If it succeeds in providing such students with a clearer perspective against which to judge the grave issues of the twentieth century he will feel his hours of labor well repaid. Of the inadequacies of the work he is only too conscious; whatever virtues it may possess are due in large measure to the inspiration he has received from such masters of the discipline as Professor Carl Becker and Professor Preserved Smith of Cornell University, and to the criticism and encouragement of his colleagues in the Department of History at New York University. To all of these he is happy to express his gratitude and his thanks.

GEOFFREY BRUUN

NEW YORK

Contents

SECTION A
EUROPE IN THE AGE OF LOUIS XIV
(1660–1715)

CHAPTER

1 EUROPE IN THE MIDDLE OF THE SEVENTEENTH CENTURY   5
     1 THE SYSTEM OF CENTRALIZED TERRITORIAL STATES
     2 THE EUROPEAN STATES IN 1660
     3 LIFE IN THE SEVENTEENTH CENTURY

2 LOUIS XIV DOMINATES FRANCE AND ASPIRES TO DOMI-
NATE EUROPE   20
     1 FRANCE AT THE ACCESSION OF LOUIS XIV
     2 HOW LOUIS XIV CONDUCTED HIS GOVERNMENT
     3 THE COURT OF THE SUN KING
     4 THE "GREAT AGE" IN LITERATURE AND ART
     5 WHY LOUIS XIV PERSECUTED THE JANSENISTS AND
       HUGUENOTS
     6 THE WARS OF LOUIS XIV

3 THE TRIUMPH OF PARLIAMENTARY GOVERNMENT IN ENG-
LAND   40
     1 CHARLES II: A DESPOT IN DISGUISE
     2 JAMES II: A DESPOT IN DIFFICULTIES
     3 THE GLORIOUS REVOLUTION OF 1688
     4 ENGLAND AND SCOTLAND BECOME GREAT BRITAIN
     5 SIGNIFICANCE OF THE SEVENTEENTH CENTURY IN
       ENGLISH HISTORY

[xi]

CHAPTER

4 THE DECLINING EMPIRE OF THE HAPSBURGS . . . 54

   1 THE AUSTRIAN HAPSBURGS
   2 THE TURKISH MENACE
   3 SPAIN IN DECLINE
   4 THE ITALIAN STATES
   5 SUMMARY OF THE PERIOD, 1660 TO 1715

SECTION B

THE EIGHTEENTH CENTURY (1715–89)

5 THE EMERGENCE OF RUSSIA 67

   1 THE RISE OF MUSCOVY
   2 PETER THE GREAT OF RUSSIA
   3 THE GREAT NORTHERN WAR (1700–21)
   4 THE SUCCESSORS OF PETER THE GREAT
   5 CATHERINE THE GREAT (1762–96)
   6 THE DISMEMBERMENT OF POLAND

6 THE RISE OF PRUSSIA 82

   1 THE ELECTORATE OF BRANDENBURG
   2 FREDERICK THE GREAT (1740–86)
   3 THE WAR OF THE AUSTRIAN SUCCESSION (1740–48)
   4 THE DIPLOMATIC REVOLUTION
   5 THE SEVEN YEARS' WAR (1756–63)
   6 FREDERICK THE GREAT IN TIME OF PEACE

7 OVERSEAS EXPANSION AND THE STRUGGLE FOR COM-
MERCE AND COLONIES 93

   1 THE SIXTEENTH CENTURY: SPAIN AND PORTUGAL EX-
     PLOIT THE WEALTH OF THE TWO INDIES
   2 THE SEVENTEENTH CENTURY: COMPETITION OF THE
     DUTCH, THE FRENCH, AND THE ENGLISH FOR COLO-
     NIES AND TRADE (1588–1688)
   3 THE EIGHTEENTH CENTURY: THE DUEL OF FRANCE
     AND BRITAIN FOR COLONIAL SUPREMACY (1689–1763)

CONTENTS

CHAPTER

    4 THE BRITISH COLONIES IN AMERICA WIN THEIR IN-
      DEPENDENCE
    5 THE ABATEMENT OF COLONIAL RIVALRY AFTER 1783

8 THE INTELLECTUAL REVOLUTION 107
    1 THE BEGINNINGS OF THE SCIENTIFIC REVOLUTION
    2 THE PROGRESS OF MATHEMATICS
    3 THE EXPERIMENTAL METHOD
    4 THE SCIENTIFIC ACADEMIES
    5 THE INTELLECTUAL REVOLUTION

9 GOVERNMENT AND SOCIETY UNDER THE OLD RÉGIME . 121
    1 DIVINE-RIGHT MONARCHY IN THEORY AND PRACTICE
    2 THE PRIVILEGED AND UNPRIVILEGED CLASSES
    3 LEGAL AND FINANCIAL ABUSES
    4 THE CRITICISM OF THE PHILOSOPHERS
    5 THE ENLIGHTENED DESPOTS
    6 ROUSSEAU AND THE DOCTRINE OF POPULAR SOVER-
      EIGNTY

SECTION C
THE ERA OF THE FRENCH REVOLUTION
AND NAPOLEON
(1789–1815)

10 THE FRENCH PEOPLE DESTROY THE RELICS OF FEUDAL-
ISM AND OVERTURN THE MONARCHY 141
    1 THE STATES GENERAL IS SUMMONED
    2 THE STATES GENERAL MEETS
    3 THE CAPTURE OF THE BASTILLE
    4 THE DESTRUCTION OF FEUDALISM AND THE DECLARA-
      TION OF THE RIGHTS OF MAN
    5 THE MARCH TO VERSAILLES
    6 THE CIVIL CONSTITUTION OF THE CLERGY
    7 THE CONSTITUTION OF 1791
    8 THE LEGISLATIVE ASSEMBLY (1791–92)

CONTENTS

CHAPTER

11 THE FIRST FRENCH REPUBLIC AND ITS STRUGGLE TO SURVIVE 160
  1 THE NATIONAL CONVENTION (1792–95)
  2 THE ORGANIZATION OF VICTORY
  3 THE JACOBIN DICTATORSHIP
  4 THE THERMIDORIAN REACTION
  5 THE DIRECTORY (1795–99)
  6 THE ACHIEVEMENTS OF THE REVOLUTION (1789–99)

12 NAPOLEON AND FRANCE 171
  1 THE ADVENT OF BONAPARTE
  2 COLLAPSE OF THE SECOND COALITION
  3 NAPOLEON RECONSTRUCTS FRANCE
  4 THE IMPERIAL ADVENTURE
  5 RESULTS OF NAPOLEON'S RULE IN FRANCE

13 NAPOLEON AND EUROPE 184
  1 THE REVOLUTION SPREADS
  2 THE RECONSTRUCTION OF ITALY
  3 THE REORGANIZATION OF THE GERMANIES
  4 NAPOLEON AND ENGLAND
  5 THE RUSSIAN DISASTER AND THE WAR OF LIBERATION
  6 THE HUNDRED DAYS

14 THE VIENNA CONGRESS 196
  1 THE CONGRESS ASSEMBLES
  2 THE POLITICAL SETTLEMENTS
  3 THE CONCERT OF EUROPE
  4 DEFECTS OF THE VIENNA SETTLEMENT

SECTION D
THE GROWTH OF NATIONALISM AND LIBERALISM IN THE NINETEENTH CENTURY
(1815–71)

15 THE ERA OF RESTORATION AND REACTION 209
  1 THE REACTION FROM THE AGE OF RATIONALISM

CONTENTS

CHAPTER

    2 THE ROMANTIC MOVEMENT
    3 THE TRIUMPH OF CONSERVATISM: AUSTRIA AND RUSSIA
    4 THE BOURBON RESTORATION IN FRANCE
    5 TEMPORARY REACTION IN GREAT BRITAIN
    6 THE FIRST RIFTS IN THE CONSERVATIVE SYSTEM

16 THE BOURGEOISIE SECURE CONTROL IN GREAT BRITAIN AND FRANCE 224
    1 THE INDUSTRIAL REVOLUTION
    2 THE FACTORY SYSTEM
    3 THE ENGLISH REFORM BILL OF 1832
    4 THE CHARTIST MOVEMENT
    5 THE FRENCH REVOLUTION OF 1830

17 THE REVOLUTIONARY MOVEMENT OF 1848–49 AND ITS COLLAPSE 239
    1 DISCONTENT IN FRANCE UNDER THE JULY MONARCHY
    2 THE FEBRUARY REVOLUTION IN FRANCE (1848) AND ITS SEQUEL
    3 THE GERMAN PEOPLE FAIL TO ACHIEVE POLITICAL UNITY (1848–49)
    4 AUSTRIA RESTORES HER HOUSE TO ORDER
    5 ITALY REMAINS IN BONDAGE
    6 THE LESSONS OF 1848–49

18 THE ESTABLISHMENT OF THE SECOND FRENCH EMPIRE: NAPOLEON III 252
    1 "THE EMPIRE IS PEACE"
    2 ALL THINGS TO ALL MEN
    3 THE LIBERAL NEMESIS
    4 THE SECOND EMPIRE AT WAR: THE CRIMEAN CONFLICT (1854–56)

19 THE POLITICAL UNIFICATION OF ITALY 262
    1 THE NATIONAL SPIRIT STIRS (1815–48)
    2 THREE CONFLICTING PROJECTS FOR UNIFICATION

[xv]

CONTENTS

3 THE DEFEATED HOPES OF 1848–49

4 CAVOUR CONTRIVES

5 GARIBALDI MARCHES

6 THE WINNING OF VENICE AND ROME

7 THE ROMAN CATHOLIC CHURCH IN THE NINETEENTH CENTURY

20 THE FORMATION OF THE GERMAN EMPIRE 277

1 THE DECADE OF REPRESSION AFTER 1848

2 THE EXPANSION OF GERMAN INDUSTRY

3 THE PRUSSIAN SYSTEM

4 OTTO VON BISMARCK (1815–98)

5 THE AUSTRO-PRUSSIAN WAR

6 THE NORTH GERMAN CONFEDERATION

7 OPPOSITION OF FRANCE TO GERMAN UNIFICATION

8 THE FRANCO-PRUSSIAN WAR

21 RUSSIA IN THE NINETEENTH CENTURY 292

1 THE AFTERMATH OF THE CRIMEAN WAR

2 THE EMANCIPATION OF THE SERFS

3 OTHER REFORMS OF ALEXANDER II

4 THE REACTION IN THE LATER YEARS OF ALEXANDER II

5 THE SPREAD OF ANARCHISM, NIHILISM, AND TERRORISM

6 ALEXANDER III AND THE POLICY OF RUSSIFICATION

7 NICHOLAS II AND THE REVOLUTION OF 1905

22 THE LESSER STATES OF EUROPE IN THE NINETEENTH CENTURY 305

1 THE SCANDINAVIAN COUNTRIES

2 HOLLAND, BELGIUM, AND SWITZERLAND

3 SPAIN AND PORTUGAL

4 THE CRUMBLING EMPIRE OF THE SULTAN (1815–78)

CONTENTS

SECTION E

THE NEW INDUSTRIAL ERA: THE CONFLICT OF CAPITAL AND LABOR, AND THE RIVALRY OF THE IMPERIALIST POWERS
(1871–1914)

CHAPTER

23 THE NEW WORLD WHICH SCIENCE AND INDUSTRY HAVE CREATED 319

    1 THE MARCH OF SCIENCE

    2 NEW CONCEPTIONS OF MAN'S PLACE IN NATURE

    3 THE NEW ENVIRONMENT WHICH SCIENCE AND INDUSTRY HAVE PROVIDED: THE "CIVILIZATION OF CITY DWELLERS"

    4 THE INDUSTRIALIZED SOCIETY: THE CONFLICT BETWEEN CAPITAL AND LABOR AND THE RIDDLE OF SOCIAL JUSTICE

    5 THE INDUSTRIALIZED STATE: THE COMPETITION AMONG THE GREAT POWERS FOR COLONIES AND MARKETS

24 THE SOCIAL CONFLICT WITHIN THREE INDUSTRIAL STATES: GREAT BRITAIN, FRANCE, AND GERMANY (1871–1914) . . 339

    1 THE MARCH OF DEMOCRACY IN GREAT BRITAIN (1867–1914)

    2 GREAT BRITAIN (1871–1914): THE QUEST FOR SOCIAL JUSTICE

    3 FRANCE (1871–1914): CONSOLIDATING THE BOURGEOIS REPUBLIC

    4 FRANCE (1871–1914): THE SPREAD OF SYNDICALISM AND SOCIALISM

    5 THE GERMAN EMPIRE (1871–1914): FOUNDATION AND EXPANSION

    6 THE GERMAN EMPIRE (1871–1914): ECONOMIC AND SOCIAL PROBLEMS

25 THE COMPETITION AMONG THE INDUSTRIALIZED STATES: THE RACE FOR COLONIES AND MARKETS (1871–1914) . . 361

    1 THE NEW IMPERIALISM AFTER 1871

[xvii]

CONTENTS

2 THE BRITISH EMPIRE IN 1871

3 BRITISH ACQUISITIONS (1871–1914)

4 FRENCH COLONIAL ENTERPRISE

5 ITALY ENTERTAINS IMPERIALISTIC DREAMS

6 GERMANY ENTERS THE RACE FOR COLONIES

7 THE RIVALRIES OF THE POWERS IN AFRICA

8 THE RIVALRIES OF THE GREAT POWERS IN ASIA

26 THE GROWTH OF ALLIANCES: INTERNATIONAL TENSION
AND THE ARMED PEACE (1871–1914) 379

1 THE GERMAN HEGEMONY AFTER 1871

2 THE TRIPLE ALLIANCE

3 FRANCE SEARCHES FOR ALLIES

4 ANGLO-GERMAN RIVALRY

5 THE TRIPLE *ENTENTE*

6 INTERNATIONAL CRISES: MOROCCO

7 INTERNATIONAL CRISES: THE BALKANS

8 THE GROWTH OF ARMAMENTS

SECTION F
THE WORLD WAR AND THE PROBLEMS
OF THE POST–WAR PERIOD
(1914–35)

27 THE WORLD WAR 397

1 THE COMING OF THE WAR

2 THE WAR ON LAND (1914–17)

3 THE WAR ON THE SEA

4 THE WAR ON LAND (1917–18)

5 THE COST OF THE WAR

28 THE PEACE SETTLEMENT OF 1919 416

1 IDEALS AND REALITIES

2 THE TREATY OF VERSAILLES

3 THE SETTLEMENT WITH AUSTRIA-HUNGARY, BUL-
GARIA, AND TURKEY

[xviii]

CONTENTS

CHAPTER

    4 THE FATE OF THE FOURTEEN POINTS

    5 THE LEAGUE OF NATIONS

29 RUSSIA UNDER THE RULE OF THE SOVIETS   . . . 433

    1 THE MARCH REVOLUTION

    2 THE BOLSHEVIKI IN POWER

    3 THE PHILOSOPHY AND PROGRAM OF THE RUSSIAN COMMUNISTS

    4 THE STRUCTURE OF THE SOVIET GOVERNMENT

    5 ECONOMIC PROGRESS AND THE FIVE-YEAR PLAN

    6 FOREIGN RELATIONS OF RUSSIA (1917–35)

30 FASCIST ITALY 447

    1 POST-WAR CONFUSION IN ITALY

    2 BENITO MUSSOLINI

    3 THE CORPORATE STATE

    4 BENEFITS OF THE FASCIST ADMINISTRATION

    5 FOREIGN POLICY OF FASCIST ITALY

    6 THE FASCIST STATE AND THE PAPACY

31 THE UNITED KINGDOM AND THE BRITISH EMPIRE COMMONWEALTH 460

    1 THE BRITISH ECONOMIC DILEMMA

    2 BRITISH POLITICAL PARTIES (1919–35)

    3 THE IRISH FREE STATE

    4 INDIA

    5 EGYPT, IRAK, AND PALESTINE

    6 THE SELF-GOVERNING DOMINIONS

32 FRANCE SEEKS SECURITY 472

    1 THE WORK OF RECLAMATION

    2 THE REPARATIONS TANGLE

    3 THE SEARCH FOR SECURITY

    4 THE PEACE PACTS

CONTENTS

CHAPTER

33 GERMANY SEEKS EQUALITY 483

    1 THE ORGANIZATION OF THE GERMAN REPUBLIC
    2 ECONOMIC CHAOS AND RECOVERY
    3 STRESEMANN AND THE SPIRIT OF CONCILIATION
    4 HITLER AND THE SPIRIT OF RECALCITRANCE
    5 THE TOTALITARIAN STATE
    6 GERMAN FOREIGN POLICY AFTER 1932
    7 CONCLUSION

APPENDIX A.   GENEALOGICAL TABLES i
APPENDIX B.   LIST OF RULERS vii
APPENDIX C.   BIBLIOGRAPHY xi
INDEX   xli

Illustrations

A MODEST SEVENTEENTH-CENTURY DWELLING 17
LOUIS XIV OF FRANCE 25
THE PALACE OF VERSAILLES 31
CHARLES II OF ENGLAND 43
PETER THE GREAT OF RUSSIA 71
FREDERICK THE GREAT OF PRUSSIA 89
SHIPS OF WAR OF THE SEVENTEENTH AND EIGHTEENTH
    CENTURIES 101
SIR ISAAC NEWTON 111
VOLTAIRE 129
JEAN-JACQUES ROUSSEAU 135
STORMING OF THE BASTILLE 149
NAPOLEON BONAPARTE 173
WILLIAM PITT, THE YOUNGER 189
ARTHUR WELLESLEY, DUKE OF WELLINGTON 197
LOUIS PHILIPPE, KING OF THE FRENCH 235
NAPOLEON III, EMPEROR OF THE FRENCH 255
CAMILLO DI CAVOUR 269
OTTO VON BISMARCK 285
ALEXANDER II OF RUSSIA 295
CHARLES DARWIN 325
GRAPH: ESTIMATED INCREASE IN THE POPULATION OF EUROPE
    DURING THE LAST THREE CENTURIES 328
KARL MARX 333
DAVID LLOYD GEORGE 345
MODERN INDUSTRIAL PLANT 356
FIELD MARSHAL PAUL VON HINDENBURG 405
WOODROW WILSON 417
NICOLAI LENIN 435
BENITO MUSSOLINI 449
ARISTIDE BRIAND 481
ADOLF HITLER 489

Maps

[Inserted maps are listed by the number of the page which immediately precedes them.]

EUROPE AFTER THE TREATY OF WESTPHALIA (1648) . *Frontispiece*

EXTENSION OF THE FRENCH FRONTIERS, 1552–1766 . . . 36

GROWTH OF RUSSIA TO 1725 75

PARTITION OF THE KINGDOM OF POLAND 79

EXPANSION OF PRUSSIA UNDER FREDERICK THE GREAT . . 87

THE COLONIAL SITUATION ABOUT 1689 96

NAPOLEONIC EMPIRE AT ITS HEIGHT 192

EUROPE IN 1815 200

UNIFICATION OF ITALY 262

ASIA, 1914 362

AFRICA, 1914 370

EUROPE, 1900 388

GERMANY AFTER THE TREATY OF VERSAILLES . . . 423

EUROPE OF TODAY 426

Volume Two

SINCE 1660

Section A

EUROPE IN THE AGE OF LOUIS XIV

(1660–1715)

There is no date of which it may be said: Here modern European history begins. The transition from medieval to modern times in Europe was a slow and painful evolution still far from complete in the middle of the seventeenth century, the point at which this volume opens. The political map of Europe, it is true, had already acquired a distinctly modern appearance, with England, France, Spain, and Portugal enjoying approximately the same boundaries as today. Dynastic and commercial rivalry had superseded religious or feudal disputes as a primary incentive to war, and the unity of medieval Christendom had yielded to a system of national territorial states under secular control. But much that was characteristic of the medieval centuries — relics of half-discarded institutions, social distinctions, legal codes, customs and habits of thought — still profoundly influenced European society.

A political fact of importance that should be noted about this Europe of 1660 was the ascendancy of France. Spain was in decline, the Austrian Hapsburgs were embarrassed by the Turkish menace, the Germanies had not recovered from the devastation of the Thirty Years' War, and England had recently been disturbed by a revolution. These favoring factors made it possible for Louis XIV of France, as head of the strongest and most highly centralized state on the Continent, to play a dominant rôle in European affairs during his long reign. Because Louis, who began his personal rule about 1660, was supreme in France, and France was unquestionably the first state of Europe, the period from 1660 until his death in 1715 has been distinguished as the Age of Louis XIV.

CHAPTER ONE

EUROPE IN THE MIDDLE OF THE SEVENTEENTH CENTURY

This is the Generation of that great LEVIATHAN . . . to which we owe, under the Immortall God, our peace and defence.

THOMAS HOBBES (1651).

IN 1660, after nearly a century of civil and international warfare, the peoples of Europe enjoyed once more the almost forgotten blessings of a general peace. By the Treaty of Westphalia (1648) the terrible Thirty Years' War in the Germanies had been brought to a close. Rivalry between the Bourbon and Hapsburg dynasties kept France and Spain in conflict for eleven years longer, until they reached an agreement which was embodied in the Peace of the Pyrenees (1659). So weary had the nations grown of warfare and its inseparable evils that the powers determined to stamp out the last embers of the general strife, and Sweden, Poland, and Brandenburg, which were still engaged in a three-cornered struggle among themselves, were persuaded to end their hostilities by the Treaty of Oliva (1660).

The era thus brought to a close, the century of tumult between 1560 and 1660, is often termed "The Period of the Religious Wars." It had opened with the revolt of the Dutch against their Spanish masters, had included the religious wars in France and the defeat of the Spanish Armada by the English, and it culminated in a great struggle which devastated the Germanies from 1618 to 1648. Religious fanaticism had done much to provoke these wars, but trade rivalry and dynastic ambition had urged them on. It is obvious that a series of conflicts which spread across the breadth of a continent and lasted for generations must have gathered strength from many sources. The phrase "Religious Wars" emphasizes one issue unduly, an issue which, as the struggle matured, was overshadowed by the rivalry of Bourbon and Hapsburg and the dynastic ambitions of the German princes. A better title for this period might therefore be "The Century of General Readjustment." *The Century of General Readjustment*

For it becomes clear, from our point of observation in a later century, that what the European states passed through between 1560 and 1660 was a period of brutal and convulsive reorganization. During the fifteenth and sixteenth centuries tremendous forces were unloosed which broke up the ordered habits of the medieval world. In the Middle Ages land had been the chief source of wealth, but with the expansion of commerce and the voyages of discovery, merchants became more wealthy than feudal lords. This social and economic change brought such far-reaching results that it has been called "The Commercial Revolution." At the same time the intellectual revival which came at the close of the Middle Ages, the renewed interest in the classical literature and art and in secular learning, which is known as the Renaissance or rebirth of the European mind, swept out a number of old ideas and swept in a multitude of new ones. In the sixteenth century the Protestant Reformation, following closely upon the impact of these earlier forces, shattered the unity of the Roman Catholic Church and divided Europe into hostile religious camps. By 1560 these three great movements — the Commercial Revolution, the intellectual revival, and the Protestant Reformation — had largely spent their force, but they had filled Europe with wreckage and confusion. The three foremost institutions of the Middle Ages, the Universal Church, the Holy Roman Empire, and the Feudal System, were crippled and disrupted. It required a hundred years of repair and readjustment, of civil and religious and dynastic struggle, to reduce European society to some degree of stability and order once more.

1. THE SYSTEM OF CENTRALIZED TERRITORIAL STATES

In the end a new Europe was hammered out upon the iron anvil of war. Turn to the map of Europe (frontispiece) and note how modern it is in appearance. All the wars and revolutions from that day to this have changed the boundaries of the states surprisingly little, for by 1660 Europe was divided into territorial areas which correspond to the European states of today. No such centralized territorial states existed in the Roman Empire or during the Middle Ages. They had emerged slowly as the Middle Ages waned, and as slowly organized themselves. It was not until the seventeenth century that the concept of Christendom as a united whole yielded definitely to a state system composed of autonomous (that is, self-governing) territorial units, and for this reason modern history is often said to begin in the seventeenth century. To the political philosopher, Thomas Hobbes (1588–1679), the sovereign state appeared so portentous a social organism that he called it a *Leviathan*, a "mortall God." In his opinion citizens submitted to the authority of the state, wielded by an absolute monarch, because they realized that such despotism was their only sure protection against anarchy, and in a condition of anarchy the life of man would be "solitary, poore, nasty, brutish and short." Like most of his contemporaries, therefore, Hobbes considered monarchy the best form of government, and held that the sovereign expressed in his august person the concentrated will, authority, and majesty of the state.

Thus two important facts are to be noted about Europe in 1660. The first is the existence of these autonomous states. The second fact concerns the form of government common to these states: they are all, or almost all, absolute monarchies. The sovereign power, in the great majority of cases, is vested *Divine-right monarchies the rule* in a prince who claims to rule by divine right. It need hardly be explained that this triumph of the kingly power was not obtained without a struggle. In France, nobles tenacious of their independence resisted the growth of the royal authority until their last revolts were crushed by Richelieu and Mazarin and Louis XIV. In the Germanies, the dukes and electors subdued their subjects and fought their overlord, the Holy Roman Emperor, until they won what amounted to sovereign independence for each of them. In Spain and Portugal the people were taught to accept the will of the king without protest, even if he proved wicked or incompetent. Only the English had dared to flout the divine right of kings, but, although they sent Charles I to the block (1649), they received back his son Charles II eleven years later as "King by the grace of God." In 1660, monarchy was the accepted form of government everywhere in Europe, with the exception of Switzerland, which was a republic, and Holland, where an elected officer exercised the power of a king under republican forms.

The new organization of Europe, consolidated during the Century of Readjustment, proved remarkably stable. For a hundred and thirty years the settlement endured without essential changes, while Europe continued to progress within the lines laid down by 1660. Though the balance of power between one state and another shifted from time to time, a general equilibrium was maintained. No civil wars or serious revolts threatened the European monarchs, who continued to rule by divine right, except in England where the ruler was made responsible to Parliament. The Century of Readjustment, it seemed, had produced an order of things that possessed the virtues of stability and permanence.

Unfortunately, the new order also brought grave evils. The most important characteristic which the national states held in common was a lust for self-aggrandizement. Though religion had been eliminated as a cause of international strife (the Thirty *Nationalism* Years' War was the last of the religious struggles), war remained a persistent scourge none the less. Like the monster in the fable, it seemed to have grown three heads for one that was stricken off. If states no longer clashed over religious differences, they found more imperious issues, such as greed for territory, jealousy over each other's trade, or the desire to monopolize the new lands discovered across the seas. More than once an ambitious king plunged Europe into war to advance the claims of his dynasty. So bitter and so relentless have national antagonisms proved in the modern state system that the system itself has been called "Ishmaelitish nationalism," the term being borrowed from the story of Ishmael in the Old Testament, whose "hand was against every man and every man's hand against him."

The danger that as the states developed the wars between them would grow more frequent and more destructive alarmed far-seeing statesmen and philosophers before 1660. Sully, the able minister of Henry IV of France, formulated in his master's name a "Grand Design" for uniting all the European states in a permanent alliance. General councils were to arbitrate all international disputes, and war was to be restricted to campaigns against the infidel Turks. In 1623, a French scholar, Émeric Crucé, in a book called *The New Cyneas*, proposed that armies should be abolished and a world court created to adjust disputes. Two years later, the great Dutch jurist, Hugo Grotius (1583–1645), published a treatise *On the Law of War and Peace* in which he attempted to distinguish between just and unjust wars, urging that if war proved unavoidable the nations engaged should at least pledge themselves to abstain from needless barbarities such as the massacre of the wounded. Unfortunately, to most practical statesmen the "Grand Design" and the suggestions of Crucé and Grotius appeared idealistic and unenforceable. Believing that no nation could expect to escape a war once in every generation, these men held it wisest to prepare for the stern eventuality by making their respective states as self-sufficient as possible, by building up armaments and seeking allies for the expected struggle.

The result was the formation of alliances for purposes of offense and defense, a process which often went forward until the states of Europe *Balance of power* were aligned in two hostile groups. If these groups were evenly balanced, the outcome of a war between them was difficult to predict, a fact which the diplomats extolled as the best possible guaranty of peace. So long as a just balance of power was maintained, few states would be reckless enough to invite a war which they stood an even chance of losing. Moreover, small countries would be preserved from the rapacity of powerful neighbors by other powers interested in maintaining the international equilibrium. This somewhat optimistic ideal, which had been invoked in the sixteenth century (and earlier), became in the seventeenth century the guiding principle of international diplomacy.

The gravest flaw in the political state system of seventeenth-century Europe was this perpetual threat of war. A second defect was to be found within the states themselves, and was inherent in *Defects of* their form of government. Divine-right monarchy is *absolute* successful if the monarch is equal to his task, but not *monarchy* otherwise. Political thinkers who had witnessed the evils that sprang up to plague a nation during a civil war or interregnum declared that people were safe and happy only when their ruler had adequate power to maintain order, and could hand on that power without interruption to his successor. As they found these two qualifications implicit in absolute monarchy, they praised it as the best system of government. But there is a Latin proverb to the effect that the best, when corrupted, becomes the worst. Under a capable king monarchy might justify itself admirably, but under a bad one it was almost certain to prove execrable. Unfortunately, not every prince who inherited a throne also inherited a talent for ruling. For one king born with genius there were ten who were mediocre if not actively mischievous. If the ministers of a stupid or wicked king were too servile to restrain him, a whole nation might suffer for his mistakes. His subjects had no redress against the injuries he did them, for in theory the king was answerable for his acts to God alone. The people might pray to God to soften his heart and enlighten his understanding; but if their prayers proved unavailing there was nothing they could do, except, as one writer has wittily observed, "to give thanks for the evil which the king neglected to do."

2. THE EUROPEAN STATES IN 1660

Had an Englishman of 1660 decided to take advantage of the restoration of peace in Europe to make a grand tour of the Continent, he could have learned much in a year of travel and adventure. Desiring to visit as many countries as possible, he might plan to sojourn a month or two in France, travel through Holland to the Germanies and Scandinavia, and then turn south to Austria and Italy. From Genoa he could, if he wished, take a ship to Spain, explore the Iberian Peninsula until the time came to board a merchantman at Lisbon, and conclude his year of wandering by a sea voyage to London. The stages of his journey may be followed with ease by referring to the frontispiece.

If we suppose our imaginary traveler to have started from London in June, 1660, he must have left behind him a city gay with flags. The

England English people were celebrating the return of Charles II. Weary of the grim austerities of the Puritan régime, the nation hailed the restoration of the monarchy as an omen that England was to be "Merrie England" once more. Theaters were reopened, dancing and card-playing came back into fashion, and fine clothes were no longer frowned upon as a mark of vanity. The wit and affability of the new king pleased his subjects and earned him the title "The Merry Monarch." Beneath his charming manners he concealed thoughts that were selfish but sagacious. England, with a population of some four and a half million people, together with Scotland and Ireland, formed a kingdom no monarch need spurn. Charles had determined to escape if he could from the limitations set upon his authority, but to defer to Parliament if necessary rather than "start again upon his travels."

Leaving London to welcome its new king, our traveler of 1660 caught a coach for Dover. Recently inaugurated, these coaches were intro-

France ducing a revolution in land transportation, for they ran more or less on schedule and jogged men and baggage over the vile English roads at the surprising average of four miles an hour. The traveler was much relieved, after crossing the Channel, to find the French roads much better. A few days' journeying brought him to Paris, which was rapidly becoming the foremost city in Europe, as France was becoming the foremost state. In June, 1660, the Parisians were celebrating the marriage of their king, Louis XIV, to Maria Theresa, daughter of the Spanish king, Philip IV. This wedding was solemnized with a pomp and luxury remarkable even for an age which loved sumptuous display, for Louis XIV, then in his early twenties, was the most powerful monarch in Europe. For over half a century he was to maintain his position as the most dreaded, the most flattered, and the most troublesome figure on the European stage.

On the northeastern frontier of France lay the provinces of the Spanish Netherlands which Louis coveted; and beyond these the popu-

The Dutch lous cities of the Dutch Republic whose inhabitants Louis *Republic* despised. Yet his contempt for the Dutch merchants was mixed with envy, for they were the wealthiest merchants and traders in Europe. Our traveler, who paused a few days in Amsterdam, was amazed to see the harbor so dark with the masts of ships that it looked like a level forest. It was said the herring trade alone brought the Dutch more wealth than Spain had drawn from all the mines of the Indies. All the nations shared the envy felt by Louis XIV at the spectacle of Dutch prosperity, but Louis had two additional reasons for disliking his neighbors. He disliked them because they were Protestant and he disliked them because they were republican.

Leaving Holland behind and ascending the river Rhine, the traveler soon found himself in the heart of the Palatinate. The Thirty Years' War had ended in 1648, but traces of its ravages were ap- *The* parent everywhere, so that an Englishman might well be *Germanies* thankful his own country had escaped such a visitation. This wave of destruction which had overwhelmed the Germanies helps to account for the ascendancy gained by France in the seventeenth century. German civilization had been thrown back a hundred years; large areas were swept as clean as a desert, and more than half the population of the empire had perished from the sword or plague or famine. With the re-establishment of peace, the German princes took up the task of restoring prosperity to their shattered domains, the most successful being Frederick William of Brandenburg, known to German history as the "Great Elector" (1640–88). By his political and military reforms Frederick William laid a foundation for a strong Prussian state in northern Germany. Settlers were drawn from all parts of Europe to people his depleted villages through the promise of good government and freedom from religious persecution. Hearing of the Great Elector's statesmanlike rule, our traveler decided to visit Berlin. He found the future capital of Germany a grim and cheerless town of ten or twelve thousand inhabitants, situated in the midst of a desert-like countryside, and his disappointment led him to hasten on for a view of the Scandinavian countries.

Five states disputed the control of the Baltic Sea in 1660: Sweden, Denmark, Russia, Brandenburg, and Poland. As a temporary truce had been concluded, the traveler was able to visit Copen- *The Baltic* hagen, the capital of the united kingdom of Denmark- *states* Norway, and to linger in Stockholm, the capital of Sweden. It astonished him to learn that these kingdoms, which desired to play the rôle of great powers, had a population of only a little over a million each. Remembering how Brandenburg was developing, and pondering what he had heard of Russia, a vast and little known country on the eastern fringe of Europe, the Englishman decided that Sweden and Denmark were unwise to waste their resources fighting each other when they might soon have such much more powerful rivals. Being tactful, however, he kept his opinion to himself, and resumed his journey down the Baltic to Danzig and thence across Great Poland on his way to Vienna.

In that ancient city on the Danube, the Emperor of the Holy Roman

Empire, Leopold I, had recently celebrated his election.   His reign
Austria   (1658–1705) was to prove a critical half-century in Austrian
        history.   Despite his grandiose titles, the emperor's power
was crumbling: the Peace of Westphalia had virtually terminated his
authority over the German princes, France was powerful and aggressive
in the West, and the Turks, having overrun Hungary, were pressing up
the Danube toward Vienna.   Twenty years later, as we shall see, they
were to besiege the city, from which Leopold fled in panic.   Only the
heroic action of John Sobieski, King of Poland, saved eastern Europe
for the cross.   With a small relief force of Poles and Germans, Sobieski
hastened to the aid of Vienna, and routed a Mohammedan host that
outnumbered his own by three to one (1683).

In the cathedral of Saint Stephen the grateful Viennese intoned the
text, "There was a man sent from God whose name was John"; but
Poland   for the timely aid Sobieski had rendered, the proud Haps-
        burgs showed scant gratitude.   Poland, in 1660, was a
loosely organized kingdom that occupied an area as large as France.
A little over a century later, as we are to learn, it disappeared from the
map of Europe completely, partitioned and annexed by the rapacious
rulers of Austria, Prussia, and Russia.

It is recounted that in the hour of their defeat before the walls of
Vienna, the Turks were dismayed to see the shadow of an eclipse blot
The Turks   out the crescent moon from the evening sky.   The crescent
        was the emblem of Mohammedan power, and the Islamic
Empire for a thousand years had stretched from Asia Minor across
Africa to Spain, a menacing crescent with its horns closing on Christian
Europe.   The western horn had been blunted at the battle of Tours
(732) and broken off when the Spaniards ended the Moorish power in
Spain (1492).   But in the same century the fall of Constantinople
(1453) saw the eastern horn of the crescent plunged into the heart of
the Hapsburg Empire.   The siege of Vienna in 1683 marked the farthest
gain in this advance.   Thereafter the Turkish power in the Balkan
Peninsula was doomed to ebb with the centuries like a slowly receding
tide.

The summer of 1660 changed to autumn while the traveler lingered in
Vienna, but before the snows could deepen in the Alps he hastened across
Italy   the Brenner Pass, and saw the waters of the Adriatic for
        the first time at Venice.   The city of the doges, once the
greatest commercial port of Europe, had lost its supremacy with the
development of the Atlantic sea lanes, and its glory was waning.   Had
the traveler been a Catholic, he might have continued his journey from

Venice through the Papal States to Rome, where he could have paid his respects to the pope; but, as he was an Englishman and a Protestant, he visited instead the lovely cities of northern Italy, stopping in Bologna, Mantua, Milan, and Pavia, before he embarked at Genoa in a swift galley that carried him to Barcelona in Spain.

On his way across the valleys and plateaus which separate Barcelona from Madrid, the traveler came to understand why Spain, the dominant nation of Europe a century earlier, had fallen into decline. *Spain* The peasants appeared lazy, disliking to work more than a few hours a day, although one day in four was a religious holiday. The irrigation systems by which, in Moorish times, farmers had coaxed produce from the arid soil were no longer tended. The only roads in many parts were the water courses, impassable after rains when streams had the right of way. Trade languished, for the government, which had driven out the industrious Moors and Jews, was also ruining Christian merchants by exorbitant taxes. Remembering how commerce was encouraged in his own country, the Englishman confessed his astonishment at this, but the noble hidalgo to whom he revealed his thoughts explained that in Spain shopkeeping was considered a mean pursuit in which no gentleman would stoop to engage. If the merchants were heavily taxed, he added with a shrug, they doubtless fared as well as they deserved.

Madrid proved to be a medieval city with a multitude of beggars in the narrow and noisome streets. The government was constantly in financial straits, while many noble families had little or nothing left except their pride. Even that had been damaged by the recent national misfortunes, such as the capture of Jamaica by the English (1655) and the concessions extorted by the French in the Peace of the Pyrenees (1659). A further reverse demanded acknowledgment, for Portugal, united to the Spanish crown in 1580, had revolted in 1640, and the Portuguese were making good their independence under John IV, a king of their own choosing. The Spaniards, however, remained loyal to their own royal line, although inbreeding and degeneracy were soon to bring it to an end. In 1661, an heir was born to Philip IV, a diseased and sickly prince who astonished his doctors by surviving the maladies of childhood. He was to astonish all Europe by living until 1700 as Charles II, last of the Spanish Hapsburgs.

An overland journey of some weeks carried the traveler from Madrid to Lisbon. The Portuguese, in their struggle for independence, had developed friendly commercial relations with England, and he had little difficulty in discovering a merchantman bound for London. A year of wandering had taught him much about the life led by the European peoples of his day. It will be interesting to imagine some of the conclusions he may have reached.

3. LIFE IN THE SEVENTEENTH CENTURY

From England to Italy and Prussia to Spain, the traveler must have found three fourths of the people leading miserable lives without leisure or luxury. In the cities most of the inhabitants subsisted on the verge of destitution, toiling as artisans or apprentices, as servants poorly paid and overworked, as porters or ostlers, linkboys or lackeys, peddlers or beggars. But there were few cities in Europe of even fifty thousand inhabitants, and the great majority of Europe's eighty or ninety million people lived amid rural surroundings, their horizon bounded by the limits of the local hamlet or feudal estate. The open countryside, when it did not begin at their doorsill, was within sight or walking distance and this was one great advantage which they possessed. But in most other respects their lives were wretched, burdened as they were by a host of inescapable hardships, by intermittent famines and plagues and unceasing toil.

The difficulty and cost of transportation confined the poor to their native community: thousands of people lived and died without traveling
Difficulty of fifty miles from their birthplace. The roads were often
transporta- no more than mud ruts, impassable for months in the year.
tion This absence of easy means of transport or communication kept society in the country districts "frozen" as it were. Many hamlets still preserved the same spirit of self-sufficiency and semi-isolation which they had possessed in the Middle Ages. Attention was confined to local affairs; the villagers had little incentive to speculate about the world beyond the horizon, for their days were filled with a multitude of duties, and when they paused to gossip it was of personal concerns. The passage of a regiment of soldiers on the highroad some miles away, or the sojourn of a nobleman overnight at the inn, were casual echoes of the great world that disturbed them little.

In that era before the advent of labor-saving machinery, life presented an endless succession of inescapable tasks. The farmer had his stock to feed and his fields to tend. Tools called for resharpening, roofs had to be rethatched, there was always wood to be hewn or water to be drawn, so that little leisure was left for amusement or study. Few outside of the professional classes ever learned to read, but news circulated about the community by word of mouth or was announced at the church on Sundays, and the illiterate masses carried a store of ballads and tales, as well as the details of local history, in their memories. Everyone in a village knew everyone else, his uncles and his cousins and his aunts, and the fact that families had dwelt in the same neighborhood and inter-married for generations bound the community together. The status of each person was thus fixed by custom and known to all; few had the opportunity to rise above their class; and the occupation a man inherited from his forbears might determine, not only his place and duties in village life, but his name also, as the Bakers, Millers, Taylors, Smiths, and other common surnames still bear witness.

To hold some settled position, to "belong" in the community, was then a matter of pride, and families clung tenaciously to ancient priv-ileges and pretensions however humble. The craving for distinctions and honors was particularly strong among the rising bourgeois class, and it has been estimated that in some towns one half the population purchased minor rôles or offices of one kind or another in the administra-tion. In a society where the position of everyone is well known and defined, strangers are usually viewed askance, and it is not surprising to find in the seventeenth century that most localities maintained special laws against "rogues, vagabonds, and sturdy beggars." Gyp-sies, traveling tinkers, and strolling players were treated with suspicion as immoral and dishonest vagrants, a prejudice that has been slow in dying out. The wars of the seventeenth century flooded Europe with disbanded soldiers and other masterless men who begged or stole as the mood pleased them, and against such "sturdy beggars" the laws were particularly severe.

In the Middle Ages poverty, or at least a contempt for worldly riches, had been considered an admirable quality, and begging assumed the dignity of a profession. But this tolerant attitude toward *Harsh laws* mendicancy had changed by the seventeenth century, especially in Protestant countries. A new sense of the dignity of useful labor had developed, and merchants and guild masters who needed workers for their shops and factories urged severe laws against idleness. Able-bodied men who declined to work were cured by whipping, forced labor, or, if they proved incorrigible, by transportation to the colonial plantations. For graver crimes the laws were proportionately harsher. Thieves, bandits, smugglers, and murderers might incur penalties which ranged from a term in the galleys, branding or mutilation, to hanging or breaking on the wheel. Executions were public, the condemned were urged to make edifying speeches at the gallow's foot for the benefit of the audience, and the bodies of criminals were left hanging from the

[15]

gibbets as a warning to other evildoers. Unfortunately, these cruel laws were administered in so clumsy and unequal a fashion that they proved more ferocious than salutary; yet few people protested against the stupidity of the system, for it was in the spirit of the time to take the evil with the good and accept the established customs in government or society without much questioning.

It must be remembered, too, that the coarseness and crudity of living conditions three centuries ago bred in the mass of the people an indifference to suffering which today would be considered inhuman. Some old European towns still preserve a whipping-post in the market-place to recall the days when misdemeanors were punished by a public flogging. Bear-baiting and cock-fighting were popular sports, and the wretched inmates of the insane asylums were sometimes exposed in cages for the amusement of visitors who might poke and tease them as if they were animals. Pain and suffering were such commonplace things in an age before anesthetics, when surgical and dental methods were elementary, that people grew insensible to the thought of them. Death and disease carried off every second child before it was ten years old and struck down the strong man in his prime. The air was full of "farewells to the dying and mourning for the dead," and the resultant sense of helplessness, of the mystery of life and the imminence of death, partly explains why people then cherished their religion more closely, for the clergy alone presumed to offer an answer to the enigma of existence.

The peasants and laborers who made up the larger part of the population in every European state clung to their established mode of life with dogged and unenlightened conservatism. The prejudice against changes and innovations was so strong that frequently new and better methods of doing things, of planting crops or breeding cattle, were rejected simply because they were new. Forks were a long time coming into fashion because people were accustomed to lift the food to their mouths with their fingers. The belief that night air was harmful led people to seal up doors and windows at night. All the members of a family often slept in a single room, huddled together on a straw mattress, or stretched on the level top of a brick oven for the sake of its comfortable warmth. The dwellings were frequently no better than barns, with earth floors and thatched roofs. Water had to be drawn from a well or stream; there were no baths, and bathing was a luxury it was easier to forgo. The poorer classes could not afford to buy meat and subsisted chiefly on coarse vegetables; inadequately nourished, they were less fitted to resist the diseases and plagues to which their unsanitary mode of life exposed

[16]

A MODEST SEVENTEENTH-CENTURY DWELLING

Millions of peasants and artisans in the seventeenth century occupied houses less comfortable or commodious than this one. Note the barrel set to catch rainwater, and the garage-like annex for stabling animals. Peter the Great of Russia lived in this cottage for a short period in 1697, when he was studying shipbuilding in Holland.

them, and they lacked the reserve of energy and courage which might have moved them to rebel against their condition.

This picture of life in the seventeenth century, as it was lived by the majority, is a dark one, but there were signs even then that a change *Signs of* was coming, though it was coming all too slowly. The *change* era of exploration and expansion which had begun as early as the fourteenth century gradually brought to Europeans a widening horizon and a richer life. New dress materials, such as muslin and calico, were introduced from the East; cotton cloth was developed as an addition to wool; and new foods, such as potatoes, tomatoes, and sugar, supplemented the monotonous diet. Coffee and tea were added to the list of common beverages in the seventeenth century, and the habit of smoking, or "drinking tobacco" as it was called, was acquired from the American Indians. The rich were the first to enjoy these innovations, but, as they grew cheaper and more common, the new types of food and clothing became available for the poorer classes also.

Yet most of the wealth created by the revival of trade remained concentrated in a few — too few — hands. While the lot of the poor had improved but little since the close of the Middle Ages, the prosperous merchant had begun to enjoy luxuries unknown to princes a few centuries earlier. The clean and comfortable interiors of Dutch houses, with their handsome furniture, polished utensils, pictures on the walls and rugs on the floors, as they are preserved in many a seventeenth-century painting, prove that well-to-do people had learned in that day how to surround their lives with comfort and charm. The country château of many a noble, the town houses of many a merchant prince, were crowded with rich collections of silver plate, carved furniture, and woven tapestry. But the enjoyment of such possessions was a privilege reserved for the rich and the powerful, and for one man who drank his wines from a silver goblet and amused himself with the intricate variety of a thirty-course dinner there were a hundred who called themselves blessed if they had a chicken to put in the pot on Saturday night.

All these impressions and many others might have crowded through the mind of our imaginary traveler as he concluded his grand tour. But not the most thoughtful and intelligent observer could have been expected to detect in the Europe of 1660 the dynamic forces which were to enable Europeans, in less than three centuries thereafter, to dominate the world. Europe, the smallest of the continents and by no means the most ancient in its civilization, which in 1660 possessed less than one seventh of the world's population, was destined to reduce four larger continents to subjection and tribute. The story of this amazing expansion, which was to carry the impress of European civilization to every quarter of the globe, is the main theme of modern history. The Europeans had never been peacemakers, but they were to come nearer than any other people had ever done to inheriting the earth.

CHAPTER TWO

LOUIS XIV DOMINATES FRANCE AND ASPIRES TO DOMINATE EUROPE

Homage is due to kings, they do what pleases them.
(Maxim from the young Louis XIV's copybook.)

IT IS the fortune of some men to personify so fittingly the dominant spirit of the period in which they live that they give their name to their age. Louis XIV of France was such a figure. The spirit which he exemplified was royal absolutism, and so impressively did he play his part as king, by the grace of God, of the leading European state of the time, that the latter half of the seventeenth century is still called the Age of Louis XIV.

1. FRANCE AT THE ACCESSION OF LOUIS XIV

Louis's long reign lasted from 1643 to 1715, and fate ordained that its glory should exceed even its length. Three factors combined to heighten the unique prestige of the *Grand Monarque*. The first was the general state of Europe in the seventeenth century. As explained in the previous chapter the turmoil and dissension of the religious struggles, followed by the civil war in England and the internecine strife known as the Fronde in France, aroused a profound longing among European peoples for peace and stability. If a king sought to gratify this wish, he would have to maintain a balance between the turbulent nobles, ambitious bourgeois, and oppressed peasants, by proclaiming himself the symbol of the state and raising the state above faction. The century thus offered an astute monarch a rare opportunity to demonstrate the saving virtues of royal absolutism as a method of government, and Louis made the most of this opportunity.

The second factor which helped to augment his prestige was the happy combination of royal supremacy with national supremacy. With Germany ruined and half-depopulated by the Thirty Years' War (1618–48), England torn by civil war (1642–49), and Spain already in decline, France under Louis XIV stood forth as the leading European power. The labors of Richelieu and Mazarin in consolidating the royal power had made the authority of the French king more extensive and more absolute than that of any other contemporary monarch. Louis became arbiter of France at the moment that France was becoming arbiter of

Europe, and this second factor largely explains his historical importance.

The third factor was the king's personality. Historians have long debated whether Louis XIV deserved to be called great, and the verdict, paradoxically enough, seems to be that he was not a great *Character of* man, but he was a great king. In appearance he was of *Louis XIV* average height, endowed with natural grace and dignity and by some accounted handsome. In youth he revealed no precocious talents and as a man he was by no means learned, for he possessed little more than a smattering of history and Italian and enough Latin to construe Caesar's *Commentaries*. But if his intelligence was mediocre, his character had elements of grandeur. A lonely and diffident childhood had taught him to be self-sufficient, to discipline his feelings and conceal his thoughts; and he reached manhood with the determination to devote all his faculties to the business of kingship. There is something attractive in the picture he has left of himself at twenty-two when Mazarin's death called him to command the ship of state. Outwardly, he knew, he must reveal nothing but calm resolution, but within he was beset with qualms and uncertainties. To his relief this timidity vanished once he set his hand to the task. "I really seemed to myself," he wrote later, "to be a king, and born to be one. I experienced a delight, in fact, which it is difficult to express." Unfortunately, years of flattery dissolved away his early sense of modesty and moderation, and made him selfish and bigoted.

Believing himself chosen as God's vicegerent to guide the destinies of France, Louis accepted his power as a serious responsibility. He schooled himself to evaluate character, to choose able *The divine* subordinates, and to weigh decisions. If he lacked genius, *right of* he possessed the best substitute for it, which is an infinite *kings* capacity for taking pains. The multifarious details of the kingly trade engrossed him, he toiled at them relentlessly, and not even in sickness or defeat would he permit the routine of councils and ceremonies to be interrupted. For over fifty years Louis sustained without faltering the exacting rôle for which he had trained himself, and history, as a reward for the technical perfection of that performance, has awarded him the title of the "Grand Monarch." To contemporary Europe, his example was a practical proof of the divine right of kings, for no demagogue lifted to power by the will of the populace and no conqueror who might "wade through slaughter to a throne" could hope to sway a scepter with so sure a hand as this legitimate and consecrated king. Among a host of writers who flattered Louis by proving that God had ordained kings to rule and endowed them with peculiar gifts for the task, the most eloquent was the Bishop of Meaux, Bossuet (1627–1704), who based his arguments on the Holy Scriptures. Those who presumed to criticize or resist the Lord's anointed were declared to be not only political rebels but heretics and blasphemers, for, as Bossuet proclaimed, the king's power was without limits and he was answerable for the use he made of it to no one on earth.

When Cardinal Mazarin, who had governed France during the minority of Louis XIV, died in 1661, the young king announced that *Absolutism* he would thenceforth take upon himself the duties of first *of Louis* minister. He was determined to preside over the councils *XIV* of government in person and guide with his own hand the destinies of the first state of Europe. There was no force in France strong enough to dispute his wishes. Louis XIV enjoyed greater powers than any of his predecessors because every faction in France which might have resisted him had been reduced to impotence or taught to serve the royal will. The king had become much more than the executive head of the state; he was the center of all authority and order, a sun radiating light and warmth to every corner of the realm. His most important vassals and ministers were no more than satellites, circling in their orbits about his august person, reflecting his glory, but forbidden to approach too near. Louis chose the sun as his symbol because it was a unique body of matchless power and radiance, and its dominant position in the heavens suggested the rôle which he felt himself called upon to assume in France. The methods by which he reduced the kingdom to an obsequious obedience offer a fascinating study in statecraft.

The threefold division of society into clergy, nobles, and commoners still survived in seventeenth-century France. The clergy were known *Position of* as the First Estate, and occupied an anomalous position, *the First* for as Frenchmen they were subjects of the king, while as *Estate, the* churchmen they were servants of the pope. It is not *clergy* difficult to foresee that under a king as jealous of his power as Louis, the exact division of authority between the king and pope was likely to become a subject of dispute. Louis was anxious to be esteemed orthodox, as befitted one who bore the title "His Most Christian Majesty," but he disliked to see the pope interfere in French affairs. His predecessors on the throne of France had wrung a number of concessions from the papacy, so that the Gallican Church (as the Roman Catholic Church in France was called) enjoyed a semi-independent position. Among the privileges assumed by the French kings was that of collecting the income from certain clerical offices

[22]

whenever they were vacant, a custom extended so broadly by Louis XIV that in 1673 his claims were repudiated by Pope Innocent XII. As the quarrel deepened, Louis allowed Bossuet to draw up a declaration which defined the "liberties of the Gallican Church," asserted the king's independence of the pope in temporal affairs, and proclaimed that a general council was superior to the papal authority. To this declaration the French clergy gave their consent (1682), but the threatening schism was composed ten years later when Louis, having won his way in the matter of appointments, permitted the bishops to withdraw from the unorthodox position he had persuaded them to assume (1693). The strong can afford to be generous and Louis had come to the conclusion that the pope would be of more service to him as an ally than as an adversary.

Like the clergy, the nobles were taught to accept the royal authority. Under Louis XIV the great feudal vassals finally lost the power to rebel. They had been the architects of their own ruin, for the long *The Second* story of their selfishness, treason, and dissension had con- *Estate, the* verted the French people to the belief that the rule of one *nobility* despot was preferable to the misrule of many. The days when a powerful noble could maintain his private army, wage his private wars, and even defy from his impregnable castle the anger of his impotent king, were past. Under Richelieu and Mazarin royal troops crushed the last revolts and royal orders leveled many of the provincial castles to the ground. The rebellion of the Fronde represented in its main aspect the last convulsive struggle of a decadent feudalism before it yielded definitely to the shackles of the kingly power. Throughout his reign Louis XIV was resolute in withholding from the nobles all political or military authority. Stripped of such power they were harmless, and he had no wish to humble them further. Their titles and honors he left intact and even multiplied, his policy being to domesticate these feudal lions rather than to destroy them. Summoning to his capital the leading nobles of France, he consoled them with pensions and flattered them with empty but impressive duties at court. Ruin or imprisonment would have made these erstwhile rebels the objects of popular sentiment and the heroes of a lost cause, so Louis bound them to him astutely with golden chains. Like the giant Antaeus in the Greek fable, their strength drained away when their feet no longer trod their native earth, for their real power was derived from their lands and their armies of loyal retainers. Cut off from these, they became parasites at the court of the Sun King. Like the orange trees in silver tubs which graced the Hall of Mirrors at Versailles, they were decorative and expensive, but they no longer served any useful purpose.

The Third Estate, although it included over nine tenths of his subjects, Louis found by far the easiest to manage, for the commoners had *The Third* never been accustomed to the exercise of political power. *Estate* From this class he drew his most trusted councilors and officials, knowing such men would be dependent upon his whim and powerless before his wrath. The subservience of the Third Estate in France is most interesting, especially when compared with the arrogance of the English Commons, which proved strong enough in the seventeenth century to get rid of two unpopular kings. In France, however, the continuous expansion of the royal power had stunted the growth of representative institutions. Yet the French monarchs, though not obliged to consult the wishes of their subjects, could not altogether ignore them. One organ through which they might learn of popular opposition to a new edict was the *parlement de Paris*. This body was not a "parliament" in the English sense. It was the most important of several similar legal courts, and one of its privileges was to register royal decrees. The councilors of the *parlement* interpreted this to mean that they might on occasion *refuse* to register a law which appeared to them contradictory or unconstitutional, but the king could silence all objection by summoning the councilors to a *lit de justice* (bed of justice) and commanding them to accept the disputed decree as an expression of his will. As further opposition would not hinder the promulgation of the law, the *parlement* usually yielded at this point, though occasionally the members persisted in their opposition and were banished from Paris as a sign of the royal displeasure. Louis XIV was so jealous of the royal prerogative that even this shadow of resistance annoyed him, and early in his reign the *parlement de Paris* was deprived of the right of protest.

Because he controlled the national income and well-paid clerical appointments, and was not dependent upon appropriations granted by a jealous parliament as were contemporary English monarchs, Louis XIV could bind the great nobles of France to him by gifts, reserving the most lucrative church offices for members of the leading families. The rising prices of the sixteenth and seventeenth centuries had impoverished many a knight and baron whose feudal income was fixed by custom, and many a titled bankrupt was happy to retrieve his fortunes through the king's generosity. But although Louis willingly bestowed sinecures at court upon such nobles, or rewarded younger sons with clerical appointments, he preferred to entrust political duties to able

LOUIS XIV OF FRANCE
1638–1715

*This portrait of Louis (from a painting by
Rigaud, Louvre) in his robes of state suggests
the poise and self-confidence which made him a
model for the lesser despots of his age.*

members of the Third Estate. More than one ambitious bourgeois served the king loyally as councilor or intendant, in the hope of winning a title thereby, and he usually paid a goodly sum into the royal exchequer in addition when he received the coveted coat of arms. These new "nobles of the robe" were scorned by the older "nobles of the sword," but they acted as a counterweight in preserving the social equilibrium, which answered the king's purposes excellently. Favored by circumstances, Louis XIV thus evolved a system in which the old nobility were paid to be subservient, the ambitious bourgeois, subservient and industrious, paid to become nobles, and the bishops and the abbots of the Gallican Church, chosen from the ancient nobility, subordinated the church to the accessory rôle which Louis intended it to play in his absolutist state.

2. HOW LOUIS XIV CONDUCTED HIS GOVERNMENT

The administrative system over which Louis presided was a highly centralized and complicated mechanism. The executive power was
The four councils of government exercised through four royal councils, which met regularly each week and dispatched their business under the king's direction. The council of state decided questions of foreign policy, peace and war, etc. The council of dispatches regulated the internal affairs of the kingdom, but left matters of a fiscal nature, such as taxation and tariffs, to the council of finances. The privy council was a court of the king's justice, but possessed extraordinary powers so that it could act as a final court of appeal and could arrest or withdraw a case from the inferior courts at its discretion. The power of these councils reached into the farthest corners of the kingdom, where financial and judicial matters were entrusted to royal officials known as intendants, each of whom administered a province in the king's name, and corresponded regularly with the council of dispatches. All the business of the kingdom was thus supervised from Versailles; all important decisions (and many that were unimportant) came before the king for his signature, with the natural result that officials preferred to evade decisions and contented themselves with obeying orders. Thus summarized, the machinery of government sounds comparatively simple, but as it had grown up haphazardly there was actually an endless confusion and overlapping of authority; the lower officials lacked independence and initiative, and an increasing burden of details was thrown upon the central councils. An energetic king and capable ministers could force the machine to function with a certain majestic

[26]

ponderosity, but it was, for all that, a desperately wasteful and inefficient system.

In the first part of his reign Louis XIV was fortunate in commanding the services of Jean Baptiste Colbert (1619–83), perhaps the greatest financial administrator in French history. Appointed *Colbert* controller general of finance in 1661, Colbert doubled Louis's revenue within ten years, not by increasing the taxes, but by cutting down the wastage and defalcations. A dour and friendless man, consumed by a passion for work, Colbert had the acuteness to realize that most systems of raising revenue ended by killing the goose that laid the golden eggs. Too many finance ministers thought only of pleasing their royal masters by filling the treasury, and cared little where the burden fell; but Colbert worked with four aims in mind, all praiseworthy. He sought (1) to collect an adequate revenue by the most honest and efficient system; (2) to expend the sums collected wisely and economically; (3) to distribute the burden of taxation upon those classes best able to sustain it; and (4) to stimulate with exemptions and subsidies those branches of farming and manufacture in which the nation was deficient so that it might grow more self-sufficing and independent of its neighbors.

The last point embodies the most significant element in Colbert's policy. The doctrine that a state which is politically independent should make itself economically independent also is known *Mercantil-* as "mercantilism," or sometimes, in honor of its greatest *ism* exponent, as "Colbertism." As applied by Colbert, the theory rested upon two main suppositions: (1) In peace, and more especially in war, a state should be able to produce within its borders or draw from its colonies all the commodities necessary for its national existence. (2) To prosper, a state should sell its surplus commodities to foreign countries, but should buy as little as possible in return, for if the value of its exports always exceeds that of its imports, the difference must be paid by the purchasers in gold, so that a store of the precious metal will accumulate in the coffers of the state adhering to mercantilist principles.

Mercantilism, though a selfish and egotistic policy, appealed strongly to the rulers of the new nationalistic states. To make France economically independent, Colbert imported skilled artisans from all parts of Europe so that they might teach the French workmen to manufacture Dutch cloth, Venetian lace, Flanders tapestries, English steel, Italian pottery and blown glass and mirrors. To protect the new industries from foreign competition, he erected high tariffs against foreign commodities; French subjects were warned that it was "unpatriotic" to

[27]

buy abroad, and were forbidden to send gold out of the country. Colbert hoped to raise French manufactures to such a level of excellence that they would outsell Dutch goods in Amsterdam and Venetian goods in Venice. To hasten this end he enforced exacting regulations and punished careless workers. His paternal efforts improved French industrial processes enormously and French trade profited from his improvement of roads, canals, and harbors. But there were some qualities which he could not create by legislation, qualities of initiative, of imagination and daring, and for lack of these some of his greatest schemes went astray. The great trading companies which he founded in the fond hope that they would rival the Dutch and English East India Companies failed after a few years. The navy which he built up at great expense to extend the French colonial empire in India and Africa and America could not compete successfully with those of England and Holland. The tariffs he enforced to protect French industry provoked other nations to similar measures against French goods and created a tradition of economic hostility so intense that every war in which France has been engaged since Colbert's time has been in part at least a tariff war. But the basic cause for the failure of Colbert's grandiose schemes is to be found in the conflict between his aims and those of Louis XIV. The resources of France, though great, would not permit her to seek commercial supremacy on the seas and military supremacy on land at the same time. To lay the foundations of a world empire or to snatch at the military hegemony of Europe were the two courses open to Louis, and nursed upon traditions of conquest he chose the latter. For France, for Europe, and for the world it was a momentous decision.

The evil genius whose influence was largely to nullify the achievements of Colbert was the minister of war, Louvois (1641–91). Under

Louvois   his direction the French army became the most efficient in Europe. France was the first state to keep a standing army in the modern sense, drilled, uniformed, and paid by the government. To promote discipline Louvois held frequent inspections, punished breaches of order, and berated indolent officers. Every branch of the service felt the impulse of his brutal and dynamic spirit, and he increased the reserves until the French army reached the total of two hundred thousand effectives. Louis was delighted with the toy which his energetic minister had placed at his command. In Condé and Turenne he possessed the foremost generals of the age; in Vauban he had the greatest master of siege warfare in all time. A city defended by Vauban, ran a popular saying, is impregnable; a city attacked by Vauban is doomed. With such resources France was secure from any threat of invasion, but Louvois was not content to see his weapon rust in peace. He played upon the king's love of "glory" and urged him along the path that led to conflict, well knowing that war alone could demonstrate the excellence of the army he had fashioned and assure his triumph over his great rival Colbert.

3. THE COURT OF THE SUN KING

To provide a suitable stage upon which the Grand Monarch might live and move and have his being, the foremost artists and architects of Europe were pressed into service. Henry IV had held *Versailles* his court in the Louvre, close by the Seine, but Louis XIV never liked Paris. He remembered from his childhood the insolence of the Parisians during the wars of the Fronde, and early in his reign he moved his residence to the small hamlet of Versailles, eleven miles southwest of Paris. There on a low crest of rising ground he had constructed a palace and gardens so vast they became the wonder of Europe, and so costly (the expense has been calculated at one hundred million dollars) that Louis ordered the accounts destroyed. At infinite labor water was pumped from a nearby river to supply the fabulous fountains and fill a "Grand Canal" two hundred feet wide and a mile long. The clipped hedges, statuary, arbors, and shaded walks made the garden an ideal setting for the fêtes and masquerades in which the courtiers delighted; while the palace itself, when finally completed, contained a theater, a chapel, a "marble court," with long connecting halls and glittering galleries, as well as sumptuous apartments for the king and his officials.

The modern visitor is likely to find the desolate splendor of Versailles oppressive, and to feel disappointed at the monotony with which the palace and parks are laid out. Tastes change, and Versailles today is like a lantern with the light extinguished. Yet even in the seventeenth century there were critics courageous enough to declare that this royal residence (and the later palace built for Louis XIV at Marly) demonstrated nothing except the king's "invariably bad taste" and his delight in "doing violence to nature." To its admirers, however, the beauty of Versailles consists in the harmony and proportion of the whole design. The architect Mansart and the landscape artist Le Nôtre studied to subordinate each part to the classic ideal of order and restraint, so that nothing alien or exotic was introduced to mar the purity of the general pattern. Versailles embodies the spirit of an age. Its virtues were the virtues of Louis XIV himself: it was formal, orderly, and elegant;

but its limitations reveal no less surely the limitations of Louis's character. Even at its best Versailles had grandiosity rather than grandeur; it was crowded with unoriginal artificialities; it was, in a word, dull, for it lacked cloudy perspectives, and the lift of distant horizons to set the spirit free.

As his reign advanced, Louis indulged his love of ceremony until his smallest daily acts were encrusted with ritualistic observances. On *Court ritual* rising from bed in the morning (the king's *lever*) he was attended by a roomful of privileged nobles who esteemed themselves honored if they were awarded the distinction of holding one arm of his shirt or adjusting his shoe buckles. His meals, his drives, his promenades were each an affair of state; and when he retired, he was assisted to bed by courtiers eager to attend the king's *coucher*. The burden of such regulated pomp would have amused some men, and wearied most, but Louis found the business of kingship "grand, noble, delightful." He was at once the high priest and the idol in this cult of majesty and he succeeded in persuading his courtiers that they enjoyed their part in it, too, so that existence away from Versailles was "a living death." If a noble displeased him, Louis might banish the man to his country estate, where the poor wretch was likely to fill his days petitioning friends at court to secure a revocation of the sentence before he died of ennui. Flattery explains in part this exaggerated anxiety to remain close to the king; vanity explains it in part, too, for Versailles was the center of fashion; but greed was the most potent incentive. Only those who caught the king's attention could hope to profit by his generosity. When besought to aid some needy noble who seldom appeared at court, Louis was wont to answer, "That is a man I rarely see. I have forgotten him."

Seated at the pinnacle of the pyramid of state, and worshiped almost as a divinity, Louis must sometimes have found life a little lonely. Yet *Louis's* he allowed no inner doubts to ruffle the serenity of his *mistresses* manner; even in the darkest days his fortitude sustained him, and the hand that held the scepter, though it might grow weary, was never seen to waver. Nor was he always serious; in his younger days especially he delighted in entertainments and the court exhausted its resources to amuse him. His wife, the worthy but stupid Maria Theresa, daughter of Philip IV of Spain, was an uninspiring consort, and even before her death in 1683 Louis had permitted himself a succession of mistresses. The gentle and nunlike Louise de la Vallière was followed by the dazzling Marquise de Montespan, who had wit and beauty and the taste necessary to encourage great artists. In 1679

THE PALACE OF VERSAILLES

This engraving illustrates the elegance and order which distinguished French court life in the Age of Louis XIV. The cost of laying out the palaces and gardens at Versailles was so enormous that Louis ordered the accounts destroyed.

there was a new favorite, a Mademoiselle de Fontanges; but by this time Louis was coming more and more under the influence of his children's governess, Madame de Maintenon. The king was growing sedate and middle-aged; he liked the grave demeanor and earnest piety of this unassuming woman, and in 1684 he secretly married her. "Madame de Maintenon," a witty historian has said, "was not so much Louis's last mistress as his companion in repentance, and it might almost be said, a part of his penance." By encouraging his zeal for the Catholic faith she was to help him toward the greatest blunder of his reign, the Revocation of the Edict of Nantes.

4. THE "GREAT AGE" IN LITERATURE AND ART

Louis XIV was not only the greatest king of his age, served by the most brilliant diplomats and the most invincible generals; he also *Corneille,* patronized artists and writers whose work was the ad-
Molière, miration of Europe. Pierre Corneille (1606–84), the *Racine* greatest of French tragedians; Molière (1622–73), whose satirical comedies still delight audiences today, and Racine (1639–99), the noblest of French dramatic poets, brought such prestige to the French stage that it remained the model for over a century. The critical Boileau (1636–1711) helped to purge the language of barbarisms and laid down the rules of elegant diction. Before the reign of Louis XIV ended, French plays, French novels, and French manners had been adopted by cultured people everywhere, and a knowledge of the language was indispensable to any who hoped for a social or diplomatic career.

There was one rôle which the polished nobles at the court filled with honor and distinction: they patronized — and sometimes created —
Saint- great literature. Few writers have wielded a pen so steeped
Simon in malice, so cruel yet candid in the details of its portraiture, as that with which the Duc de Saint-Simon wrote his memoirs of Louis *Madame* and his court. The letters, too, which Madame de Sévigné *de Sévigné* composed for her daughter, relating with delicious wit and irony the gossip of Versailles, are still used as models of epistolary
La Fontaine style. The *Fables* and *Contes* of La Fontaine are miracles of art for which he often compressed hours of labor into a single naïve but inimitable line; and the caustic, patrician wit of the *La Roche-* Duc de la Rochefoucauld preserved the observations of a
foucauld lifetime in a book of *Maxims*, each polished like a jewel at the hands of a master lapidary. These, and a score of other writers

whom there is not space to mention, helped to refine the French taste at the court of Louis XIV and to sustain the traditions of elegant intercourse for which French salons have long been famous.

Royal patronage profoundly influenced the art of the "Great Age." The indefatigable Colbert (among a host of other offices he held that of minister of fine arts) issued charters for an Academy of *Royal pa-* Painting and Sculpture, an Academy of Architecture, and *tronage of* an Academy of Music. Music was, indeed, the only art *art* for which Louis XIV possessed any real taste, and the first French operas date from his reign. For the rest, the official, not to say officious, interest of the government in matters artistic, the rules and definitions laid down by the academicians, the prizes offered for poems in praise of Louis, and the pensions accorded men of art, stimulated the production of much sycophantic craftsmanship. Yet an age in which Mansart designed the dome of the Invalides, in which Lebrun produced his admirable battle scenes and portraits, and Poussin his poetic and delightful landscapes, must always rank high in the annals of art, nor must it be forgotten that all these men were pensionaries of the Grand Monarch.

5. WHY LOUIS XIV PERSECUTED THE JANSENISTS AND HUGUENOTS

To many European thinkers the Wars of Religion, so profitless in other respects, had taught one valuable lesson. They demonstrated conclusively that it was impossible to heal religious schisms *Limits of* by the sword. Persecution had failed to reunite all Chris- *seventeenth-* tians in one belief; bloodshed had only intensified the hatred *erance in* existing between the sects, until rulers were driven, re- *religion* luctantly, to tolerate divergent creeds and make the best of it. But in the seventeenth century such tolerance was regarded, not as a virtue, but as a necessary evil. Where tolerance appeared, it was the fruit of exhaustion or of expediency, for religious passions were still narrow and strong and few men were really tolerant by conviction. The wise statesmanship of Henry IV, who consolidated France by extending protection and liberty to his Protestant subjects in the Edict of Nantes (1598), gained him many critics and few admirers. The absence, in the seventeenth century, of that genuine tolerance which recognizes every man's right to seek God after his own fashion must be kept in mind in judging the religious policy of Louis XIV.

To Louis the fact that a minority of his subjects clung to beliefs which he disliked indicated that they were self-willed to the point of treason. His desire to see all Frenchmen orthodox Catholics was not inspired by zeal for Rome; during most of his reign he was on hostile terms with the papacy; but he considered that to be one hundred per cent French and one hundred per cent royalist, a subject must share the religion of his king. His conviction that to be unorthodox was to be disloyal — a conviction, be it noted, that often had some foundation — goes far to explain why Louis persecuted both the Jansenists and the Huguenots.

The Jansenists were a group of austere and dogmatic enthusiasts who derived their name and much of their teaching from a certain Jansen, *The Jansen-* Bishop of Ypres (1585–1638). Their somewhat unortho-
ist contro- dox views of salvation brought them into conflict with the
versy Jesuits and were condemned by a papal bull in 1653. But the movement took on new life when Blaise Pascal, the famous scientist (1623–62), defended it in his *Lettres Provinciales* in 1656, so that the controversy between the puritanical doctrines of the Jansenists and the more worldly teaching of the Jesuits stirred all France. In 1661, Louis determined to suppress the Jansenists. He had little patience with their austere morality, considered them hair-splitting trouble-makers, and knew that many of them had sympathized with the Frondeurs. The effort to silence them was only partly successful; toward the end of his reign Louis was driven to invite the assistance of the Pope, Clement XI, who obligingly condemned the Jansenist doctrines in 1708 and again in 1713, while Louis had the convent at Port-Royal, a center of Jansenist piety near Paris, leveled to the ground. He preferred his subjects to be religious without too much enthusiasm; and he never forgot, as his memoirs attest, that some of the Jansenists had once engaged in anti-royalist activities.

The same spirit actuated Louis in his treatment of the French Protestants. The right to garrison a number of towns, a right which had been
Revocation accorded these Huguenots by the Edict of Nantes (1598),
of the Edict had been rescinded by Richelieu, but they still retained
of Nantes their freedom of worship and the full liberties of French
(1685) citizens. Unhappily, influences were at work which convinced Louis by 1680 that he owed it to his greatness to convert this recalcitrant minority among his subjects to the Catholic faith. He was engaged at the time in his controversy with the pope, and it was a politic method of proving that although he might disagree with Rome he had the propagation of the faith at heart. Moreover, his orderly mind disliked exceptions, and he was afraid that the Huguenots might find their loyalty divided when France was at war with a Protestant

[34]

power. So he acquiesced in a campaign of conversion. The Huguenots were gradually stripped of their schools and places of worship. Gifts of money were offered those who accepted Catholicism, but professional proselytes discredited this method by their repeated conversions. Then harsher means were invoked, and the minister of war, Louvois, encouraged his officers to quarter dragoons and other troops in Huguenot homes, with instructions to make their presence as unpleasant as possible. That Louis knew of the indignities to which many industrious and law-abiding citizens were subjected during these *dragonnades* is improbable. He was surprised and pleased at the number of conversions that followed, and in 1685, believing that there were few Huguenots left, he was persuaded by Madame de Maintenon and his Jesuit confessor to revoke the Edict of Nantes.

The result was a loss to France of some two hundred thousand of her worthiest citizens. They fled for refuge to Holland, to England, to Prussia, and even to America, taking with them what they could of their wealth, but taking also an even more precious gift to the countries they reinforced, their skill in trade and manufacture, their industry and their courage. The emigration of these trained artisans was a severe blow to the progress of French industry which Colbert had so zealously fostered, but this was not the only evil. The poorer Huguenots, who could not afford to flee, took up arms in defense of their faith and defied from their fastnesses in the Cevennes all the royal efforts to crush them. Their resistance did not end until after the death of Louis XIV, when they were finally pacified by a grant of toleration. The bigotry of the Great King not only failed to bring about that religious uniformity which he desired for his kingdom, but weakened France and enriched her enemies. Yet such was the spirit of the age that the Revocation of the Edict of Nantes was widely hailed in Catholic countries as the most statesmanlike, the most courageous, and the most glorious act of Louis's reign.

6. THE WARS OF LOUIS XIV

The greatest defect in Louis's character, greater even than the bigotry which impelled him to revoke the Edict of Nantes, was his love of martial glory. The predominance of France made that nation secure from foreign attack, therefore the wars which Louis precipitated were wars of deliberate and undisguised aggression. Where there is a will there is always a way to find a subject for international dispute: the most fertile

The doctrine of the natural frontiers of France

cause of conflict in the seventeenth century was the Bourbon-Hapsburg rivalry, and Louis revived that by asserting the need of France to realize her "natural frontiers." The map on the opposite page will show that Nature has set certain geographical barriers which might be taken to represent natural boundaries for the French kingdom, the most important being the river Rhine, the Alps, and the Pyrenees. To appreciate how conveniently the doctrine of "natural frontiers" accommodated itself to the furtherance of Louis's dynastic policy, it should be noted that in order to reach the Rhine the French would have to annex Franche Comté, the Rhenish Palatinate, the Spanish Netherlands, and about one fifth of the Dutch Republic, all of which (except the last-named) were territories under the sovereignty of Spanish or Austrian Hapsburgs.

A clause in the Peace of the Pyrenees (1659) had provided that Louis XIV should marry Maria Theresa, eldest daughter of the Spanish king,

The War of Devolution (1667–68) Philip IV. Philip died in 1665, leaving one other daughter, and (by a second marriage) a sickly son who succeeded him as Charles II. Louis promptly claimed the Spanish Netherlands as his wife's share of the Spanish Empire, advancing a doubtful argument known as the "principle of devolution," which was based upon the legal rule that property (in some provinces of the Netherlands) descended exclusively to children of a first marriage. The Spanish replied that an empire was not landed estate, and repudiated Louis's demands, whereupon he found stronger arguments. In 1667, he conquered a number of towns in the disputed territory, and the following year his armies overran Franche Comté. The European states regarded these martial parades with growing apprehension. England and Holland forgot a trade war which they had been waging shortly before, and joined with Sweden in a Triple Alliance against the warlike French king. Louis decided to make peace before a general conflict ensued, and agreed to restore Franche Comté, but retained eleven towns in Flanders, including Lille, Tournai, and Charleroi (Treaty of Aix-la-Chapelle, 1668).

The sturdy Dutch boasted somewhat arrogantly that their promptness in forming the Triple Alliance had checked the Sun King in mid-career.

The Dutch War (1672–78) Louis had no love for these "maggots" whom he disliked for their republican institutions and their Calvinist theology. Moreover, the Dutch had recently introduced retaliatory tariffs damaging to French trade. So Louis shrewdly prepared his revenge. Sweden was detached from the Triple Alliance by liberal bribes; English neutrality was purchased by pensioning the venal

**EXTENSION OF THE
FRENCH FRONTIERS, 1552-1766**

SCALE OF MILES

0   25   50   75   100

Gains of Henry IV, 1601-1643

Gained by Treaty of Westphalia, 1648

 "   "   "   " the Pyrenees, 1659

Gains of Louis XIV, 1668-1697

Gains of 1697-1766

Charles II (Treaty of Dover, 1670). In June, 1672, without warning, Louis hurled his well-trained army against Holland. The Dutch opened the dikes and flooded the countryside to delay the invaders, and in their desperation they murdered their grand pensionary, John de Witt, whom they blamed unjustly for their predicament. The defense of the republic was then entrusted to William, youthful head of the house of Orange, who was thus initiated at twenty-two into his lifelong task of humbling Louis XIV.

Sympathy for the Dutch and fear for themselves soon drove other European states to oppose France. The Emperor Leopold and the Elector of Brandenburg came to the aid of Holland; Den- *Treaty of* mark, Spain, and finally England joined the alliance; and *Nijmegen* by 1678, Louis was ready to make peace. Although the *(1678)* French soldiers under Condé and Turenne had won brilliant successes against the allies and earned the title of Huns by the ferocity with which they had devastated the Palatinate, France was suffering from exhaustion. By the Treaty of Nijmegen (1678) Louis retained Franche Comté and exchanged some frontier positions in Flanders to his advantage. He had taken another step toward the Rhine, once more at the expense of Spain; but the Dutch had escaped his vengeance, and even managed, in the final treaty, to extort from France a more favorable tariff for their goods.

Changing his tactics, Louis now strove to establish legal claims to the territories which he sought to conquer. He appointed special courts, or "chambers of reunion," to resurrect forgotten titles of sovereignty on the strength of which his armies *The "gnaw-* would quietly occupy the disputed ground. In 1680, the *ing peace"* cities of Metz, Toul, and Verdun were declared annexed to France; in 1681, the imperial city of Strasbourg was seized; and in 1683, it was the turn of Luxemburg. To resist the unscrupulous projects of the French king, Spain, the Holy Roman Empire, Holland, Sweden, and Bavaria united to form the League of Augsburg (1686), and when Louis attempted to seize the Rhenish Palatinate (1687), he precipitated a third war.

The opening of the war in 1689 was marked by an event which augured ill for France. In 1688, the English drove out James II (who had succeeded his brother Charles II in 1685) and wel- *War of the* comed William of Orange as their king. This "Glorious *League of* Revolution," which is related in the subsequent chapter, *Augsburg* *(1689–97)* united the resources of Holland and England under a man who had proved himself the most patient, the most skilled, and the most implacable of Louis's opponents. England promptly joined the League of Augsburg, and the struggle which ensued showed that the preponderance of France was passing. The French navy, which Colbert had dreamed of making the strongest in the world, was outfought by the English and Dutch; the French army failed in the later years of the war to repeat its early successes. In the Peace of Ryswick (1697), Louis was compelled to restore almost all the territories adjudged him by the chambers of reunion except Strasbourg; to abandon Lorraine and his claim to the Palatinate; to recognize William of Orange as King of England; and to concede a favorable commercial treaty to the Dutch.

In 1700, the long-expected demise of Charles II of Spain brought to the fore the question of the Spanish succession. With death at his *Philip of Anjou ascends the Spanish throne* elbow, Charles had summoned strength to dictate a testament naming Philip of Anjou, grandson of Louis XIV, as his successor. The will was a triumph of French diplomacy, but Louis knew that his enemies would never permit such aggrandizement to befall the house of Bourbon without a struggle. Nevertheless, he accepted the bequest, and bade his grandson mount the throne at Madrid. As if he was determined to make war unavoidable, he then seized some border fortresses in the Spanish Netherlands, and proclaimed the exiled Stuart Pretender (the son of James II) King of England. As a result his adversaries organized a "Grand Alliance" against him, which by 1702 included Austria, England, Holland, and Brandenburg. Thus opened the War of the Spanish Succession, the last and most exhausting of the wars of Louis XIV.

William of Orange (William III of England after 1689), who had been the moving spirit in forming the Grand Alliance, died at the opening of the war (1702), but the English possessed an even more brilliant soldier in John Churchill, Duke of Marlborough (1650–1722), whose victories at Blenheim (1704), Ramilies (1706), Oudinarde (1708), and Malplaquet (1709) drove the French out of the Germanies and wrested the Netherlands from their control. In the south the French halo of invincibility was likewise stripped away by the inspired tactics of Prince Eugène of Savoy, for the duchy of Savoy, which guarded the passes into Italy, had also joined the Grand Alliance. The resulting exhaustion and misery of France forced the Grand Monarch to sue for peace in 1709, but, finding the allies' terms too severe, he appealed to the French and Spanish people to continue the fighting. In 1710, the Whigs, the war party in England, were overthrown, and England practically withdrew from the struggle. The next year a worse embarrassment confused the councils of the Grand Alliance. They had been planning to place the Archduke Charles of Austria on the Spanish throne after expelling the Bourbon, Philip V, but by 1711 a succession of unexpected deaths in the Hapsburg family made Charles heir to the Austrian and imperial thrones also. The English and Dutch were profoundly dissatisfied to think that they had fought a ten years' war in order to replace a Bourbon preponderance by a Hapsburg hegemony.

In the peace settlement France profited by the disagreement among her enemies. The treaties which concluded the War of the Spanish Succession were negotiated in 1713 and 1714 and are known collectively as the Peace of Utrecht. The terms of this settlement, which brought Europe thirty years of comparative peace, may be summarized as follows.

Peace of Utrecht (1713–14)

(1) Philip V was allowed to retain the Spanish throne on condition that the crowns of France and Spain were never to be united.

(2) In compensation the Austrian Hapsburgs received the Spanish (henceforth to be known as the Austrian) Netherlands, and Milan, Naples, and Sardinia.

(3) The Dutch were reinvested with the "barrier fortresses" against France, and were granted a trade monopoly of the river Scheldt.

(4) The Elector of Brandenburg acquired Spanish Guelderland, and was permitted to assume the title of "King in Prussia."

(5) The Duke of Savoy was rewarded with the title of king and the addition of Sicily to his domains. (In 1720 he exchanged Sicily for Sardinia and styled himself King of Sardinia.)

(6) England was not interested in continental lands, though she kept Gibraltar and Minorca which she had wrested from Spain. Her prizes were the French colonies: Newfoundland, Acadia, and Hudson Bay, supplemented by such commercial privileges as a preferential tariff with Spain, the right to send one ship a year to the Spanish colonies to trade, and a monopoly of the lucrative traffic in slaves.

France was still a great nation, but her ascendancy no longer threatened Europe. War had exhausted the state and impoverished the people. Louis XIV outlived his most capable servants, outlived his son and his grandson, and almost, one might say, outlived himself. "My child," the dying monarch exhorted his great-grandson, five years of age, "you are going to be a great king. Do not imitate me in my taste for building, nor in my love of war. Strive, on the contrary, to live in peace with your neighbors. . . . Make it your endeavor to ease the burden of the people, which I, unhappily, have not been able to do. . . ." The sentiment was excellent, but it shared the fatality that attends most good resolutions in that it came too late. And Louis XV was too young to profit by it.

Death of Louis XIV (1715)

CHAPTER THREE

THE TRIUMPH OF PARLIAMENTARY GOVERNMENT IN ENGLAND

In all cases where government subsists, the legislature is the supreme power.
JOHN LOCKE (1690).

WHILE Louis XIV was dazzling Europe with his brilliant and irresponsible display of power, across the Channel in England the cause of royal absolutism suffered a reverse. The English had never taken kindly to the rule of a despot, and the same years which saw the French monarchy reach its apogee witnessed in England the triumph of the Parliament over the king. By 1715, France and England had come to represent two divergent types of government. In France an absolute king, with the support of the privileged aristocracy, claimed the right to make the laws by the will of God; in England, a Parliament controlled by the ruling classes of the kingdom limited the royal prerogative and allowed the sovereign to make laws only "by and with the consent of the lords, spiritual and temporal, and the commons."

It is not easy to account for this divergence. One important factor to note, however, is that the French had found it necessary to concede arbitrary power to their kings as the best security against the invasion or disunion of their country, and the greatness of the monarchy had come to symbolize for patriotic Frenchmen the glory of France. The English kings, although they furthered the national growth, were never in the same degree essential to it, for the island kingdom was practically secure from invasion and possessed a geographic unity. Hence, while in France the right of maintaining a large army, of collecting and spending the revenue, and even of borrowing and repudiating debts, were left to the king's discretion, in England these privileges were gradually curtailed by a critical Parliament. When Charles I, misunderstanding the situation, attempted to rule like a despot, he precipitated a civil war and paid for his misconception with his head (1649).

Yet the English people were royalist at heart. A decade of kingless rule under the stern and militaristic Protector, Oliver Cromwell, left *Restoration* the nation weary of the Puritan Commonwealth. Crom- *of Charles II* well's death in 1658 prepared the way for the restoration of the Stuart line, and in 1660, Charles II (son of Charles I) was acclaimed king "by the grace of God." At the same time he agreed to

[40]

limit his power and promised to summon Parliament regularly, with the understanding that he was to levy no taxes and make no changes in religion without parliamentary approval. This was a reasonable compromise and might have proved a durable one if Charles, and his successor James, had been honest in keeping their part of the bargain.

1. CHARLES II: A DESPOT IN DISGUISE

The general desire for harmony prevalent in 1660 assured the settlement a fair trial, but its perpetuation until after Charles's death in 1685 is a tribute to that monarch's duplicity. Though he *Charles II* played the rôle of a Protestant and constitutional ruler, *(1660–85)* Charles was a Catholic and absolutist in his secret convictions — if so shifty a character may be said to have convictions. This witty, affable, indolent Stuart was one of the most capable conspirators that ever held a throne. Confined in his prerogatives by a jealous and watchful Parliament, he plotted for twenty years by bribery, by adroit encroachments, even by treason, to win to absolute power, and he had reached the point of success when death cut short the fruition of his plans in his fifty-fifth year.

The haughty Louis XIV chose for his motto, *Nec pluribus impar* (not unequal to many, or a match for all), but Charles II followed the more cautious precept, *Divide et impera*. To "divide and rule" the various political factions until he could play one against another and make himself master of all was the cue to his patient policy. There were four major factions in England under the Restoration: (1) The Anglicans, who wished to see the Church of England the state church, and opposed the tolerance of dissenters. (2) the "squirearchy," country squires and gentry who had, many of them, opposed the despotism of James I and Charles I, but, finding the civil war and the Puritan Commonwealth even less to their liking, had welcomed the restoration of Charles II. These first two groups were closely identified. In addition there were: (3) the merchant and trading classes of the cities which desired to control Parliament in order to supervise taxation and direct foreign policy; and (4) the "dissenters," a term applied to members of various Puritan sects who were denied civil and military offices because they "dissented" from the teaching of the Anglican Church. Nor must the Roman Catholics be forgotten, of whom a minority still persisted in England despite persecution, while by far the greater number of the Irish people were of that faith.

[41]

For the first ten years of his reign Charles trod warily, for he found the "Cavalier" Parliament, elected in 1660, loyal but headstrong. *The "Cavalier" Parliament (1660–79)* This Parliament was dominated by the squirearchy and the supporters of Anglicanism, who promptly applied their power, the country gentlemen to obtain remission of the remaining feudal dues levied on their lands and the Anglicans to restore the Church of England to its full privileges and to punish dissent. All who were not Anglicans were barred from a share in municipal government (Corporation Act, 1661); two thousand Puritan clergy were expelled from the church for refusing assent to the prescribed Prayer Book (Act of Uniformity, 1662); and dissenters who persisted in attending nonconformist services were condemned to imprisonment or transportation (Conventicle Act, 1664). Charles himself had little patience with this persecution; his secret desire was to make not Anglicanism but Catholicism triumphant; but he bent for the time to the wishes of Parliament.

In 1665, the "Great Plague" carried off thousands of people in London, to be followed a year later by the "Great Fire" which destroyed half the city. To many a Puritan these disasters were signs of God's anger against a wicked and immoral king, for Charles set the example for a licentious court and was held responsible, as well, for the persecution which Parliament enforced against the dissenters. In 1667, a third misfortune occurred when a Dutch fleet sailed up the Thames to London and burned a number of English ships.

England had begun a second trade war with Holland in 1665 (the first was fought in 1651–54 under Cromwell). The scepter of commercial supremacy was passing from the Dutch to the English and London had become the great trade rival of Amsterdam. *Expansion of English trade* In his languid way Charles helped to promote this development. The Navigation Acts, limiting British colonial trade to British ships, were renewed, the navy improved, new possessions acquired (Tangiers and Bombay), and in 1664, New Amsterdam was captured from the Dutch and renamed New York. Dissenters, persecuted at home, swelled the population of the colonies, while city traders and courtiers eager for profit organized companies, such as the Honorable Company of Gentlemen Adventurers Trading into Hudson's Bay (better known as the Hudson's Bay Company), which was chartered in 1670. As the various companies, encouraged by the English, French, Dutch, and other national governments, often held conflicting charters, the traders frequently descended to acts of war and piracy at the expense of their rivals. In this somewhat unscrupulous contest the English were

[42]

CHARLES II OF ENGLAND
1630–1685

This Stuart monarch was indolent and sensual,
but he had affable manners and a shrewd mind.

destined to outstrip all competitors and secure the lion's share of the spoils. And the spoils were a world empire.

The extraordinary prosperity of the Dutch in the seventeenth century made England and Holland inevitable trade rivals, but the two states *Third war* had also two strong sentiments in common: both were *between* Protestant and both feared and hated France. It was *England and Holland* therefore logical that the two maritime powers should *(1672–74)* draw closer together as the lengthening shadow of a French hegemony spread across Europe. How deeply the English people feared France and Catholicism, Charles II failed to comprehend. By the secret Treaty of Dover (1670) he promised to aid Louis XIV in the attack the latter contemplated against Holland, and agreed to restore the Catholic faith in England in return for a subsidy that would make him practically independent of parliamentary grants. Charles's first step was to issue a declaration of indulgence for dissenters including Catholics (1672). To his surprise there was an immediate protest, rumors of a Catholic plot began to spread, and Parliament insisted upon the withdrawal of the indulgence. Though the English were hoodwinked into joining in the war on Holland (1672), their conviction grew that in so doing they were furthering the sinister designs of Louis XIV and in 1674 they withdrew from the conflict.

Fear of a popish plot, once roused, continued to terrify the nation. James, Duke of York, brother of Charles and heir to the throne, con-*The popish* fessed himself a Catholic and became the hope of that *plot (1678)* party, but Charles, more astute, took refuge in hypocrisy. In 1678, an adventurer named Titus Oates announced his discovery of a conspiracy to murder Charles and set his brother in his place with the assistance of a French army. Conspiring of a sort there had undoubtedly been, though it is doubtful if Oates knew anything about it, but his perjured testimony sufficed in the frenzy of popular fear to send a score of innocent Catholics to death. And Charles, who "believed not one word of what was called Oates's plot," signed the warrants.

In the tension of feeling excited by the popish plot, political leaders ranged themselves more definitely in two opposing parties and the *The Exclu-* shadow of a second civil war hung over the land. Those *sion Bill* who supported the king and the Anglican Church were *(1679)* nicknamed Tories,[1] while the faction which favored a constitutional monarchy under a Protestant king, with toleration for

---

[1] Those who sought to preserve the prerogatives of the crown were called Tories by their opponents, the term being borrowed apparently from the Irish, who applied it to certain outlaws professedly royalist.

dissenters, came to be known as the Whig Party.[1]   In the elections of 1679, the Whigs swept the country, ending the eighteen-year rule of the Cavalier Parliament.   They promptly proposed an exclusion bill to bar James from the throne as a Catholic.   Charles thereupon dissolved Parliament; but a second Whig Parliament was elected and passed the bill (1680), only to see it thrown out by the House of Lords. A third Parliament met at Oxford with the Whigs blustering and arming. "Like father, like son," they declared, and prepared to fight for their liberties in the spirit of 1642.   But they overreached themselves; hatred of military rule was still strong in England and the country was not prepared to follow the Whigs into another civil war.   If war was the only alternative to despotism, the nation preferred the genial despotism of Charles and respected him when he dissolved the unruly Oxford Parliament as soon as it assembled.   The only point the Whigs had won in their campaign to limit the king's power was their passage of the Habeas Corpus Act (1679), which provided that no subject accused of crime was to be held at the king's pleasure, but must be brought before a judge within a specified time and the charge against him indicated.

After 1681, Charles felt strong enough to rule alone and refused to summon another Parliament.   Left in this way without any constitutional means of resistance, some of the more desperate Whigs plotted to assassinate Charles and James and set the Duke of Monmouth, an illegitimate son of Charles, on the throne.   *Charles rules alone (1681–85)*   The discovery of this Rye House Plot (1683) led to the execution or exile of the principal Whig leaders.   With the opponents of the crown thus discredited, Charles was secure in his despotism and the Tories helped him to stifle self-government in the towns and suppress free speech.   A subsidy from Louis XIV permitted him to meet expenses and increase his army.   But the plan to re-establish Catholicism he dropped from his program: that was the price he had to pay for Tory support and Charles was too shrewd to miscalculate the temper of the nation a second time.   After twenty years of trimming, he had found a way to rule without Parliament and without serious opposition from the country, but death cut short his triumph in 1685.

2. JAMES II: A DESPOT IN DIFFICULTIES

When James II (1685–88) ascended the English throne, he had many circumstances in his favor.   Although he was known to be a Catholic,

---

[1] The Whigs were Scottish Presbyterians who defied the royal power in defense of their religion.   Hence the name was applied derisively to the party which desired to limit the royal prerogatives and tolerate dissenters in England.

it was supposed that he would make his faith a private matter and confirm the privileges of the Anglican Church. In return for such protection, the churchmen were prepared to teach the doctrine of non-resistance, i.e., that it was wicked and blasphemous to resist the king, because he was ordained of God. So long as James was careful to retain the support of the Tory Party (the Anglican clergy and the country squires), his throne was reasonably safe; for many Whigs hesitated to oppose the legitimate king; others wanted the Duke of Monmouth in his place; while still others favored William of Orange, Stadholder of the Dutch Republic, who had married James's daughter Mary. Divided in this fashion, the Whig Party was powerless to prevent the coronation of James.

Nevertheless, in June, 1685, simultaneous revolts were organized in England and Scotland by followers of the Duke of Monmouth, Charles's *Monmouth's* illegitimate son. Both failed and were followed by the *rebellion and* famous "Bloody Assizes" under Judge Jeffreys, in which *death (1685)* over a thousand suspected persons were condemned to death or transportation. James rewarded Jeffreys's zeal with the lord chancellorship, and sent Monmouth, who had been taken prisoner, to the block. Nothing could have been better calculated to strengthen the cause of the opposition faction; the bloody reprisals disgusted many people, while the death of Monmouth left the Whig malcontents no choice but to unite in support of William and Mary. At the same time the Revocation of the Edict of Nantes sent thousands of French Huguenots to England, where the vivid tale of their sufferings taught Englishmen what they might expect at the hands of a Catholic king.

Charles II had discovered that the English people might be made to endure absolutism, but would never accept Catholicism, but James was blind to the handwriting on the wall. As if determined to alienate every element in the nation, he proposed to maintain a permanent standing army, to repeal the Test Act which barred Roman Catholics from office, and the Act of Habeas Corpus also. When the Parliament which he had summoned protested, he prorogued it (November, 1685). Catholics were admitted to the privy council, granted commissions in the army, and even appointed to high office in the Anglican Church and the universities. In 1687, James issued a declaration of indulgence offering all his subjects the free exercise of their religion. The High Church Tories, even those who had preached that it was wrong under any circumstances to resist the lawful sovereign, found that these proceedings overstrained their loyalty, and James thus alienated many who, aside from the religious issue, were his stanchest partisans. Nor were the dissenters grateful to him for the indulgence as he had hoped; in England and Scotland nonconformists joined in denouncing an act which granted freedom of worship to Catholics. Still blind to consequences, James persisted in uniting the realm against him. A second declaration of indulgence was issued in 1688, and when seven bishops of the Anglican Church ventured to draw up a petition against it, James had them tried for libel and sedition. All England waited anxiously for the decision, and the news that the jury had voted for acquittal was the signal for wild rejoicing. It was ominous for James that even the royal army, which he had assembled near London to keep his capital in awe, cheered the verdict.

In the same month (June, 1688) a son was born to James and the news crystallized the discontent into active opposition. Many had been prepared to endure James's misrule, because he was over fifty and would be succeeded on his death by his Protestant daughter Mary. The birth of a son who would be raised in the Catholic faith ended this hope, and political leaders from both the Whig and Tory Parties dispatched a secret invitation to William of Orange to come and take the throne. William's life purpose was to defend Holland against the attack of Louis XIV; as King of England he might be able to combine the forces of both countries against France, and this argument persuaded him to accept the challenge. It was a dangerous stroke; the odds appeared to be all against success; but he displayed prudence and decision. At the news that William had landed (November 5, 1688), the English turned to him as a deliverer and James found himself deserted. William purposely allowed him to escape to France, for he had no wish to make his father-in-law a prisoner.

3. THE GLORIOUS REVOLUTION OF 1688

James's flight enabled a Convention Parliament, which met promptly, to offer the throne to William and Mary on the pretext that "King James ... having violated the fundamental laws, and *The Bill of* having withdrawn himself out of the Kingdom, had ab- *Rights* dicated ..." But the English had no intention of giving *(1689)* themselves into the power of a new despot; Parliament had learned at last not to put too much trust in princes and drew up a settlement which was enacted into law as the Bill of Rights. It provided: (1) That the sovereign had no power to suspend or dispense with the laws, to erect special courts of justice, maintain a standing army, or levy taxes without the consent of Parliament. (2) That Parliament should meet frequently, the members to be freely elected and allowed freedom in their debates. (3) That subjects were entitled to petition the monarch without fear of prosecution, that those charged with crimes could not be refused jury trial, nor could they be exposed to cruel or unusual punishments.

The religious settlement was embodied in the Toleration Act (1689), which granted freedom of worship to all except Catholics and Unitarians. This act did not establish religious equality; the Anglican Church remained the privileged state church, and the Test and Corporation Acts still barred dissenters and Catholics from civil and military office. Nevertheless, a long stride had been made toward genuine toleration, for after 1689 the government ceased to persecute, imprison, or transport people on religious grounds and the mobs lost their zest for Jesuit-hunting.

Unfortunately, this statesmanlike moderation was not applied to Ireland. Cromwell, it may be recalled, attempted to keep the Irish in subjection by dividing the land among Protestant proprietors, thus reducing the native Catholic Irish to a position of social and economic bondage. The plan failed because the English settlers were too unpopular and too few in number. James II determined to restore the Catholics to power and his overthrow grieved his Irish subjects as deeply as it delighted the English. In 1689, an uprising of the Irish broke the Protestant yoke, and in 1690, James came over from France to lead the rebellion and if possible to invade England with a French and Irish force. William III realized that his newly won throne was in danger. The French fleet, having defeated the English and Dutch at the battle of Beachy Head (June, 1690), was free to land an army on the English coast itself. To control Ireland and restore James II were to Louis XIV but preliminary moves in his vast struggle for the hegemony of Europe. The success or failure of an Irish revolt was thus transformed into a matter of European significance, and when William defeated James at the battle of the Boyne (July 1, 1790), it meant that Louis XIV had lost the first round in the War of the League of Augsburg which was just opening.

For the Irish the battle of the Boyne spelled further subordination and exploitation at the hands of their stronger neighbors. Irish com-
The Irish problem merce was regulated and sometimes ruined for the advantage of English trade, while all but a minority of the inhabitants of the unhappy isle were shut out from a share in their own government because they were Catholics. This determination to hold the native Irish in subjection was founded in the fear that Ireland might

otherwise join any European power that attacked England, a danger
that has always warped the Englishman's mind when he considered the
Irish question. This sacrifice of justice to expediency has sown a bitter
heritage of discord between the two countries and the Irish have never
forgiven their centuries of tutelage and subjection.

4. ENGLAND AND SCOTLAND BECOME GREAT BRITAIN

Between England and Scotland a happier settlement was achieved.
Following the "Glorious Revolution" those Scottish clans still favorable
to James were offered a chance to make peaceful submission and swear
allegiance to William, although one which was dilatory in complying
was given over to cold-blooded slaughter as an example — an infamous
episode known as the "Massacre of Glencoe." The tie which united
England and Scotland was in reality a frail one; an accident had made
James VI of Scotland James I of England (1603), but each state retained its separate parliament and its peculiar laws. When William
and Mary replaced James II, the dynastic tie was weakened and it appeared more than probable that the nations would drift apart. The
Scots, who numbered less than a million, were distrustful and envious
of their southern neighbors who had five times the population and a
world-embracing trade, but the English, who dreaded lest Scotland
desert to the side of France, were prepared to offer generous terms, to
achieve a "more perfect union." Under William's successor, Anne,
this end was attained by the Act of Union (1707), which *Act of*
provided that the two kingdoms were to be known as *Union*
Great Britain, the Scots sending forty-five representatives *(1707)*
to the English House of Commons and sixteen to the House of
Lords. Presbyterianism was recognized as the established faith in
Scotland.

The Act of Union, like most of the developments in English politics
during these years, was an indirect response to the French threat.
During twenty of the first twenty-five years that followed the expulsion
of James, England was fighting Louis XIV, in the War of the League
of Augsburg (1689–97) and the War of the Spanish Succession (1701–13).
Throughout this period James II (and after his death in 1701, his son
who took the title James III) threatened to invade England and regain
the throne with the aid of a French army. A Stuart restoration thus
became inseparable from the idea of national humiliation and defeat, a
consummation few Englishmen were prepared to applaud. It is a fact
not without irony that, by aiding the Stuarts, Louis XIV, the supreme

absolutist of the Continent, did more than any other single individual to assure the triumph of Parliament in England.

The political leaders who had invited William and Mary to take the throne, in order "to save the liberties and the religion of England,"
Act of Settlement (1701) felt it best to safeguard the revolutionary gains won through this act of usurpation by regulating the succession. It was provided that if William and Mary died childless, the throne should pass to Mary's sister Anne and her descendants. Unfortunately, Anne's children died young, and the fear that her own death would leave the crown to the Pretender moved Parliament to decree as her successor her nearest Protestant relative, the Electress Sophia of Hanover.[1] By this Act of Settlement, Parliament once again arrogated to itself the right to select the sovereign and to define the conditions under which he must rule. In an age of legitimacy, such an act appeared to many, even in England, an illegal and revolutionary decision. The Pretender had his partisans, and the whole revolutionary settlement still hung on the question whether, on Anne's death, the Tories would proclaim the Pretender as James III or the Whigs would bring in the Hanoverian line. In the outcome, despite Jacobite [2] plots, Whig principles triumphed. On Anne's sudden death (1714), George, son of the Electress Sophia, was proclaimed King of Great Britain and Ireland. A rising in Scotland in 1715 in favor of the Stuart Pretender was put down and the rule of Parliament assured under the king that Parliament had chosen.

5. SIGNIFICANCE OF THE SEVENTEENTH CENTURY IN ENGLISH HISTORY

In the century which ended in 1715 the English people had overturned, re-established, and remodeled their monarchy until they had reduced it to a pattern which satisfied them. In the same period they had fought strenuously on land and sea, laying the foundations of a colonial empire and commercial supremacy. It is not always easy for a student who follows the crowded events of these years to distinguish the main lines of development, so that it may be helpful to pause at the date 1715 and decide what were the really significant and durable achievements of the seventeenth century in English history.

In politics the nation had succeeded after two revolutions in reducing

[1] See the Genealogical Table of English Rulers in the Appendix.

[2] Those who favored the Pretender were called Jacobites from the Latin word for James, *Jacobus.*

the royal power within clearly stipulated limits. The sovereign had become dependent upon Parliament for his revenue, he could *Political* not raise an army without parliamentary approval, nor could *achievements* he any longer deprive a subject of his liberty or property at pleasure, for the laws guaranteed anyone accused of crime a fair and public trial before a jury of his fellow citizens (Habeas Corpus Act, 1679; Bill of Rights, 1689). Citizens were no longer to be persecuted for their religious beliefs (Toleration Act, 1689); but the Bill of Rights provided that no one who was a Roman Catholic or married to a Roman Catholic might occupy the English throne, and Parliament asserted this principle by excluding the legitimate Stuart claimants and choosing the Hanoverian line to succeed Anne (Act of Succession, 1701). When George I ascended the English throne in 1714, he became king by the will of Parliament, and he knew it; English sovereigns thenceforth were to *reign* but not to *govern*, and the rule of Parliament was assured. In analysis, this meant the rule of the nobles, the country gentry, and the merchant classes, for these were the groups which dominated Parliament.· Under William and Anne it became the custom for the sovereign to select Whig or Tory leaders to compose the royal council, according to which party held a majority in the Commons, and the council thus chosen exercised the executive power in the king's name, but in response to the wishes and subject to the approval of Parliament.

The seventeenth century was also for England an age of swift economic development. New companies were chartered, new colonies seized or founded almost yearly. For the aid which the English *Commercial* rendered in checking the power of Louis XIV, they received *expansion* a generous reward. The Peace of Utrecht transferred Acadia, Newfoundland, and the Hudson Bay region to English rule, as well as Gibraltar and Minorca. Great Britain was rapidly becoming the foremost mercantile and colonial power in the world, which helps to explain why the country was able to establish a dozen settlements in America, to challenge the maritime supremacy of the Dutch, and finally to endure the enormous burden of the struggle against Louis XIV, without serious privation, while France, a nation with more than three times the population of England, was reduced to the verge of bankruptcy.

Part of the explanation for the English victories must be sought in the financial expedients to which the government resorted to meet the cost of the wars with France. The annual revenue proving *Financial* insufficient to cover the expenditures of the war years, bor- *solidarity* rowing was found to be the best solution, with the result that the national debt rose by 1715 to the hitherto unimagined figure of £50,000,000. In

1694, the Bank of England was founded and invested with banking privileges in return for the loans it advanced to the government. At first sight this extensive borrowing might appear reckless and improvident, but it had certain advantages. Without it the nation could not have prosecuted the war to a successful conclusion and reaped the rewards of victory. A precedent was established and a credit structure developed which was to serve the government needs admirably in later wars; England's financial strength has often proved the mainstay of her allies. Moreover, the thousands of people with capital to spare who invested it in government bonds did so with the confidence that Parliament (which the moneyed class largely controlled) would see to it that principal and interest were repaid. Only defeat or a Stuart restoration could endanger the national debt, so these creditors had a powerful motive for supporting the existing régime. When a responsible Parliament backed a bond, it meant more than the word of an absolute king. The English government was able to borrow all the funds it required at six and seven per cent, while Louis XIV found it difficult to secure loans even when he offered fifteen to twenty per cent. As observers began to contrast the success and prosperity of Great Britain with the losses and impoverishment of France, they grew less confident that absolutism was really the ideal form of government. In the eighteenth century, as we shall discover later, Frenchmen conceived a profound admiration for the system of government which the English had established. Their desire to reshape their own absolute monarchy until it resembled the English model was one of the causes which brought about the great French Revolution that broke out in 1789.

In literary achievement the close of the seventeenth century fell short of its opening years — "the spacious times of great Elizabeth." The *Achievements in literature and art* political and religious controversies which absorbed the energies of the nation colored the work of even the greatest writers. John Milton (1608–74), who had given his best years and worn out his sight in the service of the Puritan Commonwealth, withdrew at the restoration of Charles II, "blind, old, and lonely," to compose his majestic epics *Paradise Lost* and *Paradise Regained*. The poet laureate of the Restoration was John Dryden (1631–1700), who produced a number of poems, satires, and dramas to amuse the dissolute court of Charles II, at which it became the fashion to ridicule the sober habits and bigotry of the Puritans. Despite this mockery, the most widely read work of the age came from the pen of a Puritan tinker, John Bunyan, who wrote his *Pilgrim's Progress* while in jail for preaching without leave. The common sense and moderation which distinguished the civil and religious settlement of 1689 are admirably represented in the writings of the philosopher John Locke (1632–1704), particularly his *Letter on Toleration* and *Two Treatises of Government*. The controversies of the seventeenth century stimulated the rise of pamphlet literature and created a class of readers in England capable of criticizing public affairs. To keep this class informed was the task of the journalists, who consequently demanded "freedom of the press," and finally won it in principle after 1694. Pamphlets and periodicals multiplied, and by the reign of Anne they had attained a vast influence and a high standard of literary excellence, a development not surprising when it is remembered that the sardonic humor of Jonathan Swift (1667–1745), the author of *Gulliver's Travels*, as well as the wit of Joseph Addison (1672–1719), borrowed this means of expression.

In architecture the outstanding figure of the period was Christopher Wren (1632–1723), to whom the Great Fire of London in 1666 proved a generous patron, for it brought him innumerable commissions. He is credited with designing over fifty churches, including Saint Paul's Cathedral, where he is buried beneath the inscription, *Si monumentum requiris, circumspice* — "If you seek [my] monument, look about you." The arts of painting and music throve but meagerly under the Restoration, for Charles as a patron had little taste or discrimination, while the Puritan spirit which still animated the middle and lower classes was inimical to art. In England the true intellectual greatness of the late seventeenth century must be sought among those minds devoted to science and mathematics. The development of modern science, however, is not a national but an international movement, and the achievements of such men as Sir Isaac Newton will be discussed in a later chapter where they can be more conveniently linked up with the contributions of Newton's illustrious contemporaries in other lands.

CHAPTER FOUR

THE DECLINING EMPIRE OF THE HAPSBURGS

The dear old Holy Roman Realm,
How does it hold together ...
GOETHE, *Faust*, Part I, Scene v.

AS ALREADY explained, the aggrandizement of France in the seventeenth century involved a corresponding decline in the fortunes of the Hapsburg dynasty. Part of Flanders, of Lorraine, and the whole of Franche Comté were seized by Louis XIV; and after 1700, Spain, under a Bourbon prince, became the constant ally of France, the two powers being bound together by a common hostility toward Austria and toward England. The title of Holy Roman Emperor, though still retained by the head of the Austrian Hapsburgs, had become an illusory honor, for the empire was little more than an historical fiction kept alive by the force of tradition. These vicissitudes in the fortunes of a once dominant dynasty have already been described in part. The present chapter will trace the history of the Hapsburg dominions in greater detail through the years 1660 to 1715, and relate at the same time the contemporary developments in Italy and eastern Europe.

1. THE AUSTRIAN HAPSBURGS

The Emperor Leopold I (1658–1705), whose long reign filled the greater part of the period under discussion, was a timid and irresolute man, no match in either war or diplomacy for his aggressive cousin Louis XIV. As Archduke of Austria, and King of Bohemia and of Hungary, Leopold was hereditary ruler of dominions which, had they been better organized, would have constituted a powerful state of some nine or ten million people. In addition, he enjoyed the elective title of Holy Roman Emperor, which meant that he was the nominal ruler of the twenty-five million people living within the boundaries of the empire.[1] In this rôle he symbolized the unity of Germany, and the Hapsburgs might, under happier circumstances, have transformed the empire into a national German state, the most populous and powerful in Europe. But two persistent forces frustrated this project, although it was a consummation toward which many patriotic German hearts secretly aspired. The first obstacle was the jealous particularism of the German princes (especially the rulers

[1] See frontispiece.

[54]

of Brandenburg-Prussia), who clung to their semi-independent status and would not sacrifice it to consolidate the German-speaking peoples into one great nation. The second obstacle was the jealousy of France. It was a cardinal principle of French foreign policy to promote German disunity lest France be endangered by the formation of a powerful neighbor across the Rhine. In prosecuting this policy, France often allied herself with Prussia and other recalcitrant German states.

The machinery of government whereby the emperor sought to impose his will upon his federal empire had been out of joint since the Protestant Reformation. The imperial court (*Reichkammergericht*), to *Weakness of* which the princes sent representatives, had grown insolent *the imperial* and unmanageable; the imperial council (*Reichshofrath*), ap- *government* pointed by the emperor himself, was more tractable, but its decrees were often evaded or disregarded. Concerning all important matters which related to the empire as a whole, it had become the custom to consult the Diet, a sort of parliament composed chiefly of the leading German princes and representatives from the free towns. But in this assembly likewise the princes held the real power and would never vote the emperor the quota of men or money he demanded for fear that they might give themselves a real master. Their contributions for the defense of the empire were so niggardly that the imperial army often took the field with less than one fourth of its nominal strength. Not even the emergency created by the Turkish advance up the Danube could subdue the selfishness of the princes, and Leopold was obliged in 1663 to accept the aid of thirty thousand men in French pay to repel the invaders; while in 1683 he had John Sobieski and his Poles to thank that Vienna was saved from capture. The lack of support offered by the princes can be explained in part by the fact that many of them were Protestant and saw no advantage in strengthening a Catholic emperor, who might, if he gained the power, suppress the Protestant faith as an earlier emperor had essayed to do in the Thirty Years' War.

Not even in his hereditary domains could Leopold exercise the control of an absolute monarch. The provinces most securely in his power were Styria, Carinthia, Carniola, the archduchy of Austria, *The Haps-* and the county of Tyrol. In Bohemia he ruled as king, *burg Empire* with the assistance of a Diet, while in Hungary (nine tenths of which was held by the Turks in 1660) he found it expedient to confirm the ancient liberties of the nobles. Ineradicable barriers of language, of custom, and of topography contributed to the disunity of the Hapsburg lands. The disruptive forces of feudalism had survived too long, the havoc of the religious conflict had left wounds too deep, the lure of im-

[55]

perial pretensions had distracted the emperors too persistently from the task of consolidating their local domains, until the opportunity of building up a national state escaped them. Certainly the problem of unifying these mosaic possessions defied the mediocre talents of Leopold I. He clung inertly to his throne through the vicissitudes of the late seventeenth century, and, if the closing years of his reign witnessed a revival in Hapsburg prestige, the credit for this must be given to Austria's allies for their aid, and to her enemies for their blunders, rather than to any vigorous activity within the Austrian lands.

2. THE TURKISH MENACE

From the fourteenth century to the seventeenth, the Danube Valley was a vast battlefield where it seemed as if the resistance of the Christian inhabitants was destined to be slowly crushed by the power of the Turkish invaders. The western European nations, preoccupied with their own politics, remained amazingly indifferent to this threat from the East. Had the Turks possessed the ability to *govern* as well as the ability to *conquer*, half of Europe might have been theirs for the taking, and the future of the European peoples profoundly altered, but fortunately for the Christian states the Mohammedan Empire was a prey to internal ills which frequently paralyzed its armies in the hour of victory.

The chief limitation from which the Turks suffered was an inability to assimilate and organize their conquests. They remained always an *Characteristics of Turkish rule* alien military caste in Europe, living on the tribute they extorted from the conquered in the form of money, recruiting their armies from the tribute they extorted in men: for it was their custom to conscript boy children whom they raised as Mohammedans and trained for military service. Knowing better how to destroy than how to create, they left matters of trade and details of local administration to their subject peoples. At its core their government was an oriental despotism in which the reign of a strong sultan was usually characterized by pitiless autocracy, the reign of a weak one by harem intrigue and military anarchy. Such a system of despotism presents one great advantage, for it affords the really capable ruler unlimited power to energize the state. This fact largely explains the vicissitudes of fortune which have attended the march of the crescent, for, as "Sultan after Sultan with his Pomp abode his Hour or two and went his way," the prosperity of Islam fluctuated according to his capacity or that of his vizier.

The latter half of the seventeenth century witnessed a revival of the

Mohammedan offensive under the leadership of the Kiuprili family. As the power behind the throne, Mohammed Kiuprili (and later his son Achmed) stamped out anarchy and united all "true believers" in a war to the death against the Christians. *Turkish offensive (1655–83)* An attack on Hungary was repulsed at Saint Gothard (1663) by an imperial army aided by French troops; but in 1669, Crete was captured from the Venetians, and the Ukraine annexed from Poland in 1676. To crown these successes by a blow that would astonish Christendom, the grand vizier planned an irresistible drive against Vienna. With an army of one hundred and fifty thousand, he reached the walls of that city in 1683, but the arrival of John Sobieski with reinforcements led to the overwhelming defeat of the besiegers, and the Turkish tide ebbed as swiftly as it had risen. When peace was re-established between the emperor and the sultan by the Treaty of Carlowitz (1699), the Hapsburgs had recovered the greater part of the fertile Hungarian plain, and the suzerainty over Transylvania.[1] Corruption and anarchy had begun once more to devitalize the Mohammedan Empire and it settled into a slow decline. The crescent had made its last conquests from the cross.

In a second conflict — the dynastic duel with the Bourbons — the emperor was fortunate in finding powerful allies. Marlborough and Prince Eugène saved Vienna from the French in 1704 as Sobieski had saved it from the Turks in 1683. But, although the allies were victorious over France in the War of the Spanish Succession, the Hapsburgs lost the Spanish throne. Reluctant to acknowledge this reverse, the Emperor Charles VI[2] attempted in 1712 to continue the war against France unaided, although it was clear that France, even in exhaustion, was more than a match for Austria, and the Spaniards were ready to defend their Bourbon king devotedly. In 1713–14 the allies, whose assistance in the war had saved Austria from ruin, showed themselves equally generous in the peace.[3] Spain they could not restore to the house of Hapsburg, but in compensation Naples, *Peace of Utrecht (1713–14)* Milan, Sardinia, and the Spanish Netherlands were handed over to the emperor, so that he was consoled for the loss of Spain by a practical hegemony in Italy. Recognizing at the same time that the house of Austria was too feeble to prevent further French aggression, the diplomats provided that the Dutch should garrison certain "barrier for-

[1] See frontispiece.
[2] Leopold I died in 1705 and was followed by Joseph I, whose death in 1711 brought to the Austrian throne the Archduke Charles, Hapsburg claimant to the Spanish throne also.
[3] The treaties of Utrecht, Rastadt, and Baden are styled collectively the Peace of Utrecht.

tresses" in what were to be thenceforth the Austrian Netherlands, so that France might be held in check, while at the same time Savoy was organized as a buffer state between Bourbon and Hapsburg frontiers in the south.[1]

The house of Austria thus emerged, after the most critical half-century in its history, victorious over the Ottoman Turks, with extensive gains in Hungary, and suzerainty over half of Italy. Of his imperial pretensions little was left to the emperor beyond the shadow of a great name, the Holy Roman Empire having ceased, in Voltaire's famous phrase, to be either holy or Roman or an empire; but in compensation he found himself the personal ruler of some twenty million people dwelling in a federation of rich and lovely provinces which possessed almost every blessing save that of national unity. For two hundred years the Hapsburg monarchs were to dedicate themselves to the heroic task of preserving this mosaic "Empire on the Danube" from the dissolution to which it was predestined.

3. SPAIN IN DECLINE

In the sixteenth century, under Charles V and Philip II, Spain had played the dominant rôle in European politics, but before the end of the seventeenth century, the Spaniards had seen this ascendancy transferred to France, while their own country sank to the position of a second-rate power. After 1700, the reforms of the Bourbon kings induced a slight revival, but the Spanish nation did not recover the energy, the prestige, or the intellectual vigor which distinguished it in the age of gold. The explanation for this decadence appears to lie in the character of the Spanish people and in the unsound economic principles which the monarchy enforced to the detriment of Spanish trade.

For many of the ills afflicting Spain the misguided policy of the government may be held responsible. In 1609, His Most Catholic Majesty, *Economic decline* Philip III (1598–1621), ordered the Moriscos (descendants of Christianized Moors) expelled from the country, a measure which strengthened the religious solidarity of the realm, but crippled many trades and handicrafts in which the Moors had specialized. Trade was further hampered by the *alcabala*, a tax of ten per cent on all sales, by the debasement of the coinage, and by the monopolies and restrictions enforced by the unenlightened sovereigns. By the reign of Charles II (1665–1700), all manufacture save that of a few necessities had come to an end; beggars multiplied and privation increased, until many, even

[1] See frontispiece.

of Spain's half-million nobles, were reduced to a degree of poverty the more tragic because their pride forbade them to confess it.   Charles II, or Charles the Sufferer as he was named out of pity for his numerous ailments, the heritage of that inbreeding too long pursued by the Hapsburg clan, was the tragic symbol of a monarchy and a nation which appeared to have reached the nadir of exhaustion.   Rapacious neighbors waited impatiently for Charles's death as a signal to partition imperial Spain and confiscate its possessions, while within the kingdom misery increased, trade and population continued to decline, and the credit of the state foundered in a sea of bankruptcy.

The decline in agriculture was no less serious.   Too much property was owned by absentee landlords whose agents neglected it.   Large areas which might have been rendered productive were *Decline of* used as pasture for sheep-raising, an occupation which at- *agriculture* tracted the indolent class of Spaniards and helped by its *and of population* promise of easy profits to discourage the virtues of industry, thrift, and foresight required for successful farming.   The agricultural districts were gradually deserted and the fields abandoned.   The population of Spain declined steadily throughout the seventeenth century, for the colonies lured the most venturesome spirits in each generation, while the ten thousand convents and monasteries withdrew the most devout from the stream of national life.   The result of this double depletion is clearly to be traced in the progressive deterioration of the Spanish character, a consequence more fatal in its ultimate effects than the twenty per cent loss in population.

The most un-European of European peoples, the Spaniards clung tenaciously to their peculiar customs and revealed slight susceptibility to foreign influences.   Little affected by the Renaissance, *Intellectual* and still less by the Protestant Reformation, they kept a *decline* distinctive culture which in the sixteenth and early seventeenth centuries was imitated by other nations because of Spain's commanding position as a colonial and military power.   This golden age of Spanish civilization was the prelude to a swift decline.   Art degenerated, literature grew pompous and empty, the universities became strongholds of medieval theology, and the Spanish Inquisition discouraged free speculation and scientific inquiry.   The great Spanish novelist Cervantes (1547–1616), writing at the opening of the seventeenth century, created in Don Quixote a character which exemplified many of the virtues and vices of his countrymen.   Brave, loyal, and courteous, Don Quixote was also stubborn, superstitious, and impractical, and failed lamentably in the daily business of life because his fancy was encumbered with the lingering figments of fairy tales, feudal lore, and medieval superstitions. Like him, many Spaniards preferred to live amid the ghosts of the past rather than grapple with the commercial and industrial problems of an age that had forsaken medievalism and chivalry. Bound by the dictates of a religious zeal corrupted by mysticism and materialism, they clung complacently to outmoded methods, and fortified themselves against the impact of newer forces or the winds of agnostic speculation.

The death of Charles II in 1700 and the accession of Philip V, followed by the European struggle over the Spanish succession, stirred the Spaniards rudely and awakened them to a show of resistance. The Portuguese, allied with the English,[1] invaded the western provinces, while to the east Catalonia was occupied and Madrid captured (1706). Spanish pride resented the attempt of the allies to force the Archduke Charles upon the nation. In the outcome Philip V remained, and his reign (1700–46) witnessed the introduction of some moderate reforms. The government of Spain and the colonies was better centralized, local laws and special statutes were abolished in favor of a national code, while trade restrictions were broken down somewhat by the *Asiento* Treaty (1713), which yielded a share in Spanish colonial trade to the English. Throughout the eighteenth century, Spain was to exhibit a slow but measurable progress.

4. THE ITALIAN STATES

Italy, the "Mother of arts, as once of arms," had, like Spain, subsided in the seventeenth century into a mournful decadence. It seemed as if the initiative and fecundity of the great Renaissance masters had exhausted the race, for the gifted Italian people had declined by 1700 from a position of leadership in the arts and sciences to a condition of intellectual apathy and political impotence. Three causes contributed to this decline: (1) the languishing trade of the Mediterranean ports which suffered when the discovery of the New World turned European commerce into the Atlantic sea lanes; (2) the Counter (or Catholic) Reformation, which consolidated the power of the Roman Catholic Church in Italy, and produced an atmosphere unfriendly to the pagan spirit of the Renaissance with its secular interests and unfettered thought; (3) the conflict in Italy of French, Austrian, and Spanish forces, each seeking to dominate the peninsula and transform the Italian states into pawns to be controlled by diplomats sitting in Madrid or Paris or Vienna. This

---

[1] The Methuen Treaty (1703) allied Britain and Portugal in a friendly commercial and political understanding.

third factor was the most evil in its effects, for it reduced Italy to a battle-ground to be ravaged by contending armies, reduced many Italian states to subject provinces that were "robbed rather than governed" by their alien masters, and condemned the Italian people to play an insignificant rôle, not only in the period 1660 to 1715, but throughout the eighteenth and a large part of the nineteenth century.

From the Treaty of Cateau-Cambrésis (1559) to the Peace of Utrecht (1713–14), the Spanish dominated Italy, for they held the Milanese, Naples, and Sicily. Their oppressive rule produced two *Period of* serious revolts in Naples and Messina during the seven- *Spanish* teenth century, revolts which were followed by reprisals as *control* stupid as they were ferocious. When the Spanish throne *(1559–1713)* passed to the Bourbon line, Spain's Italian possessions were handed over to the Austrian Hapsburgs,[1] but the change involved little that was new for the Italian inhabitants in these states except that they were to be governed thenceforth from Vienna instead of from Madrid.

Of the Italian states which still managed to preserve their independ-ence in this period, four — Tuscany, Genoa, Venice, and Savoy — deserve passing notice. Florence had degenerated from an *Florence* intellectual center, the Athens of Italy in the high Renais-sance, to a provincial capital where the later Medici princes held their court as Grand Dukes of Tuscany. The memory of Dante and Machia-velli still shed luster upon the city of their nativity, and beauty still lingered untarnished, but the days of Florentine greatness were done. Genoa fared little better, though it preserved its republican institutions, and its banking business still assured it a moderate pros- *Genoa* perity. In 1684, a French fleet bombarded the city on slight justification, and Louis XIV rebuked the independent pretensions of the citizens by imposing a humiliating peace.

In spite of the fact that Venice had been declining for two centuries, the doge and his councilors managed by skillful diplomacy to maintain the dignity of the waning republic, and even carried on an *Venice* intermittent war against the Turks from 1645 to 1699. Venice in decay was still "Europe's bulwark 'gainst the Ottomite," but the Turkish power also, it must be remembered, was on the wane, and although the Treaty of Carlowitz (1699) brought Venice a portion of Dalmatia, Greece, and the Aegean Islands, it was in reality a peace of exhaustion between crippled giants whose strength was spent. As the

---

[1] The Hapsburgs acquired Milan, Naples, and Sardinia by the Treaty of Utrecht, but in 1720 they exchanged Sardinia for Sicily and thus held all of Spain's former possessions in Italy.

main stream of European commerce shifted more and more decisively to Amsterdam and London, the erstwhile "Queen of the Adriatic" became a city of empty palaces and desolate splendors, retaining to the last, however, the fantastic beauty which had crowned her in more prosperous days, when "the exhaustless East poured in her lap all gems in sparkling showers."

The only truly progressive and independent state in seventeenth-century Italy was Savoy, which had been welded into a compact duchy by *Duchy of* the genius of its duke, Charles Emmanuel (1580–1630). *Savoy* With territory strategically placed so that it commanded both the coast route into Italy and the famous Mont Cenis pass over the Alps,[1] the dukes of Savoy could prove useful allies to any power which aspired to the control of Italy. Bargaining astutely between the French and Spaniards, they had strengthened their position and added to their territory. Victor Amadeus II joined in the War of the League of Augsburg against France to his profit; but it was the War of the Spanish Succession that gave him his real opportunity and raised Savoy to the position of a European state. Siding first with France, Victor Amadeus had the foresight to desert Louis XIV in 1703, and his army, brilliantly led by Prince Eugène, aided materially in the ultimate defeat of the French. For this assistance the allies rewarded Victor Amadeus with the island of Sicily and the title of king. In 1720, he exchanged Sicily for Sardinia, and the duchy of Savoy was generally known thenceforth as the Sardinian Kingdom. In the nineteenth century the house of Savoy was destined to head the movement for Italian unity and provide the first king of a united Italy.

The States of the Church in central Italy shared the general decline in papal prestige which made Rome less important as a diplomatic center *The papacy* in the seventeenth century than Paris, Vienna, or even London. Seven popes occupied the chair of Saint Peter in the years 1660 to 1715, but none was noteworthy. Innocent XI (1676–89) was the most upright and possibly the most capable. He defended his prerogatives against Louis XIV, and aided with subsidies in the defeat of the Turks in 1683. But the mediating power which the popes had once wielded over Europe was gone; their pleas for peace passed almost unheeded in the clash of the dynastic wars that disfigured the close of the century, and Clement XI (1700–21), who at first upheld the claims of France in the War of the Spanish Succession, was compelled by the allies to reverse his judgment under threat of invasion and deposition. The eighteenth century held no better days in store for the papacy; in-

[1] See frontispiece.

deed, it was to see the authority of the church still further weakened and that venerable institution reduced to the nadir of its fortunes.

5. SUMMARY OF THE PERIOD, 1660 TO 1715

When the major political developments that filled the period, 1660 to 1715, are passed in review, it becomes clear that the balance of power between the European states was perpetually shifting because several states were in decline and threatened to disintegrate. Thus Spain, the Holy Roman Empire, the Italian states (except Savoy), the papacy, Sweden, Poland, Turkey, and even Holland were stationary or decadent. France, on the other hand, despite its reverses, was still an aggressive power of the first rank, while Great Britain was developing vigorously. It was not difficult to foresee that these two leading powers might clash severely; by 1688, England had recognized France as her most dangerous commercial rival, and a titanic struggle between the two for commerce and colonies was to provide the leading drama of the eighteenth century.

By 1715, religious issues had been subordinated to political expediency and no longer constituted a serious cause for war. On the other hand, trade rivalries had grown more intense. Dynastic greed remained an active force, ready as ever to promote hostilities for its own profit. The long duel between Bourbon and Hapsburg lost much of its bitterness with the decline of the Hapsburg power, but new antagonists were waiting to crowd upon the stage. In the Germanies the meteoric rise of Prussia was to upset the balance of power by adding a first-class military state to the European system, while farther east Russia was about to emerge and claim its share of influence. The five great powers of the eighteenth century include, therefore, three states already familiar to us — France, Austria, and England — and two new powers, Prussia and Russia. The wars of the eighteenth century grow out of the conflicting interests of these five powers. Their methods and motives will be found to differ little from those described in the preceding section. Each state seeks to consolidate and aggrandize itself, the weaker form alliances against aggressive neighbors, and the diplomats defend the principle of the balance of power as the surest guaranty of peace and equilibrium. In all this the eighteenth century differs scarcely at all from the period just studied. But the emergence of Prussia and Russia modified the structure of European politics so sharply that their entry marks a new period and merits a new section, while the progress of new ideas among the enlightened classes gives to the eighteenth century an intellectual temper distinct from that of the seventeenth.

Section B

THE EIGHTEENTH CENTURY
(1715–89)

Although the seventy-four years between the death of Louis XIV and the outbreak of the French Revolution filled in reality less than three fourths of "the eighteenth century," they constitute a distinct period in European history for which no better name suggests itself. This period was marked chiefly by a balancing of forces. The threat of French domination had been checked, and the diplomats labored to maintain a more or less stable equilibrium among the powers. This political equilibrium was preserved with fair success to the end of the period, despite such disturbing developments as the rise of Prussia to the rank of a first-rate power, the decline of Austria and Turkey, and the westward expansion of Russia.

It proved less easy, however, to preserve a balance of forces between the social classes. As the power and wealth of the middle class increased, and the influence of the privileged orders, the nobles and clergy, declined, stress and discontent developed which could only be eased by radical social and political readjustments. The failure to carry through the necessary reforms promptly and peaceably resulted, after 1789, in the outbreak of the Great Revolution in France, the prelude to a quarter of a century of tumultuous and far-reaching change which affected every country in Europe.

Section B

THE EIGHTEENTH CENTURY

(1715-89)

CHAPTER FIVE

THE EMERGENCE OF RUSSIA

Our greatest enemy is space. Russian proverb.

NO STUDENT who studies the map of Europe can fail to note how markedly the western part of the continent is divided into segments. The British Isles, Italy, and the Iberian Peninsula possess a geographical unity of their own, while for France the ocean, the Alps, and the Pyrenees form a natural boundary for the greater part of the frontier. Western Europe thus enjoys a wide diversity of scenery and of climate, and the rising national states there have found the seacoast and the mountain ranges a protection behind which each could develop its culture and its institutions more or less unmolested.

The geography of eastern Europe is surprisingly different. Instead of an irregular coastline and snow-capped peaks, there stretches a vast and monotonous plain. From the Baltic to the Black and the Caspian seas, from the Carpathian Mountains on the border of Hungary to the Ural Mountains on the border of Asia, this great inland plain extends, large enough to contain *The Great Plain of eastern Europe* England, France, and Spain together. In the north there are many swamps and thick forests of coniferous trees; the central belt produces a mixed deciduous growth; the plains of the southland are semi-arid and bare. These bare, uncultivated steppes of the south, stretching above the Black and Caspian seas into the heart of Asia, provide an undefended route down which the Asiatic nomads have swept at intervals, to break like a destructive wave on the frontiers of eastern Europe.

To the Romans the broad steppes beyond the Carpathian Mountains and the Black Sea were known as Sarmatia. The Romans traded with the natives for furs and amber, but they cared little what happened in such a cold and forbidding region which for them lay shrouded in a twilight beyond the bounds of their empire. In the fifth century the Huns rode out of this shadowy East, to devastate the weakened provinces of Rome, and, although they retired after the death of their leader Attila (453), other Mongols continued to threaten Europe with new invasions throughout the Middle Ages. Yet the trade routes in this region were kept open even after the fall of Rome; Viking adventurers from Scandinavia penetrated the steppes and gave their name to part of the area (*Russ* was originally a Finnish name for Swede); and Byzantine merchants from Constantinople continued to traverse the territory and to navigate the rivers. Throughout the dark ages the dwellers of the Great Plain were thus exposed to the stimulus of Norse enterprise and Byzantine culture. But it was difficult for them to raise cities or cultivate the arts in an area where Roman civilization had laid no foundations, where natural frontiers were lacking, and the possibility of new invasions from Asia was a constant threat.

It is not surprising, therefore, that the Slavic peoples of eastern Europe remained politically backward and semi-barbarous while the Latins *Slavic char-* and the Germans were making substantial advances. The *acteristic* original home of the Slavs is believed to have been the basin of the Pripet River, whence they migrated across the Great Plain, or filtered into the Balkan Peninsula. The earliest accounts picture them as an agricultural people, generous and hospitable in character, fond of music, and deeply religious. Most of these characteristics still distinguish their descendants.

1. THE RISE OF MUSCOVY

In the ninth century the impact of a new wave of Asiatic invaders split the Slavs into several groups. The eastern Slavs, who were to lay the foundations of the Russian state, built up a principality with Kief, on the Dnieper River, as its center, but after two centuries Kief declined before a fresh wave of invaders from Asia. Thereupon the eastern Slavs established new cities within the forest zone to the north, of which Moscow proved the most important. Here they were better able to resist the horsemen of the plains, and Norse adventurers and traders helped them to organize a federation of feudal principalities. Until the fifteenth century, the Mongols, who had established their capital at Sarai on the Volga, continued to levy tribute on the eastern Slavs, but in 1480, Ivan the Great, Prince of Moscow, defied the Khan of the Golden Horde, as the Mongol ruler was termed, and his supremacy was broken.

Ivan the Great (1462–1505) married Sophia Paleologus, niece of the last Byzantine emperor, Constantine Paleologus, who perished when the *Byzantine* Turks captured Constantinople in 1453. Ivan considered *influence* himself heir to the Byzantine traditions, called himself Czar (Caesar) and successor of Augustus, and Protector of the Orthodox (Greek) Church. Moscow became the "Third Rome." This assumption of imperial dignity by a Slavic prince is more easily understood when it is realized that missionaries from Constantinople had converted the eastern Slavs to the Greek faith, and a strong Byzantine influence tinctured the culture of the Russians. Their mosques and their icons, their

The Russian word for church is "Cerkov"

calendar, and even their alphabet, were borrowed from Constantinople. It was an interesting anomaly, this adoption of the outworn, sophisticated, and highly conventionalized art of Byzantium by a race of vigorous barbarians who still retained many of the oriental customs of their Asiatic conquerors. The blend of these diverse influences was to make the Russians unlike any other European people.

The slow task of consolidating and extending the principality of Moscow, or Muscovy, engaged the energies of successive czars. Ivan IV, also known as Ivan the Terrible (1533–84), subdued his boyars, or vassals, with ruthless cruelty, conquered the last Tartar strongholds in European Russia, and pushed his frontiers eastward to the Ural Mountains and westward until he clashed with the Poles and the Swedes. In the seventeenth century, under a new dynasty, the Romanovs, this westward expansion was resumed. The absence of any natural barrier made it possible for the Muscovite state to expand in all directions, but the nations of western Europe remained indifferent to this rise of a new power in the East. So long as Sweden and Poland stood as buffer states, the Russians could not interfere directly in European affairs, and the English, French, and Italians thought of Russia as an Asiatic rather than a European country.

By the close of the seventeenth century, however, both Poland and Sweden were in decline, and they yielded before the inexorable pressure of the Russian advance. A glance at the map on page 75 will indicate how rapidly the Russians pressed forward. In 1660, they were still shut off from the Baltic Sea, for the Swedes held the littoral provinces from Finland to the mouth of the Dwina River, where the Polish dominions began. But Sweden, with a population of a little over a million, was unequal to the burden of guarding her empire. Even with the aid of French subsidies, the Swedish kings found it difficult to hold their Baltic provinces against the rapacity of Poland and Brandenburg.

2. PETER THE GREAT OF RUSSIA

The decline of Poland and Sweden invited further Russian expansion, and the westward advance of the Muscovites was renewed under the restless and autocratic czar, Peter the Great (1682–1725). Ambitious to see his backward and semi-barbarous subjects acquire the culture and the institutions which made France, England, and Holland powerful and respected nations, Peter determined to hasten the "Europeanization" of Russia by opening "windows to the west." By windows he meant ice-free seaports through which European trade, European travelers, and European culture could enter Russia, and before he died in 1725, he had secured outlets on both the Baltic and the Black seas.

Peter's youth, and his later career, too, ran in channels of intrigue and violence. Moscow was the scene of much factional strife in the last *Youth of* years of the seventeenth century, and the impressionable *Peter the* young czar saw more than one of his friends murdered be- *Great* fore his eyes. He was proclaimed joint ruler with his weak-minded stepbrother Ivan in 1682, but he had to wait until 1689 to overthrow the regency of his stepsister Sophia. The death of his mother in 1694, however, followed by that of Ivan in 1696, left Peter sole lord of Muscovy. Over six and one half feet in height, dexterous with his hands, and consumed with a quenchless curiosity concerning ships and navigation, machinery, and all technical processes, the new czar was destined to change the current of Russian history. His first taste of success came in 1696, when he captured Azov from the Turks with the aid of a fleet constructed by foreign shipwrights under his command. Although the Turks later regained this Black Sea port (1722), the czar's desire for further conquests was whetted by this campaign of 1696.

The following year Peter set out on a tour to study the civilization of Europe for himself. Mathematics, physics, chemistry, anatomy, and engraving claimed his attention by turns, but it was the art of warfare and particularly naval warfare that absorbed him most. In Holland and England he worked in the shipyards, and he dispatched five hundred artisans to Russia to instruct his subjects in the newer technical methods. In Vienna his tour was interrupted by the news that revolt had broken *Revolt of* out at home among the *streltzi*, or royal guards. Hastening *the* streltzi back to Moscow, Peter revealed the less amiable side of his character by condemning two thousand of the rebels to torture and death, as a lesson to his subjects on the futility of resisting his will.

Then the Russian people were startled from their fatalistic conservatism by a succession of imperial reforms. With his own royal hand Peter clipped the beards of his nobles, and tailors stood ready to shorten their long oriental robes, for the czar desired to initiate European dress and habits. The women were summoned to court from their domestic seclusion, but being unused to social freedom they huddled modestly at one end of the hall while their lords and masters drank themselves under the table at the other. Peter comprehended that his *ukases* or decrees, even when they were emphasized by knout and scaffold, could not change his people so swiftly as the penetrative influence of European ideas. To provide closer contacts he fostered trade agreements, sent young Russians abroad to study, and invited Europeans to

PETER THE GREAT OF RUSSIA
1672–1725

The old-fashioned armor and ermine cloak are merely the trappings of royalty, and the artist has idealized Peter's features. As a despot this Muscovite giant was by turns pious, cruel, resourceful or naïve, for he possessed a disharmonic but forceful personality.

sojourn in Russia. When his alien innovations led to conspiracies among his discontented subjects, he punished the rebels mercilessly, his own son being numbered finally in the list of victims. Believing many churchmen, and especially the monks, hostile to his reforms, Peter created a holy synod, or council, responsible to himself, placed it in charge of religious affairs, and abolished the office of patriarch (1700). Other departments of the government were likewise reconstructed and rendered more efficient, despite the fact that the czar possessed so few trained officials that he was compelled at times to employ Swedish prisoners of war in administrative posts.

It is difficult to exaggerate the importance of Peter's reforms. The calendar was improved, the western system of enumeration introduced, *Peter's* printing presses set up, and schools and hospitals estab- *reforms* lished. Peter even founded a Russian Academy of Sciences, composed, perforce, almost entirely of foreign savants. But there were some projects that could not be achieved by peaceful means. The annexation of a port where the ships of all nations might come freely to trade cost Peter twenty years of warfare, a hazardous struggle in which he was opposed by the most brilliant, the most daring, and the most erratic monarch of the age, Charles XII of Sweden.

3. THE GREAT NORTHERN WAR (1700–21)

The famous French writer, Voltaire, who composed an *Histoire de Charles XII*, observed shrewdly that Charles carried all his virtues to *Charles XII* such an excess that they became more dangerous than *of Sweden* their contrary vices. Charles crowned himself King of Sweden in 1697, at the age of fifteen, showing immediately a temper so imperious and abilities so precocious that the *Riksdag*, or Parliament, dispensed with a regency and voted him absolute powers. He thus became master of Sweden, with its million and a quarter inhabitants, at almost the same time that Peter assumed full control in Russia, and the stage was set for a contest between the two young autocrats and the two empires.

In 1700, Russia, Saxony, and Denmark took advantage of Charles's youth and presumable inexperience to attack Sweden, but the boy-king speedily astonished Europe by the daring of his counterstrokes. In a single campaign he forced the Danes to sue for peace; then, marching with eight thousand men to the relief of Narva, in Esthonia, he hurled his veterans through a blinding snowstorm upon the Russian lines and routed the czar's army of forty thousand men. These victories won for

[72]

Charles the sobriquet "The Lion of the North," but their ultimate effects were disastrous for his character and for Sweden. Instead of following up his victory at Narva, he chose to regard the Russians as vanquished, and turned to deal with his third enemy, Saxony.

Frederick Augustus I of Saxony (1694–1733) was also by election King of Poland (1697). Charles speedily deposed him from the latter throne and had a rival candidate, Stanislaus Leszczynski, elected in his place. The young Swedish king was now the arbiter of northern Europe, for the western powers were occupied by the War of the Spanish Succession (1702–13), but his blind and imperturbable self-confidence drove his enemies to unite and exasperated his friends. Moreover, the five years which he spent in reordering Polish affairs permitted Peter the Great the needed leisure to reknit the Russian armies, so that by 1707 they were able once more to press to the shores of the Baltic Sea.

This insolent advance of the Russians goaded Charles into attempting a project at which Napoleon was to meet disaster a century later: he marched on Moscow. Scattering a Russian army at *Battle of* Holowczyn (1708), the Swedes pressed on through a country *Pultawa* stripped bare of provisions by the retreating foe. But to *(1709)* reach Moscow proved impossible, and rather than retreat, Charles turned his devoted army southward, and sought an alliance with the Cossacks of the Ukraine. The terrible winter of 1709 harassed his ragged veterans more pitilessly than the Russian horsemen, and when summer came, Peter was able to crush the remnant of Charles's army at Pultawa (1709). Charles took refuge with the Turks, stirred them up repeatedly to attack the Russians, and finally, after incredible adventures, returned to Sweden in 1714.

Although his country was exhausted, the defiant monarch insisted upon maintaining the struggle against Russia, Prussia, Poland, Saxony, Hanover, and Denmark. But in 1718 he was killed while attacking the Danes, and Sweden sank to the level of a third-rate power, while the victorious allies seized her empire. Russia was the last to make peace, and Peter had the satisfaction of adding Ingria, Esthonia, and Livonia to his empire by the Treaty of Nystad (1721).[1]

As early as 1703, Peter the Great had begun the construction of a new capital for his dominions on the marshy ground where the river Neva drained into the Gulf of Finland. Despite the constant *Founding of* danger of Swedish reconquest, of floods, and of fevers, *Saint Peters-* Saint Petersburg rose slowly from the treacherous lagoons, *burg* and in 1712 it was recognized as the new seat of government. Moscow,

[1] See frontispiece and map on page 75.

symbol of the old Russia, was humbled before the splendor of this "western" city, where Peter established his court and assumed the novel and grandiloquent title "Emperor of all the Russias." Alone of all the great powers, Russia was to have its capital city, not near the center of the country, but upon the frontier; not in an ancient town with long traditions, but in a modern seat of administration, built upon conquered ground, the least Russian of all the Russian cities. Yet so well had Peter labored that not even his premature death in 1725 could undo his life-work, and for good or ill the destiny of Russia had been joined with that of Europe.

4. THE SUCCESSORS OF PETER THE GREAT

As Peter had married twice, and left descendants by both marriages, it is not surprising that the first sixteen years following his death were filled with disputes concerning the succession. In 1741, however, his daughter Elizabeth began a reign of twenty years and the empire regained a comparative degree of tranquillity. But there was still a deep conflict between the old and the new forces in Russia, and a deep resentment among the conservative classes at the spread of foreign ideas and the elevation of foreigners to high posts in the state. This opposition between a pro-Russian party and a pro-European party remained a permanent heritage in Russian politics from the time of Peter the Great, for many Russians felt that their country possessed a peculiar and distinct culture of its own which could not successfully be blended with or remodeled after that of the western European nations.

During Elizabeth's reign this conflict between old and new forces produced a deadlock, but foreign influences, particularly French, con-

The Czarina Elizabeth (1741–62) tinued to win an ascendancy. Russian policy, both at home and abroad, gained during these years but mediocre successes. Despite the political stagnation, however, the arts and sciences progressed, education was encouraged for the upper classes, and the Czarina Elizabeth, though a dissolute woman herself, endeavored to elevate the morals of her subjects and to ameliorate the ferocious penal code.

A minor conflict with the enfeebled Swedish state brought Russia additional gains in Finland by the Treaty of Abo (1743); and in 1756, Elizabeth joined France and Austria against Prussia and England in the Seven Years' War (1756–63). The Russian armies penetrated East Prussia and won several victories, but their sacrifices were in vain, for on Elizabeth's death in 1762 her nephew and successor Peter III (grand-

GROWTH OF
RUSSIA
TO 1725

Scale of Miles
0 100 200 300 400

ARCTIC OCEAN

NORWAY

SWEDEN

Lapland

FINLAND

Gulf of Bothnia

White Sea

Archangel

Dwina

BALTIC SEA

G. of Finland

St Petersburg

Novgorod

Riga

Niemen

Vilna

POLAND

AUSTRIA-
HUNGARY

Dniester

BESSARABIA

Bug

Odessa

RUMANIA

Crimea

Sea of Azof

BULGARIA

BLACK SEA

Batum

Moscow

Volga

Nijni-Novgorod

Kazan

Orenburg

Ural

Poltava

Donetz

Don

Volga

Astrakhan

CAUCASUS MTS.

CASPIAN SEA

URAL MOUNTAINS

Ob

Kiev

Dnieper

Oural

TURKEY

PERSIA

Long. East 40 from Greenwich 50

Grand Duchy of Moscovy in 1480
Territory acquired   1480-1689
"   "   1689-1725
Boundary of Russia in 1914

son of Peter the Great) arbitrarily reversed the alliance, and came to the aid of Frederick II of Prussia in time to save that hard-pressed monarch from ruin.[1] Peter's admiration for Frederick and his readiness to fling away the fruits of Russian victories to gratify his personal whims speedily excited a palace revolution, and before the close of the year 1762 the erratic and vicious young czar had been deposed and murdered. In his place the guards acclaimed his wife Catherine "Autocrat of all the Russias."

5. CATHERINE THE GREAT (1762–96)

Sophia Augusta Frederica, better known to history as Catherine the Great, was the daughter of a Prussian general, Prince Christian Augustus

Catherine's character

of Anhalt-Zerbst. Married to the despicable Czarevich Peter at the age of sixteen, and received into the Orthodox Church under the name of Catherine, this German princess passed several lonely years at the Russian court, where she had few friends and was shamelessly neglected by her husband. She consoled herself with wide reading, learned the Russian language, and identified herself so loyally with the interests of her adopted country that she was chosen to succeed her degenerate husband in 1762. Indiscriminate in her love affairs, and often Machiavellian in her politics, Catherine was none the less a woman of remarkable sagacity and proved an inspired ruler. Under her shrewd guidance Russia once again played a rôle equal to its importance, recaptured its waning prestige, and took a leading part in the affairs of northern Europe. Whenever possible, Catherine appointed Russians rather than foreigners to office, and showed herself at all times deeply devoted to the glory and greatness of Russia. But she introduced reforms after the European pattern when she could do so without stirring up discontent, and proved herself, especially in her foreign policy, the real executor of Peter the Great's bequest.

Catherine's long reign (1762–96) lasted until after the outbreak of the French Revolution in 1789. She was thus a contemporary of Frederick

Catherine the Great as an enlightened despot

II of Prussia (1740–86), Joseph II of Austria (1780–90), Gustavus III of Sweden (1771–92), and other rulers of the second half of the eighteenth century who are often styled the "enlightened despots." These monarchs were all inspired by a conscientious desire to improve their realms and to make their subjects happy, and something more will be told about their reforms later. Catherine was exceedingly anxious to be considered

[1] See below, page 90.

an "enlightened despot" herself, but her title to the honor is a little dubious. Of her good intentions there can be no question; she wrote to Voltaire, Diderot, d'Alembert, and other illustrious critics of society and government, inviting them to advise her how best to make her subjects contented and civilized. With her own hand she drew up a liberal plan for revising and codifying the Russian laws (1766), in the hope of making them at once more inflexible and more humane. She dreamed of establishing schools in every town and village in order to elevate her people to the responsibilities of citizenship. She encouraged artists and writers, and permitted radical books, which the authorities in France had condemned as dangerous and seditious, to circulate freely in Russia.

Among the noblest monuments to her kindliness of heart were the hospitals and orphanages erected under her patronage. She submitted herself to vaccination so that her subjects might be en- *Limits of* couraged by her royal example to accept this newly dis- *Catherine's* covered preventive against smallpox. For the millions *reforms* of serfs toiling on the lands of Russia she expressed deep commiseration, and she hoped that some day they might be liberated. But she took no serious steps to free them. Between Catherine's wishes and her acts there was often a wide divergence, for she had a kind heart but a calculating mind, and it was the dictates of her shrewd brain that guided her. Her sympathy for the serfs did not prevent her granting large estates to her courtiers, which further increased serfdom. When she divided Russia into fifty provinces, she professed to wish each district to control its own local affairs, but she kept the real power in the hands of a governor appointed by herself. Thus, despite her pretensions of benevolence, the practical results of her administration revealed more despotism than enlightenment.

For her failures in this respect Catherine must not be blamed too harshly. In politics one seldom does the best or even the next best thing: one does the best one can. Because her power rested upon the loyalty of the nobles she had to please them; hence the grants of land and the increase of serfdom. Her orders might be humane and wise, but if unsympathetic officials disdained to enforce them, she dared not rebuke them too sharply. Her desire to play the part, or at least to *appear* to be playing the part, of an enlightened ruler was genuine enough, but she was too clear-headed a realist to forget for a single moment that she had been called to govern an empire of barbarous peoples by the methods they had been trained to understand, the methods of an oriental despot.

6. THE DISMEMBERMENT OF POLAND

The expansion of Russia in the seventeenth and eighteenth centuries helped to weaken and finally to destroy the kingdom of Poland. When *Poland in* Catherine II ascended the Russian throne in 1762, Poland *decline* was already enfeebled and disorganized. The Poles, like the Russians, were of Slavic origin, but they had been converted to the Roman Catholic instead of to the Greek Orthodox faith, and were thus affiliated by ties of religion and culture with the western rather than the eastern European peoples. In the fourteenth century, Poland had been united to Lithuania, and by the sixteenth the Polish dominions extended across the plains between the Black Sea and the Baltic in a loosely knit kingdom almost twice as large as France. In that golden age of Polish history the able rulers of the Jagellon dynasty were strong enough to resist the pressure of the Muscovites in the east and the Turks in the south, but in the seventeenth century, Poland was weakened by the attacks of Turks, Tartars, Swedes, and Russians. Although King John Sobieski (1674–96) arrested the decline momentarily, and even rescued Vienna from the Turks (1683), the greatness of Poland had passed and the eighteenth century witnessed the extinction of the kingdom.

The decline and final dismemberment of Poland was the result of (1) indefensible frontiers and (2) political anarchy. The accident of geog- *Political in-* raphy which made their homeland a level plain left the *stability* Poles no natural barriers, such as high mountain ranges, behind which they could rally to check an invasion. The wide steppes, transected by slow-moving rivers which favored navigation, made it possible for Poland to expand rapidly in the days of her power, but also left her open to the inroads of her enemies in the days of her decline. Worse, however, than this territorial instability was the political instability of the kingdom. The government of the country was so wretchedly organized that it has been called "a legalized anarchy tempered by rebellion." The Polish Kingdom was in truth little more than a loose federation of feudal principalities somewhat like the Holy Roman Empire, and the people did not even possess unity of religious faith, being predominantly Catholic in Poland, Greek Orthodox in Lithuania, and Protestant in the area adjoining East Prussia. By the eighteenth century the royal authority had been dispersed, the power of the Diet all but nullified, and the state reduced to impotence, a process deliberately hastened by the watchful and rapacious neighbors of Poland.

Perhaps the worst enemies of the unfortunate country were the Polish nobles. The monarchy was elective, and these vassals were unwilling

PARTITION
OF THE
KINGDOM OF POLAND

Scale of Miles
0   50   100 150 200

Russia   Prussia

Austria

—·· "CONGRESS POLAND" Polish
Territory taken from Prussia, and
Austria and given to Russia by the
Congress of Vienna.

——— Boundary of the Republic of
Poland in 1925.

to give themselves a master who might call them to account for their misrule. They saw to it that the elected king lacked sufficient authority to curb them, sometimes extorting pre-election promises from him, sometimes choosing a French, Saxon, or Swedish prince unfamiliar with Polish affairs. Denied an income or an army large enough to defend his position, the king was often a sorry figure. But if the royal rôle was ignominious that of the Polish Diet was even more futile. Controlled likewise by the nobles, the Diet was incapable of effecting any reforms because its decrees were binding only when they were passed unanimously. Any member might block a bill or dissolve the chamber by exercising a privilege known as the *liberum veto*. Under this fantastic constitution, the selfish nobles, who had nothing to fear from Diet or king, exploited their serfs mercilessly. Poland had been known as the "Peasants' Hell" in the Middle Ages and continued to deserve the title. The townsmen, also, lacking political power, were unable to protect their interests, and Poland drifted steadily toward economic and political ruin, with the nobles blocking every suggestion for reform.

With the rulers of Russia, Prussia, and Austria eager to acquire more territory, the fate of Poland could not long remain in doubt. In 1772, *The parti-* Catherine came to an understanding with Frederick II of *tioning of* Prussia and the Empress Maria Theresa of Austria that *Poland* each should annex a small share of the enfeebled kingdom. Too disorganized to resist, the Poles saw a fourth of their territory snatched away. Sobered by this experience, the nobles made a belated effort to strengthen the kingdom and repair the disorder, but the three neighboring powers deliberately encouraged further confusion in order to have an excuse for renewed intervention. In 1793, Russia and Prussia seized coveted sections in a second partition, and in 1795, Austria, Prussia, and Russia divided what remained, despite the heroic resistance offered by a small army of Polish patriots under Kosciusko. Few transactions, even in that age of callous diplomacy, could equal this heartless obliteration from the map of Europe of a proud and independent state, but it must be admitted that the Poles had invited such a fate by the suicidal anarchy to which they had reduced themselves.

By the successive Partition Treaties, six million subjects and 183,000 square miles of territory were added to the Russian Empire. Russia had become a neighbor of both Austria and Prussia, and had acquired an interest in German affairs. In the south also Catherine saw her power extended as the result of two wars against the Turks. By the Treaty of Kuchuk-Kainardji (1774) she won Azov, and the right to protect the Christian subjects of the sultan, ten years later the sultan ceded her the Crimea, and the Treaty of Jassy (1792) brought her the lands on the Black Sea lying between the Bug and Dniester rivers. With this Catherine had to content herself, although she had cherished the dream of expelling the Turks from Constantinople, and making the czars of Russia masters of the (Eastern) Roman Empire in the ancient Byzantine tradition. Her second grandson was baptized Constantine in anticipation of the hoped-for triumph, and the dream of reaching Constantinople, unrealized in Catherine's time, persisted as a glittering legacy to spur the ambition of later czars.

CHAPTER SIX

THE RISE OF PRUSSIA

It is the unfailing rule of princes to aggrandize themselves as greatly as their means permit.

FREDERICK THE GREAT.

BY THE middle of the seventeenth century, it will be recalled, the medieval German Empire of the Holy Roman Emperors had crumbled into more than three hundred political fragments. The main causes for this dissolution may be traced to (1) the system of electing the emperors, which resulted in the passing of the imperial title from one princely house to another and prevented any one family from knitting the Germanies into a dynastic state; (2) the conflict between the popes and emperors, which weakened the imperial power and stimulated the disruptive forces of feudalism; (3) the Protestant Reformation, which might have developed into a movement for national unity under a sympathetic emperor, but encountered instead the stubborn opposition of Charles V. Left half-Catholic and half-Protestant, the Germanies were doomed to a century of religious strife which culminated in the terrible Thirty Years' War (1618–48). When the Peace of Westphalia ended this struggle, the country was half-depopulated and wholly disorganized, with the emperor's authority damaged beyond repair. Thenceforth "Germany" or the "German Empire" as a political entity had no real existence and it is customary to speak instead of "the Germanies."

Inevitably, the lack of a central authority exposed the Germans to the attacks of aggressive and better organized neighbors. France took Alsace during the Thirty Years' War, and Sweden annexed Pomerania. At a time, too, when Spain, Portugal, France, England, and even Holland and Sweden, were establishing colonial empires beyond the seas, the Germans, because of this fatal lack of political cohesion, were denied a chance to participate. The seventeenth century was thus a melancholy interlude in German history, when the imperial machinery which had lent a ponderous grandeur to the medieval empire had finally broken down, when society itself appeared to be on the verge of dissolution, and the new forces which were to shape from this chaos a modern national state had not yet made themselves apparent.

[82]

1. THE ELECTORATE OF BRANDENBURG

Nevertheless, the forces of national reconstruction were already at work. The nucleus about which they centered was the little North German state of Brandenburg, where a competent prince, *The Great* Frederick William I, better known as the Great Elector, *Elector* had begun his reign (1640–88) toward the close of the Thirty *(1640–88)* Years' War. His forbears, of the Hohenzollern family, had been rulers of Brandenburg for over two centuries, but none had inherited problems more grave or discouraging. Like the rest of the Germanies, Brandenburg had been laid waste by the war. Frederick William's possessions were disorganized and disunified, for, in addition to his title of Elector of Brandenburg, he was Duke of (East) Prussia, and he had acquired by the Treaty of Westphalia the cities of Magdeburg and Minden and a part of Pomerania, and annexed shortly thereafter (1666) three little duchies near the Rhine — Mark, Cleves, and Ravensburg.[1] Being an administrator of patience and insight, he realized that his primary task was to link his scattered domains together as firmly as possible by means of a centralized bureaucracy, establish a single treasury to administer the revenue, and build up an army strong enough to maintain a vigorous defense. The chaotic state of the Germanies made the maintenance of a strong army an indispensable precaution, and the Great Elector spent every thaler he could spare upon his splendidly drilled regiments.

His prudence, economy, and skill made Brandenburg-Prussia the foremost state in the Germanies. In 1701, his son and successor, Frederick, took the title of King in Prussia, and the scattered *Organization* Hohenzollern dominions came to be known thereafter as *of the Prus-* the kingdom of Prussia.[2] The grandson of the Great *sian state* Elector, King Frederick William I (1713–40), was a bluff, soldierly disciplinarian, who continued the consolidation and annexed Swedish Pomerania from Sweden. When he died, he left Prussia with an army that ranked fourth in Europe, a well-filled treasury, and a deserved prestige. Destiny had selected the Hohenzollern dynasty to retrieve Germany from disintegration, and to point the way later toward a national resurrection. But the duties of such leadership are grave and the Hohenzollern princes no less than their subjects were sternly disciplined for their task. In its struggle to survive and expand in those anxious times, Prussia became (1) the most militaristic state in Europe,

[1] See map, page 87.

[2] Frederick was styled "King *in* Prussia" because East Prussia lay outside the bounds of the Holy Roman Empire. Within the empire he was nominally Elector of Brandenburg. Under his successor the title "King of Prussia" came to be used indiscriminately.

and developed (2) a highly efficient, centralized bureaucracy. Further-more, the prominent rôle played by strong rulers in the rise of Prussia fostered (3) a deep-rooted tradition of paternal despotism. It is highly important to bear these formative influences in mind in order to under-stand the trend of later German history.

See dates of his reign on preceding page.

2. FREDERICK THE GREAT (1740–86)

Exactly one hundred years after the ~~death~~ *accession* of the Great Elector, his great-grandson ascended the throne as Frederick II. This keen-witted prince was to play an even more important rôle in the eighteenth century than his illustrious ancestor had played in the seventeenth. His brilliant talents, unceasing labors, and enlightened rule won him the title of Frederick the Great, for he not only raised Prussia to the rank of a first-class power, but he made the force of his personality and his example felt throughout the Germanies, so that his career, like that of a Richelieu or a Napoleon, is part of the history of his age.

There seemed little in Frederick's youthful character that was pro-phetic of future greatness. His father, bluff old Frederick William I,
Frederick's youth feared that his son would prove a disgrace to the house of Hohenzollern. *Der Fritz ist ein effeminerter Kerl* (Fritz is an effeminate fellow), he lamented, disgusted by the lad's preference for flute-playing and French poetry. When Frederick attempted flight, to escape the rigorous discipline which his father imposed, he was imprisoned for a year, and was compelled to witness the execution of a friend who had aided him. Then for ten years the youth suffered a drastic training in the business of statecraft, toiling like any clerk over minute details of civil and military administration. Few rulers have had such exemplary training, and fewer still have possessed the genius to profit by it. When Frederick ascended the Prussian throne at twenty-eight, he was ad-mirably equipped for his duties, and the severe training had tempered and toughened him. The poet who had once planned to write great dramas had become a prince who aspired to act them, a Machiavellian prince who had learned to conceal his feelings and had grown daring and cynical. The change is not wholly to be regretted. Frederick made an inspired ruler: he would almost certainly have made an uninspired poet.

It is a permanent rule with princes to aggrandize themselves to the
The Euro-pean balance of power limit of their power, the young prince decided in 1738. Even at twenty-seven his shrewd mind penetrated the web of European intrigue with an ease that surprised older states-men. Austria, he perceived, was decadent and crumbling. A war

[84]

between the Bourbons and Hapsburgs over the Polish Succession (1733–36) had demonstrated to all Europe the weakness of the Hapsburgs, who had purchased peace by sacrificing the duchy of Lorraine to France. Yet the decline of Austria, if carried too far, might leave Europe at the mercy of "these modern Romans" as Frederick styled the French. The lesser powers would be safer if they could preserve a balance between Austria and France, and so maintain an equilibrium in the body politic of Europe. "It is like the human body" — Frederick was drawing upon his dubious knowledge of physiology — "which can only subsist by the commixture of equal parts of acid and alkali...." But secretly he hoped to raise the Hohenzollern prestige until he could claim an equal position with the two older dynasties, adding some Prussian iron to the French acid and the Austrian alkali, as it were. Within a few months of his accession he found an opportunity for a bold stroke of self-aggrandizement.

3. THE WAR OF THE AUSTRIAN SUCCESSION (1740–48)

In an age of keen dynastic rivalries a disputed succession is a fertile source of conflict. The death of Charles II of Spain, it will be remembered, plunged Europe into the War of the Spanish Succession (1702–13), a vacancy on the electoral throne of Poland precipitated the War of the Polish Succession (1733–36), *Frederick seizes Silesia* and the death of the Hapsburg emperor, Charles VI, without a male heir, had the same melancholy result in 1740. Charles wished his daughter, Maria Theresa, to inherit the Hapsburg lands intact, and he labored during the last years of his life to assure her succession by means of a Pragmatic Sanction which he bribed or persuaded the European powers to accept. Two hundred thousand fighting men would have been a far better guaranty, in the opinion of the cynical Frederick II, who took prompt advantage of Charles's death to seize the province of Silesia. For Frederick saw no profit in keeping a pledge which other princes were plotting to break. His house held plausible titles to a part of Silesia, and this seizure of the upper valley of the Oder strengthened and enriched the Prussian kingdom.[1] To the Silesians he explained that he was guided by his concern for their liberties, which Austria (ironic truth) was not powerful enough to protect. These explanations were designed, of course, to conceal Frederick's true motive, which was a ruthless desire for self-aggrandizement. But this was something which he could hardly be expected to confess, even to himself. "We are all," he admitted,

[1] See map, page 87.

"the sophists of our passions." It is a permanent rule with princes, he might have added, to find good motives for bad acts.

Lured by the hope of spoil, France, Spain, Saxony, and Bavaria joined Prussia in attacking Austria. Great Britain, already at war with Spain,[1] thereupon became the ally of the empire of the Danube.

Peace of Aix-la-Chapelle (1748) The War of the Austrian Succession was therefore two wars in reality, (1) a commercial and colonial conflict waged by France and Spain against Great Britain, and (2) a continental struggle in which Maria Theresa fought to retain her hereditary dominions against the rapacity of Prussia, France, Spain, and some lesser states. In both contests the outcome of the fighting was surprisingly negative. The maritime struggle ended in a restoration of the *status quo* (Treaty of Aix-la-Chapelle, 1748), while Maria Theresa, "a woman with the heart of a king," repulsed her aggressors and emerged from the contest with her empire almost intact. Almost, but not quite, for Frederick, by the Treaty of Dresden (1745) retained possession of Silesia.

4. THE DIPLOMATIC REVOLUTION

Frederick's plan to advance Prussian prestige had succeeded almost too well, for the unscrupulous use which he had made of his powerful army alarmed both Bourbons and Hapsburgs. The rise of a new power in northern Europe drove Austria and France together, and eight years after the Treaty of Aix-la-Chapelle these perennial enemies became allies. Maria Theresa's passionate desire to be revenged on Frederick made her welcome the new combination, and Louis XV of France was converted to the project by his strong-willed mistress, Madame de Pompadour, whom Frederick had antagonized. To seal Frederick's fate, the Czarina Elizabeth of Russia, who hated the Prussian king for his satirical verses, also joined the coalition. The mischief which these three women were plotting against him was no secret to Frederick: he felt, he declared maliciously, as if he were pursued by the Three Furies, and he placed his armies in readiness to meet an attack.

The machinations of his enemies had left him without an ally on the Continent, but Frederick hoped for assistance from Great Britain.

The "Diplomatic Revolution" For hostilities between the English and French had already broken out again in America with the commencement of the French and Indian War (1754), neither side being satisfied with the indecisive peace of 1748. The renewal of war with

[1] The War of Jenkins's Ear. See below, pages 98–99.

EXPANSION OF PRUSSIA
UNDER
FREDERICK THE GREAT

Scale of Miles

0   25   50   75   100

Prussia in 1740

Additions by
Frederick the Great

France, however, meant that French armies might embarrass the British government by invading the German electorate of Hanover, to which the English (Hanoverian) kings still retained the title. When Frederick the Great offered to protect Hanover with his veterans in return for a treaty of mutual defense with England, the British readily agreed (Convention of Westminster, 1756). Thus, between 1748 and 1756 a double reversal of alliances took place. In the War of the Austrian Succession (1740–48) England and Austria fought France and Prussia, whereas in the Seven Years' War (1756–63) England and Prussia were to fight France and Austria. This realignment of the powers, which brought France and Austria, enemies of two hundred years' standing, into the same camp, marked such a complete change of established policy that it is called the "Diplomatic Revolution."

The motives which inspired the powers to change their partners for the Seven Years' War are more easily understood when this second war is seen to be really two wars, just as the War of the Austrian Succession had been. Great Britain and France carried their struggle for colonial supremacy in India and America to a decision, while Austria and Prussia engaged once more over the disputed province of Silesia.

5. THE SEVEN YEARS' WAR (1756–63)

Frederick II was not the man to wait passively while Austria, Russia, and France prepared to dismember his kingdom. Instead, he forced the issue by a sudden descent upon Saxony, for he knew the elector of that state was plotting with the coalition. His hope was to crush the Austrians before the French could come to their aid, but a reverse in Bohemia compelled him to fall back on the defensive. What followed after that is too intricate to describe in detail. For five years Frederick campaigned back and forth across his ravaged dominions, as desperate and cunning as a wolf at bay. The English furnished him with subsidies but little military aid, and Prussia, with four and a half million people, had to hold off the forces of three empires with a combined population twelve times as great.

That Prussia survived the ordeal must be attributed to its possession of three great advantages: (1) The Prussian troops could be moved from *Advantages* one scene of battle to another more rapidly than those of *of Prussia* the allies because they possessed what are termed the "inside lines." (2) The Prussian State was admirably organized and unified in its efforts, while the allies were often at odds and failed to concert their attacks. (3) The Prussian armies were commanded by

[88]

FREDERICK THE GREAT OF PRUSSIA
1712–1786

*Frederick had a cynical mind, a bitter tongue,
and a contemptuous opinion of what he called
"this damned human race"; but he rose early
and toiled late for the welfare of his subjects.*

one of the most audacious tacticians of the age in the person of Frederick II.

Having routed a French army at Rossbach (1757) and relieved the pressure in the west, Frederick swept east into Silesia in time to over-
Prussia whelm the Austrians at Leuthen. Next it was the turn
survives of the Russians, who were repulsed at Zorndorf (1758) after
the war ten hours of bloody carnage. These were victories won by inspired generalship against odds that were never less than two to one, but they could not continue indefinitely. At Kunersdorf (1759) Frederick's daring overreached itself disastrously, but the Austrians and Russians neglected to profit by their victory, and complete his ruin. In the two years that followed he continued to slip back and forth between the encroaching armies with ever dwindling forces. Yet even when England withdrew her support, Frederick refused to capitulate, hoping against hope for a turn of fortune, until in 1762 it came. The death of the Czarina Elizabeth brought to the Russian throne the erratic Czar Peter III [1] whose admiration for Frederick led him to propose a generous peace. The coalition had shattered itself against the obduracy of the Prussian king and all the contestants were weary of war. By the Peace of Hubertsburg (1763), Frederick not only extricated his kingdom intact, but forced Austria to acknowledge permanently his title to Silesia. In the separate Treaty of Paris of the same year, England secured the greater part of the French colonial empire.[2]

6. FREDERICK THE GREAT IN TIME OF PEACE

In the years of peace after 1763, Frederick, who was already illustrious as the most brilliant general of his age, gained new laurels as the model of enlightened despots. To heal the wounds of war he remitted taxes in stricken districts, set cavalry horses to the plow, and distributed free seed grain to destitute farmers. Canals and roads were constructed, bridges built, and fifteen hundred square miles of marsh and waste land reclaimed under his direction, so that he could well boast that he had thereby "added a province to his kingdom." To increase the population new villages were founded, and settlers drawn to them from all parts of Europe, encouraged by the promise of just laws, religious toleration, and financial assistance.

In his efforts to stimulate manufacture, Frederick resorted to protective tariffs, and encouraged backward industries by royal patronage. The results were not uniformly successful. To gratify the king's desire

---

[1] See above, pages 74–76.   [2] See below, page 100.

to see Prussia economically self-sufficient, silkworms were imported, mulberry trees grown for them to feed on, and a silk industry *Frederick's* artificially developed despite the unsuitable climate. But *mercantilist policies* Frederick's attempt to discourage his subjects from drink- ing coffee because it could not be grown at home, and was not, as he assured them, so healthful as beer soup, led to wholesale smuggling and damaged his popularity. Money spent outside the country he regarded as lost, his idea being to make the Prussian people provide all their essential commodities, sell the surplus abroad, but import as little as possible in return. This was the one certain method of increasing the wealth of a state according to the precepts of Colbert, the minister of Louis XIV, who had extended the principles of the mercantile system in the previous century. All the states of Europe were striving, more or less successfully, to follow this system in the eighteenth century, and Frederick accepted the prevailing ideas.

With inexhaustible patience Frederick forced himself to dispatch the tiresome details of administration. Often he was at work by five in the morning, and indolent or inefficient subordinates lived in *"The first* terror of his critical eye which appeared to overlook nothing. *servant of the state"* The remotest corners of the kingdom were quickened by the energy of his example, for he visited all the provinces in person, checking errors and correcting abuses. To enforce the laws more firmly and justly, he had the legal codes unified and simplified, forbade the use of torture to extract confessions, and warned the judges that cases must not be permitted to wait indefinitely for a decision. Toward his subjects Frederick played the part of a kindly, though somewhat despotic, father, guarding the welfare of children who were well-meaning but ignorant and stupid. He labored, and expected others to labor, for the glory of Prussia as he saw it, never permitting himself to forget that his duties were proportionate to his rank, and that a king was, in his own phrase, "the first servant of the state."

In 1772, the annexation of West Prussia from Poland added a new province to Frederick's kingdom, as large as Silesia and almost as valuable. The decline and dismemberment of Poland have been de- scribed in the previous chapter. The Prussian share in the First Parti- tion, though considerably smaller than that of Austria or Russia, pro- moted the solidarity of the kingdom, for it united East Prussia to Brandenburg.[1] With a population swelled to five million, and an army of two hundred thousand, Prussia had become a first-class power, the dominant state of the Germanies and a rival of Austria. Frederick's

[1] See map, page 87.

[91]

prestige made him not only a Prussian but a German hero; his achievements wakened a patriotic pride among all the German-speaking people; and one of his latest triumphs, before his death in 1786, was the formation of a league of German princes, organized for mutual defense against Hapsburg aggression. In thus consolidating German sentiment, he was unknowingly establishing the foundation of a greater Germany, but another century was to pass before the project of political unity could be realized.

In the lighter intervals between his official labors, Frederick found time to compose melodies for his flute, to indulge his literary bent (his *Frederick and Voltaire* writings fill thirty volumes), and to enjoy the company of philosophers, poets, and scientists. "Philosophers should be the preceptors of the world and the masters of princes," he declared; and he invited the great French satiric genius, Voltaire, to be his honored guest at his palace, *Sans Souci*. There were amusing supper parties at which Frederick and his companions discussed life and literature in witty and often irreverent fashion, ridiculing the frailties and superstitions of men and exalting the advantages of a free, unprejudiced, rational mind. Unfortunately, Frederick and Voltaire discovered that even rational men do not always agree, and Voltaire's visit ended in a scandalous quarrel between them. But for Voltaire's writings Frederick retained the liveliest admiration, for strangely enough this Prussian king, who was a national hero to the German people, preferred to speak and write in French. He regarded his native tongue as uncouth and undistinguished, and his preference for the French classic style completely blinded him to the brilliant literary revival in the Germanies which marked the closing years of his reign. Compared with the tragedies of Corneille and Racine, the early work of the young Goethe seemed to him a "detestable imitation" of the "abominable plays of Shakespeare."

In 1786, Frederick the Great died quietly in his armchair at *Sans Souci*. He had raised Prussia to the rank of a great power, made it the acknowledged rival of Austria in the direction of German affairs, doubled the army and the area of the Prussian State, and afforded Europe a dazzling example of the success which a despot might achieve if his genius and industry were equal to his opportunities.

CHAPTER SEVEN

OVERSEAS EXPANSION AND THE STRUGGLE FOR COMMERCE AND COLONIES

We will go on, even if we have to eat the leather on the ships' yards.
FERDINAND MAGELLAN.

IN THE Middle Ages the people of Europe did not speculate very much about what lay beyond the boundaries of their small continent. They knew less of geographical science than the ancient Greeks and Romans. India, with its millions of inhabitants, was a land of fable to them, and the vague wonders which they had heard of China (Cathay) and Japan (Cipango), they dismissed as travelers' tales. Of North and South America, and Australia, they knew nothing whatever. Their ignorance, of course, was due not so much to a lack of curiosity as to a lack of the means for gratifying it. Travel was slow, costly, and dangerous. Not until the revival of commerce made it profitable to visit distant lands for trade did the Europeans find it worth while to seek new continents.

1. THE SIXTEENTH CENTURY: SPAIN AND PORTUGAL EXPLOIT THE WEALTH OF THE TWO INDIES

With the voyage of Columbus to America (1492), of the Portuguese captain Da Gama around Africa to India (1497–98), and of Magellan's expedition around the globe (1519–22), the people of Europe came to realize that hitherto they had known less than one quarter of the earth. They were delighted and amazed by the discoveries of that time very much as people might be excited today by the return of explorers from the moon or the planets. No report concerning the wonders of the new lands was too incredible to win belief, whether it concerned Eldorado, the mythical "Golden City" supposed to exist somewhere in South America, or a fountain of perpetual youth hidden in the Florida wilds.

Among the many fabulous things reported about the new realms of Asia and America, two facts particularly impressed the Europeans of the sixteenth century. The new lands contained immense *Motives inspiring the* riches, so that the "treasures of the Indies" became a by-word for unimaginable wealth, and they were peopled by *explorers* races less aggressive and less skilled in warfare than the Europeans. It followed that the natives might be subdued with the aid of firearms, and

[93]

robbed with ease, or at least compelled to sell their products cheaply. A thirst for gold, and for the silks and spices that were worth their weight in gold, lured the explorers on; but in some cases they had a loftier motive, their desire to serve God by bringing the blessings of Christianity to the heathen. The conquest and colonization of the Americas reveals both these motives at work, so that the record presents a strange pattern of courage and cupidity, piety and piracy, martyrdom and massacre, interwoven, as the opportunities of the new land excited the noblest or the basest instincts of the conquerors.

Spain and Portugal took the lead in promoting the earliest voyages of exploration, so that they seemed destined in the sixteenth century to divide the heathen world between them. Such a twofold division of the non-Christian portions of the globe was actually promulgated by Pope Alexander VI in 1493. Spain received a title to North and South America, while Portugal inherited Africa, India, and the Spice Islands of the East. The papal line of demarcation was subsequently declared to run from the North to the South Pole through a point three hundred and seventy leagues west of the Cape Verde Islands, and this gave Portugal the eastern half of Brazil also. These vast possessions brought enormous wealth to the Iberian peoples, but they also excited the envy of the Dutch, the French, and the English, who not unnaturally coveted a share of colonial trade and territory. By 1600, the Portuguese in the East and the Spaniards in the West had built up empires of measureless extent and wealth. It remained to be seen whether they could maintain their dual monopoly of the new lands.

The empire which the Portuguese established in the East Indies was an empire based upon trade. Fortifying themselves at convenient *The Portuguese Empire* points — at Ormuz, Goa, and Diu in India, at Malacca, the Spice Islands, Java, and Sumatra — they monopolized the commerce and grew rich on its profits. But they sent out few white settlers, for the lands of the East were already densely populated, and their missionaries converted a very small proportion of the natives to Christianity. The "unchanging East" accepted their presence and their extortions, but their empire was an artificial one, without roots. It had been created by the genius of the viceroys, Almeida and Albuquerque, who broke the naval power of the Arabs in the Indian Ocean and substituted that of Portugal (1505–15). While their supremacy held, the Portuguese shipped yearly their rich cargoes to Lisbon, spices and rare fabrics from the East, gold and ivory from Africa, sugar, emeralds, and dyestuffs from Brazil. Then, after 1600, the Dutch and English tracked the Portuguese wealth to its sources, invaded the Indian Ocean with superior naval forces, and divided the vulnerable Portuguese Empire there between them.

During the same period the Spaniards in America were laying the basis of an empire of a different and more enduring kind. Finding the western world sparsely populated, they embarked upon *The Spanish* a policy of wholesale conquest and colonization. In 1519– *Empire in* 21, the redoubtable Cortez overthrew the Aztec Empire in *the Americas* Mexico; ten years later, Pizarro, with equal daring, made himself master of the Inca cities in Peru. The enormous treasure which these conquests yielded drew a stream of adventurers to the New World. Central and South America were parceled out as viceregal provinces; the Indians were subdued and converted to the Catholic faith; and the forests, mines, and plantations were soon yielding their tribute to Spain. When Philip II, coveting the Portuguese trade also, united the crowns of Spain and Portugal in 1580, he made himself master of an empire upon which the sun never set, and Europe trembled at the power of a monarch who could draw upon the wealth of the two Indies. But the vast imperial structure, reared by Spanish and Portuguese sea power in less than a century, lacked inward strength and was not destined to endure.

2. THE SEVENTEENTH CENTURY: COMPETITION OF THE DUTCH, THE FRENCH, AND THE ENGLISH FOR COLONIES AND TRADE (1588–1688)

The beginning of the Spanish decline was marked by the loss of the Dutch Netherlands. Many Dutch merchants had already grown wealthy as middlemen, buying cargoes of Portuguese spices and reselling them throughout Europe, before the Dutch provinces broke into revolt against Spanish control (1566). In their struggle for independence the Dutch found that they could enrich themselves and cripple their foe by preying upon Portuguese and Spanish shipping. The English, already jealous of Spanish maritime power, aided the Dutch, and the destruction which overtook Philip's Invincible Armada (1588) proclaimed the fact that Spain had passed the zenith of her greatness.

The first maritime nation to profit by the decline of Spain was the new Dutch Republic. By 1600, Dutch ships had rounded the Cape of Good Hope and the oriental empire of Portugal was at their *Decline of* mercy. A Dutch East India Company was formed (1602), *Dutch* and within ten years the hardy Hollanders had made them- *maritime* selves masters of the eastern trade. Spanish and Portu- *power* guese ships were unable to face them on the Indian Ocean or the Atlantic, and for a time a Dutch expedition even occupied the Brazilian coast. These spectacular successes, and the commercial prosperity which they brought to the United Provinces, made the Dutch the envy of all Europe, but their supremacy lasted barely half a century. After 1650, England on the sea and France on land almost crushed Holland between them. In a series of trade wars (1652–54, 1665–67, 1672–74) the English captured a share of the eastern trade and annexed New Amsterdam, which they renamed New York. Further weakened by the attacks of Louis XIV, the Dutch were driven after 1674 to seek an alliance with their later despoiler, England, as the only means of resisting the French preponderance. The accession of a Dutch stadholder to the English throne, in the person of William III (1689), cemented this alliance, and the ambitions of Louis XIV were successfully curbed. But the Dutch had lost ground in the struggle and their maritime supremacy had passed to Great Britain.

The English colonial empire, which was ultimately to surpass all others, included in the seventeenth century only some islands in the *English settlements in America* West Indies and a strip of coast in North America stretching from Maine to South Carolina.[1] To this may be added a disputed claim to Newfoundland and to the little known regions of Hudson Bay. But the English, like the Dutch, took advantage of the Spanish decline to organize an East India Company (1600), and several associations were formed in the following years to promote English trade and colonization in North America. Religious persecution at home helped to swell the colonial population, for nonconformist exiles founded Plymouth in 1620, and Roman Catholics flocked to Maryland after 1632. By 1700, the English colonies on the mainland had a population of well over three hundred thousand souls, imbued with a hardy, aggressive, and independent spirit.

The French colonists in North America were only about one tenth as numerous, but they had extended their settlements from the mouth of the Saint Lawrence River to the Great Lakes, and had established a claim to the Valley of the Mississippi. The accompanying map reveals how this extension of French influence confined the English settlements, preventing expansion to the north, the west, or the south. A thoughtful observer might easily have foretold, in 1700, that the century would bring a long struggle between France and Britain for the control of the Ohio and Mississippi Valleys.

The great Colbert, minister to Louis XIV of France from 1661 to 1683, had striven earnestly to build up the French navy and merchant marine

[1] See map on next page.

THE COLONIAL SITUATION
ABOUT 1689

British possessions   Dutch possessions
French   "   Portuguese "
Spanish possessions

NORTH

Hudson
Bay

BRITISH
ISLES

DUTCH RE

AMERICA

NEW FRANCE

England

NEWFOUNDLAND

ATLANTIC

FRANC

LOUISIANA

India

PORTUGAL

SPAIN

AZORES IS.

Gibraltar

NEW SPAIN

TEXAS

MADEIRA IS.

CANARY IS.

Bermudas

Florida

Bahama Is.

Cuba

St. Domingo
Hispaniola
Porto-Rico

Guadeloupe

A

C. VERDE IS.

Gorée

PACIFIC

Martinique
Granada

Barbados

OCEAN

Caracas

New
Granada

Cayenne

Cape Coast Castle

OCEAN

PERU

SOUTH

BRAZIL

ST. HELENA

AMERICA

CHILE

C. o.

FALKLAND IS.

C. Horn

160   140   120   100   80   60   40   20   0

60   40   20   0

60

40

20

0

20

40

60

in order to win control of the seas and their trade. But Louis, preferring the vision of European dominion, wasted his resources in continental wars, and England, victorious at sea, gained Acadia (Nova Scotia) and a clear title to Newfoundland and the Hudson Bay territory from France in the Treaty of Utrecht (1713–14), which ended the War of the Spanish Succession. From Spain, the ally of France, the English gained Gibraltar and Minorca in the Mediterranean, the right to send one ship a year to trade with the Spanish American colonies, and the highly lucrative privilege of supplying these colonists with negro slaves. This agreement was known as the *Asiento.* = agreement.

The decline of Spain and Holland had left France and Britain to dispute for the crown of maritime supremacy. In this keen contest France had the advantage of a larger population, but the English were able to throw more energy into the struggle. They could devote all their resources to naval development because a strong fleet was at once the best defense from *The advantages possessed by the English* invasion and the best protection for their shipping. Great Britain possessed, moreover, a parliamentary government which was responsive to the demands of the influential merchant class. Parliament favored commerce and had freed it from the restrictions and the crippling supervision which still burdened French traders. In other words, England had evolved into a mercantile state, with the requisite economic machinery — banks, joint-stock companies, an independent merchant class, and a strong maritime tradition — while France remained largely an archaic feudal state with rigid institutions unadapted to control and direct the new forces to the best advantage. The French colonies in Canada were laid out like transplanted feudal fiefs, and the settlers, despite brilliant leadership, never acquired the energy and initiative of the English colonists. Similarly, the French trading companies, organized and subsidized by royal decree, failed to compete profitably with rival ventures which owed their existence to the enterprise of Dutch or English merchants.

3. THE EIGHTEENTH CENTURY: THE DUEL OF FRANCE AND BRITAIN FOR COLONIAL SUPREMACY (1689–1763)

In the quarter of a century which followed the Peace of Utrecht (1713–14), the French made the most determined efforts they had so far shown to check the British in India and America. Of the lost Portuguese Empire in the East, the Dutch had *The French in India* taken the islands while tacitly relinquishing India to British enterprise.

Eager to gather some of the profits of the India trade themselves, the French entered the race, and speedily alarmed the English by their competition. They had organized a French East India Company (1664); now they established posts and factories in India, defended them with forts and garrisons, and concluded treaties with the native princes. Trade, however, was by no means the sole attraction which drew European adventurers to India. It was a much more lucrative venture to aid the Indian rulers in their wars against one another, for the presence of a small European force with its superior weapons could decide important campaigns, and the rajahs were ready to pay for such aid with a king's ransom. When, after 1741, the able and ambitious French governor general, Dupleix, began to recruit and drill Indian troops and meddle in the affairs of the Great Mogul's Empire, the British were convinced that he planned to make French influence supreme and expel them from the peninsula.

Between Spain and England also a hostile spirit reigned, for the Spaniards wished to monopolize the trade of their South and Central American colonies. *Anglo-Spanish rivalry* The Treaty of Utrecht, which permitted the English to sell the colonists slaves, and to send one trading ship a year to the Isthmus of Panama, revealed to them how profitable commerce with New Spain might be, and they coveted more of it. Had it been possible, they would have seized the Spanish cities in the New World, but the empire of Spain was vulnerable only on its fringes. Stretching from the Rio Grande to the Rio de la Plata, with its ports of entry well guarded, New Spain has been compared to a tortoise which hides under its shell and defies its enemies. The English had to content themselves with the gains they made by bribing the Spanish authorities and so carrying on a smuggling trade with the colonists. This equivocal state of affairs created ill-feeling on both sides. When, in 1739, a Captain Jenkins came before the English Parliament avowing that his ship had been boarded and his ear cut off by the Spanish officials, a conflict developed between Spain and England known as the "War of Jenkins's Ear."

The following year (1740) Frederick II of Prussia seized the Austrian province of Silesia and plunged Europe into the War of the Austrian *War of the Austrian Succession* Succession, in which England and Austria were allied against Prussia, France, and Spain. The European aspects of this struggle, which left Prussia in possession of Silesia, have been described already.[1] In India and America the French and English fought with varying fortune but indecisive results. By the

[1] See pages 85–86.

Treaty of Aix-la-Chapelle (1748), England, France, and Spain restored all conquests, and the English consented to abandon the *Asiento* in return for an indemnity of £100,000.

The interval of peace which followed 1748 was only a breathing spell in the colonial struggle, a preparation for a definitive test of strength between France and Great Britain. To the victor would go the mastery of the seas and a colonial empire without parallel in history, yet even this glittering prize failed to excite the French to a supreme effort. Under the indolent Louis XV, they turned their attention more willingly to Polish or German problems than to the needs of their colonies. Brilliant leaders like Dupleix in India and Montcalm in Canada worked heroically for the glory of France, with inadequate resources and scant encouragement, while the national revenue was being gaily squandered by the courtiers at Versailles. In America, especially, the French commanders displayed foresight and energy in their efforts to hem in the English by a line of forts stretching from the Valley of the Saint Lawrence down the Ohio and Mississippi rivers to the Gulf of Mexico. But too many Frenchmen thought with Voltaire that Canada was only "a few acres of snow," and failed to appreciate that the expenses of a single campaign on the Rhine might have secured half a continent across the ocean.

Hostilities between the French and English broke out again in America in 1754, where the new struggle was to be known as the French and Indian War. Its European phase began in 1756, and was *The French* marked by the heroic defense which Frederick the Great *lose Canada* of Prussia maintained against France, Austria, and Russia.[1] While the Prussian king waged his desperate campaigns year after year, his ally, England, was concluding the colonial duel with France. Fortune proved unfavorable to British arms in the first campaigns; a force under General Braddock was ambushed and almost annihilated near Fort Duquesne on the Ohio River; and expeditions directed against the French forts at Niagara and Crown Point were unsuccessful. But in 1757 the British were inspired to new efforts by the great war minister, William Pitt (the Elder), and their victories broke the French resistance. In 1759, in a battle which cost both leaders their lives, Wolfe wrested Quebec from the French veteran Montcalm, and Canada, with its sixty thousand settlers, was lost to France. The British flag seemed destined to wave undisputed from the Gulf of Mexico to the Arctic Ocean.

In India the success of the English was no less complete. The ambitious projects of Dupleix were frustrated by the military skill and

[1] See above, pages 88–90.

He was merely a clerk working for the East India Company

audacity of a young commander, Robert Clive, whose astonishing feats with insignificant forces broke the French influence. The southwest coast of India (the Carnatic) as well as the rich province of Bengal were brought under British control. When the Seven Years' War ended in 1763, French naval power had been shattered and French commerce had all but disappeared from the seas.

The stakes in this most arduous and exhausting colonial war yet fought had clearly gone to the English. Yet it would be a mistake to imagine that the extension of British influence and the annexation of new lands benefited all Englishmen equally. The classes which profited directly were the investors who drew larger dividends from the fur trade with the American Indians, the colonists and land speculators who could exploit the rich territory beyond the Alleghanies now freed from French control, and the adventurous officials in India whose lucrative meddling in native affairs now met no serious competition. These were the classes which had done most to provoke the war, and had pressed Parliament most vigorously to carry the struggle to a victorious conclusion.

The Treaty of Paris (1763) reflected the magnitude of the British triumph. It left England in control of French Canada, and of Florida *Treaty of* which was ceded by Spain. As compensation, the Spaniards *Paris (1763)* received a title to the lands, only partly explored, lying between the Mississippi and the Pacific Ocean. In India the French retained some of their trading posts, but their activities were so restricted that they could no longer offer any effective opposition to British expansion. The Treaty of Paris assured Great Britain the position of the world's leading commercial and colonial power, a position which her less successful rivals found it difficult to contemplate without envy. Smarting from their losses, and from British arrogance, the French, the Dutch, and the Spanish all nursed a hope of revenge. They were to find an opportunity to gratify it shortly by helping to disrupt the British dominions in America.

4. THE BRITISH COLONIES IN AMERICA WIN THEIR INDEPENDENCE

In the eighteenth century colonies were valued chiefly because they provided non-European commodities, such as rice, sugar, and tobacco, for consumption in the home country, and thus helped to render it independent of the products of other nations. This attitude toward colonies was an extension of the prevailing Mercantile System, formulated in the belief that a great power should accumulate gold by selling

SHIPS OF WAR OF THE SEVENTEENTH AND EIGHTEENTH
CENTURIES

*Insignificant as these sailing ships appear when compared to a modern dreadnaught,
they enabled the European nations, two centuries ago, to dominate the oceans of the
world and build up large colonial empires.*

to its neighbors while buying as little as possible in return. As early as 1650, the English Parliament passed more stringent Navigation Acts, which declared that only English ships could bring colonial products to English ports. Later edicts commanded the English colonists to trade only with the mother country, and forbade them to compete with manufacturers in England. For instance, the colonists were forbidden to make hats for sale in England, while the English people were forbidden to raise tobacco which was a colonial monopoly. It irked the merchants of Boston and Philadelphia that they were expected to sacrifice potential profits by trading only with English firms, when they could obtain tea from the Dutch or molasses from the French at cheaper prices. The regulations were frequently evaded and a smuggling trade developed which the British government made little serious effort to repress. This tolerant attitude eased the friction which might otherwise have developed, and the colonists were reasonably satisfied as long as the government at London pursued a policy which has been defined as "salutary neglect."

After the Seven Years' War this tolerant state of affairs underwent a change, and the British government assumed a more despotic tone in matters of colonial administration. With the establish-

Great Britain "oppresses" the colonists

ment of peace in 1763, the prime minister, George Grenville, prepared to regulate colonial trade more vigorously. New import duties were imposed upon coffee, wines, calico, etc., entering the colonies, and although the duty on foreign molasses was reduced (1764), a determined effort was made to keep the American merchants from smuggling it in duty free as they had been doing. The colonists had been in the habit of selling their products in the foreign West Indies, buying in return the sugar and molasses from which they manufactured cheap rum to exchange for Indian furs and African slaves. When this form of exchange was checked by the British regulations, the colonists found themselves running short of hard money wherewith to buy British goods; and when they sought to issue paper currency to supply the shortage, Parliament restrained them (Currency Act of 1765). To British statesmen, conscious that England had incurred heavy expenses in order to win the Seven Years' War, it appeared no more than just that the colonists should pay in part for their defense. The effort to suppress smuggling and increase the customs revenue reflected this policy, and the government sought to raise further funds by a Stamp Tax (1765), requiring all pamphlets, newspapers, and legal documents to bear a stamp. The colonists, however, argued that they could not legally be taxed by a Parliament sitting in London, to which they elected no representatives, and so loudly did they raise the protest of "no taxation without representation" that the Stamp Tax was withdrawn in 1766.

Nevertheless, the British government still insisted upon its right to levy duties if it saw fit to do so. The colonists were requested to provide for the maintenance of British garrisons stationed in America for their defense, and additional duties on imports were introduced to meet this expense (Townshend Acts, 1767). Twenty years earlier the colonists might have furnished such a contribution willingly, for they needed the protection of British regulars while the French still menaced their settlements. But the Seven Years' War had transferred Canada to England and broken the French power in the West. This newly won security fostered a spirit of independence and self-confidence in the British colonists, and they found it easy to convince themselves that the policy of George III and his ministers was a despotic infringement of their liberties.

When the British attempted to employ coercive measures, they excited armed resistance (1775). Both sides were determined not to compromise, and the colonists prepared to fight for their rights *The Declaration of Independence (July 4, 1776)* and if possible enlist outside support. In 1776, a Continental Congress representing all thirteen colonies assembled in Philadelphia and issued a Declaration of Independence. In taking this extreme step the delegates were strongly influenced by the knowledge that the French government might aid them materially if they gave proof that they sought complete separation from England. But the new nation thus ushered into existence was at first neither free nor united. The British were determined to hold the empire together by all the armed force at their command, while in America many colonists, known as "loyalists" or "tories," were opposed to the complete separation demanded by the "patriots."

The Declaration of Independence attributed the outbreak of hostilities to the tyrannous rule of George III, but the true causes were deeper and more complicated. The Americans, who numbered about two million in 1775, were accustomed to managing their own affairs. By toil and daring they had subdued and colonized a strange land. To survive and prosper under such conditions required courage and initiative and bred a spirit of self-assurance and independence. A clergyman writing in 1781 estimated that the English settlers had killed eighty-six thousand Indians in fifty years; and on the lands thus cleared they had set busy towns and rich plantations. It was perhaps no more than natural that these Americans should resent the orders of a cabinet in London, which understood little about their problems and had long treated them with comparative indifference and neglect. The removal of the French menace, as already explained, gave the colonists a new sense of strength and security; the attempts of the British officials to regulate their trade and supervise their affairs more straitly crystallized their discontent; and the treatment accorded to the newly conquered French Canadians added a final grievance. For by the Quebec Act (1774) the British government extended the boundaries of Canada south to the Ohio River (territory the American colonists coveted for themselves), and promised the French Catholics the full privileges of their religion, customs, and laws, measures which gratified the Canadians as deeply as they affronted the New England Puritans. Thus the ties which bound the English colonists to the mother country had been progressively weakened before the Declaration of Independence broke them.

At first it appeared improbable that the Americans could maintain the independence which they had proclaimed. When, after three years *Britain is* of campaigning, the tide of success began to turn in their *attacked by* favor, France came to their aid (1778) and was joined by *France,* *Spain, and* Spain (1779) and Holland (1780). Great Britain could not *Holland* maintain a successful struggle against this coalition. The high-handed use which the British had made of their maritime supremacy had left them without a friend in Europe, and they were willing by 1782 to purchase peace at the price of concessions. The thirteen colonies were recognized as independent [1] and became the United States of America; the territories of the new nation extended from the Atlantic seaboard to the Mississippi, and from the Great Lakes to Florida. Florida itself Great Britain retroceded to Spain, while France regained some posts in India, two islands in the West Indies (Saint Lucia and Tobago), and Senegal and Gorée in Africa. The British had tasted the medicine of defeat and their prestige had been somewhat reduced, but Great Britain still remained the foremost colonial and maritime power of the world.

5. THE ABATEMENT OF COLONIAL RIVALRY AFTER 1783

By the end of the eighteenth century, the Spanish, Dutch, French, and finally the English had discovered that it was easier to found settlements overseas than to retain them. Colonies, as one French statesman observed, were like fruits: they dropped from the parent tree as soon as they were ripe. To waste blood and treasure establishing such colonies, only to see them fall into other hands or assert their independence,

---

[1] Treaty of Paris, 1783.

seemed a dubious investment, especially because most of the islands and coastal areas in the New World had been claimed, and the further exploitation and colonization of the interior promised to be an even more costly and hazardous enterprise. This mood of disillusionment may explain in part why the powers relaxed their colonial rivalries for nearly a century after 1783. Wars were not for that reason less numerous or less destructive, but they were inspired by events in Europe itself and were little affected by colonial questions. Not until after 1870, as we shall note later, did new factors drive the nations to revive their interest in overseas empires, and the spirit of a "New Imperialism" make colonies once again a major source of armed conflict.

The reverses suffered in America might have provided British statesmen with valuable lessons in the art of colonial administration, but there is little evidence that they derived much conscious profit *British colonial administration* from them. Their attitude toward French Canada remained benevolent but conservative. The Quebec Act of 1774, as already explained, conciliated the *Canadiens* by preserving their customs and religion, and this statesmanlike treatment of the conquered kept French Canada loyal while the thirteen colonies revolted. In 1791, representative assemblies were established in Upper and Lower Canada (Ontario and Quebec), but the Canadians had to stage a minor rebellion (1837) before they obtained a measure of genuine popular government, and not until 1867 were the scattered provinces knit into a self-governing Dominion.

Ireland likewise, though granted a local parliament in 1782, was deprived of this privilege in 1801 when England was struggling against Napoleon, and the Irish remained bitterly discontented with British rule throughout the nineteenth century. In India a somewhat more liberal and conscientious policy prevailed after 1784, when the East India Company was brought under stricter government supervision lest it abuse its great power, but there also a bloody rebellion, the so-called Sepoy Mutiny of 1857, was needed to awaken the British administrators to the importance of reform.

The mercantilist philosophy, the application of which had helped to disrupt the British Empire in America, held its ground for some decades after 1783, but yielded slowly to the newer doctrines of *Decline of mercantilist theories* free trade. Many economists, especially in France, had come to believe that governmental regulation of trade by means of monopolies, tariffs, and bounties was artificial and constrictive, creating more evils than it cured. To govern better, they argued, it was necessary to govern less, for trade languished under arbitrary

[105]

rules and could prosper to best advantage only when it was allowed to follow a normal or natural development. The most able exposition of the new theory was propounded by the Scotsman, Adam Smith (1723–90), in a monumental study entitled *An Inquiry into the Nature and Causes of the Wealth of Nations.* By a coincidence, Smith's work, which was to become a bible for those who advocated a liberal trade policy, appeared in 1776, the year the American colonists proclaimed their independence. The mercantilist theory thus received two blows, one in the practical and one in the theoretical field, during the same year. When the liberal bourgeoisie secured control of the English Parliament in the nineteenth century, they were to lead the way in advocating the doctrine of non-interference with trade, or *laissez-faire*, and to see their theories apparently vindicated by the unequaled prosperity which British commerce and industry enjoyed throughout the greater part of the century. But this prosperity was founded upon a combination of favoring circumstances which could not endure indefinitely, and in the twentieth century even the British, as we shall discover, found that free trade could become unprofitable in practice.

CHAPTER EIGHT

THE INTELLECTUAL REVOLUTION

True philosophy expounds nature to us; but she can be understood only by him who has learned the speech and symbols in which she speaks to us. This speech is mathematics, and its symbols are mathematical figures.
GALILEO GALILEI (1564–1642).

If I have seen farther than Descartes, it is by standing on the shoulders of giants.
SIR ISAAC NEWTON (1642–1727).

T HE most significant changes in human history, developments fraught with incalculable results for the destiny of mankind, have sometimes passed all but unnoticed in their time. To European people in the seventeenth and eighteenth centuries the misery of the Thirty Years' War, the troublesome ambitions of Louis XIV, the rivalry of France and England for colonies or of France and Austria for conquests, seemed matters of the highest importance. And so, in their time, they were. But the historian who looks back on those centuries can detect a movement of another kind, a movement which proceeded without thunder of cannon or fanfare of trumpets, yet was destined to change the course of history more profoundly than all the wars from that time to the present. This development was the progress made in the study of natural science.

1. THE BEGINNINGS OF THE SCIENTIFIC REVOLUTION

The Italian Renaissance in the fifteenth century had liberated a remarkable outburst of creative energy, and the Protestant Reformation in the sixteenth had shaken the power of the universal *Rise of the* church and weakened the hold of tradition. More men had *scientific* begun to think for themselves, and by the seventeenth cen- *spirit* tury they were looking about them with a new self-confidence, a new audacity, a new inquisitiveness. Rejecting accepted beliefs, natural philosophers in all parts of Europe turned to probe Nature for her secrets with sharpened curiosity, and the result was a flood of discoveries. In a few generations men learned more truths about the universe in which they lived than their ancestors had brought to light in all previous history. Linking one discovery to another, formulating bold hypotheses and then confirming them by observation and experiment, scientists created a new heaven and a new earth, sweeping into the discard many of the most venerable beliefs which they had inherited from previous

[107]

ages. Compared with this revolution in thought, the social and political changes of the period were insignificant, but the new theories were unintelligible to most people and were consequently ignored by them. Then as now scientific speculation proved too abstruse to be grasped by the lay mind, and the progress of science depended upon the labors of a small class of experimenters and specialists.

Some of the earliest and most brilliant victories of the new scientific method were won in the field of astronomy. Although in ancient times several Greek astronomers had taught correctly that the earth revolved about the sun, during the Middle Ages the people of Europe believed that the earth was the immovable center of the universe, and that round it the other heavenly bodies revolved once in twenty-four hours. This theory had been expounded so convincingly by an astronomer of Alexandria, Claudius Ptolemaeus, who lived in the second century of the Christian era, that it is still referred to as the Ptolemaic theory.

For thirteen centuries this fallacious view prevailed, until in 1543 a learned Polish astronomer, Nicolas Copernicus (1473–1543), offered a *Copernicus* new theory to explain the movements of the heavenly bodies. He suggested that the sun was the center of the system, that the earth and planets revolved about it, and that the earth also rotated on its axis once every twenty-four hours. This view, which we accept today as self-evident, is termed the Copernican theory because it was first advocated in the work Copernicus prepared *On the Revolution of the Heavenly Bodies*.

As this book was written in Latin, and was difficult to understand, only scholars paid any attention to it at first. Some found it convincing and declared that a more patient and exact observation of the heavens would confirm its thesis. Others rejected the whole theory as fallacious, even asserting that it was dangerous and blasphemous to publish views which seemed to contradict the Bible and the teaching of the church. But the stars in their courses were fighting for the new theory and unprejudiced astronomers were gradually convinced. By the opening of the seventeenth century, a sharp conflict had developed between the champions of the Copernican theory and the orthodox defenders of the Ptolemaic system.

In 1600, an Italian philosopher, Giordano Bruno, was burned at the stake by sentence of the Inquisition, for teaching the new astronomy and *Kepler* other heresies. Yet the movements of the planets had by this time been calculated so carefully that a German astronomer, Johannes Kepler (1571–1630), was able to formulate mathematical laws for them. He showed (1) that each planet in its orbit around the sun does not describe a perfect circle, but an ellipse of which the sun is one of the foci; and (2) that the speed of each planet changes, growing swifter as it passes nearer the sun and slower as it swings around the more distant segment of its orbit, so that its radius vector traverses equal areas in equal times.   These conclusions led Kepler to his supreme discovery or third law.   (3) The time interval which a planet requires to complete its journey around the sun depends upon its mean or average distance from the sun.   This dependence Kepler reduced to the formula: the square of a planet's periodic time is proportional to the cube of its mean distance from the sun.

The invention of the telescope at this time brought fresh evidence to support the Copernican hypothesis and justify it as a system.   In 1610, the Florentine scientist, Galileo Galilei (1564–1642), turned *Galileo* this new instrument upon the heavens and disclosed a suc- *Galilei* cession of marvels.   For the first time the mountains of the moon, the rings of Saturn, the moons of Jupiter, and the phases of Venus were made visible to the eyes of men.   Doubters who had found it easy to scoff at theories were shaken by observable facts.   Yet to many it still appeared wicked to teach that the earth, far from being the center of things, created by God's special care as the stage for the drama of man's fall and re-demption, was in reality no more than a ball of mud spinning on an endless spiral through infinite night.   Galileo was warned by the In-quisition that in defending the new astronomy he was weakening Chris-tian belief and the respect due to established authority.   When he per-sisted, he was summoned before the Inquisition, compelled to forswear his belief in the movement of the earth, and forbidden to teach the theory thenceforth.   Had he refused to yield, he might have been imprisoned for life or burned at the stake like Bruno.

Despite discouragement and opposition, however, the scientists intensified their speculations and experiments, spurred on by the conviction that the heavens had further secrets to yield.   The order and permanence which prevailed in the solar system drove them to ponder what force could hold the moons and planets to courses of such undeviating regularity.   In 1600, an Englishman, William Gilbert (1540–1603), suggested that the earth might be regarded as a huge magnet which attracted bodies to itself by magnetism or gravitation. Kepler developed this idea, arguing that the force of attraction exer-cised by a body increased with its mass and extended far beyond that body, so that the earth, for example, must exert a constant attraction upon the moon which the moon resisted through some equivalent counter-force.

It remained for the English mathematician, Sir Isaac Newton (1642–1727), to reduce these inferences to order and explain the movements *Sir Isaac* of all the celestial bodies as consequences of one general *Newton* law of gravitation. In 1687, in his immortal *Principia*,[1] Newton formulated his conclusion that the force of attraction between two bodies varies directly as the sum of their masses and inversely as the square of the distance between them. To test his hypothesis he had applied it to explain the movement of the moon about the earth, and when he found his figures working out correctly, he was so deeply stirred by the splendor of his discovery that he had to ask a friend to finish the calculations for him. For further verification he extended his computations to the planets, to the tides, even to the apparent vagaries of comets, and found that all proclaimed the universality of the law his genius had discerned.

In the century and a half following the death of Copernicus scientists had stripped most of the mystery from the heavens. Inexorable laws were found to govern the movements of all sidereal bodies, so that the smallest comet hurtling through the darkness of outer space could not vary a hair's breadth from the path prescribed for it by mathematical calculations. Edmund Halley, a friend and disciple of Newton, was able to compute the orbit of a comet which appeared in 1682 and predict its reappearance in seventy-seven years. Halley's comet not only justified this computation by reappearing in 1759; it returned in 1835 and 1910, and may be expected again about 1986. The medieval superstition that comets were sent to announce an approaching disaster or the death of a king was thus forced to yield, like many another superstition, to the matter-of-fact explanation of the scientists. It is not difficult to understand why opposition grew between those people who chose still to believe in omens and miracles and the rationalists who insisted there was no place for miracles in a universe governed by inflexible laws.

While the study of astronomy advanced thus with giant strides, the other sciences were not standing still. In physics, chemistry, *"The Cen-* anatomy, and a score of related fields, investigators only *tury of* a little less illustrious than Galileo or Newton pressed on *Genius"* to new discoveries. In their search they found it necessary to invent tools more delicate and more accurate than the human senses, like the telescope, microscope, thermometer, and barometer. Unfortunately, there is no space to tell here how William Harvey (1578–1657) discovered the circulation of the blood, how Anton van

[1] The full title is *Principia Philosophiae Naturalis Mathematica*.

[110]

SIR ISAAC NEWTON
1642–1727

The painter has represented Sir Isaac Newton with a globe beside him and a book, apparently filled with geometrical figures, to suggest Newton's outstanding contributions to natural philosophy and mathematical science.

Leeuwenhoek (1632–1723) first observed bacteria under his microscope, or how Robert Boyle (1627–91) formulated the law that the volume of a gas varies inversely with the pressure. Merely to list the outstanding discoveries of these eventful years would require several pages. So productive were the experiments of these fathers of modern science, so profound their speculations, that the seventeenth century has been well named "The Century of Genius." Of the many triumphs only the epic of the astronomers has been related in any detail because it reveals best of all two *habits* which the scientists had cultivated, to which they owed their amazing success. These were (1) the habit of translating all calculations whenever possible into a new and special language, the language of mathematics; and (2) the habit of basing all conclusions upon observation and experiment instead of appealing to ancient writers or to popular belief for the truth. Both these practices were so important and so revolutionary that they demand explanation.

2. THE PROGRESS OF MATHEMATICS

The scientists of the seventeenth century first clearly perceived that "mathematics is the skeleton of God's plan of the universe."

The "Language of Nature" The most brilliant achievements of the astronomers, from Kepler's discovery of what he well named *The Harmony of the Heavens* to Newton's law of gravitation, were all expressed in mathematical formulas. It delighted these natural philosophers to think that they had at last stumbled upon the language in which Nature wrote her secrets. "This language," proclaimed Galileo, "is mathematics, and the characters are triangles, circles, and other mathematical figures." A peculiar charm invested this language of numbers, for it was flexible, accurate, and international.

The development of modern mathematics is the most original achievement of the human intellect. Although the ancients had laid down many of the first principles of the science, their legacy, in comparison with the progress of modern times, is like the simple melody of a flute contrasted with the intricate harmonies of a hundred-piece orchestra.

Decimals To this science of numbers "The Century of Genius" made four pre-eminent contributions: (1) The introduction of decimals, first written with a decimal point in 1616, saved vast labors in the handling of fractions. (2) Of even greater value was the conception of logarithms, announced by a Scotsman, John Napier, in 1614. Because they offered a short cut through cumber-

Logarithms

some calculations, logarithms doubled the lives of astronomers by halving their labors.   (3) A further advance in method is associated with the name of the French philosopher, René Descartes (1596– *Analytic* 1650).   In 1637, Descartes revealed in his analytic geometry *geometry* how facts ascertainable in geometry may be translated into algebra, and *vice versa*, thus offering a dual method of attack whereby stubborn problems could be outflanked.   (4) A fitting culmination to these previous gains was the formulation after 1680 of the differential cal- *Differential* culus, developed independently by Sir Isaac Newton and *calculus* the German philosopher Leibnitz, and acclaimed as "perhaps the most important step in the progress of mathematical science."

3. THE EXPERIMENTAL METHOD

The second habit to which the scientists owed much of their success was their practice of appealing to observation and experiment as the surest test of truth.   No statement, though repeated by ancient and venerable sages and long accepted by the mass of mankind as too obvious for argument, was to be accepted if it contradicted established facts. Copernicus, for instance, rejected the opinions of men of learning and the evidence of his own senses, all of which assured him that the earth was immovable.   But because this theory failed to explain the motions of the planets, he abandoned it, observed the phenomena, pondered them, and then devised a new theory which would include and account for the motions of all the heavenly bodies.   Reasoning in this way from a number of particular cases to a general conclusion is called *induction*. The triumph of Copernicus was one of the first in a long series of successes won by the method of experiment, observation, and induction.

Scholastic thinkers of the Middle Ages had been disposed to spin fine theories while ignoring facts, or to interpret facts in such a fashion that they would appear to support established theories.   Be- *Authority* lieving, for example, that the sun was a perfect, unchanging *vs. experi-* body because the Greek philosopher Aristotle had said so, *ment* the later schoolman offered this statement, which they could not prove, as a refutation of the Copernican theory.   When the newly invented telescopes revealed spots on the sun which moved across its face, the Aristotelians declared the notion inadmissible and argued that the flaws must be in the telescope because they could not be in the sun.   Similarly, the scientists demonstrated by dissection and experiment that accepted beliefs in anatomy or physics were wrong, but they found it difficult to convince orthodox thinkers, who rebuked them for their

[113]

irreverence and repudiated the evidence submitted to them. Some theologians even affirmed that the Devil mixed himself in scientific experiments and falsified the results in order to confuse men and shake their faith in true principles. In the face of such obscurantism it is not altogether surprising that advocates of the newer sciences learned to feel contempt for the scholastic philosophy and for its defenders.

The experimental method, on the other hand, seemed to promise man infinite possibilities for bettering his lot and controlling his destiny. The English lord chancellor, Francis Bacon (1561–1626), thought so highly of it that he drew a prophetic picture of the glories of the future in his *New Atlantis,* and scorned the hoary errors of the past. In breaking with tradition the new thinkers came to prize independence of judgment above mere book learning. Thomas Hobbes (1588–1679), who sometimes acted as secretary to Bacon and later wrote dogmatic works on political philosophy, was wont to boast that if he had read as much as most men he would probably know as little. "Reasoning from the Authority of Books," he declared, in his caustic fashion, " ... is not Knowledge, but Faith." Descartes found so many errors in the works on anatomy which he consulted that he turned to Nature for the truth. "These are my books," he told a visitor, pointing to the bodies of animals which he was dissecting. But these scientists, though they sometimes scorned the learning of earlier centuries, understood the value of sharing their discoveries with each other. "If I have seen farther than Descartes," admitted Newton, who lived half a century later, "it is by standing on the shoulders of giants."

4. THE SCIENTIFIC ACADEMIES

It was, therefore, by means of learned journals, correspondence, travel, and exchange of views that the earliest scientists sought to keep alive the flame of curiosity, which, while it sometimes burns brightly in one lonely genius, is never so productive as when it feeds upon the combined enthusiasm of many workers. In their impetuous search they were like mountaineers who attack a mighty peak from many sides, convinced that they were destined to converge until they met together at the summit and found that all truth was ultimately one. Newton had compared himself to a child playing on the seashore with the great ocean of truth all undiscovered before him, but many of his followers were less modest and more sanguine. Already they had learned how a discovery in physics might supply the clue to an obscure problem in astronomy, and this in turn depend for solution upon a recent advance in mathematics. The most versatile genius could not excel in all fields, but he might utilize the principles and proofs established by gifted contemporaries if he could avail himself of them. By such borrowing a scientist was in a position to follow experiments in a hundred laboratories at once, observe the stars from every corner of Europe on the same night, and help himself to the answers which the labor of others had wrung from arduous computations. Such collaboration speedily became a habit with the scientists, as fruitful in its results as the habit of using observation and induction to seek new truths and the habit of expressing them in mathematical terms when found.

The easiest way to share ideas is by personal contact, and societies organized for discussion and experiment were one of the first proofs that the scientific revolution had begun. An "Academy *The Royal* of the Lynx-Eyed" was formed at Rome in 1601, and *Society* an "Academy for Experiment" made its appearance at Florence in 1657. After 1660, when war ceased for a time to absorb the major attention of princes, several new societies were established under royal patronage. The most distinguished were the "Royal Society for Improving Natural Knowledge" incorporated at London in 1662, and the French "Académie des Sciences" chartered by *Académie* Louis XIV in 1666. To record their deliberations and *des Sciences* experiments these academies published scientific journals, and to encourage research they collected funds to build libraries and observatories and to purchase retorts and furnaces, telescopes and microscopes, chronometers, barometers, air pumps, and all the other paraphernalia which laboratory workers had discovered they needed in their pursuit of "Natural Philosophy."

By the eighteenth century, scientists were no longer persecuted; they were honored and rewarded. Galileo had been silenced by the Inquisition for his novel opinions, but when Sir Isaac *Eighteenth-* Newton died in 1727, less than a century later, he was *century in-* buried with honors befitting a king. Science had begun *terest in* to capture the popular imagination. Even people who did *science* not understand much about it were persuaded that it provided a new and marvelous method for unveiling Nature's secrets. Cultured ladies and gentlemen read books explaining Newton's laws and attended lectures on astronomy. Some wealthy men equipped laboratories of their own and conducted experiments in the hope of adding to the sum of human knowledge. And the sum of knowledge continued to grow. In chemistry the elements hydrogen, nitrogen, and oxygen were isolated and their general properties analyzed; in physics valuable progress was made in studying the nature of heat and sound; in zoology, Buffon (1707–88) and Linnaeus (1707–78) reduced the study of animals to a descriptive science. Benjamin Franklin demonstrated that bolts of lightning were not hurled by Satan as many people still believed, but were discharges of electricity which could be turned harmlessly aside by a lightning conductor. Astronomy, anatomy, biology, geology, and mineralogy likewise had their triumphs and flourished apace, so that although the seventeenth century takes rank as "The Century of Genius," the eighteenth has been well named "The Scientific Renaissance."

5. THE INTELLECTUAL REVOLUTION

In every age the great majority of people are too absorbed in their private affairs, in trade, or crops, or home-making, to pay much attention to the progress of abstract ideas. Few Europeans in the seventeenth and eighteenth centuries, for instance, were aware that their habits of thought were changing, for the changes came in slow and subtle ways. Nevertheless, each generation brought some modification of ancient beliefs and outworn ideals, each decade contributed some new discovery, until all educated Europeans, without being aware of it, had passed through a revolution. This revolution was in no way sudden or violent, but it was a revolution none the less. For it overturned a hierarchy of intellectual values, freed civilized men from many obsolete prejudices, knocked the shackles from their minds, as it were, and turned their thoughts from the past to the future. Above all, it filled them with an intoxicating wine, the wine of a new self-confidence.

A very old and intelligent man, looking back let us say from the year 1760, might have observed that within his own lifetime people had altered many of their ideas. A man of unusual perception might even have noted that this change could chiefly be distinguished as "a waning of fear." With each generation it seemed as if men had less dread of the wrath of God, less reverence for the wisdom of the ancients, less awe respecting Nature and her unknown forces. How was this change coming about and what factors promoted it? Whence arose this skeptical and arrogant spirit in the hearts of men which is such a striking component of the modern temper? It will be an interesting task to try to answer these questions.

With the rise of natural philosophy, theology was displaced from its proud position as "Queen of the Sciences." The Great Schism, the Revival of Learning, and the Protestant Reformation *Decline of* had all tended to weaken the unity and authority of the *theology* medieval church, and the religious wars which racked Europe for a hundred years, sapped by their futile fanaticism the faith of many Catholics and Protestants alike. By the eighteenth century religious fervor was yielding before the spirit of tolerance or indifference. It was no longer the custom to burn witches, or to martyr as heretics those who wished to seek heaven in their own fashion. Theologians who threatened the unorthodox with rack and fagot were denounced for their bigotry and obscurantism, and enlightened monarchs no longer insisted that their subjects must all profess the same faith as the king. Secular concerns and worldly pursuits had obscured the sense of intimate dependence upon religion which people had felt so keenly in earlier centuries. Some skeptics dared to repudiate all belief and to deny that the theologians were or ever had been the custodians of divine truths which could guide men to salvation.

The new learning offered man a more vainglorious picture of himself, and rooted itself in his pride, whereas his religious beliefs had been the fruit of his humility. Man was a miserable creature, the *Rise of* theologians had taught, condemned, because of his corrupt *rationalism* nature, to err and suffer endlessly unless he were rescued by divine grace and intervention. But the rationalists were moved to question this view. Perhaps, they suggested, man was intended to control his own destiny, instead of bowing fatalistically to the will of an inscrutable Providence. If God granted him intelligence, there could be nothing blasphemous in using it. It might be that the plagues and miseries from which he suffered were not after all the righteous punishment for his sins, but only the logical consequences of his folly. Instead of being "born to trouble as the sparks fly upward," he might be born to improve his lot on earth far beyond his hopes or dreams. The "original sin" which brought woe to men might not be the sin of Adam, but the sin of their own stupidity. These and similar arguments of the philosophers, disseminated by a few bold minds, won converts and leavened the consciousness of European society because they were suited to the temper of the new age.

The decline of theology was reflected in the waning faith in miracles. If God had established majestic and inflexible laws for the *Growth of* movement of the stars and other phenomena of the physi- *deism and* cal world, it seemed illogical to suppose that He would in- *skepticism* terfere arbitrarily with the working of them. To imagine that God

[117]

could be swayed by human passions or prayers, so that He would make the sun stand still, conjure up a hurricane to punish a blasphemous sailor, or overwhelm a wicked city by a specially invoked earthquake, appeared to the rationalists both stupid and irreverent. They preferred to conceive of God as a remote and impersonal deity, a First Cause or First Principle, or an ideal constitutional monarch who never violated the laws which He had established for the government of the natural realm. Thinkers who embraced this view were termed deists, but some went so far as to deny the existence of a deity altogether, and thereby proclaimed themselves atheists.

A waning reverence for the wisdom of the ancients has been cited as the second symptom of the Intellectual Revolution. In the general *"Quarrel of* assault upon authorities and institutions long established, *the Ancients* the reputation of the classical authors suffered consider-*and Mod-* ably. Under Louis XIV some French savants, proud of *erns"* the greatness of their own age, dared to challenge the title of superiority commonly accorded the great men of Greece and Rome. Half the conclusions of Aristotle, they pointed out, had been disproved by modern students of science; Plato, the "divine Plato," was after all no more than human; Virgil, for all his suavity, was somewhat cold and barren; and even the great Homer could sometimes nod — and make readers nod — with his tedious digressions. At this blasphemy the champions of the "ancients" sharpened their pens and hastened to combat these audacious "moderns." Seas of ink were spilled and the controversy dragged well into the eighteenth century without reaching a decision. But thinking men in general came to feel that the moderns were partly right; that in mathematical and scientific progress, and perhaps in music also, their own age was supreme, though they were willing to concede that ancient masterpieces in art and literature might remain unsurpassed. This "Quarrel of the Ancients and Moderns," a small affair in itself, was one more token that the western world had come of age. For over a thousand years Europeans had looked backward with a sense of nostalgia and tragic loss to the fading gleams of the Age of Gold. They had hoarded the crumbs of wisdom from the classical times as mankind's rarest heritage of culture, for, in the barbarism of the dark ages, such veneration was not altogether misplaced. Now they were escaping from this tutelage of the past and learning to anticipate such glorious progress in the future that all previous accomplishments would seem but a prelude to it.

The third and possibly the most important change which the Intellectual Revolution brought to western man was a new attitude toward

[118]

Nature. Medieval students neglected the natural sciences, and scarcely one important discovery in physics or chemistry, in astronomy or mechanics or medicine, was made during the Middle Ages. This failure to investigate Nature does not prove that medieval thinkers were necessarily less intelligent or *The medieval attitude toward Nature* industrious than modern scientists; it does indicate, however, that their values were different, that they reasoned from different premises and pursued a different aim. They neglected the study of Nature, because they conceived the chief end of man to be that he should live in accordance with God's will and strive for eternal salvation; and they subordinated all lesser studies to that of theology, because theology taught how men might be saved. Compared with the world of the spirit, the world of matter was corrupt and transitory. Undue concern with earthly affairs diverted the soul from God and might lead to damnation. The investigator who dabbled successfully in alchemy, astrology, or other pseudo-sciences, became to the popular mind a wizard or magician who had doubtless purchased his uncanny art by selling his soul to the devil. To the majority of people in the Middle Ages, illiterate, ignorant, and superstitious, the world was like a haunted house, in which they moved about cautiously and timorously, respecting the jealous whims of the unknown beings, and trusting to the aid of the saints and angels to save them from the devils and goblins.

When the austere wind of scientific speculation blew away the mists of medieval fantasy, it disclosed a universe built on a grander scale and a different plan from that previously imagined. To the eye of the scientist Nature emerged as a vast and intricate machine of severe and geometric beauty. All fear of supernatural forces seemed idle to the rationalist because for him there were no supernatural forces, no miracles, no angels, and no devils. The great machine was governed by eternal and immutable laws. To suppose that such a universe could turn from its course to strike a man to earth for presumptuous questioning, or that the sea would part and allow him to cross it dry-shod in his need, was to yield to a naïve and implausible presumption. "In Nature there are neither rewards nor punishments, there are only consequences." And it appeared to follow that if man had faith in himself and in science, if he applied himself to the study of Nature and mastered her secrets, he could learn to avoid evil consequences and assure good ones, thus becoming the arbiter of his destiny. Such at least was the dazzling promise held out by many apostles of the new enlightenment.

This optimistic faith in man's capacity for progress inspired the Age of Reason. Liberal thinkers everywhere urged that manners, morals, modes of education, of government, of religion, should be analyzed *The Age of* rationally, brought to perfection, or discarded. Once the *Reason* existing laws and institutions had been perfected, the rationalists felt confident that humanity would undergo a miraculous regeneration. This conclusion appeared to follow logically from the teaching of John Locke (1637–1704), who had proclaimed in his *Essay Concerning Human Understanding* (1690) that man's knowledge and beliefs are the fruit of his training and environment and are not predetermined by innate ideas or the curse of original depravity. The mind of a newborn child Locke compared to a blank sheet of paper. "Let us suppose the mind to be, as we may say, white paper, void of all characters, without any ideas — how comes it to be furnished?" he asked, and answered his own question with the one word "Experience." It appeared, therefore, that children born into a just and equitable society, children trained in right thinking under a rational régime, could not fail to grow into good citizens. The first step toward reform was to abolish all irrational practices, all abuses, all myths and superstitions, and to establish wise principles, just laws, and rational institutions.

In thus insisting that man must be freed from all myths and superstitions, the philosophers overlooked the possibility that to cling to myths and superstitions might be part of his nature, and in their relentless war against prejudice and error they failed to take account of their own delusions. They erred concerning the past, particularly the Middle Ages, the significance of which they misunderstood and underrated; and they erred even more seriously concerning the future, for they evinced a touching faith in human perfectibility and underestimated the obstacles to human happiness which still confronted them. They imagined that the millennium was at hand because they had found a fruitful method for investigating the physical sciences, and they leaped to the false conclusion that this method could be applied to the social sciences with the same success. Some ages ask questions, others answer them. The eighteenth century was of the latter type. Its intellectual leaders were of the opinion that they could find the answers to all the problems of society, they burned to apply them, and infected all classes with their contagious enthusiasm. It is not difficult to understand why the eighteenth century was loud with projects of reform, nor surprising that it should have ended with a revolution.

CHAPTER NINE

GOVERNMENT AND SOCIETY UNDER THE OLD RÉGIME

I should have wished to be born in a country in which the interest of the Sovereign and that of the people must be single and identical; to the end that all the movements of the machine might tend always to the general happiness.

JEAN-JACQUES ROUSSEAU.

THE system of government and the organization of society under which the European peoples lived before the great French Revolution broke out in 1789 is commonly spoken of as the *ancien régime* or old régime. It was an outmoded and inefficient system with glaring deficiencies. The wreckage of feudalism still weighed like an incubus upon society, and governments functioned in a makeshift and haphazard fashion, for none of the states had developed administrative machinery adequate to deal with the complexities of a mercantile era. It is the purpose of this chapter to reconstruct a picture of life under the old régime, and to emphasize the defects and abuses which incited the French people to rise against the system. As France was in many respects the typical land of the old régime, the discussion will deal with France in particular, but the student may think of the conditions described as prevailing with local variations throughout most of Europe.

1. DIVINE-RIGHT MONARCHY IN THEORY AND PRACTICE

In the Middle Ages two small but powerful classes, the clergy and the nobles, had come to dominate society. Above these, as the separate states organized themselves, rose the power of the king. By the seventeenth century, in almost all the European states, monarchs had made their authority supreme in theory and in fact. What the king willed was law; his peculiar function was to be at once the benevolent father of his people and the dread sovereign who animated and directed the life of the state. The laws were executed in his name, the coinage was stamped with his image, the nobles enjoyed his bounty and the priests offered prayers for his preservation. For a subject to refuse homage, or to question why one man, who might be endowed with no particular brilliance of mind or nobility of character, should enjoy royal honors, was considered sedition. The king held his office through hereditary right, an office glorified by tradition and sanctified by religion. The throne was revered as the altar was revered, because

[121]

both were regarded as symbols of God's divine authority governing the world through His instruments.

In practice, needless to say, the absolute power of the king was modified by a thousand contingencies. He was dependent upon a *The royal* host of subordinate officials who supplied him with in- *government* formation and exercised delegated powers in his name. Even an industrious monarch like Louis XIV of France, the model of absolute despots, could not supervise all the business of the state; under his indolent successor, Louis XV (1715–74), France was governed in reality by the ministers of the royal council. These councilors sometimes met together with the king presiding, but more often assembled in smaller committees, as the council of state, council of dispatches, council of finance and commerce, and council of war. As the functions of the councils were not very clearly defined, there was much confusion and business piled up more rapidly than it could be dispatched. The councilors were often compelled to waste their time on trivial matters while important issues waited, but they hesitated to delegate the decision to subordinates for fear of sacrificing their jealously guarded authority.

Confusion in the capital bred chaos in the provinces. The royal government in France had extended itself gradually, as it was super- *Chaos in the* imposed by successive rulers upon the relics of feudalism *provinces* and upon the vestiges of local institutions older sometimes than the monarchy. The kingdom had been acquired by fragments and organized by fits and starts. At one time it had been divided into *baillages* and *sénéchausées*, later into *gouvernements*, and finally, under Richelieu, into *généralités*. Each *généralité* was controlled by a royal official known as the intendant, and the power of the intendants had grown so great that they were called in the eighteenth century the "thirty tyrants" of France. Yet the governors of the provinces still held office, as relics of an older organization, and some of the provinces preserved a shadow of independence under their local assemblies, or estates, and were known as *pays d'état* to distinguish them from provinces which lacked this privilege, the *pays d'élection*. Finally, the country was further separated into segments for ecclesiastical administration, segments which bore little relation to the political subdivisions, and into judicial districts which bore little correspondence to anything, even to one another.

The centralization of authority in the hands of the bureaucracy had stifled the initiative and enterprise of local officials, who found it easiest to refer every difficult decision to their superiors. An army of civil servants was required to handle the flood of reports, dispatches, and petitions which poured in from the provinces. The royal government of France was no worse than that of Spain or Austria; it was served by many hard-working and intelligent administrators; but their efforts were of little avail in a system which seemed to have been specially devised to perpetuate confusion and procrastination. When advisers warned Louis XV that reforms were desperately needed, the pleasure-loving king replied that the machine would last out his day. He left it to his ministers to make minor repairs and readjustments and to keep the machine running.

What the state required was a radical and exhaustive reconstruction in every branch of the administration. The partial and often capricious reforms instituted by the ministers in the hope of clearing *Disorder in* a way through the disorder only added to the confusion. *the adminis-* Their instructions were commonly so involved, so lengthy, *tration* and so loaded with amendments that their subordinates found it impossible to master them. Worst of all, where a sound and simple statute existed which might have served as a guiding principle, it was speedily corrupted by a list of exceptions each more complicated than the original. Critics of the old régime in every state in Europe were agreed that the reform of paramount importance was the preparation of a simple and unified code of laws. An absolute monarch, it was urged, might bring order out of the existing chaos by defining the duties and functions of his government in a few logical and invariable rules. Or, if the prince neglected his duty, the people themselves might prepare a constitution which would safeguard their liberties by establishing the government on true and inflexible principles. Throughout society, from the king's councilors to the petty tradesmen in provincial towns, irritation at the administrative disorder was growing into a passion.

2. THE PRIVILEGED AND UNPRIVILEGED CLASSES

The feudal stratification of society into three classes, the Clergy, the Nobility, and the Third Estate, had become iniquitous and illogical by the eighteenth century. In France, a country with perhaps twenty-five million people, the clergy and nobility together constituted less than two per cent of the population, yet they enjoyed the income from the richest lands of the kingdom, were exempted from the most onerous taxes, and occupied by right of rank the highest and best paid offices in the government, the army, and the church.

[123]

The Roman Catholic Church in France owned approximately one fifth of the land. Its income was enormous, one half as great as the *The French* royal revenues according to some estimates, and was de- *clergy* rived from two main sources. The estates of the church brought in the modern equivalent of $200,000,000 a year, and a sum almost as large was furnished by the tithe. This was a tax, theoretically one tenth but in practice more often one fifteenth or less, commonly levied upon the annual yield from land cultivated by laymen. The church itself paid no taxes to the king on its property, but the clergy voted "free gifts" to the royal exchequer from time to time as a partial substitute. Part of the revenue of the church went for charitable purposes, part as salary for the 130,000 clergy; but the salaries were very unevenly distributed. Many abbots and bishops, nobles by birth in most cases, disposed of princely incomes, but the humble and hardworking parish priests were often little better off than the peasants among whom they labored. The impending revolution was to prove that many village *curés* had less loyalty to the First Estate to which they nominally belonged than to the Third Estate whose grievances they understood.

The second privileged class, the nobles, numbered about 110,000 souls, and likewise enjoyed the income from about one fifth of the *The privi-* land. As a rule this land was cultivated by tenants who *leges of the* paid the noble owner rent and services for the privilege. *nobility* Some of the nobles did not even reside on their estates, preferring the more amusing and expensive life at court. Bailiffs collected from the tenants the income which these absentee landlords often squandered on gambling and display. There was a further injustice in the fact that the nobles who enjoyed this unearned revenue, amassed by the toil of others, were free from the more burdensome taxes which the impoverished peasant still had to pay. It was the dream of many a wealthy bourgeois to win his way into this privileged caste, and members of the Third Estate occasionally gained patents of nobility through purchase or distinguished service. Such newcomers were termed the "nobility of the robe" to distinguish them from the prouder "nobility of the sword" whose titles often dated from feudal times. In addition to their exemptions and the income from their estates, many nobles received pensions from the king, while others, who had ruined themselves through extravagance and failed to secure a share of the royal charity, had to retire to their mortgaged lands and a life of penurious obscurity.

The millions of unprivileged subjects who made up the Third Estate scarcely needed the writings of the philosophers to persuade them that the system under which they lived was out of joint. *The Third* *Estate* The simple peasant, who plowed his land and dreaded the visits of the tax collector, might not understand much about political economy, but he had grievances that were concrete and specific. It irked him that when he had scattered his seed in the furrows the pigeons from the lord's dovecote might scratch it up again; that he was forbidden to molest the deer when they nibbled his vegetable garden because they were maintained for the nobleman's pleasure; that when his tender crops which represented weeks of care and toil were trampled by a hunting party from the castle, he had no means of claiming compensation. It was troublesome, too, that he had to carry his grain to the lord's mill to have it ground, and leave part of it as payment when he had too little for himself, or that he might be summoned to work on the road (the *corvée*), or to draw wood to the castle, when his threshing was overdue and his apples were rotting in the orchard because he had no time to press the cider.

The heavy and unequal taxes were a special source of bitterness. All the ranks of the unprivileged, the upper middle class, the lower middle class, the artisans, the servants, the peasants, down to the thieves and vagabonds of the highway, hated the fiscal system. This was not surprising since the burden of taxation rested most heavily upon those least able to support it and crushed the peasant most cruelly of all. For in addition to the rent and services paid to the lord of the manor, and the tithe paid to the church, poor Jacques had to discharge a land tax (the *taille*), a poll tax, an income tax, and a salt tax (the *gabelle*). Peasants too poor to buy food were still compelled to purchase salt at exorbitant prices, and if they attempted to smuggle enough for their need in order to avoid paying the royal revenue on it, they were punished with barbarous severity. Many of them deliberately sank into a state of destitution, knowing that to improve their dwellings or increase the yield of their lands would only expose them to higher assessments and heavier taxes.

The middle-class dwellers in the towns, though better off than the peasants, were even more critical and discontented. The professional and business classes, the bourgeoisie, included the most *The bour-* cultured, the most intelligent, and the most progressive *geoisie* elements in the nation. From the bourgeois class came the most competent officials in the king's service; it included the bankers who tided the government over its financial crises with their loans, and the business men who increased the prosperity of the state by their commercial and industrial enterprise. Yet this energetic and intelligent class was denied political power, and its members were forced to accept a position of inferiority, while the highest offices in the church, the army, the law courts, and the diplomatic service were bestowed upon men whose only claim to preference was their noble birth. Knowing their own worth and importance, conscious that in wealth, ability, and education they were the equals of the titled few, ambitious members of the bourgeoisie hated the system which denied them their deserts. They possessed both the intelligence and the motive for starting a revolution, and they fed their discontent by studying the abuses in the government, particularly those connected with the administration of law and the collection of taxes.

3. LEGAL AND FINANCIAL ABUSES

The confusion of authority under the old régime is well illustrated by the condition of the law courts. Instead of a uniform code of laws in force throughout the nation, France was burdened with some three hundred and sixty differing codes, with the inevitable result that jurisdictions overlapped, decisions conflicted, and litigation grew to interminable proportions. Moreover, an offense punishable in one court by a fine might earn branding or ten years in the galleys from another, although it was obvious, as the rationalists pointed out, that there could not be several penalties for the same crime and all of them just. The humane spirit of the age was further shocked by the barbarous practices of judicial torture, mutilation, branding, and breaking on the wheel. It was not unknown for judges to dismiss guilty criminals brought before them rather than inflict the brutal sentences prescribed by the statute books. But the worst terror in this legal jungle was the arbitrary power of the king and his ministers, who could imprison any citizen without warning, without trial, and without appeal, and on the sole authority of a royal *lettre de cachet* confine him in a secret dungeon "at the king's pleasure."

Harsh laws

Another active cause of discontent was the stupid and oppressive legislation which fettered the expanding trade and industry of the age. Interior customs lines restricted the normal flow of commodities, feudal overlords still levied toll on certain goods passing through their dominions, and town wardens stopped merchandise at the gate for an entrance fee. A load of wine on its way to Paris, for instance, might be assessed for duty over twenty times, with much consequent waste and delay. In industry, progress

Obstructions to trade and industry

was checked by the obstructive and antiquated guilds, which guarded their monopolies jealously. Artisans were, forbidden to change from one trade to another, and better and speedier methods of manufacture were frequently outlawed because of ancient ordinances which had outlived whatever usefulness they once possessed.

Had the government of Louis XV pursued an energetic and successful policy abroad, Frenchmen might have overlooked their domestic ills. But in the wars of the eighteenth century, France *Evils of the* was singularly unfortunate, and by 1763 the country had *tax system* lost all but a remnant of its colonial empire, and amassed a heavy debt. Frenchmen knew that their country was one of the most populous, most favored and wealthy in Europe, yet every year they saw the national indebtedness increase, until bankers hesitated to lend money to the state even at twenty per cent interest. One grave fault of the fiscal system was the custom known as "farming out the taxes." A group of wealthy men would advance a sum of money to the king in exchange for his permission to reimburse themselves by collecting the taxes due. As they often collected more than they had advanced, this practice of discounting the revenue meant in reality that it was carried to the king as it were in a leaking bucket. A second grave fault was the absence of a budget. The monarch treated the national revenues as a private credit account, and might squander upon his mistresses and his amusements the resources which should have been devoted to urgent national needs.

4. THE CRITICISM OF THE PHILOSOPHERS

Against these numerous abuses the rationalists of the eighteenth century leveled a stream of brilliant, satirical, and destructive criticism. With the Intellectual Revolution a spirit of rationalism *The philoso-* and skepticism had spread among the enlightened classes *phers of the* of society. In France the movement was particularly *eighteenth century* strong, for it was led by a unique group of writers who are known as the *philosophes* or philosophers. No tradition or institution, however ancient or venerable, was sacred to these critics, who delighted in holding up to public ridicule the stupidity, hypocrisy, and irrationality of existing customs, and who pleaded, in the name of humanity and right reason, for a program of intelligent reforms.

The most famous of the *philosophes* was François Marie Arouet, better known as Voltaire (1694–1778). Like the other *philosophes*, Voltaire was not a philosopher in the English sense of a profound, original and

[127]

systematic thinker.   Rather he was a popularizer of ideas, an inspired
journalist, whose tireless and sarcastic pen never rested.
Voltaire
The ninety volumes of his collected writings show him
in every mood from delicate irony to thunderous denunciation and
fully explain why he found it necessary to pass much of his life beyond the borders of France.   Against the theologians in particular
Voltaire delighted to turn the flood of his mockery.   He was the self-
appointed champion of all victims of bigotry and injustice and he
made Europe a court which rang with his appeals.   Religion had
originated long before priests, he believed, but it had been exploited
ever since "the first knave met the first fool."   To break the power of
a corrupt and intolerant priestcraft Voltaire considered a service to
humanity; he raised the battle cry, *écrasez l'infâme!* (destroy the infamous thing!) insistently, for to him organized religion symbolized all
that was stupid, irrational, and degrading in the old régime.   A "natural
religion," he pointed out, was one that would "enjoin us to serve our
neighbors through love of God," but we had been led by intolerance
and bigotry into the monstrous error of "persecuting and butchering
them to His greater glory."

Scarcely less influential than Voltaire was Denis Diderot (1713–84),
who edited an encyclopedia to which almost all the philosophers contributed.   The encyclopedia proved an arsenal of argu-
Diderot
ments for the rationalist cause and was completed in 1765
after repeated efforts had been made to suppress it by the clergy and
the censors.   While avoiding controversial subjects as far as possible,
the encyclopedists wrote to convince the thoughtful reader that science,
and the growth of a tolerant spirit, had contributed more to the happiness of mankind than the tenets of a thousand warring religious faiths.
Theological doctrines were not excluded from the work, nor were they
openly combated, but they were overshadowed and robbed of significance by the space and emphasis devoted to more practical and secular
matters.

No evil stirred the philosophers more profoundly than the inequality
of the laws, for they were almost all members of the Third Estate and
resented the immunities enjoyed by the privileged orders.
Beccaria
Also, they had personal grievances, for several of them
(like Voltaire) had been imprisoned for audacious writing, or (like
Diderot) had seen their books burned by order of the censor.   Furthermore, the spectacle of criminals going to execution was a constant
reminder of the barbarous codes in force.   In 1764, an Italian *philosophe*,
the Marquis Beccaria, published *An Essay on Crimes and Punishments*,

VOLTAIRE
1694–1778

*Jean François Marie Arouet, better known by his pen-
name, Voltaire, was the most brilliant and versatile
writer of the eighteenth century.   In this likeness of him,
the sculptor, Jean-Antoine Houdon, has managed to suggest the keenness of wit, self-conceit, and genius for
mockery which made Voltaire a tireless critic of the irrational customs and stupid abuses of the Old Régime.*

in which he denounced the use of torture and the infliction of cruel and outmoded punishments. Beccaria even ventured to urge the abolition of the death penalty, arguing that "crimes are more effectively prevented by the *certainty* than the *severity* of the punishment." His essay was translated into several European languages and exerted a strong influence on theories of criminal jurisprudence.

In view of the disorder prevailing in the national finances, it is not surprising that some of the philosophers were attracted to problems *The physio-* of political economy. François Quesnay (1694–1774), court *crats* physician to Louis XV, became the leader of a group of thinkers known as the physiocrats because they believed all governments should conform to "the natural order of things." They regarded most legislation as a curse rather than a benefit, insisting that trade, for instance, developed most vigorously when least interfered with, since artificial regulations constricted it. Hence, "To govern better, govern less." The mercantilist theory that a state grew wealthy by accumulating gold they declared unsound; the wealth of a society was the *produit net*, the surplus of agricultural, mineral, and other natural products accruing from the labor of its citizens. Agriculture they considered the most vital interest of a nation and they believed it important to improve the lot of the French peasantry because "poor peasants make a poor kingdom."

To dedicate oneself to the task of rooting out abuses and destroying the obstacles to human happiness is a noble adventure. The philosophers liked to think of themselves as knights-errant of humanity, and could be flattered to tears at the picture of a grateful posterity raising a statue to their memory. They did not doubt that mankind was on the threshold of a new age, in which right reason would triumph, and all citizens would enjoy their natural and imprescriptible right to life, liberty, and the pursuit of happiness. Some oversanguine dreamers even anticipated the installation of a Utopian society which would assure prosperity and contentment to all classes under laws so reasonable and so just that the people "could not choose but be good."

This hope of achieving social harmony was based in part on the deepening reverence for natural law. It seemed impossible that Na-*Faith in* ture, or Nature's God, could have *intended* confusion and *"natural* disorder to reign in human affairs, for the rest of the uni-*law"* verse, to the orbit of the farthest star, obeyed majestic and inflexible laws. There must be a *natural* order of society, the principles of which had been lost or ignored, and it was the business of the legislators to regenerate society by discovering and applying these natural principles. Once enunciated, the new precepts would be accepted by all right-thinking people. Some of these natural and axiomatic laws the philosophers believed they had already discovered, but they lacked the authority to put them into force. They appealed, therefore, to the princes of Europe, urging them to employ their despotic authority to inaugurate the new régime. So successful was the appeal, and so readily did the rulers lend an ear to the proposed program, that in 1768 Diderot declared enthusiastically, "There is no prince in Europe who is not also a philosopher." Monarchy was to have a last chance to justify itself as "enlightened despotism."

5. THE ENLIGHTENED DESPOTS

The European rulers of the eighteenth century were for the most part earnest and benevolent princes. In recognition of their high sense of responsibility, and their sincere desire to improve the lot of their subjects, they have been styled the "enlightened despots," and the middle and later years of the eighteenth century constitute "the monarchs' age of repentance." These princes strove to undo in one century the mistakes their ancestors had committed in five. Had they succeeded, benevolent despotism might still be accepted as the ideal form of government in Europe, but their intelligence was not equal to their intentions, and several of them, in their attempts to improve matters, ended by making them worse.

The most brilliant exponent of enlightened despotism was Frederick II of Prussia (1740–86). Many of his reforms anticipated the writings of the philosophers, and, although he delighted to honor *Frederick* these illustrious thinkers whom he called the "masters *the Great* of princes," his success as a ruler was due less to their *of Prussia* advice than to his own practical sense, his energy, and his genius for administration. The improvements he wrought in Prussia have already been described,[1] as well as his military triumphs which won him the title of "the Great."

Catherine II of Russia and her attempts to pose as an enlightened despot have also been mentioned, as well as the obstacles which vitiated her reforming zeal.[2] The admiration which Catherine felt *Catherine II* for the philosophers, and the interest she took in their *of Russia* recommendations, led her to invite several of them to her court. But Catherine, like Frederick II, was a practicing politician rather than a

[1] See above, pages 84–92.
[2] See above, pages 76–81.

political theorist, and she never made the mistake of regarding the philosophers as seriously as they regarded themselves.

The most sincere and least successful of this group of benevolent princes was the Emperor Joseph II of Austria (1780–90). It was *Joseph II of Austria* Joseph's ambition to transform the disunited Hapsburg possessions into a centralized military state on the Prussian model. His program embraced many admirable reforms; he wished to liberate the serfs, codify the laws, balance the budget, and stimulate trade; but his personality and his methods stirred up a surprising opposition. "Joseph always wishes to take the second step before he has taken the first," was the shrewd judgment of Frederick the Great. In Belgium, Hungary, and the Tyrol the people revolted against the emperor's proposals to unify the imperial administration and make German the official language. The nobles resented his attacks upon their privileges, Pope Pius VI protested against his interference in religious affairs, and the jurists criticized his attempt to improve the legal code. Even his councilors grew discontented and insolent. The mounting opposition only increased Joseph's determination. "The father of a family," he declared, "who holds the welfare of his children at heart, must not allow himself to be turned from a salutary course because of ill-judged complaints."

Failure attended his foreign no less than his domestic policies. An attempt to exchange the Austrian Netherlands for Bavaria was frustrated by Frederick the Great who was ever vigilant to combat any extension of Austrian power in the Germanies. Seeking aggrandizement in another direction, Joseph allied himself with Catherine of Russia and commenced a war with the Turks in 1788. Lacking military talent, he met with reverses, and in 1789, broken in health, he returned to Vienna to die. The thought of his failures obsessed him and in his last months he withdrew all his reforms. "Here lies Joseph II" was the epitaph he composed for himself, "who, with the best intentions, was unsuccessful in everything that he undertook." The judgment of history has been more generous. Peasants long remembered him as their friend, and Protestants and Jews in Austria blessed his memory for his tolerance in lightening the restrictions under which non-Catholics labored.

Of the lesser European states, scarcely one escaped the rough hand of the reformer in the eighteenth century. In Spain the conscientious *Spain and Portugal* Charles III (1759–88) curbed the power of the Inquisition and expelled the Jesuits from the kingdom (1767). Religious bigotry, lawlessness and economic decay were too deeply rooted in Spanish life to be extirpated in a single reign, but Charles sought by wise legislation to reduce the effects of these evils. Like measures were pursued in the neighboring kingdom of Portugal by the autocratic Pombal, minister of Joseph I (1750–77). Pombal secured the expulsion of the Jesuits from Portugal in 1759, and the Society of Jesus, already widely unpopular, was suppressed by a papal decree in 1773. It was Pombal's patriotic aspiration to reinvigorate the Portuguese Empire by sending the life blood of trade coursing once more through its enfeebled frame, but his arbitrary temper won him many enemies and he fell from power in 1777.

The prestige of Sweden, which had suffered eclipse in the great northern war,[1] was partially restored during the enlightened reign of Gustavus III (1771–92). This versatile monarch possessed a magnetic personality and labored with zest to reform *Sweden* the finances, improve agriculture, promote education and religious tolerance, and ameliorate the harshness of the laws. Unfortunately, he excited the opposition of various privileged groups, and in 1792 he was assassinated by some discontented nobles.

In Denmark-Norway,[2] Count Struensee, able minister of the king, Christian VII, likewise paid with his life for his presumptuous attempt to play the enlightened despot. As the power behind the *Denmark-* throne from 1771 to 1772, Struensee reorganized the ad- *Norway* ministration and attacked everything that was corrupt in the state of Denmark, until his enemies combined to impeach him and send him to the block. But the memory of his reforms survived him, for legitimate ideals and aspirations are more difficult to silence than their mortal advocates.

It was a curious anomaly that while French writers everywhere led the attack upon the abuses of the old régime, and French philosophers taught the princes of Europe the axioms of good govern- *France* ment, the glaring evils in French administration went unreformed. Louis XV (1715–74) was too selfish and too indolent to work at the arduous rôle of enlightened despot, and his ministers contented themselves perforce with a policy of palliatives and expedients. The peasants continued to groan beneath the burden of their taxes, the bourgeoisie murmured, and the government debt mounted steadily, while the privileged few continued to revel in the golden splendors of the court like butterflies which dream the summer has no end.

---

[1] See above, pages 72–73.

[2] The kingdoms of Denmark and Norway were united under the same crown from 1397 until 1814.

The accession of Louis XVI in 1774 brought a promise of better days, for one of his first acts was to appoint the able and courageous Turgot controller general of the finances. Turgot was a friend of the philosophers and favored many of the reforms which they had proposed. "Give me five years of despotism," is a saying attributed to him, "and France shall be free." The danger of insolvency he met with the bold policy: "No bankruptcy, no increase in taxation, no loans." Only a rigid curtailment of expenditures could make the plan a success, yet, when Turgot attempted to introduce economies in order to balance the budget, he created a host of enemies, from the extravagant young queen, Marie Antoinette, to the holder of the smallest sinecure. "There is no abuse that does not give someone a livelihood," he admitted bitterly, but he held to his course. Fresh opposition greeted his proposal to relieve the peasants of the hated *corvée* and to suppress the obstructive trade guilds; the clergy were unfriendly because he favored religious toleration; even the *parlement* of Paris, popular with the people because it was considered a check on royal absolutism, joined in blocking his reforms. Had Louis XVI supported him firmly, he might have fought his way through, but in 1776 his enemies won the king over and Turgot was dismissed after twenty months in office. "Do not forget, sire," was his final prophetic plea, "that it was weakness which brought the head of Charles I to the block." But Louis was too confused and too irresolute to profit by sage advice. Turgot's fall sealed the fate of the French monarchy, for under his successors in office the old expedients were revived, new loans were floated, expenditures increased, and the ship of state drifted steadily toward the rocks of revolution.

Turgot

6. ROUSSEAU AND THE DOCTRINE OF POPULAR SOVEREIGNTY

When intelligent Frenchmen saw the king and his ministers delay so long in carrying through the needed reforms, they began to ask themselves whether there was not some other authority in the state to which they might appeal. They knew that in the previous century the English people had grown impatient with their monarchy, had sent Charles I to execution (1649), and later had driven James II from his throne and kingdom (1688). These acts had shocked Europe in an age when almost everyone accepted the principle of the divine right of kings, and the English revolutionists had endeavored to justify their unconventional procedure. The philosopher John Locke (1632–1704)

JEAN-JACQUES ROUSSEAU
1712–78

*The sensitivity, and the feeling of personal mal-
adjustment, which made Rousseau the most eloquent critic of eighteenth-century society, with
its artificialities and inequalities, are clearly
discernible in this likeness of him.*

argued very reasonably that governments were instituted by the people to protect their lives and property; that when a government failed to fulfill these functions, or a king abused his power, the sovereign people had the right to change their government for a better one. This was what the English had done in 1688–89 when they expelled the absolutist James II and invited William and Mary to reign in his place as constitutional monarchs.[1] They found comfort in Locke's doctrine, which assured them that, far from being rebels, they had in fact acted as honest and courageous citizens defending their natural rights.

John Locke did not originate this idea of the sovereignty of the people, but he was one of the first writers to present it clearly and make it popular. Any people desiring to throw off allegiance to an unpopular monarch could now find an argument to justify the act. In the American War of Independence, the "patriots" invoked Locke's philosophy to prove that the tyranny of George III had absolved the colonists from their allegiance to the English king, and that they were asserting no more than their "natural rights" in setting up an independent government. The idea that the people were not created to obey the king, but that kings were merely executive magistrates responsible to the sovereign people, was indeed a revolutionary concept. In France, where it was to precipitate the greatest revolution of all, the new philosophy found an eloquent advocate in one of the most moving and passionate spirits of the century, Jean-Jacques Rousseau.

Rousseau was born in Switzerland in 1712, but first achieved fame as a writer in Paris when he composed a prize essay in 1749. He fol-

Jean-Jacques Rousseau (1712-78)

lowed this with several works wherein he attacked the evils of society and government, not coldly and rationally as more philosophical critics had done, but with a fresh and emotional style that charmed his readers. Rousseau's contempt for the frivolous and artificial society of the time was partly a defense to cover his morbid sensitiveness; his passion for quiet pastoral scenes and lonely walks verged on misanthropy, and his sympathy for the poor and unfortunate was sincere largely because they belonged to the one class he could find no reason to envy. To the *blasés* and superficial frequenters of the salons, however, his artistically written diatribes seemed outpourings of passionate honesty and they wrought a revolution in sentiment. Fine gentlemen neglected their cards and their dice to take lonely walks and commune with Nature, the queen and her ladies-in-waiting played at being dairymaids, and courtiers

[1] See above, pages 47–50.

and commoners alike began to cultivate deep but voluble emotions like the characters in Rousseau's novels.

In *The Social Contract* (1762) Rousseau formulated his philosophy of government, and pictured the state as a corporate body of citizens who subordinate their individual aims to the "general will." The sovereign power resides in the citizens, but it is indivisible, and the government derives its authority from the consent of the governed. The concept of the "general will" baffled many readers, but they applauded Rousseau for his fearless defense of popular sovereignty, and understood his meaning without difficulty when he wrote: "The depositors of the executive power are not the people's masters but its officers ... it can set them up or pull them down when it likes."

Rousseau's Social Contract

The revolutionary nature of his doctrines brought Rousseau into trouble with the authorities and he was obliged to flee from France. But the ideas he had voiced and the criticism poured out by the *philosophes* continued to circulate through men's minds, dissolving like a subtle acid the presuppositions upon which the old régime was founded. By 1789, people had been so widely converted to the new philosophy that a great historian has ventured to declare: "The French Revolution was accomplished before it began."

Section C

THE ERA OF THE FRENCH REVOLUTION AND NAPOLEON

(1789–1815)

The French people were the first to raise the cry of Liberty, Equality, Fraternity, and to challenge in radical fashion the right of a small group, the nobles and clergy, to enjoy wealth, privileges, and immunities while the vast majority of Frenchmen were shut out from such favors and from all political power. In 1789, the leaders of the middle class prepared to sweep away the old régime with its inequalities and abuses, but they ended by sweeping away the French monarchy also, and plunged their newly proclaimed republic into a war with the rest of Europe. The issues at stake in this struggle, the fashion in which the revolution influenced neighboring states, and the succession of events which made Napoleon Bonaparte master of France, and of a great part of Europe, form the subject matter of this section. Although the revolution failed to usher in the social Utopia of which its early protagonists dreamed, it broke through the entrenchments of the old régime, liberated the middle classes in the greater part of the Continent from irritating disabilities and obsolete restrictions and the peasants from the burdens of an outmoded feudal servitude. The revolutionary years marked the appearance in Europe of a new social order in which the middle class, the bourgeoisie, were destined to hold the dominant position.

[139]

CHAPTER TEN

THE FRENCH PEOPLE DESTROY THE RELICS
OF FEUDALISM AND OVERTURN
THE MONARCHY

The end of every political association is the preservation of the natural and imprescriptible rights of man. These rights are liberty, property, security, and resistance against oppression.
Declaration of the Rights of Man and the Citizen (1789).

WHEN revolutions occur, they do not necessarily break out in the most backward countries, or among the most miserable and most oppressed people. As explained in the foregoing chapter, the inequalities and restrictions of the old régime weighed upon the unprivileged classes in every state on the continent of Europe. As it happened, the French people were the first whom a sense of injustice and a desire for reform goaded into revolution, but the reason for this was not because the French were the most brutally governed or the most unhappy nation, but rather because they were the most enlightened and most eager for reform. The unprivileged classes in France toward the close of the eighteenth century were on the whole better treated than in some neighboring states, and in general their lot was improving. But for this very reason they were less disposed to tolerate abuses, less inclined to put their implicit trust in princes, and less willing to wait indefinitely for the reforms which their leading thinkers had propounded with so much brilliance and conviction.

1. THE STATES GENERAL IS SUMMONED

By 1788, the French monarchy was threatened with bankruptcy. All other expedients for raising money having failed, Louis XVI yielded to the advice of his councilors and agreed to convoke the ancient representative body of the French nation, the States General. His finance minister, Necker, announced the decision to the people as "a New Year's gift" for 1789, and it excited fervent enthusiasm. For the first time in nearly two centuries the French people were to be consulted on the management of their national affairs. When it was learned that the "good king" had agreed in addition to grant the Third Estate double representation, the people "bathed the edict with tears of gratitude."

One hundred and seventy-five years had passed since the previous

[141]

meeting of the States General in 1614. Dusty records were searched to discover the forgotten modes of procedure, and royal instructions were issued to the puzzled electors. From February to May, 1789, the elections went forward, in orderly fashion for the most part, although all classes of the nation were stirred by the flood of pamphlets and the passionate debates. They were stirred, too, by a spirit of loyalty to the king, their friend and counselor, and by a spirit of generosity which infected even the privileged orders. In this early and idealistic phase of the revolution the mutual enthusiasm frequently transcended class distinctions and some of the leading advocates of reform were men of noble birth. The Marquis de Lafayette, for instance, had fought in the American War of Independence, and had waited impatiently for the day when he might aid the French people also to gain their rights and liberties.

While choosing delegates the electors of the three orders, in each town or parish, were permitted to draw up instructions for them. The king had invited the people to list their grievances, and the *The cahiers* result was a flood of memorials filled with advice, complaints, and remonstrances, which are known as the *cahiers*. The peasants begged for relief from the salt tax, from the hated *corvée* or forced labor on the roads, from the destruction wrought by the hunting privileges of the nobles, and from the feudal dues paid to the overlord. Men of the middle class had other grievances: the law courts were costly and often corrupt, trade and industry were checked by stupid restrictions, all high offices in the army, the church, and the government were reserved for the sons of noblemen. The *cahiers* suggest that the twenty-four or twenty-five million Frenchmen who constituted the Third Estate were in substantial agreement: (1) that the privileged orders, the clergy and nobles, would have to surrender their immunities and pay their full share of the taxes, and (2) that France must have a definitive constitution, a written charter of liberties which would limit the irresponsible powers of the government, guarantee each citizen against arbitrary arrest, assure him justice in the courts and protection of his life and property. On the other hand, the nobles and clergy, while approving the convocation of the States General, were disposed to argue that France already possessed an unwritten constitution sanctioned by custom and precedent. They favored some revision and minor concessions, but they expected to remain in a position to safeguard their interests and preserve their social preeminence.

As the spring approached, Louis XVI viewed with mounting dis-

trust the wave of popular enthusiasm that his proclamation had called
forth. Even his liberal minister, Necker, the idol of *Divided*
those who prayed for reform, was alarmed by the spirit *aims at*
of lawlessness that burst out frequently into acts of violence. *court*
Many of the courtiers who surrounded Louis in his palace at Versailles
were hostile to the idea of change, and warned him not to make any
definite promises. To them, the convocation of the States General
was merely an expedient to raise money. If more gold could be found
to grease the wheels, they felt certain that the old machine of government would run smoothly enough. But the friends of reform in the
royal council had another aim. They hoped to use the indignation of
the people as a threat whereby they could compel the nobles and clergy
to tax themselves, and to this view they had more or less converted
Louis. Tired of the selfishness of the privileged orders, he was prepared to coerce them a little, but his ideas went no further than that.
If he could have brought himself to recognize the force of the popular
movement, have deserted the elegant but useless nobility, and gone
over whole-heartedly to the side of the Third Estate, he might have
saved his throne. But such a step was no part of his program.

The truth is, he had no definite program. Slow-witted, irresolute,
and unmanageable, Louis XVI was tragically unfit to command in a
time of crisis. He had virtues of a high order, physical *Louis XVI*
courage, morality, genuine religious conviction, and deep
affection for his family. As a private citizen he might have rounded
out an obscure and honorable life; but he had neither talent nor liking
for the business of kingship. In council he found it difficult to keep
awake; pageants and parades bored him; his chief enthusiasm was
hunting, and his chief aptitude leaned apparently toward mechanics.
Because he was troubled with a conscience he endeavored spasmodically
to fulfill the duties of royalty, but he had neither the will nor the interest to sustain long the rôle which he had inherited and could not
resign.

On the queen, Marie Antoinette, more severe judgments have been
passed. Beautiful, extravagant, and indiscreet, she made herself the
center of a coterie at court and the object of considerable *Marie*
scandal. By birth she was a daughter of Maria Theresa, *Antoinette*
and she had been betrothed to Louis to strengthen the Austro-French
alliance which dated from the Seven Years' War.[1] The alliance had
never been popular in France and neither was the Austrian-born queen.
Her interference in affairs of state helped to split the court into cabals,

[1] See above, pages 86–88.

[143]

whereby the queen, the king's brothers (the Count of Provence and the Count of Artois), and the ministers of state conspired and maneuvered to control the vacillating mind of Louis to their own advantage. This was a tiresome task, and as difficult, the Count of Provence admitted, as holding together a handful of oiled ivory balls. For Louis it was a species of martyrdom that drove him on occasion into fits of irrational obstinacy. His moods added the final erratic touch to policies already enfeebled by duplicities and contradictions.

2. THE STATES GENERAL MEETS

On May 5, 1789, the deputies of the three estates assembled at Versailles to hear the proposals of the king and his ministers. In a short speech by Louis and a long speech by Necker, they

Vote "by head" or "by order"?

were lectured on a fact which they already knew: that the government was faced by a financial crisis. But concerning the question of reforms and a constitution nothing definite was said; and the problem of the vote "by order" or the vote "by head" was left unsettled. For the Third Estate this last was a vital issue. Hitherto, the three estates, when assembled, had been in the habit of meeting separately, and presenting their separate petitions and responses to the throne. If this rule were maintained, the deputies of the Third Estate, although they represented over ninety-five per cent of the nation, might find themselves opposed and outvoted by the two privileged chambers. They had hoped that the "good king," in doubling their representation, had intended the deputies of the three orders to sit together and vote their decisions by head, for in a single chamber the six hundred delegates of the Third Estate, with the aid of friendly nobles and priests, would hold an assured majority. But this, they gathered, was not to be, and they left the royal session with a sense of injury and disappointment.

Sullenly they declined to organize as a separate body. Twice they invited the nobles and clergy to meet with them. The offers were

The Tennis Court Oath (June 20, 1789)

declined, but on June 13 three parish priests joined them. Others followed, and on June 17 the Third Estate took a momentous step: it proclaimed itself the National Assembly. The whole theory of a democratic revolution was implied in this step which set the dignity of numbers against the dignity of caste. Two days later, a majority of the clergy voted for fusion, and some of the nobles were yielding. The reactionaries at court decided to call a halt to these irregular proceedings. On the morning of June 20, when the deputies of the Third Estate assembled for their daily debates, they found their meeting-place closed while carpenters prepared it for a royal session to be held on the twenty-second.   Alarm and indignation seized the representatives.   Believing that their session had been intentionally prevented, they hastened to an indoor tennis court nearby, determined to hold it there.   On the proposal of Mounier, one of their number, they swore that they would not separate, and would meet whenever necessary, until they had given France a constitution.   This was the famous Tennis Court Oath of June 20, 1789.

Louis, under pressure from conservative advisers, had resolved to be firm with his obstinate commoners.   At the royal session held (a day late) on June 23, he scolded the deputies of the Third Estate for wasting time, and warned them that he might lose patience and send them home.   There must be no further resistance to his decree.   "Gentlemen," he stated in conclusion, in his rough, unmusical voice, "I command you to dismiss immediately, and to assemble tomorrow morning each in the chamber allotted to your order."   He left the hall, the nobles and clergy followed, but the Third Estate remained, irresolute yet defiant.   Before them appeared suddenly the master of ceremonies, the Duc de Brézé, to remind them of their duty.   "Gentlemen, you have heard the king's intentions."   Then the tempestuous Mirabeau, a noble born, but sitting as a deputy of the people, poured out the accumulated indignation of his colleagues upon the startled functionary.   "Go tell your master," he thundered, "that we are here by the will of the people, and that only bayonets can drive us forth."   De Brézé sought the king to learn his wishes; the regiments were within call; but Louis as always was unequal to a decision.   He allowed the commoners to hold their ground in defiance of his expressed orders.   It was the first step on a road which was to carry him within three years to the guillotine.

It may be that Louis hesitated to call upon the soldiers because the government no longer trusted its own troops.   Several of the regiments stationed in Paris had been infected with the revolution- *The specter* ary fever, and the soldiers declared openly that they *of counter-* would never fire upon the people.   So four days after his *revolution* unsuccessful attempt to overawe the deputies, Louis conceded their demands, and reversing his previous decision, he ordered the privileged classes to sit with the Third Estate.   Meanwhile, fresh regiments were summoned to surround Paris, Swiss and German mercenaries whose discipline could be relied upon.   By July 8, twenty thousand soldiers were encamped near Versailles, and the deputies of the Assembly, watching in apprehension, petitioned the king to withdraw them. Louis responded that the troops were there only to repress disorderly members of society. If *they* felt alarmed, they could remove themselves to some other city. The deputies thought the reply ironic, but Louis was probably sincere. The queen and the Count of Artois had persuaded him that it was necessary to curb the growing riots, and he had yielded to the argument that a large body of troops would be the surest guaranty against bloodshed. Secretly, the Count of Artois was less sanguine and less squeamish. "If you want an omelet," he confided to a friend, "you must not be afraid of breaking eggs."

Paris was in a ferment. Much still remains obscure regarding the disorder that spread among the people in the early days of July, but *Philip of* some historians have come to believe that anarchy was *Orléans* deliberately fostered. Rich bankers who had lent money to the government saw in the National Assembly the one power likely to stabilize the finances, and therefore urged the mob to defend it. There is some evidence to suggest that the food supplies in Paris were deliberately withheld, so that famine might add to the exasperation of the populace. One person who played a dubious rôle in the preliminaries to the revolt was the king's cousin, Philip, Duke of Orléans, the head of a collateral line of the Bourbons descended from Louis XIII. Orléans early espoused the people's cause and made the gardens of his residence, the Palais Royal, a rendezvous for the politically disaffected. Some of his adherents hoped to set him on the throne if Louis XVI were forced to abdicate, and they purposely aggravated the general discontent to further this end. It is unwise, however, to overemphasize such influences. Throughout the revolution there were many men who, like Orléans, sought to fish for their own advantage in the troubled waters. But the movement was too vast and too complicated to be charged to the designs of any individual, and the conspirator who attempted to control it for his own profit found himself in the position of a man who has summoned up an earthquake to grind his axe.

On the eleventh of July, the king, who had come under the influence of the reactionaries, curtly dismissed Necker and three other liberal ministers. The news stunned the Assembly, where the most radical deputies saw the shades of a prison house already closing about them. They protested earnestly, they debated eloquently, but they were bitterly depressed, for they knew that in reality they were powerless against a royal *coup d'état*. On the populace of Paris the news had a more stimulating effect. For weeks dark rumors had been spreading that the court planned a Saint Bartholomew's Massacre of the patriots, and through the hot July days the storm of revolt had been gathering. With the news of Necker's overthrow it burst.

3. THE CAPTURE OF THE BASTILLE

Word of Necker's dismissal reached Paris on July 12. At the Palais Royal a young journalist, Camille Desmoulins, harangued the people on their danger and the alarm spread rapidly. Mobs began to pillage the gunshops to secure arms, and were joined by mutinous soldiers from a friendly regiment, the French Guards. At the Hôtel de Ville a new municipal government organized itself, with the backing of the middle class, in an effort to curb the mounting anarchy. A civic militia, later to become famous as the National Guard, was created to patrol the streets, for many better-class Parisians felt with reason that they had as much to fear from the thieves and cutthroats running loose with the mobs as from the disciplined soldiery of a kindly though ill-advised king. The establishment of this illegal communal government, with a Parisian deputy, Bailly, as mayor, was the bourgeois reply to the mob violence on the one hand and the court project for a *coup d'état* on the other.

In their search for arms and powder the emissaries of the people, on the morning of July 14, demanded entrance to the prison of the Bastille. This ancient castle of the king was garrisoned by over a *July 14,* hundred soldiers; grim and ill-omened, it stood in the midst *1789* of a more modern Paris, a fit symbol of the old régime, with frowning walls and narrow dungeons, in the depths of which innocent victims of the royal displeasure were believed to languish. When the commander, De Launay, courteously declined to lower the drawbridge, the anger of the mob crystallized. An assault began and was carried on with considerable loss to the besiegers. The garrison could have held out, but agreed to capitulate, and the mob streamed in. Only seven prisoners, and none of them altogether innocent, were discovered, and De Launay and some of his men were massacred after they had been disarmed. This rather ugly episode of mob violence was immediately embroidered with legends and became one of the vital myths of the revolution.

The first news of the storming of the Bastille filled the National Assembly with deeper gloom. Nevertheless, the lawless citizens, by their audacity, had broken the force of the counter-revolution. Warned by the outbreaks, the Count of Artois left France, and a number of conservative nobles followed. The council of state was reorganized

[147]

and Necker recalled to office. Realizing their debt to the populace whose violent intervention had saved them, the deputies resolved to applaud an act which filled many of them with secret misgiving; and they even condoned the butchery of defenseless men. "Was the blood that they have shed then so pure?" one deputy named Barnave demanded. Before long many of these legislators were to find smooth phrases for still less agreeable facts, and to speak unctuously of the salutary justice of the people, and the need of watering the tree of liberty from time to time with the blood of tyrants.

On July 17, Louis XVI paid a visit to his rebellious capital. He came in peace, once more the "good king," and he donned a red, white, *Louis condones revolt* and blue cockade to signify his acquiescence in the recent developments. The crowds, suspicious at first, cheered him when he reached the Hôtel de Ville, and restored him to a sort of conditional popularity. Had he possessed the art or the acumen he might still have deserted the privileged orders who were deserting him, have flung aside his empty feudal title of King of France, and become the King of the French, but the rôle was beyond his skill. He had taught the bourgeois to distrust him and had driven them into an alliance with the common people, an alliance fraught with grave implications, which threatened to carry the revolution farther than the average bourgeois had any real desire to see it go.

4. THE DESTRUCTION OF FEUDALISM AND THE DECLARATION OF THE RIGHTS OF MAN

Not only in Paris, but everywhere throughout France, revolts seemed to break out spontaneously in the spring and summer of 1789. The *"The Great Fear"* storming of the Bastille gave this progressive disintegration of order a swift impulsion. The fabric of society appeared visibly to rend itself apart and the structure of government threatened to dissolve in the rising tide of anarchy. The peasants, many of whom had imagined that their feudal dues had been abolished with the election of deputies, grew impatient at the delay and rose to reckon with their masters, dragging out the records of their obligations in order to burn them, and sometimes burning the lord's château as well. Reports spread that bands of brigands were abroad; in some villages the inhabitants armed themselves for self-protection while in others they locked themselves in at nightfall, oppressed by a terror so vague yet so widespread that it has been called "The Great Fear." Without doubt, under cover of the disorder and dismay, real brigands

STORMING OF THE BASTILLE

*The Bastille, part of which dated from the fourteenth century, was a gloomy fortress
and prison standing in the suburb of old Paris known as the Faubourg St. Antoine.
As political and other prisoners were sometimes confined in its dungeons, the edifice
acquired a sinister reputation, and the Parisians, looking up at its frowning walls,
may well have come to regard it as a symbol of the Old Régime.   There is no proof,
however, that the mob which attacked it on July 14, 1789, had any motive beyond the
desire to procure arms.   When, after a short defense, the commander agreed to
capitulate, he and several of the garrison were massacred by the mob.   This dubious
episode was transformed into a heroic legend by revolutionary poets and orators,
because it symbolized so satisfactorily the popular idea that the French people had
risen in generous wrath and freed the victims of tyranny.   As a matter of fact, only
seven prisoners were discovered in the Bastille, all of whom had been sentenced to jail
for adequate reasons.*

were active; but in most cases the violence was a consequence of the illimitable expectations of the spring, of the hopes of reform too long deferred, and of the economic hardships which the political disruption had augmented.

By the opening days of August reports of these disturbances were pouring into the Assembly from all quarters. To the anxious deputies *Session of* it seemed as if the whole of France was lurid with the *August 4–5* light of burning châteaux. Among the great landowners the conviction was growing that it would be a wise and humane move to surrender their personal privileges voluntarily, but they hoped to obtain adequate compensation for their real rights. On the night of August 4, while the Assembly was debating measures to calm the provinces, the Viscount de Noailles proposed that the nobles should renounce their seignorial privileges and so abolish the injustice of the feudal system by a single edict. Even the conservative leaders of the privileged orders were prepared to make some concessions, but as the evening advanced enthusiasm swept the Assembly into a series of extraordinary decrees which constituted the death warrant of the feudal system. Nobles vied with churchmen in renouncing traditional rights and immunities, but personal calculations were not entirely forgotten. The landlords anticipated financial compensation for their losses, and many consoled themselves with the thought that the peasant outbreaks had reduced their prerogatives to a dead letter in any case. At dawn, the deputies, with an enthusiasm as sincere as it was illogical, proclaimed Louis XVI the Restorer of French Liberties, and dispersed to their lodgings, drunk with fatigue and emotion.

The legislation of August 4 extended the scope of the revolution and added a social and economic program to the political reforms. For in abolishing feudal obligations, suppressing serfdom and the game laws, commuting taxes such as the *aides*, the *gabelle*, and the *tithe*, and proposing civil equality, equality of taxation, and an equal opportunity for public service to all Frenchmen, the National Assembly transformed the French people from subjects to citizens. If the full implications of these decrees were carried into effect, it meant the end of the old social system with its corporate groups and classes vested with special rights, and the end of the old economic system with its guilds, industrial monopolies, and feudal prerogatives. Finally, it meant that the National Assembly would have to prolong its session indefinitely in order to draft the detailed legislation required to carry through this complicated program.

Humanity, which had lost its birthrights, was now on the way to recover them, and it seemed wise that they should be written down for all men to read.   In the remaining days of August the deputies prepared a table which listed the inalienable rights of free citizens.   The formulas chosen for this famous *Declaration of the Rights of Man* Declaration of the Rights of Man and the Citizen were suggested in part by English and American models, and were permeated by the democratic philosophy of Rousseau.   Every citizen was declared to be born free.   He could not be arrested or imprisoned except by due process of law, and in the making of the laws which he had to obey he was entitled to participate directly or indirectly, since a valid law was the expression of the general will.   Furthermore, the citizen was entitled to enjoy religious liberty and freedom of speech and of the press. All officials who helped to govern a state were the responsible servants of the sovereign people, and if they abused their trust, the people had the right to resist and to depose them, however exalted their rank. It is unnecessary to point out the conflict between such teaching and the theories of absolute despotism.   The Assembly had traveled far in four months, but the philosophers had been preparing the ground for over forty years.

The Declaration of the Rights of Man and the Citizen was intended to serve as a preface to the constitution upon which the deputies were busily laboring.   In the debates on this subject, however, certain differences of opinion had already betrayed themselves, suggestive of a cleavage between the ideals of the *Divisions within the Third Estate* people of moderate wealth and the poorer folk who owned no property.   The middle class, the bourgeoisie, desired the revolution to stop short with political and legal reforms, which would leave them in charge of a responsible constitutional monarchy.   But the laborers in the towns and the peasants in the fields had been inspired by radicals and demagogues to hope for a social revolution, which would introduce a genuine egalitarianism.   They had a confused idea that men were to be equal, not only in rights and liberties, but in education, in opportunity, and even in wealth.   Among the deputies themselves there were some ecstatic dreamers who believed that it was possible by enlightened edicts to legislate poverty and ignorance out of existence, and to render all citizens virtuous and happy.   Men engaged in a herculean effort, such as a war or a revolution, are often seduced by vague and shining ideals which help to blind them to the uglier aspects of the work they have to do.   The French Revolution produced more than one leader who was prepared, in his attempt to construct a Utopia, to sacrifice his own head and a hundred thousand others with it.   To

[151]

such men, and to the credulous masses which heeded them, the revolution could not fail to bring the bitterness of disillusionment.

5. THE MARCH TO VERSAILLES

The fever in Paris, which had been eased a little by the blood-letting in July, threatened to mount again with the autumn. The National Guard, under the command of the Marquis de Lafayette, endeavored to hold the riotous elements of the populace in check, but the news from Versailles was disturbing. Louis, it was learned, had again been corrupted by evil counsels. He had withheld his approval to the Declaration of the Rights of Man and was furtively concentrating troops. In the last week of September, the Flanders Regiment arrived, and the officers demonstrated their loyalty to the king by trampling under foot the tricolor cockade of the Revolution. Marat, a popular leader and the editor of a journal called *The Friend of the People*, rushed out to Versailles to investigate for himself the truth of these rumors, and returned filled with alarm, "making as much noise," his fellow journalist Desmoulins wittily averred, "as four trumpets on the Day of Judgment." The crowds were ready to follow any leader, for back of these inflammable rumors was the hard reality of hunger, to render men and women furious at a king who vacillated and an assembly which theorized, while starvation stalked the streets. If the king dwelt in Paris, it was argued, instead of twelve miles away in Versailles, he would understand better the needs of his people and do something to alleviate them.

Accordingly, on October 5, an unorganized mob composed largely of women started a march to Versailles to petition the king to reduce the price of bread. Louis made gracious promises, but the crowd remained encamped near the palace. In the evening Lafayette arrived with the National Guard, but the precautions which he took were insufficient to prevent assassins slipping into the palace before dawn in an unsuccessful attempt to murder the queen. The majority of the visitors, however, had no murderous intentions; they were appeased and gratified when Lafayette, acting a doubtful rôle as intermediary, persuaded the royal family to return with them to Paris, and they escorted the carriage back on the morning of October 6, shouting that they had brought with them "the Baker, the Baker's wife, and the Baker's little boy." By noon, Louis had taken up his residence at the Tuileries, in the heart of his capital. Thenceforward he was to be a hostage of the people.

This removal from Versailles to Paris exercised a profound effect upon the course of the revolution. For the National Assembly considered it expedient to follow the king, and a long bare riding-school near the Tuileries, the Salle de Manège, was furnished for its sessions. With its rows of mounting benches sweeping around the walls, and a cleared space in the center, the new home of the Assembly suggested an arena, and such it was to prove. In the upper galleries space was provided for visitors, and the common people soon swarmed there, to criticize the debates and applaud vigorously their favorite orators. During more than one grave crisis, in the days that were approaching, groups of disorderly onlookers, full of brandy and patriotism, were to render calm deliberation impossible and force the Assembly to measures from which a majority of the deputies secretly recoiled.

6. THE CIVIL CONSTITUTION OF THE CLERGY

The threat of bankruptcy, which had led to the convocation of the States General, proved one of the most difficult problems which faced the Assembly. In the general confusion taxes could not be collected, and the Assembly found it necessary to borrow over two million livres for current expenses. The economic plight of the government drove the deputies to undertake a measure which proved in many respects a serious mistake. The lands held by the church and by the various monastic orders in France were valued at about three billion livres, which was approximately the amount of the national debt. On November 2, 1789, the Assembly decided to appropriate these lands for the needs of the nation, and to issue paper currency, or assignats, for which the church property would serve as security.

Having in this way relieved the clergy of their wealth and their income, the Assembly then assumed responsibility for their support. As part of the political program, France was to be cut up into some eighty-three new *départements,* and the ancient ecclesiastical dioceses were reconstituted to coincide with these new divisions. Priests and bishops became *"The Civil Constitution of the Clergy"* salaried servants of the state, and were to be chosen by election like other public officials, which meant that Huguenots, Jews, freethinkers, and other non-Catholics might help to choose them. Monks and nuns were urged to forsake their cloisters and find some secular occupation. All members of the clergy were required to swear an oath that they accepted the new settlement which was styled "The Civil Constitution of the Clergy," and those who refused were deprived of their offices and persecuted as non-jurors (French *jurer*, to swear). The civil constitution turned half the French clergy into non-jurors, and also made many laymen bitter opponents of the revolution. Unfortunately, too, the confiscation of the church property failed to solve the financial problems of the state, for the land sold slowly, and the assignats, which were issued with reckless prodigality, declined in value to fifty, then to thirty, and by 1795, to less than two per cent of their face value. However, the paper money helped somewhat to provide for government expenses during a critical period, and the sale of the lands, though slow, gradually created a class of landowners who could be counted upon to support the revolution because the restoration of the old régime would have meant the loss of their newly acquired estates. In its final effects this break-up of the landed estates and the transference of ownership to members of the middle and lower classes was perhaps the most significant change wrought by the revolution, and, coupled with the ultimate abolition of all feudal dues without redemption in July, 1793, it dissolved the economic foundations upon which the old régime had rested.

7. THE CONSTITUTION OF 1791

The members of the National Assembly had sworn in the Tennis Court Oath (June 20, 1789) to provide France with a constitution.
The monarchy limited The main features were settled in 1789, and by the spring of 1791 the momentous document, which was to transform France from an absolute to a limited monarchy, was completed. The powers which the king had formerly exercised were transferred to a legislative assembly elected by the people. Louis was no longer to make laws or to collect taxes. He lost his right to appoint and dismiss at will the local administrative officials throughout France, for henceforth these men were to be elected by the people and paid by the nation. Nor could he declare war or make peace without the vote of the legislative assembly which represented the nation. This assembly was to consist of a single chamber, the members of which were to be chosen by election every two years, and the king had no power to dissolve it. A few rights, however, had been left to him. He could choose the ministers who composed his council; could supervise the conduct of foreign affairs; and might veto a law passed by the assembly if he disapproved of it. His veto, though termed suspensive, was all but absolute, for a law had to pass three successive legislatures to become effective in the face of his opposition.

Thus, in less than two years, the nobles had been stripped of their privileges, the church of its wealth, and the king of the greater part of his authority, which had passed to the representatives *Persistence* of the nation. Yet the nation as a whole was not satis- *of discontent* fied. The humbler classes, the people who had no wealth or property, were beginning to suspect that they were being cheated, that the Revolution was not destined to fulfill their hopes. The new constitution established liberty for all, but it did not establish equality. Despite the assurance of the Declaration of Rights that every Frenchman was entitled to assist, directly or indirectly, in the making of the laws, the people found that only those citizens who paid a direct tax equal to three days' wages were to be given a vote, while none but citizens of comparative wealth would be eligible to sit in the legislative assembly. Popular leaders were quick to point out that under such a constitution the middle class would control the government. Some radicals even went so far as to denounce the deputies of the National Assembly as traitors, because they had betrayed the interests of the people as a whole into the power of the propertied classes.

To a certain extent this charge was justified. The members of the National Assembly were nearly all middle-class men, loyal to their group and its traditions. Many of them sincerely be- *The power* lieved the most ignorant class of citizens unfit, without *of the middle* further training, to exercise the responsibility of electors. *class* "The veil that hides the dazzling figure of Liberty," they argued, "must not be torn away too suddenly." In the early days of the revolution, the deputies of the National Assembly had allied themselves with the people through fear of the court; but after the relics of feudalism had been destroyed and the royal power reduced, the middle class, the bourgeoisie, was left supreme in the state. The Constitution of 1791 represented an attempt of the bourgeoisie to arrest and stabilize the revolution at this point. The attempt failed (1) because Louis XVI was untrustworthy and hated the rôle of a constitutional monarch; (2) because the Parisian populace was determined to see the revolution continue until it brought equality as well as liberty; and (3) because a radical minority in the new assembly, as well as counter-revolutionaries in France or in exile, and the apprehensive princes of Europe, all desired (though for different reasons) to see the settlement fail.

Although Louis had accepted the reforms which had been forced upon him, he was not reconciled to them. On June 21, 1791, when their labors were almost completed, the deputies of the National As-

sembly were dismayed to learn that the king had fled from Paris.
The flight to Varennes His plan was to join with loyal troops in the east and north of France, win the support of the provinces, and return to his capital as master once more. Such a step had been suggested to him earlier by the great orator Mirabeau, who had been brought secretly into the pay of the court. But Mirabeau died in April, 1791, and Louis had no other adviser with sufficient statesmanship to manage the project. The attempt at escape miscarried; the royal family were recognized *en route* and arrested at Varennes; and within a week they were brought back to Paris as prisoners.

The deputies of the Assembly were in a quandary. Their new constitution called for a king; if they definitely deposed Louis and *Republic or monarchy?* set up a regency or a republic, the move might throw the revolution into the hands of the people. For the moment they compromised by suspending the king from his functions. When a crowd assembled on the Champ de Mars, on July 17, to petition for the removal of the king, the National Guard dispersed it with musketry. The Assembly, growing daily more conservative, decreed that Louis should be restored to his throne, and that there should be no further change in the constitution for at least ten years. Confident that these measures would check the democratic movement, the deputies resigned their places, and closed their last session with the announcement (ironic prophecy) that the revolution was at an end.

Their labors had earned them the right to rest. In a session of a little over two years the National (Constituent) Assembly had in-
Achievements of the National Assembly (1789–91) augurated the most startling program of destruction and reconstruction in modern history. (1) It had decreed the doom of feudalism and serfdom in France, although the liquidation of the old system remained incomplete. (2) It had obliterated the old, bewildering patchwork of provincial, judicial, fiscal, and ecclesiastical divisions in France and replaced them by eighty-three approximately equal departments. (3) It had suppressed the chaos of the conflicting legal tribunals, *parlements*, and feudal courts which had complicated the administration of justice under the old régime, and supplanted them by a graduated system of judicial courts with elected judges. (4) It had stripped the church and the monastic orders of their wealth and power and made the clergy the servants of the state. (5) It had relieved an absolute monarch of the greater share of his authority and confided it to an assembly of the sovereign people. The following months were to decide whether the revolution could be arrested at this point.

8. THE LEGISLATIVE ASSEMBLY (1791-92)

The retiring deputies of the National Assembly had decreed themselves ineligible for immediate re-election, with the result that the new legislature was composed very largely of obscure men with little political training. They arrived in Paris, as one observer noted, "discontented to find the farce over and the curtain down," for many of them "were eager to win glory by destroying something" — an ominous portent, since there was nothing great left that they could destroy except the throne. From its first sessions the Legislative Assembly found itself divided into a party of the Right, which sought to preserve the constitutional settlement, and a party of the Left, which criticized the king and sought to lead the revolution into greater extremes. Among the leaders of the Left were several brilliant young deputies from the Department of the Gironde, and from them the whole group, which was aggressive in its tactics and republican in its sentiments, came to be known as the "Gironde" and its adherents as the "Girondists."

The most momentous step which the Legislative Assembly took was to plunge France into a war with Austria and Prussia in the spring of 1792. The first reforms of the revolution had been greeted with applause from all parts of Europe, but as the months passed this early approval changed to doubt and then to hostility. Three issues in particular provoked ill-feeling between France and her neighbors. (1) The *émigrés* (French royalists who had "emigrated") found refuge chiefly in the Germanies, where they plotted a counter-revolution and intrigued for foreign aid. (2) The abolition of feudal tenure deprived some German landlords of their rights in Alsace and they demanded compensation. (3) The National Assembly, at the request of the citizens of Avignon, had annexed that city to France (1790), although it was a part of the papal possessions. When Austria and Prussia joined in a demand for satisfaction on the last two points, the Girondists decided upon a war. "It may be," one deputy opined complacently, "that the revolution has need of a war to consolidate it." The struggle so light-heartedly begun was destined to last, with breathing spells, for twenty-three years, and before it ended France was to send her armies through the capitals of all her enemies on the continent of Europe.

Opening of the revolutionary war (1792)

With the outbreak of hostilities the position of the royal hostages in Paris became desperate. The Girondists openly accused the king and queen of sympathizing with the enemy, and the charge had a basis of truth. Louis hoped that the invaders would hasten to *June 20,* Paris and restore his powers, and Marie Antoinette trans-*1792* mitted information concerning the French plans to her Austrian fellow countrymen. Excitement and suspicion flamed up in Paris at the news of French reverses, and on June 20, 1792, a rowdy mob stormed into the Tuileries "to pay a visit to the king." Louis faced his unwelcome visitors calmly and courageously, drank a glass of wine to the revolution, and had the relief of seeing them finally disperse. Nothing had been smashed except a few window-panes. The indignity to the king even caused a brief reaction in his favor, and the Assembly, which considered king-baiting its peculiar prerogative, stopped scolding Louis in order to scold the mob. These eloquent legislators, who loved to hurl audacious and inflammatory phrases from the tribune, were suddenly sobered when they saw a mob translate their suggestions into acts.

Louis's throne was already tottering when the *émigrés* decided to come to his aid, and all was lost. On July 25, these short-sighted parti-*The Bruns-* sans persuaded the Duke of Brunswick, commander of the *wick Mani-* invading armies, to issue a manifesto to the French nation. *festo* In bombastic language it warned all Frenchmen, if they still refused to lay down their arms, that they would be treated as rebels to their king, and promised, if any harm befell Louis or the queen, that Paris would be handed over to total annihilation. It seemed impossible to doubt any longer that the king was in collusion with the enemy. The Parisians decided that the monarchy would have to be destroyed; a revolutionary committee took charge and directed matters from the Hôtel de Ville; the sections vomited forth their hordes of "patriots," and on August 10 the mob attacked the Tuileries.

The royal family, having been warned in time, retired to the hall of the Legislative Assembly for protection, but the king's Swiss Guard, left *Fall of the* to defend an empty palace, was sacrificed to the fury of the *throne* mob, which massacred and mutilated its victims in ghastly *(August 10,* fashion. The leadership of affairs had passed into the *1792)* hands of the revolutionary committee which had organ-ized itself at the Hôtel de Ville, under the direction of a violent but patriotic lawyer named Danton. In obedience to this committee the Legislative Assembly suspended the king, and then summoned a new and special convention to decide the fate of France and con-struct a second constitution.

In the interval between August 10 and September 21, 1792, Danton and the insurrectionary commune provided the only real impetus behind the dislocated national government. With pro- *The Sep-* digious energy Danton spurred on the work of recruiting *tember* soldiers to resist the invading armies. To cow opposi- *massacres* tion all aristocrats and enemy sympathizers were sought out in a house-to-house search. The prisons of Paris were soon crowded, and the populace feared the prisoners might break out and massacre the good citizens while the soldiers were away at the battle-front. This served as an excuse to exercise "the salutary justice of the people." Self-appointed judges visited the prisons; hired executioners accompanied them; and over a thousand victims, after the shadow of a trial, were butchered in the prison yards. For three days the massacres went on, while the deputies of the Legislative Assembly waited nervelessly, and Danton with culpable negligence forbore all protest. The annals of the revolution offer no darker page or more sanguinary example of popular violence than these prison massacres of the first days of September, 1792.

CHAPTER ELEVEN

THE FIRST FRENCH REPUBLIC AND ITS STRUGGLE TO SURVIVE

The French Republic is one and indivisible.
Constitution of 1793.

BY OVERTURNING the throne on August 10, 1792, the people of Paris ended the first phase of the revolution. The constitutional monarchy had failed and the king was a prisoner. To meet the crisis a National Convention was summoned and held its first session on September 21, 1792. Three problems of the utmost importance confronted the new assembly: (1) What was to be done with the dethroned king? (2) How was France to be saved from her invaders? (3) What form of government should be devised to replace the monarchy? The fate of France and of the revolution depended upon the answers which the members of the National Convention found for these questions.

1. THE NATIONAL CONVENTION (1792–95)

At their opening session the deputies of the Convention lost no time in declaring royalty abolished in France. A few days later, with considerably less enthusiasm, they decided to style France a "republic." Their hesitation reflected the general uncertainty of the time. Although some radical leaders in Paris had urged a republican form of government as early as 1791, after Louis's flight to Varennes, and most educated Frenchmen professed admiration for the city-republics of ancient times, the idea of transforming France into a republic did not appeal very strongly to the nation in 1792. Conservative members of the bourgeoisie feared such a step might deliver the government into the control of the populace, and many people in the provincial centers were still attached to the monarchy, although they had lost confidence in Louis XVI. The proclamation of the new régime was accepted as a more or less unwelcome but logical alternative to the discredited monarchy, but even the champions of the republic were constrained to admit that its birth occurred in a manner obscure and unpropitious.

France becomes a republic (September, 1792)

So long as the ex-king lived, it seemed inevitable that the royalists would plot to overthrow the republic and restore him to power, and this danger made it the more necessary to decide his fate promptly. An

[160]

active group of deputies seated high on the benches of the left in the assembly hall (the "Mountain") were determined to con- *Louis XVI* demn the king, and they found support in the Jacobin *guillotined* Club, a powerful political society dominated by ardent revolutionaries, which had affiliated itself with local groups throughout France. Maximilien Robespierre, popular and radical deputy of Paris, carried the verdict of the Jacobins to the Convention. "I demand," he proclaimed from the tribune, "that Louis XVI shall be condemned to death." The Girondists, the party which had dominated the Legislative Assembly, made half-hearted efforts to win a reprieve, but were out-maneuvered by their Jacobin opponents on the "Mountain." In the final test vote, Louis was condemned to death by a small majority. His execution (January 21, 1793) deeply shocked the courts of Europe and made the new French Republic an Ishmael among the nations.

By this drastic solution of one problem, the Convention greatly aggravated a second, the question of national defense. The Austrian and Prussian forces had withdrawn from France temporarily *First coali-* after suffering a reverse at Valmy (September 20, 1792), but *tion against* they planned a new invasion for the spring of 1793. After *France* the execution of the king, Great Britain, Spain, Holland, *(1793)* and some lesser states joined the coalition against France. The allied monarchs pledged themselves to avenge the death of Louis and to destroy the revolution, believing that the superiority of their resources assured them an easy victory. Yet, although France was to fight alone against the greater part of Europe, the contest was less unequal than it appeared. Oppressed classes in every country were stirred by the French example, and to them the National Convention made appeals urging them to rise against their tyrants. It was against governments rather than against embattled nations that the revolution had to struggle in these early years. The allied powers, moreover, were far from maintaining a close accord, and the allied statesmen neglected at first to give the French situation the serious attention which it warranted.

Nevertheless, the dangers threatening France in the spring of 1793 might have sobered the most sanguine patriot. They failed, however, to silence the quarrel in the Convention, where the two factions, *Quarrel of* the Girondists and the Jacobins, wasted precious months *the Giron-* wrestling for leadership. The Girondists drew their chief *dists and* *Jacobins* support from the provinces, were opposed to the dominant rôle which Paris had assumed in the affairs of France, and were disliked by the Parisian populace. They accused their political opponents, the Jacobins, of currying favor with the mob and of planning to confiscate private wealth for the benefit of the indigent. The Jacobins retorted that the Girondists wished an "aristocratic republic"; that their project for exalting the departments would destroy the unity of France, and that at heart they were secretly royalist. These charges and counter-charges masked a quarrel which was at bottom a fight between two revolutionary groups for control of the new government. In the end the people of Paris settled the issue by a fresh insurrection (May 31 — June 2, 1793) which crushed the Girondists. Several of the proscribed deputies escaped to stir up armed revolts in the provinces, but their cause was speedily compromised by royalist overtures. The victorious Jacobins consolidated their victory by drafting a popular constitution and submitting it to the voters. On obtaining a favorable response, they laid aside this Constitution of 1793 and chose to regard the result of the referendum as a justification of their high-handed rule.

Thus, by the midsummer of 1793, the Jacobins had won control of the central government, but the republic appeared to be on the point of dissolution. The army was disorganized, for many of the officers (nobles by birth) had deserted. The administration was dislocated, the allied troops were advancing from the east while royalist or Girondist insurgents held the chief western departments. It seemed all but certain that Paris would fall before the converging forces and the revolution end in defeat and obloquy.

2. THE ORGANIZATION OF VICTORY

In this critical summer of 1793, the allies proved themselves the unintentional saviors of France. Coalitions are notoriously inept in concentrating their forces; each of the powers had selfish ends to serve and each preferred to let its allies bear the brunt of the fighting. Austria and Prussia were less interested in crushing France than in securing further remnants of Poland, for that unhappy kingdom had just undergone its second partition (1793). As a result, the invaders advanced too cautiously, and failed to destroy the French armies and seize Paris while they had the chance. Twenty years were to pass before such a favorable opportunity recurred.

Strong winds extinguish a small fire, but they feed a large one, and the misfortunes which beset the French Republic in 1793 fanned the *The Spirit of '93* fervor of the revolutionaries to a white heat. Though civil war raged in the Vendée, though Lyons, Marseilles, and Toulon had risen against the Convention, though the fortresses of the north, Condé and Valenciennes, fell before the allied advance, these reverses proved to be hammer-strokes which fashioned a new France on the anvil of war. In their inconclusive attempts to blow out the torch of the revolution, the monarchs fanned it to a mighty conflagration. Patriotic Frenchmen of all classes flocked to the armies, prepared to die for *la liberté* and *la patrie*. Too late the allies were to learn they had provoked a volcano to pour its molten lava across Europe.

Fortunately for France, the National Convention, controlled by the Jacobin element, provided the iron leadership necessary for a nation in arms. An executive cabinet, the "committee of public *The organi-* safety," assumed dictatorial powers. It dispatched deputies *zation of* to the departments to supervise the organization of the *victory* defense; it called all able-bodied men to the colors to swell the "fourteen armies of the republic," and appointed young and audacious generals to positions of command with the warning that a defeat might cost them their heads. This energetic policy swiftly turned the tide. By the close of 1793, the royalists in the Vendée had been checked, Toulon recaptured, and the Austrians and Prussians thrown upon the defensive. In 1794, the French armies swept on to further triumphs. France was cleared of her invaders, her generals took the offensive, and Lazare Carnot, the military genius of the committee of public safety who had directed the campaigns, was acclaimed "The Organizer of Victory." But the victory had been dearly bought. It will be well to pause here to note how the struggle for national defense in 1793 and 1794 militarized the revolution and deflected its aims.

3. THE JACOBIN DICTATORSHIP

Although the National Convention remained in power for three years (1792–95), it failed in the primary task for which it had been summoned; i.e., to provide a permanent and satisfactory constitution for France. The Constitution of 1791, it will be recalled, had been cast aside when the king was deposed. Consequently the National Convention was an "extraordinary" or "revolutionary" assembly with no constitutional limits to its authority. It conducted the affairs of the nation with despotic assurance, repressing criticism, crushing its opponents, and spurring the citizens to supreme efforts. The French people submitted to this tyrannical war-time régime because they believed it was "a bridge of bronze" by which they would pass from a corrupt monarchy to a regenerated republic.

But the war wrenched the revolution from its course and the "regenerated republic" remained an unrealized dream, though for this

the war was not wholly to blame. Almost from the first an inner
The bour- conflict checked the progress of reform measures, a conflict
geoisie and between the bourgeoisie and the classes without wealth or
the citizens
without property. The bourgeoisie wished the revolution to end when
property the control of the government had passed from an autocratic
king and a selfish nobility to the hands of an enlightened middle class;
i.e., to themselves. But among the poorer classes there were many
enthusiasts who construed liberty, equality, fraternity, more literally.
They thought equality meant not only equality before the law, but
equality of birth, of opportunity, and of wealth. A political revolution
was not enough for them, they wanted a social revolution, which would
extinguish poverty by distributing the property of the wealthy among the
poor. Against such egalitarian doctrines the bourgeoisie fought relentlessly, asserting at every opportunity that private property must be
considered sacred and inviolable.

Not even Robespierre, who posed as the champion of the poor, and
earned by his scorn of wealth the title of "The Incorruptible," dared
openly to attack the sanctity of private property. "Souls of mud," he
upbraided those who accused him of such an aim, "I do not wish to touch
your wealth however unclean its origin." Nevertheless, under the pressure of the war, he urged the National Convention to adopt measures
which penalized the rich to benefit the poor. The assignats, the paper
money so recklessly issued by the revolutionary assemblies, declined in
value until it was almost worthless. To meet expenses the Convention
seized the property of *émigrés* nobles, and forced rich citizens to "lend"
money to the state, part of which was used to relieve the poverty of
"indigent patriots." When the poor complained at the cost of bread, the
Convention attempted to fix the price of necessities at a fair level, and
threatened profiteering merchants with the guillotine. Such experiments
in what, today, would be termed state socialism helped to placate the
populace and were accepted by the bourgeoisie as temporary war-time
measures.

In the same acquiescent spirit the French people accepted the extraordinary decrees passed against traitors and enemy agents. A
The Reign special revolutionary tribunal was established (1793) to
of Terror judge "enemies of the people," and as the struggle grew
more intense the list of victims mounted. The queen, Marie Antoinette,
the Duke of Orléans who had joined the revolutionaries and renamed
himself Philippe Égalité, revolutionary generals accused of incompetence,
leaders of the defeated Girondist Party, all took their turn on the guillotine. Nor did humbler victims escape. Seamstresses who ventured

to sigh for the days of the monarchy when business was better, and loyal servants convicted of concealing a noble master, met the same fate. By the spring of 1794, the condemned were dispatched to the Place de la Révolution in batches of thirty and forty a day, there to make their bow before what Danton, with wry humor, referred to as the representative of the *executive* power.

Danton's grim jest possessed its element of truth, for the executive committee of public safety was using the guillotine as a political weapon. In March, 1794, it destroyed the Hébertists, a radical group which desired to push the revolution to further excesses, under the leadership of Hébert, editor of a scurrilous journal *Le Père Duchesne.* A few weeks later the committee struck at an opposing group, the "Indulgents," because they sought to retard the revolution and arrest the Terror. Having dispatched Danton and other leaders of the indulgent faction to the guillotine (April, 1794), the committee of public safety was master of the field, and Robespierre was regarded in France and abroad as master of the committee. What use would the Incorruptible make of his extraordinary prestige?

In Robespierre's narrow mind one ideal burned clearly. He aspired to establish a Utopian republic in which all citizens would possess pure morals, high ideals, and unselfish patriotism. But France *The Repub-* was growing weary of his exalted creed. As the victories *lic of Virtue* of the republican armies dispelled the threat of invasion, Robespierre found himself blamed for maintaining the Terror when the excuse for it had passed. He felt the decline of idealism and the waning of his popularity, and it seemed to him that the revolution was losing momentum at the very moment when the goal was in sight. "My reason," he confessed, "though not my heart, is at the point of doubting that Republic of Virtue of which I have traced the plan." In July, 1794, he appealed to the Convention to support him in a further "purification" of the government, but the men of property were beginning to distrust him and his enemies declared he aspired to establish a dictatorship. The Convention voted him under arrest with several of his friends, and although the Parisian populace, through their representatives at the Hôtel de Ville, attempted an insurrection in his favor, the movement failed and Robespierre perished on the guillotine.

4. THE THERMIDORIAN REACTION

From 1789 to 1794 the revolution had been dynamic, gaining momentum with each year that passed. The overthrow of Robespierre

on the Ninth of Thermidor, as the date was styled in the revolutionary
Decline of calendar (July 27, 1794), was followed by a period of re-
revolution- action. From 1795 to 1799 the revolution appears "frozen"
ary idealism or "stagnant." The men who destroyed Robespierre had
been concerned chiefly with saving their heads, but they found themselves hailed as heroes who had ended the Terror. The prisons were
emptied, the committee of public safety and the scarcely less powerful
committee of general security were stripped of their despotic authority,
and the Jacobin Club was closed. A spirit of frivolity, extravagance,
and dissipation supplanted the austere ideals of the Reign of Virtue.
Fortunes which had been acquired by speculation and profiteering were
spent in gambling and amusements. Social life in Paris had never
appeared more vivacious, but the gaiety, the glitter, and the immorality
disguised a mood of cynicism and disillusionment.

The destitute, however, had no superficial gaieties to alleviate the
sharpness of their misery. Feeling that the revolution had betrayed
their hopes, they began openly to regret the passing of Robespierre, and
attempted to assert once more the "sacred right of insurrection." In
April, 1795, and again in May, mobs invaded the Convention demanding
bread and a constitution. But the nation as a whole was weary of
radicalism and terrorism and breathed more easily when these outbreaks
were crushed. The Jacobin ideals had been discredited, the leading
terrorists of 1793 and 1794 were dead or in hiding, and a desire for
a strong and permanent government inclined many Frenchmen to
favor a restoration of the Bourbon monarchy. This sentiment was
stimulated by priests and royalists, who, finding the laws against them
somewhat relaxed after 1794, ventured to slip back into France.

Two powerful groups, however, opposed a return to the Bourbon rule.
The first included men who had grown rich and acquired confiscated
Profiteers property during the revolution, and knew their fortunes
and regi- would vanish if the republic fell. A second group, the
cides regicides, stood to lose even more. For if the Count of
Provence ever ascended the French throne as Louis XVIII,[1] those
deputies of the Convention who had voted the death of Louis XVI would
face death or exile. So these two groups, the speculators and the
regicides, united to hold the revolution from retrograding. Clinging to
power, they struck alternately at the radicals and the royalists, using the
army to preserve their unpopular régime. From 1795 to 1799 the

---

[1] The dauphin, son of Louis XVI, died in Paris, in prison, a year and a half after
his father's execution. Although he never reigned the royalists styled him Louis
XVII.

balance of power in the government remained in the hands of this coalition of trimmers.

Any subterfuge provided these opportunists with an excuse to remain in office.[1] When the National Convention was driven to prepare a constitution and dissolve itself (1795), it decreed that two thirds of its members must be re-elected to the chambers of the new assembly and would take their places whether they were elected or not. Furious at this parody of popular representation, the Parisian sections rebelled, but the insurrection was promptly suppressed by the army. Among the officers who aided materially in crushing this revolt of Vendémiaire 13 (October 5, 1795) was a young Corsican captain of artillery named Napoleon Bonaparte, to whose shrewd mind it must already have been clear that the real control in France was slipping slowly but surely into the hands of the army leaders.

5. THE DIRECTORY (1795–99)

So the great Convention which had guided France through three years of war and tumult passed into history and the nation sullenly accepted the new government provided by the Constitution of the Year III (1795). This new régime was known as the Directory because the executive power was vested in a committee of five directors. The legislative branch consisted of a Council of Ancients (with two hundred and fifty members) *Franchise* and a Council of Five Hundred, chosen by the voters who possessed the *limited.* requisite property qualifications. The leading director was Paul Barras, a profligate and unscrupulous man of mediocre ability, and, despite the fact that both chambers contained many deputies of patriotism and talent, the moral tone of the Directory was corrupt and sordid. Society became increasingly cynical, dissolute, and heartless as the revolution lost the impulse of its early ideals. Dishonest politicians and profiteers amassed fortunes at the public expense and spent them in wasteful display, while starving thousands cursed them. The directors did little to relieve the famine and suffering, for they were chiefly intent upon safeguarding their power against royalist intrigues and popular revolts. When the elections of 1797 returned a number of reactionaries to the legislature, the regicide directors called in the army once more to "purge" the chambers of royalists lest they muster a majority and invite the Bourbons back.

While the political prestige of the Directory sank, the army pursued its successes abroad. Trained and tempered in the school of war and

[1] The Constitution of 1793 (see page 162) had never been applied.

condemned to be brilliant or to face the revolutionary tribunal, the

Collapse of the first coalition (1795–97) young republican generals had developed a tactical audacity which numbed their opponents. As the French in their turn became the invaders, the proud coalition formed against France in 1793 fell to pieces. Prussia, Holland, and Spain made peace with France in 1795, and Napoleon Bonaparte, appointed to command the French army in Italy, brought Sardinia to terms (1796) and compelled the Austrians to sign the Treaty of Campo Formio (1797). Of the imposing combination of powers which had threatened to dismember France three years earlier, only Great Britain remained at war, and the British were on the defensive.

France had thus secured for herself an ascendancy in Europe unequaled since the time of Louis XIV. The government of the Directory used this advantage to "revolutionize" neighboring states, surrounding France with a ring of sister republics. Belgium was annexed outright; Holland (the Batavian Republic) was bound to France by a close alliance; the left bank of the Rhine was in French hands, while in northern Italy French influence erected the Cisalpine Republic with Milan as its capital and the Ligurian Republic which included Genoa. These new states were not only tied to France by treaties; they paid a heavy indemnity and subscribed to the support of the French armies which had conquered (or "liberated") them. If the citizens complained that the burden of tribute was too heavy, the cynical directors assured them that the French had brought them liberty and "it is impossible to buy liberty too dearly."

6. THE ACHIEVEMENTS OF THE REVOLUTION (1789–99)

It will be useful at this point to enumerate the most important changes wrought in France by a decade of revolution. Feudal privileges had

The rule of the middle class been cancelled, the church stripped of its property, the monarchy abolished, the ancient historic provinces of the kingdom carved into new departments, the anarchy of the old legal system replaced by simpler codes and elected magistrates. Unfortunately, this mighty work of destruction had not always been followed by constructive labors of equal magnitude. Too often the new institutions remained impressive sketches, distinguished by nobility of concept rather than by practicality. The revolution had signally failed to establish a government founded upon liberty and equality, for liberty had little meaning under the Directory which was in reality a corrupt and unpopular oligarchy sustained by military power. The bourgeoisie had flouted the principle of equality by entrenching themselves in a position of social and economic privilege, while denying even a vote to the poorest citizens. But the protests, and even the revolts, of the masses had little effect. "The revolution is not finished," declared the popular leader Babeuf, "for the rich monopolize all the wealth and govern exclusively, while the poor toil like veritable slaves, languish in misery, and count for nothing in the state." Babeuf was voicing a protest which in the nineteenth century was to become the leading argument of the socialists, but his ideas were premature and the conspiracy which he organized against the Directory brought him to the guillotine (1797).

Politically, therefore, the revolution had done little more than to shift the control of the government from an inept king and a selfish aristocracy to a vigorous bourgeoisie, but in other fields of endeavor the *Educational* results were somewhat more heartening. Through the *reforms* labors of enlightened thinkers like the philosopher Condorcet, a system of public instruction had been adopted which made the state responsible for the education of children. At first the new primary schools in particular were gravely handicapped by the insufficiency of funds and of teachers, but a start had been made in the great task of training all Frenchmen to become patriotic and literate citizens. Unspectacular reforms of this nature are the most easily ignored because they require many years to reveal their benefits; and the same is true of such innovations as the metric and decimal system of weights and measures, introduced by the National Convention to replace the confused standards of the old régime, but adopted all too tardily by a populace wedded to more cumbrous and diversified methods of calculation.

Legal reform, that favorite project of the eighteenth-century rationalists, was likewise greatly advanced by the revolutionary assemblies, though it remained for Napoleon to cap with his codes the *Legal* structure they erected. The new legislation recognized the *reforms* peasant's freedom from onerous duties and the artisan's liberation from obsolete guild restrictions. Merchants and manufacturers were encouraged by the legal abolition of internal customs and the freedom allowed to business initiative. Perhaps most far-reaching of all in their social effects were the new laws of inheritance which assured all the children of a family a share in their father's estate, a policy which tended to break up large estates and foster the wider distribution of property.

The printing of the assignats, continued by the National Convention with injudicious prodigality, reduced France to financial *Economic* chaos, and by 1798 this paper money had become practically *reforms* worthless. But the currency inflation, while it worked great hardship

[169]

on many people, also furthered the sale of property confiscated from the church and from "enemies of the republic," and throughout the years of the revolution this property tended to pass into the possession of bourgeois and peasant purchasers until France numbered a larger class of independent landed proprietors than any other European country. The poorest peasants and day laborers were seldom in a position to profit by this unusual opportunity, but many a well-to-do farmer or townsman realized his dream of becoming a landowner and blessed the revolution for it. The comparative stability of French society since the revolution has been due in no small measure to the existence of this numerous and conservative group of citizens with "a stake in the country."

The effects of these changes were not easily perceived in 1799 after a decade of tumult and confusion, and to most Frenchmen it appeared that the revolution had been a costly failure. But the dubious successes achieved at home were partly offset by the brilliant triumphs on the battlefield. The war of defense upon which France had entered in 1792 had been changed by 1794 into a vigorous offensive. Yielding to the lure of imperial conquests, the French speedily established a military hegemony which destroyed the balance of power in Europe. The government of the Directory, unpopular at home, sustained itself by the revenues extorted from Dutch, German, and Italian provinces, and prolonged the hostilities because the conclusion of peace would bring the republican generals back to Paris, victorious and insubordinate. The directors had no definite policy other than to postpone the day when they might be called upon to account for their corrupt and inadequate rule. The government was at the mercy of the army leaders, and the first ambitious general who fully comprehended this fact might brush aside the incompetent Directory and make himself master of France.

CHAPTER TWELVE

NAPOLEON AND FRANCE

We must not pass through this world without leaving traces which may commend our memory to posterity.

NAPOLEON.

NAPOLEON BONAPARTE was born in 1769 on the island of Corsica, which had become a French possession the previous year. At the age of ten he was sent to a military school in France, a shy, uncouth boy, who spoke French awkwardly and envied his schoolmates their more polished manners and larger in- *Napoleon's* comes. Lacking a title or a powerful patron, he would most *youth* probably have remained a lieutenant or captain under the old régime, but the revolution threw open the gates of opportunity. The desertion of the nobles created many vacancies in the staff of the republican armies, and Bonaparte, a second lieutenant of artillery in 1789, had been promoted to be a general of brigade by 1794, mainly as a reward for his services in the recapture of Toulon. Suspected as a partisan of Robespierre, he suffered a brief arrest after the latter's fall, but was soon released. In 1795, he was in Paris seeking a new appointment when the insurrection of Vendémiaire broke out. Called upon, with other available officers, to defend the Tuileries, Bonaparte collected some batteries of artillery and met the insurgents with "a whiff of grapeshot." There were, as he later explained laconically, "certain splashings," and the revolt collapsed. His presence of mind made a favorable impression on his superiors and his name was on everyone's lips. Napoleon had entered history with a salvo of artillery.

1. THE ADVENT OF BONAPARTE

From the new government of the Directory, which he had thus helped into power, the young general received further promotion. Appointed (1796) to command the Army of Italy, he left his newly *First* married wife, Josephine, and led his thirty-five thousand *Italian* ragged French troops across the Alps. The Austrian and *campaign* *(1796–97)* Sardinian armies holding northern Italy were taken by surprise, and the King of Piedmont speedily agreed to an armistice. Turning swiftly against the Austrians, who still outnumbered his forces two to one, Bonaparte laid siege to Mantua, captured it (February, 1797), after defeating the Austrian armies sent to its relief, and pursued the discomfited enemy to within a hundred miles of Vienna. Threatened by a second French army in southern Germany, the Austrians sought peace, and Bonaparte, turning diplomat, persuaded them to acknowledge the French annexation of Belgium, offered them Venice (which his troops had lately seized) as compensation for their losses, and demanded recognition for his Italian conquests which he organized as the Cisalpine and Ligurian Republics. When he returned to Paris, the populace turned out to see him present this successful Treaty of Campo Formio to the directors. France was delighted with this young general of twenty-eight who knew not only how to wage war but how to conclude peace.

Finding his presence an embarrassment, the directors appointed him commander of the Army of England. But to cross the Channel with an *The Egyptian expedition (1798–99)* army Bonaparte judged too hazardous. England and Russia were the "great intangibles": to the end of his reign both were to evade the full power of his smashing blows. Not yet strong enough to make a bid for supreme power, and fearful that he would be forgotten if he let his sword "grow rusty," Bonaparte proposed a plan to the directors whereby he might strike at Britain indirectly. His imagination turned to the East; he planned to conquer Egypt and thence attack the British posts in India. "I saw myself," he confessed later, "on the road to Asia, perched on an elephant, a turban on my head." But this romantic dream of following in the footsteps of Alexander the Great led him to the borders of disaster. Though Egypt was easily overrun, Bonaparte's fleet was destroyed by the English admiral Nelson (battle of the Nile, August 1, 1798), which severed his connections with France. His invasion of Syria carried him no farther than Acre. The proposal to invade India by land had been from the first a piece of incredible audacity as Napoleon now realized. "I allowed my imagination to interfere with my practice..." he admitted. "I shall take good care not to let it run away with my judgment again." He could appraise himself with the same cold rationality which he employed in judging his subordinates.

In Europe, meanwhile, the situation had changed to the grave disadvantage of France. In 1798, Great Britain, most implacable enemy *The second coalition* of the republic, drew Austria and Russia into a new coalition, designed to check French conquests in Italy and the Mediterranean. Within a few months the French forces in Italy had been routed by an Austro-Russian army (battle of Novi, 1799), and the Rhine frontier laid open to invasion. Then the French rallied. Masséna checked the Russians at Zurich; and to fire the reviving French hopes

NAPOLEON BONAPARTE
1769–1821

This portrait of Napoleon as a young man emphasizes the stern, relentless and unsympathetic elements in his character. His likeness was not an easy one to transfer to canvas, for his moods shifted rapidly and he was a consummate actor. When it suited his purpose few men could appear more frank, winning or persuasive.

came the news that Bonaparte had landed at Fréjus, October 9, 1799. Leaving his marooned army to waste away in Egypt, he had slipped through the British blockade and returned at an auspicious moment. A month later he was to be master of France.

The government of the Directory was tottering. Discredited, bankrupt, and incompetent, it had thrown away the fruits of Bonaparte's Italian victories and involved France in new wars. Both Jacobins and royalists were plotting to overturn it, while moderate republicans under the lead of Sieyès looked about for a soldier to help them "revise the constitution." Bonaparte's arrival in October, 1799, could not have been better timed.

A plot was formed which called for Sieyès, Ducos, and Barras, three of the five directors, to resign (November 8). Under the pretense of *The coup d'état of Brumaire* checking a Jacobin conspiracy, Bonaparte's friends proposed that he should be given command of the Parisian troops. Then the Council of Ancients and the Council of Five Hundred were persuaded to adjourn to Saint-Cloud to deliberate on the crisis (November 9). The conspirators hoped to give their *coup d'état* the appearance of legality by persuading the two chambers to approve the necessary changes, but the Council of Five Hundred grew suspicious and were on the point of voting Napoleon's arrest when his brother Lucien, president of the Five Hundred, appealed to the soldiers to clear the chamber. Lucien's presence of mind and the bayonets of the guard saved the conspirators. Of this, however, no mention was made in the proclamation posted in Paris the following day, which announced to France that the constitution would shortly be revised, and that in the interval Bonaparte, Sieyès, and Ducos would act as consuls. From their first meeting Bonaparte presided.

The man who thus at thirty became master of France was to bestride Europe like a Colossus for fifteen years. Innumerable books have been *Napoleon's character* written to explain the peculiar genius and temperament of Napoleon Bonaparte, but there is space here for only the briefest summary of his character. In appearance he was short, with an olive complexion, sharply cut features, and a penetrating gaze. The qualities which make a ruler — knowledge of men, an untiring capacity for work, a rarely failing memory for detailed facts, the power of instant and inspired decision — he possessed in a unique degree, and these very largely explain the success of Napoleon the man. But he added to them a personal magnetism that could exact the utmost in devotion from his followers, an imagination incredibly romantic in its wild sweep, and a sense of the dramatic which made him the architect of his own legend.

These help to explain Napoleon the myth. For a great many people the myth has obscured the man, transfiguring all his defects of judgment and character and investing him with attributes almost superhuman. "People will often give me credit," Napoleon prophesied, "for a great deal of depth and sagacity on occasions which were, perhaps, most simple in themselves; I shall be suspected of plans which I never formed." In his own lifetime people had begun to confuse the man and the legend.

That Napoleon was a master of military tactics and political finesse is conceded by almost all authorities. But he was no such universal genius on a throne as some admirers pretend. His taste in art and literature was mediocre; his knowledge of the sciences (aside from mathematics) was dubious and second-hand; his command of history was capricious and his economic beliefs were marred by disastrous errors. His character was inferior to his intellect and a deficient moral sense permitted him to stoop to ignoble deceptions and the basest tricks of Machiavellian polity. Nevertheless, with all his limitations he remains the most dominant and arresting personality in modern history, and the years from 1800 to 1815 are justly named the Era of Napoleon.

2. COLLAPSE OF THE SECOND COALITION

Frenchmen welcomed Bonaparte's ascent to power because they believed he would put an end to internal disturbances and conclude the war which had burdened France since 1792. Other republican generals — Hoche, Pichegru, Moreau, Masséna — had proved that they could win victories, but Bonaparte had crowned his Italian campaign with the Peace of Campo Formio. Knowing that the desire for peace was widespread, the First Consul opened his régime with proposals for a general truce. On Christmas Day, 1799, he dispatched conciliatory overtures to London and Vienna, but he strained every effort none the less to be prepared for further hostilities. The British response was vague, and the reply from Vienna left Napoleon in no doubt that the Austrians would never yield France the advantages she desired without a struggle.

The First Consul settled the issue with his customary speed. "Napoleon," admitted a contemporary, "is the only man in Europe who knows the value of time." Crossing the Alps in May, 1800, he *Second* snatched victory from defeat with the aid of Desaix and *Italian* Kellermann at Marengo, and concluded a second Italian *campaign (1800)* campaign even more decisive than his first. The following December, Moreau defeated the Austrian army in the Germanies at

[175]

Hohenlinden and peace was assured. The Treaty of Lunéville practically recapitulated the terms arranged at Campo Formio four years
earlier.

The defeat of Austria broke the second coalition. Negotiations with
the Czar Paul I (1796–1801) ended in the withdrawal of Russia in 1801,

French hegemony in Europe and Great Britain was left to carry on the struggle against
France alone. For a year these wary adversaries bargained
and finally signed a grudging peace.[1] The French Republic
had established a political hegemony in Europe. Belgium, the left
bank of the Rhine, and Piedmont had been annexed outright. Holland
(the Batavian Republic) and Switzerland (the Helvetic Republic or
Swiss Confederation) were bound to France by a close alliance that
amounted to vassalage. In Italy, the Ligurian Republic (Genoa) and
the Parthenopean Republic (Naples and Sicily) were under French control, while the Cisalpine Republic (renamed the Italian Republic)
acknowledged Bonaparte as president. The French justified their
acquisitions on the ground that the inhabitants of the annexed territories
welcomed union with France, and that the people of the subject states,
the Dutch, the Swiss, and the Italians, regarded the French as allies and
liberators. To a certain extent this was true; but the liberators were
also conquerors, and the other European powers, disregarding subtler
distinctions, complained that republican France had pursued with
unexampled success the foreign policy of Richelieu and of Louis XIV.

The English in particular found it difficult to accept this French
expansion. They deplored the fate of Belgium, for Antwerp in enemy

English hostility toward France hands was "a pistol pointed at the heart of England," as
Napoleon clearly appreciated. The subjugation of the
liberty-loving Swiss and the fall of the Venetian Republic
after centuries of glorious independence inspired the poet
Wordsworth to eloquent protests. The English merchant classes,
disappointed that the Treaty of Amiens did not open Europe to their
commerce, and alarmed because Bonaparte proposed to revive French
colonial activity in the West Indies, in Louisiana, and in India, complained that peace was more disastrous than war. The French on their
part likewise nursed grievances which they attributed to English perfidy,
and neither party executed its treaty promises in full. It is not surprising, therefore, that the general peace with which Bonaparte gratified
France proved to be an illusory peace of the briefest duration. The
causes which led Britain and France to renew hostilities in 1803 will be
discussed in the following chapter.

[1] Treaty of Amiens, 1802.

3. NAPOLEON RECONSTRUCTS FRANCE

In December, 1799, the French people approved by 3,011,007 votes to 1526 the "Constitution of the Year VIII." This interesting document provided for a dictatorship under the guise of a democratic republic. As First Consul, Bonaparte was to wield the executive power for ten years. A second and third consul, *Constitution of the Consulate* a council of state appointed by himself, and a senate filled with his supporters, assisted in his decisions. To preserve the appearance of popular sovereignty for which Napoleon had no real sympathy — "Your Rousseau was a madman," he asserted privately — provision was made for two elective chambers, the tribunate and the legislature. The tribunate had the privilege of discussing laws, but could not vote on them; the legislature might vote, but could not discuss them. This arrangement, coupled with the fact that legislation was to originate with the First Consul and the council of state, placed the legislative as well as the executive power in Bonaparte's hands. This negation of popular rule, to gain which the French had just waged a revolution, was not easily apparent to the people because all male citizens retained the right to vote. But this, too, was rendered illusory. The electors of each commune chose one tenth of their number to form a communal list; members of all the communal lists in each department then chose one tenth of their number for the departmental list; and the departmental delegates chose one tenth of their membership for the national list. Public officials and members of the tribunate and legislature could then be appointed by Napoleon and the council of state from the national list, a system which left the voters free to cast their ballots and Napoleon free to promote only those men whose loyalty to himself assured their co-operation in his aims. Actually, most appointments were made before the lists were complete.

If the French people lost their political liberty and initiative, they gained a government of unparalleled efficiency and vigor. The farmer who had paid two and even three fifths of his income in taxes under the old régime now paid one fifth, yet the state revenues had doubled. New and more competent judges stiffened respect for the law, and special courts curbed the widespread disorder and brigandage. Ruined roads and bridges were restored, harbors dredged and canals deepened. The consolidation of the national debt and attainment of a balanced budget by 1801 revived business confidence, and trade expanded under an administration which proved it could assure tranquillity. After ten years of political vicissitude France enjoyed a competent, honest, and energetic government, and the merchant in the city and the peasant on the farm gave Bonaparte the credit. To assure permanence for the new régime the constitution was amended (1802) making him consul for life with the right to nominate his successor, and the French people approved this extension of power by 3,568,885 "ayes" to 8374 "noes."

The First Consul's most popular reform was his solution of the religious problem. The breach between republican France and the papacy
Concordat
(1801) created by the Civil Constitution of the Clergy [1] grieved a majority of the French people who were still Catholic in sentiment. In 1801, a *concordat* was negotiated, whereby Pius VII agreed to renounce all claim to church property confiscated and sold by the revolutionary assemblies, and to permit the French government to nominate French bishops who would in turn appoint the lower clergy. In return the Roman Catholic faith was declared the religion of the great majority of Frenchmen and the constitutional clergy (i.e., those who had defied the pope and accepted the civil constitution) were replaced by priests duly consecrated. This settlement meant: (1) that the ten-year schism between Rome and the Gallican Church had ended with the spiritual authority of the pope unimpaired; (2) that the purchasers of confiscated church lands might for the first time consider their titles strictly valid; and (3) that the French clergy would prove submissive to the consular government because the selection of bishops and the payment of salaries had become a function of the state. Though ardent republicans disliked this compromise and called it a step backward, the mass of Frenchmen welcomed reunion with the Church of Rome. Those Catholics who had opposed the revolutionary settlement on religious grounds were mollified by the *concordat*, which remained in force for over a century.

Critics had frequently protested, both before and during the revolution, that France would never be tranquil until the laws had been re-
The Code
Napoléon duced to a clearly formulated code. Napoleon considered it his chief claim to glory that under his direction this gigantic and confusing task was completed. He drove his committee of lawyers relentlessly until by 1804 the main principles of the revolution concerning persons and property had been embodied in a civil code. Four additional digests followed, on civil procedure (1806), commerce (1807), criminal instruction (1808), and the penal code (1810). Of the five the civil code was by far the most influential and forms today the basis of civil law, not only in France, but in Belgium, Holland, Italy, and parts of Germany.

[1] See above, pages 153–54.

A law passed in February, 1800, went far to reconstruct the centralized bureaucracy familiar to Frenchmen from Bourbon times. In the departments the authority of elective councils created by *Centralized* the revolution was subordinated to that of a prefect ap- *administra-* pointed by the first consul. Similarly, a subprefect directed *tion* the affairs in each district and a mayor in each municipality. This relatively simple and centralized administrative system has survived in France up to the present day very much as Napoleon left it, demonstrating its efficiency through four changes of government.

The leaders of the revolution, having closed up the church schools, had planned to replace them by a system of national education. This project also Napoleon carried to completion with his *Education* customary genius for organization. The Imperial University (1808) crowned a state school system which embraced primary schools, high schools, and colleges. The curriculum was rigidly designed to train good citizens and the pupils learned their duty to the head of the state more thoroughly than they learned anything else. To Napoleon's mind the youth of France might have been so much raw material, to be manufactured into civil servants or soldiers as the need required. Even the adult population remained in a sort of tutelage, reading only censored journals and official *communiqués*, or attending plays specially designed to inculcate "sound principles." Napoleon was fulfilling the *philosophes'* dream of a paternal despot to a degree perhaps undreamed of in their philosophy.

All his reforms — the legal codes, the centralized administration, the obedient church, the schools that trained his councilors, and the barracks that disciplined his cannon fodder — all had been erected to the greater glory of Napoleon. Moralizing in his captivity at Saint Helena, Napoleon declared his constant motto had been "Everything for the French People." But if he made France the most efficiently ruled and the most powerful state in Europe, it was less from love of France than from love of power. "Power is my mistress . . ." he confessed with truer insight. "I love it as an artist." So, despite the glory he won for France, his popularity waned. In reducing thirty million Frenchmen to be the instruments of his will, he did violence to human nature, for man does not wish to be regarded as a means to an end, but as an end in himself. Under Napoleon's barrack-room methods the finer flowers of the human spirit, art and literature, were slow to blossom. In the end his system failed in its primary purpose, for it did not provide administrators so efficient nor officers so inspired as the revolution had bequeathed to him. "The men of 1812 were not the men of 1792," he complained, criticizing his second generation of officials for their lack of initiative. Perhaps he had drilled it out of them.

4. THE IMPERIAL ADVENTURE

The Constitution of the Year VIII (1799) had made Bonaparte consul for ten years, the Constitution of the Year X (1802) made him consul for *Plots against* life. His ambition, however, was not yet satisfied. He *the life of* began deliberately to surround himself with a royal etiquette *Napoleon* and ceremonial and took up his residence in the palace of the Tuileries where Louis XVI had held his court. In 1804, the obedient senate was persuaded to offer him the title of emperor. Several attempts had been made upon his life; agents of the exiled Bourbons and of the British government were plotting his removal; and the French people were troubled that such a beneficent régime should depend upon the safety of one man. To establish a Bonaparte dynasty appeared the surest way to perpetuate his reforms. At the same time, to deter conspirators, Napoleon had the Duke d'Enghien seized near the French borders, tried before a military court, and shot, a stroke which filled Europe with horror, but ended the plotting of the duke's Bourbon kinsmen. Several republican generals, including Moreau and Pichegru, were also arrested on the charge of conspiracy, and these drastic measures silenced all effective opposition to the establishment of the empire.

At Napoleon's invitation, Pope Pius VII journeyed to Paris to assist at the coronation of the first "Emperor of the French." The imposing *The impe-* ceremony took place in the Cathedral of Notre Dame *rial hier-* (December 2, 1804), but instead of waiting to receive his *archy* crown from the pope, Napoleon set it upon his own head and then crowned his wife Josephine empress. High-sounding titles were invented to honor a new hierarchy of imperial officials. Napoleon's elder brother, Joseph, became grand elector. Leading generals were promoted to be marshals of France, leading statesmen became grand dignitaries with the title of "Highness," while even senators were to be addressed as "Excellency." The creation of a new order for distinguished service, the Legion of Honor, enabled Napoleon to flatter the vanity and reward the merit of loyal followers by distributing ribbons and medals carrying with them a comfortable annuity for the recipients. Thus, after purging itself of one privileged caste in the fires of revolution, the French people beheld the formation of another, but the new nobility differed in one important respect from the old. The aristocrats of the old régime claimed their titles and privileges by right of birth, but the imperial notables won their promotion on the basis of service. Napoleon's motto remained as it had been, "Careers open to talent," and he boasted that any private in his armies "might carry a marshal's baton in his knapsack." "It was my intention," he maintained, looking back on these crowded years from the loneliness of Saint Helena, "to put an end to all feudal institutions in Europe by reconnecting the idea of nobility with that of public service, and detaching from it all prescriptive or feudal notions."

Those who served the Emperor of the French successfully might hope for a title, a dukedom, even a royal crown. Not from France alone, but from all parts of Europe men hastened to learn the commands of the Man of Destiny whose aspirations seemed limitless, whose good fortune appeared inexhaustible. Napoleon in the plenitude of his power suggests Shakespeare's description of Mark Antony:

> in his livery
> Walked crowns and crownets, realms and islands were
> As plates dropped from his pocket.

But unlike Antony, he lacked magnanimity. Toward failure he had no pity, and he insisted that to serve him was to serve France, a presupposition which grew increasingly dubious as he staked the security of France and the lives of his soldiers more and more recklessly on his foreign ventures.

Nor was Napoleon always just in his distribution of awards. As his empire extended itself, he yielded to an excessive nepotism, showering undeserved honors upon the members of his family. His *Napoleon's* stepson Eugène (Josephine's son by her first marriage to *nepotism* General Beauharnais) he appointed Viceroy of the Italian Kingdom. One brother, Joseph Bonaparte, became successively King of Naples and of Spain, another brother, Louis, he made King of Holland, a third, Jerome, King of Westphalia. His sisters acquired titles and estates and his mother a princely income. As a family the Bonapartes possessed more than ordinary talents, but none to warrant such promotion. Moreover, Napoleon displayed partiality even in his nepotism, for Lucien, next to himself the ablest of the family, was left to languish in the cold shades of the imperial disfavor because he dared to marry against the emperor's wishes.

It was a source of deep concern to Napoleon that his first wife, Josephine, bore him no children. In 1810, he divorced her for *The impe-* reasons of state, and married the Archduchess Marie Louise *rial succes-* of Austria. In 1811, a son was born and received the *sion* title "King of Rome," for Rome had become the second city of Napoleon's international empire. With the imperial succession assured, Napoleon predicted that his reign was about to enter a second and even more glorious chapter. In reality his star was approaching a disastrous eclipse, the causes of which will be explained in the succeeding chapter.

5. RESULTS OF NAPOLEON'S RULE IN FRANCE

Napoleon called himself "the son of the revolution"; he even said, "I am the revolution"; and he never ceased to remind Frenchmen that they owed to him the preservation of all that was beneficial in the revolutionary program. It will be interesting to decide how far his claim was justified.

In the political sphere Napoleon's work was reactionary. He not only ended the republic; he re-established hereditary monarchy and revived

Political reaction many distinctive features of Bourbon rule. His prefects ("emperors on a small scale," he termed them) were replicas of the former intendants; his council of state was the royal council remodeled. His censorship regulations and his police agents had little to distinguish them beyond their greater effectiveness from those of the old régime. Behind a screen of popular deceptions he restored absolutism in France both in theory and practice, an absolutism buttressed by institutions more efficient and more highly centralized than those fashioned by Richelieu or Louis XIV. An incomparable army, a highly organized administrative bureaucracy, a state-controlled church, a standardized educational system — these were the instruments of his will, and the legacy he bequeathed to France. But these instruments were scarcely the product of the revolution, although the revolution had cleared the way for them. Rather they approximated to the ideal of government endorsed by Frederick the Great or Joseph II of Austria, just as Napoleon himself approximated to the ideal of an enlightened despot. The French people accepted him because he was successful and because his régime provided an escape from ten years of revolutionary strife, but they never quite forgot and never quite relinquished the democratic dreams of 1793 which had beckoned like an apocalyptic vision before the clouds of disillusionment tarnished them.

Napoleon discarded liberty, but he preserved that other great revolutionary watchword, equality. The class privileges, the iniquitous taxa-

Civil and economic gains tion, the feudal obligations of the old régime, disappeared along with the archaic modes of punishment and the arbitrary administration of justice. The *Code Napoléon* assured all Frenchmen equality before the law regardless of rank, riches, or religion. Furthermore, proprietors who had acquired land confiscated from the church or from exiled nobles could thank Napoleon for confirming and legalizing their titles of ownership. Business men applauded the abolition of internal customs barriers, the improvements in roads and harbors, the benefits of a uniform system of weights, measures, and coinage, revolutionary projects which Napoleon perpetuated. The peasants were grateful for the abolition of feudal dues, for the suppression of disorder and brigandage, and for the restoration of the Catholic faith. In fact, there was no class in France which did not have some substantial reason for blessing Napoleon's régime. He undid much of the political work of the revolution, but he preserved and extended the civil and economic reforms.

The revolution had killed feudalism in France: Napoleon buried it and reared a new order of society upon its tomb. But beyond the French borders feudalism was still alive, and the privileged classes would fight until their last battlement had fallen. For if the revolutionary notion of equality triumphed, it meant the ruin of the old aristocracy. The dues their peasantry paid them, the rent from inherited estates, the sinecures gained through family connections, and the promotions assured by right of birth — all these the spreading revolution would destroy. Even the laws which had long fortified the aristocrats in their pretensions would be changed to the advantage of the vulgar. Custom had hitherto reserved the most lucrative positions in the state, the church, and the army for the nobly born, but few aristocrats could hope to win such offices if the more capable commoners could compete for them on equal terms. It is not difficult to understand why the privileged classes throughout Europe resisted the revolution as an impious and subversive movement, or why Napoleon, in extending it, found them among the most implacable of his enemies.

As the son of the revolution, he was condemned to extend it, and he believed that "every man must fulfill his destiny." When the powers leagued themselves against his spreading influence, he fought and defeated them. "I always appear to be attacking," he complained more than once, "yet what I am doing is defending myself all the time." The student will be better able to decide how much reliance to place on this statement after reading about Napoleon's European projects and campaigns.

CHAPTER THIRTEEN

NAPOLEON AND EUROPE

Throughout my whole reign I was the keystone of an edifice entirely new, and resting on the most slender foundations. Its duration depended on the issue of my battles. I was never, in truth, master of my movements; I was never at my own disposal.

NAPOLEON.

IN 1802, the wars which had grown out of the French Revolution came to a momentary close. The French had proved by force of arms that they would suffer no interference from the other powers, and the monarchs of Europe, weary of bloodshed, abandoned their plan to crush the revolutionary movement and restore the Bourbons to the French throne. Unfortunately, this temporary truce did not endure. Fighting broke out again in 1803 and continued with mounting casualties until Napoleon was finally defeated and sent into exile. It is the purpose of the present chapter to explain why, between 1800 and 1812, Napoleon was able to extend his control over the greater part of Europe, and why, after 1812, his empire collapsed.

1. THE REVOLUTION SPREADS

When Napoleon became First Consul in 1799, the French Republic had already secured control of several states beyond its legitimate boundaries. Belgium and the left bank of the Rhine had been annexed, while Holland, Switzerland, and northern and southern Italy were regarded by the French as part of their "system" of allied republics. Napoleon had to maintain and defend this extension of French influence or risk his popularity. Because of his military genius he was able to conclude a general peace by 1802 without making any concessions, but the peace was not likely to endure if he attempted further conquests, for England and Austria were intensely jealous of the French success. If Napoleon had sincerely desired peace, he might well have rested content with the laurels won, but he had a passion for reconstructing and reorganizing things. One country was too small for his ambition, and looking abroad he decided that the people of Italy and Germany would be happier if he brought to them a few of the masterly reforms which had already been introduced in France. It was easy to find a pretext for interfering because many Italians and Germans admired Napoleon for what he had done in France and were willing to defer to him and to welcome his assistance.

So Napoleon disregarded the warnings of Austria, of England, of Prussia and Russia, and continued to extend his power by extending the work of the revolution. At first he had on his side the *Admiration for revolutionary France* force of public opinion and the force of arms. Many Europeans outside of France sympathized with the ideals of the revolution and regarded Napoleon as its directing genius. People of the middle class in particular envied the French bourgeoisie who had thrown off the stupid and oppressive rule of priests and nobles and made themselves the dominant class in the state. Of course kings and nobles everywhere were opposed to any extension of revolutionary principles, and they could set the armies of Europe in motion, but Napoleon believed himself a match for them. The French battalions were the better organized and were commanded by a group of generals without equals in Europe, while at their head rode one of the greatest military strategists of all time. Moreover, Napoleon knew he would be fighting foreign governments rather than the nations they ruled and he believed he could easily turn his foes against one another.

2. THE RECONSTRUCTION OF ITALY

An Italian by descent, Napoleon knew that the people of Italy had learned during four centuries of oppression to hate the rule of the foreigner. He engaged their support by promising them liberty and self-government, and he prophesied that before long Italy would take her merited place among the powers as a strong and united nation. When he became president of the Cisalpine Republic (1802), he changed the title to Italian Republic, and the name stirred a patriotic response in the hearts of his new subjects. It seemed a further proof that the First Consul was working for Italian independence, and this hope long steeled the Italians to endure his exactions and to furnish men for his wars.

But in Italian affairs as elsewhere there was a wide divergence between Napoleon's pretended and his actual aims. Julius Caesar, it will be remembered, described Gaul when he first invaded it as divided into three parts. The modern Caesar returned the compliment, for he divided Italy into three parts and maintained the division. It had been a maxim of statecraft since Roman times that a country is more easily held in subjection when it is partitioned, and Napoleon feared that a strong and united Italian state, once formed, would prove difficult to control.

In 1805, the Italian Republic became the Italian Kingdom, but it still included only about one third of the peninsula. Napoleon came to

Milan as a modern Charlemagne, to be crowned with the iron crown of the Lombard kings, and he designated his stepson, Eugène Beauharnais, as viceroy. In the following year the Parthenopean Republic was transformed into the Kingdom of Naples and Sicily with Napoleon's brother Joseph as king. The remaining Italian states were gradually annexed to France, Piedmont in 1801, the Ligurian Republic (Genoa), Parma, Piacenza, and Guastella in 1805, Tuscany and the Papal States including Rome in 1809. The map following page 192 shows the limits of the Italian Kingdom, the Kingdom of Naples, and French Italy, in 1810, when Napoleon's power was at its height. Note that the Illyrian Provinces, seized between 1806 and 1809, were not added to the Italian Kingdom, but were annexed to France.

Though Napoleon treated Italy as a vassal state, he introduced many beneficial reforms. The Inquisition was abolished, the feudal régime *Benefits of* swept away, taxation more equitably apportioned, and *French rule* justice administered according to the new codes. The bands of brigands which had long terrorized sections of Italy, particularly Naples, were ruthlessly suppressed. An attempt was made to reduce the illiteracy and superstition of the Italian masses by establishing a state school system, improvements in agriculture and in public hygiene were introduced, and roads, bridges, and parks constructed for public use. But ten years of enlightened administration could not cure the corruption and inertia into which Italy had declined, and the French reforms, like the promise of national unity, remained more of a hope than a reality. With Napoleon's downfall Italy once again found herself chained by the forces of reaction.

3. THE REORGANIZATION OF THE GERMANIES

The three hundred or more states, large and small, which composed "the Germanies" were likewise destined to benefit from Napoleon's passion for rearrangement. His plan at first was merely to weaken Austria by strengthening lesser German principalities such as Bavaria, Württemberg, Baden, and Hesse-Darmstadt. As France had annexed nearly a hundred small states on the left bank of the Rhine, he encouraged the German princes, dispossessed by these changes, to seek "compensation" by seizing ecclesiastical lands and free cities on the right bank. After Austria had been induced to consent (Peace of Lunéville, 1801), the German Diet authorized the procedure by a decree known as the *Reichsdeputationshauptschluss* (1803), and by 1806 two hundred small German states, too weak to defend themselves, had been swallowed up by their larger neighbors. There were still nearly a hundred separate states in the empire, but a long stride had been taken toward a political consolidation of the Germanies.

Napoleon had no intention of welding Germany into a powerful and united empire any more than he planned to transform Italy into a single kingdom. But he knew that if the South German States owed their political aggrandizement to France, they would prove valuable allies in the event of a new war with Austria. He did not believe the Hapsburgs would allow him to usurp their leadership in German affairs without striking another blow, and when the new war came he wished to be prepared for it.

With Great Britain hostilities had broken out again in 1803. The English prime minister, William Pitt (the Younger), was a son of that resolute minister who had helped to strip France of her colonies in the Seven Years' War.[1] The Younger Pitt proved an equally implacable foe of French ascendancy. Napoleon, when he found a renewal of war inevitable, *The war of the third coalition (1805–06)* determined to concentrate a fleet of transports at Boulogne and other French ports for a blow against England. "If we are masters of the Channel for six hours," he boasted with undue optimism, "we are masters of the world." To deflect the impending blow, Pitt stirred up resistance on the Continent, and pouring out gold with a lavish hand he persuaded Austria and Russia to join in the formation of a third coalition. Whether Napoleon seriously meditated a descent upon England has been doubted by some historians. If he did, he abandoned his campaign projects against his principal enemy without hesitation, and marching his divisions toward the Rhine with incredible rapidity he overwhelmed an Austrian army of fifty thousand men at Ulm (October 20, 1805).

One day later (October 21, 1805) an English fleet under Admiral Nelson (1758–1805) destroyed the combined French and Spanish [2] squadrons off Cape Trafalgar, a victory which cost Nelson his life, but assured the English control of the seas to the end of the war. Once again, as in Egypt, Napoleon had felt the might of British sea power, and once again he pressed on undeterred. December 2, 1805, the anniversary of his coronation as emperor, he attacked an Austro-Russian army at Austerlitz and completely defeated it. For the third time he had forced Austria to a humiliating peace. By the Treaty of Pressburg the South German States which had aided France were enlarged and declared independent, Bavaria and Württemberg becoming kingdoms.

[1] See above, page 99.   [2] Spain had been the passive ally of France since 1801.

Napoleon now made his German policy clearer by organizing these new kingdoms and a dozen lesser states into the Confederation of the Rhine, with himself as protector. The princes of the confederation agreed to support France in the field with sixty thousand men, and to renounce all connection with the Holy Roman Empire. On Napoleon's assertion that he no longer recognized a Holy Roman Emperor, Francis II agreed to abandon that title and style himself Francis I, Emperor of Austria, instead (1806). Such was the ignominious end of that impressive medieval empire, the rulers of which had traced their authority to Charlemagne and Augustus.

End of the Holy Roman Empire (1806)

The battle of Austerlitz shattered the third coalition and hastened the death of Pitt. "Roll up that map," he is reported to have said, pointing to a chart of Europe. "We shall not need it these ten years." Yet, as Napoleon complained, he had no sooner broken up the third coalition when a fourth threatened him. While pushing on his reorganization of the Germanies, Napoleon had kept Prussia neutral by promising Frederick William III Hanover and the leading rôle in a North German Confederation. Realizing by 1806 the hollowness of these promises, the Prussian war party persuaded Frederick William to defy France. But at Jena and Auerstädt, a double battle fought October 14, 1806, the Prussians learned that their army, famous since the days of Frederick the Great, was no match for the revolutionary tactics of the French. By the end of October, Napoleon was in Berlin. Pushing on he encountered a Russian force at Eylau (February, 1807) and fought it to a sanguinary draw. For the moment he was checked, but the following June he sought out the Russians again at Friedland and won a victory as conclusive though not so dramatic as that of Austerlitz or Jena.

Intervention of Prussia (1806)

The young Czar Alexander I was ready for peace, and Napoleon, who had learned to respect the fighting qualities of the Russians, was prepared to be generous. By flattering Alexander and offering him a free hand in dealing with Turkey and Finland, he won Russia to his side. But for Frederick William III of Prussia, who had so rashly yielded to warlike advice and defied him, he had no pity. Stripped of half its territory, Prussia became a second-class power with an army limited to forty-two thousand men. Prussian Poland Napoleon reconstructed as the "Grand Duchy of Warsaw," and the Prussian possessions west of the Elbe River he joined with some lesser states to form a new "Kingdom of Westphalia" for his brother Jerome. At the same time he secured control of the North German coastline to the Baltic,

Peace of Tilsit (1807)

WILLIAM PITT, THE YOUNGER
1759–1806

*Precocious political talents made Pitt prime
minister in 1784 at the early age of twenty-five.
After the outbreak of the French Revolution his
resolute opposition to the expansion of French
influence led the revolutionaries to proclaim him
"the enemy of the human race."*

including the free cities of Hamburg, Lübeck, Bremen, and Danzig. North as well as South Germany was now in his control.[1]

The Peace of Tilsit marked the high tide of Napoleon's fortunes; after Tilsit, it has been said, he "began to attempt the impossible." Even
Napoleon corrupted by power his splendid mind was not immune to the insidious and corrupting influence of an unmeasured despotism. Hitherto he had extended his control less by conquest than by converting others to his projects, harmonizing their selfish aims with his own grand designs. Now he grew increasingly irritable at any form of criticism or opposition, and, while multiplying his own exactions, showed himself less willing to concede the desires of his allies and his vassals. He should have recalled how foreign interference after 1792 excited France to a militant protest, and have realized that his rough treatment of other nations must soon provoke them to a similar resentment. But this he failed to appreciate, misled very likely by the readiness with which the Austrian Netherlands, Italy, the Rhineland, and Poland had submitted to his control. These territories, disunited and misgoverned by their rulers, welcomed a change of masters, but when he humiliated independent national states such as Prussia, Spain, Portugal, and Russia, he unleashed the wrath of their people and united them behind their governments in a patriotic crusade.

4. NAPOLEON AND ENGLAND

The Nemesis of the Napoleonic Empire was Great Britain. With their colonial and commercial supremacy at stake, the English could not
The Continental System afford to compromise, and, as Napoleon found it impossible to strike at them directly, he decided to ruin this "nation of shopkeepers" by cutting off their trade. As master of the Continent he sought by his Berlin Decrees (1806) and Milan Decrees (1807) to close all European countries to English merchandise. By ruining the commercial classes which controlled Parliament he was confident he could bring the English government to sue for peace or face bankruptcy and revolution. He dared to stake the solidity of his empire on a test of strength and endurance, but the gamble was a gigantic one. It compelled him to close all the continental ports against England, and to stifle the hostility of Europe's millions who would be deprived of the English goods they desired to purchase.

The British struck back by issuing decrees known as "Orders in Council," by which they hoped to regulate trade so as to force their own

[1] See map following page 192.

wares upon Europe while strangling the export trade of France and her allies. The French emperor believed that Britain, if unable to sell goods, would have to pay for necessary purchases abroad in gold, thus depleting her reserves, straining her credit, and dislocating her economic structure, while unsold products glutted her warehouses. The outcome belied his hopes. Though suffering severely from the curtailment of markets, British merchants and manufacturers still managed to defy the Continental System. Napoleon on his part found that the system was enormously difficult to maintain, and it led him into expedients which undoubtedly hastened his fall.

The principal points of entry for British goods were the German ports such as Hamburg, Lübeck, and Bremen, the Dutch ports, and Lisbon in Portugal. These Napoleon endeavored to control, but goods were still smuggled into Germany, Louis Bonaparte enforced the system leniently in Holland, and the Portuguese refused to drive the English ships from Lisbon. Napoleon, therefore, dispatched an army to Portugal (1807). The following year he forced the stupid Spanish king, Charles IV, to resign, and appointed his brother Joseph Bonaparte to the vacant throne. To subjugate Spain would require some twenty-five thousand men, he imagined, and take only a few months. But he underestimated three serious obstacles: (1) the mountainous nature of the country which favored guerrilla tactics; (2) the stubborn patriotism of the Spanish people; (3) the military assistance which Great Britain might render to the Spaniards. In the end Napoleon found ten times twenty-five thousand men insufficient to quell the Spanish resistance, although he came in person to supervise operations. The expeditionary force which the English sent to Spain, brilliantly commanded by Sir Arthur Wellesley, later Duke of Wellington, contributed in no small measure to the decline of Napoleon's military hegemony, particularly after 1810.

From Spain Napoleon was summoned hastily to the Danube (1809), where Austria, somewhat prematurely as it proved, had proclaimed a war for the liberation of the Germanies. Although he seized Vienna (May, 1809), Napoleon suffered a check at Aspern *The Austrian war of 1809* and had to call up reserves before he repaired his hazardous plight by the victory of Wagram. In the Treaty of Schönbrunn, Austria yielded territory to Russia, to Bavaria, and to the Grand Duchy of Warsaw, and acknowledged the French annexation of the Illyrian Provinces.

Nevertheless, Napoleon recognized that for a moment his fortune had wavered. He was impressed by the refashioned Austrian battalions (the Archduke Charles was learning by defeat) and angered at the bad *The Austro-* faith of the Russians. Alexander had failed as an ally, for *French* it was in his power to keep Austria harmless if he really *alliance* willed it. These circumstances moved Napoleon to substitute Austria for Russia as the pivot of his European system. In 1810, after divorcing his first wife, Josephine, he married Marie Louise, daughter of the Hapsburg Emperor Francis I. Two years later, France and Austria contracted a defensive and offensive alliance, but this union of the youngest and the oldest dynasties in Europe had a touch of the fantastic about it. The Hapsburgs might overlook the humiliation of Campo Formio, of Lunéville, of Pressburg and Schönbrunn, but they could not forget the traditions of a thousand years wedding them to the old régime.

5. THE RUSSIAN DISASTER AND THE WAR OF LIBERATION

The Franco-Russian Alliance, born at Tilsit in 1807, dissolved rapidly after 1810. Dislike of the Continental System and of Napoleon's Austrian marriage; resentment at the French annexation of the North German coast which dispossessed the czar's relative, the Duke of Oldenburg; apprehension at the choice of a Napoleonic marshal, Bernadotte, as heir to the King of Sweden — all these factors poisoned Alexander's friendship. But the gravest injury was the secret hope Napoleon held out to the Poles that they might recover their independence, for Russia held the greater part of Poland and Alexander had no intention of yielding it.

Nor did Napoleon lack grievances on his side. He reproached Alexander for failing in his promise to exclude all English products from *Rupture of* his dominions, and he was alarmed when the czar stole *the Franco-* a march on him by offering the Poles independence under *Russian* Russian protection (1812). He had come to view his erst-*alliance* while friend as a "shifty Byzantine," and abandoning negotiations he concluded a military alliance with Austria and moved half a million men toward the Russian frontier. "What is the road to Moscow?" he demanded of the last of Alexander's envoys. "Sire," was the proud rejoinder, "one takes the road to Moscow at will. Charles XII chose the route by Pultava." [1] Napoleon knew the fate of the mad Swedish king who had marched on Moscow a century before, but he disregarded the lesson.

Through the heat and dust of summer the Grand Army pressed forward, defeated the Russians at Borodino (September 7, 1812), and found

[1] For the Russian campaign of Charles XII, see page 73.

NAPOLEONIC EMPIRE
AT ITS HEIGHT

SCALE OF MILES

0   100   200   300

Empire of Napoleon

Dependent States

SCOTLAND

Glasgow   Edinburgh

NORTH

Belfast

Castlebar

IRELAND

Newcastle

York

SEA

Dublin

HELIGOLAND

Cork

ENGLAND

WALES

Cambridge

DENMARK

Chris

Ham

Bre

DUCHY OF OLDENBG.

WES

London

G.D OF BERG

CONF

Osna

Cassel

Plymouth   Portsmouth

Dover

Flushing

Antwerp

Cologne

Brussels

Waterloo

Fra

ATLANTIC

Cherbourg

CHANNEL IS.

Bologne

Quatre Bras

Ligny

Jemappes

Namur

Kaiserslautern

KG

Reims

Verdun

Metz

Brest

Seine

Versailles

Paris

Valmy

Chalons

Nancy

BADEN

WURTE.

Fontainebleau

OCEAN

Nantes

Loire

Chaumont

Basle

FRENCH

Neuchatel

Zurich

SWITZERLAN

Rochefort

Lyons

Chambery

Bordeaux

Rhone

LOMB

Turin

Milan

C.Finisterre

Corunna

Ferro

Bayonne

San Sebastian

Orthez

Vitoria

Pamplona

Toulouse

Marseilles

Marengo

Spezi

Toulon

EMP

Oporto

Burgos

CORSICA

Ajaccio

Bussaco

Almeida

Douro

Salamanca

R.

Ciudad Rodrigo

Fuentes d'Onoro

Madrid

Saragossa

Gerona

Barcelona

PORTUGAL

Vimeiro

Torres

Vedras

Lisbon

Elvas

Talavera

Tarragona

SPAIN

MINORCA

KINGDOM OF

Albuera

Valencia

BALEARIC IS.

MAJORCA

SARDINIA

C.St.Vincent

Cordova

Baylen

IVIZA

Seville

Cartagena

C.Trafalgar

C.Spartel

Gibraltar

(Br.)

MEDITERRA

Algiers

Longitude West   Longitude East   5

Moscow a deserted city. For five weeks Napoleon camped in the Russian capital waiting for overtures of peace from Alexander which *The retreat* never came. Fires of mysterious origin leveled three quarters *from Mos-* of the city, provisions ran low, and disorder spread through *cow (1812)* the ranks, until on October 18, Napoleon reluctantly gave the order to withdraw. The slow retreat became a nightmare of horror as hunger and frost decimated the ragged troops while Cossacks rode out of the blizzard to cut down the stragglers. When Napoleon recrossed the river Niemen in December, less than one fifth of the Grand Army remained to him. Some of his men were captives, many had deserted, but a quarter of a million had paid for his mad gamble with their lives.

The Russian campaign destroyed the myth that Napoleon was invincible. In 1813, with a hastily conscripted army, he found himself defending his hegemony in the Germanies against Russia, *"War of* Prussia, and finally Austria. After their defeat at Jena in *Liberation"* 1806, the Prussians had set quietly to work under the *in the Ger-* *manies* patriotic Baron vom Stein and Chancellor Hardenberg to *(1813)* reform their army, abolish serfdom and other social abuses, and prepare themselves, despite Napoleon's watchful eye, for a "War of Liberation." At the "Battle of the Nations" (or battle of Leipzig), October 16–19, 1813, Napoleon was decisively defeated by the allies and compelled to retreat across the Rhine. His grand empire collapsed almost overnight, his confederates deserted him, and the opening months of 1814 found him on the defensive in France itself, attacked at five different points by armies which totaled over four hundred thousand men.

Before the battle of Leipzig, Napoleon might have had peace if he would have contented himself with retaining France and her natural frontiers; after that, with hope almost gone, he fought on in *Abdication* a defensive campaign as brilliant as it was desperate. His *of Napoleon* fortunes had changed, but not his character, and the *(April,* *1814)* egotism, the audacity, the gambler's faith in his luck which had extricated him from earlier dilemmas now became vices which betrayed him, lending a deeper truth to his boast that "Character is Destiny." On March 31, the allied forces entered Paris, and Napoleon, who was a few miles away at Fontainebleau, agreed to abdicate. He was granted a pension of two million francs a year and sovereignty over the little island of Elba, near his native Corsica in the Mediterranean Sea. The French Senate decreed the restoration of the Bourbon line, in the person of Louis XVIII, brother of the unfortunate Louis XVI who had been guillotined in 1793. The little dauphin, son of Louis XVI, who died in a Paris prison in 1795, had been styled Louis XVII by the royalists, although he had never reigned.

6. THE HUNDRED DAYS

This settlement satisfied the victorious powers, Britain, Russia, Prussia, and Austria. They allowed France to retain the boundaries of 1792, and imposed no indemnity, fearing to excite further resistance from that exhausted but still redoubtable nation. Moreover, since they had decided to restore the Bourbons, they could not very plausibly have offered them a dismembered state. Louis XVIII was urged to be moderate. He acknowledged the impossibility of undoing the work of the revolution and granted his new subjects a constitutional charter. There was to be a lower chamber elected by limited franchise and an upper chamber of hereditary peers after the fashion of the English Parliament. Louis retained the efficient bureaucracy established by Napoleon, and preserved almost unchanged the administrative centralization, the system of finance and taxation, and the legal codes which he found in force. He also did what he could to soften the hostility between the royalist followers who returned with him from exile and the imperial officials who had risen to power under Napoleon.

Many high dignitaries of the empire had foreseen Napoleon's fall in time to negotiate with his enemies. The urbane Talleyrand regained the portfolio of foreign affairs, although Louis XVIII could not forbear to remind him that he had dug the grave of three previous administrations. Talleyrand acknowledged the imputation. "There seems to be an inexplicable something in me, sire," he hinted, "that brings bad luck to governments that neglect me." But, however readily courtiers might turn their coats and serve a new master, the middle class and the peasants of France learned within a very few months to dislike and distrust the restoration government. They found Louis XVIII a colorless figure after Napoleon's fiery energy, and they feared to see the returning *émigrés* and priests regain the privileged position they had enjoyed before 1789. France had been thoroughly weary of Napoleon at the time of his abdication, but after nine months of Bourbon rule, people began to think more kindly of him, and to contrast his glorious achievements with the mediocre compromises of a king who had returned "in the baggage wagons of the allied armies."

This change in sentiment offered Napoleon the chance for a last fling at fortune. In February, 1815, he slipped away from Elba, and landing at Cannes, March 1, he started for Paris on what proved a veritable

[194]

tour of triumph. The troops dispatched to arrest him deserted to his standard, the Bourbons fled at his approach, and by *Last flight* March 20 he was back in his capital. His belief that the *of the eagle* French would support him had proved right; his hope that the allies would not oppose him proved wrong.

For at Vienna, where the diplomats were already quarreling over the spoils, the news of Napoleon's escape brought swift unanimity. Prussia and Russia had been on the verge of war with Austria and England, but the four powers hastily composed their differences and concentrated their forces. Realizing that he must fight to keep his throne, Napoleon set feverishly to work organizing an army. To rally France to his side he outdid himself with promises. The Bourbons "had learned nothing and had forgotten nothing," but for himself he swore he had profited by past errors and would initiate a liberal régime and abandon wars of conquest. But he knew that his fate must first be decided on the battlefield, and that his only chance was to repulse his foes separately.

On June 16 he hurled back a Prussian corps advancing through Belgium, then turned to face a second army gathered near Brussels under the command of the Duke of Wellington. "I tell you *Battle of* Wellington is a poor general, the English are poor soldiers, *Waterloo* we will settle the matter by lunch time," he insisted to his *(1815)* marshals. "I sincerely hope so," responded Soult, who had faced Wellington in Spain and knew better. Throughout the day Wellington held his position against the most desperate assaults, the Prussians under the redoubtable Blücher returned in time to aid him, and by nightfall Napoleon's army was completely routed. This was the battle of Waterloo, June 18, 1815.

Abdicating a second time, Napoleon chose to surrender to the English. "I come, like Themistocles," he wrote the prince regent, "to claim hospitality at the hearth of the British people." For the security of Europe, the British government decided to imprison him on the lonely island of Saint Helena in the South Atlantic. There he beguiled the oppressive days dictating memoirs to explain and justify his career, and there, on May 5, 1821, he died.

CHAPTER FOURTEEN

THE VIENNA CONGRESS

Universal expectation has perhaps never been raised to such a pitch. Men had promised themselves an all-embracing reform of the political system of Europe, guaranties for universal peace; in a word, the return of the Golden Age.
... The real purpose of the Congress was to divide amongst the conquerors the spoils taken from the vanquished.

FREDERICK VON GENTZ.

THE overthrow of Napoleon brought the revolutionary era to a close. For twenty-five years Europe had been convulsed by war and social ferment, many landmarks of the old régime had been swept away, thrones had toppled, church lands had been secularized, nobles had lost their estates, while hitherto unprivileged commoners climbed to power and office. The new aristocracy which Napoleon created, as already pointed out, was an aristocracy of talent. His ablest marshals rose from the ranks, his officials won their promotion by ability and not by birth. It was largely for this reason that the administration of the empire functioned with an energy and efficiency unknown in the older governments of Europe, and it was natural that Napoleon, with his love of order, should have endeavored to extend the revolutionary reforms throughout the Continent. To do for Europe what had been done for France, to link the disparate states by a uniform code of law, a universal system of weights and measures and coinage, to free trade from frontier tolls and promote it by transcontinental highways, to end national wars by establishing a Roman peace under the hegemony of France — such was the imperial dream at which the Corsican had clutched. But the hostile powers had no faith in his design and refused to submit to it. His titanic struggle with Great Britain corrupted the scheme and the national resentment which he stirred up in Spain and the Germanies ruined it. Europe, weary of this inveterate trouble-maker with his mania for rearranging things, banished him to the lonely island of Saint Helena for the last six years of his life.

1. THE CONGRESS ASSEMBLES

In combining against Napoleon, the associated governments had proclaimed him the enemy of peace and of humanity, and laid upon his head all responsibility for the suffering and bloodshed. In fighting him, the people were assured, they were fighting to end tyranny and social injustice. Many believed this, and made the sacrifices demanded

[196]

ARTHUR WELLESLEY, DUKE OF WELLINGTON
1769–1852

*The leading traits in Wellington's character
were his remarkable self-discipline and moderation, which inspired the British poet laureate,
Alfred Tennyson, to laud him as*

> *Rich in saving common-sense,
> And, as the greatest only are,
> In his simplicity sublime.*

of them in a high spirit of idealism. They looked to the Congress of
Hopes Vienna not only to re-establish peace, but to remake Euro-
vested in the pean society and lay the foundations of a fairer world. Such
peace con- idealistic hopes are needed to sustain men in the heat of a
ference great struggle. Frederick von Gentz, a Prussian statesman
who acted as secretary for the congress, noted these golden expectations
in a passage quoted at the head of this chapter, and being a shrewd man
he knew that they could never be fulfilled. Whatever settlement the
congress reached was certain to disappoint a great many people. The
evil that wars do lives after them, leaving a heritage of hatred and
jealousy to becloud the peace discussions and corrupt whatever generous
intentions the delegates may possess. The Vienna Congress was no
exception to this rule. It was, moreover, an assemblage of statesmen
and rulers; the common people had no voice in it, no legitimate
means to make their wishes known, or to show their approval or disapproval of the decisions taken. The princes and their ministers were
to make the peace and the people would have to put their trust in
princes.

For, with the tempest of war and revolution over, "kings crept out
again to feel the sun," and many nobles and churchmen, remembering
how pleasant life had been (for them) in the days before 1789, planned
a return to the old régime. They hoped to re-establish the obsolete
class distinctions of an older day, to rebuild the forts of privilege, restore
society to its ancient foundations, and make the world safe from democracy. Europe, wearied by too many and too rapid changes, was to
plunge from an era of revolution into an era of reaction.

In this temporary triumph of conservatism over liberalism, Austria
played a leading part. The empire of the Hapsburgs was still a land
Recovery of of the old régime. Stricken repeatedly by Napoleon's swift
Austria blows, Austria had emerged toughened and consolidated by
her reverses, and had been able to hurl her forces against the "Son of the
Revolution" with decisive energy in 1813 when he was already wavering
in the saddle. The choice of Vienna as the seat of the peace conference
was a tacit recognition of this revival in Austrian prestige, for it seemed
natural and fitting that a congress of reactionaries should choose for their
sessions the capital of the most reactionary state in Europe.

The leading Austrian statesman in 1814 was Klemens Wenzel
Rôle of Nepomuk Lothar, Prince von Metternich (1773–1859), the
Prince self-appointed spokesman of the reactionary forces of the
Metternich day. As host to his fellow delegates at the conference, Met-
ternich had an opportunity to display his unrivaled diplomatic gifts and

to labor for a settlement which would undo the work of the revolution while exalting the position of his imperial master, Francis I. Metternich was an egotist who believed that he had been selected by Providence to re-establish the fortunes and the security of the Hapsburg Empire on a firm foundation. But as Austria was a land of the old régime, it could be preserved in tranquillity only if Europe were rendered as static as possible, with the privileged classes once more in power. Metternich sided, therefore, both by policy and inclination, with those who regarded the French Revolution as an unparalleled disaster inspired by false and irresponsible reasoning. Liberty and equality, as preached by the Jacobins, he recognized as subversive and disintegrating ideals which might have destroyed the Austrian Empire if they had not been checked. In politics, therefore, he argued that the safest methods were those which had been tried and tested; innovations, even when they promised great benefits, were likely to prove dangerous because they outran control and often destroyed what they sought to improve. As the old proverb had it, "the best is often the enemy of the good." Beguiled by the siren voices of demagogues and dreamers, the French people had attempted to introduce radical reforms with the result that Europe was plunged into twenty-five years of confusion and bloodshed. To repair the damage and to guard against a recurrence of such disorders, Metternich regarded as a practical duty. "To the dreamers," he admitted frankly, "I have never belonged."

With one notable exception his princely colleagues at the conference shared the Austrian chancellor's views. The exception was Alexander I of Russia (1801–25). A grandson of that enlightened empress, Catherine the Great, Alexander had been tutored in *Czar Alexander I* his youth by liberal thinkers. The desire of the Poles for national unity and of the French for constitutional government struck a responsive chord in his heart which caused Metternich grave apprehension. It seemed incongruous that a prince born to rule despotically over a great empire like Russia should harbor genuine sympathy for popular causes. To his fellow monarchs Alexander's character appeared a curious blend of piety and hypocrisy, of mystical concern for the welfare of humanity and hard-headed political acumen. His importance compelled them to treat the whims of this "crowned Hamlet" with deference, but in private they distrusted and feared him.

The mediocre Prussian king, Frederick William III (1797–1840), was particularly subject to Alexander's influence. The czar had promised to help Prussia to obtain Saxony if Frederick William supported the Russian plans for Poland. The interests of Great Britain were ably defended at the congress by the astute foreign minister, Castlereagh, and by the Duke of Wellington, who had defeated Napoleon at Waterloo. To represent France the newly restored Bourbon king, Louis XVIII, dispatched to Vienna the subtle and audacious Talleyrand. A bishop of the church under Louis XVI, and foreign minister under Napoleon, Talleyrand had offered his services to secure for France the best terms that could be wrung from defeat. For although loyalty to princes might be with him, as he confessed blandly, "a matter of dates," his loyalty to France did not falter.

The delegates of the lesser states were doomed to play an insignificant rôle, for the representatives of the "Big Four," Austria, Russia, Prussia, and Great Britain, formed an inner circle and decided the most important questions with small regard for minority opinions. Into this charmed circle Talleyrand edged his way with the convenient principle of "legitimacy," a strange password in his mouth, but one which found favor with the victors. It should be the aim of the congress, Talleyrand suggested urbanely, to restore the states of Europe wherever possible to the control of their former rulers. This principle served France and the Bourbons well, for even after the "Hundred Days" the congress abstained from seizing territory "legitimately" French, and punished the nation instead by demanding an indemnity of seven hundred million francs on the payment of which all foreign troops were to be withdrawn. On the whole this was generous treatment to accord a defeated power, especially if it be compared with the terms meted out to Germany by the victorious allies a century later.

2. THE POLITICAL SETTLEMENTS

It was not France, therefore, but her allies that paid a territorial forfeit. The great powers, while professing at Vienna their earnest desire for a just settlement, were in reality guided (1) by their greed for compensation to defray the enormous costs of the war, and (2) by their anxiety to erect safeguards against a fresh wave of French expansion. The final act of the congress, embodying these aims, was signed June 9, 1815, and a brief survey of its provisions will reveal how the spoils taken from the vanquished were divided among the victors.

Austria acquired once again a deciding voice in the affairs of Italy and the Germanies as well as increased territory. The Austrian Nether-

Austria lands (Belgium) were not restored; but in compensation Austria gained Salzburg and the Tyrol, the Illyrian Provinces, and (in Italy) Venice and Milan and dynastic control over the

EUROPE
IN 1815

SCALE OF MILES

0   100   200   300   400   500

P = Parma   M = Modena

ICELAND
(Den.)

ATLANTIC   OCEAN

FÄROE IS.

SHETLAND IS.

ROCKALL

ORKNEY IS.

HEBRIDES

SCOTLAND

Belfast
Edinburgh

NORTH
SEA

BRITISH
ISLES

Dublin
IRELAND

Cork

Liverpool
Manchester
Birmingham
ENGLAND
London
Southampton
Dover

St. George Chan.

English Channel

CHANNEL IS.

Brest

BAY OF
BISCAY

C. Finisterre

Oporto

Burgos
Ebro R.
Saragossa

Salamanca

Madrid

Toledo
Valencia

SPAIN

PORTUGAL

Lisbon

C. St. Vincent

Seville

Granada

Str. of Gibraltar
Tangier
Gibraltar
(Br.)

Malaga

Oran

Metilla

Fez

MOROCCO

BARBARY

Bayonne
Toulouse
Marseilles

Bordeaux

FRANCE

Loire R.
Lyons
Geneva

Seine R.
Paris
Strassburg

Havre
Lille
Luxemburg

NETHERLANDS
Brussels
Antwerp
KINGDOM

Amsterdam
The Hague
Bremen
Hanover

Hamburg

OF
Berlin

PRU

Bergen

Trondhjem

Christiania

Gothenburg

Sto

SWEDEN

NORWAY

DENMARK
Copenhagen

HELGOLAND.

BALTIC

Danzig

Dresden
Leipzig
Prague
Brësl

GERMAN

Nuremberg
Munich

SWITZERLAND
Bern

Milan
LOMBARDY-VENETIA
Genoa

KINGDOM OF SARDINIA

CORSICA (Fr.)

SARDINIA

Brünn
Vienna

CONFEDERATION

Graz

EMPIRE

Trieste
Venice

BOSNIA

ADRIATIC SEA

TUSCANY

Rome
STATES OF THE CHURCH

Naples

KINGDOM OF THE TWO SICILIES

Palermo
Messina
C. Spartivento

C. Passaro

MALTA
(Br.)

IONIA
SE

Barcelona

BALEARIC IS.

MEDITERRANEAN

ALGERIA

Algiers
Tunis

Tripoli

TRIPOLI
STAT

Longitude   West   0°   10°   Longitude

THE POLITICAL SETTLEMENTS

duchies of Parma, Modena, and Tuscany.[1] No attempt was made to revive the defunct Holy Roman Empire. Instead, the thirty-eight German states were loosely organized into a Germanic Confederation at the Diet of which the Austrian delegate presided.

Many liberal and patriotic Germans had hoped to see their fatherland take its place among the powers as a strong and united empire. But the petty jealousies of the German princes and the ancient *The Ger-* rivalry of Austria and Prussia rendered the fulfillment of *manies* this dream impossible at the time, although the cause of German unity had received a powerful stimulus during the revolutionary era. Politically, the Germanies had been reduced from over three hundred states to thirty-eight, a long step toward ultimate unity. A spirit of national patriotism had developed rapidly during the War of Liberation against Napoleon, and had found expression in the teaching of philosophers like Johann Gottlieb Fichte, in the poems of Theodor Körner and Ernst Moritz Arndt, and the broad-visioned labors of statesmen like the Baron vom Stein. Napoleon, by his aggressive interference, had hastened the political consolidation and stimulated the national spirit of the Germans. Indirectly and unwittingly he had made himself the godfather of the later German Empire. But in 1815 the time was not yet ripe and the ideal of a united Germany remained a frustrated dream.

The peace conference was delayed for a time in its discussion of German affairs by the immoderate demands of Prussia. The Saxon king, Frederick Augustus, had been slow in deserting Napoleon, *Prussia* and to punish him the Prussian government proposed to annex the whole of Saxony. Austria, France, and Great Britain were prepared to oppose such a step by force of arms if necessary, and Prussia in the end received only two fifths of Saxony, but gained Swedish Pomerania on the Baltic and further possessions on the lower Rhine. It was hoped that these Rhineland annexations would make it possible for Prussia to maintain a "watch on the Rhine" and protect the German people from the danger of a new French invasion. The rulers of the house of Hohenzollern thus acquired a tutelary rôle in the affairs of the North German States which was equivalent to an international recognition of their leadership.

The handsome and enigmatic young Russian czar, Alexander I, helped himself to an immodest share of the spoils. Finland, seized from Sweden in 1809, and Bessarabia, conquered from Turkey in 1812, *Russia* he proposed to retain; while Poland was to be reconstructed as an independent kingdom under Russian protection, with himself as

[1] See map following page 200.

[201]

king.   Austria firmly declined to cede her Polish territory for such a purpose, but the czar gained a slice of Prussian Poland, added it to the lion's share which he already possessed, and announced himself king of a united Poland.   He even bid for the loyalty of his Polish subjects by granting them a constitution, to the disgust and apprehension of Metternich who distrusted such concessions to popular desires.

For Great Britain, as banker of the successive coalitions, the wars had proved enormously expensive.   The British national debt quadrupled *Great* in a quarter of a century, largely as a result of loans to other *Britain* countries which were never repaid.   The British rewarded themselves, however, by expanding their trade and adding to their colonies.   Malta and the Ionian Islands in the Mediterranean Sea, Tobago, Trinidad, Saint Lucia, Honduras, and part of Dutch Guiana in the New World, Capetown in South Africa, Mauritius and Ceylon in the Indian Ocean — all passed under the British flag.   The Congress of Vienna failed to regulate the abuse initiated by British men-of-war of searching neutral vessels on the high seas.   Nor, although this highhanded practice had precipitated a war between Great Britain and the United States in 1812, was the "right of search" defined when these two countries concluded the Treaty of Ghent in 1814.   The British had secured an unparalleled predominance upon the Seven Seas, and they were determined to brook no curb upon the exercise of their naval supremacy.

In readjusting the claims of the lesser states, the diplomats evinced a callous disregard for national aspirations and popular preferences, *The fate of* bartering and subdividing densely inhabited areas as if they *the lesser* had been so much vacant real estate.   To strengthen *states* Holland, for instance, and compensate the Dutch for the loss of Capetown and Ceylon (which the English declined to restore), Belgium was joined to Holland to form the Kingdom of the Netherlands under William I of the house of Orange (1813–40).   The Belgian provinces, which had been administered successively by Spain, Austria, and France, thus passed under Dutch control despite the opposition of their inhabitants.   In the same fashion, Sweden received Norway, having lost Swedish Pomerania to Prussia and Finland to Russia; but in compensating the Swedes the diplomats paid scant attention to the wishes of the Norwegians.   Norway had been administered by the Danish kings for over four centuries, but the Dano-Norwegian Kingdom was split as a punishment to the Danes for supporting Napoleon overlong.   Even worse treatment awaited the Italian people whose desire for self-government and national unity was completely overridden.   Only the Kingdom of Sardinia survived as an autonomous state under the house of Savoy, strengthened, indeed, by the addition of Genoa the better to serve as a check on French expansion in the south.   Of the remaining Italian provinces, Venetia and Lombardy were in Austrian hands; Parma, Lucca, Modena, and Tuscany were restored to princes who looked to Vienna for their instructions; the States of the Church passed again under the theocratic rule of Pius VII; while Naples and Sicily accepted the return of that despicable scion of the Spanish Bourbons, Ferdinand I, of the Kingdom of the Two Sicilies.   The principle of legitimacy was extended to Spain also, where the crafty and unscrupulous Ferdinand VII (1813–33) hastened to re-establish the Inquisition, welcome back the Jesuits, and surround himself with all the symbols of despotism which the French had suppressed.

3. THE CONCERT OF EUROPE

To maintain peace and safeguard the Vienna settlement, Austria, Russia, Prussia, and Great Britain extended their wartime coalition into the post-war era, and pledged themselves to preserve *The* a common agreement in international affairs by means of *Quadruple* frequent congresses.   After 1818, France was admitted *Alliance* to a sort of conditional membership and the Quadruple Alliance became in reality a Quintuple Alliance.   This putative attempt at a League of Nations is usually called the Concert of Europe and it functioned with comparative success for several years after 1815.   Congresses called under this plan assembled at Aix-la-Chapelle (1818), at Troppau (1820), at Laibach (1821), and at Verona (1822), but already by 1820 the divergent policies of the great powers had crippled the co-operative project, and it finally broke down for reasons to be explained in the following chapter.   Great Britain, never friendly to the idea of permanent alliances, was the first of the powers to resume a position of diplomatic isolation; further rifts developed among the remaining members of the concert, and by 1825 the British minister Canning was able to declare with satisfaction, "Europe is once more back to the situation in which every nation is for itself, and God for all."   His words might serve as an epitaph for the Concert of Europe, and marked the dissolution of one more attempt at international co-operation.

Because it appeared to stand for the preservation of legitimacy and the *status quo*, the Quadruple Alliance was bitterly hated by *The Holy* all apostles of liberty and progress.   In their denunciations *Alliance* they sometimes confused it with a second league formed at the same time and known as the Holy Alliance. The concept of the Holy Alliance, propounded by Alexander I in one of his more mystical and pious moods, was accepted by his deferential fellow monarchs with considerable skepticism. The czar proposed in all seriousness that the princes of Europe should pledge themselves "to take for their sole guide the precepts of the Holy Religion, namely the precepts of Justice, Christian Charity, and Peace ...''; and that they should base their reciprocal relations as well as their conduct toward their subjects "upon the sublime truths which the Holy Religion of our Saviour teaches. ...'' Unlike the Quadruple Alliance, which was a political compact between nations, the Holy Alliance was no more than a moral pledge subscribed to by the monarchs. Though Castlereagh expressed the general opinion when he called it "a sublime piece of mysticism and nonsense," all the princes of Europe signed the text except the Prince Regent of Great Britain, the pope (who declined to enter such an agreement with non-Catholics), and the Sultan of Turkey whom it was considered superfluous to approach. Despite its lofty phrases this "sonorous nothing" had no discernible effect upon the cynical diplomacy of the time, and liberals and republicans denounced it as a nauseating example of princely hypocrisy. Yet it would be unfair to Alexander and some of his colleagues to doubt that they were sincere in their wish to see a new era of human brotherhood succeed the slaughter and sacrifice of the war years. Great wars instill such a vivid impression of their horror and destructiveness that they are always followed by an earnest desire to avoid future conflicts. It is the tragedy of such good resolutions that they always come too late and are forgotten too early.

In 1815, the tragedy of war had burned itself so deeply into the hearts and minds of men that the generation which had witnessed the retreat from Moscow and the slaughter at Leipzig could never be tricked into thinking of war as a romantic and chivalrous game. The impression of its horrors, however, faded with the years; already by 1830 a new generation was growing up to which Napoleon was almost a myth and war an untried adventure; but it was not until 1854 that Europe beheld again the outbreak of a major conflict between the great powers. That forty years' interval of comparative peace is the longest in modern European history. Part of the credit for it must go to the statesmen who shaped the Vienna settlement, for if the primary purpose of a peace conference is to make a peace as permanent as possible they were unusually successful. The merit of their work, however, has been ignored because it was overshadowed by the defects; the problems they solved are obscured by the problems they failed to solve or for which they found the wrong solution.   This is natural, for it is the unsolved problems that focus attention on themselves and make subsequent history.

4. DEFECTS OF THE VIENNA SETTLEMENT

Most of the diplomats who assembled at Vienna were unaware that the eighteenth century was over.   They had been trained to serve the dynastic interests of princes, had inherited the aristocrat's disdain for the masses, and saw no reason to consult by a plebiscite or other democratic device the peoples whose fate they were deciding.   This disregard for democracy and contempt for national sentiment betrayed the congress into a succession of blunders the rankling injustice of which undermined the stability of the international settlement.

In five important cases where the congress sought to fix political frontiers in defiance of national sentiments, its work was later reversed. The enforced union of Belgium and Holland lasted only fifteen years, for *Somewhat* Belgium broke away in 1830.   Norway, unhappy in its union with *inaccurate* Sweden, finally secured its independence in 1905.   The Italians, resenting the rule of the restored Hapsburg and Bourbon princelings, drove them out and succeeded in realizing their dream of a free and united Italy by 1870.   In the same year the German people, doomed by the congress to disunion and impotence, saw the triumph of their deferred hopes in the proclamation of a German Empire.   Last of all, Poland, the iniquitous dismemberment of which the congress perpetuated, emerged again in 1919 as the independent Polish Republic.   The diplomats of 1815 lacked the foresight and the courage to provide for these developments because they underestimated the force of nationalism.

The attempt to defend legitimacy and to preserve what remained of the old régime against the rising tide of democracy proved equally futile in the end.   It was not difficult, in the wave of reaction, to place princes back on their thrones, but no settlement could have been devised in 1815 to make those thrones secure.   All that the Congress of Vienna and the governments of the restoration could do was to check the revolutionary movements for the moment, drive them underground, and usher in a decade or two of severe reaction.   The next chapter will trace the history of Europe during these years of reaction from 1815 to 1830, when the conservatives labored with maximum success to keep society "frozen" and to chain the forces of liberalism and nationalism.   The attempt was foredoomed to failure because liberalism and nationalism were the most vital and dynamic forces of the nineteenth century and they were working from the first to disturb the Vienna settlement.

Section D

THE GROWTH OF NATIONALISM
AND LIBERALISM IN THE
NINETEENTH CENTURY

(1815–71)

Inspired by the example of the French revolutionists, the unprivileged classes in other European countries agitated for similar reforms during the turbulent era, 1789–1815, and the victories of the French armies spread the influence of the revolution across Europe.   But in their struggle to preserve and to extend the new ideals, Frenchmen became extremely nationalistic. Napoleon's ruthless treatment of neighboring countries, even when it led to beneficial reforms, stimulated the patriotic resentment of Germans, Dutch, Spaniards, etc.   When the revolutionary era closed with Napoleon's overthrow, it left behind as a heritage to nineteenth-century Europe an intensified and mounting spirit of nationalism, and a conquering faith in liberalism, · which, though it was temporarily checked by the Restoration, was destined to revive and spread.   When the bourgeois class had rallied and consolidated their victory, they were to dominate nineteenth-century society.

It is important to note, however, that the typical bourgeois, although liberal in principle when fighting for power, was generally conservative in his attitude toward the lowest classes, especially the city proletariat, when these in turn demanded full political recognition.   This division of interests frequently paralyzed the liberal movement at critical moments.   Note also that the sentiment of nationalism, which tended to grow more intense among all the European peoples during the nineteenth century, sometimes worked in harmony with, sometimes in opposition to, the spirit of liberalism.

CHAPTER FIFTEEN

THE ERA OF RESTORATION AND REACTION

In striving to reweld the chain of time, broken by a fatal interlude [i.e., the French Revolution], we have expunged from our memory — as we would that they might be expunged from History — all the evils which have afflicted the country during our absence.

LOUIS XVIII, *Preamble to the Charter of 1814.*

Yet, Freedom! yet thy banner, torn but flying,
Streams like a thunder-storm against the wind;
Thy trumpet voice, though broken now and dying,
The loudest still the tempest leaves behind.

LORD BYRON (1818).

WHEN the news of the capture of the Bastille first spread through Europe in 1789, it excited many favorable comments. Few contemporaries foresaw, in that bright dawn of the revolution, the profounder implications of the movement, or guessed that the thunder of its repercussions would soon shake the entire continent. But the mob violence, the Reign of Terror, and the long ordeal of the revolutionary wars brought discredit upon the whole movement and taught people to undervalue its real achievements. This change of mood made the more stable society of the old régime appear almost attractive in contrast to the turbulence and slaughter the revolution had brought with it, so that many people, after Napoleon's fall, were ready to welcome a period of restoration and reaction.

1. THE REACTION FROM THE AGE OF RATIONALISM

One of the first statesmen to sound a note of warning on the developments in France was Edmund Burke (1729–97), whose *Reflections on the French Revolution* (1790) attacked the principles on which the revolutionary ideologists built their hopes. They erred, Burke submitted, in their conviction that society *The philosophy of conservatism* could be radically transformed in a brief period, that ancient institutions could be remodeled overnight as it were. In their impatience with the old and their zeal for the new they had allowed themselves to be carried away by the belief that it was possible to tear out the scribbled pages of the past and start humanity afresh with a clean sheet. To confront this revolutionary or cataclysmic theory of reform, Burke offered the sober principle of the continuity of history. Each generation, he reasoned, is but one link in a lengthening chain. It is not for us, the creatures of a day, to decide what part of the heritage of

[209]

the ages we will preserve, what part we will remodel or destroy. We are not the owners, but only the custodians, of humanity's baggage. It would be presumption on our part to discard old customs and institutions because their purpose is not clear to us; no one generation should set itself up as judge of society's future needs; the ties which knit together a state or a people have a mystical sanctity, and the rationalist who strikes right and left in a fanatical desire for progress may end by destroying the vital but intangible forces which preserve a civilization. To Burke, Reason did not seem an entirely safe guide. "We ought to venerate where we are unable presently to comprehend," he insisted. He distrusted the revolutionaries because they envisaged man, not as he was, but as he might be or ought to be; they were ideologists who expected human nature to perfect itself to fit their formulas. But "the lines of morality are not like the ideal lines of mathematics," Burke pointed out, and his challenge marked the waning of the Age of Reason.

As the revolution spread and its excesses mounted, the conservative classes of Europe found Burke's arguments more and more convincing, and his masterpiece became a bible for the reactionaries. The revolution, its enemies contended, might seem to promise advantages, but experience proved them illusory, for in the outcome the sacrifices outweighed the gains. Revolutionists made the old mistake of the dog in the fable, which, crossing a bridge with a piece of meat in its mouth, saw reflected in the brook below another dog with a morsel even more juicy and attractive. Dropping its own prize, the dog plunged into the water, sacrificed the substance for the shadow, and emerged with neither. In similar fashion the Jacobins had clutched at the vision of liberty, equality, and fraternity, and plunged Europe into chaos.

Between 1789 and 1815 this distrust of radical experiments filtered through all classes and the people of Europe underwent a change of *Distrust of* mood. The monarchs who returned to their thrones after *the intellec-* Napoleon's downfall were convinced that Louis XVI had *tuals* ended his life on the guillotine because he yielded to liberal advice. They blamed the enlightened despots of the eighteenth century also for preparing the way to revolution by experimenting with reforms and encouraging the radical doctrines of writers like Voltaire and Diderot. That day was now past. After 1815, liberal writers who dared to comment freely upon political abuses were viewed with hostility. Princes no longer honored them nor read their books; instead they suppressed such criticism and persecuted the authors of it. Painters, sculptors, and musicians were tolerated because their work did not lend itself readily to propaganda, but so long as the fear of the great revolution endured (and it lasted far into the nineteenth century), all liberal poets, philosophers, and pamphleteers were viewed with suspicion and treated with official disfavor.

The statesmen of the restoration believed likewise that the decay of organized religion in the eighteenth century, the prevalence of skepticism, deism, and atheism, had done much to weaken *Revival of* morals and promote revolution. In restoring Pius VII to *organized* his Italian domain, the Congress of Vienna sought to revive *religion* the former authority of the Roman Catholic Church. The Society of Jesus, suppressed in 1773, obtained permission to reorganize; ecclesiastical censorship grew more severe; and many secular governments renewed obsolete statutes against blasphemy and heresy. In Spain and Italy this revival of orthodoxy stifled audacious speculation, and the schools, restored to the supervision of the priesthood, remained inadequate and unprogressive. Even in France, home of revolutionary principles, Catholicism had a powerful revival, the writings of François-René de Chateaubriand (1768–1848) and the arguments of Joseph de Maistre (1754–1821) converting many to the defense of papal absolutism. But ultramontanism — that is, the practice of appealing "beyond the mountains" (the Alps) to the pope at Rome as the supreme authority of the Catholic world — did not find favor with secular rulers. Monarchs might be anxious to renew the historic alliance of "altar and throne" against the forces of revolution which threatened both, but in reviving the spiritual authority of the church, they had no intention of restoring the political authority also, as it had functioned in medieval times. They regarded religion as a convenient handmaid of absolutism, and they expected the clergy, for favors received, to teach the people submissiveness and gratitude toward their rulers.

In Protestant countries a new awakening of religious fervor had already stirred the common people in the eighteenth century. The German Pietists repudiated dogmatism and lifeless ritual *Protestant* in pursuit of a more intense and personal faith, and re- *sects* animated the Lutheran Church with their pure zeal for the Christian life. In England the passionate preaching of John and Charles Wesley spread the movement known as Methodism and induced many people to experience the sense of a "new birth." These religious revivals helped to elevate the morals of the poorer classes, to stir compassion for the sick and needy, and to direct attention to the wretched inmates of prisons and asylums. In their humanitarian zeal (though in little else) the revivalists were in harmony with the rationalists. "Humani-

[211]

tarianism" was the only tenet in the creed of the *philosophes* which survived the revolution unimpaired and won favor with the society of the restoration. The strength of the sentiment is manifested in the abolition of the slave trade by the Congress of Vienna, in the spirit animating the text of Alexander's Holy Alliance, and the abandonment of branding, flogging, and other "cruel and unusual punishments" in the prisons.

Cfr. Art. "Romanticism" in Encycl. of the Soc. Sci XIII, 426

2. THE ROMANTIC MOVEMENT

Another reaction to the Age of Rationalism took the form of a vital outburst of artistic and creative energy known as the "Romantic Movement" or the "Romantic Revival." No simple formula will describe this dynamic outburst, which included revolutionary and reactionary elements and drew its strength from many sources. In one sense it was a revolt against the formal classical style of the seventeenth and eighteenth centuries. Poets of the romantic school deliberately broke away from the discipline of classical forms, turned back to Shakespeare with his "monstrous irregularities" and to the makers of medieval ballads for inspiration, extolled the joys and sorrows of the common man and the beauty and majesty of Nature as the authentic subjects of great verse. Sincerity and passion meant more to them than a precious style, for they sought to appeal to the emotions rather than the intellect. "For all good poetry," declared William Wordsworth, one of the first of the English romantic poets, "is the spontaneous overflow of powerful feelings...." Wordsworth chose characters from "humble and rustic life" and wrote about them in a simple, unadorned style, because, as he explained, "My purpose was to imitate, and, as far as possible, to adopt the very language of men."

Forewarnings of the romantic revolt appeared in the eighteenth century when tales of mystery and imagination achieved enormous

Romanticism attracts the middle class

popularity, and the generation which had worshiped the cynicism of Voltaire turned with even greater enthusiasm to the sentimentalism of Rousseau. As the claims of the heart reasserted themselves against the dominant rationalism, the century abandoned the pompous odes and "rocking-horse meter" of the classicists in favor of the "unpremeditated art" of the newer bards. Middle-class readers of average education could appreciate the common touch and the direct appeal of romantic poetry even better than sophisticated courtiers, and its democratic flavor pleased them. The spread of the Romantic Movement coincided with the rise of the bourgeoisie to social and political dominance. For in its reassertion of personal values and its emphasis on the dignity of the common man, romanticism harmonized with the political tenets of the revolutionary age. In Germany much of the early work of Johann Friedrich Schiller (1759–1805) and Johann Wolfgang Goethe (1749– 1832) echoed revolutionary sentiments, and the English poets, George Gordon, Lord Byron (1788–1824), and Percy Bysshe Shelley (1792– 1822), were ardent champions of political liberty.

But the Romantic Movement also had its reactionary side. In the novels of Sir Walter Scott the old régime and the Middle Ages lived again under a veil of romantic glamor, for Scott had a *Romanti-* "feudal soul" and found much to admire in the so-called *cism and* "Dark Ages." This romantic interest in the past linked *Reaction* itself readily with the deepening national sentiment of the time. The decades after 1815 saw the foundation of new state historical societies and the publication of great collections of documents, as scholars labored to trace the slow and painful steps whereby the national institutions, laws, and languages of the various European peoples had evolved. Men who appreciate how deeply all contemporary culture is rooted in the past are inclined to distrust sudden and revolutionary changes, and in this respect the study of historical continuity exerted a conservative influence upon political thought.

It will not be possible to trace here the effect of the Romantic Revival upon music and painting, although the wide range of the movement, its search for new themes and new forms, its tempestuous vigor and emotionalism, invaded and enriched these and other departments of art equally with literature. Not until the second quarter of the nineteenth century did its impetus abate, and it left a vital heritage. From Russia to Spain artists had responded to the new intellectual quickening so that the Romantic Revival may almost be ranked with the Renaissance and the Intellectual Revolution in the richness and variety of its contributions to modern culture.

3. THE TRIUMPH OF CONSERVATISM: AUSTRIA AND RUSSIA

The distrust of "French ideas" after 1815, the revival of organized religion, and the shift toward more conservative lines of thought were related phases of the general reaction which found its most vigorous expression in the policies of the restoration governments. In this swing toward the right, Austria and Russia became the chief protagonists of conservatism for reasons which must now be more fully explained.

In the ill-assorted empire of the Hapsburgs, which lacked racial, geographical, and even linguistic unity, the principal bond holding the diverse provinces together was their common allegiance to the imperial crown. Hapsburg rulers possessed "an almost inexhaustible influence and invulnerable prestige"; they treated their subjects with paternal benevolence, but they guarded the privileges of their dynasty with jealous hands. Austria remained, even in the nineteenth century, a feudal rather than a national state, with a nobility powerful and privileged, a middle class slight in number and influence, and a passive peasantry living chiefly as tenants on entailed estates. To foreigners the empire on the Danube appeared artificial, an anachronism with the dusty flavor of medievalism about it, a "mummy" preserved in a lifelike semblance by the strong tincture of tradition. The great personal authority of the ruler, the haughty and languid spirit of the officials, the disjointed and ponderous machinery of administration suggested an oriental satrapy rather than a European state. Even Metternich had been known to complain that "Asia begins on the *Landstrasse*," the eastern suburb of Vienna. Yet, despite handicaps, Austria possessed greater vitality than its enemies appreciated, and so long as the dissolving forces of nationalism and liberalism could be shut out it was capable of sustaining the rôle of a great power.

Character of the Austrian Empire

But Austria could not remain immune to revolutionary experiments if liberal agitation stirred again in neighboring states. The most rigid censorship of books and journals, the most careful scrutiny of travelers' baggage and papers, could not prevent ideas from filtering across a border. Self-preservation drove the Austrian government to urge the repression of radical movements everywhere, and Metternich, as the high priest of conservatism, labored to unite all the monarchs of Europe in a common resistance to revolutionary changes. He helped to dissuade Frederick William III from granting the Prussian people the constitution which they had been led to expect, and he constantly warned the other German princes, through their representatives in the Diet of the Germanic Confederation, to be perpetually on guard against secret revolutionary activities.

Unfortunately, minor disturbances in the Germanies soon provided Metternich with an excuse for further repression. In several universities the students had organized societies pledged to advance German liberty and unity. These fraternities, or *Burschenschaften*, held a congress at the Wartburg in 1817. The date was the fourth anniversary of the battle of Leipzig and the castle had been made famous by Martin Luther at the commencement of the Protestant Revolt three centuries earlier. After patriotic demonstrations, the students imitated Luther's burning of the papal bull, and flung into a bonfire the copies of several reactionary books, the *Code Napoléon*, and a corporal's staff, to indicate their contempt for political and military tyranny. Two years later an unbalanced student named Karl Sand assassinated the dramatist Kotzebue, believing him to be a Russian agent whose death would help to liberate Germany from the influence of the Czar.

Nothing more was needed to convince the German rulers that revolution threatened. They dissolved the *Burschenschaften* and ejected liberal-minded professors from the universities, while a council of ministers meeting at Carlsbad (1819) narrowed the laws of censorship and spurred the police on their hunt for radicals. These Carlsbad Decrees mark the high tide of repression in the Germanies and their stupid and unnecessary harshness added to the grievances of the discontented masses. *Carlsbad Decrees (1819)*

In Russia, likewise, the pendulum swung toward reaction after 1815. Alexander I (1801–25) was a handsome and gracious prince, but he lacked the patient and inflexible character needed in executing the reforms of which he dreamed. With the aid of a practical minister, Michael Speranski, he opened his reign by consolidating the departments of government and even drafted a constitution for Russia. Face to face with fundamental issues of reform, however, his decision failed him. The intricacy of Russian affairs, and the dishonesty of the officials for which he could find no cure, drained away his enthusiasm. Not unwillingly he turned his attention from domestic difficulties to the long and absorbing duel with Napoleon. The annexation of Finland (1809), Bessarabia (1812), and further portions of Poland (1815) gratified the practical side of his nature, and it flattered his mystical temperament to picture himself as an instrument of the Divine Will in the stirring drama of Napoleon's downfall. *Reaction in Russia*

Yet a tincture of liberalism remained sufficiently strong in Alexander's complex nature to cause Metternich moments of uneasiness at the Congress of Vienna. The Holy Alliance, although it came to be viewed as a conspiracy of tyrants, originally reflected a sincere effort of the czar, under the influence of the religious mystic, Baroness von Krudener, to infuse a more humane and Christian spirit into political affairs. But once again the pressure of events proved too strong for Alexander's unstable enthusiasms. The ingratitude expressed by the Poles at the constitution which he granted them, a mutiny in the imperial regiments, and the murder of his agent Kotzebue, cured him of his liberal fancies. At the Congress of Troppau (1820) he confessed his conversion to Metternich. "You are not altered. I am. You have nothing to regret. I have." Thenceforward, Alexander aligned himself with the protagonists of reaction until his death in 1825.

The Grand Duke Constantine, legitimate successor to Alexander I, preferred to resign his throne to the youngest of the three brothers,

Nicholas I Nicholas. In the temporary confusion of the interregnum
(1825–55) a group of Russian army officers organized a revolt at Saint Petersburg in favor of "Constantine and the Constitution" (December 26, 1825). Nicholas easily crushed this uprising of the "Decembrists" and punished the leaders with death or imprisonment. He had none of Alexander's sympathy for liberalism; trained as a soldier he based his faith upon discipline and autocracy; and he succeeded throughout a thirty-year reign in keeping political movements in Russia stagnant. To ensure this end he created the famous "Third Section," a special division of the imperial government organized to combat agitation and discontent. Nicholas could favor improvements in administration, as his codification of the Russian law (1832) and reform of the finances attest, but only if they left intact his autocratic powers. So successfully did he preserve his "system," even when his brother monarchs were driven to compromise, that he enjoyed the admiration of conservatives and the detestation of liberals throughout Europe.

Political stagnation, however, could not altogether dam the intellectual currents of the age. Russian writers escaped from their earlier

The Russian dependence upon French and German models and de-
novel veloped in the nineteenth century a literature distinctively national. Wherever cultured people foregathered, at city salons or rural villas, new developments in music, painting, or architecture evoked animated discussion. New novels above all were read with emotion and criticized with tireless enthusiasm. For in the hands of such masters as Gogol (1809–52), Turgenev (1818–83), Tolstoi (1828–1910) and Dostoievski (1821–81) the Russian novel gave expression to the fervent political and social speculation of the day. Questions which could not be debated in parliament, because none existed, nor aired in the daily press, because of the censorship, found voice in works of fiction which were often political pamphlets thinly disguised. Permitted to indulge their mania for discussion, many Russian intellectuals developed radical and revolutionary theories, the more so because they were denied the opportunity to influence the government of the empire

[216]

or to learn the sobering lessons of practical politics. It is an ominous portent for any régime when the intellectual classes become persistently hostile. In Russia, as in eighteenth-century France, the interminable discussions and philosophical ferment were to be the prelude to a revolution.

4. THE BOURBON RESTORATION IN FRANCE

However greatly the statesmen of the restoration might desire to turn back the clock, the achievements of the French Revolution could never be wholly undone. Particularly in France too many momentous changes had intervened for Louis XVIII to see his wish realized that all the evils of the previous twenty years might be "expunged from history." Being an intelligent man, Louis recognized the facts and prepared to compromise. Napoleon's gibe that the Bourbons "had learned nothing and had forgotten nothing" was only partly true. The charter Louis granted his subjects in 1814 embodied the best of the revolutionary gains and made France the most liberal monarchy in Europe, for it promised a bicameral legislature consisting of a Chamber of Peers and a Chamber of Deputies, the latter to be chosen by about one hundred thousand voters. The best of Napoleon's achievements were likewise preserved; his centralized bureaucracy still functioned smoothly, the Bank of France continued to stabilize the admirable fiscal system, the schools were much as he left them, the *concordat* remained in force. Most important of all, the *Code Napoléon* assured all citizens equality before the law and all the children in a family a share in their father's possessions.

Nor could the church lands which had been confiscated and sold, and the estates of the nobles which had passed into other hands, be returned to their former owners. The revolution had *Social and* created a solid class of peasant proprietors, men who held *economic results of* their farms free of feudal dues, conservative citizens desir- *the revolu-* ing peace and order. The law of primogeniture had *tion* previously conserved entailed estates by transferring them intact to the eldest son or next male heir, but the revolutionary legislation provided that all the children must receive a share. By subdividing the land into smaller and smaller holdings, the new laws of inheritance induced an unexpected decline in the French birth rate. For a tradesman or peasant whose patrimony would barely provide for one family could not split it among several children and leave each an adequate means of livelihood. The most simple solution was to have only one or two children, and for this and other reasons large families became less common in France. During the last hundred years the birth rate has steadily declined until the population has become almost stationary. In this way the French have achieved a social solidarity and compactness unrivaled by any other nation. Freed from the problems of an expanding population, France does not need to ship her surplus sons to the colonies, nor do many Frenchmen emigrate to other lands.

Thus the major social and economic results of the revolution proved remarkably effective and stable, but political stability was a goal *The ultra-* more difficult to attain. Throughout the nineteenth cen-*royalists* tury the French people oscillated between the opposing ideals of an autocratic monarchy and a democratic republic. Though Louis XVIII sought to steer a middle course as a constitutional monarch, the ultra-royalists (followers more royalist than the king) drove him toward a policy of reaction. In 1820, the Duke of Berry, the king's nephew, who stood in the line of succession to the throne, fell before the dagger of a fanatic, and the resulting wave of popular indignation brought the ultras into power. They proceeded to shackle the press and revise the electoral laws so as to strengthen the party of the Right, and having secured an overwhelming majority in the Chamber of Deputies, they decreed that the Chamber should remain in office for seven years.

With the accession of the Count of Artois as Charles X (1824), the ultras found a king after their own hearts. More honest and more *Charles X* scrupulous than Louis XVIII, Charles was also more stiff-*(1824-30)* necked and despotic. The aristocrats, never reconciled to the loss of their confiscated estates, now pressed for reimbursement to the extent of a billion francs (1826). By converting the rate of interest on the national debt from five to three per cent, the government proposed to save twenty-eight million francs a year and apply it toward this indemnification. Capitalists and middle-class holders of national bonds would forfeit two fifths of their income from this source to benefit an undeserving nobility. A proposal to re-establish primogeniture in defiance of the Charter of 1814 increased the resentment of the bourgeoisie to the danger point, but Charles X persisted in his course, blind to the signs of popular discontent. In 1829, he attempted to override the parliamentary opposition by appointing as premier the stiff-necked and unpopular Prince de Polignac, thus violating the principle of responsible government. The consequences of his folly — the French Revolution of 1830 — will be described in the succeeding chapter.

5. TEMPORARY REACTION IN GREAT BRITAIN

Even in England, which Britons considered the historic home of political liberty, the period after 1815 proved an era of reaction. With the return of peace came economic depression and the *Reaction* evils of unemployment. The parliamentary system had *(1815–22)* ceased to be representative, owing to the shifts in population, and it had never been democratic, but distrust of the masses and of "French ideas" made the governing classes hostile to reform. When riots broke out in 1816, the government suspended the Habeas Corpus Act, the Englishman's guaranty of fair and speedy justice. When police and soldiers found it necessary to break up a mass meeting in Manchester with the loss of several lives (the so-called "Massacre of Peterloo"), the ministry succumbed to panic. They hastened to draft the Six Acts (1819), repressive enough to have pleased even Metternich, which curbed the long-established right of freedom of speech, muzzled the press, and limited the extent and purpose of public meetings.

Not until 1822 did the panic wane and more liberal policies prevail. It was a sign of better times when the draconic penal code, which prescribed the death penalty for such offenses as stealing a *Beginning* sheep or picking five shillings from a pocket, was amelio- *of liberal* rated in accordance with the more humane spirit of the *reforms* age. Another concession long overdue was the removal of religious disabilities. Formerly candidates for almost all important offices in the state had to be members of the Church of England, a rule which excluded Roman Catholics and dissenters (members of Protestant sects other than the Anglican) from a share in the government. The abolition of these restrictions in 1828 and 1829 gave the English people, who had boasted religious freedom since 1689, the wider tolerance of religious equality. The Catholic Emancipation Bill (1829), passed reluctantly by the bigoted English Tories, was a particular boon to the Irish, for it enabled this predominantly Catholic people for the first time to elect representatives of that faith to the English Parliament.

Though conservative at home during the years that followed Waterloo, Britain was often the champion of liberalism abroad. Such discrepancy between the domestic and foreign policies of a great power is not uncommon, and statesmen who sought to curb the popular demands in England actually aided the people of Greece and Belgium and South America to rebel against the governments that ruled them. In return Britain gained the gratitude — and the trade — of the

[219]

liberated states, but displeased conservative powers like Prussia and Austria. It was, in fact, Britain's refusal to co-operate with her late allies in suppressing revolutionary outbreaks that introduced the first serious schism in the councils of the Quadruple Alliance and prepared the way for the disruption of Metternich's system.

6. THE FIRST RIFTS IN THE CONSERVATIVE SYSTEM

Driven underground by the official repression, European liberals after 1815 planned new revolts in the name of liberty and democracy. *Liberal agitation* Kings sat uneasily upon their thrones, remembering the fate which had overtaken Louis XVI, and spurred their police to burn revolutionary pamphlets and hunt down conspirators. Nor was this dread of secret societies without foundation. In Italy, the famous *Carbonari* (or "Charcoal Burners") numbered thousands of members pledged to abolish tyrants and establish a free and united Italy. In Spain, the attempt of the restored Bourbon monarch, Ferdinand VII, to reconquer his rebellious American colonies, led to a revolt among the troops embarking for that purpose. Thoroughly alarmed, Ferdinand hastened to grant his subjects a constitution and made lavish promises of a liberal régime. Taking heart from this example, revolutionists in Naples compelled Ferdinand I of the Kingdom of the Two Sicilies to accept a constitution likewise. The following year the liberals of Piedmont won a smaller concession, forcing King Victor Emmanuel I of Sardinia to resign the throne to his brother Charles Felix.

Without loss of time the apprehensive monarchs united for a counter-offensive. At the Congress of Troppau (1820), to which all the great *The Troppau Protocol (1820)* powers sent delegates, the governments of Russia, Prussia, and Austria pledged themselves to intervene, by armed force if necessary, in any state rent by a menacing revolt, and to restore the legitimate government to power if it had been overthrown by a revolution. The following year at the Congress of Laibach the Austrian government was commissioned to suppress the Neapolitan liberals, and Ferdinand I, restored to absolute power, took a barbarous revenge upon his late advisers, who paid with their lives for the folly of trusting their prince's oath. As the Sardinian government had failed to suppress the revolt in Piedmont, an Austrian army invaded that state also and extinguished the embers of rebellion. As a means of combating liberalism and maintaining the *status quo*, the principle of armed intervention had scored a brilliant success, and Metternich could congratulate himself that his system had shown itself "trium-phantly fireproof." Because of its zeal in hastening to extinguish revolts, the Austrian army was derisively dubbed "the fire brigade of Europe."

Although Great Britain declined to endorse this international prac-tice of armed intervention, the Congress of Verona (1822) decided to extend the principle to Spain. This time France received the man-date of the powers to intervene, for France had been admitted to the councils of the Quadruple Alliance in 1818 at the Congress of Aix-la-Chapelle. To prove that the French people had repented of their revolutionary debauch and had been converted to conservative ideals, Louis XVIII dispatched an army across the Pyrenees to subdue the Spanish liberals. In 1823, the French captured Cadiz, and Ferdinand VII, shamelessly revoking his promises, condemned hundreds of his subjects, who had been implicated in the revolt, to exile or execution. Master once more in his own house, he begged the powers to assist him further to bring his Central and South American colonies, which had broken away from Spain during the Napoleonic Wars, back under his control.

The prospect of extending their war on rebels and republicans to the New World was not unpleasing to the allied monarchs, but here for the first time their reactionary zeal encountered a *British attitude on armed intervention* definite check. The British government had protested with increasing force at the alacrity with which the allies rushed troops across Europe and disregarded national frontiers. Ignoring the British attitude, the autocrats had had their will upon the Continent, but to transport an army to South America might prove a hazardous undertaking if the Mistress of the Seas seri-ously opposed it. As the British had established a profitable trade with the independent Spanish-American republics, they had no in-clination to permit a restoration of the Spanish monopoly.

Furthermore, the foremost power of the New World, the young United States of America, regarded an attempt of the allied monarchs to extend their repressive measures to this continent as a *The Monroe Doctrine* threat to all republics. In 1823, President James Monroe made it clear in a message to Congress that interference with the liber-ties of any independent American republic by a European power would be construed "as the manifestation of an unfriendly disposition toward the United States." In the face of British and American opposition, the absolutist powers did not venture to proceed.

The rift thus opened in the Concert of Europe steadily widened.

The spirit of revolt could not be exorcised, and the fitful outbreaks
Greek War of Independ- ence (1821-29)
of 1820 and 1821 had scarcely been suppressed when a new insurrection threatened. Embittered by centuries of oppression, the Greeks opened a sanguinary war against their Turkish masters. Cultured Europeans everywhere, who had received a classical education, felt a lively sympathy for these modern Hellenes, regarding them as the heroic descendants of the ancient Athenians and Spartans. Metternich insisted, however, that they were none the less rebels against their "legitimate" ruler, the Sultan of Turkey, and he urged that the revolt be allowed to "burn itself out beyond the pale of civilization." By 1826, the Greek resistance seemed broken, the murderous and energetic Ibrahim Pasha having depopulated the Morea in an apparent determination to make a solitude and call it peace. But the powers had finally decided to bestir themselves, Russia because of her traditional hostility toward the Turks, Britain from sympathy, and also because her bankers, having backed the Greeks, were anxious to collect, France because it had long been her policy to play a rôle in Mediterranean affairs, and all of them because none would trust another to intervene unsupervised. Having attempted in vain to resist the will of these powers, the sultan was forced to grant complete independence to the Greeks (Treaty of Adrianople, 1829).

The Greek Revolution illustrates better perhaps than any other event of the time the essential weakness of the Concert of Europe. Russia, as a signatory to the Protocol of Troppau, should have been willing to suppress the Greek revolt, but Russia was traditionally committed to the policy of hastening the dismemberment of the Turkish Empire. Austria, though opposed to revolution, was equally hostile to Turkey. Great Britain, on the other hand, favored in a general manner the preservation of Turkish integrity, but the English statesmen, with their classical education, sympathized with the Greek insurgents, and English banking and shipping interests stood to profit if Greece became independent. The consequence of this division of motives and clash of national policies was a series of blunders and half-measures at the end of which Greece emerged as an independent state.

The guiding principle of the conservative system, the joint action of all the powers against any people which sought to change its government by revolutionary means, had broken down. The outcome of the Greek War of Independence displeased strict legitimists, but they found some consolation in the fact that the Greeks were not permitted to set up a republic, but accepted a monarchy instead, with a Bavarian prince mounting the new throne as Otto I of Greece. Nevertheless, it was an ominous portent for the defenders of the established order that the ideal of political immobility had been openly violated by governments pledged to maintain it. The system had suffered a serious blow, and the events of the year 1830 were to strain it still more severely.

CHAPTER SIXTEEN

THE BOURGEOISIE SECURE CONTROL IN GREAT BRITAIN AND FRANCE

In the silence one can hear a soft monotonous dripping. It is the dividends of the capitalist continuously trickling in, continuously mounting up. One can literally hear them multiply, the profits of the rich. And one can hear too, in between, the low sobs of the destitute, and now and then a harsher sound, like a knife being sharpened.

HEINRICH HEINE (1842)

ANY fundamental change which affects a large number of people, altering their mode of living, their habits of thought, or their form of government, may be styled a revolution. The progress of natural philosophy in the seventeenth century was described in an earlier chapter as the "Intellectual Revolution" because it induced thoughtful people to revise their ideas about God and Nature. The action of the French nation after 1789 in destroying the monarchy and substituting a republic is an outstanding example of a political revolution. In this present section a third type of revolution is to be discussed, a revolution caused by the substitution of machinery for hand labor in many manufacturing [1] processes. The new machines changed conditions in the handicraft trades so radically and multiplied the output so enormously that they produced an Industrial Revolution the accelerating consequences of which still dominate our modern civilization.

1. THE INDUSTRIAL REVOLUTION

For reasons not yet fully understood, the eighteenth century brought an unusual increase of population to the European countries. This

The quickening of trade after 1750

can be explained in part by the improvement in living conditions, the stricter sanitation and cheaper food. Between 1750 and 1800, the English population rose from six to nine million and the French from nineteen million to twenty-six. The same years saw a rise in the general standard of comfort, so that sugar, chocolate, coffee, tea, furs, and silks came to be looked upon as necessities rather than luxuries in the homes of the well-to-do, while even the poor were enabled to vary their diet with new vegetables like cabbages and carrots, and to afford cotton and

---

[1] It is interesting to note that "to manufacture" meant originally, not to produce by machinery, but to make by hand. The word derives from the Latin *manus*, a hand, and *factura*, a making, from the verb *facere*, to make.

linen clothing. The normal consequence of this increased demand was a marked quickening in trade, especially colonial trade, and a speeding-up of all business life. Anvils rang and spinning wheels hummed to a swifter tune, roads and canals were bettered that goods might travel with greater dispatch, and sailing ships bound for distant markets crowded on more sail in the hope of a fleeter passage.

Rising demands meant greater profits, and the urge to speed production led manufacturers to experiment with new methods. When English foundry-owners discovered that they could not satisfy the orders for iron because sufficient wood was lacking to smelt the ore, they found a way to use coke instead. This meant more business for the mine-owners, but they were handicapped by the water in the mines, until they solved the problem with a steam-driven pump invented by Thomas Newcomen and improved by James Watt.

In like fashion, when spinning and weaving by hand proved too slow and costly a method of producing cotton fabrics for an expanding market, an improved loom was constructed by John Kay *Effect of* (1733) and a swifter method of spinning devised by James *machinery* Hargreaves (1764). Five years later, Richard Arkwright *on the cotton trade* invented a still better spinning frame, only to see it superseded within ten years by Samuel Crompton's mule, a machine which, under one worker, could equal the output of two hundred hand spinners. To eliminate the tiresome task of picking all the seeds from the raw cotton by hand, an American, Eli Whitney, invented the cotton gin (1793). For motive power to turn the spinning and weaving machines the owners first tried dogs and horses, then water power, and finally, where streams were lacking, Watt's steam engine was found to provide the needed energy. A fabulous increase in the production of cotton goods was the result. By 1790, Great Britain imported thirty million pounds of raw cotton a year, and the acceleration of the new processes was such that by 1810 this sum had quadrupled.

Similar mechanical improvements in the weaving of silk and woolen goods, and the knitting of hosiery and lace, came more slowly, but in these industries also Great Britain attained an unques- *Why England led in* tioned supremacy, possessing by 1812 more than twice as *the Industrial Revolution* many knitting frames as could be found in the remainder of *trial Revolu-* Europe. A unique combination of favoring circumstances *tion* explain this British leadership. (1) Nature had endowed the British Isles with the rich coal and iron deposits indispensable in the production of industrial machinery, and had provided in addition the damp climate most suitable for cotton spinning. (2) The wars of the eighteenth century left England with a colonial empire from which to draw raw materials and a maritime supremacy which enabled her ships to carry the manufactured product to every market. (3) Even before 1750, England led in the textile industry; her business men possessed surplus capital to purchase the new and costly machinery; and the extension of new farming methods, which drove many workers from the land, provided in this way a supply of cheap labor for the new factories. (4) Lastly, the disruption of economic life on the Continent resulting from the wars of the revolutionary era (1792–1815) favored British trade, spurring it to feverish activity and unparalleled expansion. Helped by these circumstances, Britain not only survived the financial burden of the struggle with Napoleon, but emerged in 1815 as "the workshop of the world."

2. THE FACTORY SYSTEM

Unfortunately, the Industrial Revolution possessed a dark as well as a bright side. In many trades, which had formerly demanded skill *Evils of* and craftsmanship, the introduction of machinery reduced *the system* the worker to an automaton, whose duties consisted of twisting together an occasional broken thread or periodically throwing a lever. The pride which an artisan had once felt in his handicraft vanished when he saw a machine supersede him and he became that machine's attendant, condemned to repeat motions of stultifying monotony all day long. Previously, under the so-called "domestic system," spinners and weavers had worked by their own firesides, receiving the raw material from merchants or middlemen who later called and paid for the finished product. But the factory system ended this casual part-time labor and herded the workers together for long hours in ugly and humid workshops. No longer their own masters, the spinners and weavers learned to hate the pitiless machines and their equally pitiless masters. Forced by the changing conditions to abandon the farming and other domestic activities which had brought them a living, and to toil for starvation wages in wretched factories, many workers held the machinery to blame for their plight and for the mounting unemployment after 1815. In a burst of vengeance as pitiful as it was futile, they fell to wrecking frames and power looms, and were speedily hanged or transported for their folly. They might as well have sought to sweep back the tide with a broom.

If men found the factory conditions cruel, for women and children they were all but insupportable. Yet women and children, it appeared, could tend machines as capably as men and would work for lower wages. Parsimonious employers hired wards from orphan asylums for their keep, and forced them to labor ten, fifteen, and even eighteen hours a day. It was not unknown *Employment of women and children* for such children to be chained to their machines and locked up at night to prevent their running away. Overworked and usually underfed, without schooling, exposed to the brutal and promiscuous habits of the older hands, such children could hardly fail to grow up anemic and vicious. A few philanthropic employers attempted to better conditions, notably Robert Owen, who established a model industrial community at New Lanark in which the employees had a share in the ownership and profits of the factories. But the majority of owners were heartless or indifferent and the conscience of the nation remained numb.

Men who are growing rich, and who see their country growing rich, through their efforts, seldom fail to find good arguments to justify the existing conditions. Employers not only defended the factory system as wholesome and profitable; they fought all *Laissez-faire ideals* efforts of the government to investigate or improve the lot of the workers. Business prospered best when let alone, the economist Adam Smith had argued in his *Inquiry into the Nature and Causes of the Wealth of Nations* (1776). Business men pointed to the expansion of British industry as proof that a *laissez-faire* (i.e., non-interference) policy, without tariffs, regulations, or other trade restrictions, was the soundest course for a government to pursue. It was, they agreed, most regrettable that so many people lived on the margin of starvation, but inexorable economic laws ordained that it must be so. "Population," Thomas Malthus proclaimed in 1798, "has a constant tendency to increase beyond the means of subsistence." If war and disease failed to curtail a nation's growth, he went on to explain in his *Essay upon the Principles of Population*, actual starvation would keep it within the limits determined by the food supply. Another political economist, David Ricardo, applied similar reasoning to the problem of the laboring classes. If wages rose above the margin of subsistence, he argued, the workers took advantage of their increased income to raise larger families. This soon produced a surplus of unemployed laborers who, underbidding those with jobs, brought wages back to the subsistence level. It was not the greed of employers but the inexorable weight of economic laws which decreed that the poor must be damned for the greater glory of Mammon, a doctrine which naturally found favor with the governing classes.

Commencing as an economic phenomenon, the Industrial Revolution precipitated social and political changes of the highest importance. *Capital and* It raised two classes to new prominence and widened the *labor* gulf between them. On the one hand stood the men of wealth, men with the capital and the initiative to build factories, play for the high stakes offered by the rapidly expanding industries, and win for themselves the rank of an industrial aristocracy. On the other hand stood the workers, or proletariat, a class waxing in number, but without property, without any share or direction in the industry that employed them, and without the means to better their condition. In the years after 1815, years of economic adjustment and social strain, both these classes grew conscious of their importance and both began to seek political power.

3. THE ENGLISH REFORM BILL OF 1832

Though admired by Europeans as the home of representative government and political liberty, Great Britain in 1815 possessed institutions far from liberal. The government may best be *Abuses in* described as a "plutocracy," for the wealthy classes ruled *the English* the Parliament, particularly the city merchants, ship-*system* owners, landlords, and country nobility. As only one person in thirty-two had the right to vote, it was possible in many "rotten" boroughs to buy a seat in Parliament by bribing a majority of the local electors. In others, termed "pocket" boroughs, the most powerful local landowner controlled the election, nominating a candidate and persuading or intimidating the voters to support his choice. As the ballots were recorded publicly, a tenant openly invited his landlord's displeasure if he opposed the latter's selection. Under these circumstances it was inevitable that the House of Commons should represent the English governing classes rather than the English people. Nor must it be forgotten that two highly privileged groups, the peers and the bishops of the Anglican Church, sat in the House of Lords and exercised through that chamber a potential veto on all legislation. Clearly the plutocracy held all the entrenchments of power.

Projects for the reform of Parliament, designed to make it more popular and more truly representative, had been debated forty years earlier, but the outbreak of the French Revolution filled the ruling classes in England with panic and discredited democratic ideas. When the war with France ended in 1815, the Tory government embarked upon a policy of repression, fearing that any concessions might encourage revolts and revolts lead to revolution. Within a decade, however, as described in the previous chapter, this reactionary mood weakened. The amelioration of the penal code and the passage of the Catholic Emancipation Act [1] indicated that liberal sentiment was gaining the day.

At this point (1830) the Whig politicians, political opponents of the Tories, came forward as the champions of parliamentary reform. At heart the Whig leaders had little sympathy with demo- *Unequal* cratic ideals, but they allied themselves with the discon- *representa-* tented workingmen because they hoped by reform to keep *tion* themselves in power. The Tories drew much of their strength from the "rotten" and "pocket" boroughs, particularly in the south of England. They enjoyed the support of the great country landowners, and deserved it by the manner in which they favored and protected the agricultural interests in Parliament. The Whigs, on the other hand, were more closely identified with the middle-class dwellers of the cities, with merchants, traders, bankers, factory and mill owners. As already noted, the Industrial Revolution had rapidly increased the importance and wealth of the industrial aristocracy, causing factory towns to spring up around the coal-fields of the western counties. But the unreformed Parliament ignored this shift in population and denied important manufacturing centers, such as Manchester, Sheffield, and Birmingham, a single representative, although ancient and decayed boroughs, shrunken to a few families, continued to send a member to London. The first item on the Whig program was, therefore, a redistribution of seats, which would increase the representation of the new cities at the expense of depopulated counties.

The second item of reform which the Whigs proposed was an extension of the suffrage. Hitherto less than four per cent of the population had enjoyed the right to vote. If this right were *Extension of* extended to all householders who paid the equivalent of *the suffrage* ten pounds rent a year, many of the lesser bourgeoisie of the towns and leaseholders in the counties could share in the elections, increasing the number of voters from 435,000 to 656,000. As this was roughly one in twenty-two instead of one in thirty-two of the population, it will be seen that the measure stopped far short of genuine democracy. A majority of the laborers on the farms and workingmen in the cities were to be left no better off than before.

Nevertheless, the struggle for reform enlisted the ardent support of the city workers, who demonstrated, by mass meetings, riots, and

[1] See above, page 219.

occasional acts of violence, that they had reached a dangerous mood. The Whigs could also count upon the support of the intellectual radicals, a small but distinguished group of writers and scholars led by the philosopher Jeremy Bentham (1748–1832) and John Stuart Mill (1806–73). These Benthamites, or Utilitarians, believed the purpose or utility of a government should be gauged by the degree to which it afforded "the greatest good to the greatest number." To fulfill this function it should be genuinely representative; hence the Utilitarians favored universal manhood suffrage, but they were willing to endorse the Whig program as a step in the right direction. Prospects brightened when the news that the French had driven out the absolutist king, Charles X, precipitated a cabinet crisis in England which caused the fall of the Tory Party and brought the Whigs into office (1830). The moment for an experiment in constitutional reform had arrived.

The Whig prime minister, Earl Grey, found the House of Commons divided on the merits of the proposed bill and called for a general *The Reform* election to discover the wishes of the electorate. The *Bill passes* Whigs were returned to power with a large majority, but *(1832)* their second bill, though it passed in the Commons (1831), was rejected by the House of Lords. In 1832, therefore, the Commons passed a third reform bill. Again the Lords rejected it. Popular indignation had risen to the verge of revolution at this persistent frustration of the nation's expressed will. Yet when Earl Grey resigned as a protest, the stubborn king, William IV, called upon the Tory Duke of Wellington to take office. But not even the Iron Duke's resolution, which had defeated Napoleon at Waterloo, could stem the liberal tide. After a few days the king found it necessary to recall Grey to power, with the assurance that if no other means sufficed, the Crown would create enough new peers to break the deadlock in the House of Lords. The threat proved sufficient. Rather than see their august rolls defaced by a host of new titles minted for the occasion the Lords yielded, and the Reform Bill became law in June, 1832.

A revolution had been accomplished by constitutional means, and the strength of the old régime in England definitely broken. In effect, the Reform Bill of 1832 elevated the industrial aristocracy to a level with the older landed nobility and divided the control of the government between them. In a more final sense, however, it meant the triumph of the manufacturing interests over the agricultural. The clearest proof of this is to be seen a few years later in the repeal of the Corn [1] Laws. The tariff on grains had assured the great land-

---

[1] In England the term "corn" is applied to oats, barley, wheat, etc.

owners a profit on their crops. The abolition of this tariff proved a
blow to agriculture, but a boon to the city workers for whom it meant
cheaper bread. And the city dwellers had to be served, for they had
become the most important element of the population. By 1846, for
the first time in English history, over half the people lived in towns,
outranking in wealth and number the dwellers of the countryside. This
rapid increase in the urban population was the most startling social
change introduced by the Industrial Revolution.

4. THE CHARTIST MOVEMENT

Their somewhat hesitant espousal of the Reform Bill (1832) won
for the Whigs the distinction of being the "Liberal" Party in England
throughout the remainder of the nineteenth century, while *Liberal*
their Tory opponents became known as the "Conserva- *reforms*
tives." The Liberals used their ascendancy after 1832 *after 1832*
to hasten further reforms which reflect both the idealism and the
selfishness of the middle class. Having won control of Parliament, the
Liberals proceeded to reorganize the town governments also, to assure
middle-class control in local affairs (Municipal Corporations Act, 1835).
Trade and industry profited by a reduction in the tariff rates, by the
construction of better roads and canals, the extension of steam railway lines, and the institution of a "penny post" system (1840). The
abolition of slavery throughout the British colonies with compensation
to the slaveholders (1833) stands out as a triumph of humanitarian
sentiment, and the same spirit dictated further amelioration of the
penal code and more humane treatment of criminals. But where the
impulse toward kindliness warred too sharply with business profits,
the middle-class legislators showed themselves less generous. A new
Poor Law (1834) saved the taxpayers' money, but subjected paupers
to a régime so harsh that it made them feel that poverty had become
a crime. Slaves on the plantations overseas might celebrate their
liberty, but the factory workers at home too often appealed in vain
for a lightening of their economic serfdom. Employers insisted that
for the government to interfere in, or even to investigate, the lot of
the workingmen, would be a violation of that *laissez-faire* policy under
which business prospered best.

The workers who had paraded and petitioned for reform in 1832
thus found that they had gained little by it. Their hope that a further
extension of the franchise would soon follow was rudely shattered,
and Earl Grey himself declared the Reform Bill was "final." Too late

the workers comprehended that they had helped to place in power a
Disillusion- class actually hostile to their own interests. The "conserv-
ment of the ative" Tories were more disposed to help the factory
workers workers than were the "liberal" Whigs. It was a Tory peer
who proposed that children under ten years of age should not be worked
over nine hours a day (Factory Act, 1833); and a Mines Act (1842)
prohibiting the employment in the mines of women, or children under
ten, passed with Tory support. Such reforms, however, were but
feeble palliatives for a deep-rooted evil.

Though strong in numbers the working class was weak in organization. Since a Parliament dominated by landowners and business men
Chartism might remain permanently indifferent to their needs, they
determined to force further democratic reforms, secure
the right to vote, and send their own delegates to Westminster. They
drew up a People's Charter embodying six demands which became
known as the "Six Points of Chartism" (1838). These were: (1) universal manhood suffrage; (2) secret balloting; (3) annual Parliaments;
(4) equal electoral districts; (5) no property qualification for members
of Parliament; (6) a salary for members of Parliament. This program
would have transformed Great Britain into a genuine democracy, but
the Chartists failed to secure its adoption by "moral" pressure and
hesitated to resort to armed revolt. In 1848, the movement reached
its climax. Several years of poor harvests and business depression
had caused grave suffering among the submerged classes, and a monster
petition, reported to bear six million signatures, was prepared for presen-
tation to Parliament to support the Chartist demands. When Parliament rejected it, the resulting disorders were easily put down and the
Chartist Movement collapsed.

Yet it is interesting to note that the Six Points, considered radical
in their day, have almost all been adopted since in all democratic
countries. The Chartist Movement itself lost force largely because
of the growing prosperity which affected all the leading industrial states
after 1850. Railways and steam navigation quickened transportation.
The construction of steel ships made England not only the workshop of
the world, but the mistress of its carrying trade also, and so rapidly
did capital increase that London became the banking center of the
world. In this flood tide of prosperity the "benevolent bourgeoisie"
conceded better terms to the workers and eased the tension between
the two classes. The workers themselves, discouraged in their plans for
political representation, turned instead to the formation of stronger trade
unions and bargained directly with their employers.

[232]

5. THE FRENCH REVOLUTION OF 1830

In France, the Industrial Revolution developed later than in Britain and wrought no such swift and startling transformation. The English migration to the cities, which increased the population of Manchester and Birmingham forty per cent between 1820 and 1830, had no parallel across the Channel, where a majority of the French people continued to cultivate the fertile earth and to remain content with the rewards of agriculture.

It has been estimated that in 1815 no more than fifteen steam engines were serving French industry and that most of these had been set up to drive mine pumps. The importation of machinery from England was prohibited until after 1825, and the poor quality and scattered distribution of French coal offered a further difficulty, but by 1830 the fifteen engines had increased to six hundred, and a small group of factory-owners and a growing class of factory-workers added to the problems of the Bourbon régime. The owners reinforced the discontented bourgeoisie, the workers joined the discontented proletariat of the cities.

The reactionary policies of Charles X (1824–30) gravely displeased the French middle and lower classes. Charles's determination to strengthen the privileges of the old nobility and to restore royal absolutism in France have been discussed in a previous chapter.[1] His policies, if fully successful, would have robbed the bourgeoisie of the broad advantages which they had gained since 1789. In 1829, Charles betrayed the principle of responsible government by appointing the Prince de Polignac prime minister despite the opposition of the Chamber of Deputies. Dissolving the obstinate Chamber, Charles called for an election (1830), but the new Chamber threatened to prove still more recalcitrant. Refusing to accept the verdict of the electors, the stubborn monarch prepared four summary ordinances: (1) The liberty of the press was severely limited. (2) The new Chamber was declared dissolved before it assembled. (3) Three fourths of the electors lost their right to vote. (4) A new election was decreed. The posting of these ordinances (July 26, 1830) stirred Paris to revolt, the royal forces proved unable to curb the movement, and after three days of fighting Charles fled to England.

Overthrow of Charles X

Success so sudden and so unexpected left the Paris revolutionaries divided in their aims. Radical leaders of the populace demanded a democratic republic such as the Jacobins had attempted to establish

[1] See above, page 218.

in 1793. Bourgeois moderates urged a constitutional monarchy. A

Louis Philippe becomes king republic, they pointed out, could not hope to survive in a Europe dominated by the spirit of reaction, for the monarchs would unite their forces in opposition to it. The middle class won the day, and the Chamber of Deputies offered the vacant throne to Louis Philippe, Duke of Orléans. Orléans was the son of the notorious Philip of Orléans of revolutionary fame who changed his name to Philippe Égalité, was elected a member of the National Convention, and voted for the death of Louis XVI. In 1830, the son was living quietly in Paris like any middle-class gentleman. His fellow citizens admired his simple tastes and bourgeois virtues; they recalled that he had fought for the French Republic in 1792, and they felt certain that if they placed him on the throne he would make an excellent "citizen king." The aged Lafayette, the hero of two worlds and three revolutions, used his influence to persuade his fellow citizens to accept the compromise which seemed happiest under the circumstances, and the "July Revolution" ended with the tricolor replacing the white flag of the Bourbons while Louis Philippe accepted the title "King of the French."

Like the English radicals after 1832, the Paris radicals and workingmen felt that they had been cheated. To shed their blood upon the barricades that the middle class might set up a bourgeois monarchy appeared to them a mockery of their hopes. They had not even secured to themselves the right to vote, since this privilege was restricted to some two hundred thousand "men of property." In 1830 they had to yield, however, because they realized that they were not strong enough to set up the republic they desired, but they continued to dream of democracy, and their discontent slowly undermined the foundations of the "July Monarchy."

Word that the French had again dethroned a legitimate king ran like an electric spark throughout Europe. Monarchs trembled on their thrones as if they had heard an echo of republican armies chanting the *Marseillaise.* "Gentlemen, saddle your horses," said Nicholas I when the news reached Saint Petersburg, "France is in revolution again." Liberals, on the other hand, hailed the event with delight, and prepared to rise in arms for a general war of liberation. The Poles, counting upon French aid, prepared to cast off the yoke of Russia, and the Belgians, who hated the union with Holland decreed for them by the Congress of Vienna, proclaimed their independence. At this resurgence of liberalism the monarchs of Europe took hurried counsel, fearing France was about to loose a new wave of revolutionary fury upon them. But their appre-

LOUIS PHILIPPE, KING OF THE FRENCH
1773–1850

Caricaturists opposed to the July Monarchy delighted in drawing Louis Philippe with a pear-shaped head, thus emphasizing his heavy expression, somewhat narrow forehead, and fleshy jaw.

hension proved groundless. The French middle class did not wish a war which might dislocate trade, and Louis Philippe assured his fellow monarchs that France would lend no aid to revolutionaries in other countries. This cautious policy proved a second disappointment to the French republicans, who, still fascinated by the great days of 1792, believed France owed it to her destiny and to Europe to take the lead in a general movement against the tyranny of kings.

This lack of French aid or intervention partly explains why the revolts of 1830 in the Germanies and Italy met with small success. A few

The Germanies and Italy

secondary German states — Brunswick, Saxony, and Hanover — won limited constitutions, but Prussia remained unshaken, and Austria, the stronghold of reaction, stood so solidly amid the general unrest that Metternich was able to spare an Austrian army to quell the revolts in Italy. Rome was recaptured from the hands of a group of radicals who had proclaimed an Italian republic there; Parma and Modena received back their petty despots; and Italian liberals who had sprung to arms in the hope of liberating their country were hanged, imprisoned, or exiled.

Even more tragic was the fate of Poland. The constitution granted by Czar Alexander I in 1815 failed to satisfy the Poles, and the news of

Polish Revolt (1830–31)

the French Revolution of 1830 crystallized their discontent and spurred them into a futile stroke for freedom. Nicholas I (1825–55) had far less sympathy for Polish national aspirations than his brother Alexander had shown, and he encouraged his armies to crush the revolt without pity. When, after a brave and desperate defense, the kingdom lay at his mercy, he proceeded to punish the patriot leaders, abrogate the constitution, and incorporate Poland into the Russian Empire. Its cities acknowledged Russian garrisons, and Russian officials controlled the administration. As Prussia and Austria both held small fragments of Polish territory, their governments felt no regret at this extinction of Polish nationalism. France, under the citizen king, Louis Philippe, declined to interfere, and Great Britain, though sympathetic toward the Poles, possessed no adequate motive for intervention. The British government preferred to reserve its special attention for the troublesome question of Belgium.

In joining Belgium to Holland in 1815, the diplomats had sought to compensate the Dutch for colonies lost to England, and at the same

The Belgian question

time to strengthen them against a possible renewal of French aggression. The Belgians resented this union with a stronger, Protestant state, for they feared that their Catholic faith, their liberties, and their language might be endangered. The stern policies of William I, as King of the United Netherlands, increased these apprehensions. In 1830, therefore, the Belgians took their cue from the French and repudiated the rule of an unpopular king. Frenchmen of all classes favored the cause of Belgian independence, although the new bourgeois government was not prepared to risk a war in support of it. British merchants looked to Belgian independence to benefit their trade. Accordingly, in 1831, the great powers signed an agreement at London recognizing Belgium as a separate state. It was necessary to find a king for the Belgians, republics being in disfavor, and a German prince, Leopold of Saxe-Coburg, accepted the crown. William I of Holland clung to his Belgian provinces stubbornly until forced to yield by French military intervention and a British blockade. Holland did not, in fact, formally renounce her claims until 1839, whereupon Britain, France, Prussia, Austria, and Russia pledged themselves to respect the perpetual independence and neutrality of Belgium, a treaty which remained in force until the German government violated it in 1914.

By 1830, the conservative system, or as it is often called, the system of Metternich, had suffered some severe reverses. The success of the Greek Revolt, the overthrow in France of the legitimate king, Charles X, and the proclamation of an independent Belgium were all developments which violated the established order and the principle of legitimacy. For these setbacks the allied monarchs could largely blame Britain for lack of co-operation, for had the British government so chosen, its navy could have hindered the revolt of the Belgians and have assured the collapse of the Greek Revolt. But in each case the British government had thrown its influence on the side of the rebels, just as it had been the first to recognize Louis Philippe's usurpation of the French throne. It would be a mistake, however, to assume from these instances that the British cabinet was liberal and favored revolutions: on the contrary, its policy from 1815 to 1832 was, as already explained, one of repression and reaction. Nevertheless, the British government often found it profitable to press a liberal policy abroad in the interests of British trade. The creation of small independent states, in South America, in Greece, or in Belgium, favored British manufacturers and merchants who could not exploit these markets so easily while they were in the control of a strong and monopolistic power. In this sense, the exigencies of trade triumphed over political principles, and the Industrial Revolution became one of the most dangerous foes of the conservative system. The old feudal-monarchical order of society which the diplomats had labored to patch together at Vienna could not hold in check the growing pressure of national and liberal sentiment, especially when this was reinforced by

[237]

the transforming influences of the factory system. The new forces were destined to crack open a static society as irresistibly as a great tree pushes its way through the walls of a crumbling house.

It is interesting to study the gathering of the new forces, especially after 1830. Wherever factories increased the numbers of the urban workers, the republican party gained ground. Wherever railways spread across the countryside, they transformed and quickened the industrial and social life, facilitating travel and the interchange of ideas and goods. The new faith in progress, the increase in material wealth, the opening of new vistas and new opportunities made men more and more impatient with the obsolete class distinctions, outworn regulations, and inefficient methods of administration. The Revolution of 1830 and the Reform Bill of 1832 assured the new middle class the lead in the two most progressive European countries, France and Great Britain. A generation later the expanding forces gathered strength for a fresh explosion and another wave of revolution passed over Europe in the years 1848–49. How the wave gathered and how it broke will be described in the following chapter.

CHAPTER SEVENTEEN

THE REVOLUTIONARY MOVEMENT OF 1848–49 AND ITS COLLAPSE

The Revolution had come before its time.
PIERRE JOSEPH PROUDHON.

THE Paris insurrection on July, 1830, gave France a "citizen king" in the person of Louis Philippe,[1] but it did not go far enough to please the working classes or the republicans. The new régime represented, and was supported by, the bourgeoisie, and it made the promotion of business prosperity its chief aim. From 1830 to 1848, "Peace and Order" were to be the official watchwords in France. As war would have involved a disruption of trade, the government pursued a discreet and unaggressive foreign policy, and so far abandoned that authoritative stand customarily assumed by *la grande nation* in the affairs of Europe that ultra-patriots characterized the course as "peace without honor." In 1840, Louis Adolphe Thiers (1797–1877), who had attempted to revive French prestige by an aggressive policy in the Near East, had to resign his office to the more conservative François Guizot (1787–1874). The policy of caution had triumphed, and under Guizot's ministry, from 1840 to 1848, the unprogressive character of the régime became more and more apparent. Restrictions muffled all attempts at outspoken criticism, the government gratified the timid bourgeois with a foreign policy which eschewed glory but assured peace, and society grew daily more dull and respectable. The German poet Heinrich Heine shrewdly observed that Guizot's main qualification for office was the high degree to which he had perfected the art of immobility. "He does nothing," Heine wrote in 1842, "and that is his secret of preservation."

1. DISCONTENT IN FRANCE UNDER THE JULY MONARCHY

So long as its opponents remained divided, the government of Louis Philippe had little to fear. At least five factions desired its overthrow, but of these the Legitimist followers of Charles X and his line wasted no love on the Bonapartists who sought to revive the Napoleonic tradition, the Clericals resented chiefly the weakened authority of the church under a usurping king and had no sympathy for the Republicans who clung to the hopes betrayed in 1830, while the Socialists, though growing

---

[1] See above, page 234.

in number, alarmed all the other factions by their projects for establishing a communist society. Of the five groups the Legitimists counted least and had few serious adherents outside of the Faubourg Saint-Germain in Paris, where the ancient aristocrats lived in decayed elegance with their memories. The Bonapartists likewise lived on memories, but the Napoleonic legend had vitality, and when the ashes of the emperor were brought from Saint Helena to Paris in 1840, people could not help comparing the vigorous rule of Napoleon with the mediocre government of the citizen king.

The third group, the Clericals, were more than a political clique, yet could scarcely be termed a party. The clergy, who had formed the *The Clericals* privileged First Estate under the old régime, regained a share of their lost power and wealth on the restoration of the Bourbons in 1814. They erred, however, in linking their fortunes to the legitimist line, for, with the fall of Charles X in 1830, they lost their chief protector and most of their privileges. Excluded from teaching in the schools, the priests became opponents of the July Monarchy and assailed the secular schools as godless institutions that would corrupt the youth of France. The bourgeoisie paid little heed to this clerical criticism, but the peasants still reverenced their priests and resented the official discrimination against them. Among them the priests built up an intangible but powerful sentiment against the July Monarchy.

To the Republican standard rallied a number of young intellectual radicals disgusted with the existing government and its static ideals. *The Republicans* The ministers of Louis Philippe turned a deaf ear to proposals for reform, and agitators who urged a wider franchise so that they might enjoy a share in the government won from Guizot the curt advice to work harder, grow rich, and so gain the ballot. As the administration solidified, the governing class became a closed official caste and the hope of constitutional reform steadily waned. It seemed as if nothing less than a revolution could break the torpid hold of the bourgeois régime, and young Republicans read eagerly the histories of the great French Revolution which poured from the press. Statesmen of that day prepared to make history by writing it. Thiers had first won fame by a *History of the French Revolution*, Alphonse Lamartine (1790–1869) composed a *History of the Girondins*, Louis Blanc (1811–82) wrote a *History of the French Revolution* and attacked the existing government in his *History of Ten Years*, while Guizot was the author of a voluminous *History of France* and a *History of the Revolution in England*. Reading of the great days of 1793 and 1794, the young republican ideal-ists of the 1840's were fired with impatience to emulate the heroes of the past.

Eager to find allies for an attack upon the royal government, the Republicans turned to the Socialists, and in 1843 the two groups joined forces in a fusion party. The Republicans sought a wider *The* franchise and an abolition of the property qualifications *Socialists* which barred many of them from a part in politics. The Socialists had more radical demands and loftier dreams. The earliest Socialists, Henri de Saint-Simon (1760–1825) and François Marie Fourier (1772–1837), concocted visionary schemes for the reorganization of society, and dreamed of establishing ideal communities where the citizens would live lives of simplicity and harmony blessed by the dignity of labor. The working classes for whom these Utopian schemes were specially devised paid them scant respect, preferring the more practical suggestions of Louis Blanc, who understood their grievances and made himself the fearless champion of their hopes. The state, Blanc declared, was responsible for the welfare of the poor, and ought to abolish unmerited poverty by organizing the great industries of France on a co-operative basis as "national workshops," with employment assured to all who sought it. This doctrine violated the *laissez-faire* principles popular with the capitalist employers, but it seemed just and reasonable to the workers and the radical intellectuals.

2. THE FEBRUARY REVOLUTION IN FRANCE (1848) AND ITS SEQUEL

As its following increased, the reform party in France, like the Chartists in England, advertised its demands by monster petitions, mass meetings, and parades. By 1847, this agitation had taken the novel form of political banquets, and a "Banquet Campaign" grew to proportions that alarmed the government. Still true to his principle of immobility, Guizot refused concessions, and the civil authorities attempted to halt the agitation by forbidding a banquet scheduled for February 22, 1848. The thwarted populace reacted indignantly and the following day barricades blocked the streets of Paris. Too late, Guizot resigned, and Louis Philippe offered concessions, but the revolt grew more serious and on February 24 the king abdicated. The Chamber of Deputies yielded the control of the state to a group of popular Socialist and Republican leaders who formed a provisional government.

The success so speedily achieved as speedily revealed the anomaly of the Republican-Socialist coalition which had made it possible. Afraid at first to antagonize the working classes, the moderate Republicans admitted four Socialists to a place on the provisional government, and reduced the working day in Paris from eleven to ten hours. But it soon became apparent that the majority of the French people had little real interest in social experiments. Louis Blanc's demand for the immediate establishment of national workshops was held up by his less radical colleagues. Instead, a substitute program, a parody of Blanc's project, was entrusted to an unsympathetic minister who hired thousands of unemployed at two francs a day and set them to work digging ditches. The burden on the state of this wasteful and stupid work persuaded many taxpayers that Blanc's scheme was a costly failure, a deception easily propagated because the middle classes and the conservative farmers were already frightened by the nightmare of socialism.

In the elections of April, 1848, clericals and aristocrats, peasants and bourgeois united to choose a Constituent Assembly of distinctly moderate *Defeat of* temper. Beaten at the polls, the Paris radicals resorted to *the Social-* the futile alternative of a bloody insurrection (June 23–26, *ists* 1848) which ended with the execution or deportation of eleven thousand of the insurgents, the suppression of the Socialist newspapers, and the abandonment of the plan for national workshops.

With the Socialists crushed, the Assembly soon completed a constitution for the Second French Republic. The right of free speech and a free press, security from arbitrary arrest, and permission to assemble peaceably and to petition the government, won legal recognition. The constitution further provided for a single legislative chamber of seven hundred and fifty deputies, to be selected by universal manhood suffrage, and a president to be chosen in the same broad and direct fashion. The moderates believed it safe to entrust the vote to all male citizens because they counted upon the peasant majority to offset the influence of the radical city proletariat and elect a "Party of Order."

The results more than justified these expectations. Of three leading candidates competing for the presidency, the Socialist Ledru-Rollin *Election of* was feared as the standard-bearer of a party identified with *Louis Na-* the madness of the June revolt, while General Cavaignac, *poleon* hope of the middle-class Republicans, was disliked because *Bonaparte* he had crushed that revolt by shedding the blood of Frenchmen. This illogical division of feeling, characteristic of electorates, defeated two capable men and opened the way to a third candidate, Louis Napoleon Bonaparte, who represented the Party of Order. He was (if legitimate) a nephew of the great Napoleon, his parents being Louis Bonaparte and Hortense de Beauharnais, the stepdaughter of

Napoleon I through his marriage to Josephine de Beauharnais. The death in 1832 of Napoleon's son, born of his second marriage to Marie Louise of Austria, left Louis Napoleon Bonaparte heir to the imperial succession. In 1848, monarchists, Catholics, militarists, patriots, peasants, and workers combined to elect, by a majority of five and a half out of seven million votes cast, an adventurer about whom they knew little save that he bore the name Napoleon.

It was an ominous portent for the stability of the Second Republic that the "prince-president" had already made two comic-opera attempts (in 1836 and 1840) to seize control of France by a military *coup d'état*. Imprisoned by the government of Louis Philippe after the second escapade, he finally escaped to England, where he was living in exile when the Revolution of 1848 brought him his opportunity. During the years of waiting, Louis Napoleon had published a book on *Napoleonic Ideas* in which his uncle emerged (somewhat unrecognizably) as the champion of peace and liberty. He also wrote on military science to prove that he had inherited soldierly interests, and even cultivated Socialist support by a work on *The Extinction of Poverty*. When, at forty, he assumed the executive rôle in the Second Republic, he felt himself under a fatal impulsion to follow in his uncle's footsteps. France had grown sated with mediocrity, and Louis Napoleon, if he would justify his name and his opportunism, was "condemned to be brilliant." But behind his enigmatic pose he possessed little of his uncle's genius or energy; his leading traits were a mystical faith in what he called his "destiny" and a fund of shrewd political sense.

From the outset of his rule, Louis Napoleon used his presidential office to build up a following for himself, especially in the army. As the Assembly declined to consider an extension of his term beyond the four years for which he had been elected, he prepared a military *coup d'état*. The date chosen was $\text{Coup d'état of December 2, 1851}$ December 2, 1851, anniversary of the great Napoleon's coronation and of his victory at Austerlitz. Without warning, the leaders of the Monarchist and Republican parties in the Assembly found themselves arrested, and Paris awoke on December 3 to the rule of martial law. Despite resistance and bloodshed in Paris and some of the larger towns, the French nation ratified the president's stroke by an overwhelming plebiscite. In 1852, the Second Republic gave place to the Second Empire, and the European monarchs debated whether or not they ought to compromise their dignity by addressing Napoleon III, Emperor of the French, as "brother."

The story of the Second Empire and the rôle which Napoleon III attempted to play in Europe between 1852 and 1870 will be related in the chapter which follows. First, however, it will be useful to note the repercussions which the French Revolution of 1848 exerted upon the rest of Europe.

3. THE GERMAN PEOPLE FAIL TO ACHIEVE POLITICAL UNITY (1848-49)

Attention has been called before this to the political disunion which weakened the Germanies. The breakdown of the Holy Roman Empire, *Particular-* the heritage of feudalism with its disruptive tendencies, the *ism in the* jealous independence of the German princes, and the rivalry *Germanies* of Austria and Prussia from the seventeenth century onward, combined to delay German unification until late in the nineteenth century. Napoleon I gave a great impetus to the work of consolidation by encouraging his allies among the more powerful German rulers to annex the smaller states, bishoprics, and free cities, a task which they performed with such alacrity that by 1815 three hundred and sixty states had been reduced to thirty-eight. But the Congress of Vienna showed no disposition to complete the amalgamation. Instead, it disappointed the friends of union by instituting a Germanic Confederation so loose and ineffectual in its structure that the thirty-eight fragments all enjoyed a practical autonomy. Poems and pamphlets pleading for closer political bonds were suppressed, and the princes displayed their loyalty to the spirit of the past by discouraging all sentiment in favor of liberty or unity.

For a time these methods of repression proved successful. The German people could not have a revolution, as the poet Goethe humorously declared, because the police would not permit it. When the French rebelled in 1830 and drove out the unpopular Charles X, German liberals reacted in several states of the federation to the extent of demanding a larger share in the government and freedom of the press, but their agitation led to no serious violence and to few important reforms. Nor did it advance the national movement. The German people, because of their political impotence and disunion, seemed destined to forfeit indefinitely the important rôle which they deserved to play in European and world affairs.

Yet economic forces were drawing them together, though political *The Zoll-* bonds failed to knit. The multiplicity of tariffs erected by *verein* thirty-eight separate governments proved a severe hindrance to trade, so great that in 1818 Prussia adopted a uniform customs

[244]

policy and invited her neighbors to merge their policies with hers. By 1834, seventeen German states had entered this *Zollverein* or customs union, and six others shortly followed. German manufacturers profited by the disappearance of internal trade barriers and by the common tariff which partly protected them from French and British competition. The exclusion of the Austrian Empire, with its mixed population, from this economic alliance, foreshadowed the unification of the strictly German states under Prussian leadership.

The success of the *Zollverein* convinced the business classes that political unification would prove a further boon to trade, for they saw that it would make possible a simpler postal, currency, and *The Frank-* banking system and a single code of law. Professors urged *fort As-* it in the lecture room and journalists pleaded for it in the *sembly* press. When, following the February disorders in France, *(1848–49)* a revolutionary wave broke over Europe in 1848, German liberals and nationalists believed that the auspicious moment had arrived to realize their hopes, and called an assembly at Frankfort to prepare a constitution for a federated commonwealth. All Germany anxiously followed the deliberations, but the delegates found themselves challenged from the first by two issues that defied a satisfactory solution: (1) Should the proposed German commonwealth be a republic or a monarchy? (2) Should the Austrian lands be included or excluded from the union? A third problem, which threatened for a time to precipitate a general European war, concerned the inclusion of Schleswig and Holstein, for these provinces, though largely German in population, were subject to the Danish king. Finally, the determination of the Prussian government to bring its segment of Poland into whatever German union might be formed raised another racial difficulty.

When, in the preliminary discussions at Frankfort, the delegates voted to make the greater Germany which they planned a constitutional monarchy, seventy-nine republicans walked out in disgust. *Failure of* From that point a fatal division weakened the national cause. *the Frank-* On the second problem, concerning the inclusion of Austria, *fort As-* the Assembly attempted to compromise. Since the Slavs, *sembly* Magyars, Czechs, Poles, and Italians in the Hapsburg Empire could not properly be included in a Germanic union, only the German provinces of Austria were invited to join. The Austrian government, hostile to any federation it could not aspire to dominate, rejected the compromise and recalled its representatives from Frankfort. Still hopeful of forming a smaller German Empire under Prussian leadership, the Assembly offered the imperial crown to Frederick William IV of Prussia (March,

[245]

1849). His curt refusal, with the intimation that he might accept it from his fellow princes, but could not take a crown from the hands of a revolutionary assembly, extinguished the last hopes of the Frankfort delegates. Most of them dispersed in disillusionment, and the handful of extremists who attempted to resort to radical measures were driven out by force.

The aspirations of the German nationalists, so promising in 1848, had changed by 1849 to a sense of ignominious failure. In 1850, the old *Prussia wins a deceptive constitution* Germanic Confederation was re-established, a signal victory for Austria and for conservatism. Nevertheless, Germany had heard the call to union, and liberals could find a few grains of comfort in the fact that constitutional privileges had been extended in several states, while Prussia, hitherto a stronghold of autocratic principles, acquired a measure of representative government. For during the riotous days of 1848, Frederick William IV had been intimidated into promising his subjects a constitution, and he fulfilled his word, although the charter which he granted could not be called liberal. It created a House of Representatives, but the deputies possessed little power beyond the right to reject new taxes. It assured universal suffrage, but nullified its effect by dividing all the voters into three classes according to the amount of taxes they paid. As each class chose the same number of deputies, the very rich and the moderately wealthy controlled the parliament, while the third group, including the millions of peasants and workers, had a minority representation. In 1854, Frederick William established an upper chamber, or House of Lords, the noble members of which were to hold their seats by hereditary right or by appointment for life. This insincere constitution, so cleverly designed to wear the appearance of democracy while checkmating its effects, possesses more than a passing importance because it later became the constitution of the German Empire.

The failure of the revolutionary movement of 1848–49 sobered the German liberals and turned their thoughts from finespun theories about the ideal form of union to a consideration of indissoluble, brute facts. They saw more clearly now that if Prussia was to unify the German-speaking people, it could only be accomplished in defiance of Austria, probably as the result of a military decision in which Austria suffered defeat. For such a test of strength between the two leading powers in the Germanies, the time was not ripe in 1849, but the problem had been clarified and the issue defined. Within twenty years the Germans were to unite their fatherland, despite domestic feuds, and in the face of French and Austrian opposition.

[246]

4. AUSTRIA RESTORES HER HOUSE TO ORDER

No European dynasty was more firmly wedded to conservative principles in 1848 than the house of Austria. From his palace in Vienna the ageing Metternich watched with disapproval the resuscitation of democratic ideas, as firmly convinced as ever that government by the people would lead to anarchy, and that the spirit of nationalism agitating the Italians, the Germans, and the subject peoples of the Hapsburg Empire formed the gravest threat to the peace of Europe. Like Guizot in France he sought to preserve his immobility in a world that ebbed and shifted, but his deep-seated conviction that any change in political or social relations was likely to prove dangerous can be ascribed to something more than prejudice. Metternich may well have foreseen, what subsequent history has made clear, that the triumph of liberalism would ultimately destroy the old régime in Austria and that the triumph of nationalism would result in the dissolution of the polyglot empire. He fought to preserve the dynasty he served, and the empire he administered, from forces which threatened both with destruction.

Despite all his precautions, however, the revolutionary fever of 1848 invaded Austria. A popular uprising in Vienna forced him into exile, while the liberals wrung the promise of a constitution from the feeble emperor, Ferdinand I (1835–48). In Bohemia the Czechs demanded local autonomy with their own elected Diet, while the Magyars prepared to establish Hungary as an almost independent kingdom. This last proposal roused opposition among the repressed Slavs who split the Hungarian Kingdom in two by proclaiming a Southern Slav State to include the Croats and Serbs. All the new governments demanded recognition from the paralyzed ministry at Vienna, and all adopted liberal programs, promising the peasants relief from feudal dues, the middle class freedom of speech and the press, and all the citizens the benefit of a representative government. Metternich's apprehensions had crystallized into facts; the bulwarks of absolutism in the Hapsburg Empire were tottering, and the empire itself seemed on the point of dissolution.

Then the tide turned. The insurgent factions fell to attacking one another and the conservative forces seized the opportunity to strike back. Rivalry between Germans and Czechs in Bohemia enabled Prince Windischgrätz to recapture Prague for the imperial government. In Italy the veteran Austrian general, Radetsky, suppressed the Italian outbreaks in Lombardy and Venetia. These victories encouraged the emperor's advisers to suggest a counter-

Defeat of the Austrian liberals

stroke against the liberals in Vienna. As a feud had already developed in the reform ranks between the middle-class moderates and the more radical workingmen, Windischgrätz found it possible to reoccupy the capital in October, 1848. Ferdinand resigned the throne to his nephew, Francis Joseph I (1848–1916), who dissolved the revolutionary assembly, threw out the newly completed constitution, and restored much of the conservative régime. The indifference with which the Austrian people accepted this defeat of the liberal experiment proved that the movement had excited little real support outside Vienna.

Though threatened for a time, the old régime in Austria had demonstrated its capacity to withstand revolutionary change. Where the liberal cause had joined forces with the national urge, however, as in Hungary, a fiercer blaze had been kindled and one more difficult to extinguish. But the imperial court, long adept at the game of playing one national faction against another, cleverly selected Count Joseph Jellachich, leader of the Southern Slavs, to head a campaign against the rebellious Magyars. Windischgrätz followed with a second imperial army, and in 1849, Czar Nicholas I marched a Russian force to the aid of Francis Joseph and helped to destroy the Hungarian Republic in the interests of legitimacy. Weakened by dissensions and crushed by superior forces, the Hungarian patriots under the heroic Louis Kossuth were compelled to yield, and the Hapsburg ruler could congratulate himself that he was master in his own household.

The prestige which accrued to Austria from these triumphs over the forces of liberalism and separatism enabled the government at Vienna

Metternich's system "triumphantly fireproof" to adopt a decisive tone in German affairs also, and to oppose successfully the project for the unification of the Germanies under Prussian leadership. Austria had once again shown herself the vigilant champion of conservatism, and Metternich, though he did not resume the office of chancellor, returned to Vienna to write his memoirs, consoled by the assurance that his life-work had proved itself "triumphantly fire-proof" in the years 1848 and 1849.

5. ITALY REMAINS IN BONDAGE

In Italy as in Germany the events of 1848 roused the nationalists and *National uprising in Italy (1848)* liberals to action. Hatred of the rule of foreign despots had been growing steadily in the Italian states since 1815, but the revolutionary factions possessed no central committee and no concerted plan. In 1848, an uprising of the Milanese forced the Austrian garrison to withdraw, and the Venetians likewise expelled the Austrian authorities from their city and proclaimed it a republic. A surge of national defiance swept the peninsula as Charles Albert of Sardinia took the field and prepared to drive Radetsky's white-coated contingents from Italian soil. Even the pope, Pius IX, and the reactionary Neapolitan king, Ferdinand II, sent troops to aid in the War of Liberation. The Austrian government, paralyzed at home by the liberal outbreak in Vienna and the revolts in Bohemia and Hungary, could hardly be expected to maintain a firm hold upon its Italian provinces.

Yet, despite these hopeful circumstances, the Italians signally failed to break the Austrian yoke. Pius IX and Ferdinand II soon recalled their contingents from the struggle, and Charles Albert of Sardinia, defeated by the Austrians at Custozza and again at Novara, resigned his throne (1849). Reaction swept Italy as it was already sweeping Europe. Constitutions were revoked, popular assemblies dismissed, and Italian liberals hanged, jailed, or exiled. Austria had displayed unexpected strength, but the real fault for their failure lay with the Italians themselves. The excesses of the republican radicals in Milan, in Naples, and especially in Rome, where they drove the pope from the city and set up a Roman Republic, brought discredit upon the idea of "government by the people" and disgusted moderate-minded men. If the alternative to Austrian or papal absolutism was to be the murderous anarchy of a Roman mob or of Neapolitan brigands, sober citizens found that they preferred to live in reasonable security under princely despots. This division between the outlook of middle-class Italians who favored constitutional monarchy and radicals who sought to set up democratic republics so disrupted and crippled the national-liberal movement that the Austrians found it easy to reoccupy Milan and Venice, while a French expeditionary force (dispatched by the newly elected prince-president, Louis Napoleon Bonaparte) restored Rome and the Papal States to the rule of Pius IX. In Italy as elsewhere the revolutionary movement of 1848 had ended in failure in 1849.

6. THE LESSONS OF 1848-49

In fact, few upheavals of equal magnitude in the history of Europe have produced such apparently negative results. The Second French Republic, established in 1848 on the ruins of the monarchy, after destroying the Socialists was itself destroyed that an imperial adventurer, Napoleon III, might restore the throne. The Frankfort Assembly, summoned to unite the Germanies in 1848, closed its sessions in ridicule and failure in 1849. The widespread revolts in the Austrian Empire produced little in the way of permanent reform beyond the belated abolition of the remnants of serfdom in central Europe, while the Italian campaign for liberty and independence collapsed in defeat and anarchy.

Yet of these hopes betrayed in 1849 fully half were to be realized within a generation. By 1871, the French had proclaimed a Third Republic, destined this time to endure; the Germans had transmuted their dream of unity, so long deferred, into an actuality; the Italians had won their independence and a constitutional government. Note, however, that these were mainly nationalist causes, and that they triumphed largely because nationalism had the support of the industrial and mercantile classes. The social program of 1848, in so far as it sought the emancipation of the workingmen, ran counter to the powerful interests of employers and the prejudices of the wealthy, and this partly explains why socialism faltered while nationalism advanced. The propertied classes had, in fact, been so gravely alarmed by the socialist and communist menace in 1848 and 1849 that they cast about for measures to combat it, and in several states (France, Austria, Prussia) the government and the middle class repented the curbs which they had imposed upon the Roman Catholic Church and welcomed it again as a useful ally in combating socialist heresies.

Among Socialists and Republicans the collapse of their hopes produced a profound sense of disillusionment. Yet all the expense of blood *Socialism* and spirit had not been vain, for through defeat they *discredited* achieved a more realistic and more practical comprehension *after 1848* of their task. The Russian liberal, Alexander Herzen, recorded this change of mood. "It is a strange thing: since 1848 we have all faltered and stepped back, we have thrown everything overboard and shrunk into ourselves, and yet something has been done and everything has been changed. We are nearer to the earth, we stand on a lower, that is a firmer, level, the plow-cuts more deeply, our work is not so attractive, it is rougher — perhaps because it really is work." The romance of dreaming a social revolution was over; the work of preparing one had begun. But for some years after 1849, socialism languished, partly because it had suffered a setback, partly because the 1850's brought an era of business prosperity that exorcised the specter of unemployment and eased the lot of the worker.

Nor were signs lacking that the bourgeoisie might learn benevolence and soften the hostility between capital and labor by reasonable concessions. It was a favorable omen that the plight of the working classes had already attracted the sympathy of essayists and novelists who held up a mirror to society and pricked the consciences of the wealthy by descriptions of slum life and the degradation of poverty. In England the novels of Charles Dickens (1812–70) pleaded in all keys from humor to pathos the case of the wretched and impoverished. Thomas Carlyle (1795–1881), the Scottish historian and philosopher, launched flaming indictments against the evils of the factory system which rotted the hearts and souls of rich and poor alike. Across the Channel, Honoré de Balzac (1799–1850), perhaps the greatest of French novelists, depicted with dispassionate skill in his *Comédie Humaine* the ambition, selfishness, and avarice that infect a society ruled by the love of money, and revealed how petty and soulless life may become for people who know (like Oscar Wilde's cynic) the price of everything and the value of nothing.

The influence of such literature, though slow in its effect, could hardly fail in time to sensitize the rich to the problems of social justice. Books are more powerful than bombs in pleading a just cause. The violence of the radicals of 1848 and 1849, who sought to remake society by force, defeated its own aims because it welded the conservative classes together more solidly against the urban workingman. In all European countries the proletarian groups of 1848 were minority factions, and for this reason their successes, if they won any, were certain to be bloody and impermanent and to leave a heritage of obloquy upon their perpetrators. The anarchist Proudhon perceived this when he lamented that "the revolution had come before its time." It remained for established governments and conservative statesmen to make halting concessions to the popular demands after 1860.

CHAPTER EIGHTEEN

THE ESTABLISHMENT OF THE SECOND FRENCH EMPIRE: NAPOLEON III

I believe that from time to time men are created whom I will call providential, in whose hands the destinies of their countries are placed. I believe myself to be one of those men.

LOUIS NAPOLEON BONAPARTE.

STUDENTS who delight in the conviction that history repeats itself often note remarkable similarities between the First French Empire created by the great Napoleon and its counterpart erected half a century later by Napoleon III. Like his more famous uncle,

Parallel between Napoleon I and Napoleon III

Napoleon III transformed a republic into an empire, allied himself with the Roman Catholic Church, promised peace and made war, nurtured vast colonial dreams, fought an Italian campaign against the Austrians, sent an army to invade Russia, attempted to interfere in the Germanies, lost his throne and empire on the battlefield, and died in exile. To insist too far, however, on these striking resemblances between the two reigns would prove dangerously misleading. History never repeats itself without significant variations. The Second French Empire was no more a re-creation of the first than Louis Napoleon was a reincarnation of Napoleon I. The points of comparison suggest a case of historic plagiarism rather than historic repetition, and the Second Empire as a political experiment can be most profitably judged if it is judged by itself.

1. "THE EMPIRE IS PEACE"

As explained in the previous chapter, the *coup d'état* of December 2, 1851, by which Louis Napoleon made himself master of France, was confirmed by an enormous majority of the French voters. A second plebiscite, announced officially as 7,839,000 "ayes" to 253,000 "noes," sanctioned the establishment of an empire. In approving this move the French peasants remembered that an earlier Napoleon had secured them their property, reduced their taxes, and maintained public tranquillity; they forgot that he had also consigned their sons to slaughter on distant battlefields. The French middle class welcomed a strong government that would cope with the threat of socialism, though they dreaded that the name Bonaparte might spell military hazards for France and for business. Such fears the new emperor sought to dispel by a public denial. "In a spirit of mistrust certain people say 'The Empire is War.' I say 'The Empire is Peace.'" Whereupon he outlined the peaceful aims to which he hoped to dedicate his reign: the construction of railways, canals, and harbors which would create work for the unemployed, the expansion of commerce, the stimulation of agriculture, and the development of the French colonial empire. Nor did he forget the enrichment of culture and the propagation of the Catholic faith.

In his plans to promote the prosperity of his subjects, Napoleon found himself favored by extraneous circumstances. The decade between 1850 and 1860 was a period of great business activity, especially in France. Prices rose steadily, farmers and manufacturers found a ready market for their commodities, and workers found employment without difficulty in the expanding industries or the public projects inaugurated by the imperial government. Frenchmen told themselves that they had lost nothing by surrendering some of their liberties to an autocrat, for at least the emperor knew how to give them security and prosperity. In actual truth, the business "boom" was due to many complicated economic factors, such as the quickening effect of the Industrial Revolution in France, improvements in the methods of manufacture and transportation, and the discovery of gold in California (1848) which increased the world supply of that precious metal and made commodity prices appear to rise as gold became cheaper. But as few people understood such complicated matters, Napoleon III received more credit than he deserved for his efforts on behalf of better business.

France had become bored, to borrow a famous expression of the poet and historian Lamartine, by the unimpressive appearance and mediocre policies of Louis Philippe. Napoleon III studiously avoided this danger by entertaining his subjects with lavish displays and dramatic actions designed to keep the person of the emperor constantly in their thoughts. He toured the country delivering political addresses full of high-sounding platitudes, dedicated town halls and hospitals and railway stations to the public service, and laid corner-stones with eloquence and dexterity. The Parisian populace soon learned to shout *Vive l'empereur* as he drove past with a clattering escort of guards, and crowded to watch him when, dressed in a brilliant uniform, his moustaches waxed to a point, he distributed decorations to his loyal soldiers.

To make Paris a more beautiful capital for the Second Empire, Napoleon had the city modernized under the direction of his able friend Baron Haussmann. At enormous expense beautiful *Moderniza-* boulevards and broad squares replaced many of the city's *tion of Paris* ancient and crooked streets. The program of reconstruction provided

THE SECOND FRENCH EMPIRE: NAPOLEON III

labor for the unemployed and made Paris the most elegant and spacious capital in Europe, but it also made the task of the troops easier in case of insurrection. Broad boulevards are less convenient to barricade than narrow lanes, and crowds in open squares are defenseless before gunfire or cavalry.

At an exposition held in 1855 to celebrate the progress of French art and industry, visitors were dazzled by the beauty and gaiety of the city. *Prestige of the Second Empire* Paris had become once more what it had been under Louis XIV and Napoleon, the world center of art, fashion, and diplomacy. At the palace of the Tuileries the Empress Eugénie, a beautiful young Spanish girl whom Napoleon III married in 1853, presided gracefully over the imperial court. French writers, under the leadership of Gustave Flaubert (1821–80), set the standards for a new realist school of fiction which supplanted the romantic tradition of the preceding generation. All Europe acknowledged in Charles Augustin Sainte-Beuve (1804–69) the dean of literary critics. *Carmen* by Prosper Mérimée and *La Dame aux Camélias* by Alexandre Dumas the Younger, both destined to serve as the inspiration for famous operas, were written in these years, while Victor Hugo, a giant surviving from the romantic era, published his novel *Les Misérables* and much of his greatest poetry during the Second Empire. Frenchmen were proud to feel that their country had resumed again that leading position in art, literature, diplomacy, and military prestige to which *la grande nation* was entitled.

2. ALL THINGS TO ALL MEN

It has been said of Napoleon III that even upon the throne he remained a conspirator at heart. His diplomacy always had a hint of the subterranean about it, and his idea of government was to divide the nation into a multiplicity of factions all bound to him by private understandings while he alone held the strings. There is some justice in this criticism, but the same charge may be leveled with more or less truth against every successful politician. It is but another way of saying that Napoleon was a practicing politician upon a throne, and a very proficient one at that, until his many promises and diverse commitments combined to trip him up.

To win the support of the French Catholics, Louis Napoleon, before his *coup d'état,* had dispatched a military force to Rome to restore the *The Catholics* Papal States to the rule of Pius IX after the outbreaks of 1848. In 1850, the Legislature of the Second Republic passed the Falloux Law which placed French schools under the super-

NAPOLEON III, EMPEROR OF THE FRENCH
1808–1873

*The dull gaze and enigmatic expression which
made Napoleon III seem a sphinx to his contemporaries are well suggested in this portrait.*

vision of the clergy. The panic created by the Socialist agitation in 1848 and 1849 had softened the hostility of the anti-clerical bourgeoisie toward the church and convinced them, as already noted, that religious instruction could best check the spread of radical and subversive doctrines among the masses. So the Empress Eugénie busied herself with Catholic charities, Napoleon posed as the champion of that faith, and felt confident that, so long as he maintained a garrison at Rome to safe-guard the papal dominions and preserved the favored position of the clergy in France, he could count upon Catholic support. Nor was he mistaken.

The bourgeoisie were disposed to endorse any government which promised peace and order. In addressing this class Napoleon disavowed
The bourge- any warlike intentions and promised economic prosperity
oisie and liberty of trade. Through the establishment of a sort of government bank, the *Crédit mobilier*, which lent large sums of money for business projects, Napoleon encouraged the extension of railway, steamship, and telegraph lines. Industry throve, profits mounted, and the business classes applauded the emperor for his sage administration throughout a decade of unparalleled expansion (1850–60). In 1859, on his own authority, Napoleon negotiated a free-trade agreement with Great Britain which speedily doubled French exports, but angered many French manufacturers because it swept away the tariff protection which had shielded them from British competition. Through this interference in trade he had offended a group, numerically small, but powerful in the business world, an omen of the increasing difficulties which were to beset him in the later years of his reign.

The peasants had little fault to find with a régime which protected their religion and assured cheap transportation and a ready market
The peas- for their produce. To them the fifty per cent rise in the
ants and the cost of commodities which came after 1850 proved a bless-
workers ing, for it meant a higher reward for their labors, but to the city working class it meant that food grew dearer while wages lagged. Napoleon succeeded to some extent in raising wages and reduc-ing unemployment by his program of public works, and he sought to combat the evils of poverty by organizing insurance societies which would encourage the poor to save, and by rebuilding the tenement districts at public expense. The government reformed the pawnshops which had preyed upon the poor, the Empress Eugénie devoted herself to charity, the emperor constantly protested his deep concern with social problems. But socialism continued to spread among the city proletariat none the less, for the workers judged the régime less by its promises than by its fruits and saw that too few of the fruits fell to them.

Officers and men in the military services knew that with a Bonaparte at the head of the state they would not be forgotten.   No dictator can afford to estrange his army; Napoleon had relied upon it for *The army* the *coup d'état* of 1851; and the beat of distant drums was to persist like a fateful chorus throughout the twenty years of his reign, growing louder and more ominous as the Second Empire drifted toward the final tragedy of Sedan.   While protesting that the empire meant peace, Napoleon raised the prestige of the army and fed it with expectations.   Nationalists, ashamed of the "peace without honor" policy that had been pursued by the government of Louis Philippe, applauded Napoleon when he dispatched troops to Rome (1849) to prove that France as well as Austria could meddle in the affairs of Italy.   In 1853, he ·sought to please Catholics and nationalists alike by challenging Russia in a dispute over the holy places of Palestine, a controversy which involved France in the Crimean War.[1]   At the same time an aggressive foreign policy led to an extension of the French influence in Algeria, the transformation of Cambodia (in Indo-China) into a protectorate, and the acquisition of islands in the Pacific, so that France came to rank second only to Great Britain as a colonial power, although the penalty of such imperialism was a constant danger of war.   But Napoleon believed in his destiny, and destiny for a Bonaparte spelled war. Despite his own preference for peace and the assurances he had given that he would maintain it, war proved the deciding factor in his fortunes.

3. THE LIBERAL NEMESIS

The emperor's attempts to reconcile all factions failed to win over many clear-sighted intellectuals, or to appease the ardent republicans and socialists.   These groups would not forgive Napoleon his usurpation of power, nor the bloodshed, the arrests, and the deportations by which that illegal usurpation had been consecrated.   Official manipulation of the elections, official supervision of the press, and official suppression of liberal courses in the universities reduced the opponents of the imperial régime to impotence, but intensified their resentment.   France, the liberals held, had betrayed the high cause of Liberty, Equality, and Fraternity, and made herself the slave of one man.   The army, the clergy, and the commercial classes might support Napoleon the Little, as Victor Hugo named him, but an unreconciled minority of his subjects still insisted that his throne was built upon sand and must dissolve in the rising tide of European liberalism.

[1] See below, pages 259–61.

Napoleon was prepared, if he could, to conciliate the liberals also. In 1860, he compromised his absolutism by political concessions and *The Liberal* opened the second phase of his reign, the Liberal Empire. *Empire* A general amnesty for political prisoners freed the bitterest foes of his régime from captivity, an opposition press was permitted to appear, and the Chamber of Deputies gained the right to criticize Napoleon's ministers, to control the budget, and to make public its debates. This ingenious attempt to harmonize absolute with parliamentary government produced little except an opposition party supported by various discontented factions, by Legitimists and Orléanists, by Catholics antagonized when the emperor helped the Italians toward unity, by manufacturers who suffered by the commercial treaty with Great Britain, by the persistent Republican minority and the radical Socialists. Napoleon, prematurely aged, with his health failing, lost his faculty for reconciling discordant elements. He continued to make concessions to the growing liberal demands until his empire had become by 1870 a constitutional monarchy. Still the republicans and socialists harassed him, determined that the throne itself should be overturned and the republic restored. This rising menace which threatened his rule and the succession of his son, the prince imperial, was one reason why Napoleon in 1870 gambled on a war with Prussia in the effort to regain his waning prestige.

But in foreign as in domestic affairs fortune had deserted him after 1860. The subsequent pages will outline the foreign policies of the Second Empire, and endeavor to explain the complex motives which led Napoleon III to seek a war with Russia which added to his prestige, to provoke a war with Austria which added to his perplexities, and to accept a war with Prussia which overturned his throne.

4. THE SECOND EMPIRE AT WAR: THE CRIMEAN CONFLICT
(1854–56)

Throughout the nineteenth century, European statesmen, particularly British statesmen, were haunted by an almost superstitious fear of Russia. The enormous size of the Muscovite Empire, larger in area than all the rest of the European states together, was in itself an alarming reflection. Napoleon's disastrous march on Moscow in 1812 furnished seeming proof of Russian invulnerability, and Alexander I, by his determined stand at the Congress of Vienna, had indicated that the great Slavic power was not yet satiated and lusted for more territory. As if driven by an irresistible pressure, the Russian frontier moved eastward until it reached the Pacific Ocean. By 1860, the province north of the Amur River had been wrested from China, and Vladivostok ("The Conqueror of the East") founded as a Russian port on the Sea of Japan. At the same time Russian armies in the Middle East pressed into Mongolia and overran Turkestan to the borders of Afghanistan and India. In the Near East the shadow of the Russian giant hung like a dark threat above the crumbling Turkish Empire, and the czar's forces waited only for a favorable opportunity to seize Constantinople.

British merchants were convinced that their Mediterranean trade would suffer if Constantinople fell to Russia, and the British people persuaded themselves that an army of Cossacks might soon be pouring through the passes of the Hindu Kush to compete for the control of India. A deeper knowledge of the internal weaknesses of the Russian Empire would have dispelled much of this anxiety, but few western Europeans had traveled there and the czar's subjects could not journey abroad without special permission. So to foreigners Russia remained shrouded with the vague menace which always invests an unknown and unpredictable force.

Even peaceful overtures from Saint Petersburg aroused misgivings. "We have a sick man on our hands," declared Nicholas I in 1853, referring metaphorically to Turkey; and he proposed to the British ambassador that, as chief beneficiaries of the Ottoman bequest, England should establish a claim to Egypt while Russia "inherited" the sultan's Balkan provinces. *Turkey the "sick man" of Europe* The British cabinet doubted the czar's good faith, but Nicholas apparently took their refusal for a diplomatic "yes."

Thereupon Russian armies anticipated the "sick man's" demise by occupying the Turkish provinces of Moldavia and Wallachia [1] and the British government prepared to aid the Turks. Meanwhile, a dispute had developed between France and Russia concerning the claims of Roman Catholic and Greek Orthodox monks to control and exhibit to pilgrims certain holy places in Syria. Napoleon III needed the prestige of a successful war; he was annoyed at Nicholas because the latter had declined to greet him as "my brother" when he made himself Emperor of the French; and he hoped to please the Catholics in France by claiming the right to protect Catholics in Turkey. So Napoleon deliberately fostered a conflict for which there was little cause and no justification, and Britain joined France in order to fight for the preservation of the Ottoman Empire in Europe.

In 1854, the two powers dispatched an expedition to the Black Sea

[1] See map following page 200.

to besiege the Russian fortress of Sebastopol on the Crimean Peninsula. *Siege of Sebastopol* After heavy losses and terrible suffering on both sides, Sebastopol was evacuated by the Russians (September, 1855) and the allies (France, Great Britain, Turkey, and the Kingdom of Sardinia, which had joined them in 1855) agreed to suspend hostilities. The British, who had conducted their share of the war with heavy casualties and tragic inefficiency, would willingly have continued it, but Napoleon III was satisfied with his victory such as it was. As for the Russians, they had never really desired the war, and had been disillusioned by the hostile attitude of the Austrian government, which had accepted Russian aid in crushing the Hungarians (1849), but failed to reciprocate in Russia's hour of need. Gratitude was never a Hapsburg virtue.

So the Crimean War was terminated by a congress of diplomats who met at Paris to work out a new settlement for the Near-Eastern Question. *The Treaty of Paris (1856)* To hold Russia in check the victors ordained: (1) That no great power should construct fortifications or maintain warships in the Black Sea. (2) That Moldavia and Wallachia (modern Rumania), which Russia had occupied in 1853, and later evacuated, should become an autonomous principality while remaining under Turkish suzerainty. (3) That the Danube River should be open to the trading ships of all nations. The Congress of Paris had the further significance of admitting Turkey for the first time to a recognized place in the European concert of nations, and of formulating a "Declaration" defining the rights of neutrals and the question of protecting neutral property in time of war. The attempt to limit the destructiveness of warfare and to impress a respect for certain humane conventions upon all the belligerents marked a distinct advance in the evolution of international law. Though frequently violated since, the "Declaration" of the Congress of Paris, because of the ban it placed upon privateering and the limits it set upon the right of blockade, has proved the most permanent benefit of the war.

For in so far as it represented an attempt to settle the Near-Eastern Question the Treaty of Paris proved a tragic failure. The sultan, after swearing to grant equal justice to his "Christian cattle," conveniently forgot his promise. After a few years Russia coolly ignored the provisions prohibiting armaments on the Black Sea, and a generation later a new congress had to be convoked to protect Turkey from the Russian advance. For this negative result, Britain, France, and Russia had shattered a truce which had restrained the great powers from war with one another for thirty-nine years; for this a sum equivalent to two billion dollars had been poured away, and half a million lives sacrificed to war, disease, and negligence. But Napoleon III had won the honor of presiding over a peace conference in Paris; British traders could sleep more soundly in their beds because for the moment the Russians ceased to threaten Constantinople; and Cavour, who had plunged Sardinia into an alien conflict to gain the friendly interest of Napoleon, could turn that interest to his own astute ends.

A new period of armed conflict had opened in Europe, for the Crimean War proved the first of five struggles which disturbed the great powers between 1853 and 1871. The second, which broke out in 1859, found Napoleon leading an army into Italy to expel the Austrians. Napoleon's reasons for engaging in this Italian war of 1859 were numerous and complicated. His mind was a strange crucible in which generous impulses and humanitarian ideals blended obscurely with dynastic aims and political calculations. As a youth he had campaigned with the Italian patriots in their ill-starred uprising of 1830, and as an emperor he continued to declare his sympathy for suppressed peoples, Poles, Germans, or Italians. To drive the Austrians from Italy and replace their influence by a French hegemony, as the first Napoleon had done, must certainly have appealed to him as an undertaking that would shed luster upon French arms and strengthen his throne. But he took no active steps to aid the liberals in Italy until, in 1858, an impatient Italian patriot named Orsini threw a bomb at his carriage to refresh his memory.

Far from deterring Napoleon, Orsini's conspiracy crystallized his resolution to aid the Italians. He knew that the only state in Italy strong and independent enough to take the offensive in a war to expel the Austrians was the Kingdom of Sardinia. With elaborate secrecy he arranged a meeting with Count Camillo di Cavour, the tireless and far-sighted Sardinian diplomat who was the most ingenious statesman of his time. The two agreed that Austria should be tricked into attacking Sardinia, whereupon a French army of two hundred thousand men would hasten to the aid of the Sardinians. Italy was to be freed from "the Alps to the Adriatic," and France as a reward would annex the province of Savoy and the city of Nice. Privately, Napoleon felt confident that a victory would enable him to make French influence supplant Austrian domination in the Italian Peninsula.

It will be convenient at this point to pause in the discussion of the Second Empire, and turn back to trace the drama of Italian unification up to 1859 in order to appreciate better how skillfully Cavour had prepared the stage for Napoleon's entry.

CHAPTER NINETEEN

THE POLITICAL UNIFICATION OF ITALY

Italy is one nation; unity of customs, language, and literature must in a period more or less distant unite her inhabitants under one sole government, and Rome will without the slightest doubt be chosen by the Italians as their capital.
NAPOLEON I, at Saint Helena.

DISREGARDING the national aspirations which had stirred in Italy during the era of Napoleon I, the Congress of Vienna sought in 1815 to restore the Italian people to that condition of disunity and subjugation under which they had languished before the *Italy in* French Revolution. How well the congress succeeded may *1815* be seen by comparing the status of Italy in 1648 and in 1815. Old states and old governments reappeared, and princes long in exile returned to claim their privileges in the name of legitimacy. In the south Ferdinand I, despicable scion of the Spanish Bourbon line, assumed the crown of the Kingdom of the Two Sicilies. Central Italy, from Rome to Ravenna, was reconstituted as the States of the Church under the temporal rule of Pius VII. In the Grand Duchy of Tuscany and the neighboring duchies of Parma, Lucca, and Modena, petty despots, most of them Hapsburg dependents, returned to their thrones. North of the Po the new map differed slightly from that of 1789, because Austria now held both Lombardy and Venetia, while to the west the congress strengthened the Kingdom of Sardinia by incorporating with it the late republic of Genoa. Those patriotic Italians who cherished the dream of a free and united Italy in 1815 found the prospect disheartening. The nine fragments into which the peninsula had been redivided were not linked by even a loose confederative bond, and most of them were ruled by princes of foreign extraction who had no sympathy for the ideal of Italian unity and independence.

1. THE NATIONAL SPIRIT STIRS (1815–48)

Nevertheless, though the map of Italy might be redrawn on the eighteenth-century model, the Italian people had acquired a new spirit, *National-* new memories, and new ideas. Everywhere in Europe the *ism* revolutionary epoch had quickened national feelings. The Poles, the Germans, and the Italians, who possessed no independent fatherland of their own, had grown fiercely conscious of their right to liberty and unity. In Russia and Spain the appearance of Napoleon's

UNIFICATION
OF ITALY

SCALE OF MILES

0   50   100   150

The dates are those of annexation
to the Kingdom of Sardinia, and after
1861 to the Kingdom of Italy.

armies had aroused the people to deep patriotic resentment. The intensification of the feeling of nationalism during the years of war and revolution made it the most dynamic political force in the modern world. How this vital sentiment can spread among a people, converting them to a belief in their own uniqueness, their common historical and cultural heritage, and their right to political unity and self-government, is well illustrated by the story of the Italians.

The Italian people had never forgotten that in ancient times Rome was the mistress of the known world, and that a thousand years later the scholars and artists of the Renaissance made Italy the "mother of arts." Unfortunately, with the discovery of *The Risorgimento* the New World, Mediterranean trade declined and the Italian cities lost the primacy which they had enjoyed, many of them falling under the thralldom of French, Spanish, or Austrian masters. By the eighteenth century little remained of Italy's former greatness save her "fatal gift of beauty." Yet when Napoleon, to serve his own purposes, sounded the call of Italian freedom, he wakened a spirit which survived his fall. Though subjected again to the rule of foreign despots, Italian patriots refused to abandon their dream of liberty. Secret societies, such as the famous *Carbonari*, plotted against the Austrians; poets and dramatists like Alessandro Manzoni (1785–1873) and Giacomo Leopardi (1798–1837) celebrated the past glories and the undying genius of the Italian people, while all classes felt the stir of a genuine resurrection of the Italian spirit, a rebirth, or *risorgimento*. If Italy could but win liberty and unity, the patriots urged, she would take her merited place among the great nations of the world and lead the march of civilization.

In 1820, the spirit of revolt blazed up in Naples, and in 1821 in Sardinia, but these ill-planned and sporadic outbreaks lacked direction and co-ordination and were easily extinguished by Austrian *Abortive* intervention. Uprisings in Parma, Modena, and the *revolts* Papal States in 1831 produced the same negative results. The conspirators, hunted down by the Austrian police, were sentenced to death or imprisonment. Their failure, however, and their fate, fanned the fervor of other Italians, who perceived more clearly each year that there could be no liberty anywhere in Italy until the Austrian yoke was broken. Their hatred for the Austrians was well depicted by Robert Browning, whose *Italian in England* exclaims:

> I would grasp Metternich until
> I felt his red wet throat distil
> In blood thro' these two hands...

2. THREE CONFLICTING PROJECTS FOR UNIFICATION

The liberals, though eager to end foreign influence, could not agree upon the best form of government to establish in Italy when the nation attained freedom.   Joseph Mazzini, one of the most in-spiring leaders of the *risorgimento* in the years after 1830, hoped to sweep away the vestiges of the separate monarchi-cal states and to found a democratic republic in Italy, and devoted his whole heart to the project.   An idealist swayed by the loftiest motives, Mazzini preached the gospel of liberty and democracy with the ardor of an apostle, proclaiming that humanity stood on the threshold of a golden age, when all peoples, having established free governments, might dwell together in peace and justice.   The English poet Swinburne, in his *Songs Before Sunrise*, hailed Mazzini as

Joseph Mazzini (1805–72)

the world's banner bearer
Who shall cry the republican cry;

but both Swinburne and Mazzini were dreaming of a sunrise that never came.   An ideal society requires ideal citizens, and not even Mazzini's burning faith could endow his fellowmen with the unselfishness, the generosity, and the fair-mindedness of which he believed them capable.

Exiled in 1831 by the Sardinian government for his revolutionary activities, Mazzini organized Young Italy, an association dedicated to the establishment of a free and democratic society in defiance of prelates and princes.   Scores of generous-hearted Italian youths, fired by his eloquence, risked their lives in fruitless insurrections which wasted precious blood without advancing the cause of liberty.   Despite his sincerity and his personal magnetism, Mazzini lacked the qualities of a practical leader.   His unitary demo-cratic state appealed chiefly to the lower classes, for his dogmatic re-publicanism alarmed conservative Italians, and his denunciations of the Catholic faith as an outworn superstition offended many of his orthodox fellow countrymen.

Young Italy

As an alternative to Mazzini's republicanism, many Italians, es-pecially members of the propertied classes and the aristocracy, favored the idea of uniting the states of Italy in a confederation with the pope as president.   This project found an earnest advocate in Vincenzo Gioberti, who wrote a lengthy and widely read work *On the Moral and Civil Supremacy of the Italians* (1843).   The great virtue of Gioberti's plan lay in its solution of what was called "The Roman Question"; that is, the problem of founding a united

The Roman Question

[264]

Italy without antagonizing the pope, who naturally declined to surrender the States of the Church to the rule of a secular government. For centuries it had been the consistent policy of the papacy to oppose the establishment of any government in the Italian Peninsula strong enough to threaten the papal patrimony. By conferring upon the head of the church in perpetuity the office of president of the proposed Italian confederation, it seemed probable that this opposition could be overcome, for in this way the pope could be assured of the power to maintain a theocratic rule in his temporal dominions.

The election to the papal chair of the winning and charitable Pius IX (1846) gave a powerful stimulus to the plan. Pius opened his pontificate by an amnesty for many political offenders, dismissed his Swiss Guard, and appointed popular ministers to his council. These reforms won him an enthusiastic *Accession of Pius IX (1846–78)* following, particularly among liberal Catholics who were good churchmen and also good friends of Italian independence. But republicans and anti-clericals expressed a doubt that the pope's liberalism could be either deep or sincere, and continued to work for a secular state without religious affiliations.

Advocates of yet a third project of unification looked to the Kingdom of Sardinia [1] to lead the movement. As the only independent Italian principality ruled by a native dynasty, the Piedmontese state enjoyed a unique position in Italy. With *The Sardinian Party* its hard-working peasantry, influential middle class, and well-trained army, it ranked as a third-class power, and might aspire to play the rôle in Italy which Prussia was playing in the Germanies. Ardent revolutionaries like Mazzini distrusted the Sardinian king, the enigmatic Charles Albert (1831–49), believing him a traitor to liberal ideals because he had refused his subjects a constitution and hesitated to challenge Austria in a war for Italian liberation. To a large body of moderate liberals, however, the thought of unifying their country under the sober-minded Sardinian king seemed an admirable solution, for what they most desired for Italy was a secular government that would be independent of Austrian and of papal influence. Believing in the old Latin proverb that middle roads are safest, such men could be counted upon to support the Sardinian government if it steered a sane middle course between radical republicanism and clerical domination.

[1] The student should understand clearly that "Kingdom of Sardinia" refers not to the island but to Savoy and the Piedmont. See the map following page 262.

3. THE DEFEATED HOPES OF 1848–49

At the opening of 1848, that year of revolutions which saw the throne of Louis Philippe overturned in Paris and Metternich driven from *Italian* office by an outbreak in Vienna, Italy was shaken by spon-*uprisings* taneous revolts from Venice to Sicily. Charles Albert at *of 1848* Turin, Ferdinand II at Naples, Pius IX at Rome, and the Grand Duke of Tuscany at Florence, all endeavored to pacify their rebellious subjects by granting constitutions. Nationalism and liberalism seemed on the point of obtaining a mutual triumph as the Venetian populace expelled the Austrian garrison and established a republic under the liberator Daniel Manin, while at Milan leaders of the national movement proclaimed the independence of Lombardy. The Austrian government was paralyzed at home by revolts in Vienna, Bohemia, and Hungary,[1] and this knowledge encouraged the Italians to attempt a general war of independence. Even the papal and Sicilian governments yielded to the popular fervor and contributed detachments to swell the gathering army of liberation.

With belated zeal, Charles Albert of Sardinia rallied to the head of the national movement. *"L'Italia farà da se"* (Italy will do it *"Italy will* herself) he announced proudly, and launched his army *do it her-* against the retreating Austrians. But the weakness and *self"* the unharmonized ideals of the Italians betrayed them. As the first flush of enthusiasm passed, the papal and Neapolitan contingents were recalled, for Pius IX and Ferdinand of Naples recollected their duties to the side of tradition and legitimacy. At the same time, the Austrians, rallying strongly under their octogenarian field marshal, Radetsky, defeated Charles Albert's mixed forces at Custozza (July 24, 1848). With the failure of moderate leadership, the more radical of the Italian insurgents swung to the left and set up republics (1849) in Florence and Rome. Pius IX fled from the Vatican as Rome passed under the control of a popular government headed by Mazzini and defended by the tireless knight of liberty, Giuseppe Garibaldi.

But the Italian people were unprepared for a sharp transition to democracy, and the Roman Republic could hardly have survived in *Collapse of* any case amid the general reaction of 1849. Its death *the republi-* warrant, however, was signed by Louis Napoleon, newly *can move-* elected president of the Second French Republic, who *ment (1849)* dispatched an expeditionary force to Rome which overcame the heroic resistance of Garibaldi's republican guard and re-

[1] See above, pages 247–48.

established the papal government by means of French bayonets. At the same time Austria aided the lesser Italian despots to remount their thrones and revoke the constitutional guaranties which they had granted in the first months of the popular movement. By the close of the year 1849, the most determined and widespread effort yet made to free Italy from foreign oppression and domestic tyranny had ended in the blackest failure.

Yet one Italian state conserved its dignity even in defeat. Crushed by the Austrians at Custozza, and a second time at Novara (March 23, 1849), Charles Albert resigned his throne to his son Victor Emmanuel II, who concluded a hard treaty with the victors. *Sardinia remains independent* One concession, however, the new king refused to make. Neither by threats nor by promises of easier terms could the Austrians induce Victor Emmanuel to revoke the Sardinian *Statuto*, or constitution, proclaimed the previous year. This loyalty to a contract which other princes were breaking without a qualm won for him the title "the honest king" and endeared him to all Italians who hated the despotism of Austria.

Two lessons might be drawn from the failures of 1848–49. The first suggested that neither the Republican nor the Clerical Party would succeed in uniting Italy. The collapse of the Roman Republic left Mazzini and his colleagues, not exactly *Republicans and Clericals lose ground* leaders without a party, but certainly leaders of a discouraged and diminished party. The Catholic liberals, on the other hand, now found themselves a party without a leader, for Pius IX had returned to Rome completely cured of his liberal sympathies. With the party of the Right and the party of the Left losing ground, it became clear that the party of the Center might yet win the day, and make the Kingdom of Sardinia the nucleus of a resurrected Italy. This was the first lesson to be learned from the events of 1848–49. But there was a second conclusion to be realized, a bitter one for Italian patriots to accept. Italy could not "do it herself." The Italian people possessed neither the forces nor the co-operation needed to drive out the Austrians; to attempt the task unaided was to invite further failure. Fortunately for the cause of Italian freedom, there was at least one statesman in Italy capable of appreciating both these lessons. His name was Camillo di Cavour.

4. CAVOUR CONTRIVES

Cavour was born in Turin in 1810, the second son of a noble family. After graduating from military school at the age of sixteen, he obtained

a commission in the Sardinian army, but his dabblings in liberalism
Camillo di and his indiscreet comments upon the backward political
Cavour condition prevailing in Piedmont got him into trouble, and
(1810–61) after a brief imprisonment he resigned his commission.
His liberalism had made him a marked man, and the Austrian police
in nearby states were warned that he was "deeply corrupted in his
political principles." From 1831 to 1848 he pursued private interests,
experimented with new methods of agriculture, studied, traveled, and
accumulated a fortune, but his mind was constantly absorbed with
political affairs in which he was denied a part. Then, in 1848, conditions changed abruptly. Charles Albert granted his subjects a constitution, and Cavour was elected to the recently created Sardinian
Parliament. In 1850, the new king, Victor Emmanuel II, appointed
him minister of commerce and agriculture, an office which permitted
him to display at once his extraordinary grasp of political and economic
questions.

Few people would have guessed from Cavour's appearance that he
was one of the dominant personalities of the nineteenth century. With
his stocky figure, plain garb, and metal-rimmed spectacles, he looked
a shopkeeper or clerk. His life-purpose was to free Italy and give the
Italian people a parliamentary government on the liberal English
pattern, but he made no passionate speeches about the rights of man
like Mazzini, nor did he lead the van of hopeless and heroic charges
like the fearless Garibaldi. His unique talent consisted in his ability
to grasp realities, to move only as fast as events permitted, to take
practical advantage of the political forces at work in Europe and quietly
direct them to his own ends.

The first step in Cavour's program was to make the Sardinian Kingdom known as a liberal and prosperous state to which all other Italians
Cavour's would look with pride and envy. His wide study and
ministry observance had made him an authority on commerce and
agriculture, on railroads, finance, the methods of parliamentary government, and the conduct of foreign affairs. Once in office he pushed
his reforms with implacable deliberation. The Sardinian Parliament
ordained that marriage should become a civil contract, and forbade
the gift of further property to the church, a policy aimed at curbing the
influence of the clergy. Commercial treaties with other nations and
a revision of the tariffs benefited the poorer classes. While assiduously
cultivating the friendship of France and Britain, Cavour maintained
a firm and cool attitude toward Austria, so that Sardinia came to be
recognized as a state guided by liberal counsels where men dared to

CAMILLO DI CAVOUR
1810–61

*Cavour was often careless in his dress, and his appearance
was not impressive, but he proved himself the most astute
and successful diplomat of his day.*

plan the liberation of Italy. This was precisely the impression Cavour wished to convey to the discontented citizens in other Italian provinces, and to Mazzini's republican insurgents.

Few of Cavour's contemporaries understood the intricacies of his foreign policy, yet his aim was comparatively simple. Believing that *Cavour finds* the Italians must have the aid of a great power to help *an ally* them to expel the Austrians, he sought for such an ally and found it in France. How he joined Britain and France in the Crimean War has been mentioned already.[1] Sardinia had no real quarrel with Russia, but the intervention won Cavour a seat at the peace conference in Paris, where he had an opportunity to impress Napoleon III and to bring the Italian question before the European diplomats. Three years later, Cavour and Napoleon held a secret interview at Plombières, and the stage was set for the War of Italian Liberation. Napoleon insisted upon two stipulations: Austria must appear to be the aggressor, and France must receive the county of Savoy and the city of Nice as compensation for the aid rendered. Cavour hated to sacrifice a portion of the Piedmontese realm, but he knew that the population in the disputed sections was more French than Italian, and that France could not be expected to fight a war for pure altruism. Cavour was a realist.

A policy of astute provocation incited Austria to declare war against the Kingdom of Sardinia in April, 1859, and Napoleon III fulfilled his promise by leading an army of two hundred thousand men into Italy. But after the Austrians had been driven from Lombardy in the bloody battles of Magenta and Solferino, and half Europe feared to see the French emperor follow up his successes as brilliantly as his uncle had done sixty years earlier, Napoleon III suddenly abandoned the campaign and signed a truce with the Austrians.

What were the motives which moved Napoleon to end the war before Italy had been freed from "the Alps to the Adriatic"? Well, for one *Napoleon* thing, he had been appalled by the carnage of the battle-*abandons* fields. A second and weightier reason was the growing *the war* hostility of the Prussian government which had mobilized its army and could threaten France with an attack on the Rhine. Then, too, Napoleon had come to suspect that he had underrated the strength of the Italian movement for independence, which now seemed likely to create, not a loose Italian federation which he could dominate, but a unified state which might menace France in the south. Finally, if the Italians succeeded in forming a united kingdom, they would

[1] See above, pages 260–61.

seek to include Rome as their capital, a course which must deprive the pope of his temporal possessions and cause French Catholics to blame Napoleon for endangering the papal patrimony after he had promised to safeguard it.

Accordingly, to prevent the developments from outrunning his aims, Napoleon made peace with the Austrian emperor, Francis Joseph (Truce of Villafranca). As the Austrian forces remained strongly entrenched in the circle of fortresses known as the Quadrilateral (Mantua, Peschiera, Verona, and Legnago), Francis Joseph could still bargain, and although he agreed to surrender Lombardy he insisted that the rulers of Modena and Tuscany should retain their thrones. The two emperors also decided to promote the formation of an Italian federation under the presidency of the pope, a step which Napoleon counted upon to placate the French Catholics.

Overwhelmed with disappointment at this desertion of his ally before the successful completion of a war from which he had hoped so much, Cavour for once lost his good sense, demanded *Enlarge-* that Sardinia carry on the struggle alone, and, when Victor *ment of the* Emmanuel prudently refused, threw up his office. Equally *Sardinian* *Kingdom* chagrined at the developments, but more level-headed, the Sardinian monarch acquiesced in the terms arranged at Villafranca, which at least promised to bring him Lombardy. But this inadequate settlement, so galling to Italian pride, was destined to be speedily superseded. Seized with patriotic enthusiasm, the people of Parma and Modena, as well as the population of the Romagna, in the Papal States, voted for unification with the Kingdom of Sardinia. The Romagna formed part of the patrimony ruled by Pius IX, which Napoleon had agreed to protect. Nevertheless, he offered to approve the enlargement of the Sardinian Kingdom on condition that France obtain Savoy and Nice, for, although he had failed to keep his full promise made to Cavour, Napoleon still desired his reward. After the inhabitants of the districts concerned had signified their approval through plebiscites, France incorporated Savoy and Nice, while Sardinia annexed Lombardy, Tuscany, Parma, Modena, and the Romagna (Treaty of Turin, 1860).

Cavour, recovering from the bitter mood into which Napoleon's separate negotiations had driven him, returned to office in time to complete these diplomatic exchanges with a masterly hand. His policy, though not wholly successful, since Venice still remained to the Austrians, had doubled the area and population of the Sardinian Kingdom. But many patriots, Garibaldi among them, denounced him as a traitor because he had relinquished Savoy and Nice to France.

5. GARIBALDI MARCHES

Giuseppe Garibaldi (1807–82) ranks with Mazzini and Cavour as the third in the great triumvirate of Italian liberators. While still in *Giuseppe* his twenties he joined Young Italy, and plunged, with *Garibaldi* the courage of a lion and the heart of a child, into the war *(1807–82)* against tyrants. In 1834, he was sentenced to death, but escaped to South America, where he fought for the liberty of alien republics until the outbreaks of 1848 afforded him another chance to strike a blow for Italy. The following year he defended Mazzini's Roman Republic, and barely escaped with his life, to resume his career of adventure and exile. The War of 1859 found him back in Italy, leading a free-lance company against the Austrians once more. The involutions of politics and the sagacious statesmanship of Cavour he neither understood nor approved. What he did understand was the nobility of taking up arms in the cause of liberty and fighting side by side with honest men. An alliance with a despot like Napoleon III, or the bargain by which Cavour traded Nice to France, appeared to Garibaldi, who had been born in Nice, an act of treason.

It is not surprising, therefore, that when Cavour wished to rest in 1860 and consolidate the Sardinian gains, Garibaldi insisted that the *"The* struggle must continue until all Italy was free. Organiz- *Thousand"* ing an expedition, the famous "One Thousand," he sailed from Genoa on May 5, to attack the Kingdom of the Two Sicilies. Francis II (1859–61) had an army of over one hundred thousand men, but many of his subjects hated him and his soldiers were half-hearted in their allegiance. Within six months Garibaldi's "red shirts" had conquered the island of Sicily in the name of Victor Emmanuel, and crossing to Naples they entered the city in triumph on September 7, after Francis II had fled. The south of Italy had been won for the Italian Kingdom, and the next step, logically, was to march on Rome. But Cavour, fearing that such an affront to the pope must bring a French army to his rescue, frustrated Garibaldi's impetuosity. With the tacit consent of Napoleon III, Victor Emmanuel led a Sardinian force across papal territory into the Neapolitan State, and completed the conquest of it; but at the same time he eased the tension by taking the leadership out of Garibaldi's hands. It is possible Garibaldi felt somewhat slighted, for, although he agreed to drive through the streets of Naples with Victor Emmanuel, the only favor he asked for his great services was that Cavour should be dismissed, and when this was refused, he retired to his farm on the island of Caprera.

[272]

By the close of 1860, Sicily, Naples, and the papal provinces known as the Marches and Umbria,[1] had voted for union with the other states now ruled by Victor Emmanuel, and the following March *Death of* the Sardinian monarch was proclaimed king of a united *Cavour* Italy, although the kingdom remained incomplete. But *(1861)* the enormous labor, the hopes and the disappointments of the crowded years 1859 to 1861 had exhausted Cavour, and he died on June 6, 1861. In his last hours he consoled himself with the thought, *L'Italia è fatta* — Italy is made.

6. THE WINNING OF VENICE AND ROME

Italy was made, but it was not yet complete, for the papal government still ruled at Rome and the Austrians held Venetia. The successors of Cavour had to wait for a favorable moment to add these "unredeemed" segments to the Italian Kingdom. One such chance came in 1866, when Prussia fought Austria in the "Seven Weeks' War." [2] The Prussian statesman Bismarck arranged an alliance with the new Italian Kingdom, which joined in the attack and attempted to seize Venetia. Although they were defeated by the Austrians on both land and sea, the Italians received Venetia for their assistance when the triumphant Prussians negotiated the Treaty of Prague after their victory over the Austrians at Königgrätz.

To crown the new kingdom by the acquisition of Rome as its capital had now become "an inexorable necessity." Twice Garibaldi led a force of volunteers to seize the Eternal City, but he was *Occupation* checked by Victor Emmanuel's troops (wounded "by an *of Rome* Italian bullet" he complained) on the first attempt (1862), *(1870)* and defeated by the French garrison at Rome on the second (1867). Diplomacy seemed powerless to achieve a settlement of the "Roman Question," yet the Italian government feared that if the pope were dispossessed by force he might summon the Catholic nations to his assistance. In 1870, however, the outbreak of the Franco-Prussian War directed international attention elsewhere, and compelled Napoleon III to recall the French guard at Rome for home defense. The moment was too auspicious to overlook. On September 20, 1870, Italian troops marched into Rome, and the citizens voted, by a majority of 134,000 to 1500, for incorporation into the Italian Kingdom. Cavour's great project had been completed nine years after his death.

[1] See map following page 262.
[2] See below, pages 282–83.

7. THE ROMAN CATHOLIC CHURCH IN THE NINETEENTH CENTURY

Stripped of his temporal possessions, Pope Pius IX retired within the environs of the Vatican, where he chose to regard himself as a prisoner. In 1871, the Italian Parliament passed a Law of Papal Guaranties recognizing him as a sovereign within this tiny domain, and offering him a sum equal to $650,000 as compensation for the territory which had been seized. This offer Pius refused, and he and his successors [1] preferred to remain voluntary prisoners rather than recognize a government which they regarded as guilty of an act of inexcusable and illegal usurpation.

From the days of the great French Revolution, when the National Assembly confiscated the church lands in France, the papacy had shown

Conflict of liberalism and clericalism itself more opposed than ever to liberal and revolutionary doctrines. After the Congress of Vienna restored the States of the Church, which Napoleon had seized, to the rule of Pius VII, the church allied itself with the conservative governments of Europe during the Era of Reaction. Catholics were warned to be on their guard against the seduction of liberal notions, which, as experience had recently proved, often led to revolution and tragic social excesses. Yet, although liberals were denounced as atheists and enemies of society, liberal and national ferment continued to spread despite all efforts at repressing it. The outbreaks of 1848 and 1849, which shook conservative governments everywhere and drove Pius IX from Rome, not unnaturally convinced him that all revolutionists, whether they called themselves liberals, socialists, or republicans, were a menace to the established order. Nor was the pope alone in this opinion. Napoleon III greatly strengthened the position of the Roman Catholic clergy in France as the best defense against socialism. The Austrian government signed a *concordat* with the papacy (1855), and several lesser states restored to the clergy the control which they had previously exercised in matters of censorship and education. The panic over socialism which followed the revolutions of 1848 had modified the hostile attitude of the bourgeoisie toward the church. The clergy, it was now felt, might prove invaluable allies in the combat with radical thinkers, who were misleading the people by their attacks upon religion and their demands for the confiscation of private property. When the liberals, socialists, and other rebels who dreamed of remaking society found the church entrenched upon the side of the propertied

[1] Until 1929, see pages 458–59.

classes and the established governments, they assailed it as the greatest obstacle to progress, and denounced it much as the eighteenth-century *philosophes* had done. Throughout the greater part of the nineteenth century, the liberals were inclined, not without reason, to regard the clericals as their most ingenious and most consistent foes.

The policies of Pius IX (1846–78) did much to confirm this widespread impression that the church would always be found on the side of the conservatives and the reactionaries. In 1864, Pius *Pontificate* issued an encyclical, *Quanta cura*, accompanied by a *Syllabus* *of Pius IX* *of Errors*, in which he reaffirmed the independence of the Catholic Church and its supremacy over all secular governments, condemned all those who favored granting toleration to other sects, those who advocated civil marriage, lay schools, or curtailment of the privileges of the clergy, and those who sought to deprive the pope of his temporal possessions. Pius thus arrayed the church against liberalism and nationalism, the dominant social and political ideals of the day, at a time when a more cautious and more conciliatory diplomat might well have hesitated to antagonize and add to the anti-clerical forces.

For the opponents of organized religion in the middle of the nineteenth century had already opened a fierce and dangerous attack from another quarter. The spread of scientific doctrines con- *Growth of* cerning the age of the earth and the origin of man [1] ap- *skepticism* peared to contradict the teaching of the church, while a *and agnosti-* more critical study of history and of comparative religion *cism* led many people even in Catholic countries to question the authority of the pope, to deny the validity of religious dogmas concerning the fall of man and the divine revelations of the Gospels, to repudiate, in fact, the whole structure of theology, which supported the Christian faith, as a complicated mythology inadmissible to minds steeped in the truths of science. In every country a growing number of people, especially among the educated classes, found their faith weakened, and many became frank agnostics or atheists in matters of religion.

In meeting this attack upon the intellectual front, Pius IX displayed the same firmness and consistency which had inspired his unequivocal condemnation of so many political and social currents of *Vatican* the age. The sharpest answer to those who presumed to *Council* question the papal authority was furnished by the Vatican *(1869–70)* Council which met at Rome in 1869. Before it was prorogued in 1870, the council declared it to be a dogma "divinely revealed" that when the pope officially pronounced upon a question of faith cr morals he

[1] See below, pages 323–24.

was endowed with infallibility. Thus, in the same year that his temporal possessions were reft away, Pius IX was invested with spiritual claims as absolute as any exercised by his mighty predecessors Gregory VII or Innocent III in the Middle Ages.

To the theologians who proclaimed it, the dogma of papal infallibility was a definition of, not an addition to, the papal prerogatives. *Leo XIII* Among the laity, particularly among non-Catholics, it *(1878–1903)* excited opposition, distrust, and ridicule. The *Kulturkampf* in Germany, the breach between the Italian government and the papacy, and the conflict of church and state in France, as well as the feuds of clericals and anti-clericals elsewhere, were all intensified by the misapprehensions aroused by the papal claims. To Leo XIII, who succeeded Pius IX in 1878, fell the task of healing estrangements and harmonizing the position of the church with the existing forces and realities of the modern age. While retracting nothing, Leo endeavored with tact and skill, and with considerable success, to reveal the possibility of a working compromise on the political and intellectual issues which had separated the church from most of the secular governments and dug a gulf between religion and science. The careers of Louis Pasteur and Gregor Mendel were cited as proof that it was possible to be a great scientist and a good Catholic, and the Vatican archives were opened to accredited historians in the hope that a more thorough study of the early centuries of the church would tend to reconcile the secular with the orthodox interpretations. In this way part of the opposition to clerical authority was skillfully dissipated, and the opening years of the twentieth century found the Roman Catholic Church performing its historic mission with renewed vigor, to the surprise of many prophets who had been prepared thirty years earlier to predict its imminent collapse.

CHAPTER TWENTY

THE FORMATION OF THE GERMAN EMPIRE

*... Not by speeches and majority votes are the great questions of the day decided
— that was the mistake of 1848 and 1849 — but by blood and iron.*

OTTO VON BISMARCK.

THE panic which seized the governing classes throughout Europe during the revolutionary outbreaks of 1848 and 1849 made itself felt with particular force in the Germanies. After 1849, the Austrian government, strengthened by its military victories over the Italians and the Hungarians, turned its forces to the congenial and familiar task of stamping out the last embers of revolt. The proposals for German unification sponsored by the Frankfort Assembly had fallen to the ground, largely because of Austrian hostility to the project; and a Prussian scheme to organize a federation of states excluding Austria met with the same haughty opposition, with the result that Prussia abandoned the plan (Humiliation of Olmütz, 1850). In 1851 the old inept Diet of the Germanic Confederation of 1815 resumed its sessions, and the Austrian chancellor, Schwarzenberg (Metternich's successor), advised the German princes how best to cancel the liberties which they had conceded to their subjects during the popular turmoil of 1848. In the test of strength between Prussia and Austria, for leadership in central Europe, the hesitant Frederick William IV (1840–61) had been steadily outmatched by the purposeful Schwarzenberg, and the Prussians, unprepared for war, had been forced to concede the dominance of Austria and to stomach a diplomatic defeat.

1. THE DECADE OF REPRESSION AFTER 1848

For German liberals the decade from 1850 to 1860 was a tragic era. Their books censored, their letters opened, their homes searched, they endured the bitterness of official persecution until many of them were literally hounded out of the country because of their political convictions. Hardest to bear of all their misfortunes was the knowledge of their failure. They had come so near to establishing a constitutional government in a united Germany that the reaction covered them with the blacker discredit. Convinced in their disillusionment that democracy could never thrive in the poisoned soil of Europe, with its rooted prejudices and ancient hatreds, thousands emigrated to shape their lives anew in the freer air of the New World. Of these many found homes in

[277]

the United States and contributed in substantial fashion to the growth of the American Republic.

Those who remained behind found that a change came over the spirit of their dream. A harder note of cynicism, a readiness to face essential facts, replaced the tendency toward metaphysical specula-*The German spirit changes* tion and sentimental eloquence which had paralyzed the Frankfort Assembly. The German people had long been noted for the dreamy and philosophical bent of their thought. "The English inhabit the sea, the French the earth, and the Germans the air," Napoleon observed at the opening of the nineteenth century. But after 1850 a more practical and realistic tone asserted itself in Germany. Scientific experiments attracted a generation which had lost faith in philosophical vagaries; business prosperity and the progress of industry opened a new avenue of advance to a people depressed by the frustration of their national hopes. The common-sense methods by which Cavour fused the Italian states together made a deep impression upon the Germans, who perceived more and more clearly that Prussia was the only state strong enough to play for them the rôle assumed by Sardinia in the drama of Italian liberation. Able historians, such as Johann Gustav Droysen and Heinrich von Sybel, wrote scholarly works extolling Prussian achievements in peace and war, and the conviction grew, among nationalist groups, that the Hohenzollern rulers of Prussia had been chosen by the logic of history to lead the cause of German unity. Liberals might still plead the principles of democracy and urge the German people to unify themselves, but the liberals were losing ground, while the national cause, drawing its strength from other and more conservative sources, forged steadily ahead.

It is true that after 1858 the spirit of repression abated somewhat, but liberals gained little by the change. William I, who succeeded his brother on the Prussian throne in 1861 (he had been regent since 1858), possessed a more open mind than Frederick William IV and a firmer character, but he had no less faith in authority. Austria, defeated in the Italian War of 1859, still championed the cause of reaction, though with diminished prestige. Yet the tide was slowly turning in favor of the German nationalists and they renewed their efforts with zeal. The business classes in particular, aware of the advantages they would derive from closer political ties, worked for the day when Germany, as a great power, would acquire the position and the prestige to safeguard and extend their commercial interests at home and abroad. But before unification could be achieved the Germans had to reckon with Austria and France, and the reckoning was to be settled on the battlefield.

2. THE EXPANSION OF GERMAN INDUSTRY

Industrially, Germany had lagged behind Great Britain and France; the people had remained conservative because German society, as late as the middle of the nineteenth century, was still dominated by agricultural and feudal concepts. But the decade 1850–60 saw the beginning of a dynamic change. Banks were organized, factories built, new railway lines transected the countryside, and Old-World towns expanded into modern cities. If the Industrial Revolution came late to Germany, it made up for the delay by its unparalleled acceleration. All the available statistics reflect the same trend after 1850, but as the major effects of the industrial awakening were not felt until the last decades of the century they will be described in a later chapter.

Of the many factors which combined to promote this mid-century prosperity in the German lands, the *Zollverein* or customs union deserves mention because it reduced internal trade barriers, while the *Rise of* gold discoveries in California (1848) and Australia (1851) *German* provided an increase in bullion and tended to raise prices by *industry* making gold cheaper. Eager to take advantage of advancing prices, industrialists borrowed the money which was readily available, to install newly invented machinery and adopt improved processes for speeding manufacture, and the general prosperity of the period encouraged such speculation and richly rewarded the business enterprise of the rising capitalists. The German people made excellent industrial workers, for they were frugal, diligent, patient, and intelligent. They showed special aptitude for the technical trades, and the schools hastened to equip the young with the practical knowledge required in their elected professions. In every field of manufacturing technique, research specialists collaborated with the business men, until the Germans excelled the British, the French, and the Americans in the fruitful alliance which they developed between modern science and modern industry.

Politically, the influence exerted by the new industrialists became a powerful force working for national unity. As business men, the manufacturers, mine-owners, steel barons, and railway builders desired the uniformity of laws, of taxes, tariffs, postal service, currency, weights and measures, which would follow political union, and they desired even more the support and protection in foreign lands which a powerful government could command for them. Familiar, moreover, with the traditional efficiency, economy, and vigor of the Prussian administrative system, the leaders of trade and manufacture were disposed to favor the establishment of a national government under the initiative of Prussia and on the Prussian model.

3. THE PRUSSIAN SYSTEM

What was this Prussian system to which its advocates pointed with such admiration? Since the days of the Great Elector (1640–88) the government of Brandenburg-Prussia had been a military and bureaucratic despotism in the best sense of the term. Supported by loyal and intelligent officials and a resolute army, the Hohenzollerns had transformed their scattered heritage into a powerful, well-governed state. Defeated and humbled by Napoleon, the Prussian ruling class profited by the lessons of adversity, rooted out abuses and remodeled the army, with the result that Prussia emerged after 1815 with territory increased and prestige restored. Yet how could this small kingdom continue to play the rôle of a great power when its population was less than eleven millions, its lands divided and largely unfertile, its industries backward, its merchant marine undeveloped? The answer was to be found in the Prussian System. A scrupulous economy in every department of government provided a surplus for the exorbitant expense of a first-class army, conscripted by compulsory military service. Even in time of peace Prussia became a state disciplined for war, a militarized machine served by competent officers and obedient subordinates. The ranks were filled by the peasants, laborers, and artisans; the officers and administrators were drawn chiefly from the noble landowning families of East Prussia (the "Junker" class) or from the bourgeois group of the cities. At the threat of war the Prussian armies could take the field and strike with swift and deadly precision; but in a prolonged struggle the kingdom was certain to suffer from its lack of economic resources.

This inescapable deficiency in its economic reserves partly explains the inactivity of Prussia after the Napoleonic Wars: it was the quiescence of *Prussian* recuperation. From 1815 to 1848, Austria dominated the *Constitution* Germanies and Prussia followed the Austrian lead. But a *deceptive* rift developed between the two states in 1849 when Frederick William IV granted his subjects a constitution and maintained it in force despite Austrian disapproval. As a constitutional state and leader of the *Zollverein* (which excluded Austria) Prussia made a stronger appeal to German liberal and national sentiment than the Vienna régime, which was dedicated to reaction and anchored in the past. It is an error, however, to imagine that Prussia had become liberal in any true sense: the government remained intrinsically an enlightened military despotism.   Under the new constitution the parliament consisted of an elected (but not truly representative) Chamber of Deputies and a permanent upper Chamber, but its powers remained exceedingly dubious.[1]   The king continued to rule "by the grace of God" and retained the right to choose his ministers.   He could levy established taxes, but could not impose new ones.   Such an ill-defined compromise between king and parliament, between responsible government and absolute despotism, invited a crisis to determine on which side the real authority lay.   The test came when William I ascended the Prussian throne in 1861, a test the outcome of which profoundly influenced the future of Prussia, of Germany, and of Europe.

A soldier's training had confirmed in the mind of William I the belief that authority should come from above, and had given him a special fondness for the army.   While still regent he nominated *King* vs. Hellmuth von Moltke head of the Prussian general staff and *parliament* Albrecht von Roon minister of war, and these inspired appointments demonstrated his shrewd knowledge of men.   In 1860, he approved a plan to reduce exemptions under the military service law and double the reserve period for conscripts, thereby increasing the Prussian army to 190,000 men in peace-time and 450,000 in war.   The Chamber of Deputies fought this project stubbornly, agreed finally to vote the extra appropriation it necessitated for one year, but refused to extend it in 1862. Rather than yield on a measure which he considered indispensable if Prussia was to fulfill the destiny marked out for her, William I was prepared to resign his throne.   His resignation had been already written out when he changed his mind and determined to hold resolutely to his course.   For he had found a minister, Otto von Bismarck, who shared his views and was prepared to defy popular opinion and overrule the parliament in order to carry through the military reforms.

4. OTTO VON BISMARCK (1815–98)

The Bismarck family, dwellers in the Elbe Valley since the fourteenth century, had furnished many capable soldiers and servants of the state. The future chancellor of the German Empire inherited his faith in absolutism and militarism from ancestors who had learned to venerate those principles under the Great Elector and Frederick the Great.   Even during the liberal days of 1848 and 1849, the young Bismarck remained a frank reactionary, openly voicing his contempt for parliamentary govern-

[1] See above, page 246.

ment and his admiration for the inflexible conservatism of the Austrian régime.

But this admiration faded when, as Prussian ambassador to the Diet of the Germanic Confederation, Bismarck studied Austrian diplomacy at closer range. Between 1851 and 1858 he came to view a war between Austria and Prussia for control of the Germanies as inevitable, and he pressed toward it so fervently that William I (then regent) "put him on ice," as he expressed it, by transferring him to Saint Petersburg. As ambassador to Russia, Bismarck set himself to strengthen the friendly feelings between Prussia and Russia, for he knew how invaluable the czar's friendship would be to the Prussians when the moment came for them to fight Austria.

Such was the determined and experienced man whom William I appointed as his chief minister in the crisis of 1862. For the next four *Bismarck's* years Bismarck overrode the opposition of the Prussian *methods* parliament, muzzled the press, and took from the treasury the funds required for army reform. Few men have been so fiercely denounced, so bitterly hated and vilified, but attempts at impeachment and even at assassination left him unmoved. He had set his talents to the task of making Prussia supreme in Germany and Germany supreme in Europe, and he held no illusion that such a triumph could be achieved by compromise or persuasion. The great questions of the day, he affirmed in a statement which became famous, were settled "by blood and iron."

5. THE AUSTRO-PRUSSIAN WAR

With such a man directing Prussian policy it is not surprising that the German Empire was forged in the flame of war, of three wars, in fact, all *The Danish* fought within a period of six years. In the first conflict *War (1864)* Austria and Prussia united to wrest the provinces of Schleswig and Holstein from Denmark, cutting with the sword of war a Gordian knot of tangled diplomatic claims. The two duchies, though peopled largely by Germans, had long been subject to the Danish kings. But in 1864 they were overrun by the Austro-Prussian forces despite a courageous resistance, and Christian IX of Denmark had to relinquish his claims to the conquerors (Treaty of Vienna, 1864).

Although they had united temporarily for the purpose of despoiling Denmark, Austria and Prussia fell to quarreling again after the conclusion of peace. A sharp dispute over the disposal to be made of the conquered duchies brought them to an open breach in 1866. Austria controlled the Diet of the Germanic Confederation and could count upon support from the South German States. Prussia had a secret alliance with Italy, but even so the odds appeared to be against her, and few people doubted that Austria, so much superior in wealth, area, and population, would have the victory. But the Prussian troops carried a newly invented "needle gun" which was three times as deadly as the old muzzle-loading type, and their tactics were devised by the greatest strategist of the age, Hellmuth von Moltke. What followed was a stunning demonstration of Prussian efficiency. Austria's German allies proved of little assistance, for the capitals of Hanover, Saxony, and Cassel fell within two weeks; the opposition of Bavaria, Württemberg, Baden, and Hesse-Darmstadt collapsed almost as swiftly. Three Prussian columns converged upon the Austrian army in Bohemia and shattered it on July 3, 1866, in the decisive battle of Königgrätz. Within five weeks the war was virtually at an end.

The Seven Weeks' War (1866)

Instead of marching on to Vienna, Bismarck persuaded William I to offer Austria a generous peace. By the Treaty of Prague (August 23, 1866) the Italians, who had collaborated by attacking the Austrians in Venetia, received that province for their assistance;[1] Prussia annexed Schleswig and Holstein; and the Germanic Confederation was formally dissolved, leaving Prussia to control the Germanies. Bismarck spared the Hapsburgs all undue humiliation, anticipating a time when the friendship of Austria might prove helpful to his projects. Wisely he forbore to prolong the conflict or to take ruthless advantage of a victory which had already alarmed the other powers. Napoleon III, lulled into neutrality by the half-promise of Belgium or other territorial compensation on the Rhine, realized over-late that he had missed a rare chance to hold the scales between the combatants. To retrieve prestige he began to press for his "concessions," and Bismarck, who had no real intention of gratifying him, was happy to extricate the Prussian armies from Bohemia before a French offensive could materialize.

Peace of Prague (1866)

The "Seven Weeks' War" definitely ended Austrian interference in both Germany and Italy, the two countries which the Hapsburgs had so long sought to dominate for their own advantage. This curtailment of inflated pretensions, though a blow to their pride, actually strengthened while it constricted the empire on the Danube. Convinced at last of the need for internal reforms and liberal adaptations, Francis Joseph granted the seventeen Austrian provinces a constitution in 1867, establishing responsible par-

Austrian reconstruction after 1866

[1] See above, page 273.

[283]

liamentary government with a bicameral legislature chosen by indirect suffrage. At the same time Count Beust, the Austrian imperial chancellor, and Francis Deák, a Hungarian leader, worked out an agreement whereby the relationship between Austria and Hungary was readjusted. This *Ausgleich* or Compromise of 1867 established Hungary as a semi-independent kingdom with a separate constitution and parliament. Francis Joseph remained Emperor of Austria and King of Hungary, and in addition to possessing the same monarch the two states were represented by a joint ministry for the conduct of foreign affairs, war, and finance. This curious Dual Empire established in 1867 survived for fifty years despite its seemingly cumbrous and impracticable form, for the settlement satisfied the German element, which retained a dominant position in Austria, while the Magyars controlled Hungary. But the subject races, the Czechs, Slavs, Poles, etc., grew increasingly restless as their national ambitions steadily mounted while the autonomy which they demanded was as steadily refused. This discontent, particularly among the Slavs, many of whom dreamed of uniting with Serbia and Montenegro to form a pan-Slav kingdom in the Balkans, had become a serious danger to the solidity of the Austro-Hungarian Empire by 1914. It will be explained later how the resultant antagonism between Austria and Serbia produced the incident which precipitated the World War.

6. THE NORTH GERMAN CONFEDERATION

The strong can afford to be generous. Not only toward Austria, but toward the German liberals also, Bismarck displayed a spirit of patience *Bismarck's* and conciliation after the victory of Königgrätz had vindi- *popularity* cated his policies. From the Prussian parliament, in which *after 1866* for the first time he enjoyed the support of a friendly majority, he requested a decree legalizing his former unconstitutional measures. It was voted at once, together with further appropriations for the victorious army, and substantial rewards and honors were heaped upon the leaders who had made the triumph possible.

The Peace of Prague, which closed the "Seven Weeks' War," left four South German States — Bavaria, Württemberg, Baden, and Hesse- *Prussian* Darmstadt — free to organize as they chose, but the re- *annexations* maining states, north of the river Main, were at the mercy of Prussia. Schleswig and Holstein, Hesse-Cassel, Nassau, the Kingdom of Hanover, and the free city of Frankfort, Prussia annexed outright, thereby acquiring some splendid ports on the North and Baltic seas, and a consolidated territory stretching from the Rhine to the Russian

OTTO VON BISMARCK
1815–98

*This portrait shows Bismarck as an old man,
but the strong will, keen mind, and realistic outlook which distinguished the "Iron Chancellor" can still be read in his expression.*

border.   With a population raised to twenty-four million, the Prussian
Kingdom after 1866 comprised two thirds of Germany and included
nearly two thirds of the German people.

But Bismarck desired more than the aggrandizement of Prussia: he
was aiming at the unification of Germany.   At his invitation the twenty-
*The North
German
Confedera-
tion*
one North German States joined Prussia in a new union to
replace the defunct Germanic Confederation.   After the
rulers had consented, a convention elected by universal
manhood suffrage approved the constitution of the alliance,
and the King of Prussia became president of the newly formed "North
German Confederation."   This federal state was created with a popular
chamber (the *Reichstag*) to represent the people, and an upper chamber
(the *Bundesrat*) to represent the princes.   Bismarck had been careful to
leave the component states the illusion of independence and individual-
ity, but the really vital matters, such as the direction of the military
forces and the conduct of foreign affairs, had passed under the control of
Prussia.   Through his dynastic prestige, and his authority as president
of the Confederation, the Prussian king could dominate the *Bundesrat*,
for of its forty-three members seventeen were Prussian deputies and a
sufficient number of the others subservient to his wishes to assure Prussia
a majority control.

7. OPPOSITION OF FRANCE TO GERMAN UNIFICATION

Throughout the decade 1860–70, while he was laboring to prepare the
way for the unification of the Germanies, Bismarck had constantly to be
on his guard against the possible intervention of France.   Since the time
of Richelieu, French statesmen had encouraged the existing disunion in
the Germanies by playing one state there against another, for the creation of a powerful and unified empire across the Rhine was likely to prove
a disadvantage and a danger to France.

The spectacular rise of Prussian power and prestige under Bismarck's
guidance filled many Frenchmen with alarm, and they blamed the gov-
*Bismarck
outwits
Napoleon
III*
ernment of Napoleon III for failing, either to prevent it, or
to secure reciprocal compensations.   Unfortunately, Napoleon's efforts to delay German unification brought him no
advantage and even hastened the result which he desired to
postpone.   The Prussian victory over Austria in 1866 took him and
many other European statesmen by surprise, but he hoped to derive one
advantage from the Treaty of Prague, for it left the four South German
States (Bavaria, Württemberg, Baden, and Hesse-Darmstadt) independ-

ent, and he believed he could make them allies of France. But Bismarck impressed upon the rulers of these states the dangers of isolation, showed them proofs of Napoleon's desire for German territory, and persuaded them to sign secret military treaties with Prussia (1867). At the same time they joined their commercial interests with those of the North German Confederation in a common *Zollverein* or customs union. Economically, therefore, Germany might be considered one empire after 1867, although distrust of the autocratic Prussian methods kept the South German States politically sundered for four years longer.

The diplomatic reverse which Napoleon thus suffered in the Germanies came at a time when his régime was growing more and more unpopular in France. The liberals had never forgiven his seizure of power, and his efforts after 1860 to reconcile their opposition by transforming an autocratic into a "liberal" empire failed to appease them. More than ever he felt the need of doing something truly Napoleonic.

The Polish insurrection of 1863 afforded him one chance, for French liberals and clericals sympathized with the desire of the Poles to liberate their fatherland, but Napoleon hesitated to offend Russia, *The Mexi-* Austria, and Prussia, all of which held fragments of Poland. *can misad-* Instead, he dispatched an expeditionary force to Mexico, *venture* where disturbed conditions provided the great powers with an excuse to intervene. Largely under French protection a Mexican Empire was set up (1863) and the Archduke Maximilian, brother of the Emperor Francis Joseph of Austria, accepted the crown. Napoleon hoped in this way to make Austria his ally, to conciliate Catholic sentiment by protecting church property in Mexico which the revolutionists threatened to confiscate, and to secure commercial benefits for France. The American government regarded the presence of a European army in Mexico as a violation of the Monroe Doctrine,[1] but could make no effective protest until the war between the States was concluded in 1865. Then, rather than risk the possibility of war with the veteran Union forces, fresh from their victory over the Confederate States, Napoleon withdrew his troops from Mexico, and Maximilian, who remained behind, was captured and shot by the revolutionaries. Instead of the brilliant *coup* which he had projected, Napoleon had precipitated a tragic fiasco.

In Europe, Napoleon's diplomacy proved equally disappointing after 1867. The possibility of a clash with Prussia made it at least advisable that France should come to a friendly understanding with one of the other powers, but despite negotiations nothing was achieved. The Italians would not join France so long as a French contingent remained

[1] See above, page 221.

at Rome, especially as this French garrison defeated an attempt of Italian patriots under Garibaldi to seize the Eternal City (1867). Between France and Russia the question of Poland remained a source of friction which discouraged attempts at a friendlier co-operation. Austria remained as a possible ally, and should have proved a likely one, for Austria had suffered at the hands of the Prussians in 1866. Diplomatic overtures between Paris and Vienna dragged on from 1868 to 1869, but they resulted in nothing conclusive. Meanwhile, Napoleon's difficulties at home were increasing. In 1870 he offered further concessions by enlarging the powers of the Chamber of Deputies, but far from being satisfied, the liberals and republicans increased their criticism. Several of his closest advisers, ultra-imperialists who feared for the safety of his dynasty, urged him to do something forceful to retrieve his waning prestige, preferably some clever diplomatic stroke which would humiliate Prussia. The summer of 1870 brought the opportunity for such a stroke.

8. THE FRANCO-PRUSSIAN WAR

A revolution having driven Isabella II from Spain in 1868, the Spanish people decided, after two years of confusion, to offer the throne to a *The Spanish* German prince, Leopold of Hohenzollern-Sigmaringen. *question* Fearing the possibility of an alliance between Prussia and Spain if a relative of the Prussian king should don the crown at Madrid, the French government entered a protest. The news that the young prince, unable to secure his father's approval, had declined the honor, eased the tension, and should have satisfied the French, as it afforded them a tacit victory. But the ultra-imperialists who surrounded Napoleon III wanted to humiliate Prussia in some more signal fashion. They persuaded him to ask an assurance from bluff old William I that he would promise never to authorize the candidature of his kinsman at any future time should the Spanish offer ever be renewed. This unwise action played directly into Bismarck's hands.

For behind the scenes Bismarck had been deliberately working for war. He knew that a struggle with France would consolidate the German nation and forge the bonds of a political union as noth- *The Ems* ing else could do, but it was essential for his plan that *dispatch* France appear the aggressor. He had privately encouraged the Spanish offer of a throne in order to alarm the French, and the news that Leopold of Hohenzollern had declined it (July 12) filled him with gloom because it wrecked his plans. Then the French envoy, Benedetti, sought William I at Ems, where the Prussian king was resting, and pressed the French demands for further assurances so insistently that William dismissed him with some abruptness. To Bismarck at Berlin the king dispatched a telegram recounting the incident (July 13), and in this Ems dispatch Bismarck saw his opportunity to retrieve his hopes. He condensed and published the telegram in curt phrases which persuaded the French that their ambassador had been repulsed, while patriotic Prussians were convinced that their venerable king had been insulted.

Napoleon III did not want war, but he allowed himself to be pushed into it by the ultra-imperialists. Seemingly the advantage in the approaching conflict lay with France; actually the French had a doubtful cause (interference in a neighbor's affairs), an inferior army (courageous, but obsolete in tactics and equipment), and poor leaders (Napoleon III and his second-rate ministers and marshals). On July 15, 1870, the French prime minister, Émile Ollivier, announced the imminence of war to the Chamber of Deputies, and declared that the ministry accepted the prospect "with a light heart." Misled by incorrect information on the causes of the conflict, by jingoistic oratory, and by vague assurances of support from Austria or the South German States, the Chamber voted to declare war on Prussia (July 19) while the Parisian crowds cheered and shouted "On to Berlin."

The conflict which had been accepted "with a light heart" led France within six weeks to the *débâcle* of Sedan, where Napoleon III was forced to surrender with 86,000 men (September 2, 1870). On October 27, General Bazaine handed over a second French army of 175,000 men which the Prussians had shut up in Metz. In Paris, where the régime of Napoleon III [1] had been overthrown two days after Sedan, the newly proclaimed "Government of National Defense" prepared the city to resist an inevitable siege, but starvation forced the Parisians to surrender, January 28, 1871. The newborn republic had fought desperately for five months against the forces which had destroyed the empire in five weeks, but further opposition would only have prolonged a hopeless war.

A French National Assembly, convoked at Bordeaux, elected Adolphe Thiers "Head of the Executive Power" and authorized him to negotiate for a peace settlement. By the Treaty of Frankfort, May 10, 1871, France surrendered the provinces of Alsace and Lorraine to Germany and agreed to pay an indemnity of five billion francs (about one billion dollars). The Germans were to occupy French key fortresses until the last of the indemnity had been paid. *Treaty of Frankfort*

---

[1] Napoleon III, released by the Germans in 1871, joined his wife and son who had escaped to England. He died there in 1873. Six years later his heir, the prince imperial, was killed while fighting with the British in Zululand.

It was not with Prussia but with a united German Empire that France concluded peace.   The South German States had joined the North German Confederation in the struggle with the hereditary foe, and the common patriotic effort, as Bismarck had predicted, forged the bonds of union.   In the Hall of Mirrors at Louis XIV's stately Versailles palace the German princes hailed William I as "German Emperor" (January 18, 1871) while the guns of Paris ten miles away were firing their last despairing volleys. After long delays and multiple discouragements, after peaceful projects had fallen through and liberal hopes miscarried, German unity had been finally sealed in the midst of war and under the direction of the conservative and autocratic Bismarck.

Proclamation of the German Empire (1871)

Thus the Franco-Prussian War made Germany an empire and France a republic.   Nor did this complete the changes of the historic year 1870– 71.   The withdrawal of French troops from Rome for service against Prussia made it possible for the Italians to occupy the Eternal City and complete the Kingdom of Italy by the acquisition of its predestined capital.[1]   The entrance of Italy and Germany into the circle of great powers profoundly altered the pattern of European politics, and made it difficult for France to attempt again the rôle of *la grande nation*, interfering ruthlessly in the affairs of her weak and divided neighbors across the Rhine and the Alps.   Henceforth, until the World War, five first-class powers, France, Germany, Italy, Austria, and Russia, were to strain against each other in the narrow confines of Europe while Great Britain looked on and sought to preserve a balance of power among them for her own security.

The most significant development in the troubled years between 1848 and 1870 had been this triumph of nationalism.   All the major conflicts of the period — the Italian and Hungarian revolts of 1848–49, the Polish insurrection of 1863, the Crimean War which grew in part from the Balkan ferment, the War of 1859 for Italian liberation, the Danish War of 1864, the Austro-Prussian War of 1866, and the Franco-Prussian War of 1870–71 — are traceable to the pressure of this movement for national consolidation.   After 1871 the more powerful and legitimate national aspirations had been satisfied, the Germans and Italians had achieved unity and the Hungarians had been quieted by the Compromise of 1867. That a considerable measure of solidity had been attained is attested by the fact that the conflicts which had disturbed Europe on the average of one every three years from 1848 to 1870 are remarkable for their scarcity after the latter date.   The remaining decades of the nineteenth century form the most peaceful period that Europe has enjoyed in modern times,

[1] See above, page 273.

although beneath the calm new antagonisms were deepening and frustrated national emotions gathering force, especially in the Balkans.   The year 1870 is, therefore, an important date to remember, like 1815 or 1789, because: (1) it closed a broken period marked by frequent conflicts; (2) it signalized the establishment of a new relationship among the great powers; and (3) it opened a forty-three-year period of comparative peace, of great scientific progress, and of growing imperialistic tendencies.

CHAPTER TWENTY-ONE

RUSSIA IN THE NINETEENTH CENTURY

The Russian government of this period is the most monstrous abstraction. . . .
The government exists for the sake of the government, the people for the sake of
the state . . . material force in place of an ideal, material power in place of
authority.

ALEXANDER HERZEN (1812–70).

IN THE nineteenth century as in the eighteenth the impressive expansion of the Russian Empire alarmed and disconcerted the other European powers. The costly victories achieved by France and Britain in the Crimean War (1854–56) checked the Muscovite ambitions in the West temporarily, and preserved Turkey from dismemberment, but Russian imperialism continued its drive to the east and south. In the twenty years that followed the Peace of Paris (1856), Russia gained the Amur Province from China and subjugated Turkestan.[1] This Asiatic territory, acquired in two decades, exceeded in area all the annexations that the Russians had won in Europe in two centuries. Clearly, the settled and civilized European states could withstand the Russian encroachments much more successfully than the backward and disorganized peoples of Asia.

1. THE AFTERMATH OF THE CRIMEAN WAR

Russia is a bridge between Europe and Asia, not only in a geographical sense, but in a cultural, historical, and military sense also. The Crimean War had demonstrated that the fighting forces of France and Britain surpassed the Russian armies in training, organization, and equipment as greatly as the Russians in their turn surpassed the Chinese. Throughout the czar's empire the blunders and defeats of the war produced a mood of disillusionment and discontent. The Russian army had been an object of special pride to Nicholas I (1825–55) and his last days were darkened by the reverses which it suffered on the Crimean Peninsula. These reverses could not be attributed to lack of manpower or of resources, for Russia possessed both in abundance. The common soldiers had fought stubbornly and bravely; but the collapse of the commissariat service, the breakdown of transport facilities, and the graft and corruption among high officials nullified the sacrifices of the rank and file. The war revealed defects in the Nicholas

[1] See map following page 362.

[292]

System which could not be covered up, and the army, the favorite instrument of the autocrat, lost much of the prestige which it had enjoyed since the struggle with Napoleon half a century earlier.

The spreading discontent encouraged the new czar, Alexander II (1855–81), to inaugurate an era of reforms. Autocracy, orthodoxy, and nationalism remained the watchwords, but Alexander *Character of* proposed, within limits, to bring Russian institutions into *Alexander II* closer harmony with the progressive and humanitarian spirit of the nineteenth century. He lacked his father's military firmness and had little experience in administrative tasks, but he was patient, cautious, and kind-hearted. People recalled how his uncle, Alexander I, had planned half a century earlier to play the part of a reforming czar, but had gradually abandoned the ideal. Alexander II possessed a less ardent zeal but a firmer purpose, and he was destined to carry through an administrative revolution before he, too, wearied of the mounting difficulties and relapsed into conservatism.

2. THE EMANCIPATION OF THE SERFS

Alexander's greatest single achievement was his emancipation of some forty million Russian serfs, a deed which won him the title of the "Czar Liberator." To visit a rural Russian community *Serfdom in* in the earlier nineteenth century was like stepping back into *Russia* the Middle Ages. Nine tenths of the land was held by something less than one hundred thousand noble families. The serfs, attached to the soil, could be sold with the estates to new landlords, conscripted into the nobleman's household to work as domestic servants, or even sent to the factories in the towns for their master's profit. Though some nobles exercised their authority in a kindly and paternal fashion, others overworked their serfs, flogged them cruelly for slight faults, and interfered insolently in their private affairs and family relations. A serf could not marry without his master's consent, could not leave the estate without permission, and might be pursued, brought back, and punished if he sought to escape. He lived at the mercy of his master's caprice.

This iniquitous and archaic system of human bondage was rightly resented by intelligent Russians as a stigma upon their civilization. As the landlords declined to modify the system voluntarily, Alexander II took the initiative, and after careful consideration he issued a *ukase* abolishing serfdom in 1861. Supplemented by further decrees in 1863 and 1866, this proclamation transformed the serfs into free citizens, and permitted them to retain their cottages, tools, and sufficient land for them to maintain themselves by their common efforts. The aristocrats ceded part of their estates to the peasant *mir* or community village, and for this sacrifice the government promised compensation. They also received some financial reimbursement for the loss of peasant dues and personal services, but instead of evincing gratitude for this settlement many nobles complained that they had been unjustly impoverished.

The peasants were dissatisfied also, but with greater reason. The land apportioned to the *mir* proved often an infertile tract, and the allotments inadequate. They discovered, moreover, that far from obtaining freedom they had in reality become serfs of the state, for the government expected them to pay off by a special compensation tax the enormous sums expended to reimburse the landlords. This meant in application that a serf was to purchase his land and liberty by annual payments extending over a period of forty-nine years. Many peasants found it difficult to believe that the "Little Father," as the czar was affectionately named, really intended to burden his children so heavily after treating the aristocrats so generously. It seems doubtful, however, if Alexander had it in his power to execute a fairer settlement. Despite the complaints of the landlords and the bitterness of the liberated serfs, the benefits of emancipation soon showed themselves in the form of larger crops, increased areas under cultivation, better living conditions for the peasants, and a rise in trade. The freeing of the serfs was without question the most important event in Russian history during the nineteenth century.

Discontent with the terms of emancipation

3. OTHER REFORMS OF ALEXANDER II

The emancipation edict had stripped the landlords of much of their judicial and paternalistic responsibility and had created many million new citizens. It appeared wise, therefore, to the czar and his advisers, to train the people in self-government by creating provincial and district assemblies, or *zemstvos*, composed of delegates representing the landlords, the townsfolk, and the peasants. Each *zemstvo* was to be a sort of local parliament, entrusted with the responsibility for maintaining the roads, schools, churches, and jails of the district. It had authority to levy taxes for local purposes and to relegate the execution of its decrees to a permanent committee. Admirable in theory, the *zemstvos* proved a disappointment in practice.

The zemstvos

[294]

ALEXANDER II OF RUSSIA
1818–81

Some admirers of Alexander II professed to read in his haunted glance the tragedy of a ruler who was foredoomed to die by a terrorist bomb. His enemies declared that his fishlike eyes proclaimed the callous autocrat.

The members too often lacked political training, and the imperial officials, wedded to the methods of a centralized bureaucracy, distrusted and overruled the provincial legislators. Alexander recognized the defects in the system, but he hoped it would improve with time.

In all his attempted reforms, the czar found himself gravely handicapped by a lack of honest and experienced officials. This difficulty
Judicial proved acute when he sought to reorganize the law courts.
reforms In place of the secret and arbitrary methods of the bureaucrats, he decreed (1862) a court system modeled on that of the western nations, with local justices of the peace, district tribunals, and a high court of final appeal. Criminals won the privilege of trial by jury and the proceedings in civil and criminal cases were opened to the public. Despite these improvements, the ignorance of the Russian masses left them still confused at the working of laws intended to guarantee their rights, and the ineradicable corruption and graft of the old legal system persisted and poisoned the new. Moreover, Alexander himself failed to make the new order either consistent or universal, for he preserved the infamous "Third Section" and the secret police tribunals organized by his father to punish political offenders. The Czar Liberator was like an architect who installs more spacious windows and widens the corridors in the upper floors of a feudal castle, while leaving unchanged the submerged dungeons with their dark secrets and instruments of torture.

While his zeal lasted, Alexander also sketched the plan for a system of public instruction, with primary schools, secondary schools, and colleges, supported and supervised by the state. He relaxed the strict censorship of the press, permitted Russians to travel abroad freely, and treated the Jews and other minority races in the empire with greater consideration and leniency than his father had shown. But the chorus of criticism which greeted his endeavors daunted and discouraged him. The conservatives denounced his policies as dangerously radical, the liberal intellectuals called them nervelessly moderate, while the peasants resisted all innovations with pious apathy. The fatalism that permeated the lower orders is reflected in the reply of an old *muzhik* who was urged to boil his drinking water because of the cholera epidemic. "If God wished us to drink hot water," he responded, "He would have heated the Neva." The indifference and the active opposition which he encountered checked Alexander's reforming efforts after 1865, although he still maintained a pretense of enthusiasm. But his liberalism had been more largely the fruit of expediency than of conviction and the mood had passed.

4. THE REACTION IN THE LATER YEARS OF ALEXANDER II

Undoubtedly one factor which turned Alexander II toward reaction was the Polish uprising of 1863. Stirred by the spread of liberal ideas and by their invincible dream of national independence, *Polish uprising (1863)* Polish patriots organized a revolt, but were defeated by the superior Russian forces. Determined to destroy this troublesome Polish nationalism once and for all, the Russian government executed or exiled the leaders of the revolt and sequestered their lands. Russian became the official language, and the Catholic Church in Poland was weakened by the loss of much of its land and the suppression of monasteries. From this harsh treatment one benefit resulted to the stricken people, for the confiscated lands were distributed among the peasantry, and Alexander remitted the feudal obligations in order to punish the disaffected ruling classes while securing the loyalty, or at least the gratitude, of the tenants and serfs.

An attempt to assassinate him, made by a fanatic in 1866, dispelled Alexander's last liberal sympathies. Convinced finally that in tampering with the Nicholas System he had opened the door to anarchy, the czar turned his back on reform. Thenceforth the *zemstvos*, the law courts, the journals, and the schools found their privileges steadily curtailed; vigilant police spies circulated once more among all ranks of society; and teachers, writers, and others who had hailed the reform era too eagerly felt again the chill breath of imperial disfavor. Even the great novelist and philosopher, Count Leo Tolstoy (1828–1910), confessed that he felt surprise each morning on awakening to find that he was not on the road to exile in Siberia.

A considerable group of Russians, known as Slavophiles, or Nationalists, applauded the czar's resumption of the traditional policy of autocracy, orthodoxy, and nationalism. The Slavophiles held *The Slavophiles* that Russia was a unique country, with customs, beliefs, and institutions peculiar to itself. To adopt the dress, the manners, the legal and political ideals of the western European states appeared disloyal to these ardent nationalists, whose dislike of the "westernizers" and their servile imitation of European culture dated from the days when Peter the Great had opened his "windows to the west." The innovations introduced by Alexander II, such as trial by jury and representative *zemstvos*, they were inclined to disdain as foreign importations, and when these reforms failed to work smoothly, when the Poles broke into revolt, and anarchists multiplied, they laid the responsibility upon the czar's liberal experiments instead of blaming

[297]

the evils which those experiments were designed to cure. The Slavophiles themselves had little to offer in the way of a constructive program. Their ideals were for the most part vague and negative, but they had a strong following, for their insistence upon preserving the integrity of Holy Russia appealed alike to the reactionaries, the nationalists, the orthodox clergy, and the inertly conservative masses.

Placed upon the defensive, the "westernizers" tried to argue that the late reforms had proved disappointing, not because they went too

The "westernizers" far, but because they did not go far enough. They besought Alexander to continue his liberal efforts, but they lacked any constitutional means of action aside from the crippled *zemstvos* and their petitions brought no response. Turning, therefore, from the government to the people, they planned to make war upon the dense ignorance and superstition of the masses, as the chief obstacles to progress. Hundreds of ardent young intellectuals dedicated themselves to the work of instructing the liberated serfs, hoping by daily contact and kindly example to inculcate a gospel of enlightenment. But they soon grew discouraged at this seemingly hopeless task. Crushed between the hostility of the government and the apathy of the peasants, the liberals faced a crisis which split their ranks. The more moderate continued to hope that improvements might be introduced slowly through the spread of education and administrative reforms, but the more radical, losing patience with such dilatory methods, began to advocate more direct and desperate remedies.

The "Father of Russian Liberalism" and a leading protagonist of constitutional reform had been Alexander Herzen (1812–70). From

Alexander Herzen (1812–70) his points of exile in France and Germany, Herzen had done much to encourage the liberal experiments that marked the period 1855–65, for his pamphlets and journals, smuggled into Russia despite the censorship, were read by many high officials including the "Czar Liberator" himself. But with Alexander's conversion to a more cautious policy after 1865 and Herzen's death in 1870, the more moderate program of constitutional reform lost its appeal, especially for the younger radicals, and many of them embraced new and more violent modes of revolutionary activity.

5. THE SPREAD OF ANARCHISM, NIHILISM, AND TERRORISM

This change of temper after 1870 is reflected in the activities of the anarchists, nihilists, and terrorists. The word "anarchism" was first popularized by the French writer Pierre Joseph Proudhon (1809–

65), who, believing that all government based upon physical force was iniquitous, urged an ideal order of society in which men *Anarchism* would live together in peace and liberty without governments, without a police force, and without compulsion of any kind. Proudhon's theories, which might have sufficed to govern a community of saints, appeared utterly impracticable for the guidance of a society in which most individuals are constantly seeking to enrich themselves by exploiting others. Nevertheless, his argument that the institution of private property, protected by the law, the police, and the government, is part of an iniquitous system whereby a favored group of individuals monopolize the wealth and power to the exclusion of the rest, struck a responsive chord in the heart of a Russian noble, Michael Bakunin (1814–76). If Herzen was the father of Russian liberalism, Bakunin may be considered the father of Russian radicalism.

Born in 1814, Bakunin visited Germany and France as a young man, and joined in the revolutionary movement of 1848. Arrested in Dresden and transported to Russia, he was exiled to Siberia, but *Michael* escaped in 1861, and wandered thenceforth from land to *Bakunin* land preaching his fanatical brand of anarchism. His *(1814–76)* hand was lifted against everything which imposed upon or restrained the liberty of the individual, against the God of the theologians, against marriage, and against the state. Kindly and simple in manner, Bakunin yet felt himself dedicated to a career of universal destruction and revolt, urged on by his pity for suffering humanity which he saw as crushed beneath the tyranny of existing institutions. That government, while it benefited some members of society more perhaps than others, might none the less be indispensable for the protection of all, he could not see, and in countries such as Russia, where the evils of despotism were more apparent than the advantages provided by the administration, his doctrines won many converts among the radical thinkers.

The intelligent and educated minority among the Russian population tended to form, in the later nineteenth century, a curiously rootless, irreverent, and unconventional group. Isolated from the *Nihilism* masses of peasants, denied participation in practical political affairs, the Russian intelligentsia indulged themselves in the pastime of criticizing existing conditions. Because they found little to commend in society, they repudiated government, religion, the sanctity of tradition, and the veneration usually accorded to that which is old. This iconoclastic attitude of mind, particularly admired among the younger members of the educated classes, came to be termed "nihilism," a nihilist being one who bowed before no authority without weighing its virtue, and accepted nothing on faith. The nihilists vented their disgust and ennui in passionate and pessimistic debates, arguing interminably and inconclusively upon the meaning of life, the purpose of government, and the tenets of religion. Most of them were harmless eccentrics, content to discuss philosophical dilemmas or invent theoretical projects, but a few, more ruthless and determined in their convictions, sought to compel reform by direct means. These swelled the group of the so-called terrorists.

The terrorists were apostles of action who believed that no orderly or legal cure could be found for the evils of the czarist régime. The *The ter-* government, irresponsible and autocratic, had failed to curb *rorists* its own abuses, and stubbornly refused to let the Russian people institute reforms through a representative parliament responsive to their wishes. The only method which remained, the terrorist held, was to frighten the czar and his ministers into making reforms by a deliberate policy of violence and assassination. Secret revolutionary groups, working with extraordinary patience and cunning, plotted one assassination after another, despite the incessant activity of the police. In 1879 an attempt was made to blow up the czar's train; and shortly thereafter an explosion shattered part of the Winter Palace. Alexander II was no coward, and he insisted that these revolutionaries must be crushed; but he decided at the same time to satisfy some of the popular demands by drafting important reforms. Before the program could be completed, however, he fell a victim to a terrorist bomb (1881).

6. ALEXANDER III AND THE POLICY OF RUSSIFICATION

This drastic effort to temper despotism by assassination proved a failure. The revolutionaries gained no advantage from the violent *Alexander* death of the Czar Liberator, for his son and successor, *III* Alexander III, showed himself a strong-willed despot who *(1881–94)* promptly announced his intention to avenge his father's murder and to preserve the autocratic régime. In Constantine Pobiedonostsev (1827–1907) and Venceslas de Plehve (1846–1904) he found subordinates ready and willing to carry out this policy. Pobiedonostsev, as "Procurator of the Holy Synod," directed the affairs of the Russian Orthodox Church. He had rationalized his distrust of parliaments, popular education, and the press into a veritable philosophy of reaction, and he exerted a compelling influence over the mind of the new czar. For the more practical task of running conspirators to earth, Alexander

[300]

III relied upon Plehve, who directed the state police with such ruthless efficiency that for several years revolutionary activity all but ceased.

Like most despots, Alexander III was disposed to favor a high degree of uniformity throughout his empire. This was the more difficult to attain because the advance of the Russian frontier had *Russification* brought millions of alien people under the rule of the czar, until the minorities actually exceeded the real Russians of Great Russia in number. Alexander's ambition to promote cultural, linguistic, and religious unity pleased ardent pan-Slavists and "Russifiers," but it antagonized the Poles, Finns, Jews, and other racial minorities. The Poles, since their abortive revolt of 1863, had suffered bitterly under the policy of coercion designed to make better Russians of them. The Finns, Lutheran in religion and jealous of their vestiges of independence, suffered the same encroaching pressure until Nicholas II curtailed their constitution in 1899. But the most defenseless victims of this program of Russification were the Jews, for although they numbered over five millions, they were scattered throughout western Russia, possessed no one locality which they could call their own, and were subjected to periodic *pogroms*, or murderous persecutions, which were permitted, if not actually instigated, by the imperial authorities.

Naturally these abused minorities furnished numerous volunteers for the revolutionary cause. Had all the discontented factions in Russia discovered a formula upon which they could unite, the *The Social-* autocracy would not long have survived their onslaught. *ist Revolu-* But the revolutionists were swayed by divergent ideals and *tionaries* interests. The peasants, constituting a majority of the Russian population, were primarily interested in the land question, and their hopes rested with the Socialist Revolutionaries or "S–R" Party. To destroy czardom, seize the landed estates of the aristocrats, and award a free farm to each peasant family was the S–R program, a program which any peasant could understand and support. The S–R leaders hoped to substitute a free association of communes for the existing bureaucratic tyranny, they accepted violence and assassination as a means of hastening this end, and they counted upon the assistance of the dissatisfied bourgeoisie and the workingmen of the towns in their war against autocracy.

The workingmen of the towns, however, were formulating a revolutionary program of their own. Industrialism spread rapidly in Russia in the late nineteenth century, especially after 1890, and the construction of factories and railways brought trade unions, strikes, and the recurrent clashes between capital and labor which were already common in western

Europe. The pan-Slavists opposed the new industrialism as a western

The Industrial Revolution in Russia

importation, but it spread prodigiously under the direction of Sergei de Witte (1849–1915), who was minister of finance from 1893 to 1903. Witte favored a protective tariff for the benefit of the manufacturers and social legislation for the benefit of the workers, hoping thereby to keep both classes contented. But the growing ferment, the strikes, and the spread of Marxian socialism among the new proletarian classes greatly alarmed the reactionaries, as well it might, and Witte was forced to resign in 1903.

Witte's downfall could not check the spread of the Industrial Revolution, which, for good or ill, had struck Russia with its transforming magic.

The Social Democrats

A new revolutionary class had emerged, a Russian workers' party, nursed on socialist doctrines, and more dangerous, more defiantly radical than the Socialists of France or Germany. Organized as the "Social Democrats" the Russian workingmen prepared the way for the destruction of the czarist régime by means of strikes, propaganda, and mass action. They had little use for independent acts of terrorism and assassination, and they expected little help from the peasants. To these industrial proletarians the coming revolution was to be their revolution.

7. NICHOLAS II AND THE REVOLUTION OF 1905

Alexander III was succeeded by his son Nicholas II in 1894. Nicholas was an amiable man, but narrow in his outlook and his sympathies, in-

Nicholas II (1894–1917)

termittently stubborn without perseverance, despotic in principle yet weak in will. Like Louis XVI of France, he inherited a revolution and was destined to pay with his life for the mistakes of his ancestors as well as for his own. Although his father's policy of reaction and Russification had created mounting opposition, Nicholas made no concessions. He retained Pobiedonostsev in office and multiplied the powers of the hated pan-Slavist, Plehve, until the latter's assassination in 1904.

The Russo-Japanese War (1904–05), a consequence of the pan-Slavists' ambition to enlarge the Russian foothold on the Pacific Ocean, brought

Revolutionary movement of 1905–06

rude disasters which the rotten imperial system was ill-suited to endure. As one defeat followed another, and evidence of corruption and inefficiency in high official circles came to light, a ferment of complaint, criticism, and disorder swept the empire. Assassinations multiplied, armed revolt broke out in Poland, and in Saint Petersburg a procession of petitioners led by a priest, Gapon, was fired upon by the soldiers. Revolution threatened to engulf the imperial régime and Nicholas II agreed reluctantly to offer concessions. He proclaimed religious toleration for minority sects, cancelled the arrears which many peasants still owed for their communal lands, removed unpopular officials, and promised (June, 1905) to establish a Russian parliament. This promise he reaffirmed four months later in his "October Manifesto," which guaranteed popular liberties, a limited suffrage, and responsible government under a bicameral legislature.

By 1906, the revolutionary wave had begun to ebb. The Social Democrats in the cities and the Socialist Revolutionaries in the country could not combine their efforts; many middle-class liberals *The reaction* were satisfied with the October Manifesto (and were conse- *in 1906* quently known as "Octobrists"), while others (termed the Constitutional Democrats, or Cadets), wished to press on toward a genuinely democratic government. The reactionary classes, disconcerted in 1905, began to rally their forces, and, feeling confident that the threat of revolution was waning, they urged Nicholas to withdraw his promises.

Under these circumstances it is not surprising that the first Russian Parliament, or Duma, which assembled in May, 1906, found itself powerless to control the czar's ministers. When the representa- *The first,* tives of the empire demanded a responsible ministry, the *second, and* Duma was dissolved by imperial decree. The Cadets, the *third Dumas* most defiant group among the deputies, attempted to reassemble at Viborg in Finland, and appealed in vain to the Russian people to support their stand. A second Duma was summoned to meet in March, 1907, but when it showed the same independent spirit, it likewise was promptly dissolved. Nicholas now determined to revise the electoral system in such a way that the more radical elements were curbed or disenfranchised. The third Duma, in which the moderates and conservatives predominated, proved more conciliatory and was permitted to sit until 1912. But its rôle had been reduced from that of a legislature to the feeble dignity of an advisory or consultative body, and the Russian government continued to justify Herzen's indictment that it was "material force in place of an ideal, material power in place of authority."

In 1906, Nicholas chose as his prime minister an able compromiser, Peter Stolypin (1863–1911). Stolypin was a man of firm character who dealt vigorously with political offenders, but he sought at *The third* the same time to render the government more popular by *Duma* improving the lot of the peasants and workingmen. After *(1907–12)* 1908, revolutionary agitation slowly subsided, acts of violence grew less

[303]

frequent, police reprisals less severe, but this did not prevent Stolypin himself falling victim to an assassin in 1911. This act, however, did not disturb the comparative tranquillity of the empire.

In 1912, a fourth Duma was elected and evinced the same moderate disposition as its predecessor in compromising with authority. The *Election of the fourth Duma (1912)* activities of the pan-Slavists continued to alarm the national minorities, but one pan-Slav project, the enlargement and reorganization of the Russian army, was approved by the Duma because of the growing tension in Europe between the Triple Alliance and the Triple *Entente*. Russia had achieved a momentary balance between the forces of liberalism and despotism. It remained to be seen whether, under wise statesmanship, the empire would advance peacefully along the constitutional path, or whether a new crisis would precipitate a second revolution more radical, more sanguinary, and more destructive than the inconclusive effort of 1905.

THE LESSER STATES OF EUROPE IN THE NINETEENTH CENTURY

. . . We know of no reason in the nature of things why a state should be any the better for being large . . .

SIR JOHN R. SEELEY, *The Expansion of England.*[1]

IN THE drama of modern European history the great powers have tended more and more to usurp the center of the stage and to dwarf and obscure the significance of the secondary states. The peoples of the smaller countries justly resent this subordination, but a textbook which attempted to assign equal space to the history of France and Finland, or Britain and Belgium, in the nineteenth century, would develop abnormal and confusing proportions. Of the ten or more states discussed in the present chapter, several played dominant rôles in earlier centuries, but none has exerted a decisive influence in the last hundred years. For this reason their more recent annals, though intensely interesting in themselves, have been severely and perhaps unjustifiably compressed.

1. THE SCANDINAVIAN COUNTRIES

The prominent part which Sweden played in European affairs during the seventeenth century came to an end with the Great Northern War of 1700–21.[2] Deprived of its hegemony in the Baltic, the *Sweden* kingdom declined into more peaceful days and economic decadence. The turmoil of the Napoleonic struggles, which left no part of Europe unstirred, drew Sweden into the later coalitions against France, and despite the fact that the Swedish campaigns were largely defensive the Congress of Vienna united Norway to Sweden as a reward (1814). On the death of Charles XIII (1809–18) without heirs, the Swedish throne passed to his adopted successor, the French general Bernadotte, as Charles XIV (1818–44). The Bernadotte dynasty still reigns in the northern kingdom.

Long a people of aristocratic traditions, the Swedes continued in the nineteenth century to accept the dominance of the great landowners and (with the development of mining and manufacturing activities) of the great industrialists. A constitution promulgated in 1863 did little to break this oligarchic rule, and the consequent discontent of the lower

---

[1] The Macmillan Company.   [2] See above, pages 72–74.

classes promoted the growth of socialism and helps to account for the phenomenal emigration. Over a million Swedes left their homeland between 1850 and 1900, the great majority of them settling in the United States.

The neighboring kingdom of Norway, united to the Danish crown from 1397 to 1814, was ceded in the latter year to Sweden. By approving

Norway

this decision the diplomats at the Congress of Vienna hoped to console the Swedes for the loss of Finland (seized by Russia in 1808) and at the same time to punish the Danes for aiding Napoleon. This forced political union of Norway and Sweden left the Norwegians full control of their domestic affairs, but it irked this hardy and freedom-loving people none the less, for they cherished their distinctive speech and traditions. In 1905 the Norwegian Parliament, or *Storthing*, voted for complete independence and the people confirmed this decision by a plebiscite. The Swedish king, Oscar II, gave reluctant consent to the separation, and a Danish prince mounted the Norwegian throne as Haakon VII. Further democratic amendments to the constitution abolished the royal veto and permitted women to vote on the same terms as men (1913), Norway thus becoming the first state in Europe to accord women this right. Like Sweden, Norway has suffered heavy losses through emigration. The population at the opening of the twentieth century was less than two and one half million; but the Norwegians ranked fourth among the nations of the world in the tonnage of their merchant marine.

The Danes, in their small seagirt kingdom of peninsulas and islands, endured two attacks by the British fleet (1801 and 1807) during the

Denmark

Napoleonic Wars, because they had been subordinated to French policy. The peace that followed brought a further injustice in the loss of Norway. In 1864, Austria and Prussia united to wrest the provinces of Schleswig and Holstein from the Danish monarch,[1] and the diminutive kingdom became the smallest of the Scandinavian states. Denmark retained, however, as tokens of those heroic centuries when Norse adventurers pushed their dragon-prowed vessels into unknown seas, the islands of Iceland and Greenland, forming a colonial empire fifty times the area of the Danish State, but sparsely populated with one hundred and twenty thousand settlers. In 1918, Iceland gained the status of a sovereign principality under the Danish king.

Farming, chiefly dairy farming, forms the principal source of wealth of the Danes, who export large quantities of butter, eggs, fodder, and

[1] See above, page 282.

animal products to England and Germany. The lack of mineral resources and of rivers suitable for providing hydroelectric power has retarded industrial development, but wood and textile manufactures are expanding. The campaign for political democracy, which made little headway in Denmark during the later nineteenth century largely because of the stubborn opposition of Christian IX (1863–1906), won a victory in the twentieth century with the extension of the franchise to all men and women of twenty-five or over who possess a fixed place of abode.

With their combined population of less than eleven million people, the three Scandinavian states could not play, or expect to play, a very ambitious rôle in the military, political, or economic *Scandina-* affairs of nineteenth-century Europe. But if the material *vian litera-* contributions of the Scandinavian peoples were modest, *ture* their intellectual influence was great. The foremost sculptor of the century, Albert Bertel Thorwaldsen (1770–1844), was a Dane, and Denmark could also boast of producing the greatest literary critic of his time in Georg Brandes (1842–1927). Still another Dane, Hans Christian Andersen (1805–75), made his name a household word in Europe and America by his exquisite fairy tales. The plays of the Norwegian, Henrik Ibsen (1828–1906), stirred widespread controversies by their unflinching diagnosis of social problems, and Norway also produced a world-renowned composer in Edvard Grieg (1843–1907). To list but one more name from many which might be included, the Swedish dramatist, August Strindberg (1849–1912), had no equal among his contemporaries in his capacity for bitter, pessimistic, and ironic characterization. The contribution which these men made to European culture is a fitting reflection of the high standards of intelligence and education prevalent among the Scandinavian nations.

2. HOLLAND, BELGIUM, AND SWITZERLAND

Endangered by the military might of France and the naval supremacy of Britain, Holland has invariably suffered when these two powers were at war. In the first years of the nineteenth century, *The King-* Napoleon forced the Dutch into his Continental System, a *dom of the* step which afforded the British an excuse to deprive Holland *Netherlands* of the Cape of Good Hope and Ceylon. But Dutch enterprise in the sixteenth and seventeenth centuries had built up an empire which still remains imposing despite such losses, and includes a native population (1931) of over sixty millions. It embraces Java, Sumatra, the Celebes,

Dutch Borneo, and Dutch New Guinea in the East Indies, Curaçao and some lesser islands in the West Indies, and Dutch Guiana in South America. The immense volume of trade, both colonial and international, which flows in and out of northern Europe through the ports of Amsterdam and Rotterdam, lends the Kingdom of the Netherlands an economic importance out of proportion to its size (12,580 square miles) and population (8,031,679 in 1931).

The Congress of Vienna decreed in 1815 the junction of the Belgian provinces (previously the Austrian Netherlands) with Holland, thus forming the United Kingdom of the Netherlands under William I of the house of Orange. From this union the Belgians seceded in 1830. In 1848, the Dutch adopted a new constitution providing for a responsible ministry and a restricted suffrage, but the growth of democratic sentiment throughout Europe later led to cautious extensions of the franchise until today the electorate includes all men and women over twenty-five years of age. Fear of foreign aggression induced the Dutch to increase their naval and military forces considerably after 1890.

Upon proclaiming their independence of Holland (1830), the Belgians established a constitutional monarchy with a German prince, Leopold *Belgium* of Saxe-Coburg, as their first king. To protect the new state from the designs of more powerful neighbors, the leading nations of Europe, Great Britain, France, Austria, Prussia, and Russia, guaranteed the independence and neutrality of Belgium by solemn accord in 1839. The new kingdom was soon stirred by the quickening effects of the Industrial Revolution, with a consequent exploitation of its mineral resources, and a rise in population which has made it the most densely inhabited state in Europe (estimated population in 1930, 8,129,-824). A liberal government, controlled after 1884 by the Catholic majority, promoted education, broadened the franchise, and improved the condition of the working classes through enlightened social legislation. In 1908, the immense Congo territory in Africa, which had been exploited largely through the business initiative of the astute Belgian monarch, Leopold II (1865–1909), and established as a free state under his sovereignty, was annexed to Belgium as a colony. Like the Dutch, the Belgians became increasingly apprehensive concerning their security in the tense years which preceded the outbreak of the World War in 1914 and followed the general trend in augmenting their armaments.

Until the middle of the nineteenth century, the Swiss Confederation *Switzerland* was little more, politically, than a loose agglomeration of cantons, each practically autonomous. Their inhabitants were bound together by a common love of liberty and of republican institutions, but divided by differences in customs, language, and religion. A majority of the Swiss people speak German, but French prevails in five of the twenty-two cantons and Italian in one, while some thousands of the country folk speak a Latin dialect known as Romansch. In addition to these linguistic barriers there are religious differences, for the Protestants predominate in twelve cantons and Roman Catholics in ten.

Yet, despite these racial and religious divergencies, the Swiss have found it possible in recent times to transform their loose association into a well-knit federal state. A constitution adopted in 1848 established an executive federal council and a bicameral legislature. Uniform coinage, tariffs, postal regulations, and law codes followed; and a federal militia, efficient but expensive, was created for national defense. Swiss citizens enjoy universal suffrage, manifest a lively interest in matters of cantonal and federal administration, and possess two novel constitutional prerogatives. They may, if they wish, demand a plebiscite on any important legislative measure (the referendum), or on any issue proposed and sponsored by fifty thousand voters (the initiative).

Farming, industry, and the tourist trade have combined to make Switzerland, with its four million inhabitants, one of the most prosperous states in Europe. The unrivaled Alpine scenery draws millions of visitors annually. Farming, particularly dairy farming, provides a living for almost one third of the Swiss people, while one half find employment in the manufacture of clocks, watches, silk articles, and other high-grade products. The plentiful water power supplied by the mountain torrents, a public utility controlled by the federal government, provides cheap electricity throughout the country, and permits the electrification of the greater part of the Swiss railway system, most of which is likewise state controlled.

3. SPAIN AND PORTUGAL

The history of Spain in the nineteenth century is largely a story of retarded economic development, maladministration, intrigue, and civil war. The secession of the South and Central American *Spain* colonies [1] had deprived the Spanish government by 1820 of its major source of revenue, leaving it to stagger on as best it might under a burden of insolvency. As a considerable part of the Iberian Peninsula is a semi-arid plateau too infertile for easy cultivation, Spain lacked the agricultural wealth of France and has failed to develop an

[1] See above, page 221.

independent class of sturdy industrious peasant proprietors. Industry likewise, despite the existence of natural deposits of coal and iron, has made slow progress, for the Spaniards possessed little capital and less initiative. The powerful and privileged position of the Roman Catholic Church, the devout and conservative temper of the masses, the widespread superstition and illiteracy, and the lack of modern facilities for internal communication have served to insulate Spanish society from the transforming effects of commerce and invention.

The strength of Spanish conservatism lay in the fact that it was a peculiar blend of patriotism and religious fervor. The rough attempts made by Napoleon to modernize Spanish institutions, after setting his brother Joseph on the throne (1808), intensified the national prejudice against liberalism as an alien and sacrilegious importation. Enlightened and enterprising Spaniards conceded the advantages of reform, but, in the absence of a powerful and progressive middle class, the reform movement drew its chief strength from the circle of the intellectuals and the discontented army officers. These minority groups, while active enough to stir up occasional revolts and issue *pronunciamentos* (proclamations), could not awaken the masses from their lethargy. The enterprise of a firm and enlightened monarch might have turned the scale in favor of reform, but Spain has been cursed during the past hundred and fifty years with more stubborn and incompetent rulers than almost any other European state. The reign of the despicable Ferdinand VII (1814–33) has been described already.[1] His decision to set aside the Salic law and transmit the throne to his daughter Isabella II (1833–68) led to the so-called Carlist Wars (1833–40), in which the supporters of Ferdinand's brother Charles contested the succession. Although Isabella finally made good her claim, her despotic rule and immoral life disgusted the Spanish nation and a revolutionary upheaval in 1868 drove her from the kingdom.

Between 1868 and 1875, Spain endured kaleidoscopic shifts as the Carlists, Liberal Monarchists, and Republicans battled for control. In 1870, the throne was offered to Prince Leopold of Hohenzollern-Sigmaringen, a move which excited a diplomatic crisis and precipitated the Franco-Prussian War.[2] Subsequently Prince Amadeo of Savoy, younger son of Victor Emmanuel II of Italy, was invited to become King of Spain, only to abdicate in discouragement three years later. Finally, in 1875, Alphonso XII (1875–85), son of the deposed Isabella, assumed the crown and restored peace to the distracted nation. With the aid of two remarkable statesmen, Marshal Martínez Campos and Antonio

[1] See above, pages 220–21.   [2] See above, pages 288–89.

Cánovas del Castillo, Alphonso inaugurated a happier era under a moderately liberal constitution. Following his early death (1885), the throne passed to a posthumous son, Alphonso XIII, who was declared of age in 1902. In the interval the widow of Alphonso XII, Maria Christina, acted as regent.

A stupid, tyrannical, and short-sighted colonial policy, which had already disrupted the once vast colonial empire of Spain, induced a stubborn revolt (1895–98) in the chief remaining dependency, the island of Cuba. With the intervention of the United States, Spain suffered a decisive defeat, and surrendered all *Spanish-American War (1898)* title, not only to Cuba, but to Puerto Rico, and to the Philippine Islands and Guam in the Pacific, in return for twenty million dollars compensation. The loss of these last fragments of a mighty empire deeply wounded Spanish pride, and the nation entered the twentieth century with a heritage of defeat, impoverishment, and social unrest. Past colonial misfortunes, however, did not deter Alphonso XIII and the military chiefs from embarking upon a campaign for the subjugation of the native tribes of Spanish Morocco, an essay in imperialism which brought expenses and defeats so ruinous that in 1923 revolution appeared imminent. For the moment it was averted by a *coup d'état* which established General Primo de Rivera as chief minister of the Spanish cabinet with dictatorial powers.

For eight years longer the amiable but extravagant Alphonso XIII clung to his shaking throne, but in 1931 the expected revolution broke out and the monarchy collapsed. A republican constitution, adopted December 9, provided for the confiscation of church property, suppression of religious instruction in the *Spanish Revolution of 1931* schools, and the expulsion of religious orders such as the Jesuits. All men and women over twenty-two were accorded the right to vote and a unicameral legislature established. During the first years of its existence the new republic survived serious strikes and disorders. Admirable progress was made in cutting down wasteful expenditure of the inadequate national revenue, and in promoting education, but grave problems remained to be overcome. A satisfactory solution of the clerical question proved difficult to find, and the new government's declared intention to parcel out the estates of the nobility, aggregating some fifty million acres, encountered obstacles.

A close historical parallel has long existed between the annals of Spain and Portugal. Like Spain, the smaller Iberian Kingdom *Portugal* lost its American possessions (Brazil) in the 1820's, and suffered a disputed succession and civil war in the 1830's, which left a

[311]

woman, Maria II (1834–53), on the throne. The reigns of Maria's two sons, Peter V (1853–61) and Louis I (1861–89), were marked by comparative stability and some progress, but political corruption, delay in essential reforms, and excessive taxation drove many thousand Portuguese to emigrate, and fostered the growth of anti-clericalism, socialism, communism, and anarchism among those who remained at home.

Portugal differs from Spain in retaining an extensive colonial empire which includes the Azores, the Cape Verde Islands, Portuguese Guinea, Angola, and Mozambique in Africa, Goa, Damao, and Diu in India, Macao in China, and part of the island of Timor in the East Indies. The cost of administering an empire so widely distributed and estimated at twenty-six times the area of the mother country has strained the resources of the Portuguese treasury. Portugal entered the twentieth century with a heavy burden of debt, a population two thirds of which was illiterate, a heritage of political confusion and incompetence, and a government apparently blind to the need and demand for progressive reforms.

The not surprising result was the outbreak of a popular revolution in 1910. Manuel II (whose father, Charles I, and elder brother had been *Portuguese* assassinated in 1908) fled from Lisbon, and a republic was *Revolution* proclaimed. The new constitution established a govern-*of 1910* ment resembling that of France, with a bicameral legislature, universal manhood suffrage, and a president chosen by the national deputies. The separation of church and state, confiscation of the property of religious orders, and the erection of a system of free popular schools followed; but in dealing with economic problems the new régime showed a bourgeois bent, and the government was more concerned to protect private property than to alleviate the condition of the working classes.

4. THE CRUMBLING EMPIRE OF THE SULTAN (1815–78)

The decline of the Turkish Empire, already far advanced in the eighteenth century,[1] continued in the nineteenth, with the prospect of a complete dissolution growing yearly more imminent. Each of the great powers stood ready to claim a goodly share of the Ottoman bequest, but each was apprehensive lest a rival secure a more coveted section. As a consequence the diplomats frequently protested their hypocritical anxiety to protect and preserve the integrity of Turkey, by which they really meant to protect it from each other and preserve it for themselves. It is significant to note that each successive compromise which they

[1] See above, pages 56–57, 80–81.

negotiated was preceded by a clause emphasizing the importance of preserving the Ottoman Empire intact, but each inevitably led to a further diminution of the sultan's possessions.

As a result of the Hellenic War of Independence [1] the Greek Peninsula slipped the Turkish yoke and was recognized as an independent kingdom by international agreement. The great powers considered Turkey then at the point of disintegration, and Russia pressed her military advantages so well that she was able to establish a protectorate over the provinces of Moldavia and Wallachia, and to annex the territory of Georgia in the region of the Caucasus (Treaty of Adrianople, 1829). At the same time the hardy Serbs, who had been in rebellion against their Turkish masters for years, won practical independence under their hereditary prince, Milosh I (1830). The map which follows page 388 will reveal the extent of these Turkish losses. Note that Greece and Serbia are the first fragments of the Ottoman Empire to secede as independent principalities. Russia would readily have assumed a protectorate over both these states, the inhabitants of which were most of them of the Greek Orthodox faith, but the opposition of the other powers held the Muscovite ambitions in check.

The unhappy status of the sultan's remaining Christian subjects, oppressed by special taxes and denied civil equality, provided a constant motive for foreign intervention. Members of the Greek Orthodox Church in Turkey looked to Russia for protection, while Roman Catholics commonly sought sympathy for their lot from France. The solicitude which these two powers expressed for the welfare of the "Christian cattle" of the sultan was often no more than a cloak for moves aiming at the establishment of a protectorate. In 1854, as already explained,[2] mutual rivalries led France, in alliance with Great Britain, to attack Russia in the Crimea, and the Treaty of Paris, which closed this Crimean War, solemnly guaranteed the integrity of the Ottoman Empire, frustrated Russian designs for the moment, and protected British trade in the Near East. For this respite the sultan was grateful and he made eloquent promises of reform which as usual he forgot to redeem.

In thus preserving Turkey, Britain and France were playing a rôle suspiciously like that of the dog in the manger: they would not themselves free the Balkan peoples from the sultan's misrule nor permit Russia to do so. But the spirit of nationalism which fused Italy and Germany into unified states during the *The Serbs and Rumanians* decade 1860–70 had penetrated the Balkans also, and drove the Serbs, the Rumanians, and the Bulgars to demand autonomy despite the pro-

[1] See above, pages 222–23.   [2] See above, pages 258–61.

crastination of the western powers. In 1867, the Serbian ruler, Milosh Obrenovich III, secured the withdrawal of the last Turkish garrison from Serbia, although the sultan refused to acknowledge the complete independence of that state until 1878. In the same years the inhabitants of Moldavia and Wallachia [1] voted to establish a common government, chose a noblemen, Alexander Cuza, as their prince, and proclaimed the union of the two Danubian provinces (1861). Like the Serbs, the Rumanians had to wait until the Congress of Berlin assembled in 1878 before they won acknowledgment of their status as a sovereign nation, the independent principality of Rumania.

The last of the Christian peoples of the Balkan Peninsula to escape from Turkish oppression were the Bulgars. A national and cultural *The Bulgars* revival preceded their demand for political freedom, and the Bulgars fought to emancipate themselves at one and the same time from the domination of the Greek clergy and the Turkish tax collectors. In 1870, the sultan permitted them to establish their own national church, but when they attempted to assert their political independence also (1876), they were punished by massacres so brutal and so sanguinary that all Europe was filled with indignation. Seizing the opportunity furnished by the general horror at these "Bulgarian atrocities," the Russian government intervened as the champion of the Christian minorities and declared war on Turkey (1877).

Once more the Near Eastern Question had created a European crisis. As the Russian armies advanced with Constantinople as their ultimate *Russo-Turkish War (1877–78)* objective, the British government dispatched a fleet to the Black Sea, and Austria mobilized an army to curb Russian activities in the Balkan States. To avoid a clash with either of these powers, and to secure the gains already made, the czar concluded the hasty Treaty of San Stefano with the sultan (1878). This provided for the creation of an extensive, free Bulgaria, and decreed complete independence for Serbia, Rumania, and little Montenegro. But the vigilant powers, particularly Great Britain and Austria, were not satisfied with this solution. They viewed with alarm the creation of a greater Bulgaria under Russian influence, and they insisted upon calling an international congress to revise the Treaty of San Stefano. Sullenly the Russians submitted. Berlin was chosen as the meeting-place for the diplomats, and Bismarck, who declared that Germany had no direct stake in the Near East and was therefore the best arbiter, proposed to play the part of an "honest broker" whose only desire was to reconcile his clients' interests.

[1] See map following page 388.

Not since the princely delegates hastened to Vienna to celebrate the overthrow of Napoleon in 1814 had Europe beheld a diplomatic gathering of greater moment. The powers stood dangerously *Congress of* close to war, for, although the Russians had exacted fairly *Berlin* modest concessions from the Turks, British popular feeling *(1878)* was opposed to any compromise, and the audiences in the London musichalls were chanting in belligerent fashion:

> We don't want to fight, but, by Jingo, if we do,
> We've got the ships, we've got the men, we've got the money too.

This spirit of "jingoism" as it came to be termed made a judicious settlement of the dispute extremely difficult, but in July the leading British delegate to the congress, Lord Beaconsfield (Benjamin Disraeli), was able to announce that he had brought back "peace with honor," and British "jingoists" applauded their returning prime minister and his imperialistic diplomacy.   Later, however, his colleague, Lord Salisbury, was to confess that they had "backed the wrong horse" at Berlin, for, in checking Russia, Britain had not only helped to frustrate a promising solution of the Balkan tangle, embodied in the Treaty of San Stefano, but had encouraged the advance of Austria in the Balkans.   Thirty years after the Congress of Berlin, the British had to ally themselves with the Russians to hold Austria, backed by Germany, in check.

For the moment, however, peace had been preserved by Russian concessions, and Great Britain and Austria mollified by the diplomatic device known as "reciprocal compensation."   Russia was permitted to annex the province of Bessarabia on the Black Sea between the Danube and the Dniester deltas, and also the Armenian districts of Kars, Ardahan, and Batum.[1]   In return, Austria-Hungary received the right to administer the late Turkish provinces of Bosnia and Herzegovina, and Britain, by a separate convention with Turkey, assumed possession of the island of Cyprus.   Thereupon the powers once more repeated their solemn determination to respect and to preserve intact the territorial unity of the Turkish Empire, or what remained of it.

The wishes of the Balkan peoples, who were most vitally concerned in the settlement, won scant and illogical consideration.   Bulgaria was split into three parts, the northernmost section winning practical independence, the middle section administrative autonomy, while the southern section, including Macedonia, was restored to Turkish control. For Rumania, Serbia, and Montenegro, the congress decreed complete independence and some increases in territory, but the national aspira-

[1] See map following page 362.

[315]

tions of the inhabitants were far from being satisfied. The Greeks, who were permitted to add Thessaly to their diminutive peninsula-kingdom, had the most substantial reason for gratitude.

The treaty of Berlin failed to solve the Near Eastern Question, failed to safeguard such Christian minorities as still remained under Ottoman rule, and failed to ensure the needed reforms which experience had shown the Turks might promise but would never execute. It may be that the problems involved were too intricate for solution, but in truth the diplomats revealed little honest desire to settle them equitably, being too deeply engrossed with their own plans for imperial aggrandizement to study the issues dispassionately. The Balkans remained a center of disorders, rivalries, and intrigues fermenting with national unrest, until two generations later they provided the spark which generated a World War.

Section E

THE NEW INDUSTRIAL ERA: THE CONFLICT OF CAPITAL AND LABOR, AND THE RIVALRY OF THE IMPERIALIST POWERS

(1871–1914)

In the twenty years preceding 1871, Europe had been shaken by no less than five wars, each involving two or more of the great powers. All these struggles — the Crimean War, the Italian War of 1859, the Danish War, the Austro-Prussian conflict, and the Franco-Prussian War — grew in large part out of the tension resulting from the progress of national consolidation. Italy, Germany, and to a less degree Russia, were striving to round out their territories and achieve a higher degree of political unity. By 1871, however, Italy had been organized into the Italian Kingdom, the Germanies had been welded together to form the German Empire, and Europe was permitted to settle down to a condition of relative peace and equilibrium. Twenty years of strain and frequent warfare were to be followed by over forty years of peace.

But history never stands still, and during these peaceful decades forces were at work which aggravated old problems and created new ones. The most impressive single factor affecting European civilization after 1871 was the rapid industrial development. Stimulated by new and revolutionary advances in science and technology, industry superseded agriculture as the main source of livelihood for a majority of the people in the industrialized states. But this further extension of the factory system deepened the conflict

[317]

between the owners of the machines and the workers, while the steady accumulation of capital and the need for raw materials drove the powers to exploit backward countries and expand their colonial empires. As a consequence the period from 1871 to 1914 was characterized by social conflict and the rise of socialist parties within the industrialized states, and by keener commercial and colonial competition between the industrialized states. As the tension grew, the powers were driven into two competing systems of alliances, while the people suffered the burden of ever-increasing armaments. A succession of diplomatic crises culminated, in 1914, in the outbreak of the most tragic and destructive war in European history.

CHAPTER TWENTY-THREE

THE NEW WORLD WHICH SCIENCE AND INDUSTRY HAVE CREATED

Better fifty years of Europe than a cycle of Cathay.
ALFRED TENNYSON.

EVERY student of history who peers back into past centuries will find himself drawn to certain periods with the conviction, "Here was an eventful age!" To have walked on the banks of the Nile when the Great Pyramid was rising, or through the streets of Athens in the fourth century before Christ; to have visited Cathay with Marco Polo and seen the court of Kublai Khan, or dwelt in Florence in the height of the Italian Renaissance, would doubtless have provided rich and stimulating experiences. Yet it is safe to say that at no point in the past could one find an age which, for eventfulness, for extension and diffusion of culture, rapidity of change, interest and complexity, might prove a rival to contemporary times. To have lived in Europe or America during the past half-century is to have lived in the most advanced civilization and the most extraordinary epoch in the recorded history of the human race, an epoch in which man's knowledge of the universe which he inhabits, his control over the forces of nature, his ability to produce the necessities of life and to prolong life itself, have increased more rapidly than in any comparable era of the past.

1. THE MARCH OF SCIENCE

The element in modern civilization which has made possible the dynamic changes of recent years is the progress of science and industry. An earlier chapter [1] described the beginnings of modern science in the sixteenth and seventeenth centuries, the advances in mathematical method, and the brilliant discoveries in astronomy, physics, and other fields of investigation. The scientists of the eighteenth century extended and systematized this new knowledge with such success that they made their period an Age of Rationalism, a Scientific Renaissance. But it was not until the nineteenth century that the fruits of their researches really made themselves felt in the life of the common man. A hundred and fifty years ago farmers still plowed their fields much as they had since Roman times two thousand years before. The horse provided the chief

[1] Chapter VIII, pages 107–20.

means of transportation on land, the sailing vessel on water. The swiftest means of communication was to signal a message from one hilltop to the next. Nevertheless, although the people of that age could not foresee its outcome, a revolution was at hand which speeded up the methods of communication, of transportation, and of production more effectively in a single lifetime than in all previous history. Men born in 1800 saw within the span of an average life the advent of the age of steam and steel.

In the eighteenth century it required as many days to travel the hundred and sixty miles from London to Manchester as now suffice for the
The revolution in transportation
crossing of the Atlantic or a journey from New York to San Francisco. Today goods can be shipped from England to Japan or Australia at less cost and labor than it demanded then to transport them from London to Edinburgh. The introduction of the steamship and the railway a century ago shrank this planet so surprisingly that distant continents became more accessible than neighboring states had been a few decades earlier. As a result, Europe was able to lay the world under contribution, drawing the products of every clime and every continent to her ports. The high speed and low cost of steam transportation made it possible for manufacturers to feed their factories with raw materials drawn from the ends of the earth, and to ship the finished articles back across the ocean to distant markets. The inhabitants, moreover, of the new industrial centers no longer cultivated gardens or raised their own food. For the whole world had become their garden, and from every part of it ships were racing toward them with the supplies of food which they no longer found it profitable to produce.

There is no easy comparison to be found in history for this revolutionary change. In days of old a king, perhaps, might obtain fresh fish from a lake in the next province by exhausting relays of fleet slaves, or draw melting snow from a mountain-top by the same means when he wished to cool his wine. Today every common man in a civilized community commands privileges which the king could not have imagined. The average Englishman, for example, will sit down unthinkingly to a breakfast gathered from five continents. He chooses casually between an apple from British Columbia and an orange from Tangier, coffee from Brazil or tea from Ceylon, lambs' kidneys from Australia or bacon and eggs from Denmark. The breakfast table may be of Venezuelan mahogany, the cloth of Egyptian cotton, the cutlery compounded perhaps of Canadian nickel, Swedish chromium, Chinese tin, and Mexican silver, all blended at Sheffield, England.

The newspaper folded beside his plate likewise bears witness to a revolution, not in transportation, but in communication. From every part of the world the events of the previous twenty-four *The revolu-* hours have been gleaned for his entertainment and informa- *tion in com-* tion. News of an earthquake in Tibet, a fire in Buenos *munication* Aires, or a shipwreck off the Aleutian Islands is crowded together with market quotations from Chicago and Tokyo and messages from explorers in the Amazonian jungles or near the South Pole. To draw in this medley of details a wire net has been woven from a mileage of submarine cables long enough to girdle the earth a dozen times and a length of telephone wire that would reach to the sun. The more recent devices of wireless telegraphy and radio are already accepted as commonplaces by people whose tastes are jaded with so many scientific wonders. Yet the greatest marvel of all, and the one most frequently ignored, is the fact that the inventions which make this collection and diffusion of news possible, the telegraph, telephone, and wireless systems, the linotype, and the rotary press, have all been perfected within the memory of men yet living.

While the conveyance of goods, passengers, and news was thus being speeded up, an equally momentous change took place in the methods of production. Industrial centers, able suddenly to draw upon *The revolu-* the whole world for supplies, demanded them in prodigious *tion in pro-* quantities and doubled their demands every few years. *duction* The production of iron, an essential commodity of the machine age, increased a hundred-fold in the nineteenth century, and the output of coal kept pace with it. New inventions, such as the internal combustion engine, created new demands, and the world production of petroleum after 1900 leaped ahead one thousand per cent in thirty years. To satisfy the insatiable demands of expanding industries men learned to tap pools of oil miles below the earth's crust, to draw nitrogen from the atmosphere, and to extract bromine from the sea. Power for their engines was obtained by a reckless consumption of coal, oil, or gas, or by harnessing the tireless waterfalls.

Nor did science lag in finding new ways to augment the food supply for the hungry millions. By the use of fertilizers, by experimenting with new and more nutritious types of grains and fruits, by the invention of agricultural machinery, power-driven plows, tractors, and threshing machines, the world's food supply has been augmented until in recent years the surplus has proved an embarrassment and its distribution a problem. By means of refrigerator cars and steamers millions of tons of fruit or meat can now be shipped from continent to continent, or, sealed in sterilized cans, may be preserved for years until needed. The dread specter of famine which had lurked like a lean wolf on the edge of every human community since the beginning of history seemed about to vanish at last.

This increase in material wealth has made the world a vastly more luxurious and amusing place for many people. Today the citizen of modest circumstances can afford luxuries which a Roman noble with a thousand slaves could not obtain. The electric light, telephone, and radio, the steamship, train, and automobile are at the disposal of millions. The Caesars carried no timepiece as accurate as a dollar watch, nor could their banquet table provide the variety of flavors obtainable at a modern soda fountain. Silk, once the apparel of princes, has become a household article, materials unknown or unprocurable to the ancients, such as rustless steel, aluminum, rubber, and a hundred synthetic products, have suddenly become so cheap that they are discarded after use as too worthless to salvage. Science and industry have accustomed civilized men to regard the supply of materials, raw and manufactured, as inexhaustible, so that they cast aside daily as rubbish the tons of newsprint, bottle glass, tin cans, old tires, or broken pottery which have served their purpose, indifferent to the question whether their mines and forests can long withstand such ruthless depletion.

2. NEW CONCEPTIONS OF MAN'S PLACE IN NATURE

While becoming richer and more interesting in the past hundred years, human existence has also become healthier and safer. The scientists did not rest content with exploring the inorganic universe from stars to atoms, they turned their investigations upon organic (that is, living) things as well. As a result of these researches they have been able to conquer many deadly diseases and prolong man's span of life, at the same time formulating new and revolutionary theories regarding his origin and place in nature.

In pursuing those branches of knowledge which concern man, however, such subjects as biology or psychology or politics, the scientists had to overcome a problem which had troubled them little in physics or chemistry. This problem might be called the human factor. It is an inescapable, and to the scientist a troublesome, fact, that man, who likes to put the rest of the universe under the microscope, objects to being put under it himself. For he has learned from experience that the results are likely to humiliate and bewilder him. It disturbs him little when the scientists dispute about the speed of light or the temperature of the sun, but his vanity is affronted when they tell him their evidence indicates that he is descended from the apes instead of from the angels. The poets may agree that "the proper study of mankind is man," but the scientists have found it is often considered an improper study. However warily they walk, however scrupulously they weigh their observations, they still find that their conclusions regarding man are apt to be distorted by popular prejudices and passions or invalidated by their own unsuspected loyalties.

One of the first shocks which modern science administered to human vanity was the Copernican theory.[1] If the universe was, indeed, nothing more than a vast machine, then all life on earth might be merely "the superficial phenomena of arrested radiation on the outer crust of a cooling nebula." Yet men clung to an inherited belief that the trees which bore fruits for them to eat, the lakes teeming with fish, the valleys which they plowed, and the hills to which they lifted up their eyes had been shaped to serve human needs by a benevolent Creator. How else could the mountains and the lakes, the river valleys and the fertile plains have achieved their present useful and familiar conformation?

In 1830–33, Charles Lyell attempted to answer that question in his *Principles of Geology*, explaining that the irregularities of the earth's surface were the result of natural processes still at work; *Geology* that the actions of volcanic pressure, of winds and rain and rivers, the formation of strata, and the rising and sinking of the earth's crust would, in the course of sufficient time, produce all the results now apparent. The theories of this great English scientist, which won rapid acceptance, presupposed a much greater age for the earth than the six thousand years suggested by Biblical chronology. Some modern calculations have named a figure in excess of two thousand million years.

Stimulated by Lyell's hypothesis, geologists began, by patient scrutiny and classification, to estimate the age of the various types of rock found in the earth's crust. Discovery of the fossil remains *Paleontology* of plants and animals in some of these stratified formations provided a clue to the origin of life on this planet. The earliest indications revealed the most primitive forms of organic structures, successive later strata retained the impressions of shellfish, vertebrate fish, insects, trees, reptiles, mammals, and finally of man. In 1863, Lyell published a second important work on *The Geological Evidences of the Antiquity of Man*, in which he submitted that relics of human tools and skeletons had been traced back at least fifty thousand years. Thus the geologists

---

[1] See above, page 108.

and paleontologists (that is, students of fossilized animals and plants) discovered "books in the running brooks, sermons in stones," and opened up a new and amazing vista which stretched from the portals of written history back to the first algae in the proterozoic slime.

The advances in geology set the stage for the most epoch-making conclusion of nineteenth-century thought, the theory of biological evolution. Since the time of the Greeks independent thinkers had pondered the suggestion that all life might have developed originally from a simple cell, but the proposition appeared untenable because, so far as man could observe, all living things were divided into fixed species, each producing "after his kind," as the Book of Genesis had ordained. It followed that if species were, indeed, unchanging or *immutable*, they could not all have derived gradually from the same common ancestor. But the new calculations regarding the vast age of the earth, the discovery of prehistoric forms and species now extinct, and the variations found to exist between families of living animals and their fossilized forbears provided the clue that species were not immutable after all, but were, indeed, changing imperceptibly through vast periods of time.

How the variation, progression, and multiplication of life forms not only *might* have come about, but inevitably *must* have come about, as a result of natural forces, occurred independently to two English naturalists, Charles Darwin and Alfred Russel Wallace, but Darwin reached his conclusion first and fortified it most carefully. Breeders of mice or pigeons, as Darwin knew, by mating only the dark- or light-colored offspring in successive generations, could produce in time a pure white or pure dark strain, and he reasoned that, if such a process of selection were carried on long enough, it could change the entire character of the stock. If the deer with the fleetest legs or the giraffes with the longest necks had been selected from each generation for millions of years, the cumulative effect would result in the emergence of new species. That such a process of *natural selection* had actually taken place, Darwin postulated as a corollary of the struggle for existence, explaining that the favored individuals of each species, the fleetest or the fiercest or the most intelligent, had the better chance to survive and propagate according as they were better adapted to their environment. In the course of time this principle of "the survival of the fittest" would bring about the evolution and differentiation of living organisms into an infinite variety of types and species. In 1859, Darwin offered this conclusion to the world by publishing his momentous work *On the Origin of Species by Means of Natural Selection.*

The Darwinian theories, as propagated in the philosophy of Herbert

Charles Darwin (1809–82)

[324]

CHARLES DARWIN
1809–82

*There is little in the appearance of this mild and ven-
erable figure to suggest the bitter controversy that
Darwin excited by his theories on biological evolution.*

Spencer and the lectures of Thomas Henry Huxley, aroused deep

Louis
Pasteur
(1822–95)

opposition especially among theologians. Efforts to confirm or confute them led to a more intensive study of comparative anatomy and to a more careful classification of all forms of organic life. That all living things were built out of microscopic organisms or *cells* had been demonstrated as early as 1839. Further improvements in the microscope enabled Louis Pasteur to prove that the fermentation of wine and yeast and many diseases in plants and animals were caused by minute living organisms or *germs*. For the first time physicians were given the opportunity to recognize enemies which hitherto they had fought in the dark. Pasteur demonstrated that many dangerous disease germs could be killed by such a simple device as raising the temperature of their environment (pasteurization), and that others could be combated by inoculating or immunizing human beings against their ravages. A Prussian physician, Robert Koch (1843–1910), raised bacteriology into a science, and within a decade (1884–94) the bacillus of typhoid, tuberculosis, cholera, lockjaw, diphtheria, bubonic plague, and other scourges had been identified. Although the greatest scientists were generally the most modest in their claims, enthusiasts hoped that the twentieth century would see the passing of the great plagues.

In surgery the results of the germ theory were not less important. The knowledge that infection and suppuration of wounds was due to the presence of microbes emphasized the value of antiseptics and the importance of sterilizing all the implements, bandages, etc., used in operations (asepsis). At the same time the introduction of ether and chloroform as anesthetics not only spared the patient incalculable pain, but made possible longer and far more complicated investigations. The miracles of modern surgery would be impossible without these discoveries which now save the lives of hundreds of thousands of people yearly.

Throughout the civilized world the methods popularized by Pasteur, Koch, and others led to a concerted war against disease which has had

Increase in
population
in the nine-
teenth and
twentieth
centuries

spectacular results. The medical profession, the public health authorities, and a more enlightened public adopted measures of hygiene and sanitation which in many parts of Europe cut the death rate in half in fifty years. The result has been a phenomenal increase in population, due not only to the advances in medical science, but also to the new methods, already mentioned, of producing and distributing vast quantities of cheap food. Because of the mitigation of plague and famine, the population of Europe has more than doubled since 1800. But Europe is not the only continent affected. It is estimated that during the same period the population of the earth has trebled until it stands today at two billion souls, a result made possible not so much by increasing the birth rate, but by decreasing the death rate.

This unprecedented gain in population, made possible by the achievements of modern science and industry, is the most arresting fact in modern history. It has created profound problems, for mere multiplication of the human race is not a blessing unless the newborn individuals are offered a chance to lead happy and profitable lives. It is pertinent to ask what sort of lives these added millions are condemned to live, what chance they have to find happiness, and what type of environment science and industry are providing for them. These are questions which the next section will endeavor to answer.

3. THE NEW ENVIRONMENT WHICH SCIENCE AND INDUSTRY HAVE PROVIDED: THE "CIVILIZATION OF CITY DWELLERS"

After 1870, the acceleration of the forces shaping modern life, the flood of inventions and the multifold discoveries, grew so rapid that it really constituted a second Industrial Revolution or what might better, perhaps, be termed a Technological Revolution. Successive innovations, such as the automobile, motion picture, airplane, and radio, led to the establishment of new industries overnight, industries which, like the older weaving and metallurgical trades, required hundreds of thousands of workers and were centered often in mushroom cities created to house their plants and their employees. The new methods of quantity production necessitated the co-ordination of all the processes of an industry, and of associated trades, so that the garment-makers tended to congregate in one locality, the makers of automobile parts in another. Miners crowded into dingy dwellings near the pit mouth, cotton spinners into congested towns where cheap power, a damp climate, or convenient transportation facilities had concentrated the factories. The machines demanded power to run them and raw materials to feed their tireless maw, hence it was most profitable to establish them where these essentials were easily available. Thus, in selecting the site of operations the machine was the master, and the workmen who had to tend it were condemned to live nearby. Too often this meant that thousands of mill hands had to pass their lives under the smoke-laden sky of a factory town, where the grass withered from the fumes of the blast furnaces and the streams were polluted

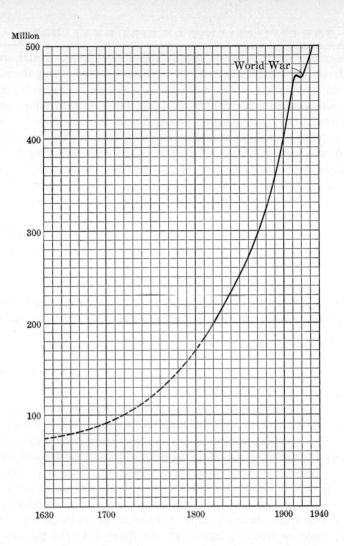

Million

ESTIMATED INCREASE IN THE POPULATION OF
EUROPE DURING THE LAST THREE CENTURIES

*No official records of European population before the last century are in exist-
ence, and even today census statistics are not absolutely dependable. Estimates
calculated from various sources indicate that there was a slow rise in the total
population from the close of the Middle Ages until the eighteenth century,
followed by the extraordinary increase of modern times.*

with the wastage of tanks and vats. The migration of the population toward the new industrial centers, a shift already observable in England at the close of the eighteenth century, continued at an increasing rate throughout the nineteenth in all the leading European countries.

The result was the growth of cities at the expense of the country districts. The most notable feature about the population in the modern industrial state is the fact that it is predominantly an *The growth* urban population. Until a century ago, and even later, *of cities* the people of the British Isles, of France, or Germany lived chiefly on the land, supporting themselves by some form of agricultural labor. England was the first state to discover, about 1850, that the town dwellers had grown to outnumber the country folk. That process has continued inexorably until today four out of every five Englishmen live in cities of ten thousand or upwards. In France and Germany the same phenomenon is to be observed, induced by the same causes, but it has not yet developed so far. The trend, however, which affects the whole of Europe, is startling enough. A century ago there were scarcely a dozen cities in Europe with a population over two hundred thousand. Today there are more than one hundred, and they are still growing.

Yet so swift has been the transformation, so recently has modern civilization become a civilization of city dwellers, that the thought, the language, the mental background of most urban inhabitants are still impregnated with rural images. City children who never visited a mill stream or plundered a farmer's orchard sing songs about the old swimming hole and the old gray mare, but they have little comprehension of these things. For most modern children know nothing of barefoot days or calling the cattle home; the world in which they are growing up has come to be a world of paved streets and angular buildings, of lighted shop windows and dark alleyways, of gasoline fumes and factory whistles. This is the environment in which the man of the twentieth century seems destined to pass the greater part of the twenty thousand days that fate allots him, divorced from the forests and the fields which were home to his grandfather, but in which a dwindling proportion of his fellow countrymen now dwell.

It follows that the proper regulation and development of those cities in which so large a part of the people elect to live must be of pressing concern to modern governments. Cities are vast agglomerations of unique and artificial growth. To police them, to safeguard their thousands or millions of inhabitants, to direct their traffic or dispose of their refuse, employs an army of public servants. Many modern cities have grown up so hurriedly and haphazardly that vast sums must later be expended to provide an adequate water supply, to create port and railway facilities, playgrounds, parks, and traffic speedways. A little foresight and foreknowledge might have solved many of these problems in advance, but the rapid changes of the machine era took governments by surprise and found even the experts largely unprepared to cope with the riddles of a dynamic civilization.

4. THE INDUSTRIALIZED SOCIETY: THE CONFLICT BETWEEN CAPITAL AND LABOR AND THE RIDDLE OF SOCIAL JUSTICE

In the Middle Ages, when land was the most important form of wealth, a man's power and riches were computed in terms of the num-

The rise of the bourgeoisie

ber of fertile acres which he possessed. His income depended upon the produce raised on his estates, part of which was turned over to him by his tenants or serfs as rent. As the yield from the soil could not be greatly increased under existing methods of cultivation, medieval wealth and medieval society tended to remain the same from one generation to the next. By the thirteenth and fourteenth centuries, however, other factors introduced a change which helped to bring the Middle Ages to an end. The story has already been told of the improvements in communication, the slow revival of commerce, and the rise of the towns, which raised a new class to prominence, the class of manufacturers, bankers, and traders. The wealth of these men was not in land, but in the commodities which they sold, in bills of exchange, and in money. Though scorned at first by the feudal, landowning nobles, the merchant class gained steadily in power and wealth and influence. For whereas the landowner's income was limited by the yield of his land and the rents paid him by his tenants, the commercial classes grew wealthier as their business grew in volume. In time this emerging middle class became strong enough to challenge the privileged position of the feudal aristocracy, and in the end they succeeded, with the aid of the seventeenth-century revolutions in England and the great revolution in France, in dominating state policies. By 1832, as explained in Chapter XVI, the bourgeoisie, the class composed of manufacturers, merchants, traders, bankers, professional men, and shopkeepers, had secured control of the government in France and Great Britain.

At this point, when the leaders of the new "commercial aristocracy" were tasting the fruits of political power, they tapped a new source of economic gain through the wider application of machinery. The Industrial Revolution had begun, and it proved the truth of the scriptural adage that to him that hath shall be given. For only men *The rising* who already possessed surplus capital could afford to ex- *power of* periment with and to install the new spinning and weaving *capital* machines which revolutionized the production of cotton and woolen fabrics. Men with foresight and initiative, who had capital to invest or knew where to borrow it, made surprising profits, and those who utilized their dividends for the purchase of still more machines might multiply their fortunes and lift themselves to the rank of great industrial capitalists.

But the factory system not only enriched the capitalist class; it also multiplied vastly the number of unpropertied wage-earners, the class which has come to be called the industrial proletariat. *The indus-* The machines provided wide employment for the unskilled *trial prole-* and semi-skilled laborer, but too often he found life in a *tariat* factory little better than economic serfdom. In some respects his lot was even harder than that of a serf in the Middle Ages, for the medieval peasant could not be deprived of his land or his means of livelihood, poor as it might be, but a factory worker might be discharged at any time and face starvation if he found no other work. The peasants of the Middle Ages had usually accepted their lot with resignation, but the industrial laborers of the nineteenth century, living in larger groups, could combine and protest more effectively than their thirteenth-century forbears. They agitated for better working conditions and better wages, and organized themselves in order to fight for their rights. Dissatisfied and unemployed workingmen were among the first to raise the barricades in the Paris revolutions of 1830 and 1848, and they swelled the ranks of the Chartists in England.

The attempts of the workers to organize trade unions to promote their interests met at first with strong opposition, and the unions were condemned and disbanded as "conspiracies in restraint *Trade* of trade." Labor combinations formed for the purpose *unions* of gaining better hours, wages, or working conditions did not enjoy full legal protection in England until 1871. In France, although co-operative societies were permitted, workingmen's combinations formed to bargain with employers (*sociétés de résistance*) were first forbidden, then tolerated (1868), and finally given legal status (1884). In Germany, the laborers' right to combine for the purpose of winning more favorable wages and working conditions was not recognized legally until after 1890. It is to be noted that in all three countries the statutes which forbade the combination of the workers with the object of forcing wages *up* also

[331]

contained clauses prohibiting combinations of employers for the purpose of forcing wages *down*, but in the latter case the legislation remained very largely a dead letter.

After the middle of the nineteenth century, the deepening antagonism between the capitalist or bourgeois employers and the workingmen acquired new significance through the writings of Karl Marx.

Karl Marx (1818–83)

Born in Treves, Germany, Marx enjoyed an excellent education, but his political activities on behalf of the lower classes got him into trouble in his homeland and also in France, where he joined in the revolution of 1848. So he settled in London in order to devote himself to study and to the development of those theories which have earned him the title "the father of modern socialism."

Armed with profound learning and a powerful intellect, Marx formulated a new philosophy of history, based upon his conclusion that the factor which is common to society in every age is the exploitation of one class by another. In modern society Marx found this "class struggle" exemplified in the contest between capital and labor, the capitalists being the "expropriators" and the workingmen the "expropriated," and he prophesied that the struggle would gradually split society into two hostile camps with no middle ground between. For the progress of the Industrial Revolution seemed destined to increase the profits of the machine-owners while the proletarians grew more numerous and more conscious of their violated rights. In the end the proletariat would take over the machinery of production to run it for the benefit of all, and the "expropriators" would be expropriated.

To its exponents the chief attraction of this "economic interpretation of history" lay in its logical prediction that the ultimate triumph of the proletariat must come about in the natural course of events.

Criticism of Marxism

Critics have objected, however, that at this point Marx abandons his realistic approach and becomes almost as Utopian as Fourier or Saint-Simon. For he implies that the proletarian revolution will be followed by the creation of a co-operative commonwealth without expropriating or expropriated classes. Such a conclusion appears to presuppose either (1) that the class conflict is not a constantly operative and rigidly determined principle, or (2) that the human mind, by understanding it, can alter conditions and arrest the endless series of revolutions to which the class struggle has given rise — neither of which offers a wholly logical explanation. Most socialists were encouraged, however, by the Marxian prophecy that capitalism would dig its own grave, and that, although the advent of socialism

KARL MARX
1818–83

A capacity for profound and dispassionate
thought made Marx the outstanding philosopher
of socialism, but opponents who rejected the
gospel according to Marx found that he could
also be a passionate controversialist.

might be delayed, it could not be prevented. Since the workers of all countries had the same general grievances, Marx urged them to unite in pressing the class war, disregarding national ties and boundaries, for all the workers of the world were "comrades."

In 1864, socialists from various countries attempted to organize an international movement for which Marx prepared a constitution. *The First and Second International* Weakened by the desertion of the moderates and the expulsion of the anarchists, this First International foundered in 1873, but a Second International was formed in 1889. Meanwhile, socialist groups in the leading European countries entered the political arena and socialist voters polled an increasing number of ballots. By 1914, the Socialist Parties in France and Germany had each over a hundred deputies in parliament, while in the British House of Commons the Labor Party held forty seats.

The spread of democracy in the period 1870–1914 and the extension of the suffrage to all classes naturally favored the growth of the Socialist *Evolution or revolution?* Parties. Their leaders hoped a time would soon come when the workers, as the most numerous class in each state, would control the parliaments through the deputies whom they elected, for when they secured this control they could transform the capitalist system by legislative decrees. All moderate-minded men naturally hoped that the ends of social justice might be realized by constitutional means and that the problems growing out of the class struggle would find an *evolutionary* rather than a *revolutionary* solution. The parliaments of the nineteenth century had generally avoided these problems, and, true to the bourgeois doctrine of *laissez-faire,* or "let alone," they had left the workers to the mercy of their employers. But there seemed good reason to hope after 1900 that the parliaments of the twentieth century would abandon this evasive course and grapple honestly with the task of reconciling the demands of capital and labor. Unhappily, this hope was to be temporarily blasted by the outbreak of the World War in 1914.

Like the "class struggle," the World War was very largely a product of the new forces which science and industry have let loose in society. The economic rivalries of imperialistic powers which helped to provoke this war, the machine guns, submarine boats, and poison gas which multiplied its horrors, and the airships which dropped bombs on frightened towns were no less the products of the new world which science and industry have provided than the cheap food, the rapid transportation, and the protection against plagues. The Industrial Revolution not only helped to intensify the class struggle *within* the modern states;

[334]

it also helped to intensify the jealousies existing *among* the modern states, as the next section will explain.

5. THE INDUSTRIALIZED STATE: THE COMPETITION AMONG THE GREAT POWERS FOR COLONIES AND MARKETS

In medieval times, when highways were few and poor and ships small and slow, the inhabitants of a village or dwellers on a barony had to raise the necessities of life in their own neighborhood. Meat and eggs, fruit and grain, wine and olives, were largely consumed where they were produced, for it was costly and difficult to preserve or to transport them. The same principle applied to almost all the commodities of existence. Traders had to limit their load to light and precious wares, such as salt, spices, silks, and jewels. After the revival of commerce and the voyages of exploration in the fifteenth and sixteenth centuries, the European peoples learned to enjoy many foreign products, such as coffee, tea, cocoa, tobacco, etc., but until the nineteenth century the European states still remained to a high degree self-sufficient and self-supporting.

The Industrial Revolution tended to destroy this economic equilibrium. A modern industrial state such as England, with four fifths of the people living in towns, would find it impracticable *Agriculture* if not actually impossible to raise at home the food re- *vs. industry* quired for its urban millions. Instead, the English people have learned to utilize the cheap and rapid transportation of the steam age to import vast supplies of wheat from Canada or Argentina and tons of frozen mutton from Australia. For this food, which makes good their own deficiency, they pay with shipments of manufactured articles from their humming factories, and so satisfactory did the method of exchange appear that British agriculture has been permitted to languish. In 1840, British farmers grew enough wheat to supply ninety per cent of the population of the United Kingdom, but by the close of the century their crops sufficed for only ten per cent. The German population has tended since 1870 to outgrow the domestic food supply in the same way, and, despite state encouragement and subsidies to the farmers, Germany has become partly dependent upon imported foodstuffs. On the other hand, France still demonstrates the balance which may be maintained between agriculture and industry, and has remained the most self-sufficient of the three powers, but France is not so highly industrialized as England or Germany and has a stationary or almost stationary population.

[335]

For the industrial state an equally serious problem arises from the fact that the insatiable capacity of the machines tends to outrun the *The web of* domestic supply of raw material. England, long famous *empire* for the quality and quantity of her domestic wool, was able until a century ago to provide her mills with home-grown fleece. But industrial development rendered the local supply insufficient, and today four fifths of the wool utilized in the British textile trades comes from overseas. Where the raw materials of a trade cannot be raised in England, as in cotton manufacturing, the dependence upon foreign sources may be even more complete. Great Britain's imports of raw cotton have increased from a few million pounds a year in the eighteenth century to something over a billion, and her re-exports of cotton textiles have been valued at six hundred million dollars for a single year. Yet this gigantic industry, like many others in the British Isles, is dangerously dependent upon the vicissitudes of world trade. The ships which carry these cargoes back and forth are the indefatigable shuttles weaving the fabric of British commercial greatness. If they ceased to operate, even for a few weeks, British industry would face economic paralysis, and if the tie-up lasted several months, the British people would suffer the severest privation. This danger, in a greater or less degree, faces all states which devote a major part of their energies to the profitable but precarious hazards of modern industry.

Under these circumstances the great industrial powers must be prepared to safeguard their communications and to maintain contact with the foreign markets and sources of supply without which their home industries would languish. The incoming tide of raw materials and food, the outgoing flood of manufactures, these are the life blood of empire, and the railway and steamship lines are the channels through which this life blood ebbs and flows. This is the reason why modern governments often subsidize private transportation companies, why they build railways along strategic routes in the battle for trade, and are prepared to go to war to keep control of them. It also explains in part the interest which the great powers show in colonies and markets in the so-called "backward countries" of the world.

But there is a second and less obvious reason which drove the powers to engage in an undignified scramble for control of the less civilized *The scram-* portions of the globe, especially after 1870. In all the *ble for con-* industrialized states capital was accumulating as a result *trol of back-* of business enterprise, and as the opportunities for highly *ward coun-* *tries* profitable investment at home were narrowed by competition, the masters of this disposable capital looked abroad for new fields which might promise higher returns. They "exported" their capital to the backward countries, using it to open up untapped natural resources, to build roads and railways, and to develop new enterprises under favorable conditions which assured them a high rate of interest. Frequently the local rulers, as the Khedive of Egypt or the Sultans of Turkey and Morocco, invited this influx of capital because it helped to modernize their domains. The profits to be reaped from thus opening up backward and often anarchic countries were great, but the risks were great also, for local disturbances might endanger the plant or property which the investors' money had established. It was but natural, therefore, that British investors, for example, should appeal to their government to safeguard their investments by establishing a protectorate over the area they were exploiting. In its hidden but effective fashion, this pressure which British or German or American investors might bring to bear upon their respective governments to safeguard their exported capital provided a more persistent impulse toward imperialist expansion than either the profits of colonial trade (which were often negligible to the mother country) or the need to obtain raw materials (which could usually be purchased in the world's markets).

These several motives help to explain why the vast and half-unknown continent of Africa was parceled out among the European powers in little more than a decade after 1880, and the ancient but feeble Chinese Empire carved into "spheres of influence" as the Russians, British, French, Germans, and Japanese vied for control of the oriental resources. Even scattered islands in the seas, hitherto ignored as of no value or interest, were annexed as possible naval bases or sites for a cable or wireless station. Not since the colonizing ventures of the seventeenth century had Europeans shown such zeal in planting their flags on alien shores as in this era of the New Imperialism.

The native peoples of Africa and Asia frequently resented the imposition of foreign control, and all the colonizing powers became involved in frontier wars which were settled in almost all *The threat* cases by the superiority of the white man's weapons. The *to world* New Imperialism brought with it, however, a threat of *peace* more serious conflict, of an armed struggle among the great powers themselves growing out of their clashing activities and claims. The tension already existing among the European nations was intensified by colonial rivalry and commercial competition; the result was a mutual increase in armaments which in turn increased the fear and suspicion. The final fruit of this spirit of jealousy and of international covetousness was to be a world conflict fought on a scale and with resources hitherto unimagined. The roots of this World War will be examined in the two following chapters which discuss the class struggle within the industrialized states and the national antagonism among the industrialized states during the period 1871–1914.

CHAPTER TWENTY-FOUR

THE SOCIAL CONFLICT WITHIN THREE INDUSTRIAL STATES: GREAT BRITAIN FRANCE, AND GERMANY
(1871–1914)

... Proclaiming social truth shall spread,
And justice, ev'n though thrice again
The red fool-fury of the Seine
Should pile her barricades with dead.
ALFRED TENNYSON, *In Memoriam,* cxxvi.

THE middle years of the nineteenth century were years of exceptional prosperity for the British people. As the greatest manufacturing, colonizing, and naval power of the world, Britain enjoyed a unique prestige in international affairs, a prestige which the Whig leader, Lord Palmerston, influential in foreign affairs *British* throughout the period from 1830 to 1865, maintained vigor- *prosperity* ously by brandishing a "big stick" over the lesser nations. *in the mid-* A spirit of complacency permeated the British ruling classes *nineteenth* during this "Palmerstonian Era," which neither the blunders of the Crimean War [1] nor the murmurs of the exploited masses could seriously disturb. The poet-laureate, Alfred Tennyson, might lament "the faithless coldness of the times," but the rapid industrial expansion provided employment for all who sought it, and brought wealth to a growing number of business men, who were naturally disposed to agree that all was for the best in the best possible of worlds.

1. THE MARCH OF DEMOCRACY IN GREAT BRITAIN
(1867–1914)

The Chartist Movement had collapsed in 1848, but the prophets of democracy, the liberal and radical reformers, still raised their voices to demand the franchise for all adult males. Heartening reports of progress came from abroad. The establishment of a liberal monarchy in Italy (1859–61), the emancipation of the Russian serfs (1861), and the liberation of Negro slaves in the United States (1863), were events hailed by English liberals as milestones on the road to democracy. They demanded that England, the historic land of freedom, should lead the way in vindicating the rights of man and extend the vote to the common

[1] See above, pages 258–61.

[339]

citizen. But the ruling classes remained hostile or indifferent to the idea of parliamentary reform. When, in 1866, William Ewart Gladstone (1809–98), the most popular and eloquent leader in the Liberal Party after Palmerston's death the previous year, proposed to add some four hundred thousand voters to the lists, his bill was rejected and the Liberal ministry resigned from office.

The defeat of Gladstone's bill created an outburst of popular indignation and was followed by threatening demonstrations in London and *The Reform* elsewhere. The brilliant and versatile Benjamin Disraeli *Bill of 1867* (1804–81), who succeeded Gladstone and headed a Conservative ministry, decided that if the Conservatives wished to remain in power they would have to make concessions. So in 1867, Disraeli introduced a moderate reform bill and blandly permitted Gladstone, and the aggressive Liberal, John Bright, to amend it until it became more radical than the defeated bill of 1866. As finally passed, the Reform Bill of 1867 (supplemented by similar measures for Scotland and Ireland) added a million voters to the rolls and almost doubled the electorate. Disraeli's admitted purpose was to "dish" the Whigs (i.e., Liberals) by stealing their thunder, and he hoped that the workingmen whom he had enfranchised would vote for the Conservative Party out of gratitude. In obeying such selfish calculations, Disraeli did not stand alone, for many of the Whig members also had compromised with their prejudices and supported reform in order to attract the new voters. The vitriolic Thomas Carlyle, a friend of the oppressed but not of democracy, declared in a pamphlet on the bill — which he called ominously *Shooting Niagara: and After?* — that "Traitorous Politicians, grasping at votes, even votes from the rabble, have brought it on." Stanch reactionaries, who still clung to the time-hallowed conviction that the people who own a country, the propertied classes, were the only ones sane and stable enough to be trusted with political power, viewed the change with alarm and despondency.

Whatever their several motives, Gladstone, Disraeli, and Bright had advanced the British people a long stride on the way to complete democracy. Many tenant farmers in the country and all householders in the city, as well as all lodgers paying the equivalent of ten pounds a year for rent, won the ballot. Disraeli's argument that the Conservatives had shown themselves the true friends of the people, and his attempt to build up a "Tory-Democracy," met, however, with dubious success. The growing radical party in Parliament, including many delegates of the laboring classes, preferred to collaborate with the Liberals, who returned to power in 1868.

In 1884, Gladstone introduced a further reform, extending the suffrage to include some two million agricultural laborers. The following year a Redistribution of Seats Bill enacted that each member of *Third Re-* the House of Commons should represent a constituency of *form Bill* approximately fifty thousand inhabitants, but, as this provi- *(1884) and Redistribu-* sion was not consistently applied and no device included for *tion of* redrawing the constituencies in obedience to the shifts and *Seats Bill* changes in population, proportional representation contin- *(1885)* ued to be an ideal rather than a reality.

After 1884, four out of five adult Englishmen possessed the right to vote and the House of Commons might be considered to be fairly representative of the nation. But the House of Lords remained a stronghold of class privilege. Its membership was composed of several hundred hereditary English peers, two score elected peers chosen to represent the aristocracy of Scotland and Ireland, and the leading prelates of the Anglican Church. As all legislation had to be approved by both chambers, this aristocratic body enjoyed a virtual power of veto over the acts of the lower house. Usually, as in the case of the Reform Bill of 1867, the Lords showed the good sense to yield to the popular will, but their occasional opposition to liberal measures irritated many people who had come to consider the House of Lords a feudal anachronism.

In 1909, the upper chamber excited particular indignation by throwing out a fiscal measure, although by custom all legislation concerning the budget had long been regarded as secure from such *The Parlia-* treatment. The Liberals, then in office, decided that the *ment Act of* time had come to curtail the Lords' prerogatives, and de- *1911* spite Conservative resistance they passed the Parliament Act of 1911. Under this act all money bills voted by the House of Commons were to become law after the lapse of one month, with or without the approval of the House of Lords. Other measures which the Lords opposed would become law after two years if passed by three successive sessions of the Commons. The members of the upper house could hardly be expected to approve the Parliament Act, but had they persisted in rejecting it the Liberal prime minister, Herbert Asquith, would have called upon George V to create enough new peers to change the balance, a move to which the king had pledged his agreement. As in the case of the Reform Bill of 1832, the threat sufficed and the Lords yielded.

In 1914, the Liberal program was interrupted by the outbreak of the World War. A vote for every adult male was assured, however, by the Reform Bill of 1918, and also for every woman over thirty provided that either she or her husband was eligible to vote in local elections.

Full legal equality for women followed in 1919, a tribute to their varied
Triumph of services during the war, and in 1928 they obtained the ballot
woman on the same terms as the men enjoyed. Great Britain had
suffrage become, in theory at least, a land where the will of the people
was the supreme law. The major demands of the Chartists, considered so
dangerous and radical in the 1830's, had been adopted as matters of
common practice less than a century later.

Of the Six Points of the Chartist program,[1] the abolition of the property qualification for members of Parliament had first been enacted into
The Six law (1858); then followed the introduction of the secret
Points of (sometimes called the Australian) ballot (1872), the estab-
Chartism lishment of approximately equal electoral districts (1885), a
vindicated salary for members of Parliament (1911), and universal
adult male suffrage achieved through the successive reform bills of 1832,
1867, 1884, and 1918. The provision for annual Parliaments has not yet
been adopted, but a five-year period has been set as the maximum interval that may elapse between elections.

This onward march of democracy is one of the most significant developments in British history during the past hundred years. Without
revolution, without serious disorder or bloodshed, the English liberalized
their institutions and made their Parliament, once a stronghold of the
privileged ruling classes, a flexible and responsive instrument of the
people's will. This was a truly remarkable achievement, unmarred by
violence or persecution, and Englishmen have reason to boast that theirs
is a land "Where freedom broadens slowly down from precedent to precedent." If, as many of its protagonists had sworn, democracy held the
answer to the ancient riddle of social justice, then a government which
represented all classes should have been able to resolve the conflicts
between those classes, and the legislators at Westminster, as democracy
progressed, should have seen their way more and more clearly as they
sought a remedy for the evils of the class struggle. To some extent they
did; but in several important respects they failed. The story of that
quest for social justice and its indeterminate outcome must now be told.

2. GREAT BRITAIN (1871–1914): THE QUEST FOR SOCIAL JUSTICE

From the beginning of the Industrial Revolution, the English workingmen had been confronted by two alternative programs for bettering their
condition. The first was a political program. They might agitate for a

---

[1] See above, pages 231–32.

more democratic franchise, elect delegates to Parliament, and work through their delegates for legislation that would assure them shorter hours, easier working conditions, and better wages. But such a workers' party had little chance to develop while the unpropertied classes still lacked the vote, and at first the English workingmen, especially in the years of depression which followed the Napoleonic Wars, gave little thought to politics. Instead, they favored a second program calling for more direct action. They organized trade unions or combinations whereby the metal workers or the weavers or the paper-makers might band together and extort more favorable terms from an employer by threatening a strike that would tie up his business. The law was hostile to such combinations, but they continued to operate, and the workers placed more confidence in such direct methods of bargaining than in tedious and uncertain political action. They were confirmed in this opinion when the Chartist Movement, despite the support that it received from the masses, failed to secure any parliamentary gains and broke up ignominiously after 1848.

Nevertheless, the occasional successes won by the trade unions did not obviate the fact that their members might be exposed to prosecution and their funds to confiscation under the existing laws. *Trade-* This difficulty did not disappear until after 1871, but with *Union Act* the passage of the Trade-Union Act of that year the organi- *(1871)* zation of labor in Great Britain entered a new, legalized, and aggressive phase. Strikes became frequent, employers were thrown upon the defensive, and in 1899, the British Labor Movement was consolidated by the creation of a Federation of Trade Unions.

Then came a serious setback. In 1901, the House of Lords, sitting as a court of final appeal, sustained a decision awarding the Taff Vale Railway Company £23,000 damages against the Amalgamated *Taff Vale* Society of Railway Servants for loss and destruction of *decision* property resulting from a strike. At a stroke of the pen the *(1901)* accumulated savings of all the trade unions, collected penny by penny to sustain the members through the possible privation of a strike, were placed in jeopardy. By this decision the unions would be exposed to possible suits for damages whenever their leaders ordered the members to lay down their tools.

Leaders of the Trade-Union Movement now realized that perhaps organized labor had erred in avoiding the field of practical politics. If the existing laws worked against them, the existing laws *Labor enters* would have to be changed by act of Parliament, for other- *politics* wise the gains of many years and many strikes might be undone by a

[343]

few adverse verdicts. As early as 1893, a small Independent Labor Party had been organized by Mr. Keir Hardie, and there was in addition a Social Democratic Federation pledged to work for Marxian socialism. Furthermore, the members of the Fabian Society, a group of advanced thinkers which included the witty dramatist George Bernard Shaw, H. G. Wells the novelist, and writers on political and economic questions such as Sidney and Beatrice Webb, were winning a strong following among the intellectuals and had begun to popularize socialist ideas among the liberal middle-class thinkers. These associations pressed their campaign so energetically between 1901 and 1906 that by the latter year Labor controlled twenty-nine seats in Parliament and had become a force in national politics.

The election of 1906 also brought the Liberal Party back into power after a decade of Conservative rule. By combining forces with the *The Liberal ascendancy and the era of social reform (1906–14)* Laborites and with the Irish Nationalists (a parliamentary group seeking Home Rule for Ireland), the Liberals were in a position to control 514 seats against 156 held by the Conservatives. Under the leadership of the cool-headed Herbert Asquith, prime minister from 1908 to 1916, and the eloquent, mercurial Welshman, David Lloyd George, this *bloc* carried through a series of daring social reforms.

One of the first fruits of the Liberal-Labor coalition was the Trades-Disputes Act (1906), which protected trade-union funds from the menace *Social legislation* of the Taff Vale decision. Then the "New Liberals," having partly abandoned the old *laissez-faire* principles, attacked the evils of the industrial system with legislation which their opponents rightly termed "socialistic." A Workingmen's Compensation Act (1906) compelled employers to compensate a worker (or, in fatal mishaps, his family) for injuries incurred at his trade. Stringent regulations for the health and schooling of the young, and state pensions for the indigent old, followed in 1908. To relieve unemployment a government employment office was opened in 1909 to assist able-bodied workers to find occupations suited to their talents, and the same year a Trade Boards Act established commissions to regulate the wages and protect the employees from undue exploitation in the so-called "sweatshops." The crowning achievement of this program of social reform was the adoption (1911) of a National Insurance Act. From premiums subscribed in part by the workers, in part by the employers, and in part by the state, a fund was established which gave the assurance to over two million workers that in case of unemployment they would receive an allowance of seven shillings a week. A much larger number were guaranteed free medical

DAVID LLOYD GEORGE

Dynamic energy and facile eloquence raised Lloyd George to political eminence, despite the attacks of opponents who accused him of being an opportunist devoid of sincerity or profundity.

attention and weekly allowances in case of sickness, thus exorcising to some extent the cruelest fear that haunts people of small income and no resources.

To meet the mounting state expenditures resulting from the Old Age Pensions Act, the extension of education, and other items in the list of *The Budget of 1909* social reforms, the fiery crusader, Lloyd George, proposed to tax the rich. As chancellor of the exchequer he brought in a budget in 1909, which he frankly designated "a war budget" in the campaign against poverty. It not only increased the existing income and inheritance taxes, but laid a heavy strain upon the great landowners. In parts of England where land had recently increased in value, often through no effort of the owner, the government proposed to appropriate twenty per cent of such unearned increase. Idle land, particularly acreage set aside for private parks or game preserves, incurred a two per cent levy, and royalties derived from mineral deposits discovered on private property paid a five per cent tax. The House of Lords opposed this attempt "to lay the heaviest burden on the broadest back," a stand which moved the Liberals, as already explained, to reduce the obstructive power of the upper house to little more than a temporary or suspensive veto.

To rectify an old injustice and satisfy the Irish Nationalist Party, which had over eighty members in Parliament, the Liberals also passed a Government of Ireland Bill embodying a project for limited home rule. The bill excited frantic opposition from the inhabitants of Ulster, most of them Protestant descendants of English or Scottish settlers in northern Ireland, who feared that Home Rule would leave them at the mercy of the Irish Catholic majority. The Ulsterites and the Irish Nationalists were on the verge of armed conflict when the outbreak of the World War overshadowed their dispute and caused the suspension of the Government of Ireland Bill until the close of hostilities.

The war also brought to a close the era of the New Liberalism. In the progressive years, 1906–14, the political leaders had waged an energetic campaign against social injustice, relieving poverty, educating and elevating the masses, and distributing more equitably the burden of taxation. Yet these significant innovations had been fitted, with characteristic British caution, into the existing framework of government and society. The new architects had sought to compromise with, not to uproot, the old traditions, and even the emergence of a well-organized political group, pledged to socialist principles, had alarmed conservative opinion less than it might have been expected to do, perhaps because the new group called itself, not the "Socialist," but the "Labor Party."

Viewed as a triumph of political compromise, the reforms of 1906–14 might be called a success; but measured against the high hopes which a Thomas Jefferson or a Joseph Mazzini had reposed in the *Democracy* possibilities for good which would lie within the reach of a *on trial* genuinely democratic government, they left much to be desired. Not in England only, but in all Europe, the decade before the war provided the best chance democratic statesmen had ever enjoyed to solve the conflicts within and between the different states. Some thinkers would have it that democracy failed to meet the test. Some are disposed to believe it succeeded as well as could be expected. Still others have argued that government by the people was never honestly tried, or that it failed to bring the peace and harmony expected of it because democratic institutions had been conceived in the eighteenth century when all nations were predominantly interested in agriculture, and applied in the nineteenth and twentieth centuries when the Industrial Revolution was remoulding society on different lines. All these are speculations which the student might profitably ponder as he compares the social legislation introduced in France and Germany after 1871 with that which was passed in England.

3. FRANCE (1871–1914): CONSOLIDATING THE BOURGEOIS REPUBLIC

After the government of Napoleon III disappeared like an "insubstantial pageant faded" in the *débâcle* of Sedan, the French people pursued for six months longer a war that was already lost. Hostilities between the newly born French Republic and the newly proclaimed German Empire were formally closed by the Treaty of Frankfort (May 10, 1871), whereby France yielded the best part of Alsace and Lorraine and an indemnity of five billion francs.[1]

Not yet, however, were the misfortunes of "the terrible year" at an end. The National Assembly, which had been convoked at Bordeaux in February, 1871, was monarchist and bourgeois in temper, *The Paris* and the radical elements of the Parisian populace, led by *Commune* Republicans and Socialists, repudiated its authority. Then *(April–May, 1871)* followed a second siege of Paris, in which the defenders of the Commune, as the radical city government was termed, massacred their hostages and set fire to important buildings before they were suppressed in desperate street-to-street fighting by the national troops. The victims of this fratricidal strife exceeded fifteen thousand, and all

[1] See above, page 289.

Europe stood aghast at "the red fool-fury of the Seine." The merciless suppression of the *communards*, with the wholesale executions and deportations which followed, temporarily crushed the Socialist movement in France and left the bourgeois middle class securely entrenched, but it bequeathed a heritage of hate which has continued to divide the workers from the propertied classes.

Having restored order at this terrible cost, the National Assembly should have lost no further time in fulfilling its task and creating a per-

The quasi-republic (1871–75) manent government for the republic. But the deputies were by no means certain whether they wished to make France a republic or a monarchy. The Monarchists, it is true, outnumbered the Republicans 500 to 200, but they were themselves split into Legitimists, Orléanists, and a few Bonapartists. In their dilemma they compromised by naming Adolph Thiers "President of the French Republic," as a temporary expedient, but when Thiers frankly defended the Republic as "the form of government which divides us least," the Monarchist majority replaced him (1873) by a stanch royalist, Marshal MacMahon, who could be counted upon to make way for a king at the right moment. The Legitimist pretender, the Count of Chambord (grandson of Charles X), might have mounted the throne as Henry V, but his insistence that before he did so the white flag of the Bourbons must replace the revolutionary tricolor proved a stumbling-block. Slowly the tide turned in favor of the Republican cause, which was championed indefatigably by the fiery and eloquent Léon Gambetta (1838–82). In 1875, the reluctant Assembly passed five constitutional laws which clarified the status of the quasi-republic, but the danger of a monarchist *coup* did not really wane until the elections of 1879 gave the Republicans control of the Senate as well as the Chamber of Deputies.

The Third Republic, established in this indefinite fashion, proved the most stable and enduring régime that France had known in a century.

The government of the Third French Republic A Senate, the members of which were chosen through electoral colleges, and a Chamber of Deputies elected by universal manhood suffrage assured popular control. The president, elected for a seven-year term by the senators and deputies jointly, possessed a minimum of executive authority, the real power resting with the ministry or cabinet responsible to the Chamber of Deputies. In general, from 1879 to 1914 the successive *blocs* or coalition groups which controlled the Chamber and the cabinet represented the moderate republican point of view. The powerful middle class which had created the Third French Republic held it true to bourgeois principles.

This middle-class rule was not maintained without a struggle. Two factions in France, the Clericals and the Royalists, were definitely hostile to the republican régime. They sought to discredit the leading Republican deputies by charges of dishonesty and incompetence, some of which were well deserved. Many *The "man on horse-back"* Frenchmen, disgusted with the graft and intrigue that disfigured party politics, yearned for a ruthless and efficient dictator of the Napoleonic type, a leader who would unite France and perhaps wage a war of revenge against Germany. From 1886 to 1889 General Georges Boulanger, minister of war, courted popularity and posed as the man of destiny, but Boulanger was no Napoleon and hesitated to gamble upon a *coup d'état*. When the republican government ordered an investigation of his activities, he fled from France, and the Boulangist Movement collapsed in ridicule, to the discomfiture of its supporters.

Five years later the rivalry between the friends and foes of the republic provided the passionate and dramatic setting for a new dispute. In 1894, Captain Alfred Dreyfus, a Jew and an officer in the French army, was convicted by a military court of communicating important secrets to a foreign power, and sentenced to life *The Dreyfus case* imprisonment in a penal colony off the coast of French Guiana. Members of Dreyfus's family and others who had convinced themselves of his innocence (among them the famous novelist, Émile Zola) demanded a new trial, but the anti-Dreyfusards, led by high military officials, Clericals, and Monarchists, were satisfied of his guilt. Many of them regarded him as a symbol of the corruption, treachery, and commercialism which they conceived to be ruining France under the republican rule. But when subsequent revelations (1897–99) proved that the real culprit, a Major Esterhazy, had been shielded, and the evidence against Dreyfus withheld from those who sought to reopen the case, lest the prestige of the army staff should suffer, French public opinion underwent a profound reversal. Dreyfus, brought back from Devil's Island for a retrial (1899), was again found guilty by his hostile judges, but President Loubet pardoned him, and the supreme court of France finally exonerated him completely (1906). Royalism, clericalism, and militarism had been so thoroughly discredited by the revelations of this famous case that, from 1899 until the outbreak of the war in 1914, Republicans and Socialists controlled the Chamber of Deputies.

One of the first steps taken by the Republican-Socialist "Cabinet of Republican Defense" of 1899 was to "purify" the army, too long a stronghold of royalist sympathizers, and subordinate it to the civil authority. Having thus "republicanized" the military institutions, the

[349]

cabinet attacked the more difficult task of curbing clerical activity *The republic* harmful to the republic. By the *concordat* of 1801,[1] which *triumphs over Militarists and Clericals* still remained in force, the government of the Third Republic was committed to an agreement to pay the salaries of the clergy, although the clergy might be and in some cases were actively hostile to the republic. Furthermore, the clergy had continued to supervise the training of the young, and might, it was thought, teach them to grow up reactionary Monarchists instead of ardent Republicans. The first blow struck against this clerical influence was the Associations Law (1901), which had the effect of dissolving most of the religious orders engaged in teaching and charitable work in France, and of curbing religious instruction in the schools. The second blow followed in 1905 with the repeal of the *concordat*. A Separation Law stripped the Catholic Church of its privileged position, ended the payment of state salaries to the priests, and the state appointment of bishops. The Roman Catholic Church in France was left to stand on practically the same footing as other religious cults.

Though its birth had been ill-omened and its early decades unauspicious, the bourgeois republic had attained at the end of its first thirty years a position of remarkable strength and solidity. Despite frequent cabinet crises caused by party shifts in the Chamber of Deputies, France had evolved a régime which appeared to meet her needs, with the army and the church subservient to the rule of the middle class. But in France as in England this rule of the middle class was threatened at its foundations by the growth of an organized labor movement and the spread of socialism. This development must now be considered.

4. FRANCE (1871–1914): THE SPREAD OF SYNDICALISM AND SOCIALISM

The bloody suppression of the Paris Commune in 1871 shattered the Socialist Party in France for a generation. French workingmen retained, however, the privilege of forming labor unions and could call a strike to enforce their demands. In 1876, a labor congress convened at Paris, representing unions or *syndicats* from all parts of France, and in 1884 the government granted the *syndicats* full legal recognition. Unfortunately, the labor leaders could not agree among themselves concerning their aims or their methods. Some favored the idea of working with the Socialists for legislation that would reduce the hours of labor and compel employers to improve the conditions in mines and

[1] See above, page 178.

factories. But a majority of the French workers, like the English trade-unionists, were persuaded that they could do best for themselves by direct bargaining. If we elect leaders to the Chamber of Deputies, they argued, we shall have no control over them if they choose to compromise our interests and go over to the side of our masters.

So the members of the *syndicats* told the Socialists to go ahead in their own fashion, but for themselves they considered it more profitable to organize their forces in a General Confederation of Labor *The General* (1895). In this way they planned to work for the day when *Confedera-* they would be strong enough to bring their capitalist em- *tion of* ployers to terms through a general strike, and expropriate *Labor* the expropriators as Karl Marx had prophesied that they would.

Several times between 1900 and 1910 the *syndicats* attempted to test their strength by strikes, and several times they gained concessions, but the results were not conclusive. Their most ambitious *The railway* effort, a strike of the railway workers, proved their most *workers'* signal defeat. To tie up all railway transportation even *strike (1910)* for a few days would not only cripple the industries of a modern state, but would also cut off the food supplies from the great cities. The syndicalists believed that they would have the government of France at their mercy, but when they called their strike, the government struck back cleverly and effectively. The prime minister, Aristide Briand, had formerly been a Socialist, but his sympathy for radical measures did not restrain him from proclaiming a national emergency and calling in military aid to keep the trains moving. The strikers were faced by a difficult dilemma. As soldiers in the class war, their duty was to preserve a passive resistance, but as soldiers in the French army (all able-bodied Frenchmen are liable for military service), they could be ordered to drive the trains or face a court martial. In the test military discipline triumphed over syndicalist solidarity and the strike collapsed (1910).

Through this lesson the French syndicalists learned, as the English trade-unionists had discovered a few years earlier, that they had little chance of scoring a decisive triumph with the forces of law *Socialist* and government against them. But, as in England, their *legislation* Socialist allies had been gaining political recognition during these same years, and were in a position to win concessions by less revolutionary means. In 1905, a United Socialist Party was organized in France and polled a million votes the following year. By 1910, the Socialists counted 105 delegates in the Chamber of Deputies, led by the patriotic Alexandre Millerand and the profound and witty historian and journalist Jean Jaurès. All the important measures which succeeded the *dénouement* of

the Dreyfus affair, the "republicanization" of the army and the separation of church and state, were passed by a *bloc* composed of the parties
of the Left — that is, of Republicans and Socialists. As a reward for
their co-operation, the Socialists asked the adoption of old age insurance.
Between 1905 and 1910 a compulsory pension system was worked out to
assure all men and women workers a retirement allowance when they
reached the age of sixty, the premiums to be subscribed by the workers,
their employers, and the state. The state also encouraged the introduction of accident and liability insurance on a large scale, but left the
management of it to private associations. A ten-hour day in the factories, more sanitary conditions to safeguard the workers' health, and strict
injunctions against overworking children to the detriment of their
welfare and education, were further legislative achievements resulting
from the initiative of the Socialists.

These concessions to the proletariat, in so far as they were designed
to improve social and industrial conditions, often won the approval of
The Party
of Liberal
Action
Catholic deputies on the Right as well as Socialist deputies
on the Left, though for a different reason. Heeding the
advice offered by Pope Leo XIII in 1892, a section of the
French Catholic Party rallied to the support of the republic and were
known in consequence as *Ralliés*. Organized after 1901 as the Party of
Liberal Action, this group pledged its representatives in the Chamber of
Deputies to accept the republican régime instead of opposing it as some
Catholics and monarchists still insisted upon doing, to labor for the
protection of the Catholic faith in France, and to promote legislation
favorable to the working classes. It was the hope of these leaders of
liberal clerical opinion that the spread of socialism might be curbed if
the conflict between capital and labor were eased by means of remedial
legislation which reflected a spirit of Christian charity. Despite their
efforts, however, the Socialist Party continued to grow, and in 1914
there were over 130 deputies in the Chamber who might be considered as
Socialists, although only 102 belonged to the United Socialist Party.
In France as in Great Britain this rising influence of the proletariat was
the outstanding political development of the pre-war era. The socialists defended their platform on the ground that it would assure a larger
share of the profits of industry to the workers, and they also hoped to
reduce the danger of war by curbing ruthless commercial competition
and negotiating with other socialist governments for a general reduction
of armaments. British and French socialists were encouraged by the
fact that in Germany, also, socialism was advancing, although there it
pursued a somewhat dissimilar course.

5. THE GERMAN EMPIRE (1871–1914): FOUNDATION AND EXPANSION

Bismarck's pronouncement that the great questions of the day would be decided by blood and iron rather than by speeches or majority votes had proved true of the events which led to the forging of the German Empire. The Danish War (1864) had cut short the argument whether Schleswig and Holstein should or should not be incorporated in the new Germany. The Austro-Prussian War (1866) and the Franco-Prussian War (1870–71) had repulsed and excluded outside influences, leaving Bismarck at liberty to organize the Germanies into a powerful state under Prussian leadership. These conflicts were the birth-pangs of a new international order, for the sudden emergence of the German Empire, which was created, like the goddess Athena, full grown and fully armed, replaced the existing balance of power in Europe by what amounted to a German hegemony.

Unlike Cavour, who died before Italian unity had been fully realized, Bismarck enjoyed the opportunity to direct for nearly twenty years the policies of the empire which he had helped to create. The *Constitution* leading German princes, it will be recalled, proclaimed *of the German Empire* William I of Prussia "German Emperor" on January 18, *man Empire* 1871, at Versailles. The constitution of the new federation was not promulgated until some months later and proved to be a severely practical document. The states previously allied in the North German Confederation (1867) were now joined by the four South German States. All twenty-five [1] members of the new *Bund* were to send delegates to a federal council or *Bundesrat* of 58 members, a body comparable in some respects to the United States Senate, with the difference, however, that the members were not elected, but appointed, and the state representation varied from Prussia, which held seventeen votes, to the smallest states with one apiece. There was also a popular lower chamber, the *Reichstag*, made up of 382 deputies. Outwardly, the imperial German government corresponded to the bicameral legislative systems of Britain and France, but there was one significant point of difference. Instead of providing for a cabinet of ministers responsible to the *Reichstag*, the

---

[1] The states composing the German Empire in 1871 included the four kingdoms of Prussia, Bavaria, Saxony, and Württemberg; the six grand duchies of Baden, Hesse, Mecklenburg-Schwerin, Saxe-Weimar, Mecklenburg-Strelitz, and Oldenburg; the five duchies Brunswick, Saxe-Meiningen, Saxe-Altenburg, Saxe-Coburg-Gotha, and Anhalt; the seven principalities of Schwarzburg-Sonderhausen, Schwarzburg-Rudolstadt, Waldeck, Reuss (older line), Reuss (younger line), Lippe, and Schaumburg-Lippe; and the three free cities of Hamburg, Bremen, and Lübeck. Alsace-Lorraine ranked as an imperial territory and remained without representation on the *Bundesrat* until 1911.

constitution vested all ministerial authority in a single official, the president of the *Bundesrat*, who, as imperial chancellor, held his office at the emperor's pleasure and was not answerable for his actions to the assemblies. This all-important chancellery post Bismarck reserved for himself.

It was a matter of grave import for German and European history that this constitution failed, despite appearances, to establish a govern-
The German government not truly responsible nor democratic ment that was representative of the German people or responsible to them. The chancellor was not a prime minister obedient to the will of a parliamentary majority. Furthermore, the *Bundesrat*, the members of which were nominated by the German princes, was superior to the *Reichstag* elected by the German people. The *Reichstag*, finally, did not meet the requirements of a truly representative and democratic assembly because its members were elected under the three-class franchise system already functioning in Prussia,[1] which gave the wealthy classes and the property-owners a controlling voice. In short, the government of the new empire was more nearly an autocracy or oligarchy than it was a democracy. A second point to note is the dominant position assumed by Prussia, a position so commanding that it is scarcely an exaggeration to say that the Germanies had been conquered and "Prussianized" by that militant kingdom. Bismarck had been solicitous to leave the smaller states the illusion of sovereignty; but the facts were that the King of Prussia had become German Emperor, and he appointed the all-powerful chancellor, who in turn selected the chief functionaries of the imperial government. In the *Bundesrat*, Prussia held 17 of the 58 votes and could as a rule dominate the deliberations.[2] The union of states was indissoluble and the Prussian vote could defeat any amendment to the constitution.

Powers not specifically relegated to the imperial government were reserved by the component states, which continued to handle their own
Rights reserved by the states fiscal, religious, educational, and administrative problems. So tactfully had Bismarck gathered the reins of power into his own hands that the minor states were unaware of the degree to which they had compromised their independence. The coinage, the banking system, the railways, telegraphs, and mails, and later the codes of civil and criminal law, were all harmonized and subjected to the regulation of the imperial bureaucracy. Although several states, notably Bavaria, Württemberg, and Saxony, maintained their separate

[1] See above, page 246.
[2] Subsequent to 1871, Prussia acquired the vote of Waldeck, and the two votes of Brunswick, raising her total for all practical purposes to twenty.

army contingents and even their separate consular services, these survivals of particularism steadily lost significance as the authority and efficiency of the imperial government increased.

As the disparate segments of the empire were knit into an indissoluble whole, the German merchants and manufacturers discovered that political unity was a boon to business. The federal administration of the transport and communication services made them the nerves and sinews of a new economic order, and Bismarck counted upon the effects of the industrial expansion to vindicate and strengthen his political architecture.

For the German people after 1871 encountered the full transforming force of the Industrial Revolution, that irresistible ferment stirred by mechanical innovations, which had appeared in England a *The Industrial Revolution in Germany* century earlier and had modified French society during the reigns of Louis Philippe and Napoleon III. The effects of the factory system and of machine production came still later to Germany, but for that reason they came with accelerated force. In Great Britain the mechanization of industry had been achieved in successive stages, from the eighteenth-century improvements in spinning and weaving to the technical inventions which multiplied in all trades after 1850. But in Germany the Industrial Revolution did not really manifest itself until approximately the middle of the nineteenth century. Then, borrowing the experience and the machinery of the British and French, German industrialists proceeded to overtake their rivals. In this they were enormously aided by the scientific progress made after 1870. Thus, the first wave of the Industrial Revolution (which had introduced the steam engine and the factory system in England a century earlier) and the second wave (for such the flood of technological inventions, electrical devices and chemical discoveries that began about 1870 may be called) both struck Germany in the same years. This largely explains the phenomenal development of German industry under the empire, but it must not be forgotten that the political consolidation achieved in 1871 smoothed the way for the industrial expansion which was already overdue.

6. THE GERMAN EMPIRE (1871–1914): ECONOMIC AND SOCIAL PROBLEMS

As in England and France, the spread of the factory system created in Germany a class of proletarian workers who organized trade unions to protect their rights and adopted socialistic views in politics. Until

MODERN INDUSTRIAL PLANT

Photograph by Ewing Galloway, N.Y.

The manner in which the machinery of modern industry can change and dominate the countryside is well illustrated by this photograph of German steel mills at Bremen.

1875, the German workingmen were divided, some adhering strictly to the teaching of Karl Marx, while others joined a Socialist Party formed in 1863 by Ferdinand Lassalle (1825–64). *The German Social Democratic Party* The union of these two factions into a single Social Democratic Party (1875), pledged to seek immediate legislation for the relief of the workers, and ultimate socialization of industry, alarmed the forceful Bismarck. As he had no liking for democracy or socialism, he determined to destroy the Social Democratic Party before it grew strong enough to constitute a menace.

Although the constitution rendered the chancellor independent of the *Reichstag*, Bismarck knew that he could not rule without the approval of some powerful political groups. From 1871 to 1879, *Bismarck and the National Liberals (1871–79)* while he was consolidating the new imperial régime, he leaned upon the National Liberals, a party chiefly representing the upper middle class, the business men, bankers, lawyers, doctors, professors, etc. To satisfy the National Liberals, who favored free trade and responsible parliamentary government, Bismarck proposed low tariffs and pretended to have more patience for the ideals of free speech and freedom of the press than he really felt. The National Liberals supported him in his task of strengthening the central government and he joined them in making war upon the Catholic Church in Germany. The story of Bismarck's clash with the church is interesting for the light it throws upon his prejudices and his ability to profit by his mistakes.

The German Catholics, finding themselves a minority in the new empire, organized a strong Center Party after 1871 to protect their interests. The Center Party drew most of its support *The Kulturkampf (1872–79)* from the South German States, where many people were inclined to be distrustful of Protestant Prussia and of the centralizing policy pursued by Bismarck and the National Liberals. The Catholics in Germany, however, were themselves divided in sentiment, for the pope had recently been proclaimed infallible in matters of faith and morals by the Vatican Council, a decree not altogether popular in Germany. As one group of German Catholics, known as the "Old Catholics," declined to accept the decree of papal infallibility, Bismarck encouraged this schism by supporting them against the orthodox bishops, and this opened a conflict honored by the grandiose title of the *Kulturkampf* or "struggle for civilization." In 1872, the Jesuits were expelled from Germany and diplomatic relations severed between Berlin and Rome. In 1873 and 1874, the Prussian government prohibited the appointment of anyone to a clerical office in Prussia unless he were a native German and had attended a German high school and university, and declared all clerical appointments subject thenceforth to state approval. When the Catholic clergy opposed these decrees, they were expelled or arrested, and within a few years two thirds of the Prussian Catholic bishops had been driven from their dioceses and four hundred parishes lacked pastors. But instead of disintegrating, the Catholic resistance throve under this persecution and the Centrists increased their representation in the *Reichstag*. Awake to the danger which might result if the Centrists and Socialists fused their forces in an opposition *bloc*, Bismarck decided to change his tactics and halt the *Kulturkampf*. His enemies declared that, like the headstrong emperor, Henry IV, four hundred years earlier, he had "gone to Canossa" — that is, yielded to the pope — but it would be more just to say that, like Henry IV, he had escaped from a threatening situation by an adroit move.

For, dropping his war on the Catholics after 1878, Bismarck freed his hands for a struggle with the Socialists. His aims were: (1) to cripple the Social Democratic Party by repressive decrees; (2) to placate the discontented workingmen who voted Socialist by introducing legislation which would ease their grievances; and (3) to make the imperial government financially independent of state contributions by erecting a high protective tariff on imports. To follow this new course meant a break with the National Liberals, who disliked repressive legislation and opposed high tariffs. But the chancellor believed that he could win the Center Party to his side, and he counted upon the support of the landowners and manufacturers who would profit by a tariff which would protect them from the agricultural and industrial competition of other lands.

Two attempts at assassination made against the venerable William I (1878) provided an excuse for harsh measures against all radical agita-

Social insurance   tors. They were forbidden to publish or propagate their doctrines, or to hold meetings, and were exposed to arbitrary arrest. To reconcile the working classes and give them a motive for supporting the state, Bismarck drafted a comprehensive code of social insurance. The Sickness Insurance Law (1883) provided a fund, to which the employers contributed one third of the premiums, whereby workers were assured half-pay and medical attention for six months in case of illness. By the Accident Insurance Law (1884) employers were compelled to establish a fund providing compensation to workers partially or totally disabled through accidents of their trade, and a pension of one fifth the annual wages to the dependents of a worker killed while working. Most ambitious of all was the Old Age Pension Act (1889).

Compulsory contributions from employers and workers, augmented by the state, provided a retirement annuity for all workers who reached their seventieth birthday or became incapacitated before that age. Although Socialist leaders denounced these measures as a means of insuring the capitalist system rather than the workers, and exhorted their followers not to be lulled by such pretended charity into a forgetfulness of their rights, the state insurance laws in Germany did much to alleviate the misery and anxiety of the poorer classes. Moreover, the extraordinary prosperity of German industry enabled the employers to carry their contributory burden with ease. It is not without interest to note that the autocratic and conservative Bismarck anticipated by more than twenty years the social legislation later enacted by the Liberal-Labor coalition group in Great Britain and by the Republican-Socialist *bloc* in France.

William I died in 1888 and was succeeded by his son, Frederick III, who reigned only a few months. On the latter's death in the same year the throne passed to William II (1888–1918), a prince of versatile talents, but unstable and impetuous moods. Determined to be his own chief minister, William II relieved Bismarck of his office in 1890, and the great chancellor retired with bitterness and foreboding in his heart. His successors in office, the rigid and pious Caprivi (1890–94), the aged Prince Hohenlohe (1894–1900), the supple Prince von Bülow (1900–09) and the ill-starred von Bethmann-Hollweg (1909–17), were none of them men of Bismarck's stature, and German policy, domestic and foreign, lost much of its earlier unity of will and direction. *William II dismisses Bismarck (1890)*

Disapproving of Bismarck's harshness toward the Socialists, William II allowed the repressive legislation against them to lapse, and the Social Democratic Party, which had elected 9 deputies to the *Reichstag* in 1878, and 35 in 1890, increased its representation to 79 by 1907. By 1912 the Social Democrats held 110 seats and constituted the largest party in the *Reichstag*.

Thus, despite repression, and despite the paternal legislation intended as a sop to the workers, the Socialists had gained ground as their doctrines appealed to a wider and wider circle of voters. The class which Bismarck had called "the disinherited" appeared to be headed for ultimate control in Germany as in Great Britain and France. It is important to note, however, that as socialism became more popular in these three countries it became less radical, and Socialists abandoned the call to revolution in favor of more cautious and constitutional reforms. In this way they attracted many liberal-minded people who approved of remedial legislation for the benefit of the workers, higher income and inheritance taxes aimed at the rich, and a policy of progressive socialization of industry. With respect to foreign policy, Socialists were disposed to "view with alarm" the excessive growth of armaments and to denounce the methods by which most governments acquired and exploited the lands of backward peoples principally for the benefit of capitalists and business men at home. But the acquisition of colonies and the possession of a strong army and navy pleased so many unthinking people and flattered their patriotic pride so much that the Socialist leaders met with little success when they sought to reduce armaments and curb the aggressive imperialism of the era 1871–1914. In matters of foreign policy nationalism proved a stronger force than socialism.

CHAPTER TWENTY-FIVE

THE COMPETITION AMONG THE INDUS-
TRIALIZED STATES: THE RACE FOR
COLONIES AND MARKETS
(1871–1914)

The day of small nations has passed away; the day of Empires has come.
JOSEPH CHAMBERLAIN (1836–1941).

THE nineteenth century witnessed an exodus of European peoples to other parts of the globe in a remarkable migration surpassing anything of its kind in previously recorded history. Accurate statistics are lacking on many phases of this mass movement, but competent estimates place the number of European emigrants who took up permanent residence in the Americas, Asia, or Australia between 1800 and 1900 at forty to fifty millions. The greater number of these emigrants settled in the United States or the republics of Central and South America, lands dominated by European culture, but no longer attached politically to any European empire. But part of the tide also flowed to the colonies and dependencies of the European powers and helped to build up their overseas dominions. It is the purpose of the present chapter to describe the empires overseas which were acquired by Great Britain, France, Germany, and Italy, how they were governed, and especially how the rival powers clashed more and more frequently as they competed for the unclaimed areas of the earth and sought to win them as fields for imperial exploitation.

1. THE NEW IMPERIALISM AFTER 1871

As already explained in an earlier chapter,[1] Spain, Portugal, Holland, France, and England all established overseas empires in the sixteenth and seventeenth centuries. By the close of the Seven Years' War in 1763, Great Britain had usurped the lion's share of both colonies and trade, and her rivals, defeated and discomfited, largely lost interest in the competition. For the first three quarters of the nineteenth century, the European peoples gave their chief attention to the problems arising from the French Revolution, and to the national movements which culminated in the unification of Italy and of Germany. After

[1] See Chapter VII, pages 93–106.

1871, the question of colonies came again to the fore, and Europe entered a new and dynamic phase of overseas expansion often referred to as the "New Imperialism." Like the growth of cities or the rise of socialism, the New Imperialism will be found upon examination to derive its strength from the forces let loose by the Industrial Revolution. For the highly industrialized state, colonies had suddenly acquired a new value as fields for the investment of surplus capital, as sources of raw material, as potential markets which could not be closed by foreign tariffs, and as reservoirs for the excess population of the home country.

2. THE BRITISH EMPIRE IN 1871

Following the loss of the thirteen American colonies, the slow growth of more liberal policies and democratic ideals in England inspired *The Domin-* British statesmen to administer the colonial dependencies *ion of* more tactfully. In Canada, which had been conquered *Canada* from France (1763), the settlers, predominantly Catholic and French, had been reconciled by the assurance that they might retain their language and religion undisturbed (Quebec Act, 1774). Friction between the French and incoming English colonists was difficult to avoid and discontent with the royal administration led to small revolts, but a measure of local self-government eased the tension (1840), and Canada was later raised to the status of a confederated state by the British North America Act (1867). A bicameral legislature modeled upon the British Parliament assured the Canadian people control of their own affairs, and a governor general appointed from London fulfilled the constitutional and largely nominal duties discharged in England by the king. As a self-governing dominion in the British Commonwealth of Nations, Canada has begun to develop her vast natural resources, linked up her scattered provinces with transcontinental railways, and increased her population to over ten million (1933).

The island continent of Australia first became substantially known to the English when it was visited in 1770 by the famous navigator, *Australia* Captain James Cook. The first settlement was established (1788) as a place of banishment for criminals, but during the nineteenth century five separate areas were colonized, with a sixth colony on the nearby island of Tasmania, and a seventh on New Zealand, twelve hundred miles to the east. The discovery of gold about 1850 and the profits of sheep-raising drew an increasing stream of immigrants to Australia, and in 1900 the separate provinces on the mainland joined with Tasmania to form the Commonwealth of Australia,

ASIA
1914

SCALE OF MILES
0   200   400   600   800

the second largest self-governing dominion within the British Empire. As in the case of Canada, the Australian Parliament consists of a bicameral legislature and a governor general appointed by the British crown.

The separate group of islands known as New Zealand attained dominion status in 1907. Politically the colonists have distinguished themselves chiefly by their democratic and socialistic ex- *New* periments. Universal suffrage, state ownership of rail- *Zealand* ways, state departments for life, accident, and fire insurance, old age pensions, and compensation for workers injured at their trade were all introduced in New Zealand before 1900. Both Australia and New Zealand have adopted a rigid immigration policy, so that their joint population of over eight million (excluding aborigines) in 1934 was drawn almost exclusively from peoples of European ancestry.

In India the British extended their influence inland from the trading posts, established in the seventeenth and eighteenth centuries, until they controlled the whole country with its teeming millions. *India* Until 1858, the management of this empire, continental in its vast extent, was left in the hands of the British East India Company under the supervision (after 1784) of a royal board of control known as the "India Office." The sudden outbreak of a serious revolt in the Ganges Valley (1857), led by the native troops or *sepoys* and consequently termed the Sepoy Mutiny, led to cruel reprisals by the British, but also to a more enlightened type of rule. A secretary of state for India in the British cabinet and a governor general at Calcutta, assisted by a council and by provincial governors, superseded the régime of the East India Company (1858). In several hundred states, comprising perhaps two fifths of India, the native potentates continued to govern under British supervision, but in the larger part of the peninsula the white conquerors took charge of the administration.

The benefits conferred by British rule in India, in the form of better agricultural methods, irrigation systems, highways, canals, and railways, might be more deeply appreciated by the native population if the British had shown equal solicitude in promoting education and training for self-government. But to interfere with the social and religious customs of an oriental people is a dangerous experiment, and the British have allowed nine tenths of India's three hundred and fifty million people to remain in a state of illiteracy and often of degrading superstition. In defense of this policy many Englishmen have argued that western ideals of education and democracy are unsuited to the eastern mind; that, despite the influence and prestige of the British adminis-

[363]

trators, they could not, even if they would, change the habits of an ancient and unprogressive people. Their position in India, like that of white men everywhere among less aggressive and less civilized peoples, has brought them a sort of "bewildered omnipotence" which they scarcely know how to use. They have, however, no wish to resign their authority.

Since 1900, a growing body of Indian nationalists have demanded a greater measure of self-government so that the Indian peoples may

National Movement in India learn to modernize themselves in their own way. Limited representative assemblies were conceded to most of the provinces of British India in 1909, but, despite this beginning of reform, nationalist sentiment has grown steadily and has led to acts of violence, the assassination of British officials, and consequent measures of repression. India is "the brightest jewel in the British crown," not only because of the valuable crops of cotton and wheat raised there, but also because it provides a market for textile and factory products. As a self-governing dominion, India might attempt to exclude British goods or even to secede from the empire. Naturally the possibility of such a grievous economic loss makes it difficult for the British people to view the Indian nationalist movement in a candid and impartial fashion, and they find it easy to believe that the nationalists represent only a noisy and discontented minority of India's millions and that the inarticulate masses are truly grateful for the benefits of British rule.

The lesser portions of the British Empire in 1871 included a number of crown colonies and protectorates scattered about the globe, as Gibraltar and Malta in the Mediterranean; British Guiana, British Honduras, the British West Indies, Bermuda, and the Falkland Islands in the New World; Aden, Ceylon, Lower Burma, and Hongkong in Asia; and Gambia, Sierra Leone, Cape Colony, and Natal in Africa. This impressive heritage, which the British had built up in the course of two hundred and fifty years of conquest and colonization, was destined to undergo further expansion under the stimulus of the New Imperialism.

3. BRITISH ACQUISITIONS (1871–1914)

In 1875, the imperialistically inclined Disraeli was able to increase British influence in the Mediterranean by purchasing a considerable

Egypt share in the Suez Canal, the completion of which six years earlier had opened a new and shorter sea route to India. To safeguard the canal became one of the guiding motives of

British foreign policy. When the Khedive (or ruler) of Egypt defaulted on his debts to European bankers, France and Britain established a condominium over that country (including the canal), despite the fact that it formed part of the Turkish Empire. The French government was only passively interested, but the British increased their military control, repressed an insurrection of the Egyptians (1882), and soon enjoyed a protectorate in everything but name. Anglo-Egyptian forces subdued the fierce Mohammedan tribes of the Sudan after several reverses, and by 1900 the upper valley of the Nile had been marked out as a sphere of British influence.[1]

At the headwaters of the Nile the area known as Uganda, lying to the north of Lake Victoria, was proclaimed a protectorate in 1894, and the following year the territory between Uganda and the Indian Ocean, which had already been chartered by the British East Africa Company, became a protectorate also. Though bisected by the Equator, British East Africa proved suitable for white settlers in the elevated sections. Less healthy, but valuable because of the tin, rubber, palm oil, and ivory produced there, was the lower Niger Valley, proclaimed a British protectorate in 1914, and the hinterland of the Gold Coast (Ashanti), annexed in 1886. British Somaliland, at the mouth of the Red Sea, became a protectorate in 1884, and the territory lying back of Sierra Leone was delimited as a sphere of British influence in 1889.

The most important area which the British won in the partitioning of Africa remains to be mentioned last. Since 1806, when they conquered Capetown from the Dutch, the British had made *The Boer* it a port of call for their ships on the long sea voyage to *War (1899–* India. Preferring to keep their independence, the Dutch *1902)* settlers, or Boers, moved inland and established the Orange Free State and the Transvaal Republic. But discoveries of gold and diamonds in South Africa after 1886 brought an influx of British colonists and precipitated an armed conflict between the Boer Republics and the British Empire. Such a war could end only one way, but unequal as it seemed, the struggle cost the British three years of fighting before they could break the resistance of the Boers, whose stubborn courage won the admiration of the world. By granting favorable terms, including $15,000,000 for the farms destroyed, the British government endeavored to placate their late adversaries. Seven years after the conclusion of peace, the provinces of Cape Colony, Natal, Orange Free State, and the Transvaal united to form the self-governing Union of South Africa (1909).

[1] See map following page 370.

Under the inspiration of an indefatigable empire-builder, Cecil Rhodes, the British pressed inland from their South African settlements to establish a protectorate over Bechuanaland (1885) and occupy the area traversed by the upper Zambesi River, now known as Rhodesia. With the proclamation of a protectorate over Nyasaland (1891) and the submission of the Boer Republics (1902), Rhodes's dream of a railroad that would run from Capetown to Cairo without leaving British territory seemed at the point of realization. But the proclamation of a German protectorate over the East African mainland opposite Zanzibar (1890) and the extension of this protectorate inland until it linked itself with the Belgian Congo at the head of Lake Tanganyika effectively broke the contiguity of the British possessions.[1]

In Asia, British expansion since 1871 has been largely confined to the task of consolidating and extending the frontiers of the Indian *Anglo-* Empire. To forestall Russian interference, the Indus *Russian* Valley from Sind to Kashmir had been occupied between *diplomacy* 1840 and 1850; Beluchistan was added in 1876, and Af-*in Asia* ghanistan transformed into a buffer state under British influence.[2] In 1904, the Chinese province of Tibet likewise became a "sphere of British influence"; and in 1907, Persia was subdivided into a northern (or Russian) zone, a neutral center zone, and a southern (or British) zone. The compromise over Persia reflects the more amicable spirit which developed between England and Russia after 1905. As Russia had suffered a defeat at the hands of the Japanese, and the British were alarmed at the growth of German power, the diplomats at London and Saint Petersburg were more disposed to reach an agreement over Indian frontier problems than they had been in the nineteenth century.

On the northeastern boundaries of India, the British had already conquered Assam and Lower Burma before 1871. In 1886, the native *Burma* ruler was deposed, and the whole of Burma, a kingdom larger in area than the State of California, became part of the British Indian Empire. Holding in addition the Malay States, the Straits Settlements, and the northern coast of Borneo, Britain enjoyed a dominant position on the South China Sea.

A war with China (1840–42), occasioned by the efforts of the Chinese government to forbid importations of opium, delivered the island of *Hongkong* Hongkong into British hands. The trade in opium, which *and Canton* was raised in India and sold in China to the considerable profit of the British East India Company, helped to produce a second

[1] See map following page 370.   [2] See map following page 362.

Chinese War (1856–60). By a joint offensive, Britain and France compelled the Chinese to pay a further indemnity, open new ports to trade, admit and protect Christian missionaries, and permit the traffic in opium. As a consequence of this "Second Opium War" the British gained a foothold at Canton and established another "sphere of influence" in the Yangtze Valley.

4. FRENCH COLONIAL ENTERPRISE

Since the days of the crusaders the French have maintained a persistent interest in the conditions affecting the eastern Mediterranean and the seaboard of northern Africa. Bonaparte's expe- *Algeria* dition to Egypt (1798) intensified this interest, although *and Tunis* his conquests were speedily abandoned. In 1830, however, the dispatch of a punitive expedition against an insolent Dey of Algiers brought the French the control of several Algerian ports. Years of economic penetration and military campaigns gradually subdued the great Sahara Desert, and in 1881 Tunis as well as Algeria became a protectorate of France. The impotent protests of the Sultan of Turkey, who claimed a feeble suzerainty over northern Africa, failed to delay the march of events and served but to advertise the decline of the Turkish power.

The French were in some respects more successful than the British in consolidating their African conquests, for in 1885 they linked their expanding posts on the Congo (French Equatorial Africa) *Morocco* with their West African dominions by way of the Ubangi River. Morocco, established as a French protectorate in 1912, rounded out the northeast corner of their African Empire. Including the island of Madagascar, which was proclaimed a French colony in 1896, the French African possessions had come by 1914 to exceed even those of Great Britain in area. The scramble for territory on the Dark Continent had provided France with a colonial empire larger than the whole of Europe, and much of it adjacent to the mother country.

Nor were the French possessions in Asia insignificant. In the middle of the nineteenth century, France held no more than two hundred square miles of Asiatic territory surrounding five small *French* posts on the Bay of Bengal, the most important of which, *Indo-China* Pondicherry, had been established by the French East India Company two centuries earlier. In 1858, however, the government of Napoleon III dispatched an armed expedition to Cochin China to avenge the murder of some Christian missionaries, and this province, nominally

[367]

a part of the Chinese Empire, became a French protectorate five years later. A successful policy of war and diplomacy brought Annam, Tonkin, and part of Cambodia under French control in the decades which followed. The Chinese government was forced to renounce its shadowy sovereignty over these regions, concede favorable tariff rates on goods from Tonkin, and permit the French special privileges on the railroads of southern China. In less than fifty years the French had acquired an Asian Empire as large as Texas, with an industrious population half that of France itself. By agreement with Great Britain, the Kingdom of Siam was recognized as an independent buffer state between British Burma and French Indo-China.[1] Toward the east, however, France might aspire to enlarge the boundaries of Tonkin, and the lease of Kwang-chow (1898) near the island of Hai-nan hinted at such intentions.

5. ITALY ENTERTAINS IMPERIALISTIC DREAMS

When the Italians achieved political unity in the decade 1860–70, they found their national government burdened with debt, embarrassed by the unfriendly attitude of the papacy, and confronted with the problem of educating a largely illiterate population. Yet these domestic difficulties did not deter them from the attempt to play an imperialistic rôle in imitation of older established powers. Italian patriots not only regarded the Istrian Peninsula and part of the Austrian Tyrol as territory to be "redeemed," but cast covetous eyes across the Mediterranean Sea to Tunis on the North African coast. When the French thwarted their aspirations in this direction by annexing Tunis (1881), the act created a deep and lasting resentment between the two Latin powers.

Worse fortune awaited the Italians in Abyssinia. After establishing a colony at Massowah on the Red Sea (1885), the Italian gov-

Abyssinia   ernment attempted to secure control of the inland empire of Abyssinia, or Ethiopia, a state lying between the Nile Valley and the Red Sea, ruled by the Ethiopians, a Hamitic tribe which professed Christianity. But the Italian hopes of creating a sphere of influence in East Africa went down to defeat in 1896 when the Abyssinians overwhelmed their expeditionary force in catastrophic fashion at the battle of Adowa. The protectorate was abandoned, and Abyssinia remained independent under the rule of Menelek II, the only native African ruler who had successfully repelled a European

[1] See map following page 362.

[368]

army. Italy retained, however, two strips of coastline in the neighborhood, Italian Somaliland and Eritrea.[1]

Restrained for the moment by this costly and humiliating reverse,
Italian imperialists proceeded more cautiously in their next African
venture. The provinces of Tripoli and Cyrenaica were *Libya*
marked out as fields for Italian exploitation by 1901, but
it was not until ten years later that Italy took the initiative and wrested
them from Turkey after a brief struggle.[2] The expense of improving
the new conquests and subjugating the desert tribes of the interior
proved a heavy burden for the Italian taxpayers, but their pride was
gratified by this evidence that Italy could compete successfully with
the older nations in the scramble for colonies. They named their new
possession Libya.

6. GERMANY ENTERS THE RACE FOR COLONIES

Distracted by their own dissensions and handicapped by the lack
of a competent central government, the German people took little
share in overseas exploration and colonization before 1871. While
Spain, Portugal, Holland, France, and England were fighting to found
and maintain colonial empires, the German princes remained absorbed
in the petty play of central European politics. Even after national
unity had been achieved and the victory over France had made the
new empire the leading European power, Bismarck displayed little
inclination to compete for colonies. His chief concern was to consolidate the position which Germany had won for herself on the continent of Europe. To participate in the scramble for backward countries, when the best areas suitable for white men to live in had already
been pre-empted, seemed to him a dubious game offering few rewards
and likely in the end to embroil Germany with Great Britain, the
leading colonial power of the world.

Nevertheless, the expansion of German industry and the growth of
the German maritime interests prepared the way for a more aggressive
colonial program. In 1884, after negotiations with Great *German pro-*
Britain, the German government proclaimed a protectorate *tectorates in Africa*
over South-West Africa, and annexed in the same year
a strip of coastline on the Gulf of Guinea which shortly expanded into
the German Kamerun. In 1885, German East Africa was acquired,
and proclaimed a protectorate in 1890. Though less favorable for

---

[1] See map following page 370.
[2] The Turko-Italian War, 1911–12. See below, pages 370–71.

colonization or trade than the choicer sections of Africa already claimed by other nations, the new German colonies were by no means negligible in either wealth or area.

Once embarked upon the imperialistic race, the Germans pressed forward with energy. The murder of two missionaries (1897) provided an excuse for armed intervention in Shantung, and the Chinese government was compelled to lease the port of Kiaochau to Germany with some two hundred square miles of territory attached. In Oceania, a portion of the island of New Guinea was recognized as a German protectorate (1884); the two largest Samoan Islands were acquired in 1899; and the Caroline and some lesser groups of Pacific islands purchased from Spain in the same year.

7. THE RIVALRIES OF THE POWERS IN AFRICA

The competition for colonies quickened the jealousies of the great powers, and more than once, particularly during the partitioning of Africa, their rivalry brought them to the verge of war. Between 1880 and 1914, scarcely a year passed without its diplomatic incident or minor crisis concerning some disputed sphere of influence on the Dark Continent. But African protectorates were a little too remote from the knowledge and interest of the average European citizen to appear worth a war to him; and Austria and Russia, which held no African territory, had no wish to be drawn into a struggle over colonial questions by their allies. But although the acrid disputes arising from African rivalries were all settled by arbitration, they added considerably to the international animosity and helped in this way to prepare the stage for the World War.

When France established a virtual protectorate over Tunis in 1881, disappointment and irritation induced the Italians to sign a treaty of alliance with Germany and Austria the following year. This Triple Alliance, directed against France in particular, assured Italy of support if she became involved in a war over the disposal of North African territory. Five years later (1887), Italy and Great Britain agreed to respect each other's rights in the Mediterranean; and after 1901, Italy and France achieved a partial compromise whereby Tripoli was marked out as a potential sphere of Italian exploitation, while the French strengthened their hold on Morocco. In 1911, judging the moment opportune, the Italians seized the Tripolitan ports and compelled the Sultan of Turkey to acknowledge their right of control. This acquisition of a colony five times as large as Italy provided some

AFRICA
1914
Scale of Miles
0 200 400 600 800 1000

British | Italian | Spanish | Belgian
French | German | Portuguese | Independent

compensation to Italian pride for the loss of Tunis and dispelled the Franco-Italian rivalry.

Between France and Great Britain, the two powers most active in dividing Africa, an even sharper antagonism had risen and waned. While far-sighted Englishmen were dreaming of carrying *Anglo-* the Union Jack from Egypt to Cape Colony, energetic *French rivalry —* Frenchmen were pressing eastward from the region of *the Fashoda* Lake Chad. The map which follows page 370 will show *affair* that these conflicting lines of advance must clash in the upper Nile Valley. In 1898, General Herbert Kitchener, fresh from his victory at Omdurman, where he had reconquered the Sudan for the Khedive of Egypt (and for England), learned that the intrepid Captain Marchand had hoisted the French flag at Fashoda, where the White Nile parallels the Abyssinian border. With the control of the upper Nile region at stake, both nations drifted dangerously close to a war mood, but the crisis passed when the French finally agreed to recall Captain Marchand. Following this incident, both rivals made an effort to improve their relations and avert such threats to peace in the future. The terms of the Anglo-French *Entente* of 1904 included a compromise affecting African questions, Great Britain retaining Egypt and the Egyptian Sudan, while acknowledging the right of France to win Morocco as compensation.

The active participation of the German government in the scramble for African territory may be dated from 1884, when an international congress was held in Berlin to delimit spheres of influence *Anglo-* and provide for the adjustment of rival claims. The *German* congress erected an international Congo Free State under *rivalry* the sovereignty of King Leopold II of Belgium, but sought to preserve freedom of trade and navigation on the Congo River. At the same time (1884–85), Germany took possession of Togoland and the Kameruns, secured a block of coastland farther south which became German South-West Africa, and proclaimed the German East African Protectorate.[1] As already explained, these German annexations struck a sharp blow at British hopes. South-West Africa had been considered of little value, but in German hands it might become a threat to British South Africa. German East Africa, extending inland to the shores of Lake Tanganyika, prevented the British from linking Rhodesia with their Uganda protectorate at the head of the Nile. With good grace, however, they suppressed their disappointment and concluded an agreement recognizing the new German claims (1890). In addition,

[1] See map following page 370.

Germany received the island of Helgoland in the North Sea in return for recognizing the British claims to Uganda, Nyasaland, and Zanzibar.

It will be noted that three of the lesser European states also developed African colonies, more or less under the sufferance of the great powers. The Portuguese, once foremost in exploring the coastline of the Dark Continent,[1] still preserved some trading posts in the nineteenth century which they enlarged into the protectorates of Angola and Mozambique. The Congo Free State, established as a neutral concession under international sanction (1884), was annexed as a Belgian colony in 1908. The Spaniards held, as remnants of ancient claims, a small Guinea protectorate, a stretch of northwestern coastline, the Rio de Oro, and a diminutive slice of Morocco opposite Gibraltar. Had their resources permitted the effort, the Spaniards would no doubt have subjugated the whole of Morocco, but this enterprise devolved upon the French instead. Britain was acquiescent, but Germany sought to block this French design, the result being a series of diplomatic clashes which brought the European nations close to war on three occasions.

By 1905, Morocco was entirely hemmed in on the landward side by French territory, but the sultan was still a nominally independent ruler. *The Moroccan question* The German government wished him to remain independent, or, failing that, favored some system of international control. In 1906, a conference held at Algeciras (Spain) sustained the German view, but conceded France and Spain "police powers" to enable them to maintain order in the semi-civilized sultanate. Morocco had become a pawn in a dangerous diplomatic game, for the duel between France and Germany over Moroccan independence was at bottom a test of prestige between the Triple Alliance (Germany, Austria, and Italy) and the Triple *Entente* (France, Russia, and Great Britain). A second Moroccan crisis developed in 1908 when French military police invaded the German consulate at Casablanca and arrested deserters from the French Foreign Legion. The German government entered a vigorous protest against the use the French were making of their police power, but were partly placated by an assurance that the trade of all nations would be equally protected in Morocco. The French, however, continued to push their plans for a systematic conquest of the country, and in 1911 the German government protested a third time. On this occasion Great Britain ranged herself firmly at the side of France, demonstrating that the Anglo-French Alliance had acquired new force, and the Germans agreed to a compromise. In return for one hundred thousand square miles of the French Congo they permitted the French

[1] See above, pages 93–94.

government to declare a protectorate over nine tenths of Morocco (1912).

All the colonizing powers advanced laudable motives to justify their annexation of African land, but the real forces which drove them into this form of imperialistic gambling remained hidden. Not even the citizens who paid their taxes and aided their governments in the task of conquest comprehended the cost or understood precisely who benefited when new protectorates were established. They were pleased in a general way to see new areas on the map marked out as part of their empire, and they supposed that they were doing a noble and progressive thing in bringing the Christian religion and the advantages of a higher civilization to backward peoples. But the strongest motive in most of these ventures was economic, and behind each diplomatic crisis or tribal war in which a government engaged there lurked the shadow of the bondholders and the investment brokers who were the chief and sometimes the only beneficiaries of the imperialistic game.

For by 1875, not only in Great Britain, but in France, Germany, Italy, and the United States, surplus capital had accumulated, and bankers and brokers were turning the golden flood toward *The profits* foreign fields where the interest return promised to be high. *of imperial-* Only a comparatively small group in each country drew a *ism* real profit from these imperialist enterprises — the investors who owned stock in the business or trading companies, or who bought the bonds which the Khedive of Egypt or the Shah of Persia might float in Europe, the investment bankers who made a good commission handling the bonds, and the civil and military officials who supervised or defended the undertaking. To the great majority of the people in England or France or Germany, however, these ventures brought no dividends, and might even mean higher taxes if their government yielded to the persuasion of the interested minority and fought a war or proclaimed a protectorate in order to safeguard the capital of a small group of investors. Because most of the profits derived from the imperialistic exploitation of Africa and Asia went to a small upper-class group, the socialist leaders in every European country opposed such expansion, while the bondholders, militarists, bankers, munition-makers, and others were likely to support a conservative *bloc* which would fight for an aggressive foreign policy, for imperialism, and (since interference in other countries often breeds war) for militarism. Thus the Industrial Revolution not only aligned the proletariat and the capitalist class on opposite sides in questions of domestic politics, it also separated them in much the same fashion on matters of foreign policy.

[373]

No small minority, however influential, can long control the foreign policy of a great power unless it wins some support from the masses. In *The fruits of* every country there were citizens, sometimes well-meaning, *imperialism* sometimes stupid, who played the imperialists' game for them. Many devout people thought chiefly in terms of Christianizing the heathen. Many jingoists applauded their government's foreign policy, right or wrong. The self-sacrificing missionaries, such as David Livingstone (1813–73), and the courageous explorers, like Henry Morton Stanley, who made Africa known to Europeans, were inspired by altruism or the lure of adventure rather than any hope of gain. But shrewd business men with a sharp eye for profits built on their labors and organized commercial ventures with attractive titles, such as the International African Association (1876), the German African Society (1878), the British East Africa Association (1885), and the British South Africa Company (1889). On the basis of concessions secured from the native chiefs, the agents of these companies exploited African resources, and, when blocked by rival companies or by native resistance, they appealed to their governments for protection. The result was the long succession of international disputes and rivalries already described, some of which missed war by the narrowest margin. With the native population the colonizing powers found it impossible to avoid hostilities. The French conquest of West Africa was a saga of unsung strife; the Germans had to suppress costly uprisings in South-West Africa and in East Africa; the British fought a score of frontier wars between 1871 and 1914 against the Zulus, Basutos, Ashantis, Swazis, Matabeles, and other African tribes; while the Belgian officials in the Congo Free State exploited and massacred the Bantu peoples there with a cruelty that finally aroused international protest. Yet, despite harsh incidents, the white man has brought many benefits to the native Africans, for he has curbed their tribal wars, reduced plagues, suppressed cruel and degrading practices, improved communications, and, in some colonies, fostered education.

8. THE RIVALRIES OF THE GREAT POWERS IN ASIA

As a field for imperialistic effort, the continent of Asia differed from Africa in several important respects. It had a population six times as large, and the level of civilization among the Asiatics was considerably higher than among the Negroes. Moreover, the Asiatics, notably the Japanese, revealed a marked capacity for assimilating the European arts of war and peace, and might learn in time to resent and to resist alien intervention in their affairs. But this possibility did not deter aggressive Europeans from exploiting Asia for their own purposes. The twentieth century will reveal whether in so doing they have not created a Nemesis for themselves, for Asia holds one half the world's population, and the Asiatics, if trained in the use of modern weapons of war and in the arts of machine production, might offer a serious challenge to the supremacy of the white races.

During the greater part of the nineteenth century, the chief protagonists of European imperialism in Asia were Russia and Great Britain. The Russian advance to the Pacific and to the borders of *Anglo-* Persia and India has already been described.[1] The British, *Russian* while consolidating their Indian Empire, opposed the Rus- *jealousy* sians in the Near and Middle East, fought them in the Crimean War (1854–56), and resisted their demands on Turkey at the Congress of Berlin (1878). In the Far East, Russia and England did not clash directly, but both established spheres of influence in the Chinese Empire, the British making Tibet and the Yangtze Valley a field of special interest, while the Russians penetrated Mongolia and Manchuria.

These encroachments, supplemented by the French conquest of Indo-China, made it seem probable in the last quarter of the nineteenth century that China would suffer the same fate as Africa and pass completely under the domination of foreign powers. In 1894, a new claimant to the spoils appeared when Japan wrested the Korean Peninsula and the island of Formosa from the feeble sovereignty of the Celestial Empire. This Sino-Japanese War of 1894–95 also gave the Japanese a foothold on the Liaotung Peninsula, but this the other powers compelled them to relinquish. The evident helplessness of China invited a race for concessions. Germany seized the bay of Kiaochau in Shantung Province (1897), Russia secured Port Arthur (1898) and began to construct a railway across Chinese Manchuria, while the British occupied the harbor of Wei-hai-wei. A glance at the map following page 362 will show how these acquisitions on the Yellow Sea threatened the Chinese capital at Peking. Meanwhile, the French obtained the port of Kwang-chow in southern China, close to their Tonkin protectorate.

The hatred that developed in China against the "foreign devils" led to an uprising in 1900 known as the Boxer [2] Rebellion. It had been fomented with the approval of the reactionary empress, Tzu-hsi, but was crushed by an international army dispatched by Japan, Russia, Great

[1] See above, pages 258–59.

[2] The Chinese patriots who were most active in the attempt to drive out all foreign barbarians were called "Boxers" because many of them belonged to secret societies, the most important being "The Fists of Righteous Harmony," or, as it is sometimes translated, "The Society of Harmonious Fists."

Britain, France, and Germany. Europeans who were besieged in Peking were relieved and the capital occupied by the allied troops until the Chinese government promised an indemnity of about $330,000,000 and commercial concessions to the victors. This salutary lesson convinced even the dowager empress of the need for reform, and projects were introduced for modernizing the military, political, and educational institutions of China. A proposal sustained by the United States (1899) had inaugurated an "open-door" policy in regard to Chinese trade, whereby all nations were to receive equal preference, even in those ports leased by foreign powers. The attitude of the United States, which had respected the integrity of China, and the jealousy of the other great powers, each eager to block the others, delayed the further dismemberment of China after 1900.

The astonishing rise of Japan also furnished a curb upon the spread of European imperialism in the Far East. Until 1853, the Japanese *The rise* had little contact with Europeans and desired less; but the *of Japan* visit of a naval squadron under Commodore Perry forced them to open some of their ports for trade with the United States (1854) and later with other nations. Recognizing the superiority of western methods in war and peace, the Japanese embarked upon a program of modernization unique in history. Prior to 1867, the administrative powers in the Land of the Rising Sun had been dissipated among numerous feudal vassals (the *daimios*), while a sort of mayor of the palace (the *shogun*), had grown so powerful that he overshadowed the emperor. This situation was remedied by a peaceful revolution when the enlightened emperor, Mutsuhito, began his epochal reign in 1867 by concentrating the power in his own hands. In the name of reform he abolished feudalism and serfdom, organized a national army and navy, instituted modern methods of government, industry, and education, and finally promulgated a constitution (1889). Young Japanese students were sent abroad to attend American and European universities, and instructors were invited to Japan to teach the Nipponese the arts and sciences of the western nations. So thoroughly and so successfully was the "revolution" carried out that Japan acquired in a single generation the essential distinguishing characteristics of a western power.

Having organized a splendid army, modeled partly on that of Prussia, and an effective navy on the British type, the Japanese could feel secure from foreign aggression. They could still learn from the example of the powers, however, and realized the uses to which these armaments could be put for imperialistic purposes. The rapid spread of industry increased the population and strained the limited resources of the island kingdom, so that Japanese merchants and manufacturers looked to China as a market for their products and a source of raw material. Imitating European methods, the Japanese made war upon China in 1894, freed Korea, which was later annexed to Japan (1910), gained the island of Formosa, an indemnity of one hundred and eighty million dollars, and commercial privileges in four Chinese ports (Treaty of Shimonoseki, 1895). But the Japanese remained dissatisfied because the European powers compelled them to restore Port Arthur and the Liaotung Peninsula, to "preserve Chinese integrity." Such sudden solicitude for the protection of China on the part of nations lately engaged in despoiling the Celestial Empire appeared hypocritical to the Japanese, who suspected that it was a device to cheat them of the fruits of their victory. This suspicion was confirmed a few years later when Russia obtained a lease to the coveted Port Arthur (1898).

If the Russians once made good their hold on Manchuria and fortified it, the Japanese knew that they would lose their fairest field of expansion on the mainland of Asia. The growing tension *Russo-* between the two powers brought on a war in 1904 which *Japanese* demonstrated how competently the Japanese had learned *War (1904–* their lesson. The Russians suffered defeat on land and sea, *05)* and by August, 1905, were ready to agree: (1) to transfer their lease on Port Arthur to Japan; (2) to evacuate Manchuria; (3) to recognize the special Japanese interest in Korea; and (4) to cede to Japan the southern half of the island of Sakhalin (Treaty of Portsmouth). The European nations noted with amazement this discomfiture of the Russian giant by an Asiatic state with one third the population and one fiftieth the area of the czar's empire. But the struggle had not been a true test of strength because the Russians had been taken partly by surprise, had been crippled by the impossibility of bringing sufficient men and supplies to the scene of conflict, and had yielded largely because the discontent of the Russian masses threatened to break into revolution. On the other hand, the Japanese had been thoroughly prepared, had been stirred to intense patriotism by a struggle which involved their national existence, and enjoyed a position near the seat of war where they could use their military and naval superiority in the East to best effect. A longer struggle might have overstrained their finances and ended in a less unequal peace.

The scramble among the nations to seize and exploit backward countries reached its climax about 1900. By that year almost all of Africa, a large part of Asia, Australasia, and the far-scattered islands of the Pacific Ocean had been divided among the powers. In North and South

America the European states had made no recent annexations out of deference to the position taken by the United States, which had made it clear that such intervention would be viewed as an unfriendly act.[1] But, in assuming this preponderant and protective rôle in the New World, the United States had in reality manifested a form of imperialism. In 1898, the question of Cuban independence brought on a war between the United States and Spain which ended in a Spanish defeat. Cuba became a republic under American protection, and Spain also transferred the Philippine Islands to the United States.

The Spanish-American War, the Boer War, and the Russo-Japanese War, the Boxer Rebellion, the Italian defeat in Abyssinia, and the English conquest of the Sudan all fell within the years 1895–1905. Occurring in widely separated parts of the globe, these events reflect how completely the whole world had been caught within the net of imperialism. There was no longer a country so obscure or so remote that it might not serve to awaken the spirit of covetousness and become the object of international conflict.

The competition for colonies was a grave threat to world peace because it sharpened antagonisms already existing among the European powers. The next chapter will explain why the period 1871–1914 has been named "The Armed Peace." Throughout Europe fear and misunderstanding between the states were fed by jingoistic patriots and intensified by the competition in armaments until the period ended in the most destructive war that has threatened modern civilization.

[1] See above, page 221.

CHAPTER TWENTY-SIX

THE GROWTH OF ALLIANCES: INTERNATIONAL TENSION AND THE ARMED PEACE
(1871–1914)

The factors which really constitute prosperity have not the remotest connection with military or naval power, all our political jargon notwithstanding.
NORMAN ANGELL, *The Great Illusion.*[1]

THE Franco-Prussian War of 1870–71 did much more than end an empire (that of Napoleon III) in France and consolidate a new empire (that of William I and Bismarck) in Germany. It shifted the center of gravity in European politics, increased the international tension, and augmented the spirit of militarism. Berlin superseded Paris as the diplomatic capital of Europe, and the new German Empire emerged as the dominant nation on the Continent. The old balance of power had been destroyed with disconcerting suddenness. For the neighbors of Germany it became a matter of the utmost importance to discover what use the Germans planned to make of their ascendancy. Would the Prussian forces, after winning three wars in seven years, be content to put away their weapons now German unity had been secured? And if not, which state would prove their next victim? The rapid industrial expansion, the increasing population, and the unrivaled military efficiency of the Teuton Empire filled weaker nations with jealousy and apprehension. In the tense and suspicious atmosphere of modern statecraft, a powerful neighbor is likely to be viewed as a perpetual threat.

1. THE GERMAN HEGEMONY AFTER 1871

Bismarck appreciated the general distrust which the Prussian victories had aroused. As chancellor of the German Empire he desired peace, and after 1871 he labored to prevent war as successfully as he had sought it hitherto. For he knew that the prevalent fear of Germany might easily favor the growth of a hostile coalition, and it lay in the logic of things that France, so brutally humbled in the process of German advancement, would furnish the nucleus for such a combination. Standing alone, France constituted no very grave danger, but Bismarck did not underrate the skill, patience, and patriotism of French statesmen, nor the jealousy which German success had fostered in international circles. He was haunted by the presentiment that sooner or later France would

[1] G. P. Putnam's Sons.

secure allies and assume the rôle of a Nemesis fated to destroy his life-work. The rapidity with which the French paid off their indemnity and restored their national prosperity after 1871 increased his misgiving so strongly that in 1875 he considered, but abandoned, the thought of inflicting a second and more crushing defeat upon France before that nation won wider support. Bismarck's friends chided him for enter-taining a "nightmare of coalitions," but history has revealed that his fears were later to materialize as grim realities.

That Germany was able, under such circumstances, to leave France diplomatically isolated for twenty years and to build up friendly relations *The isola-* with all the other continental powers, was partly the result *tion of* of circumstances, partly a tribute to Bismarck's moderation *France* and astuteness. He arranged treaties of alliance and good-will with Austria, Russia, and Italy before France could turn to them for aid or encouragement. These agreements, consolidating the recent Prussian military triumphs, rendered the position of Germany unas-sailable during the years that Bismarck remained in office. It will be useful to examine the Bismarckian system of alliances in detail, because they largely determined the diplomatic history of the period 1871–1914.

Bismarck's first endeavor after 1871 was to unite Germany, Austria, and Russia in a cordial understanding. Although the Austrians had *The Three* been defeated by the Prussians in 1866, they had been *Emperors'* generously treated by the victors and were ready to forgive *League* and forget; while the Russians had found Prussia friendly *(1873)* during the Polish Rebellion of 1863 and after. The three governments had several important interests in common: they were all concerned in keeping the Poles in subjection, they were all monarchies with an absolutist bent, and they were all hostile toward republican ideas. It was not a matter for great surprise, therefore, when Francis Joseph of Austria, William I of Germany, and Alexander II of Russia established a friendly compact known as the "Three Emperors' League" in 1873. Confident that this accord would assure a more stable peace, Bismarck turned his attention to projects for the internal consolidation of the German Empire, a complicated task which he was anxious to carry through undisturbed.

Unfortunately for his hopes, the Three Emperors' League soon dis-solved. Jealousy between Austria and Russia in the Balkans almost brought these powers to war in 1877. How a temporary settlement of this Near-Eastern Question was worked out at the Congress of Berlin the following year is told elsewhere.[1] Here it is sufficient to explain that

---

[1] See above, pages 314–16.

Bismarck, though he strove to be impartial, leaned to the side of Austria in the controversy and so forfeited for a time the friendship of the Russians. The Three Emperors' League lost its force, Russo-German relations grew cold if not actually hostile, and Bismarck was denounced in Saint Petersburg as a false friend.

2. THE TRIPLE ALLIANCE

Wasting no time in fruitless efforts to soften the hostile mood of the Russians, Bismarck hastened to Vienna and arranged a dual alliance between Germany and Austria-Hungary which was destined to endure for forty years. This highly important treaty of 1879 provided that Germany and Austria would make war together should either of them be attacked by Russia; if either were to be attacked by France, the other promised to observe benevolent neutrality. The effect of this agreement was to bind Germany and Austria in a close understanding directed against Russia and France, but the two latter powers were carefully left in ignorance of the arrangement. The "High Contracting Parties" specifically agreed that "This Treaty shall, in conformity with its peaceful intentions, and to avoid any misinterpretation, be kept secret..."

Austro-German Alliance (1879)

Three years later the Dual Alliance was expanded into the Triple Alliance by the admission of Italy (1882). The Italians had been irritated by the French annexation of Tunis the previous year, and welcomed the assurance of German support in the event of a war developing with France over the North African littoral. The terms of the Triple Alliance provided that if Italy or Germany were attacked by France, the three allied powers (Germany, Austria-Hungary, and Italy) would fight together, or if any one of them were attacked by two other great powers, all three would provide mutual assistance. The treaty might be renewed after five years, and its terms were to remain secret. The Italians stipulated, however, that its provisions should not be regarded as directed against Great Britain.

The Triple Alliance (1882)

Still Bismarck was not satisfied. In 1881, he had succeeded in resurrecting the Three Emperors' League, Germany, Austria, and Russia pledging each other not to join any fourth power (France, for instance) against any member of the league. But this second Emperors' League proved no more permanent than the first, and when Czar Alexander III declined to renew it in 1887, Bismarck agreed instead to a secret Reinsurance Treaty between Germany and Russia. Each party promised to remain neutral if the

The Reinsurance Treaty (1887)

[381]

other were attacked by a great power. Stripped of their ambiguities, the commitments which Bismarck had negotiated bound Austria, Italy, and Russia not to join France in a war of aggression against Germany. So long as the Bismarckian system of alliances remained in force, the French, if they opened a war of revenge, would have to enter it alone.

Even the Balkan States, Serbia and Rumania, were drawn into Bismarck's system, Serbia by a secret treaty with Austria-Hungary *Rifts in the* (1881) and Rumania by an agreement for mutual support *Triple Alli-* negotiated with the members of the Triple Alliance (1883). *ance* When the Emperor William II relieved Bismarck of his office (1890), the Iron Chancellor retired with the knowledge that he had consolidated the preponderant position of Germany and successfully frustrated for the moment the composition of a counter-alliance. Yet within the Bismarckian system dangerous rifts were already widening. Austrian pressure in the Balkans was almost certain, sooner or later, to estrange both Russia and Italy. The Reinsurance Treaty between Germany and Russia was not renewed in 1890. The loyalty of Italy could not be depended upon — "her promise will have no value if it is not in her interest to keep it," Bismarck had predicted shrewdly. Great Britain, though friendly toward Germany, might easily be alienated if the Germans pressed their commercial and naval rivalry, and their quest for colonies, too aggressively. To resolve these problems would have taxed even Bismarck's skill, and his successors in office were not his equals in diplomacy. By 1914, little remained of the Bismarckian system save the Dual Alliance of Germany and Austria, and a counter-coalition had been formed to oppose the Central Powers, a coalition more dangerous, more powerful, and more circumscribing than Bismarck's darkest apprehensions had foreshadowed.

3. FRANCE SEARCHES FOR ALLIES

Shamed by defeat, without friends, and weakened by the internal conflict between republicans and royalists, France played a minor part in international affairs from 1871 to 1890. Bismarck approved of a republican government in France for the precise reason that he opposed it in Germany, because he believed that republican institutions were unstable and unsuited to military enterprise. The political quarrels of the French factions and the frequent cabinet crises at Paris left foreign courts in doubt whether the Third Republic could long endure, but by 1890 the republican régime had acquired an appearance of permanence and French policies were accorded more serious attention as they gained in firmness and continuity.

Between 1891 and 1894, France secured her first ally, Russia. It might appear surprising that a liberal republic and a conservative autocracy should reach a "cordial understanding," but the exigencies of foreign policy often forge strange alliances. The Russo-German Reinsurance Treaty had lapsed in 1890 and the German government was disinclined to renew it. *Franco-Russian Convention (1894)* Russia, in need of capital for railroad construction and other industrial enterprises, found the French government benevolently inclined and French bankers obliging. The friendly feeling thus engendered was confirmed by a secret convention (1894) which stipulated:

(1) If France should be attacked by Germany, or by Italy supported by Germany, Russia would employ all her available forces against Germany.
(2) If Russia should be attacked by Germany, or by Austria supported by Germany, France would employ all her available forces to attack Germany.

This "rigorously secret" convention was to endure as long as the Triple Alliance remained operative, a condition which proved that it was intended as a counterweight to that alliance, which French and Russian statesmen feared the more because they were ignorant of its precise terms. It was also important to France and Russia in 1894 to present a united front in the face of British imperialism, particularly as there were rumors that Great Britain also might be drawn toward the Triple Alliance.

In 1898, the year of Bismarck's death, Théophile Delcassé became French minister of foreign affairs. He was to retain that important post for the unusually long period of seven years, and during that interval (1898–1905) he helped to bring about a *Théophile Delcassé* diplomatic revolution which nullified much of Bismarck's labor. It was Delcassé's conviction that the security of France depended upon the creation of a coalition powerful enough to defy the Triple Alliance. Faced, when he took office, by the Anglo-French crisis concerning the occupation of Fashoda,[1] he sought a peaceful solution for the affair, and after France had yielded, he strove to obliterate the memory of the clash of interests and to promote closer relations with Great Britain. The accession in 1901 of Edward VII (1901–10), who liked the French and admired Delcassé, helped to create a friendlier feeling between the two powers. Irksome colonial disputes were smoothed away by negotiation, Great Britain agreeing in 1904 to recognize French interests as paramount in Morocco, while the French in return agreed to insist no longer

[1] See above, page 371.

that the British vacate Egypt. In its secret clauses this convention of 1904 further provided that France and Britain should afford each other diplomatic support on all questions concerning North African territory.

Because of the strong British prejudice against entangling alliances, this understanding with France was termed an *entente,* and no formal treaty was signed, but the *rapprochement* was full of significance none the less. The British government, like the French, had come to feel that the peace of Europe might be rendered more secure if the preponderance of Germany and her allies could be offset by a counter-combination of powers. As Germany, Austria, and Italy had formed a Triple Alliance, France, Russia, and England might form a Triple *Entente.* Yet as late as 1900 an alliance which would bind England to her erstwhile foes, France and Russia, seemed no more than a remote possibility, and few people in England or on the Continent would have prophesied such a development. Ten years later, however, the alliance was an actuality. The motives which inspired this "diplomatic revolution" may be traced to the sharp competition which developed between Britain and Germany in commercial, colonial, and naval affairs.

4. ANGLO-GERMAN RIVALRY

Throughout the greater part of the nineteenth century, the British had been content to maintain a policy of "splendid isolation." By 1900, however, isolation began to seem less splendid. The Boer War (1899–1902) revealed to the British people their military unpreparedness and their wide unpopularity. A sense of insecurity clouded the mood of complaisant superiority which they had derived from their industrial and maritime supremacy, for that supremacy was definitely passing. After 1880, British trade had begun to falter while that of Germany forged ahead. In all the world's markets, even in the British Isles, German goods sold in mounting quantities. Germany was the most enterprising, the most aggressive, and the most successful competitor, but the British monopoly suffered further reverses through the progress of industrialization in France and the United States.

It has been said that "race hatred is founded upon international covetousness." For a few years the British endeavored to preserve an attitude of "fair play" toward their chief rivals. They acknowledged the right of Germany to acquire colonies, and they clung to the belief that British commerce could meet all competition. But when the Germans continued to overtake them, when the German steel production surpassed their own, and German ships transported German manufactures that

[384]

undersold the British in their own colonies, the note of sportsmanship yielded to one of anxiety. Unofficial British suggestions for a friendly agreement were coolly received in Berlin. After 1898, a race in naval armaments added to the tension, for the young kaiser, William II, declared that, in order to protect her growing commerce, Germany must construct a navy second to none. This challenge was promptly met by the British, who determined to launch two warships for each keel that the Germans laid down, in order that the British navy might continue to be a match for any other two fleets in the world combined. This two-power standard imposed an enormous strain upon the British taxpayer, but he accepted it as indispensable to his security, for the British Empire was founded upon sea power and any nation which could destroy its shipping in time of war could starve the island kingdom into surrender.

Between 1900 and 1914, the British admiralty steadily concentrated its forces in the North Sea to meet the German threat. Warships which had been scattered around the world to protect British *Naval* interests, which had lain anchored in Rangoon, or Nanaimo, *rivalry* or the Bermudas until they "had grounded on their own beef bones," as one authority phrased it, were either scrapped or remodeled and recalled to home waters. A treaty of friendship and alliance, signed between Britain and Japan in 1902, enabled the British to withdraw a portion of their Pacific squadron with the assurance that the Japanese would watch over their interests in the Far East. After the establishment of the *Entente cordiale* with France in 1904, the naval defense of the Mediterranean Sea was largely relegated to the French in order that the British might further strengthen their North Sea fleet. Although the public remained generally ignorant of this redisposition of naval forces, it was fraught with a deep significance for the peace of Europe, and was a part of the tragic process which was aligning all European powers into two hostile camps.

5. THE TRIPLE *ENTENTE*

The formation of a Triple *Entente* including France, Russia, and Great Britain was indirectly hastened by the result of the Russo-Japanese War (1904–05). France as the ally of Russia and Britain as the ally of Japan were both anxious to prevent the war from spreading, lest they should be drawn into it on opposite sides. The defeat of Russia proved to the English that their long-nursed fear of the Muscovite power had been largely unnecessary and exaggerated. At the same time the Russian reverse showed the French that their only ally had feet of clay and would prove no match for Germany in case of war. The revelation of Russian weakness inspired the Germans to a new truculence, while France labored to draw Russia and England to her side and unite the three in a firm understanding in order to meet the Central Powers on a more equal footing.

The outcome was the negotiation of the Anglo-Russian *Entente* of 1907. As in the case of the Anglo-French *Entente*, arranged three years

Formation of the Triple Entente

earlier, no definite treaty of alliance was signed, but the British and Russian governments smoothed away long-standing difficulties by an agreement to demarcate their spheres of influence in Persia and arbitrate any disputes that might arise concerning the frontiers of India. English sentiment toward Russia had been warmed by the promises of liberal reform made by Nicholas II after the revolutionary movement of 1905–06,[1] and the accord was further strengthened by a meeting of the English and Russian monarchs at Reval, the naval base of the Russian Baltic fleet, in 1908. Edward VII of England took a much more active part than usually falls to a constitutional monarch in the creation of the Triple *Entente*, which re-established the balance of power in Europe on a clearly defined basis. When he died in 1910, he was mourned by his subjects as "Edward the Peacemaker."

To German eyes, however, the Triple *Entente* wore anything but a peaceful aspect. It seemed rather a deliberate attempt to "encircle"

Ill-success of German diplomacy

Germany and Austria and stifle their free development. Everywhere that the Germans turned for expansion, they appeared to find themselves hemmed in by the insidious encroachments projected by *entente* diplomacy. In reality the agreements existing between France, Russia, and England were extremely vague, and were designed to operate only in the face of German aggression. Unfortunately, in a situation which would have taxed Bismarck's astuteness, the kaiser and his associates pursued a contradictory policy of overtures nullified by truculence and compromises inspired by pacific intentions, but marred by indiscreet saber-rattling. The blustering, touchy, and ill-advised attitude of the German foreign office helped more effectively than the machinations of the *entente* statesmen to forge the links in the chain that was being drawn about the Central Powers. A dozen times between 1906 and 1914, when the interests of the Triple Alliance and the *entente* powers clashed over some minor issue, the Germans had the melancholy success of driving England, France, and Russia closer together, and cementing

[1] See above, pages 302–04.

the nebulous *entente* into an effective alliance by the very methods which they had adopted in the hope of dissolving it.

6. INTERNATIONAL CRISES: MOROCCO

In the ten years that preceded the outbreak of the World War, the increasing tension between the Triple Alliance and the nations which combined to form the Triple *Entente* gave rise to a series of diplomatic shocks which might be likened to the premonitory tremors which presage a violent earthquake. Several of these incidents were connected with the French penetration of Morocco. In 1900, France and Italy reached a secret agreement relegating Tripoli and Cyrenaica[1] to Italian enterprise while the French sought supremacy in Tunis and Morocco. This understanding eased the Franco-Italian feud over North African territory, and two years later, Delcassé won a secret promise that the Italians would not join in a war of aggression against France. Spanish possessions in Morocco were delimited by a Franco-Spanish accord of 1904, and the same year Great Britain assented to the French designs in the convention establishing the Anglo-French *Entente*.

Suspecting the bent of Delcassé's intrigues, and annoyed by the conviction that German interests had been ignored, William II intervened brusquely in Moroccan affairs in 1905. The German *First Moroccan crisis (1905–06)* government had selected a favorable moment to oppose France, for Russia had suffered a disastrous defeat at the hands of the Japanese, and the French dared not risk a war until their ally had recovered some strength and morale. Reluctantly the French cabinet yielded to the German demand for an international conference on Moroccan affairs, and acceded to the German hints that Delcassé's resignation of the portfolio of foreign affairs would ease the situation. The conference met at Algeciras (Spain) in 1906, and the delegates agreed solemnly that the sovereignty and integrity of the sultanate of Morocco must remain intact. At the same time, however, France and Spain were authorized to direct the police force, protect foreigners, and maintain order.

To carry out this mandate, the French soon found it necessary to land troops in Morocco (1907). The following year French military police, searching for deserters from the Foreign Legion, invaded the German consulate at Casablanca and precipitated further trouble. A settlement was effected after the affair had been submitted to the

[1] See map following page 370.

Hague Tribunal, a permanent court of international arbitration which had been established in 1899. Germany conceded that her interests in Morocco were economic, not political, and the French government gave assurances that it would not abuse its privileges there to favor the commerce of any nation unduly. This compromise displeased many Germans, who perceived that "the power of France had spread . . . like an oil stain," until the greater part of Morocco had been subordinated to French control despite German vigilance.

When French forces occupied Fez, the chief city of Morocco, in 1911, the German government dispatched the warship *Panther* to the

Compro-
mise con-
cerning
Morocco
(1911)

Moroccan port of Agadir as a protest. For several months the threat of war hung over Europe, but the British government showed its determination to support France, and Germany accepted a compromise. The French were permitted to establish their long-sought protectorate over Morocco, and Germany received two strips of the French Congo as compensation. This settlement removed one dangerous subject of dispute which had exacerbated the mood of French and German patriots, but a heritage of ill-will remained, and the enmity between the two powers, though transferred to other issues, was not appreciably lessened by the compromise.

7. INTERNATIONAL CRISES: THE BALKANS

While France and Germany quarreled over the disposition of Moroccan territory, Russia and Austria pursued their tortuous rivalry in the

The Bagdad
Railway

Balkans. Although Bismarck had once declared that the Near-Eastern Question did not interest Germany sufficiently to be worth the bones of one Pomeranian grenadier, his successors in office modified this judgment. With the spread of industry and of transportation facilities German business men awoke to the possibility of exploiting the Turkish Empire as a commercial field of considerable importance. In 1902, they obtained concessions from the sultan's government for the construction of a railway from Constantinople to Bagdad and thence to Basra on the Persian Gulf. By linking up such a line with the German and Austrian railway system they hoped to develop important trade relations with the East, for the new overland route to the Indian Ocean would be shorter and speedier than the British or French maritime connections through the Suez Canal.

The German directors of the Bagdad Railway were willing to have

[388]

EUROPE
1900

Scale of Miles

0   100   200   300   400

the project financed and controlled as an international venture, but the British and French declined to co-operate. Fear of *The* Drang the German *Drang nach Osten,* or "drive to the east," was nach Osten growing keener in British business circles by 1902. German diplomatic influence had become paramount at Constantinople, German officers were drilling Turkish regiments, and German manufacturers were demanding preferential tariffs in order to win the markets of Asia Minor. British jingoists, who had been loud in their declaration twenty years earlier that the Russians should not have Constantinople, suddenly perceived that German control of the Bosphorus had become an even more imminent danger. A century earlier, Napoleon had affirmed (with picturesque exaggeration) that the power which controlled Constantinople could control the world. After 1900, it seemed likely that this key position of the eastern Mediterranean would fall under the sway of the Central Powers. The British lion and the Russian bear neglected their ancient rivalry to watch the shadow of the Prussian eagle, and the two-headed eagle of Austria, sweeping toward the Dardanelles.

A glance at the accompanying map will show that the fear of German influence in the Near East was somewhat exaggerated. Direct communication between Berlin, Vienna, and Constantinople *The Pan-* depended upon the attitudes of the Balkan States, particu- *Slav dream* larly Serbia and Bulgaria. The Serb population, which was predominantly Slavic, looked to Russia as the "Big Slav Brother" for sympathy and support, and Serb patriots nursed dreams of creating a Pan-Slav state in the Balkans which would include their fellow nationals living under Austrian administration in Bosnia and Herzegovina. It is scarcely necessary to point out that such a project, the success of which would threaten the integrity of the Hapsburg Empire, was resented and resisted at Vienna. Any attempt either to expand or to constrict Serbian territory was certain to bring Russia and the Central Powers face to face in a duel of prestige, and as the Pan-Slav enthusiasts were constantly active, such a clash was likely to come at almost any time.

The spirit of nationalism which had stirred the Balkan peoples spread to Turkey also. Turkish patriots were disgusted by the signs of decadence and disintegration in the Ottoman Empire, *First Near-* which in less than a century had lost control of most of its *Eastern* European provinces, and allowed France to seize Tunis *crisis (1908)* and Morocco while Britain occupied Egypt. In 1908, a Young Turk Association, inspired by the motto "Union and Progress," organized a revolutionary movement and compelled the reactionary sultan, Abdul Hamid II (1876–1909), to grant a constitution. This apparent rejuvenation of Turkey alarmed the Austrian government, for the Young Turks wished to take over Bosnia and Herzegovina which Austria had administered by virtue of the decision reached at the Congress of Berlin in 1878.[1] To forestall the Young Turk claim, Austria annexed the two provinces (1908), a move which displeased the Turks and infuriated the Serbs. For the Serbs regarded the Bosnians as fellow nationals destined to be incorporated into a greater Serbia, and the Austrian action dealt a fatal blow to their aspirations. They hastened to arm, counting upon Russian aid, but Russia had not yet recovered from the conflict with Japan, and found France and England cool toward the Serbian demands for aggrandizement. Advised "to avoid everything that might lead to an armed conflict," the Serbs yielded in sullen impotence, and the crisis passed.

Three years later, a situation of grave tension developed in the Near East as a consequence of the Turco-Italian War of 1911–12. The success of the Italians in seizing Tripoli proved to the world that Turkey was still feeble and could be attacked with impunity. Furthermore, as both the combatants, Italy and Turkey, were nominal allies of Germany and Austria, this dissension within the ranks of the Triple Alliance provided secret satisfaction for the *Entente* powers. Waiting for the repercussions that were certain to follow upon the Turkish defeats in North Africa, the European diplomats turned their scrutiny upon the Near East once more.

The repercussions soon displayed themselves and provided a second Near-Eastern Crisis in 1912–13. Heartened by the evidence of Turkish

Second Near-Eastern crisis (1912–13) enfeeblement, the Balkan states, Greece, Serbia, Montenegro, and Bulgaria, launched a campaign against the Ottoman forces. Their victories were as surprising as their cooperation, and within a few months the allied armies had almost driven the Turks from Europe. But when the time came to divide the spoils of this First Balkan War of 1912, the Bulgarians, dissatisfied with their share, attacked their late allies, and were severely defeated in the Second Balkan War of 1913. Rumania, hitherto neutral, and even Turkey, entered the conflict against Bulgaria, which was stripped of the greater part of its earlier gains. Throughout the peace negotiations, in which the great powers insisted upon taking a hand, Austria showed a firm resolve to check the aggrandizement of Serbia as far as possible. By insisting that the liberated Turkish province

[1] See above, page 315.

[390]

of Albania must be organized as a separate independent principality, Austrian statesmen denied Serbia an outlet to the Adriatic Sea.[1]

In Vienna, the Pan-Slav Movement, with the potential might of Russia behind it, was viewed with mounting alarm. In fighting it the Austro-Hungarian government was fighting to preserve the Hapsburg Empire from disintegration, for if the Austrian Slavs were permitted to secede, other minority races would demand similar privileges. Germany was *The "powder magazine of Europe"* constrained to support Austrian policy because she could not afford to alienate her only firm ally. Russian statesmen saw in the Pan-Slav Movement an opportunity to harass Austria and extend their own influence in the Balkan Peninsula. The French and British governments were anxious to preserve the existing balance of power in the Near East and to prevent either Austro-German or Russian influence from becoming paramount. With so many conflicting forces concentrating their effects in a small area, and with all the great powers ready to utilize the local rivalries and feuds to further their own designs, it is easy to understand why writers in 1913 constantly described the Balkans as "the powder magazine of Europe." Sooner or later a chance spark was likely to set off an explosion that would bring the old order in Europe crashing down in the chaos of a general war.

8. THE GROWTH OF ARMAMENTS

Nothing reflects the growing fear and tension in Europe between 1900 and 1914 more clearly than the increase in armaments. Following the Franco-Prussian War of 1870–71, all the European powers except Great Britain enforced the principle of compulsory military training for practically all able-bodied male citizens, *Military conscription* thus building up huge conscript armies, with a still larger reserve. The expense of drilling and equipping millions of men imposed a staggering burden upon the national budgets, and a secondary loss resulted because these men were necessarily withdrawn from peace-time occupations during some of the most important years of their early manhood. Yet the spirit of fear and of international distrust defeated all proposals for a limitation of armed forces, and led instead to a constant increase in the number of effectives, to extensions in the period of service, and additions to the military appropriations. In 1913, on the eve of the World War, all the great powers increased their expend

[1] See map following page 426.

itures for defense, and even lesser states like Belgium and Switzerland found it expedient to augment their forces.

Such gigantic preparations made it certain that any war which might develop would involve an unprecedented number of combatants. Wars *New* were no longer to be waged between small professional *weapons* armies, but with all the available man-power of great and populous states. Civilians might likewise be mobilized and compelled to produce food and munitions, and the danger and destruction would not be confined to the battlefields. For the new weapons which science and invention were producing promised to add new horrors to the ancient art of human massacre. Mines and torpedoes which would explode on contact, dreadnoughts with guns that hurled projectiles weighing a ton, new and deadly high-explosive shells, and machine guns that sprayed bullets as a hose sprays water, had all been brought to a high degree of effectiveness. With the invention of the airplane and the dirigible airship, as well as the submarine boat, it became possible for men to slay each other, not only on land and sea, but beneath the waves and above the clouds. Troops far back of the firing line might now be bombed in their billets and cities rocked with the concussion of explosives dropped from the skies.

The deepening conviction that war would certainly come if the nations continued to prepare for it, and the belief that it would bring *Peace* nothing but loss and tragedy to all concerned, led many *societies* earnest men and women to organize peace societies and to advocate a limitation of armaments and the arbitration of international disputes. The most important result of this widely diffused sentiment for peace was an international conference held at The Hague in 1899, at the suggestion of Czar Nicholas II of Russia. The delegates designed a formula whereby disputes between sovereign states might be submitted to arbitration, and a second conference (1907) strengthened the Hague Tribunal as an international court of justice. There was no power, however, aside from public opinion, which could compel nations to submit their quarrels to this impartial court, nor did the court have any means whereby it could enforce its decisions. Governments evinced little faith in its efficacy as an instrument for the prevention of war, and the efforts made at the Hague Conferences to effect a limitation or reduction of armaments came to nothing.

For side by side with the advocates of peace, who denounced war as unchristian or argued that under modern conditions it would ruin victor and victim alike, there stood an opposing group of thinkers who defended it as a harsh necessity of the struggle for existence. These realists, as they liked to style themselves, pointed out that history revealed that men had fought each other since the dawn of time, that in the animal world Nature showed herself "red in tooth and claw," and that mankind could not escape the call to strife because it was an inherited biological necessity. The contemporary clash and rivalry of the imperialistic powers they held to be the modern application of the ancient law of battle. Peace-loving peoples, averse to war and unprepared for it, would be herded to the wall by those nations which had conserved the military virtues and had arrayed their warriors to conquer. Since war, regrettable and destructive though it might be, was none the less a visitation likely to confront each nation at least once in a generation, the sane course for a state was to prepare for it, to maintain a large and well-trained fighting force, and if possible to secure allies. For the fate of the unprepared peoples could be read in the history books, and it was written, not in black and white, but in red.

The belief that impressive armaments, and particularly a far-flung navy, helped a power to control and exploit the backward regions of the earth, and so increase its prestige and prosperity, was a political maxim so generally accepted at the opening of the twentieth century that few people undertook to dispute it. The fact that a small state like Switzerland could hold its own in the commercial race, although surrounded by four great military powers, or that Norway, with an insignificant navy, ranked fourth among the nations of the world in the extent of its maritime tonnage, did not shake the faith of the militarists in the efficacy of armed force to promote the prosperity of a nation. Precisely how battleships or howitzers captured trade was not made clear, but the belief that they were necessary to guarantee a nation's prestige and security, and to extend its commercial and colonial ambitions, appeared to be sufficient justification for their expense. It was even argued in all seriousness that the more heavily the nations armed, the less likely they were to fight, because the more destructive war became, the less profit there would be in it for the victor. And if war did come, some militarists averred, it would be over sooner if the states were fully prepared for it; unpreparedness only delayed the decision and so prolonged the agony.

As a consequence of this contradictory and muddle-headed attitude, the European peoples prayed for peace and prepared for war. Each nation built up its armaments under the impression that *The armed* its neighbor meditated an attack, and in so doing inspired *peace* its neighbor with the same dread. These mounting fears were stimulated by the patriotic and militant utterances of such writers as Frederick von Bernhardi, who declared it to be the law of life that the strong must vanquish the weak, and urged his fellow Germans to prepare for war. But German writers were not alone in defending militarism: in Russia, France, Austria, Italy, and England writers and teachers were active, inculcating in the minds of the young men and boys the belief that to risk their lives on the battlefield in defense of their country was a supreme privilege and duty. Of course, the war envisaged was always a war of defense, for no people and very few leaders had any wish to provoke a conflict if it could be honorably avoided, but military strategists were in general agreement that the best defensive was an offensive, and the high command in each state developed plans for hurling an army across its neighbor's frontier as the first measure of self-defense. As rumors of new and secret weapons and plans for sudden attacks filtered back and forth, they created a nightmare of suspicion and fear from which there seemed to be no possible escape. If one power increased its military budget, its opponents matched the increase and lengthened the period of conscript service; a strategic railway leading toward the frontier was countered by the construction of a new line of fortifications. By 1914, all Europe was tense with the strain and the expense of the long-drawn-out competition, and for some the bursting of the storm came almost as a relief.

Section F

THE WORLD WAR AND THE PROBLEMS
OF THE POST–WAR PERIOD
(1914–35)

The outbreak of a general European war in 1914, which ultimately involved almost all the nations of the globe, marked the opening of a new and unsettled era. Despite the enormous destruction and the tragic sacrifices which it caused, the World War solved few problems and created many. Both victors and vanquished suffered irremediable losses, and the heritage of hate which the conflict bequeathed made a satisfactory settlement difficult.

From the nightmare of war the European peoples emerged into a scarcely less desperate era of political turbulence and economic confusion. Although all classes earnestly desired to safeguard the world from future conflicts, the post-war years brought a general increase in armaments and a growing fear that Fate held even more destructive wars in reserve unless the machinery of peaceful arbitration could be greatly strengthened. Politically, the most significant development of the post-war period was the challenge to democracy and to democratic ideals afforded by the establishment of a new régime in Russia founded upon communist principles, and new governments in Italy and Germany which substituted the authoritarian rule of a single well-disciplined party, headed by a dictator, for the parliamentary rule of a popularly elected and representative assembly.

CHAPTER TWENTY-SEVEN

THE WORLD WAR

We are glad, now that we see the facts with no veil of false pretence about them, to fight thus for the ultimate peace of the world and for the liberation of its peoples...
WOODROW WILSON (1917).

There never was a good war or a bad peace.
BENJAMIN FRANKLIN.

THE incident which precipitated the long-dreaded war between the European powers in 1914 originated in the Balkans. A dispute which broke out between Austria and Serbia drew in Germany, as the ally of Austria, and Russia, as the protector of the Serbs. France was bound to Russia by treaty, and Britain chose to stand by France and Russia under the terms of the *Entente*. Thus the system of alliances which was supposed to preserve a balance of power not only failed to prevent war, but made it, when it came, an all but universal tragedy.

1. THE COMING OF THE WAR

For more than a decade before 1914, the governing classes in Austria-Hungary had grown increasingly alarmed at the spread of nationalist sentiment among the Slavic peoples of the Balkan lands, *Hostility* and they were particularly hostile toward the Serbs, who *between* had taken the lead in urging the creation of a Slavic state to *Austria-* include if possible all the Balkan Slavs. The Austrian an- *Hungary* nexation of Bosnia and Herzegovina in 1908 had dealt a severe blow to these Serbian aspirations, and Austrian opposition prevented Serbia acquiring all the territory she desired after the Balkan Wars of 1912–13.[1] In revenge the Serbs waged a tariff war against Austria, their newspapers stirred up anti-Austrian feeling, and Serbian secret societies strove to excite the Slavs within the Austro-Hungarian Empire to rebellion, despite the fact that the Serbian government had pledged itself to restrain such unfriendly activities.

The Serbian plots to disrupt the Hapsburg Empire would not have constituted a serious menace if the Slavic subjects of Francis Joseph had been contented with their lot. But, although half the fifty million people living in Austria-Hungary were of Slavic origin, they possessed little political power, for the Germans and Magyars practically controlled the

[1] See above, pages 390–91.

government and were unwilling to relinquish their privileges. Some Austrian statesmen agreed that the best way to placate the Slavs and consolidate the empire was to extend greater political power to the subject Slavs, perhaps to transform the empire from a dual into a triple monarchy so that the Slavs might enjoy equality with the Germans and Magyars. Among the leaders believed to favor such a compromise was the Archduke Franz Ferdinand, nephew and heir of the Emperor Francis Joseph. The Serbian patriots, who hoped to win over the discontented inhabitants of Bosnia and Herzegovina and unite them to a greater Serbia, feared that their chance might be lost if Franz Ferdinand mounted the throne and granted concessions. Many Germans and Magyars likewise regarded Franz Ferdinand with dislike because they feared his reforms might strip them of their preponderant influence in the empire. Whatever changes the archduke may have meditated (his intentions have never been made clear), his path was certain to be hedged with difficulties.

But Franz Ferdinand was not destined to mount the Austrian throne. On June 28, 1914, he was assassinated while visiting the town of Sarajevo *Assassination of the Archduke Franz Ferdinand* in Bosnia. The assassin was a Bosnian youth, Gavrilo Princip, but it was later proved that the act had been plotted in Belgrade and that officials in the Serbian army and the Serbian government had helped to provide the means. There is even some evidence to suggest that more than one member of the Serbian cabinet knew in advance of the conspiracy.

The Austrian government, already hostile to the Pan-Slav Movement in the Balkans, could hardly fail to take advantage of the opportunity *Austrian ultimatum to Serbia* thus offered for a reckoning with Serbia. On July 23, the foreign minister of Austria-Hungary, Leopold von Berchtold, dispatched an ultimatum demanding in substance: (1) that the Serbian government suppress all anti-Austrian activity in Serbia and dismiss officials guilty of fomenting it; and (2) that Austrian officials be permitted to aid in this work of suppression and in the punishment of the conspirators who had planned the archduke's death. A reply to this ultimatum was demanded within forty-eight hours. The Serbian government yielded to the greater part of the Austrian demands, but some details they questioned, offering to submit them to a decision of the Hague Tribunal or a concert of the powers, and protesting that the active intervention of Austrian officials in Serbian affairs was inadmissible because it would violate the constitution and the law of criminal procedure. The conciliatory tone of the Serbian response of July 25 was contradicted, however, by Serbia's simultaneous mobilization for war.

The Austrian government, proclaiming the reply evasive and unsatisfactory, declared war against Serbia July 28.

The belligerent attitude of Austria was founded (1) on a promise of support from Germany, and (2) on a conviction that Russia, the natural protector of Serbia, would not intervene. But this time the *The impotence of the diplomats* Russian government was confident of French aid, for the president of the French Republic, Raymond Poincaré, had visited Saint Petersburg in July, 1914, and assured the Russian minister of foreign affairs, Serge Sazonov, of Franco-Russian solidarity. The Russians, therefore, began preparations for a general mobilization as early as July 25. On the same day, as the threat of a general war became apparent, the British foreign minister, Sir Edward Grey, proposed a conference of British, French, German, and Italian ambassadors, to avert an Austro-Russian clash. Unfortunately, neither France nor Germany would endorse Grey's proposal for fear of offending their respective allies. Privately, however, Germany was advising Austria to show greater moderation, and urged that Russian fears should be allayed by a promise from Austria to respect Serbian integrity (July 28). Disregarding the advice from Berlin, the Austrians chose that date to declare war on Serbia.

After July 28, the Serbian issue was completely overshadowed by the German alarm over the progress of Russian mobilization, officially decreed July 29 (a preparatory state of war had been proclaimed four days earlier). Mobilization made hostilities all but inevitable, and Kaiser William telegraphed Nicholas II entreating him earnestly to withdraw his order. The harassed czar thereupon "suspended" the order for mobilization against Germany, but his advisers persuaded him to renew it the following day (July 30). The kaiser, though proclaiming a "state of imminent danger of war," had delayed German mobilization while making his appeal to Nicholas. On July 31, he offered the Russians twelve hours in which to countermand their continued mobilization, waited twenty-four hours for a reply, and then, on August 1, announced that a state of war existed between Germany and Russia. From France, where mobilization had been going quietly forward since July 30, the German government demanded a statement of policy, and as no clear answer was obtainable (France had already promised Russia to fulfill her obligations as an ally), Germany declared war against France also (August 3).

If Germany and Austria fought Russia and France, could Great Britain remain neutral? The British were bound by no formal treaties, but the British fleet was pledged, by private agreement between the govern-

THE WORLD WAR

ments, to protect the northern French coasts while the French war-
The British ships patrolled the Mediterranean. Sir Edward Grey, who
attitude had negotiated this "gentlemen's agreement," considered
that Britain was bound in honor to aid France, but would the British Parliament and the British people see the matter in this light? On August 2,
Grey's painful dilemma was solved by German ruthlessness, for on that
date the German government demanded permission to march its armies
through Belgium to attack France. This permission the Belgian government courageously refused. On August 4, the British government noti-
fied the German government that a state of war would commence at
midnight unless Germany promised to respect Belgian neutrality. There
was no reply, and Britain considered herself at war. It is not easy to see
how neutrality could have been preserved in any case, for two days earlier, before Belgium had been invaded, the British cabinet had accepted
responsibility under the "gentlemen's agreement" to protect the French
coast.

Thus, within a week five great powers had plunged into a war of unpredictable dimensions. Italy, as might have been expected, deserted
the Triple Alliance and issued a declaration of neutrality on the ground
that Austria and Germany were engaged in an offensive, not a defensive,
conflict. But a sixth power came into the struggle on August 23, when
Japan declared war against Germany; and one week later, Turkey joined
the "Central Powers." At first glance the "Allies" or "*Entente* Powers," Britain, France, and Russia, together with Japan and Serbia, appeared to have a great advantage over the Central Powers, Germany and
Austria and their dubious ally Turkey. For the Allies possessed the
world's greatest sea force, the British navy, and a combined potential
man-power three times that of the Central Powers. They hoped, in consequence, to see a speedy conclusion to the war. But in modern warfare,
training, equipment, and generalship count more than numbers, and here
the superiority lay with the Central Powers and encouraged them also
to look for an early victory. Only a few farsighted realists anticipated
that the struggle might last three or four years, or apprehended the full
magnitude of the tragedy which had overtaken European civilization.

From the outset each side endeavored to lay the full responsibility for
the war upon the other, and each government in turn published an
official explanation to justify its course of action. These accounts, the
British Blue Book, the German White Book, the French Yellow Book,
etc., were presented as impartial diplomatic surveys of the events leading
to the outbreak of hostilities, but in actuality they were subtle instruments of justification and propaganda. Supported by a carefully cen-

sored and not infrequently a subsidized press, they convinced the people in each belligerent country that their government was in the right, and that they were fighting for their liberties against an unprovoked attack by scheming and unscrupulous foes. No people and no government (a few reckless individuals aside) had planned or desired war; but once war came, a wave of patriotic fervor swept the rival populations into a maelstrom of enthusiasm and self-sacrifice. This spirit was deliberately intensified by carefully circulated tales of enemy perfidy and brutality manufactured for purposes of propaganda by the governments participating. Some of the atrocities recounted were true, for war is a brutal and brutalizing affair, but most of them were inventions. In justifying their own acts and blackening the case of the Central Powers, the Allied governments enjoyed an important advantage, for they controlled the sea routes and the ocean cables of the world and were enabled to impress their version upon the neutral nations. By their indefatigable propaganda, they succeeded in fastening upon the Germans in particular a reputation for infamy and inhumanity, which the latter did much to earn by the barbarous and destructive acts they committed in their drive through Belgium and northern France. To the neutral observer, the fact that Austria had attacked Serbia, while Germany had violated Belgium and invaded France, made the Central Powers appear the aggressors and largely invalidated any explanation which they might attempt to offer.

No question in modern history has been the subject of such bitter controversy and such intensive research as this concerning the responsibility for the World War. The finger of guilt has been leveled in *The question* turn at the Austrian foreign minister, Berchtold, for his *of war guilt* imperious note to Serbia; at the Russian foreign minister, Sazonov, for encouraging the Serbs and resisting mediation; at the French president, Poincaré, who assured Sazonov of French support, but failed to urge him to take a less aggressive stand. Throughout the war the German Kaiser, William II, was represented in the Allied countries as the arch-fiend who had planned the whole desperate drama in advance, with the aid of his ministers and generals. Still other critics have blamed Sir Edward Grey, arguing that, if Great Britain had pledged support to France and Russia earlier, Germany and Austria would have backed down; but as British statesmen appreciated at the time such a pledge might have moved Russia to greater belligerence. After twenty years of debate, the question "Who caused the war?" is still unsettled, but it has become reasonably clear that all the statesmen involved did what they earnestly believed to be their duty, and served the interests of their governments and their allies in the fashion that seemed to them best. The issue therefore would appear to be not so much "Who caused the war?" as "What caused the war?" If the answer to the latter question can be found in a single word, the word is nationalism, or the juxtaposition of aggressive and imperialistic nation-states, each bent upon augmenting its power, each prepared to go to war in defense of what it assumes to be its legitimate interests, and each indisposed to recognize any authority, moral or political, as superior to itself. So long as this condition of international anarchy persists, an appeal to arms must remain an imminent possibility at all times, and the threat of war must continue to hang, like the sword of Damocles, above the apprehensive nations.

2. THE WAR ON LAND (1914–17)

The plan of the German high command called for a vast enveloping movement which would destroy the French armies in the west before the dilatory Russians could concentrate their forces in the east. *The Schlieffen plan* Five German armies were to advance through Belgium and northern France, the First Army sweeping past Brussels on a semicircle which would carry it west and south of Paris, the Second, Third, Fourth, and Fifth Armies pivoting with it on concentric arcs with Metz as a center. Enveloped by this prodigious flanking movement, the French armies were to be herded against the Alsatian frontier, where the Sixth and Seventh German Armies formed an anvil upon which they could be pounded to pieces. Time was the most vital factor in this plan, time and a powerful right wing, for the First and Second Armies on the extreme right had the longest arc to follow and the heaviest resistance to overcome. Despite the heroic opposition of the Belgian forces, the Germans swept rapidly forward, driving back the French and a small British expeditionary force of one hundred thousand men. By September 5, the German First Army was within thirty miles of Paris and ahead of its schedule. But it was weaker than the original plan, designed by Count von Schlieffen in 1906, had ordained, and the troops were wearied by long marches. On September 6, the French attacked it desperately. In defending his right, the German general, von Kluck, opened a gap twenty miles wide between his forces and the Second Army on his left. French and British troops were hurled into this opening, making the position of the Germans still more hazardous, and after four days of fierce conflict they retreated. This first battle of the Marne (September 6–12) had not only saved Paris, but had irreparably dislocated the Schlieffen plan.

Throwing up entrenchments, the Germans quickly fortified a line against which the Allied troops pounded in vain (battle of the Aisne, September 13–21). By October this line stretched from the *The dead-* North Sea coast near the Franco-Belgian frontier to neutral *lock in the* Switzerland. The Germans hoped to capture the French *west* seaports, Dunkirk, Calais, and possibly Boulogne,[1] in order to cripple communications between France and Britain, but they were blocked by the stubborn British resistance at Ypres. Before the close of 1914, the struggle in the west had changed from a war of movement to a war of position. Both sides constructed intricate systems of trenches fortified with barbed-wire entanglements and machine guns against which cavalry regiments were useless and infantry battalions hurled themselves in vain. The armies were unprepared for this type of warfare, and the commanders clung to the belief that, by wasting enough men in concentrated attacks, it would prove possible to break through the enemy lines and open a rapid deployment. In March, 1915, the British advanced one mile on a three-mile front at Neuve Chapelle, after an unprecedented bombardment, but the German lines held and the gain was dearly bought with thirteen thousand dead. A month later, the Germans surprised the Allied forces at Ypres with waves of poison gas, but this new and ghastly instrument of war failed to drive the defenders from the city and increased the reputation of the Germans for treachery and inhumanity.

The year 1916 brought still further tragic proof that the western battle-line could not be broken. From February to June, the Germans assailed the great French fortress of Verdun. They gained over one hundred square miles of shell-torn ground, throwing in reserves until their casualties approached half a million, but the French had sworn, "They shall not pass," and Verdun still stood. In the north the Allies attacked in their turn, winning an equivalent area of tortured ground at twice the cost. In these prolonged battles the defenders suffered almost as heavily as the attackers, and the terrible slaughter weakened the morale of soldiers and civilians on both sides. There seemed, at the opening of 1917, to be little hope of forcing a decision in the west.

On the eastern front the campaigns had been more dramatic, but had proved even less favorable to the Allies. As the Russians had mobilized first, and with unexpected rapidity, they were able to invade *Battle of* East Prussia on the outbreak of war. To check their ad- *Tannenberg* vance, the kaiser called from retirement General Paul von *(August 26–* Hindenburg (1847–1934), a clear-headed strategist of sixty- *31, 1914)* seven, who possessed an intimate knowledge of East Prussian topogra-

---

[1] See map following page 388.

[403]

phy. With a Napoleonic gesture, Hindenburg hurled his forces between two larger Russian armies, and won, at Tannenberg, the most decisive victory of the war. Driving the Russian Second Army into the morasses of the Masurian Lake region, he practically destroyed it, taking ninety thousand prisoners and two hundred guns; then turning against the Russian First Army, which was advancing on his left, he forced it to retreat behind the frontier. The losses suffered by the Russians were enormous, but their early drive had caused the German high command to recall several divisions needed on the western front and this depletion helped to weaken von Kluck's First Army in its decisive encounter on the Marne.

Against the Austrian armies the Russians continued for a time to compete with greater success, capturing the province of Galicia and one hundred thousand prisoners in September, 1914. But the tide

Austro-German victories in the east (1915) turned when German reinforcements under von Hindenburg and von Mackensen came to the relief of the Dual Monarchy. Between May and September, 1915, the Russians were driven from Galicia and Poland with losses so catastrophic they appear incredible; at least one million of the czar's soldiers were made prisoner, and the list of killed and wounded must have reached twice that sum. From this drain of men and material Russia never recovered. Bulgaria decided the moment had come to join the Central Powers (October, 1915), and Serbia, vulnerable from three sides, was easily overrun. Before the end of 1915, the armies of Austria and Germany dominated the Balkans and had secured a direct land communication with their ally Turkey.

Strategically the Central Powers possessed several important advantages, for they held the "inside lines" and could move their forces from

The Dardanelles campaign one sector to another with rapidity and ease. Also, they were in a position to cut Russia off from easy communication with France and Britain by blocking both the Baltic and the Black Seas. The Allies, hoping to force their way to Constantinople and open the Black Sea to their ships, prepared an attack on the Dardanelles early in 1915, but were compelled to abandon the project after a year of costly blunders. A British expedition which advanced from the Persian Gulf toward Bagdad in 1915 was likewise defeated. To offset these staggering reverses on the eastern and Turkish fronts, the Allies had the meager satisfaction of repelling several assaults which the Turks directed against the Suez Canal.

One other important development of the year 1915 was the intervention of Italy in the conflict. On May 23, after eight months of bargain-

FIELD MARSHAL PAUL VON HINDENBURG
1847–1934

As a field marshal in the World War, and later as president of the German Republic, Hindenburg displayed in marked degree the self-discipline, inflexibility of temper, and devotion to duty which have long distinguished the Prussian ruling class.

ing with the opposing camps, the Italian government declared war
Italy joins   against Austria. In return for this assistance the Allied
the Allies   Powers promised her all those sections of "unredeemed Italy"
(1915)   to the north and east of the Adriatic Sea which she coveted, and more if she could take it, for in disposing of enemy territory the
Allies could afford to be generous. Among themselves, the Allies had already agreed that when the war had been won Russia should have Constantinople, France should reoccupy Alsace and Lorraine, and Great
Britain should acquire the lion's share of the German colonies. But as
1916 succeeded 1915, bringing victory no nearer, the optimism of the
Allied nations began to fade. In the west the indecisive carnage of Verdun and the Somme decimated the conscript armies. In the south the
Italians were hard-pressed to hold their own against the Austrian offensives. In the east a valiant Russian drive in Galicia (June–July, 1916)
raised undue hopes and encouraged Rumania to declare for the Allies,
whereupon the armies of the Central Powers swiftly overran the kingdom
and seized the Rumanian harvest. Thus the closing months of 1916
found the Central Powers holding Belgium, part of northeastern France,
Poland, Serbia, Montenegro, and most of Rumania. So far as land
operations were concerned, they appeared to be winning the war despite
their costly failure at Verdun.

3. THE WAR ON THE SEA

The operations on land, however, did not tell the whole story. On the
sea the Allies had applied their superior naval forces with immediate
The naval   effect, capturing, sinking, or driving into port all ships flying
blockade   the flags of the Central Powers. Great Britain then declared all enemy territory in a state of blockade and attempted to seize
as contraband all materials useful in the prosecution of the war. As the
months passed, the British government increased the list of goods liable
to be confiscated, and even restricted the importation of merchandise
into neutral countries like Holland and Denmark on the ground that any
surplus was intended for Germany. The United States and other neutral nations protested vigorously against the British actions, which violated international agreements, and the Germans complained with justice that the Declaration of Paris [1] and later declarations concerning the
seizure of contraband in time of war were being flouted daily. To this
the British replied that the German government had been the first to
disregard international laws and treaties, and insisted that it must bear

[1] See above, page 260.

the responsibility if its civilian population suffered hardships because the supply of fuel, cotton, and foodstuffs had been curtailed by the blockade.

In addition to the strangling effect of this state of siege, which steadily reduced the morale and resistance of the German people, the Allies took advantage of their control of the sea to isolate and capture the German colonies, to transport their own supplies and men to the scene of conflict, and to maintain the shipments of food and raw material without which British industry and the British population would have slowly starved. Furthermore, England and France could purchase munitions in the United States, where factories were kept running day and night to fill their orders, while Germany and Austria were cut off from this important source of supplies. Under the circumstances it is not altogether surprising that the Germans decided upon a program of retaliation against Allied shipping, planning by means of submarine boats to enforce a counter-blockade.

Early in 1915, she German government pronounced the waters surrounding the British Isles a "war zone" in which any merchant ship of the Allied nations might expect to be torpedoed without warning. This application of a new naval weapon, the submarine boat, proved at first highly successful; British ships *The German submarine blockade* were sunk almost daily, the most important being the giant liner *Lusitania* which was torpedoed on May 7, 1915, with a loss of over eleven hundred lives. But the campaign of the undersea boats failed to stop the flow of Allied commerce, although it seriously depleted the supply of merchant ships. Moreover, it injured the German cause by inflaming neutral opinion against the Central Powers. The arrogance of the British, in searching ships on the high seas and confiscating their cargoes, appeared almost pardonable in comparison with the inhumanity of the German U-boat commanders who sank ships, cargoes, and passengers indiscriminately. Strong protests from the United States after the sinking of the *Lusitania* impelled the German government to modify its procedure for a year, but in January, 1917, it announced a policy of "unrestricted submarine warfare" under which any ship, belligerent or neutral, which entered the danger zones surrounding the coasts of the British Isles, France, or Italy, would expose itself to destruction without warning. The Germans hoped by this defiant course to destroy one million tons of shipping a month and cripple the Allied transportation system beyond salvation, but they failed in their objective and sealed their fate by drawing the United States into the war on the side of their opponents.

In the years preceding the war, an American naval historian, Captain (later Admiral) Alfred Thayer Mahan, wrote several widely read books to prove that in warfare a power which controls the sea possesses a decisive advantage over its adversary, an advantage which, if it be maintained, must almost certainly assure victory in the end. The Allied peoples found this argument a consolation during the dark days of the World War; but some German theorists retorted that, even if Mahan's conclusions had held true in the past, the submarine had changed conditions, for it gave the Central Powers a means to control the seas also. But before the war ended, the destructiveness of the submarine boats had been severely curtailed by the improved tactics and vigilance of surface craft, and flotillas of merchant ships, heavily guarded, were passed safely through the forbidden zones. Had the Germans made good their threat to destroy the ships of the Allies faster than they could be replaced, the war might have had a different ending, but since the Allies did succeed, though with difficulty, in maintaining their control of the sea, Mahan's thesis appeared to be vindicated.

Only once throughout the war did the German High Seas Fleet risk a major engagement with the British Grand Fleet. On May 31, 1916, the *Battle of* British admiral, Jellicoe, learning that the Germans had left *Jutland* port, converged upon them with superior forces, and at-*(May 31,* tempted to draw them into a trap by advancing his cruiser *1916)* squadron as a lure. When the German admiral, von Scheer, discovered the ruse, he extricated his slower fleet with exceptional skill, and after darkness had fallen slipped through a British destroyer screen to safety. Both sides claimed a victory, the Germans because they inflicted losses double their own upon a superior enemy force, the British because they remained masters of the scene of combat and held their supremacy without a second direct challenge until the end of the war. In marksmanship, maneuvering, and night fighting, however, the Germans had displayed a technical superiority which won the admiration of their foes.

The battle of Jutland probably represents the only occasion when the war could have been won or lost in half an hour. Had the English seized *Effects of* this unique chance to destroy the German High Seas Fleet, *the blockade* they could have opened the Baltic and secured their sorely needed communication with ice-free Russian ports. On the other hand, a striking German success which broke the blockade and exposed Allied merchant shipping to the risk of capture and destruction by German cruisers would have proved more paralyzing than the submarine campaign at its worst. But because Britain continued to rule the waves, and because the arrival of American naval reinforcements after April,

1917, made a further sally by the German fleet an unwise gamble, the inexorable pressure of the blockade continued. The growing shortage of rubber, oil, nickel, cotton, and many other substances necessary in the conduct of modern technical warfare, sapped the resistance of the Central Empires. The curtailment of the food supply was less vital, for by strict rationing and the use of substitutes the beleaguered peoples learned how to dispense almost entirely with the luxury of foreign products. There can be no doubt, however, that malnutrition, added to the horror and the strain of war, induced the final collapse of their morale.

4. THE WAR ON LAND (1917-18)

The war might well have ended in 1916 in a general stalemate and a compromise peace. Allied mastery on the sea largely nullified the successes won by the Central Powers on land, and all the belligerents had come to realize that a decisive victory would demand disproportionate slaughter and ruinous expense. *Peace negotiations of 1916* Yet, when the German government proposed "to enter into peace negotiations" (December 12, 1916), the Allied Powers returned a joint refusal, declaring the offer a ruse designed to create dissension in the Allied countries, and stigmatizing it as "empty and insincere." In the same month President Wilson dispatched a note through the state department of the United States, urging the adversaries to draw up an outline of their war aims. Wilson pointed out that the precise objectives for which the nations were fighting had never been definitely stated, and he suggested that an interchange of views might clear the way for a conference. To this friendly overture the Central Powers responded that they had themselves proposed an interchange of views a few days earlier. The Allied nations replied at greater length with a general but not entirely frank definition of their objectives, including "the restoration of Belgium, Serbia, and Montenegro ... evacuation of the invaded territories in France, in Russia, and in Rumania ... liberation of the Italians, as also of the Slavs, Rumanes, and Czecho-Slovaks from foreign [i.e., Austro-Hungarian] domination, [and] the setting free of the populations subject to the bloody tyranny of the Turks ...' The Allies also demanded compensation and indemnities, and adequate guaranties for the future peace of Europe.

Only definite defeat could bring the Central Powers to accept such terms, for they involved the break-up of the Hapsburg Empire. The insistence of the Allied governments that Germany and Austria were exclusively responsible for the war, and the rejection without thanks of the German peace overture, destroyed all hope of an early conference and condemned Europe to nearly two more years of bloodshed. In choosing this course the Allies were influenced chiefly by the fear that in 1916 they would enter negotiations at a disadvantage, and by the hope that by further and better concerted action they might win a decisive victory and dictate their own terms.

Following the rejection of the peace proposals, Germany turned to new and more ruthless methods of submarine warfare, for more than ever Time had become the enemy of the Central Powers.

Outbreak of the Russian Revolution (1917) The Allies planned to make 1917 a year of synchronized attacks from all sides, but their hopes were betrayed through the collapse of Russia. Demoralized by the terrible slaughter, the failure of supplies and of munitions, and the despair which had followed on their disastrous reverses, the Russian armies and the Russian people broke into a popular revolt and the forces of government dissolved in spontaneous anarchy. Nicholas II was compelled to abdicate (March 15, 1917) and a republic was proclaimed. For several months the French and British clung to the illusion that the new Russian government would press the war with fresh vigor, but after a second revolution in November, 1917 (which is treated more fully in Chapter XXIX), the radical faction known as the Bolsheviki secured control and arranged a truce extremely favorable to the Central Powers. The withdrawal of Russia from the war was formally confirmed by the Treaty of Brest-Litovsk which was signed in March, 1918.

While losing one ally, however, the *Entente* nations found another and more powerful one. The campaign of unrestricted submarine warfare, opened by the Central Powers in February, 1917, imperiled the lives of such American citizens as chose to sail on ships entering the war zones. Hostility toward the Central Powers had grown steadily in the United States. It was fostered by Allied propaganda, by sympathy for France and Belgium, and by the ill-advised activities of German agents who attempted to prevent the shipment of munitions from the United States to the *Entente* nations. The fact, too, that American financiers had advanced a billion and a half dollars in credits to the Allied governments played its part in shaping sentiment toward intervention. On February 3, 1917, the United States broke off diplomatic relations with Germany, and on April 6, Congress voted to declare war. This action meant that the enormous wealth, the industrial equipment, the natural resources, and the undepleted man-power of the American people would be available for the French, British, and Italians to draw upon. Sweeping measures were

The United States enters the war (April, 1917)

rushed through Congress extending loans to the Allied governments, mobilizing millions of men for military service overseas, and speeding up the production of ships, shells, guns, airplanes, and all the other forms of material and equipment essential to the vigorous prosecution of a modern war.

Fortune was clearly deserting the Central Powers, but the German general staff, now dominated by Erich von Ludendorff, was still confident of victory and decided to risk everything upon a gambler's chance. With Russia in collapse, and the United States unprepared to train and dispatch large forces to Europe for at least a year, the Germans possessed a numerical superiority on the French and Italian fronts at any point where they chose to concentrate their reserves. In October, 1917, they launched a drive against the Italians at Caporetto, and the resulting *débâcle* cost Italy three quarters of a million men and all but drove the nation out of the war. Then the Germans prepared for a spring offensive on the western front, a drive of unparalleled proportions by which they hoped to bring the French and British to terms. All the nations were war-weary, the spirit of defeatism had infected soldiers and civilians alike, and both the French and Italian governments had crushed serious mutinies among the troops by wholesale executions. The Germans believed that the morale of the Allied armies would break under a new assault before July, 1918, so that the American reinforcements, even if they escaped the hazards of submarine attack, would reach France too late to turn the tide of war. In March, 1918, von Ludendorff delivered his first blow in this "Victory Drive," shattering the British Fifth Army, but stopping just short of the important railway junction of Amiens. A second blow parted the British lines before Lille. The numerical preponderance which the Germans enjoyed had given them two important though not decisive victories, but the cost exacted was half a million casualties. Their third drive, against the French this time, carried them forward thirty miles to the Marne River, so that they were almost as close to Paris as during their first rush of 1914. Ludendorff now prepared his fourth stroke, which was designed to capture Reims and dislocate the Allied front so completely that it would end the war.

The German offensives of 1917 and 1918

This supreme offensive opened in mid-July, 1918. The Allied armies, recently unified under the command of General Ferdinand Foch, were learning to concert their resistance to better effect; they held firm against the fury of the German assault, and after three days they counter-attacked so energetically that the whole aspect of the war changed in two weeks. This second battle of

The German drive fails (July, 1918)

the Marne (July 15—August 2, 1918) was even more decisive than the first. With American reinforcements coming into line by the hundreds of thousands, Foch gave orders to General Haig, who directed the British expeditionary force, and to General Pershing, who commanded the American army in France, to attack the enemy along the whole line. With the advantage of numbers now turning against them, the Germans were driven slowly back, in a rearguard action of such magnitude that it cost them another half-million casualties by the middle of September. The tide had turned irreversibly and the end was in sight.

In September, Bulgaria sued for peace. An Allied army, operating from Salonica, had reconquered Macedonia and Serbia, and was threat-

Withdrawal of Bulgaria, Turkey, and Austria-Hungary (September— November, 1918) ening the Bulgarian capital. A few weeks later, the Turkish Empire collapsed. The British had entered Jerusalem (December, 1917), and, after joining forces with rebellious Arab leaders, General Allenby opened a campaign in 1918 which overthrew the Turkish strongholds from Bagdad to Aleppo. With her southern allies dropping out of the war, Austria-Hungary could not hope to resist invasion. Her subject peoples were rising in revolt and her armies falling back before the Italians when the Dual Monarchy capitulated on November 4, 1918. In reality, even while the envoys were signing the armistice, the proud Austro-Hungarian Empire had ceased to exist, for the same day the Emperor Charles VII (who had succeeded Francis Joseph in 1916) renounced his throne, and the Poles, Czechs, Croats, and Slovenes were organizing independent states.

Fully aware that the war was lost, but preserving their admirable discipline throughout the retreat, the German armies fought on stubbornly while their allies fell away from them and Foch's unremitting attacks multiplied from day to day. In the end it was the civilian population of Germany which first broke under the strain of defeat, starvation, and disillusionment. Repudiating the imperial government which had promised victory and now stood forsworn, the inhabitants of Munich and Berlin, and the sailors in the naval squadrons at Kiel, raised republican flags during the first week of November. On the tenth, William II fled to Holland, and the following day the German delegates, who had been sent to ask for an armistice, signed under protest the terms of surrender which Foch had drawn up. The reversal of fortune in the final months of the war had been so swift that the Allied Governments chose to regard the Germans' acceptance of a truce as an unconditional capitulation. Firing ceased at eleven o'clock on the morning of November 11, 1918.

5. THE COST OF THE WAR

For over three years the leading nations of the world had strained their resources to the breaking point in the work of slaughter and destruction. Before its close the World War had involved over thirty states and left no part of the planet or its population unaffected. The magnitude of the struggle blunted the comprehension even of those who lived through it, and no later description can give more than a feeble suggestion of its horrors. Statistics are but a ghostly residue of what were once flaming facts, and it is better perhaps that no ciphers on a page can ever borrow the power to clothe with reality for later eyes this greatest of modern tragedies.

Eight million soldiers, the finest of their generation, had perished, over six thousand a day for each day that the war continued. Nearly three times as many had been wounded, some in such ghastly *Loss of life* fashion that they took their own lives rather than survive as blinded, crippled, or paralyzed invalids. Losses of life among the civilian population from shell fire, air raids, submarine attacks, the hardships of the blockade, and other causes, cannot be easily estimated; and it is still less possible to find any measurement for the spiritual anguish endured, the waiting for word from the missing, the disruption of family life, the shock and the grief as the friends and relatives of eight million men faced the knowledge that the dead would not return.

For the material costs of the war the figures are too vast to bear any recognizable relation to familiar things. The property destroyed, mines flooded, trees shattered, buildings razed, ships and cargoes *Material* sunk, have been valued at thirty billion dollars. Modern *costs* methods of fighting proved far more expensive than anyone had conceived and grew more so daily, until the combatants were spending ten million dollars *an hour*, and piled up a grand total of war expenditure by November, 1918, which has been estimated at one hundred and eighty-six billion dollars. But when, to the cost of mobilizing sixty-five million men for military service, one adds the sacrifice entailed by withdrawing them from profitable and productive occupations, the loss to civilization becomes vastly greater. This expense of energy and of gold, turned into channels of peaceful accomplishment, might have replaced all the tenements in all the cities of Europe and America by model houses; might have curbed disease and provided medical service which would have saved as many lives as the war cost; might have banished illiteracy among the civilized nations and endowed free libraries in every town. Applied to more prosaic purposes, these billions would have cancelled the national debt of all the belligerent states and eased the burden of taxation, instead of leaving the governments in a state scarcely distinguishable from bankruptcy.

The scientists and inventors who had done so much to enrich and extend the life of man in recent generations were summoned by the warring governments to devise new methods of mass murder and new safeguards against it. Guns remained the principal weapons, but all types, from the light machine guns to the German long-range cannon which shelled Paris from a point seventy miles away, were developed to an extraordinary pitch of efficiency. Of new devices the most terrifying was poison gas, first utilized by the Germans, and the most effective the cumbersome armored tractors or "tanks," a British invention designed for smashing a way through entrenchments and barbed-wire entanglements impassable for infantry. Bombs dropped from the air, another innovation, were generally more spectacular than effective, but the airplane proved an invaluable aid in reconnaissance work and in directing artillery fire. The construction of underground defenses, often reinforced with sheet iron and concrete, and of fortified machine-gun stations led to a much wider demand for high-explosive shells, which were used to destroy these positions as completely as possible before the infantry attempted to pass.

In sea fighting the most novel diversion was provided by the submarine boat, but it is a truism in warfare that new weapons are met by new defenses. Before the conflict ended, the British and their allies had perfected methods for the detection and destruction of undersea craft which seriously curbed their activities. The question whether the giant battleships, which were the pride of all the pre-war navies, could survive the threat of airplanes and submarines remained open to debate, but most naval experts were satisfied that the dreadnought would preserve its relative invulnerability, and they continued to repose their trust in these floating fortresses with their armor plate a foot thick and their guns which hurl one-ton projectiles.

More than any previous struggle, the World War proved itself a war of steel and gold. Only nations which possess huge financial reserves, and can command the industrial equipment to supply the munitions required, are capable of waging a modern war successfully. The day had past, also, when a state could entrust its defense to a small professional army while the people went about their daily business. Not only the able-bodied men, but all the citizens of a society, may be conscripted for war service of one sort or another in the modern state. Nor are all the casualties confined to the firing line, as the British discovered when their merchant ships were torpedoed and German airships dropped bombs on London. With no fireside secure, and the pervasive force of official propaganda reaching every quarter of the country, it was practically impossible for any citizens to preserve an indifferent or an open mind on the issues of the struggle. Patriotism triumphed, and on both sides, as the casualties mounted, a sense of loyalty to the heroic dead demanded further sacrifices from the living.

To maintain their peoples in this exalted mood, governments resorted to every device which could stimulate a waning morale. Indeed, the "propaganda offensive" waged by all the belligerents was *War propa-* perhaps the most significant weapon which the war devel- *ganda* oped. Official spokesmen of the Allies and the Central Powers consistently idealized their own acts and objectives while unscrupulously misrepresenting the aims and actions of their enemies. In this deceptive art the governments of Great Britain and France displayed a marked superiority, impressing, not only their own nationals, but many neutral observers also, with the unimpeachable justice of their cause. They represented the war as a struggle between the forces of autocracy and democracy, between despotic rulers swayed by lust for conquest and free peoples defending their liberties, this despite the fact that Russia, most autocratic of the European governments, fought on the side of the Allies. World opinion was further impressed by the Allied claims after the United States joined in the war in the spring of 1917. Woodrow Wilson proclaimed with stirring phrases that the free peoples of the world were fighting to make the world "safe for democracy" and to secure a just and lasting peace. In warfare slogans are sometimes more effective than shells. The idealization of Allied war aims which Wilson presented as his "Fourteen Points" (January 8, 1918) not only inspired the people in all the Allied countries, but influenced the German and Austrian nationals also. When, in the autumn of 1918, the war-weary German people sued for an armistice, it was to Wilson that they appealed, and to his program. But Wilson referred their request for a peace based upon the Fourteen Points to the Allied and Associated Powers, and these powers accepted it "subject to ... qualifications." What these qualifications were will be explained in the next chapter.

CHAPTER TWENTY-EIGHT

THE PEACE SETTLEMENT OF 1919

The day of conquest and aggrandizement is gone by; so is also the day of secret covenants entered into in the interests of particular governments and likely at some unlooked-for moment to upset the peace of the world.
WOODROW WILSON (January 8, 1918).

NO PEACE conference has an easy task to perform, for the disputes which precipitate a war are seldom settled by the strife and the bloodshed, and new problems are certain to be created during the struggle. The student will recall the high hopes with which the people of Europe waited for the Congress of Vienna to assemble in 1814, and the disillusionment which followed as they concluded that the chief interest of the diplomats was not to secure a just settlement, but "to divide among the conquerors the spoils taken from the vanquished." After the World War ended in 1918, the nations, victors and vanquished alike, passed through a similar transition from hope to bitterness, and their dissatisfaction over the peace settlement of 1919 was even more profound and more general than the disappointment which succeeded the Napoleonic Wars a century earlier.

1. IDEALS AND REALITIES

There were many complex reasons why the delegates who met at Versailles in 1919 could not justify the hopes reposed in them. The
Wilson's chief difficulty, perhaps, was the gulf which had been dug
idealism between ideals and realities. While the World War raged, neither the Allied governments nor those of the Central Powers had admitted frankly and publicly the concrete advantages which they hoped to derive from victory. As early as 1916, President Wilson had proposed privately that the Allies summon the Central Powers to a peace of no annexations and no indemnities, intimating that if Germany and Austria refused this offer the United States would help to enforce it. But the Allied statesmen, bound by their secret projects for national aggrandizement, evaded the suggestion. When, a year later, the United States declared war against Germany, Wilson insisted that the American people had no selfish ends to serve. "We desire no conquest, no dominion," he averred. "We seek no indemnities for ourselves, no material compensation for the sacrifices we shall freely make. We are but one of the champions of the rights of mankind."

WOODROW WILSON
1856–1924

Wilson's enigmatic personality puzzled his associates. Some considered him a sincere humanitarian, some a clever politician, and some a dogmatic idealist; but almost all agreed that he was a difficult colleague with whom to work.

By implication, the other "champions of the rights of mankind," Great Britain, France, and Italy, were likewise fighting to put an end to armaments and the spirit of militarism, to assure the principle of self-determination to all oppressed peoples, and to organize a world league of free nations pledged to live together for the future in peace and harmony. But unfortunately, these ideals were above the level of events, as the pre-election promises of politicians are above the predatory machinations of a party eager for the spoils of office.

David Lloyd George, prime minister of Great Britain after December, 1916, and the fiery French premier, Georges Clemenceau, recognizing the enthusiasm which Wilson's peace program evoked among the war-weary population, identified themselves with it and allowed Wilson to appear the spokesman for all the Allied and Associated governments. Everywhere people came to think of Wilson's Fourteen Points as embodying the generous aims for which the Allies were fighting, and even the Germans and Austrians trusted that the United States would contribute its powerful influence to assure a just treaty in accordance with Wilson's program. It is time, therefore, to examine the famous Fourteen Points in detail, before seeking to explain what happened to them when the congress finally assembled. A summary of them follows.

I. Open covenants of peace, openly arrived at . . .
II. Absolute freedom of navigation upon the seas . . . alike in peace and in war . . .
III. The removal, as far as possible, of all economic barriers . . .
IV. Adequate guaranties given and taken that national armaments will be reduced to the lowest point consistent with domestic safety.
V. A free, open-minded, and absolutely impartial adjustment of all colonial claims . . .
VI. The evacuation of all Russian territory and such a settlement . . . as will secure [for Russia] . . . an unhampered and unembarrassed opportunity for the independent determination of her own political development and national policy . . .
VII. Belgium . . . must be evacuated and restored . . .
VIII. All French territory should be freed and the invaded portions restored, and the wrong done to France in the matter . . . of Alsace-Lorraine . . . should be righted.
IX. A readjustment of the frontiers of Italy should be effected along clearly recognizable lines of nationality.
X. The peoples of Austria-Hungary . . . should be accorded the freest opportunity of autonomous development.
XI. Rumania, Serbia, and Montenegro should be evacuated; occupied territories restored; Serbia accorded free access to the sea . . .
XII. The Turkish portion of the present Ottoman Empire should be assured

a secure sovereignty, but the other nationalities which are now under Turkish rule ... autonomous development ...

XIII. An independent Polish state ... should include the territories inhabited by indisputably Polish populations ... [and should] be assured a free and secure access to the sea ...

XIV. A general association of nations must be formed under specific covenants for the purpose of affording mutual guaranties of political independence and territorial integrity to great and small states alike.

These were lofty and unselfish aims which would, many people hoped, remove the causes that were responsible for past wars, and safeguard the world from armed conflict in the future. Of course, it was easy to foresee that some of the points, such as the demarcation of Italian or Polish frontiers "along clearly recognizable lines of nationality," might prove more complex in practice than in theory, but it was hoped that any hasty or unwise decisions compounded in the hurry of a general settlement could be rectified later by an appeal to the League of Nations. The creation of such a league, though not mentioned until the last clause of Wilson's program, remained to him the point of first importance.

What the advocates of a "just peace" failed to allow for were the national passions which propaganda and sacrifice had fanned to an irrational pitch; the distorting effect of the "war-guilt" *The secret* thesis, which had convinced millions of people in the Allied *treaties* countries that William II and his responsible subordinates ought to be punished for their "crimes against humanity"; and the malign force of those secret agreements which Britain, France, Italy, Greece, and Rumania had already concluded with respect to the disposal of the Rhineland, the Adriatic littoral, the Turkish Empire, and the German colonies.   Allied forces, chiefly British and Japanese, had conquered all the German colonies by 1918, and possession is nine tenths of international law.   French statesmen had informed London and Saint Petersburg of a project to detach the left bank of the Rhine from the German Empire in the interests of security.   Russia had been promised control of Constantinople and the Straits, although guaranties made to Russia might conveniently be revoked because that country had made a separate peace and was in no condition to insist upon the bargain. But the other parties to the secret treaty of London (April 26, 1915), to the secret accord with Rumania (August 17, 1917), and the secret conventions which drew Greece to the side of the Allies, were not likely to renounce their promised rewards.   Wilson had been too sanguine in his assumption that the day of "secret covenants," of "conquest and aggrandizement," had gone by.   The cause for which he strove was lost in advance before he sailed for Paris, and the "war to end war," as an embittered humorist remarked, seemed likely to be followed by "a peace to end peace."

2. THE TREATY OF VERSAILLES

In defiance of customary diplomatic usuage, the four defeated nations, Germany, Austria-Hungary, Turkey, and Bulgaria, were excluded from any share in shaping the treaties of peace. Nor did any of the lesser states among the thirty-two "Allied and Associated" victors play a significant rôle. The real masters of the conference were the "Big Four," the representatives of Great Britain, France, Italy, and the United States. Lloyd George, who was the idol of his countrymen and had guided England through the last two years of the war; Clemenceau, whose fierce resolution had silenced the "defeatists" in France when they abandoned hope of victory; Vittorio Orlando, prime minister of Italy, and the only one of the Big Four who spoke no English; and Woodrow Wilson, the first president of the United States to visit Europe while he was in office and participate personally in a peace congress — these were the men who formed the real deliberative committee which decided the peace.

The "Big Four"

In the Hall of Mirrors at Versailles, where the German Empire had been proclaimed on January 18, 1871, a peace conference assembled exactly forty-eight years later to signalize the ignominious defeat of that empire. By May, the treaty had been drafted and the Germans were summoned to sign it. Stunned by the severity of the terms, Count von Brockdorff-Rantzau, head of the delegation, entered an earnest protest at the contradiction between the draft of the treaty and the assurances granted the Central Powers when the armistice was negotiated. The Allied governments, however, were adamant in their hour of victory, and on June 28, yielding to necessity, the Germans accepted the treaty, acknowledging "the responsibility of Germany and her allies for causing all the loss and damage to which the Allied and Associated governments and their nationals have been subjected as a consequence of the war imposed upon them by the aggression of Germany and her allies" (Article 231).

The terms of the armistice, supplemented by the peace treaty, condemned the Germans to make restitution for property destroyed by their armies in the occupied regions. They turned over thousands of locomotives, railway cars, automobile trucks, farm machines, horses, swine, sheep, and cattle to the Allied govern-

Material surrendered

ments. They also surrendered the best part of their merchant marine as compensation for Allied shipping sunk by their submarines, and promised to construct up to one million tons of new ships for the same purpose. Substantial payments in the form of coal, dyestuffs, chemicals, etc., were likewise required of them, and the German-owned ocean cables passed under the control of the victors.

The Treaty of Versailles reduced the area and population of the German Empire by approximately one tenth. The provinces of Alsace and Lorraine were restored to France; some small districts *Territorial* (Eupen, Moresnet, and Malmédy) were transferred to *concessions* Belgian sovereignty; and the Saar Valley, with its valuable coal-mines, was placed in pawn for fifteen years, after which the inhabitants might vote for independence, for union with France, or for reunion with Germany. On the eastern frontier, Germany surrendered all the segments of Poland acquired in the eighteenth-century partitioning of that state. To provide Poland with an outlet to the Baltic Sea, a "corridor" was created which separated East Prussia from the remainder of Germany, while Danzig, with a population predominantly German, was incorporated in the Polish tariff system as a (nominally) free city. Germany also lost part of Upper Silesia to Poland although a plebiscite (1921) indicated a German majority throughout the greater part of the disputed territory. The city of Memel was finally allotted (1924) to the Lithuanian Republic; and a plebiscite in the provinces of Schleswig and Holstein gave Schleswig back to Denmark.

Article 119 of the treaty declared that "Germany renounces in favor of the Principal Allied and Associated Powers all her rights and titles over her overseas possessions." Japan acquired the *Colonies* German posts and privileges in Shantung Province, China, and all the Pacific islands north of the Equator where the German flag had flown in 1914. Islands south of the Equator passed into British control, and the British also took over German East Africa and German South-West Africa. The French added the German Kamerun territory north of the Congo to their empire in Equatorial Africa. A suggestion put forward by the Germans that the computed value of these colonies might reasonably be deducted from the reparations total was disallowed by the Allied governments.

Unable, in the few months at their disposal, to compute the total bill for reparations, the peacemakers contented themselves with stipulating that "Germany undertakes that she will make *Reparations* compensation for all damage done to the civilian population." A reparations commission, created to assess the damages and to examine the capacity of the Germans to pay, set the sum (1921) at thirty-three billion dollars. Although economists pointed out that there was no precedent for such a huge indemnity, and insisted that it could never be collected, the politicians and the Allied peoples were more sanguine, for the treaty entitled the victors to take punitive measures if the Germans fell behind in their payments, and the slogan that Germany should be made to pay to the last penny had been re-iterated too long to be easily relinquished. Ten years of economic confusion and a world-wide depression in trade and manufacturing activities supervened before the Allied governments could be per-suaded to reduce the German obligations to a sum which might be transferred without dislocating the machinery of international finance.[1]

The Allied high command maintained the economic blockade in force after the Central Powers had capitulated, an exercise of rigor
Guaranties which caused an alarming spread of tuberculosis and other diseases fostered by malnutrition among the en-feebled population of the demoralized states. This policy, insisted upon by the French, was short-sighted as well as inhuman, since it was equivalent to starving the goose which was expected to produce golden eggs in the form of reparation payments. Of further resistance from the defeated nations there could be little fear, for the Germans had surrendered their navy to the British under the terms of the armi-stice, and Allied troops held the left bank of the Rhine and the bridge-heads on the right bank at Mainz, Coblenz, and Cologne. The Treaty of Versailles exacted further guaranties that Germany would keep the peace, reducing the German army to one hundred thousand men and the navy to a handful of small or obsolete ships. No submarines or military aircraft were to be maintained, and all fortifications dismantled in the areas occupied by Allied troops and up to a line drawn forty kilometers to the east of the Rhine. Provision was made for the gradual evacuation of the occupied districts, to be completed within fifteen years, but the Allies retained the option of delaying, or even of reoccupying the left bank "to the extent regarded as necessary for the purpose of obtaining the required guaranties" (Article 429).

Repeatedly during the war the Allied spokesmen had emphasized the point that their quarrel concerned the imperial government of Germany rather than the German people. President Wilson had reaffirmed this view. "We have no quarrel with the German people," he declared on April 2, 1917. "We have no feeling toward them but

[1] See below, page 473.

GERMANY AFTER THE TREATY OF VERSAILLES

one of sympathy and friendship. It was not upon their impulse that their government acted in entering this war." Such protestations had encouraged the Germans to hope that, after they had overthrown the kaiser (November, 1918) and adopted a republican constitution (February, 1919), they would be permitted to join in the peace discussions, and to enter the League of Nations as an equal. The Socialist majority in the National or Weimar Assembly elected Friedrich Ebert provisional president of the German Republic, and this choice of a man who had begun life as a saddler, together with the democratic guaranties which distinguished the new constitution, advertised to the world that the German people had repudiated the ideals of their late masters. But this espousal of democracy gained them little appreciable advantage in the form of more lenient terms of peace. The Allied statesmen, who had professed a desire to see Germany a democratic republic, dealt the new government a deadly blow by forcing it to assume the onus of concluding a peace which patriotic Germans could never remember without a sense of humiliation. The Weimar Régime, as the republican experiment was called, never succeeded in clearing itself before the bar of German opinion for its inescapable part in "the betrayal of 1919."

The Weimar Assembly adopts a republican constitution (1919)

3. THE SETTLEMENT WITH AUSTRIA-HUNGARY, BULGARIA, AND TURKEY

Before the Peace Conference assembled in January, 1919, the Austro-Hungarian Empire had ceased to exist. The subject peoples of the Hapsburg domains had felt little enthusiasm for the war, and the defeat of the Central Powers brought them a chance to assert their independence. It devolved, therefore, upon the Peace Conference to draw geographical boundaries for the nascent states in accordance with the principle of the self-determination of nations.

The Allies embodied their terms to Austria in the Treaty of Saint-Germain (September 10, 1919), which limited the Austrian Republic to an area one tenth the size of the former Hapsburg Empire. The six and a half million Austrian Germans who inhabited the diminutive state realized that a free national existence under these restricted conditions was impracticable because of economic problems. They asked to be united to Germany, but France feared to permit this aggrandizement of her defeated foe and the treaty specifically prohibited such a fusion. Hungary suffered a similar fate

Fate of Austria and Hungary

by the Treaty of the Trianon (June 4, 1920), the once proud Magyars retaining control of a small state comprising some thirty-six thousand square miles and nine million people. Like Austria, Hungary was called upon to bear part of the burden of reparations, although the ability of either country to pay, or even to survive, in its mutilated condition was open to doubt. As the Allies refused to permit the Hungarians to recall a Hapsburg to the throne, Hungary remained a kingdom without a king.

From the peripheral areas of the defunct empire the peacemakers constructed one new state and enlarged four others. The new state, the Republic of Czechoslovakia, included over three million Germans, Magyars, and Slovenes, for the Allied statesmen proved more generous toward the demands of the Czechs and Slovaks than just toward the German and Magyar minorities. The province of Galicia, lying to the north of Czechoslovakia across the Carpathian Mountains, was transferred to Poland; and Rumania received, as a reward for joining the Allies, the extensive province of Transylvania and part of the district known as the Banat. The remainder of the Banat and the late Austrian provinces of Bosnia and Herzegovina were united to Serbia and Montenegro to form the Kingdom of Yugoslavia. Finally, the Italians received the district known as the Trentino, and claimed all the Istrian Peninsula, including the cities of Trieste and Fiume. These claims were based upon the secret understandings which Italy had reached with her allies; but President Wilson refused to approve the cession of Fiume, and the Italian delegate, Orlando, withdrew from the conference in protest. A separate agreement between Italy and Yugoslavia (Treaty of Rapallo, 1920) finally divided the disputed area and established Fiume as a free city.[1]

By the Treaty of Neuilly (November 27, 1919), the Bulgarians paid for their mistake in joining the side destined for defeat, by losing part of the gains which they had saved from the Balkan Wars *Bulgaria* and also their World War conquests. Greece and Yugoslavia (Serbia) were the principal beneficiaries, and the Bulgarians, in addition to promising reparation payments and reducing their armed forces, were obliged to see a million of their fellow nationals placed under foreign rule.

Of the four defeated powers, the Turkish Empire, which had been the first to crumble, was the most truculent in adversity. The Allies planned to divide the greater part of the Ottoman possessions among themselves as protectorates, but the Treaty of Sèvres (August 10, 1920),

[1] See map following page 426.

embodying these intentions, proved unenforceable. The Turks were

*Revival of
Turkish
power*

stirred to national resistance by the severe terms, denounced the treaty, and repudiated the helpless sultan at Constantinople who had accepted it. In 1919, the Greeks, who had been promised a share of Anatolia, landed an army at Smyrna to help in carving up the Ottoman possessions, but in 1922, this expeditionary force was driven into the sea by the armies of the newly organized Turkish Republic. The English were chagrined, the French secretly gratified by this development, for the two powers were already pursuing divided aims in the Near East, and the Turks profited by this divergence to secure their hold on Constantinople and demand recognition of the complete independence of the Turkish Republic. Even the humiliating "capitulations," which had previously defined the special privileges enjoyed by foreigners in Turkey, were abolished. Though limited to the Anatolian Cape and a small strip of European territory,[1] the new Turkish State, with its capital at Angora, has undergone a remarkable transformation under the inspiring and progressive dictatorship of Kemal Pasha.

Over the Arabian Peninsula, where the Arab tribes had been encouraged during the war to rise against their Turkish masters, France and Great Britain were more successful in establishing a tutelary control. On a rough basis of self-determination the victors carved new states from the disintegrating Ottoman realm. The French acquired a mandate over Syria, including Lebanon, the British over Palestine and Irak. The Arab principality of Trans-Jordania and the little known hinterland which stretches from Aden to the Persian Gulf are also under British supervision and protection.

4. THE FATE OF THE FOURTEEN POINTS

To demonstrate how far the final peace terms diverged from the principles laid down in Wilson's Fourteen Points, it will be of interest to consider these points one at a time and to note the fate which overtook each.

I. *Open covenants, openly arrived at.* The peace discussions of the Big Four were so rigidly guarded that even their lesser allies were ignorant of the settlement until the treaty had been completed. Even Wilson conceded that treaties could not always be openly arrived at.

II. *Freedom of the seas.* Out of deference to British prejudices on this point, it was dropped before the conference assembled.

[1] See map on the following page.

EUROPE
of Today

Scale of Miles

0 100 200 300 400 500

III. *Removal of economic barriers.* The effect of the treaties has been to increase the number and augment the importance of economic frontiers.

IV. *Adequate guaranties for disarmament.* Only the vanquished were disarmed. The victors continued to maintain armaments, more costly in many cases than those of 1914.

V. *Impartial adjustment of colonial claims.* The victors divided the spoils.

VI. *Evacuation of Russian territory and an opportunity for independent political development to be granted the Russian people.* The Allied governments interfered repeatedly in Russia (1918–20) in their efforts to overthrow the Soviet régime.

VII. *Belgium to be evacuated and restored.* This point was carried out.

VIII. *All French territory to be freed and restored, and Alsace-Lorraine returned to France.* This point was likewise carried out.

IX. *Readjustment of the Italian frontier along recognizable lines of nationality.* The final compromise placed over half a million Germans and Yugoslavs under the Italian flag.

X. *Autonomous development for the peoples of Austria-Hungary.* Carried out in the main, with the Slavs winning most disputed areas at the expense of the Germans and Magyars.

XI. *Self-determination for the Rumanians, Serbians, and Montenegrans.* Vindicated in general.

XII. *A secure sovereignty for the Turkish portion of the Ottoman Empire, and self-determination for the subject races.* The Turks finally achieved a stable régime despite interference. The self-rule permitted the subject races by the French and British is more nominal than real.

XIII. *An independent Polish State with access to the sea.* This point was realized.

XIV. *A general association of nations.* The covenant of the League of Nations was incorporated in the Treaty of Versailles.

In his anxiety to assure the principle of self-determination to subject peoples, and to win general acceptance for the idea of a League of Nations, President Wilson found it necessary to acquiesce in five significant compromises which violated his program in fact and spirit: (1) The Germans living on the left bank of the Rhine were placed under the control of France for a period which might last fifteen years or even longer. (2) Several hundred thousand Germans and Yugoslavs were incorporated into the Italian Kingdom, many against their will. (3) The German colonies were parceled out among the victors without any honest regard for an "impartial adjustment of colonial claims." (4) Instead of the just peace between equals which Wilson had envisaged, the treaty condemned the Germans and Austrians to assume the sole guilt for the war and to pay as much as they could in restitution. (5) Reduction of armaments to the lowest point consistent with domestic security (Point IV) was enforced upon the Central Powers, but wholly ignored by the victors.

The failure to disarm provided a particular disappointment for lovers of peace throughout the world, the more acute because the *The failure* Allied governments, throughout the duration of hostilities, *to disarm* had blamed the pre-war armament race upon the initiative of the Germans, and had excused their own preparations for war as unavoidable measures of self-defense. Yet with Germany reduced to impotence they still maintained, and even increased, their military forces. It was still possible to hope, however, that the sober judgment of conscientious men, exercising itself through the agency and the decisions of the League of Nations, might yet retrieve the ground lost through the unavoidable compromises, and that for each problem a final solution might be found in which the claims of justice would triumph over the forces of expediency.

5. THE LEAGUE OF NATIONS

More than once, in earlier centuries, proposals had been drawn up which aimed at the establishment of a permanent group or league *Precedents* of nations pledged to promote peace in Europe. The *for the* Duke of Sully, minister of the French king, Henry IV, *League* drafted such a plan; Napoleon aspired to end war by organizing Europe into one great empire under French leadership; and the diplomats who assembled at Vienna after Napoleon's downfall proposed to maintain peace in Europe by calling frequent congresses of the powers. But the spirit of co-operation which inspired this last suggestion, and evoked the more mystical experiment known as the Holy Alliance, soon yielded to the older anarchic spirit of each nation for itself. Although advocates of peace continued to plead the advantages that would flow from an international court created to adjust disputes between states, the only important result of their efforts was the establishment (1899) of a permanent court of arbitration known as the Hague Tribunal.[1]

The failure of the diplomats, with their system of competitive al-

[1] See above, page 392.

liances and balance of power, to prevent the World War, and the casual violation by the belligerents of many existing treaties and conventions, convinced thoughtful people more completely than ever that some organization was essential for the amelioration of this condition of international anarchy. In 1917, Wilson gave the concept new force by including the proposal for "a general association of nations" among his Fourteen Points. When the Peace Conference assembled in Paris in 1919, the organization of a League of Nations found a place in the agenda and the Covenant of the League was incorporated in the Treaty of Versailles. But here again the clash between ideals and realities compelled a number of compromises. The French statesman, Clemenceau, while endorsing the League, wished to see it an association dominated by the victors, pledged to preserve the Versailles settlement against all who might seek to disturb it. Although the French stand was later modified, the League as first constituted included none of the defeated powers and was too largely dominated by France and Britain. A second curb upon its efficiency and universality was imposed out of deference to the United States, and concerned "regional understandings." American statesmen had stood by the Monroe Doctrine for a century and had consistently opposed European interference in New World affairs, and American public opinion was not disposed to welcome League intervention in questions arising between American countries. The Monroe Doctrine was, therefore, recognized as a "regional understanding" which would be respected by the League. Other points upon which the framers of the Covenant were compelled to abandon their objectives were: (1) disarmament, (2) the recognition of the racial and religious equality of all member nations, and (3) the proposal to endow the League Council with authority to execute its decisions against recalcitrant states by invoking force. Because of the grave difficulties which had to be overcome in any attempt to settle these issues, all three were compromised or abandoned.

The Covenant or constitution of the League of Nations affirms that the member states have agreed to accept obligations not to resort to war, and have promised to observe open, just, and *The* honorable relations, and a scrupulous respect for treaties, *Covenant* in their dealings with one another. The original list of members included some forty-two states, the British self-governing dominions, Canada, Australia, New Zealand, South Africa, and India, receiving individual representation. Any self-governing state was declared eligible for admission, and any member might withdraw after providing two years' notice of its intention to do so. The cost of administra-

[429]

tion was to be met by contributions levied upon the members in proportion to their national budgets, and Geneva was chosen as the permanent seat of the League bodies.

The machinery of the League includes (*a*) an Assembly, (*b*) a Council, (*c*) a Secretariat, and (*d*) a Court of Arbitration. The Assembly includes representatives from all the member states, large *The Assembly* and small, each state casting but one vote, although it may send as many as three delegates. The most important functions of the Assembly are: (1) the admission of new states into the League; (2) the election of non-permanent members to a seat on the Council; (3) the investigation of disputes specifically referred to the Assembly for consideration. These are in general responsibilities of a secondary nature and many small states have protested that the rôle assigned to the Assembly is a lame and impotent one. In practice, however, the importance of the Assembly has tended steadily to increase.

It is true, however, that the functions of the Council appear more masterful in comparison. Composed of one member each from Great *The Council* Britain, France, Italy, and Japan, and one each from four (later increased to nine) lesser nations, the Council as originally constituted was little more than an executive cabinet dominated by the Allied Powers. As the United States declined to join the League and the Soviet Government of Russia had not been accorded official recognition, the places reserved for these powers on the Council remained vacant; but Germany was granted a permanent seat on her admission to the League in 1926. In 1933, Japan and Germany announced their intention to withdraw from membership, and in 1934, Russia was admitted, and received a permanent Council seat. The Council meets at Geneva, official headquarters of the League, at least once each year, and may deal with "any matter within the sphere of action of the League or affecting the peace of the world." Its decisions, unless otherwise specified, must be unanimous, a rule which also applies to the resolutions of the Assembly.

Much of the current work of the League is conducted by the permanent Secretariat, or by commissions. A secretary-general appointed *The Secretariat* by the Assembly directs the work of the Secretariat in conducting correspondence, investigating disputes, and registering treaties. In addition, commissions have been nominated under the League to investigate international evils, such as the traffic in narcotics, to curb the spread of malaria, cancer, and tropical diseases, to promote intellectual co-operation, to further the codification of international law, to abolish slavery and to protect minorities.

[430]

Responsibility for the welfare of backward peoples is also entrusted to special commissions, and the powers which acquired control over former German colonies, or any other regions, by the Treaty of Versailles, administer these areas as "mandates" of the League, subject to the supervision of the Commission on Mandates.

To settle disputes having to do with the legal claims of states under existing treaties and conventions, the Covenant provided for an International Court of Justice which was established in 1921. *The World Court* Like the Hague Tribunal, this World Court may accept cases referred to it for decision, and its verdicts contribute to the growing body of international law. But the most important function of the League is to find a prompt solution for the sudden disputes which arise between nations and threaten war, and this function falls upon the Council and Assembly. All members of the League are pledged to submit their quarrels to arbitration, and to abide by any decision endorsed unanimously by the Council members and accepted by the other party to the dispute. The real strength and significance of the League, therefore, depends upon the degree to which the members observe this compulsory arbitration clause (Article XII), and upon the effectiveness of the measures taken by the League to punish those members which dare to flout it.

Against defiant member states which refuse its mediation and violate the terms of the Covenant, the League may recommend punitive measures, such as a general economic boycott, or it may even invite the other members to employ their armed forces to discipline the refractory member. But it is highly doubtful that a unanimous vote (the participants to the quarrel excluded) could ever be passed through the Council and the Assembly to authorize such drastic action. The efficacy of the League in combating war rests less upon its power to punish violators of the peace than upon its ability to mobilize world opinion against such violators. The vital part played by propaganda in the World War furnishes proof that public opinion, when marshaled in support of a cause, can prove a mighty, if not a decisive, factor in achieving victory. It is the function of the League of Nations to marshal public opinion against the use of force in international disputes, and against the nation which shows itself overeager in drawing the sword or overreluctant in laying it aside.

In the first fifteen years of its existence, the League arbitrated a number of disputes, arising between lesser states, with a creditable degree of firmness and impartiality. In sharp territorial disputes which involved Sweden with Finland, Poland with Lithuania and with Czechoslovakia, and Greece with Albania and with Bulgaria, hostilities were averted, or were arrested after they had broken out, by judicious intervention. But the League proved less effective in dealing with the great powers. In 1923, following the murder of an Italian officer on Greek soil, the Italian government delivered a twenty-four-hour ultimatum to the Greeks, and, finding the reply unsatisfactory, bombarded and occupied the island of Corfu. Although Greece appealed to the League, the Italian delegate to the Council refused to approve any action, and the matter was finally decided by the Council of Ambassadors under whose authority the murdered official had been engaged in delimiting the Greek frontier. The settlement provided for the evacuation of Corfu by the Italians and the payment of an indemnity by the Greeks, although it was not proved that Greek citizens had been responsible for the murder.

In a second case involving a great power, the League Assembly displayed a resolution more creditable to its dignity. Following an investigation of the aggressive measures pursued by the Japanese military forces in Manchuria, the Assembly unanimously adopted a report condemning the Japanese policy. The Japanese delegates thereupon withdrew from the Assembly; but the Japanese government continues to hold several Pacific islands as mandates, and will undoubtedly insist upon retaining them, even though it sever all connection with the League. Such dilemmas and rebuffs must continue to beset the League so long as its decisions remain "paper verdicts."

It rests with the years, therefore, to decide whether the League of Nations, the most earnest and the most intelligent attempt so far made to curb the destructiveness of war, will survive the stresses of the postwar era, or whether it will founder, as similar projects have foundered hitherto, in the sea of international rivalries. Clearly, the mere creation of such a court can do little to curb international anarchy unless the peoples of the world can be taught to respect the League and to support it. If the World War and the peace which closed it can be said to have proved anything, they demonstrated that no mere rectification of local inequalities or emancipation of suppressed racial minorities will end the danger of war while the fundamental causes of it survive undiminished. Agitation over the fate of Frenchmen in Lorraine or Slavs in Bosnia doubtless helped to stimulate a war spirit in 1914, but today, when the map of Europe has been brought into closer correspondence with the desires of the various national groups, and several submerged minorities have acquired independence through the principle of self-determination, the danger of armed conflict is no less great, and militarism holds Europe as tenaciously as ever in its iron grip.

CHAPTER TWENTY-NINE
_____

RUSSIA UNDER THE RULE OF THE SOVIETS

We shall have a soviet government, without the participation of bourgeoisie of any kind...

NICOLAI LENIN.

THE suppression of the revolutionary movement of 1905–06 in Russia left a heritage of hatred and ferment behind which the stupid and stubborn attitude of Nicholas II did little to dissipate. Although the Russians rallied loyally to their government in the fervent patriotism of the first months of the World War, distrust soon began to undermine their allegiance. The stupendous losses which their armies suffered on the eastern front, the lack of war materials and munitions, and the graft and corruption which disgraced many sections of the high command and the supply services, ripened the mood of rebellion. Rumors that alien influences were at work in the court, the malign power which the monk Rasputin was known to exercise over the czar and czarina, and the suffering caused in many cities by the virtual blockade of Russian trade resulting from the war, combined to destroy the last foundations of the monarchy.

1. THE MARCH REVOLUTION

In March, 1917, strikes broke out in Saint Petersburg. Nicholas, who had remained blind to the realities of the situation, and had refused to heed the advice of his own ministers or the remonstrances *Abdication of* of the Duma, believed that the old methods of repression *Nicholas II* would once more prove effective. From his headquarters with the army he telegraphed orders to suppress the rioters and dissolve the Duma. But the troops refused to fire on the crowds, the Duma declined to dissolve, and the Autocrat of all the Russias suddenly found himself abandoned and helpless. On March 15, he abdicated a throne which had already collapsed.

Habits of thought often lag behind events. The Russian people did not recognize at once the magnitude of the changes which were occurring, a fact which is not surprising when the size, complexity, and *The Keren-* apathy of the Russian population is borne in mind. But *sky régime* even the political leaders at Saint Petersburg were slow at first to comprehend the depth of the movement which they had unchained. A provisional government was proclaimed, headed by a liberal nobleman, Prince Lvov, and the eloquent revolutionary, Alexander Kerensky, but

[433]

it was out of touch with the masses, its bourgeois affiliations excited distrust, and its program for continuing the war against the Central Powers aroused little enthusiasm. Kerensky's efforts to galvanize the armies for a new drive broke down before the war-weariness of the soldiers. The peasants, who coveted the estates of the nobles, grew impatient with a régime which hesitated to attack private property, and the workers in the towns began to demand a genuine social revolution instead of a mere political shift. By the autumn of 1917, it was clear that the provisional government would have to ally itself firmly with the propertied classes and defy the "confiscators" or else swing definitely to the Left and appease the land-hunger of the peasants by dispossessing the nobles. Kerensky's failure to strengthen his government played into the hands of the more radical revolutionaries. Even before 1914, the Russian Socialist Party had divided into two groups, the Mensheviki (minority) who hoped to introduce socialism by peaceful reforms and the Bolsheviki (majority) who planned to establish the "dictatorship of the proletariat" by a sudden and violent change.

After the outbreak of the revolution in 1917, the Bolsheviki urged the immediate introduction of socialistic measures, and they remained *Nicolai* defiant in their refusal to compromise with the bourgeois *Lenin* provisional government. The most important points in their program were: (1) the immediate conclusion of peace, (2) confiscation of large estates without compensation, and (3) control by the workers of the means of production. Their most intelligent leader was Vladimir Illyich Ulyanov, better known as Nicolai Lenin (1870–1924), a student of the writings of Karl Marx and a prophet of the proletarian revolution. With the collapse of czardom, Lenin had returned from his exile in Switzerland to put his profound understanding of social forces to practical use. Before his death seven years later, he was to make his name known throughout the world, and impress his ideals more forcibly upon the thought of the twentieth century than any other contemporary leader.

Throughout the summer of 1917, under the shadow of the shaky provisional government, the framework of a new order was being reared. *The soviets* The unit of the new organization was the *soviet* or council. Soviets of soldiers and workers and peasants were spontaneously organized in every regiment, factory, or village in the land, each sending delegates to higher committees, and these in turn choosing a national congress. At the First Congress of Soviets (June, 1917) the Bolsheviki were in the minority, but their strength grew rapidly. By October, Lenin's demand, "All power to the Soviets," had become a rallying cry, and the promise of land, peace, and bread made an ir-

NICOLAI LENIN

1870–1924

To those who stood in his way, Lenin seemed a modern Tamerlane, ready to sacrifice millions of victims without reason or compunction, but today his tomb is a shrine to the Russian masses.

resistible appeal to the land-hungry peasants, to soldiers weary of war, and to workers threatened with famine. Kerensky had called for the election of a constituent assembly on November 25, but the events were moving too fast for legal formalities.

2. THE BOLSHEVIKI IN POWER

At the beginning of November, the Bolsheviki prepared to seize control. They were still a minority organization of perhaps one hundred
The November Revolution thousand members, but they were resolute and unscrupulous, while their opponents, the dwindling factions of Mensheviki, and the more cautious Social Revolutionaries, were still seeking a middle path. Kerensky attempted to call in troops from the front to sustain his régime, but the railway employees refused to transport them; and on November 7, Lenin was able to tell the Second Congress of Soviets that the provisional government was at an end. A resolution was immediately adopted calling for a three months' armistice with the Central Powers and a peace with no annexations and no indemnities.

Unfortunately for the Bolsheviki, the Germans were in dire need of supplies and determined to press every advantage. With the Russian
Treaty of Brest-Litovsk front crumbling, they were in a position to write their own terms, and the Treaty of Brest-Litovsk, signed March 3, 1918, was a peace-at-any-price to the Russians and "the peace that passeth all understanding" to their disconcerted allies, England and France. Russia abandoned her claim to one fourth of her pre-war territory, including Poland, Lithuania, Estonia, Livonia, and Finland, and conceded valuable commercial and economic privileges to the Central Powers. Kars and Batum were restored to Turkey. Many Russians felt that this ignominious treaty was a betrayal, and the Bolsheviki found themselves menaced by a campaign of resistance and terrorism, but they clung defiantly to power. The National Constituent Assembly which assembled in January, 1918, declared the Soviet régime illegal, whereupon the Bolsheviki dissolved the Assembly by force. A department of secret police, the dreaded *Cheka*, was organized to frustrate all "reactionary" activity and Lenin pressed on to establish the dictatorship of the proletariat.

The peasants were invited to cultivate the land they worked free of rent, all private ownership having been abolished. Workingmen took over the management of the larger factories; the railways, banks, mines, and other enterprises became the property of the state; and the wealth of the Russian Orthodox Church was confiscated without compensation. The debts of the czarist administration, domestic and foreign, were repudiated, to the alarm and indignation of the foreign governments which had helped to finance Russia since pre-war years. Even in normal times such profound economic changes could not fail to disrupt the life of a nation, and their effect upon Russia, which had suffered more grievously than any other power from the shattering effect of the war, was to plunge the nation into a chaos from which there seemed no escape.

Nor were the Bolsheviki left free to work out a solution in peace. Their late allies, the French and British, grew steadily more hostile to the revolutionary régime, until they instituted an unofficial *The struggle* blockade and used the expeditionary forces which they had *to survive* landed at Vladivostok, at Archangel, and on the Black Sea, to attack the Soviet government under the pretense of protecting Russian minorities. Disaffected classes in Russia organized a militant resistance and "White Armies" appeared in half a dozen sections. By the fall of 1919, the Bolshevik control had been reduced to the area around Moscow and the collapse of the Soviet régime appeared to be a matter of weeks.

Then the picture changed. A Red Army organized by the indefatigable Leon Bronstein, better known as Trotsky, began to check the advances of the "White" generals. Kolchak, who had established a provisional government at Omsk, was overtaken and executed; Yudenich, operating in the Baltic area, and Denikin, who advanced from the south, were both forced back by the close of 1919. But the struggle was not yet over. In 1920, Poland declared war against the Soviet government, and a White Army from the Crimea, commanded by General Wrangel, advanced upon Moscow. Trotsky agreed to a sacrifice peace with the Poles, which left him free to turn his Red Guards against Wrangel's forces and destroy them. The Allies had abandoned their blockade early in 1920, and two years later the Japanese withdrew their forces from eastern Siberia. Soviet Russia had demonstrated its right to survive, but the sacrifice had been great. Wholesale execution of suspects and hostages by Red and White forces alike had marred the records of every campaign in the civil war, the most illustrious victims being Nicholas II and his entire family, executed at Ekaterinburg on July 16, 1918.

While crushing insurrections and consolidating their power, the Bolsheviki attempted to carry out their program to nationalize all land and industry in Russia, but by 1921, Lenin recognized that *The NEP* the task was too great for immediate execution. In many *(1921)* industries production had fallen to less than one fifth of the pre-war output. The peasants, eager enough to take over confiscated lands, were disillusioned when the government demanded that (as part of the collectivist experiment) they surrender their crops to feed the city workers. Agriculture, like industry, seemed on the point of foundering when Lenin prepared a compromise known as the New Economic Policy, or more briefly, as the NEP. The NEP restored the smaller industries, employing no more than fifteen to twenty workers, to private control, and permitted the peasants to sell their grain for profit. Furthermore, capital was obtained by extending concessions to foreigners and commerce began to revive. With economic conditions improving, the Communist Party, as the Bolsheviki had named themselves (1919), grew more and more popular, and when Lenin died in 1924 the desperate experiment which he had directed during five perilous years was on the road to success. As the Communist régime represents the most interesting social experiment so far undertaken in the twentieth century, it will be useful to examine its ideals and methods.

3. THE PHILOSOPHY AND PROGRAM OF THE RUSSIAN COMMUNISTS

In proclaiming the dictatorship of the proletariat, the Russian Communists sought to establish a state in which the workers would be the *Proletarians preferred* controlling and the favored class. They accepted the teaching of Karl Marx that wealth is the product of human labor, and they believed that the workers, instead of piling up surplus profits for their capitalist masters, should themselves be the chief recipients and beneficiaries of the wealth created by their efforts. The so-called non-producing members of society, aristocrats, capitalists, employers of labor, priests, etc., were refused a vote, and received smaller rations of food than the "workers." Society was thus deliberately turned upside down. Ex-nobles, ex-officials of the czarist government, rich bourgeois, and churchmen now formed the unprivileged class, while peasants and workers were preferred to them, receiving better food, readier accommodations on the state railways, more habitable dwellings and lighter taxes.

Needless to say, the members of what had been the property-owning classes were embittered by the change. But they were too small a *Secret police* minority to offer any effective protest, for no powerful and well-entrenched middle class had developed in Russia comparable to the bourgeoisie of England or France. Furthermore, all those who had been dispossessed were known and were watched by the

THE PROGRAM OF THE RUSSIAN COMMUNISTS

secret police. Conspiracy against the Soviet government, or even un-guarded criticism of it, was likely to be followed by arrest, a secret trial and a secret execution. The "Extraordinary Commission" created in 1917 for combating counter-revolutionary activity proved remorselessly efficient, hunting down the disaffected even more competently than the czarist police had done. By 1922 this commission, or *Cheka*, under the command of Felix Djerzinsky, had served its purpose so well that it was replaced by a new organization of political police known briefly as the *Ogpu*. A calculation of the number of counter-revolutionaries con-demned to death in Soviet Russia since 1917 is difficult to make, for estimates have varied from a few hundred to over a million. Since 1922, however, exile to Siberia has largely replaced the death penalty, and has been invoked even more extensively than in czarist times.

No institution of the old régime excited more criticism from the Communist leaders than the Russian Orthodox Church. At first the Bolsheviki were content to confiscate the property of the *The war on* church, expecting that religion would soon lose its force if *religion* deprived of wealth and official support. Finding, however, that the clergy continued to be active and even to increase their following, the government adopted repressive measures, circumscribing the activities of priests in educational and charitable work, and inaugurating a cam-paign among the people to free them from "superstitious beliefs." The hostility felt by the Bolshevik leaders toward religious dogmas was due in part to their conviction that faith in miracles and the efficacy of relics was contrary to the modern, realistic, and scientific attitude toward life which they desire to instill. But they advanced another and pro-founder objection. They had accepted the doctrine of Marx that "Religion is the opium of the people," and they wished to extirpate it because they held that the spirit of humility and resignation which the Russian priests long urged upon the masses was a device of the ruling group to keep the people fatalistically resigned to their lot. According to this view the church was no more than a subtle and successful instru-ment of propaganda for perpetuating the enslavement of the credulous peasants and proletarians by teaching them to accept their suffering as imposed by the will of God.

The children of Soviet Russia are undergoing a careful training in a new social philosophy. To fit them for a practical share in the duties of a proletarian state, they receive free instruction, are *Education* promoted on a basis of merit, and will take their places as artisans, engineers, laborers, or peasants according to their aptitudes. They are being trained also to compete with each other in the quality and quantity of their work, but to scorn the thought of toiling solely for material advantage or profit. Whether, under changed conditions, the Russian workers can be persuaded to take such pride in their labor that they will give as much effort and attention to ordinary tasks as the workers in other lands, who are stimulated by the desire for material gain, is not yet certain. The Russians, however, are indoctrinated with the belief that their fellow toilers in capitalistic countries are heartlessly exploited under an unregulated system of ruthless and selfish competition, and they believe that the proletarians everywhere, when they realize this, will take heart from the Russian example, throw off their chains, and unite in a World Federation of Workers' Republics. Because they travel very little, and have no means to contrast what they are taught with the actual conditions elsewhere in the world, most Russians believe that in the western states of Europe society is honeycombed with dry rot and the capitalistic system is on the point of collapse. The morale and faith of the hundred and fifty million people in the Union of Soviet Socialist Republics is maintained at a high pitch by means of the campaign of education, and is fortified through radio, newspaper, and pictorial propaganda circulated for the same purpose.

4. THE STRUCTURE OF THE SOVIET GOVERNMENT

The Union of Soviet Socialist Republics (or U.S.S.R.) is not a centralized empire, but a federation of many semi-autonomous states bound together by constitutional treaties. It includes over nine tenths of the Russian population. A constitution, adopted by the All-Russian Congress in 1918, and revised in 1924, defines the union as a federal state, and assures each of the participating republics the right to withdraw at will.

All men and women over eighteen who are engaged in socially useful work possess the vote and may help to choose the members of their local *Governing* soviet. District soviet congresses in turn elect delegates *committees* to a Congress of the Union on a basis of one representative for each 25,000 city electors and one for every 125,000 rural electors. The All-Union Congress of about two thousand deputies corresponds to a Russian Parliament, but most of its duties are relegated to a central executive committee of four hundred and fifty members. The central executive committee in turn appoints a presidium of twenty-seven members, and a council (or cabinet) of sixteen commissars. The titular head of the Russian government is the chairman of the presidium.

Two interesting points should be noted about this somewhat intricate political machine. The first is the concentration of legislative, executive,

[440]

and judicial functions in the hands of the central executive committee and subcommittees. There is no provision for a separation of power between a legislative chamber which enacts the laws, a supreme court which interprets them, and an executive which enforces them. The second point to note is that the constitution does not tell the whole story because it makes no mention of the Communist Party. This energetic organization of some three million members is controlled by a central committee which in turn appoints a political bureau. Three fourths of the delegates to the All-Union Congress are members of the party, and so firm and effective is the influence which the political bureau exerts upon the government that, since Lenin's death, Joseph Stalin, secretary-general of the Communist Party, has become the practical dictator of Russia, although he holds no important political office. *The Communist Party*

In a land where all national resources, lumber, minerals, etc., are held in trust by the government for the benefit of the people, the power of the commissars who control the exploitation of the resources is almost unlimited. With no opposition party to criticize their acts, and no system of administrative checks and balances to delay their projects, the council of commissars can co-ordinate their efforts and apply with ruthless determination the plans which Stalin and his economic advisers have worked out for the expansion of Russian industry and the improvement of Russian agriculture. The Communists have not only sought to transform the social philosophy and ideals of one hundred and fifty million people within a decade, but they have sought in the same space of time to modernize Russia, exploit her natural wealth, and make the Soviet State one of the richest and most productive of the great powers.

5. ECONOMIC PROGRESS AND THE FIVE-YEAR PLAN

The New Economic Policy which Lenin instituted in 1921 represented a compromise between capitalist and Communist practices. But the Russian leaders did not intend to halt halfway on the road to socialism, and in 1928, Stalin and his advisers decided that the hour had come for a new advance. The result of their determination was the Five-Year Plan, a gigantic project calling for the expenditure of over twenty billion dollars to speed up Russian industry, develop electric power, multiply mineral output, and create new factories capable of providing the tractors, automobiles, railway engines, airplanes, and other mechanical equipment necessary to a modern state. All lines of activity were to be co-ordinated, each mine or factory was given a quota to fill, and so keen was the enthusiasm of the workers that the government held out hope of realizing the Five-Year Plan in four years. The goal set for Russian industry was a general increase of 133 per cent within five years. Engineers and technicians were hired from Germany, England, and America to supervise the establishment of new factories and train Russian workers in processes about to be introduced.

A state planning commission kept the records, and cast a balance each year, commending those branches of industry which achieved their quota, *State plan-* and investigating those which had failed. The Communist *ning com-* leaders have extolled their system as a signal improvement *mission* upon the unco-ordinated competition which distinguishes the march of industry under a *laissez-faire* régime, for they can plan the future, regulating in advance the miles of railway to be built, the output of iron, coal, oil, electrical power, etc., which will be required each year, and the number of workers and of working hours needed in each unit of the gigantic whole.

For the peasants the Five-Year Plan entailed a progressive socialization of agriculture, the wholesale introduction of machinery, and the creation of state farms. The Communists had been displeased to find that their plan to divide the land into small holdings of some ten acres for each family had failed to work satisfactorily. In each rural community the more energetic and farsighted farmers had prospered, increasing their acreage, hiring helpers, and emerging as men of property, so that ten years after the great estates of the nobles had been confiscated a new class of landowners was in process of formation. Against these well-to-do peasants or *kulaks* the government opened a campaign of intimidation and suppression. Peasants were urged to merge their private holdings in collective farms, a movement which made rapid progress despite the opposition of many *kulaks*, who disliked to lose their improved status and see their farms submerged in the collective experiment.

By 1932, the "socialized sector" comprised three fourths of the cultivated land, and its total area, already vast, was still expanding. *Socialization* Under modern conditions it is much more profitable to *of agricul-* manage large farms with power-driven machinery, and the *ture* Russian government had made enormous efforts to supply the tractors, reapers, harvesters, and threshers needed to supplant the primitive methods previously followed by the peasants. To stimulate the trend toward collective management and demonstrate the efficiency of mechanized agriculture, state farms have been established in all parts of the country. Some of these include hundreds and even thousands of square miles of farmland. The workers live in model villages, possess their own newspaper, motion-picture hall, library, hospital, and recreation grounds, and share, through the delegates they elect to the local soviet, in shaping the policies of the management. But they have lost the freedom of choice which they knew briefly as independent farmers, and not all of them are happy in the change.

On December 31, 1932, a little over four years after its inception, the first Five-Year Plan was officially terminated. Not all the objectives had been achieved, but the results appeared encouraging. *Second* Unemployment had been greatly reduced, the increase in *Five-Year* the manufacture of machinery was gratifying, and the *Plan* production of coal and minerals, which had lagged behind, was speeding up. In the development of collective farms the results had exceeded all hopes. A second Five-Year Plan was drafted which projected the complete socialization of agriculture by 1937, with a fifty to two hundred per cent increase in the various crops, a doubling of the output of basic industries, and a sixfold increase in the production of electric power. These achievements were to be reflected in the living conditions of the Russian people, who were promised a six-hour working day and a threefold increase in the amount of the goods to be utilized for domestic consumption.

In attempting to judge the Soviet experiment, however, it is necessary to realize that almost all the statistics available are "official," and that governments seldom make out an unfavorable case for themselves. Thus, the Soviet factories may exceed their quota, as stated, but it is relevant to ask how many of the tractors or harvesters, for instance, break down when put to use, and how many are ruined by peasants unused to handling machinery. Under the Five-Year Plan, government figures record, the extension of collective farming surpassed expectations, but unofficial sources reveal that many *kulaks* slaughtered their domestic animals rather than surrender them, so that Russia suffered from a serious shortage of meat. The Soviet régime has undoubtedly accomplished wonders, but they are wonders chiefly because of the difficulties overcome. The efficiency of Russian industry and agriculture is still far below the standard maintained in a country like the United States, and Russian products, in cost and quality, do not equal those produced under methods of mass production in capitalistic states.

Moreover, it would be an error to invest Soviet economists with all the credit for the remarkable advances made by the Russian people since the World War. Industrial development and the mechanization of agriculture would have made some gains even under a chaotic or a reactionary régime, for the Russian masses could not have remained altogether immune to the effect of the mechanical and technological revolutions. But the Communist leaders have hastened the transformation by several decades, and have instituted the first attempt on a grand scale to establish the dictatorship of the proletariat. The success or failure of the Communist experiment in Russia will have repercussions throughout the world and may well prove the most interesting chapter in the history of the twentieth century.

6. FOREIGN RELATIONS OF RUSSIA (1917–35)

At the time of its creation in 1917, the Soviet government stood without friends in a hostile world. Not only the Central Powers with which Russia was still at war, but also the Allied nations, France, Britain, and Italy, refused their recognition to the Bolshevik régime, and lent their aid to the counter-revolutionary forces. It is not difficult to find reasons for this opposition. The Bolsheviki repudiated the debts of the czarist government, published the secret treaties to which it had been a signatory, and proclaimed a world revolution of the working classes against their capitalist masters. The Allied statesmen were embittered at the Russians because they made a separate peace with Germany, and they became alarmed when the Communists attempted to inspire proletarian uprisings in other lands. In proclaiming a blockade of Russia, the Allied governments sought both to punish the Russians and to prevent their dangerous doctrines from spreading. Even after the Soviet régime had defeated the "White" forces and proved its strength and stability, it was still refused international recognition.

Very gradually this unfriendly attitude changed. The Communists learned that the "Third International," which they organized at Moscow in 1919 for the purpose of furthering a world revolution of the working classes, made them feared and distrusted by other nations, and they found it expedient to deny any official connection between it and the Soviet government. The need of reviving Russian trade moved the Bolshevik leaders to seek commercial understandings with neighboring states; political recognition followed, first from Germany (1922), then from Great Britain (1924). By 1933, when the United States reestablished formal diplomatic intercourse, Russian foreign relations were normal and friendly once more. In addition to trade agreements the Soviet government had signed non-aggression pacts with fourteen states, and had ratified the Kellogg Pact (1928) renouncing war as an instrument of national policy.¹   In 1934, Russia joined the League of Nations and accepted a permanent seat on the Council.

In the Far East the relations of the Soviet government with Japan proved less amicable, and a non-aggression pact proposed by Russia was not ratified.   The chief source of contention continued to *The Japan-* be the Chinese province of Manchuria.   When Japan *ese in Man-* defeated the czar's forces in 1904–05, the Russians aban- *churia* doned their claims to Manchuria which remained technically a part of China.   The victory of the Japanese, however, enabled them to persevere in their economic penetration and establish a disguised protectorate.

Their aim was to make Japanese influence paramount throughout the Chinese Republic before other powers could forestall them or the Chinese Nationalist Party (the Kuomintang) could organize an *Japanese* effective national resistance.   In the midst of the World *designs on* War (1915), Japan presented twenty-one demands which *China* would have subordinated the vast Chinese realm to Japanese designs had not the other powers protested.   Frustrated for the moment, the Japanese imperialists moderated, but did not abandon, their aims.   The surprising victories of General Chiang Kai-Chek (1926), which estab-lished the power of the Kuomintang throughout the greater part of China, warned the Japanese that a strong Chinese Nationalist govern-ment would seek to reknit Manchuria to China proper.   The increasing friction moved the Japanese to launch a sudden attack on Mukden, the Manchurian capital, in 1931, and they rapidly expelled all Chinese forces from the province.   In retaliation the Chinese proclaimed a boycott of Japanese products, whereupon the Japanese attacked Shanghai (still without a formal declaration of war), but withdrew after encountering a stubborn and surprising resistance.

Spurred by an appeal from China, the League of Nations investigated and condemned the aggressive tactics of the Japanese in Manchuria and Shanghai (1933).   To disguise their suzerainty over the *Russo-* conquered province, the Japanese organized Manchuria as *Japanese* the independent state of Manchukuo under the rule of *tension* Henry Pu-yi, the boy emperor who had been deposed from the throne of the Chinese Empire by the revolution of 1911.   Although the powers declined to recognize Manchukuo, the Japanese continued to consolidate and enlarge the new state, to the grave concern of the Russians, who operated the Chinese Eastern Railway across Manchuria to Vladivostok.² After prolonged and critical negotiations, the Russians agreed to sell their share in the railway (1934) and the tension in the Far East relaxed,

¹ See above, page 479.   ² See map following page 362.

but further clashes between Russia and Japan may easily develop at any time in Mongolia or in the neighborhood of Vladivostok. In wrenching Manchuria from China, the Japanese not only defied the League of Nations, but created a Far-Eastern problem which seems foredoomed to precipitate further armed clashes.

CHAPTER THIRTY

FASCIST ITALY

For Fascism the state is an absolute before which individuals and groups are relative.

BENITO MUSSOLINI.

AMONG the Allied Powers which emerged as victors from the World War, the Italians were the least satisfied with the results and the most deeply infected by the post-war mood of disillusionment. The war effort and war losses had dislocated the economic and social life of the nation, for Italy was less highly industrialized than France or Britain and less fitted to endure the financial strain of a war. The re-establishment of peace was followed in 1919 and 1920 by growing poverty and unemployment. The cost of living rose, and the government, unable to balance the budget, drifted toward bankruptcy. Italian industry was crippled by the necessity of importing coal from foreign sources, and Italian agriculture did not produce a food supply sufficient to feed a nation of forty million people. As conditions grew worse, the failure of the government to alleviate the distress or devise remedies for the economic situation aroused widespread discontent.

1. POST-WAR CONFUSION IN ITALY

Many patriotic Italians were further incensed by what they considered the inadequacy of Italy's war gains. The Trentino and the southern portion of the Tyrol, Trieste and the Istrian Peninsula, had been added to the kingdom by the Versailles Treaty,[1] but these territorial conquests did not satisfy the ardent nationalists who had hoped in addition for the port of Fiume and the Dalmatian coast. Moreover, they had another and more legitimate grievance concerning the division of colonial spoils, for France and Britain took possession of the German protectorates and choice portions of the Turkish Empire, and established their control over these mandates while ignoring the claims of the Italians for an equal share.

For several years after the war the tide of Italian discontent continued to rise, fed by the protests of the thwarted nationalists, by Socialists dissatisfied with the bourgeois régime, and by Communists who *Growth of* hoped to overturn the government and establish the rule of *disorder* the proletariat. The nerveless and inefficient government failed signally

[1] See map following page 426.

to check the growth of opposition or to satisfy the popular demands. In 1919, the Socialists won 156 seats in Parliament, the largest number held by a single party, for the spirit of war-weariness, combined with the misery of the workers and the agricultural laborers, had turned many people toward socialism as a remedy. But in 1920, when strikes tied up the metal industries, and peasants, stirred by Communist ideals, began to seize and divide the landed estates, the fear of communism turned moderate citizens conservative, and the property-owning classes fought to protect their interests. In the midst of strikes and disorders, which affected all the larger cities of northern Italy, opposing factions rioted in the street, broke up each other's meetings, and endangered life and property by their constant turmoil.

Out of this national chaos, a new political group, the Fascists, rose to power. The Italian people desired a firm and efficient government, *Desire for stability* which would save the country from communism, re-establish industrial peace, promote national prosperity, and gratify national aspirations. After almost four years of post-war turbulence the moment was ripe for a party professing these aims to take over the government. Such a group, commanded by an extraordinarily able and energetic leader, Benito Mussolini, was already in existence and a dramatic revolution placed it in control in 1922.

2. BENITO MUSSOLINI

Born near Forli in 1883, the son of a blacksmith, Benito Mussolini rose to prominence through his own unaided efforts. By working and saving, he managed to enter the University of Lausanne, but was expelled from Switzerland in 1904 as a Marxian Socialist. When the World War broke out ten years later, he had risen to a high post in the Italian Communist Party, and was editor of the Socialist journal *Avanti*, published at Milan. His associates bitterly opposed the idea that Italy should enter the war, but Mussolini changed his views on this point, advocated war, and thereby lost favor with the Communist and Socialist groups with which he had been affiliated. Starting a new paper of his own, *The People of Italy*, he appealed to the patriotic sentiment of the Italians, and when Italy entered the war he fought in the ranks until wounded and discharged in 1917.

With the eye of a realist, Mussolini had perceived that nationalism was *The formula of Fascism* too powerful a force in Italian life to be ignored. The Socialists had won wide support by their demands for social justice and improved conditions for the workers, but they had also of-

BENITO MUSSOLINI

The personal qualities which enabled Mussolini to rise to power are ruthless will, stern self-confidence, and a gift of vehement eloquence.

fended Italian patriots by their indifference toward the question of "unredeemed Italy," by their frank espousal of pacifistic ideals and their pleas for disarmament. The formula for a successful political party, Mussolini realized, might be found by blending elements of socialism and nationalism, by combining an aggressive foreign policy with proposals to tax the rich and benefit the poor. The impotence and extravagance of the representative parliamentary régime made a strong, even a despotic, rule seem preferable, and Mussolini strengthened his appeal by demanding a moral and administrative reform of the Italian State which would purge it of bolshevism and other foreign or corrupting influences. The nation was to be purified, regenerated, and dedicated to the task of regaining that historic leadership in arts and arms which the people of Italy had attained in the days of the Roman Empire and of the Renaissance. Few patriotic Italians could remain cold to such a national appeal; Mussolini's condemnation of bolshevism and communism reassured the property-owners, and the element of socialism in his program won over many members of the working classes. He preached a composite, but a conquering faith.

In the chaotic days which followed the war, Mussolini organized aggressive groups pledged to promote the new faith. Many of his followers *The "March on Rome" (1922)* were, like himself, ex-soldiers and Socialists, and the Society called itself the *Fascio di Combattimento*, or "Union of Combat." Frequently resorting to violence, the Fascists attacked their political opponents, particularly the Communists, breaking up their meetings, smashing their printing presses, combating strikes, and in some cases compelling the strikers to return to work. It is not clear that Italy was ever in very grave danger of becoming a Communist state; the attempt to seize the factories for the benefit of the workers and set up soviets had already failed by 1922; but the Fascists claimed the credit of saving the nation from bolshevism, denounced the ineffective ministry headed by the premier, Luigi Facta, and prepared to march on Rome and take over the administration by direct action. At this point (October, 1922) the king, Victor Emmanuel III, offered Mussolini the post of prime minister, which he accepted. Although the *coup d'état* which placed the Fascists in power was irregular and perhaps illegal, it was as much a moral revolution as a triumph of force.

Declaring that the Parliament had failed ignominiously at the task *Constitutional changes* of government, Mussolini demanded and obtained a grant of autocratic powers from the intimidated deputies. A vigorous policy of economy and efficiency was adopted, Mussolini himself assuming the portfolios of foreign affairs, and of the interior, to which he later added five other cabinet posts. A new electoral law, forced through the Parliament in 1923, provided that the political party obtaining the largest number of votes cast in an election (providing these amounted to twenty-five per cent of the total) would receive two thirds of the seats in the Chamber. The following year, after some official pressure, the Fascist or government party won the election by a large majority. The Socialist minority, however, continued to oppose and criticize the Fascist dictatorship. When a Socialist deputy, Giacomo Matteotti, threatened to make public some discreditable facts concerning Fascist methods of rule, he was abducted and murdered (1924). This act produced "a profound moral oscillation" in Italy, as Mussolini himself admitted, and almost overturned the new régime. Nevertheless, the Fascists continued to consolidate their control and press forward their designs for the reorganization of the state.

The policy of silencing political opponents by violent methods, the most regrettable phase of Fascist activity before the March on Rome, continued to disfigure the record of Fascist success. System- *Fascist* atic beating, dosing with castor oil, and even worse bar- *repression* barities, awaited those rash enough to oppose the new government. Newspapers survived at the price of a humiliating subservience; teachers in schools and universities took an oath to instill Fascist ideals into their students, or lost their positions; obdurate foes of the Fascist Party who had fled the country were punished by the loss of their rights and property, while many who failed to escape were transported to a prison colony on the Lipari Islands off the coast of Sicily. As head of the state, responsible to the king alone, Mussolini ceased to be dependent upon a Fascist-controlled Parliament and could issue decrees with the effect of laws. The cabinet members were his appointees, and the *podeste*, or local officials placed in control of the communes, were dictators in miniature executing his orders. Thus the minority opponents of Fascism were left without protection and without a court to which they might appeal.

3. THE CORPORATE STATE

Between 1925 and 1928, sweeping reforms initiated under the Fascist dictatorship transformed the government of Italy into a new type of political organism which was termed the "corporate state." From the first the Fascists had made clear their desire to control or dissolve all clubs, unions, or other associations outside their own ranks, to replace the confused tangle of political parties by a single National Party (Fascist), and to bring the political, economic, social, and intellectual life of the nation into harmony with Fascist ideals. By a decree issued in 1926, the National Sydicates or unions of Italian workers were legalized by the government, and a second decree established a ministry of corporations to control their activities. Six employers' associations and seven workers' associations were to be co-ordinated under the minister of corporations, but this reorganization meant that the workers would lose the right of independent action, the syndicates would no longer have the power to declare a strike, and no new or unofficial associations could be formed. Not only industry, but agriculture, commerce, banking, etc., were to be regimented by these enactments, which made it possible for the government to curb the conflict between workers and employers, and regulate the vital productive activities of the entire nation. The liberal philosophy of the nineteenth century, which had taught that business prospered best when left alone, and that governments should interfere as little as possible in the disputes of capital and labor, had thus been abandoned in favor of a policy of strict regulation which subordinated all the individuals and enterprises of a society to the welfare of the state as an entity. Critics of the Fascist régime have objected, however, that the corporations have never really been organized, except on paper, and that they do not function, so that the workers have lost the advantage of collective bargaining and gained nothing in return.

The final transition from the parliamentary to the corporative system of government was not proclaimed until 1928. In that year a new *New elec-* electoral law went into effect which made the hierarchy of *toral system* official syndicates, directed by the minister of corporations, the "organs of the state." Universal manhood suffrage was discarded, and the right to vote limited to those men who could prove they were members of a recognized syndicate, paid one hundred *lire* in taxes, or held a position of responsibility. These provisions disfranchised some three million voters out of twelve million. The most striking innovation, however, concerned the nomination of the candidates for election. The Chamber of Deputies was reduced to four hundred members, electoral districts disappeared, and Italy became one great constituency. These measures were designed to curb the spirit of sectionalism, with the inevitable compromises and petty political bargaining which had disfigured the parliamentary régime before the Fascists came into power. Henceforth each deputy would represent, not one local district, but the Kingdom of Italy as a whole. Finally, the task of preparing a list of eight hundred candidates was confided to the executive councils of the thirteen national employers' and workers' federations. Two hundred additional nominees were chosen by professional associations, teachers, authors, artists, etc., and this list, now comprising one thousand names, was turned over to the Fascist National Grand Council (the central executive committee of the Fascist Party), which drew upon it in composing a final reduced list of four hundred "deputies designate." In the first election held under the new system (1929), the voters were invited to record their acceptance or rejection of the list of designated deputies as a whole. Out of some 8,650,000 ballots cast, only 136,000 had been marked "no." Should the official list be rejected by the voters, a second election is held for which all recognized organizations in the state with five thousand or more members prepare lists of candidates.

The effect of the new law has been to curtail greatly the importance of the electors and of the Chamber of Deputies, while augmenting the power of the cabinet ministers and especially of the "Head *Authoritari-* of the Government," as Mussolini is termed. All important *anism* vs. legislative enactments originate with the ministerial coun- *democracy* cil; and the Chamber of Deputies can be relied upon to approve them. The Senate is likewise in general harmony with Fascist policies, although a few individual members have remained unsympathetic. Senators are appointed for life, but Mussolini can assure his government a favorable majority in the upper chamber by requesting the king to appoint loyal Fascists to that body from time to time, and he has nominated nearly one hundred new senators in this fashion since 1922. The reconstructed Italian government thus represents a compromise between the authoritarian and democratic principles with authoritarianism predominating. Mussolini has contended that the new government is more genuinely democratic than the old, because it directs the welfare and furthers the aspirations of the nation as a whole, whereas the Parliament it supplanted was dominated by a cabal of lobbyists seeking advantages for selfish interests or favored classes.

The validity of such a contention can be decided only by students of political science who possess a full appreciation of its implications. Mussolini extended the argument to justify the censorship of the Italian press, declaring that under a "liberal" régime, so-called, the "free" journals are too often the lying organs of vested interests or political factions. If, he insisted, newspapers are compelled to limit their comments on controversial issues to quotations from official sources, the public will be spared much mendacious argument, special pleading, and misinformation. This is true; and under a state-controlled press, he might have added, the government will also be spared much embarrassing criticism. But criticism is sometimes good for governments, and a free press and a freely elected legislature are the best checks European political ingenuity has devised to keep a government responsible to its trust. There are undoubtedly great advantages in a system of enlightened paternalism; in times of crisis an honest and vigorous dictatorship is more efficient than the cumbrous machinery of parliamentarism with its checks and balances and delegated powers. But no method has yet been devised to guarantee that an able dictator will find an equally able successor, or that enlightened paternalism may not deviate into an unenlightened despotism.

The vigor and success of the Fascist experiment in Italy encouraged the growth of Fascist movements in other European countries. Citizens who viewed with alarm the economic dislocation which followed the war, or grew disgusted with the mediocrity of professional politicians, re-echoed Mussolini's pronouncement that good government was more important than representation, and were disposed to agree that the parliamentary system, devised by theorists in the eighteenth century who envisaged the state chiefly as an agrarian democracy, was inadequate to deal with the complex administrative problems of a modern industrial commonwealth. The Fascist doctrines appealed particularly to those people who, for one reason or another, were most strongly opposed to Socialism and Communism. Thus Russia and Italy provided Europe and the world in the post-war era with two dynamic and antagonistic political faiths, Communism and Fascism

4. BENEFITS OF THE FASCIST ADMINISTRATION

Under Fascism the Italian people have been stirred by a new spirit of pride and accomplishment. Monster mass meetings, parades, and demonstrations, inspired and directed by the authorities, serve to keep their patriotic enthusiasm aflame; the young boys are trained by courses in group calisthenics, maneuvers, and games to prepare themselves for military service; subsidiary organizations teach the girls to perfect themselves in those accomplishments which will make them good wives and mothers. A renewed sense of the purpose and dignity of life, a renewed faith in the grandeur and destiny of the country, and a deeper and more earnest response to the imperious call of duty have been bred in the hearts of Italian youths by the Fascist ideals and training.

The firm and purposeful methods of Fascist rule are designed to impose social and industrial peace upon the Italian nation. Strikes and lockouts *Justice* are forbidden and all labor disputes are settled by compulsory arbitration. Riots, disorders, and crimes of violence are rigidly repressed. The secret societies, such as the *Mafia* and the

Camorra, which had long been a scourge to honest citizens in southern Italy and Sicily, extorting payments from shopkeepers and others under threat of violent reprisals, have been broken up by wholesale arrests and severe sentences. To eliminate delay and corruption in the courts and make sure that the laws are executed promptly and inflexibly has been one of Mussolini's foremost aims. In the cities and towns, where, since 1926, the elected mayors and councils have been superseded by *podeste* appointed from Rome, the administration of local affairs has functioned with new vigor and efficiency.

On agriculture, the most vital industry of the nation, the Fascist ministers have bestowed much paternal thought. Circulars of information have been distributed to dairy farmers and improved meth- *Agriculture* ods of cultivation recommended to those engaged in wine, olive, and silk production. Reclamation and irrigation projects have added to the acreage of arable land, and experiments with new types of grains and fruits are conducted by government experts. An agricultural credit bank, established to assist farm proprietors through their financial difficulties, has enabled many farmers to expand their holdings and enlarge their crops.

In attempting to stimulate the mechanical trades the Fascist government has faced serious obstacles. To offset the dependence upon foreign coal and petroleum supplies, new power stations have har- *Industry* nessed the rivers, and three fourths of the power available for industrial purposes is now drawn from hydroelectric sources. In comparison with England or Germany, however, Italy is still a backward nation in this respect, for the industrial establishments provide work for less than one tenth of the population. Unemployment has proved a severe and stubborn problem, the number of jobless workers passing the million mark in 1932. Despite the best efforts of the government to provide work rather than doles, and to stimulate business by regulations and subsidies, the decline in world trade after 1929 had a serious effect upon Italian exports. By 1934 the annual deficit in the national budget promised to reach half a billion dollars.

Since the proclamation of the Italian Kingdom in 1861, fiscal problems have never ceased to embarrass the national government, and the Fascists inherited a burdensome legacy of debts, internal *Financial* and international. Since 1922, with the aid of a loan from *difficulties* foreign bankers, the finances have been improved, the *lira* stabilized at a little less than one fourth its pre-war value, and the gold standard re-established (1927). But the Italian people remain relatively one of the highest taxed nations of Europe, and continue to labor under the disad-

[455]

vantage of an unfavorable balance of trade. Despite the recent improvement in the agricultural yield, Italy still imports large quantities of foodstuffs as well as coal, copper, wool, seed oils, etc. This economic situation makes it difficult for the nation to sustain the heavy expenditures for armaments in time of peace, and renders it vulnerable to the effects of a blockade in time of war. The appropriations for the military, naval, and air services amount to more than a quarter of a billion dollars annually.

5. FOREIGN POLICY OF FASCIST ITALY

With its expanding population and limited resources, modern Italy has suffered more heavily than any other great power through emigration. The exodus of native-born Italians to other lands has decreased somewhat under Fascism, but many thousands still depart annually to seek work in France or make new homes overseas. Despite this, Mussolini has sought to raise the birth rate, and Italy, with little more than half the area of France, now surpasses her older Latin sister state in population. This trend of vital statistics has been cited by Fascist orators to justify an Italian policy of expansion at the expense of neighboring states. Jingoistic demands for the "redemption" of Nice and Savoy from France, for the annexation of neighboring Mediterranean islands and the Adriatic littoral, have frequently roused Italian audiences to enthusiasm and have alarmed France, Yugoslavia, and Greece. As a consequence Italian foreign policy has been watched with grave apprehension and Italy has constituted one of the dynamic and disturbing factors in the post-war diplomatic situation.

The settlements which concluded the World War, and the Treaty of Rapallo in particular,[1] gave Italy a dominant position on the Adriatic

Albania Sea, but placed nearly half a million Yugoslavs dwelling in the Istrian Peninsula and Trieste under the Italian flag. As a consequence, relations between Italy and Yugoslavia have remained tense, despite negotiated agreements. The backward and disorganized principality of Albania[2] has become a pawn in this international match, with Italy endeavoring to subjugate the Albanians to her policy. Economic penetration, loans, military assistance, and a twenty-year treaty of alliance (1927) bound Albania so closely to Italy that Yugoslavia became alarmed. Command of the Albanian port facilities would make it possible for the Italians to move an army into Albania in a few days for a campaign against the Yugoslavs in the event of war. But the possibility

[1] See above, page 425. [2] See map following page 426.

that Albania might be reduced to the position of an Italian protectorate diminished after 1930 as the Albanians acquired greater self-confidence and independence under the rule of a king of their own choosing, Skander-beg III.

These circumstances have driven the Yugoslavs to cultivate the friend-ship of France, the dominant military power on the continent of Europe since the Treaty of Versailles, and the counterbalancing *Franco-*force adequate to hold Italy in check. In 1930, France *Italian*began preparations to fortify her Alpine (Franco-Italian) *rivalry*frontier, whereupon the Italian government increased its military budget ten per cent, creating a situation tragically reminiscent of the armament rivalries which preceded the World War. But after 1932, the hostility between France and Italy was somewhat diluted by the apprehension both felt at the revival of German nationalism and the avowed determi-nation of the German (Nazi) government to rearm in defiance of the provision of the Versailles Treaty. A later chapter will explain how the Germans, like the Italians, sought to escape from economic and social confusion by adopting a strong government of the Fascist type after 1932. The student might be disposed to imagine that a Fascist Italy and a Fascist Germany would prove natural allies, but it must be re-membered that the strongest element in Fascism is nationalism and two nationalistic states seldom make friendly neighbors.

With the revival of Germany and of German dreams of expansion, the diminished and defenseless Austrian State became a pawn for control of which the powers competed. The Italians no less than the *Austria*French feared that the Austrian Germans might join with Germany, thus adding to the population and strength of the German *Reich,* and extending its borders until they touched those of Italy. In his determination to prevent such a development, Mussolini announced (1934) that he would march the Italian army into Austria if circum-stances required such a move, in order to preserve the independence of the Austrian Republic. Europe was thus presented with the spectacle of three leading powers, France, Italy, and Germany, facing each other in a tense, triangular hostility which magnified every diplomatic incident into a miniature crisis.

In the colonial sphere, the desire to join the Italian East African pos-sessions, Eritrea and Italian Somaliland, by annexing the intervening Abyssinian territory, led Italy to provoke a war with Abyssinia (Ethi-opia) in 1935. The Ethiopian ruler appealed to the League of Nations, which threatened Italy, as an aggressor nation, with economic penalties, but the Italian armies continued their subjugation of Ethiopian territory.

[457]

6. THE FASCIST STATE AND THE PAPACY

One signal triumph of Mussolini's statesmanship was the conclusion (1929) of an accord between the Italian government and the papacy. Since 1870, each succeeding pope had accepted the precedent set by Pius IX and had regarded himself as the prisoner of the Vatican. The student will recall that when the forces of the new Italian Kingdom occupied Rome, Pius IX refused to sanction this infringement of his authority or to accept compensation for the loss of his temporal possessions. This papal policy of non-recognition, awkward alike for the Italian government and for the papacy, prevailed for nearly sixty years. After 1922, the aggressive and multifarious activities of the Fascists threatened to create new emergencies and to widen the existing rift, until in 1927 Pius XI found it necessary to condemn the Fascist theories concerning the supremacy of the state.

Two years of negotiation followed during which the Fascist chiefs succeeded in softening the papal displeasure. Mussolini recognized that *Lateran Treaty (1929)* the opposition of the church might prove a serious threat to his authority in a state where nine tenths of the people professed the Catholic faith. A mutual desire for reconciliation resulted in the Lateran Treaty of 1929, which recognized the pope as temporal sovereign of the Vatican City. This minute state of about one hundred acres in the heart of Rome was to enjoy complete independence, with its own rail, postal, and coinage facilities, and its own radio station. As compensation for the loss of that larger patrimony which former popes had ruled, the Italian government agreed to make restitution to the extent of 1,750,000,000 *lire* (about $92,000,000). The government further consented to declare the Roman Catholic faith the official religion of the state, to provide for religious instruction in the schools, and to enforce the canon (church) law throughout Italy. In return the Holy See formally recognized the Italian Kingdom with Rome as its capital. To many people it appeared that the Fascists lost more than they gained by this *concordat*, but the Fascist régime was strong enough to afford concessions, and, although many points of possible friction remained, this reconciliation of church and state contributed to the tranquillity of Italian society.

Moreover, Catholicism and Fascism could work better as allied than *Fascism and Catholicism as allies* as antagonistic forces, for they possessed some common aims and common enemies. In successive encyclicals, Pius XI upheld the sanctity of private property and defended the claims of capital, while insisting with equal force that real progress in

[458]

the industrial sphere must rest upon an equitable adjustment of the burdens and rewards of industry between the owners and the workers. This solution of the class conflict accorded well with Fascist principles. Pius further stressed, as Leo XIII had done, the mutual interdependence of capital and labor, and adjured the wealthy to remember and exercise the sacred duty of charity toward the victims of economic pressure. His denunciation of birth control and divorce coincided with the Fascist drive to raise the Italian birth rate. Nor must it be overlooked that the church and the Fascist State were united by the common battle against the principles of communism, for both fought and condemned unreservedly the communistic program for the abolition of private property, the socialization of industry and agriculture, the suppression of organized religious bodies and the confiscation of their wealth.

The Fascists could not, however, derive an unmixed satisfaction from the papal pronouncements. For Pius denounced the competition in armaments and the national rivalries which threatened the peace of the world in phrases which lashed the more militant Fascists no less sharply than the ultra-patriots and jingoists of other nations. Mindful of the great influence for peace which the church exercises throughout the world, the pope issued an apostolic letter (1931) urging a crusade for the relief of the suffering and the indigent, in the hope that social and national rancors might be quenched by the pure zeal of a great religious and humanitarian effort, and that part of the funds expended so lavishly upon armaments might be diverted to more humane services.

CHAPTER THIRTY-ONE

THE UNITED KINGDOM AND THE BRITISH EMPIRE COMMONWEALTH

No Act of Parliament of the United Kingdom passed after the commencement of this Act shall extend, or be deemed to extend, to a Dominion ... unless ... that Dominion has requested, and consented to, the enactment thereof.

Statute of Westminster (1931).

TO THE undiscerning eye it might well appear that Britain had gained more by the World War than any other great power. Her most dangerous trade rival had been crushed, her naval position strengthened by the destruction of the German fleet, and the major share of the German colonies had passed under the British flag. Although nearly seven hundred thousand British soldiers had lost their lives in the various theaters of conflict, the civilian population had escaped the horrors of invasion, and the fatalities from German air and naval raids totaled less than fifteen hundred. Britain had no shell-torn fields or ruined towns to reclaim, and her vast industrial plants had expanded under the stimulus of the war demands.

1. THE BRITISH ECONOMIC DILEMMA

But there was another and less hopeful picture to be drawn. Millions of tons of British shipping had been destroyed by submarines. Government indebtedness had risen enormously, and the loans which Britain had advanced to her allies in the World War were largely uncollectible. The prosperity of the United Kingdom before the war had been a result chiefly of the Industrial Revolution, which had made Britain the workshop of the world. In addition, there was the large annual return on British capital invested abroad, and the profits derived from the British merchant marine which transported half the world's trade. Dependence upon these sources of wealth, however, made it impossible for Britain to recover from the exhaustion of the war years until world trade revived, and the political and economic chaos of the post-war era delayed such a revival. With Russia in revolution and Germany prostrate, with the reconstructed European states raising new tariff barriers, and the Indian Nationalists boycotting British goods, the anticipated revival had little chance to materialize.

Nor were these the worst features of the dilemma. In the decades before the war, British manufacturers had already found themselves embarrassed by the industrial progress of other nations and even of the British Dominions. Following the war this rivalry grew more serious. Japanese textiles competed with the product of British looms for the markets of China and India; merchandise from the United States undersold British manufactures in South America. The British coal exports, long an important source of revenue, declined rapidly, for motors driven by electricity or gasoline were supplementing the steam engine. Even at sea the British encountered a new spirit of competition, and soon express liners built in Germany and Italy were capturing the best of the Atlantic passenger trade while the shipyards on the Clyde and the Mersey lay idle. By 1921, two million workers in England were without occupation; during the decade which followed, the number was to vary from three quarters of a million to approximately three million registered unemployed, as the business tide ebbed and flowed. The problem of providing relief for these victims of economic circumstances became the gravest issue of the post-war years.

Under the stress of these abnormal conditions the social insurance acts passed by the Liberals between 1909 and 1911 [1] proved lamentably inadequate. Although in 1921 nearly three million people were *Unemployment relief* receiving annuities under the Widows', Orphans', and Old Age Pension Acts, while another million were the recipients of poor relief, and upwards of two million more received war pensions, the government found it necessary to assume the burden of relieving the unemployed to the further extent of fifty million dollars. Within ten years this aid to the unemployed had increased fivefold; and the total annual cost of social services amounted (1931) to nearly two billion dollars. The increased taxes necessitated by this expenditure augmented the burden and the difficulties under which British industry already labored, while the income, inheritance, and land taxes drove many property-owners to sell their estates or transfer their investments to other countries.

As three fourths of the inhabitants of the United Kingdom had become town dwellers by the twentieth century, British farmers were a neglected minority and the urban millions depended upon the food *Britain abandons free trade* supplies imported from other lands. How to pay for these imports, and for the raw materials consumed by the factories, when the British export trade was languishing, became a problem of the utmost gravity. The world-wide economic depression which set in after 1929 reduced British trade and credit to such a serious extent that the government abandoned the gold standard (1931) and the pound sterling depreciated thirty per cent in terms of gold currencies. This

---

[1] See above, pages 344–46.

financial crisis was followed by a frank abandonment of the free-trade principles which had dominated British commercial practices for nearly a century. With other nations raising their tariff walls against British manufactures, it became inevitable that Britain should retaliate. The Import Duties Bill (1932) levied a ten per cent duty on foreign goods entering British ports, but left the government at liberty to negotiate a lower tariff accord with countries which accepted British products on favorable terms; and to raise the import duty as high as one hundred per cent on goods produced by those nations which discriminated against British exports.

The mounting economic pressure also proved an important factor in modifying British naval ambitions. Before the World War, Great Brit-

The Washington Naval Conference (1922) ain had attempted to maintain a fleet equal to any two other navies in the world combined, but by 1922 the naval forces of the United States and Japan had increased to such a point that Britain was driven to abandon this policy. The destruction of the German High Seas Fleet, the ships of which were sunk by their own crews after their surrender, left the British an unquestioned superiority in European waters; but their Pacific squadron could no longer compete with the American and Japanese forces. Great Britain, therefore, welcomed the proposal for a conference on naval limitation set forth by the American government in 1922. The most important treaty resulting from this Washington Naval Conference provided that Great Britain, the United States, and Japan should accept a quota regulating the strength of their respective navies in the proportions of 5:5:3. At the same time the three powers agreed to maintain their fortifications in the Pacific at their existing status. The Japanese were the least satisfied with the agreement, which permitted them a navy only three fifths as strong as the two leading naval powers, but the treaty achieved its main purpose in that it postponed the prospect of an unrestricted naval rivalry at least until its expiration in 1936.

2. BRITISH POLITICAL PARTIES (1919–35)

During the last two years of the World War, Great Britain was governed by a coalition cabinet, resting chiefly upon Conservative support, but headed by the indefatigable Liberal leader, David Lloyd George. This fiery Welshman was one of the few British politicians who emerged with enhanced prestige from what he later described as "our bloodstained stagger to victory," but his popularity waned in the troubled post-war period. The mounting economic distress after 1920 found

British opinion divided regarding the best course to follow, the Conservatives generally favoring a tariff to protect the manufacturers, while a growing Labor Party demanded increased government relief for the unemployed and the progressive socialization of industry. In the national election of 1922, the Conservatives secured a majority of the seats in the House of Commons, but Labor also gained and became the official opposition party. A second election (1923) gave the Conservatives 258 seats, the Laborites 192, and the waning Liberal Party 158. By combining forces, the Laborites and Liberals were enabled to control Parliament, and James Ramsay MacDonald became the first Socialist prime minister to direct the destinies of Great Britain.

This first British Labor government lasted less than a year. MacDonald sought to lower duties, to modify the more aggressive features of British imperialism (a proposed naval base at Singapore was *First Labor* abandoned), and to conclude trade treaties with Soviet *government* Russia. But the British electorate declined on appeal to *(1923–24)* support his policies and returned the Conservatives to power with a majority of two hundred in the election of 1924.

For the next five years the Conservative government wrestled with the problems of trade and unemployment under the premiership of Stanley Baldwin. Business taxes were reduced and the pound *Conserva-* restored to par value (1925), a victory for the bankers and *tives in* the creditor class generally. But the Conservatives found *power* themselves compelled to augment the "dole" to the unem- *(1924–29)* ployed, from fear of revolution if not from more humanitarian motives. For a time the sinking coal industry was buoyed up by government subsidies, but when these were curtailed (1926), and the mine-owners attempted to cut wages, the miners went out on strike and were joined by unionized transport workers. For over a week business stood still, while the British people endured with rare common sense and good humor the discomforts of the gravest and most costly labor crisis in their history. The outcome proved a defeat for the miners; and public opinion endorsed the prompt passage of a new Trade Disputes Act which prohibited further "general" strikes, forbade picketing, and weakened the influence of the workers' combinations.

In the general election of 1929, the Labor Party came into power a second time, but once again the control of Parliament de- *Second* pended upon the co-operation of the Liberal group. In the *Labor* face of the international business depression which set in *government* almost immediately, Ramsay MacDonald, as prime minis- *(1929–31)* ter, found it increasingly difficult to obtain a balanced budget, and heavy

[463]

French withdrawals of gold from the Bank of England in the summer of 1931 precipitated a financial crisis in London. Bankers and business men blamed the fiscal dilemma of the government upon the cost of unemployment relief and other public services which had steadily increased until they cost the taxpayers two billion dollars annually; but the Labor group in Parliament, led by Arthur Henderson, refused to approve a slash in the "dole." The result of the deadlock was a dramatic and unprecedented reconstruction of the cabinet. In August (1931) a coalition government was formed, under the domination of the Conservatives, but it was still headed by Ramsay MacDonald, who had deserted the Labor Party in order to do his duty as he saw it for his country. On September 21, Britain abandoned the gold standard and the pound fell from $4.86 to $3.40.

This new coalition government or National Party appealed to the people in an election held the following month. The result proved a *The National Party triumphs (1931)* signal repulse for both Liberals and Laborites, for the National Party gained 554 of the 615 seats in Parliament. The British electorate had backed the forces of stability and given the new government a clear mandate to develop its policy of retrenchment, protection, and economic nationalism. Ramsay MacDonald again became prime minister in a cabinet dominated by the Conservatives. Thirteen Laborites had followed him into the National Party, but the Labor Party proper, weakened and disrupted by his desertion, was reduced to fifty members and formed an insignificant opposition to the triumphant Nationalists. The Conservative preponderance, however, was too overwhelming to endure unchanged, and, although business conditions improved in 1933 and both imports and exports expanded, the Labor Party showed indications that it might in time revive sufficiently to challenge the Nationalist *bloc*.

3. THE IRISH FREE STATE

Although, to the people living in post-war Britain, the crises in domestic affairs appeared to outweigh all other issues, the Parliament at Westminster was forced in these same years to decide questions which concerned the empire at large. For London is the center of a commonwealth of nations which includes one fourth of the habitable area of the world and more than one fourth of the world's population. Decisions of momentous consequence for the inhabitants of Ireland, of India, and of other portions of the British Empire were reached between 1919 and 1934, and these must now be discussed.

[464]

No problem in British history has excited more bitterness of feeling than the Irish Question. The ill fate which has frequently frustrated attempts to settle the difficulties between England and Ire- *The Irish* land did not fail to attend the Government of Ireland Bill *Question* which the Liberals passed in 1914.[1] This act was suspended because of the outbreak of the World War, and the hostility between the inhabitants of Ulster, who were largely Protestant and pro-British, and the Irish Catholic majority in the remaining four fifths of Ireland remained unappeased. Irish national feeling found its most vigorous expression in the movement known as "Sinn Fein" (Gaelic for "we ourselves"); and in 1916 a group of reckless patriots attempted to proclaim an independent Irish Republic. The swift and deadly measures adopted by the British in crushing this attempted "Easter Rebellion" made reconciliation between England and Ireland all but impossible. A majority of the Irish members elected to the British Parliament in 1918 refused to take their seats, and set up instead an independent Irish Parliament at Dublin, under the presidency of a stanch member of the Sinn Fein group, Eamon de Valera. The Irish situation had reached a point indistinguishable from civil war.

Stubbornly refusing to acknowledge the right of the Irish to self-determination, the British government endeavored to crush the irregular forces of the Irish Republic during three years (1918–21) of *Irish Free* savage ambushes, assassinations, and reprisals. The strug- *State pro-* gle, which was characterized by acts of ferocity and treach- *claimed* ery disgraceful to both sides, ended in the negotiation of a treaty between the Republicans and the British government on December 6, 1921, and the following year the Irish Free State was organized. Although fanatic Republicans favored the forcible inclusion of Ulster and repudiation of all ties with Britain, a more moderate settlement was worked out. The Irish Free State achieved Dominion status with its own Parliament (the *Dail Eireann*) and membership in the League of Nations, but deputies to the Irish Parliament were to take an oath of allegiance to the British king, and the military and foreign policy of the Free State remained a matter of proprietary concern to the British government.

It was further provided that no religious legislation should be enacted which discriminated against citizens of the Free State or Ulster. As the six counties of Ulster refused to join the Free State, they *Northern* were granted a separate government. The capital of North- *Ireland* ern Ireland is Belfast, and the six Unionist counties which thus remained loyal to the British tie contain forty per cent of the population of Ireland.

[1] See above, page 346.

The active head of the Irish Free State is not the governor general appointed by the British crown, but the prime minister, or president of the executive council, as he is termed. From 1922 to 1932, this office was filled by William T. Cosgrave, a leader of statesmanlike moderation who guided the new Dominion through its first decade of tense and troubled history. The agitation of an irreconcilable minority led by Eamon de Valera continued to disturb Anglo-Irish relations. In the general election of 1932, De Valera's party (the *Fianna Fail*) obtained a majority, and he replaced Cosgrave as president of the council. The *Fianna Fail* had pledged itself to abolish the oath of loyalty to George V, and De Valera's new administration repudiated the annuities due the British government under financial agreements ratified by the Cosgrave régime. The British government retaliated by imposing a tariff on imports from the Irish Free State, whereupon the Free State taxed imports from Britain. The chief burden of this economic war fell upon the Irish peasantry whose produce was thus excluded from its normal (British) markets. How far the Irish people are prepared to indulge national sentiment at the price of economic disadvantage remains to be determined.

4. INDIA

In recognition of the loyalty displayed by the Indian princes and peoples during the war, and as a concession to the growing Nationalist *The Diarchy* sentiment agitating India's teeming millions,[1] the British government passed a Government of India Act in 1919. Native-born civil servants who displayed the requisite ability were to be admitted to important offices in the administration. The people received a larger share of control in matters of local government, as taxation, education, and public health; and most important of all, the bill established a national government for India, to consist of a Legislative Assembly and a Council of State meeting at Delhi. In both these chambers a majority of the members were to be elected, the remainder appointed. This approach to representative government failed to satisfy the Indians, because by a division of power termed "diarchy," control of the police, the law courts, and the army, as well as the direction of foreign affairs, were reserved to the British authorities.

Instead of moderating, Indian opposition increased under the Diarchy, and an unofficial assembly known as the National Congress became the focal center of the resistance. The most influential leader of the Na-

[1] See above, page 364.

tionalist cause was Mohandas Karamchand Gandhi, known to his followers as the *Mahatma*, the holy or saintly man. Gandhi *Non-co-* adjured the Indians to win independence by passive resist- *operation* ance, and organized (1920) a movement of non-co-operation whereby all British goods, courts, laws, and institutions were to be passively boycotted. Despite Gandhi's injunctions against violence or rioting, disturbances inevitably broke out and he was jailed as an agitator (1922). From prison he continued to exhort his followers to practice non-co-operation and non-resistance; and after his release, finding that the British government still refused to make concessions, he advocated complete independence for India. In 1930, he defied the authorities by extracting salt from sea water (the manufacture and sale of salt in India is a government monopoly), and as this ostentatious act of defiance was followed by renewed disturbance, he was again imprisoned.

The calling of a Round Table Conference to meet in London for the discussion of Indian affairs eased the tension at the close of 1930, and the second British Labor ministry, then in office, sought to pacify the Nationalists with a promise of Indian autonomy. But the Indian Nationalist leaders were themselves divided concerning the relative representation to be accorded Hindus and Mohammedans in an Indian Parliament, and religious prejudice barred the way to equality for the hundred million "untouchables," the Hindus of the lowest caste. In September, 1932, Gandhi, who was again in jail, declared he would "fast unto death" unless the "untouchables" received adequate representation in the legislatures and a fair share of the official posts. These terms were conceded, and the task of drafting a more liberal constitution for India proceeded slowly during 1933. To devise a settlement acceptable to the diverse religious and social groups that make up the population of British India is a herculean task; to decide what status the semi-independent domains of the Indian princes shall enjoy in an Indian federation involves further complications, while to appease the anxiety of British capitalists, who fear to lose two billion dollars which they have invested in India, is perhaps the most difficult task of all. Any extension of Indian self-government must be approved by the British Parliament, and the Nationalist Party, which has enjoyed an unprecedented majority in Parliament since 1931, is less disposed to make concessions than the Labor group or the Liberals might be. It appears probable, therefore, that several years must pass before India can receive Dominion status on the same basis as the other self-governing Dominions constituting the British Commonwealth of Nations.

5. EGYPT, IRAK, AND PALESTINE

To the Indian Nationalists, whether they stood like Gandhi for complete independence, or were members of the more moderate *Swaraj* or

Egypt

Home Rule Party, it appeared unjust that the British should grant practical autonomy to protectorates like Egypt and Irak while withholding it from India. Great Britain had controlled Egypt for thirty years before the World War, but did not declare the ancient land of the Pharaohs a British protectorate until 1914. The resentment felt by the Egyptians at this domination led to increasing disorders, until the British consented to end the protectorate (1922), withdraw their armed forces, and permit the native population to set up a constitutional monarchy under their own sultan, who took the title Fuad I, King of Egypt. Egypt is not, however, an entirely independent state, for the British government continues to scrutinize Fuad's policies and has reserved the right to fortify and guard the Suez Canal. Moreover, the vast hinterland of the Sudan, stretching from the twentieth parallel north latitude almost to the Equator, remains under British control.[1]

As a result of military operations in the valleys of the Tigris and Euphrates, the British were able to claim Mesopotamia as a mandate

Irak

after the World War ended. The native Arab tribes, however, which had welcomed British aid in throwing off the Turkish yoke, did not wish to exchange one conqueror for another and demanded complete independence for their homeland, which they termed Irak. Accordingly, after the Emir Feisal had been proclaimed King of Irak (1921), the British agreed to recall their armed forces provided their interest in the rich Mesopotamian oil-field was safeguarded. In 1930, the official mandate was replaced by a treaty of alliance between Irak and Great Britain, and in 1932 the Irakian Kingdom became a member of the League of Nations. Irak has a population of almost three million, and its capital is located at Bagdad, the ancient city of the caliphs.

When British forces conquered Palestine from the Turks in 1917, the foreign secretary, Arthur Balfour, declared that Great Britain favored

Palestine

"the establishment in Palestine of a National Home for the Jewish People...." At the conclusion of the war, the British received Palestine as a mandate under the League of Nations with the understanding that the Jewish people would be encouraged to settle there, but the discontent of the Arabs, who desired self-government and

---

[1] See map following page 370.

resented the immigration of Jews, led to constant turmoil. Faced by seemingly unsolvable difficulties, the British government was driven (1930) to modify the Balfour Declaration, and announce that it was necessary to suspend Jewish immigration until unemployment in Palestine decreased, because the land available for Jewish settlers and for the increasing Arab population was proving insufficient. Although the proportion of Jews in Palestine almost doubled in the decade which followed the war, they still formed less than one fifth of the population, and the British, with a hundred million Mohammedans in their empire, could not afford to antagonize the latter by dispossessing the Palestinian Arabs.

6. THE SELF-GOVERNING DOMINIONS

The political tie which binds Great Britain to the self-governing Dominions, Canada, Newfoundland, Australia, New Zealand, the Union of South Africa, and the Irish Free State, has been largely transformed in recent years into an empire partnership between semi-autonomous states. As early as 1897, the prime ministers of the British Dominions (as then constituted) assembled in London for the first Imperial Conference, and numerous meetings of this empire cabinet have been held since that date. Its resolutions are recommended to the separate Dominion governments, which may or may not adopt them, and the divergent interests of the sister states not infrequently make co-operation difficult and complete agreement impossible. Nevertheless, the wisdom of allowing these major colonies to assume complete control of their own affairs has been strikingly vindicated, for the Dominions have grown increasingly loyal as the political bonds which united them to Great Britain slackened to a nominal tie.

The World War afforded effective proof of the solidarity of the British Empire. Although not technically bound by the treaty commitments of the mother country, the colonies rallied enthusiastically to *War efforts* her support, and contributed generously to the final victory. *of the* They raised nearly 1,500,000 men to support the British *Dominions* military operations and incurred heavy expenditures in the prosecution of the war. In recognition of these efforts, the self-governing Dominions received separate representation at the Peace Conference and individual membership in the League of Nations.

At imperial conferences held in 1926 and 1930, the question of the precise status of the British self-governing Dominions was further elaborated, and subsequently defined in the Statute of Westminster passed by the House of Commons in 1931. Henceforth the Dominions were to be

recognized as "autonomous communities within the British Empire,
Statute of Westminster (1931) equal in status, in no way subordinate one to another in any aspect of their domestic or foreign affairs, though united by a common allegiance to the Crown, and freely associated as members of the British Commonwealth of Nations...." In virtue of their new dignity, the Dominions have the privilege (with reservations) of contracting treaties with foreign states, and may establish direct diplomatic relations by appointing ministers to foreign capitals. As the white population of the empire overseas is increasing much more rapidly than the population of Great Britain, it is possible to envisage a time, a few years hence, when the Dominions will achieve an equality in numbers, in wealth, and in power, which will accord logically with their equality of rank.

New economic forces working for imperial unity have come into play since 1931 when Great Britain abandoned the principle of free trade.
Imperial preference While imposing a tariff upon many articles of foreign origin, the new regulations still permitted goods from the British colonies to enter the United Kingdom free of duty. The co-operation of the Dominions was invited with a view to establishing a general system of imperial preference which would help to promote imperial trade relations and make the empire largely self-sufficient and independent of foreign markets. But the Imperial Economic Conference held at Ottawa (1932) revealed the difficulties attending such a course, for the Dominions showed a disposition to protect their nascent industries against British competition, and as individual partners in the British Commonwealth of Nations they were more concerned with safeguarding their national interests than in promoting the economic unity of the empire. Nevertheless, the Ottawa accords gave Great Britain a favored position as a market for such products as Canadian wheat and Australian mutton, while the Dominions agreed to accept British coal, iron, and steel, and various commercial products, in preference to similar exports from foreign sources.

Increased liberties involve increased responsibilities, but the Dominion governments have been slow to realize this and reluctant to acknowledge
Imperial defense their dependence upon the protection afforded them by the British fleet. The forty-five million inhabitants of the United Kingdom support by their taxes the naval forces which constitute the empire's first and almost only line of defense, while the twenty million people living in the self-governing Dominions devote a much smaller proportion of their revenues and their attention to the problem of imperial armaments. Australia and New Zealand, through fear of Japan, have

[470]

displayed a greater readiness to co-operate with the mother country on this matter than Canada or the Union of South Africa, but in general the attitude of the emancipated colonies has been one of complacent acquiescence in benefits received. Their people felt, perhaps rightly, that in founding new provinces and subduing new lands to the uses of British civilization, they were serving the empire in an original fashion and in adequate measure.

CHAPTER THIRTY-TWO

FRANCE SEEKS SECURITY

If Germany will not pay up, the Treaty of Versailles affords us a remedy. Article 248 gives the Allies a priority claim against all the property and resources of the German Empire and the German states.

RAYMOND POINCARÉ (1922).

The High Contracting Parties solemnly declare, in the names of their respective peoples, that they condemn recourse to war for the solution of international controversies and renounce it as an instrument of national policy in their relations with one another.

BRIAND-KELLOGG PEACE PACT (1928).

THROUGHOUT the World War the French people fought for their national liberties in the profound conviction that they were defending their fatherland against an unwarranted and premeditated attack. This assumption that Germany and her allies were responsible for the war, that they had plotted it in a desperate gamble for European hegemony, and fought it with the systematic intention of crippling France, in particular, beyond the possibility of recovery, has colored the outlook of the French people ever since 1914 and still determines their attitude on questions of foreign policy. Believing themselves to have been the innocent victims of Teutonic fury, they emerged from the war with two fixed ideas: that Germany must be made to pay to the utmost possible limit for the loss and damage which France and her allies had suffered, and that Europe must be safeguarded in future from the danger of a second conflict precipitated by German lust for conquest.

1. THE WORK OF RECLAMATION

The French war losses, in proportion to the population and wealth of the country, were heavier than those of any other great power. The war *The devas- tated regions* dead numbered 1,385,000; the war expenditures exceeded $26,000,000,000; and the property destroyed in the devastated regions was estimated at a further $20,000,000,000 or more. Ten of the richest departments of the republic, the heart of industrial France, had suffered for over four years from the destructive effects of warfare and enemy occupation. Forests had been cut down, mines flooded, factories wrecked, thousands of towns, villages, farms, wells, and bridges destroyed, and an area as large as the State of Maryland transformed into a waste region of ruin and desolation.

[472]

Upon the conclusion of peace, the French people devoted themselves with admirable decision and energy to the work of reclaiming the devastated regions. Trenches and barbed-wire entanglements *The work of* were removed, fortifications and gun emplacements demol- *reclamation* ished, hidden mines extracted, and the poisoned earth of shell-torn fields restored to productive uses. The replacement of ruined factories and wrecked machinery provided an opportunity for remodeling and modernizing many of the industrial plants, with results highly beneficial and stimulating to French manufacturing methods. Moreover, the colossal task of rebuilding and refurnishing three quarters of a million private dwellings and other edifices provided employment for millions of workers and induced a wave of prosperity in many lines of trade. In less than ten years the scars left by the war had all but vanished and the countryside of northeastern France once more supported five million industrial workers and farmers. Only a few square miles of desert, preserved in all their desolate horror as mementoes of the conflict, bore witness to man's ingenuity in the art of destruction and served as a warning to future generations.

The enormous outlay required for this work of reclamation greatly increased the French national debt. German reparation payments were expected to cancel the expenditure, but unfortunately for the French hopes it proved impossible to make Germany pay the sums anticipated. A large portion of the French people, convinced that the Germans were deliberately defaulting, favored strong measures, and clung to the belief that full reparation could be exacted if the Allied governments preserved an implacable attitude. A stubborn conviction that Germany could pay and should pay for the devastation wrought by the invading armies blinded Frenchmen to the realities of the situation, and greatly complicated the whole question of war debts and reparations from 1919 to 1932.

2. THE REPARATIONS TANGLE

When the Treaty of Versailles was signed in June, 1919, seven months after the war ended, the Allied governments had not yet filed their complete claims for indemnification against Germany. The Germans were ordered to commence payments in money and materials, but they did not learn until 1921 their total liability, which the reparations commission fixed at approximately $33,000,000,000.[1] Financial experts pointed

---

[1] This was an approximate sum, which was to be increased if it were found that the capacity of the Germans to pay had been underrated. The Allied Governments had demanded (January, 1921) a total of $56,000,000,000.

out that no precedent existed for the transfer of such an enormous sum, and that even if the payments were spread over many years the attempt to collect them would dislocate the framework of international finance, but the cupidity of the victors rendered them deaf to the cautions of the economists.

The German nation was crippled by the strain of war and the long blockade, by the loss of valuable colonies and shipping and the cost of *Germany* supporting an army of occupation. Moreover, the Ger- *defaults* mans regarded the demand for reparations as totally unjust and had no will to contribute more than they were compelled to yield. In 1922, instead of the $180,000,000 in gold marks demanded, they paid only $112,000,000; and their payments in goods, estimated at $550,000,-000, likewise fell behind. Recognizing that Germany had been brought to the verge of a ruinous financial collapse, the British government proposed a revision of the reparations terms; but France, dominated by a Nationalist *bloc* headed by the intractable Raymond Poincaré, favored punitive measures. Declaring Germany in default, Poincaré ordered French troops to seize the Ruhr Valley, the nerve-center of German industry, and hold it until payments were forthcoming.

A catastrophic collapse of German credit followed. The mark, already inflated when the French entered the Ruhr (January, 1923), fell faster *The Dawes* than the printing presses could operate, until notes for a *Plan (1924)* billion marks were needed to pay for a single meal. Since the stabilization of German currency was an indispensable preliminary if Germany was to resume payment, the late Allies agreed to reduce the burden of reparation temporarily to $250,000,000 a year, and to arrange for a foreign loan of $200,000,000 to promote the recovery of German industry. The international committee which devised this compromise was headed by an American, Charles Gates Dawes, and the project was subsequently known as the Dawes Plan. Under this arrangement Germany paid $1,896,860,000 between 1924 and 1929. The French and Belgian troops which had occupied the Ruhr Valley were withdrawn in 1925.

In 1929, the Dawes Plan was superseded by a new project which took its title from another American adviser, Owen D. Young. The Young *The Young* Plan fixed the sum which Germany still owed on reparations *Plan (1929)* at $9,000,000,000 and provided for a scale of annual payments to run for fifty-nine years. Ratification of this new pact was followed (1930) by the withdrawal of the last Allied forces from the Rhineland, and Germany indicated her good faith by continuing her payments to the extent of $685,916,000.

In 1931, however, the world-wide economic depression led President Hoover of the United States to suggest a one-year moratorium on all intergovernmental debts, a proposal which the debtor na- *The Lau-* tions readily adopted. Recognizing that Germany would *sanne Settle-* not be in a position to renew reparation payments when the *ment (1932)* moratorium expired, the Allies concluded a fresh agreement known as the Lausanne Settlement (1932). The reparations total still outstanding was cut drastically to about $2,000,000,000, a sum which the German government might reasonably discharge in time. But subsequent developments in Germany, which will be discussed in the following chapter, made it improbable that any further remittances on the reparations account would be forthcoming.

With the Lausanne Settlement the Allied governments finally acknowledged the impossibility of making the defeated nations pay the indemnity demanded. Reparations ceased to be a vital problem in international affairs, and the fierce and acrid controversy which had beclouded the issue for thirteen years passed into history. Yet even in the ledgers Allied and German estimates continued to clash, for the Germans calculated the value of their total remittances at nearly $13,000,000,000, while their late foes credited them with less than $5,000,000,000. This eight-billion-dollar discrepancy is traceable to divergent estimates regarding the value of the "tangible assets" — ships, cars, cattle, munitions, manufactured and raw material, etc. — which Germany had surrendered.

In releasing Germany from nine tenths of the obligations specified in the Young Plan, the delegates of Great Britain, France, Belgium, and the other nations represented at the Lausanne Conference, *The war* were influenced by the hope that the United States in turn *debts* would cancel the loans advanced to the Allies during the World War. These obligations the American government had already reduced from eleven to seven billion dollars, but the debtor states sought to make further repayment conditional upon the collection of the reparations demanded from Germany. In other words, France, Britain, Belgium, etc., would pay the United States when and if Germany paid them. It followed from this argument that since Germany in 1932 was relieved of all but a small fraction of her reparation liabilities, the debts owed by the Allies to the United States should be cut in the same proportion. This confusion of reparations and intergovernmental obligations the United States refused to sanction, with the result that after 1932 all the European nations in debt to America (except Finland) made reductions in their payments, and many of them defaulted altogether.

[475]

3. THE SEARCH FOR SECURITY

After 1924, the French attitude toward Germany was characterized by greater moderation and a more conciliatory spirit. The intransigent policy of Poincaré and the Nationalist *bloc* having failed to solve the reparations tangle, a new French cabinet was formed from the parties of the Center and Left. The portfolio of foreign affairs was entrusted to Aristide Briand, whose efforts from 1924 to 1931 to promote more cordial relations among European states won him the Nobel peace prize.

But to solve the financial dilemma created by the cost of reconstruction and by official extravagance, the French turned again to Poincaré in

Poincaré, savior of the franc 1926. The franc had fallen from its pre-war value of nearly twenty cents to less than two, and France hovered on the verge of that bottomless pit of inflation which had engulfed German credit three years earlier. Poincaré's firm policies, as head of a Nationalist government, saved the day, and the franc was stabilized at approximately four cents. By 1927, France revealed signs of a brisk business recovery, and by 1931 French prosperity excited the envy of the world. With little unemployment, humming factories, a good wheat and potato crop, and an enormous gold reserve, the republic appeared immune to the general depression which had set in. But Poincaré, the "savior of the franc" as he had been named by the grateful bourgeoisie, was forced to retire in 1929 because of ill-health, and the National Union ministry which he had headed fell from power.

Despite the recovery of Alsace and Lorraine, the World War left France weaker in man-power than in 1914. The consciousness that their fatherland had a smaller population than any other great power, and that the death rate equaled, when it did not exceed, the birth rate, filled Frenchmen with apprehension for their future security. As better protection against a new invasion from Germany, they demanded that the left bank of the Rhine should be ceded to France, or at least erected into a neutral state. But Lloyd George and Woodrow Wilson opposed these claims at the Peace Conference, and Clemenceau was driven to accept instead the promise of a treaty whereby the United States and Great Britain would guarantee France against any future threat of unprovoked aggression. This Wilsonian pledge was repudiated by the United States Senate and subsequently disallowed by Great Britain. In chagrin and disillusionment the French turned to more practical measures of protection.

The war divided the European states into two main groups: those which had gained by the peace settlements and those which had lost by them. French statesmen decided, in realistic fashion, that the nations which had gained territorially, especially those which had acquired more perhaps than their just share, would be eager to stand with France against any power or combination of powers that favored revision. To encircle Germany with a coalition of states pledged to oppose any renewal of the Teuton threat became once again, as before the war, the cardinal aim of French diplomacy.

With Belgium, France concluded a secret defensive alliance in 1920. Comrades in war, the French and Belgians were also united in peace, for they had substantial interests in common, including fear of *Belgium* a German revival and the claim to a major share of the expected indemnity.

Poland, re-created by the peace treaty from territory which before the war had belonged to Russia, Germany, and Austria, likewise anticipated with misgiving the day when Germany would arise from her *Poland* defeat. A Franco-Polish Pact was concluded in 1921, providing for a common policy in foreign affairs and a concerted defense if either of the signatories were attacked. The following year France strengthened the alliance with gold links, advancing several hundred million francs for the construction of Polish armaments and other national projects. France was buying allies.

The three states which profited most extensively from the dismemberment of the Austro-Hungarian Empire — Czechoslovakia, Rumania, and Jugoslavia — were particularly concerned to avert the *The Little* possible return of the Hapsburgs to Vienna and the resurrec- *Entente* tion of the Dual Monarchy. In 1920, these succession states formed a protective alliance known as the Little *Entente*. Poland, already allied with France (1921), entered into an understanding with the Little *Entente* later in the same year. A new network of pacts and protocols was thus rapidly taking shape, to replace that which had preceded the war. France definitely bound the Little *Entente* powers to her side by contracting formal treaties with Czechoslovakia (1924) and Jugoslavia (1927). Loans for the purchase of French munitions were advanced with a lavish hand, and French officers were commissioned to assist in organizing the armies of the new allies. In knitting together this band of armed and vigilant states, which stretched from the Baltic Sea to the Adriatic, French statesmen served two purposes at once. The menace of the hostile band encircling their borders could be relied upon to keep the defeated nations (Germany, Austria, and Hungary) neutral and quiescent. But a further service of the league, no less important in French eyes, was the exclusion of Russian revolutionary influences from

Europe. The student should study the map following page 426, and note how successfully the French system of alliances served both these aims. Poland, reconstructed chiefly at Russian expense, and Rumania, which had seized Bessarabia without Russian consent, could be counted upon to maintain a jealous guard and to constitute a *cordon sanitaire* which would check the infiltration of Bolshevist propaganda into Europe.

Nor did the French neglect, while securing allies, to augment their own military forces. Their army in the post-war decade was the most power-
French ful in the world. Their air force was the largest and perhaps
armaments the best equipped. Their armament appropriations were more extravagant than in pre-war years. They spent billions of francs for the construction of defenses along their German border, and after 1930 they strengthened the fortifications along their Italian frontier also. Although Germany had been disarmed, and France had inherited the military hegemony of Europe, French statesmen were harassed by the fear that secret projects would be formed for a war of revenge, just as Bismarck, after the Prussian triumph of 1870–71, was haunted by his "nightmare of coalitions."

Uneasy lies the head that wears a victor's crown. From 1919 on, a succession of fears harried the French public: fear that Germany would become a communist state and join Bolshevist Russia in proclaiming a world revolution; fear that the Germans were secretly rearming; fear that Italy would support Germany in demanding a revision of the Versailles Treaty. It was such alarms that made a rational consideration of the reparations problem impossible, and precipitated the seizure of the Ruhr Valley (1923), with the subsequent collapse of the German mark. In 1931, a projected customs union between Germany and Austria, which might have relieved the desperate economic plight of the Austrian people by linking them commercially to their stronger neighbor, was frustrated largely through French opposition. Such a pact, it appeared to the enemies of Germany, might easily prove the prelude to a political union of the two German states, and the Treaty of Versailles had specifically prohibited such an *Anschluss*.

4. THE PEACE PACTS

Since it was the earnest desire of French statesmen to maintain the *status quo* as established by the Treaty of Versailles, they stressed the defensive character of the alliances which they negotiated, and affirmed that France was ready at all times to enter any wider accord that would guarantee greater security and tranquillity to the nations of Europe and

[478]

the world. France, and Italy also, sent delegates to the Washington
Naval Conference of 1922,[1] and both these states agreed to a limitation
of naval armaments on a ratio of 5:5:3:1.67:1.67 for Great Britain, the
United States, Japan, France, and Italy, respectively. France also supported the League of Nations in its efforts to promote peace and arbitrate
disputes (so long as the League did not recommend any revision of the
Versailles Pact), and the League's repeated attempts to find an acceptable formula for the limitation of armaments enjoyed French approval
"in principle." In 1924, Premier Edouard Herriot of France and Ramsay MacDonald of Great Britain formulated a project (the Geneva
Protocol) for the pacific settlement of international disputes, but the
agreement failed to thrive after MacDonald's Labor ministry in England
was overthrown by the Conservatives a few months later.

In 1925, abandoning for the moment the search for a general formula
against war, Aristide Briand of France and Gustav Stresemann of Germany joined in urging a conference to settle some of the *The Locarno*
outstanding controversies which threatened European *treaties*
peace. At Locarno, Switzerland, representatives of France, *(1925)*
Germany, Great Britain, Italy, Belgium, Poland, and Czechoslovakia
concluded five treaties of arbitration, the most important of which bound
France, Germany, Great Britain, Italy, and Belgium to guarantee the
existing boundaries between Germany and Belgium and Germany and
France. By this Rhine Pact, the French abandoned any proposal to set
up a buffer state in the Rhineland and the Germans acknowledged the
permanent loss of Alsace-Lorraine, a compromise which did much to
mollify the bitterness between the two nations. Furthermore, France,
Germany, and Belgium pledged themselves to refer their future disputes
to arbitration, and Germany made a similar agreement with Poland and
Czechoslovakia. Lovers of peace everywhere hailed these "regional
understandings," and pledges to negotiate, as corner-stones for the temple
of peace, but in actuality the Locarno treaties were monuments to a
momentary good-will rather than enduring evidence of a new spirit or
policy. The French, at least, saw nothing inconsistent in signing at the
same time pacts of mutual defense with Poland and Czechoslovakia.

Briand's efforts to curb war did not end at Locarno. In 1928, as a
result of diplomatic conversations which he had conducted *The Briand-*
with Frank B. Kellogg, secretary of state for the United *Kellogg*
States, an anti-war pledge was devised and submitted to the *Peace Pact*
representatives of fifteen nations meeting in Paris. This *(1928)*
Briand-Kellogg Pact (or Paris Pact as it is often termed) was ac-

[1] See above, page 462.

cepted within a short time by nearly fifty nations. The contracting governments pledged themselves to renounce war as an instrument of national policy in their relations with one another, and to seek a solution for any disputes which might arise among them by pacific means and pacific means only. In adopting this solemn and definitive agreement to outlaw war, however, each nation reserved to itself the right to take up arms in its own defense, or in order to punish a state which had violated the pact or flouted the Covenant of the League of Nations. As civilized states never resort to war save on the pretext that they are defending their rights, these reservations all but invalidated the purpose of the earlier clauses.

How little genuine trust the governments of the European states placed in the various peace pacts which they negotiated was grimly *Increase in* reflected in their armament budgets. With the exception *armaments* of Germany and Austria, compulsorily disarmed after their defeat, all the great powers increased their military and naval defenses during the decade 1920–30. Great Britain, France, and Italy had expended approximately $900,000,000 on armaments the year before the World War opened, pleading fear of German militarism as their chief excuse; yet in the ten years which followed a peace treaty which left Germany prostrate, they not only failed to reduce their expenditures for war purposes, but raised them to a total of $1,250,000,000, an increase of almost forty per cent. The secondary powers likewise felt constrained to waste their resources in the same desperate competition, to the great profit of the munitions manufacturers, who did not hesitate to foster the existing fears and rivalries in order to increase the demand for their death-dealing wares.

In the period before 1914, the era of the Armed Peace, military and naval rivalry intensified international fears and suspicions until the *World Dis-* European peoples were psychologically disposed to view *armament* war as inevitable. To many statesmen it seemed clear that *Conference* the mounting armaments of the post-war years must exert a *(1932–33)* similar baleful effect, and that the more carefully the nations prepared for war, the more certain it became that war would materialize. Peace societies and other public bodies, therefore, petitioned in favor of a world conference on disarmament, and in 1925 the Assembly of the League of Nations appointed a commission to draft the agenda for such a conference. Seven years elapsed, however, before the conference was summoned, and even then its deliberations proved sterile and profitless. Although sixty countries dispatched delegates and a variety of projects for the gradual reduction of armaments were submitted, no

ARISTIDE BRIAND
1862–1932

*The shrewdness of mind, unaffected manner, and keen
sense of humor which distinguished Briand are all suggested in this unconventional camera study.*

agreement could be worked out. In June, 1933, the conference adjourned temporarily. When it reconvened the following May, the members found the prospect of an accord more remote than ever, and promptly adjourned a second time with nothing to show for their labors.

The French representatives at this abortive arms parley favored the establishment of an international military force to preserve peace and *Persistence* maintain the existing political settlement. For France was *of French* haunted more profoundly than ever by the fear that Ger- *fears* many would rearm and demand a revision of the Versailles Treaty under threat of war — a fear fed by the rise of the National Socialist Party in Germany and the sharp resurgence of German patriotism after 1932. The failure of the French government to prevent the German recovery, or to save France from the delayed effects of the world economic depression, rendered the administration exceedingly unpopular, and scandals and abuses involving members of the government crystallized this discontent. Sharp rioting in Paris (February, 1934) was followed by the formation of a National Union Cabinet with Gaston Doumergue as premier. This fourth cabinet crisis in less than four months left France shaken but sobered, and the new ministry was able to introduce some necessary economic reforms at home and pursue a more determined policy abroad. To offset the reviving German threat, France drew closer to Italy, and signed an accord with her Latin sister at the close of the year which fortified the dubious French hegemony in Europe. But the apprehensions of the French people were not dissipated, for their strong sense of realism warned them that neither the faith of fickle allies nor the high-sounding phrases of a peace pact could offer sure or lasting protection against a more powerful neighbor endowed with a sense of wrong.

CHAPTER THIRTY-THREE

GERMANY SEEKS EQUALITY

And in this moment I can only repeat, within the hearing of the world, that no threat and no force will ever induce the German nation again to renounce those fundamental rights which no sovereign state can be denied.
ADOLF HITLER (January 30, 1934).

THE revolutionary outbreaks in Germany during the last days of the World War,[1] which overturned the imperial régime and drove the kaiser into exile, delivered the fate of the empire into the hands of the Socialists. Had the Social Democratic Party remained united, it might have commanded an unquestioned majority in the subsequent elections, but during the war it had been split into three groups. The Majority Socialists headed by Friedrich Ebert and Philip Scheidemann favored a moderate program aiming at the progressive socialization of industry; the Independent Social Democrats insisted upon the immediate socialization of industry by constitutional decree; while the radical Sparticists clamored for the dictatorship of the proletariat on the Russian model. From the resulting struggle for control after the armistice, the Majority Socialists emerged in the lead. A Sparticist revolt was harshly suppressed, and an assembly elected to prepare a constitution (January, 1919). This Weimar Assembly accepted the peace treaty dictated by the Allies, and organized a government for the German Republic.

1. THE ORGANIZATION OF THE GERMAN REPUBLIC

Under the Weimar Constitution, proclaimed in August, 1919, Germany became a democratic republic of federated states. The executive authority was vested in a president, elected by direct ballot for a period of seven years. The legislature consisted of *The Weimar Constitution* the *Reichstag*, a popular chamber of more than five hundred members chosen by universal suffrage, and the *Reichsrat*, a federal council or senate of some seventy members in which the eighteen states composing the new Germany were represented in the order of their importance. The constitution confided the control of foreign affairs, national defense, tariffs and taxation to the central parliament at Berlin, ordained that the local governments in the component states should be republican and democratic in form, guaranteed freedom of speech and of the press, and

[1] See above, pages 422–24.

[483]

promised equality before the law to all citizens. Popular rule was safe-guarded by permitting the *Reichstag* to overrule the *Reichsrat* by a two-thirds vote, and by making the federal chancellor and ministry responsible to the lower chamber. In an emergency, however, the president had power to suspend the constitution and rule by decree if the *Reichstag* consented.

Friedrich Ebert became the first president of the German Republic and Philip Scheidemann the first chancellor. A *bloc* composed of Majority Socialists, Christian Democrats (the former Catholic Center Party), and Democrats (Bourgeois Republicans) dominated the cabinet, while the Independent Socialists on the Left Wing (the People's Party) and the Nationalists on the Right Wing (Conservatives and Monarchists) sat as a divided opposition. Public opinion shifted steadily away from the proletariat to the bourgeoisie and the more radical promises of the revolutionary days were not fulfilled, but earnest efforts were made, despite the financial confusion of the early post-war years, to construct public parks, gymnasiums, swimming pools, and libraries for the workers, to shorten hours and improve labor conditions, and to replace slum districts with model living quarters at a moderate rental.

This moderate program, a "betrayal" of the proletariat in the opinion of uncompromising radicals, incited the Communists to further abortive *Nationalist* plots which the government suppressed without grave *plots* difficulty. More threatening were the Nationalist demonstrations, sponsored by ex-army officers disgusted with the rule of Socialists and liberals who had "betrayed" Germany by signing an ignominious peace. Two leading liberal statesmen, Matthias Erzberger and Walter Rathenau, who had earned the hatred of the Nationalists, were assassinated, and several attempts were made to overturn the republic by a monarchist uprising. In 1920, a group of ex-soldiers headed by Waldemar Kapp marched on Berlin, but were foiled by a general strike of the Socialist workers. Three years later, General Erich von Ludendorff and a vigorous political orator, Adolf Hitler, sought to organize a *coup* to overthrow the "inglorious republic," but were likewise unsuccessful. Hitler with several of his followers was arrested and sentenced to prison.

2. ECONOMIC CHAOS AND RECOVERY

The staggering financial burden of the war overtaxed the credit of the imperial German government and before the conclusion of peace the mark had declined to half its value. The peace terms, the sequestration of the

Rhineland, deprivation of colonies and shipping, and imposition of reparations made German economic recovery almost impos- *The infla-* sible. The paper mark, nominally worth about twenty-four *tion* cents in gold, continued to fall in value until by 1923 it became literally worthless, and a new currency had to be issued for which the agricultural and industrial wealth of Germany was pledged as security. The Dawes Plan,[1] which provided for a foreign loan of $200,000,000 to stimulate the recovery of German industry, marked a turning-point in the tide of economic distress. Thereafter business conditions improved slowly, but the inflation had ruined a large creditor class, and millions of Germans had seen their bonds, mortgages, and other securities repudiated or else paid off in paper marks which were finally redeemed at one billionth of their normal value.

Yet all was not lost. Despite the suffering, the sacrifices, and the financial *débâcle*, the German people still possessed their habits of industry and efficiency, the workers had not lost their *German* craftmanship nor the experts their technical training. With *economic* the stabilization of the currency, business revived, industrial *recovery* plants expanded, and exports increased rapidly. The annual reparations tribute of $250,000,000 payable under the Dawes Plan, though galling to national pride, was lighter than the cost of maintaining first-class armaments. Factories and shipyards worked overtime to replace the goods and ships surrendered to the Allies, unemployment decreased, and the frugal living standards in Germany enabled the manufacturers to produce their wares more cheaply and invade foreign markets despite discriminatory tariffs. By 1929, the German merchant marine was approaching the total of its pre-war tonnage, the industrial output exceeded that of 1913, and for the first time in fifteen years the value of Germany's exports surpassed that of her imports.

After 1929, however, this promising expansion of German industry suffered a series of checks. Domestic replacement and reconstruction was largely at an end; world trade declined sharply under the blight of the economic depression; foreign loans to Germany practically ceased; and several foreign nations inflated their currencies and offered sharper competition in the world markets. By 1934, the German trade balance had once more turned passive; that is, German exports fell short of German imports in value. One reason for this economic decline was the spirit of distrust and antagonism which the Germans excited among their neighbors after 1932. The political vicissitudes in Germany which gave rise to this international suspicion must now be discussed.

[1] See above, page 474.

[485]

3. STRESEMANN AND THE SPIRIT OF CONCILIATION

The heritage of hate left by the World War, and the grievance felt by all Germans at the harsh terms of peace, made it difficult for Germany to re-establish normal relations with neighboring states. Bitterness over the reparations issue culminated in 1923 when the French, declaring Germany in default, seized the Ruhr Valley. With the adoption of the Dawes Plan the following year, however, and the subsequent evacuation of the Ruhr, Franco-German relations improved. The German people continued to resent the "guilt clause" in the Versailles Treaty and to condemn the extortion of reparations; they denounced the confiscation of their colonies without compensation and deplored the humiliating and defenseless status to which the treaty had reduced them; but their economic recovery after 1924 made them more philosophical about these injustices, and they sought for peaceful means whereby they might recover the equal place among the great powers to which their population, culture, and industrial progress entitled them.

From 1923 to 1929, the portfolio of foreign affairs in the German cabinet was held by Gustav Stresemann, a statesman who displayed *The Locarno* remarkable tact in restoring Germany's international *Pacts (1925)* prestige. As a patriot and a realist Stresemann comprehended that a policy of conciliation might win favorable revision of the peace terms, whereas a policy of recalcitrance would only aggravate the evils of an unjust settlement. In 1925, he proposed that France and Germany abandon their watchful hostility by negotiating a security pact through which both would guarantee to respect the existing frontiers. Fortunately, Stresemann found in Aristide Briand, French foreign minister, a statesman no less eager to improve international relations, and the fruits of their joint labors were the Locarno treaties.[1] Germany agreed to arbitration pacts with France, Poland, and Czechoslovakia, and renounced all claim to Alsace-Lorraine. The spirit of cordiality which prevailed at Locarno proved that there could be peace among men of good-will and seemed a hopeful augury for the future of European tranquillity.

The admission of Germany to membership in the League of Nations (1926) marked a further triumph for Stresemann's diplomacy, for, in assuming an equal status and a permanent seat on the League Council, the German Republic cast off much of the stigma of isolation and defeat which since 1919 had excluded the nation from its merited place among the European states. When the Briand-Kellogg Peace Pact was pro-

[1] See above, page 479.

posed in 1928,[1] Germany was one of the first to concur in renouncing war as an instrument of national policy. In the year of Stresemann's untimely death (1929), he was able to perform a final service for his country by facilitating the negotiation of the Young Plan,[2] winning a promise that the last Allied forces of occupation would be withdrawn from the Rhineland by the following year.

The honesty and moderation of Stresemann's policies had thus wrung some notable concessions from the victor powers, and the stability and responsibility of the German Republic seemed to be assured. The German people were by no means reconciled to the position of disarmament and economic vassalage imposed by the Versailles Treaty, but they were disposed to emancipate themselves by peaceful and diplomatic means provided these promised them relief within a reasonable period. To ardent German nationalists, however, the concessions gained by Stresemann appeared too meager and too dilatory. As the memory of the war dimmed, the mood of socialism and pacifism which had dominated the first years of the republic waned also, and a mounting nationalistic fervor replaced it.

The election (1925) of Field Marshal Paul von Hindenburg as president of the republic revealed a latent veneration among the masses for those principles of discipline and authority which had distin- *Hindenburg* guished the imperial régime. Hindenburg served the *as president* republic in his new capacity with the same rugged fidelity and dignity with which he had once served his emperor, and in 1932 the German people re-elected him, at the age of eighty-five, for a second presidential term. But it was significant that the monarchists and militarists, who had supported him in 1925, found his loyalty to his oath of office and to moderate republican principles a disappointment, and in 1932 he owed his re-election to the votes of Socialists and bourgeois republicans.

4. HITLER AND THE SPIRIT OF RECALCITRANCE

Hindenburg's chief opponent in the election of 1932 was Adolf Hitler, a popular leader whose spectacular rise to power gave a new direction to German politics. Born in Austria in 1889, Hitler had served *Adolf* in the German armies during the World War, and after the *Hitler* peace had plunged into a career of political agitation. For his share, with Ludendorff, in an attempt to overthrow the republic (1923), he was imprisoned for a short term, but on his release he renewed his efforts

---

[1] See above, page 479.   [2] See above, page 474.

to organize a party modeled on the pattern of the Italian *Fascisti*. Like Mussolini, Hitler recognized that nationalism and socialism were the two strongest political forces of the day, and he attempted to fuse them into a National-Socialist program. By his impassioned oratory, and his denunciation of the "pacifist traitors" who had "stabbed Germany in the back" in 1918, in order to establish the republic, and crowned their infamy by accepting a dishonorable peace, he awakened a fierce response, particularly among youthful enthusiasts, and discredited the Weimar Constitution. Organized bands of National-Socialist (or "Nazi") agitators carried Hitler's banners throughout Germany, attacked his political opponents, especially the Communists, with violence, and committed many brutal and disorderly acts. The Jews were marked out for systematic persecution on the ground that they had evaded their patriotic duties during the war and had enriched themselves in unscrupulous fashion amid the national misery that followed it. The Nazis' use of violence, terrorism, and even assassination to promote their aims made them abhorrent to many observers, particularly outside Germany, but they continued to increase their following by exploiting the inflamed spirit of German nationalism, and by a shrewd appeal to the German middle class which had been largely reduced to ruin and impotence by the war, the currency *débâcle*, and the taxes imposed by the Socialist régime.

The successive election totals tell the story of the National-Socialist triumph. In 1928, the Nazis held only 12 seats in the German *Reichstag*.

Rise of the National-Socialists But the mounting economic difficulties deepened the indignation of the electorate, and the business depression multiplied the number of unemployed to over four million by 1930. The election of that year raised the National-Socialist representation to 95. The cabinet, resting chiefly upon the support of the Center and the People's Party, under the chancellorship of Heinrich Brüning, steadily lost ground. Had France and Britain proved more prompt in easing the reparations burden, or made some other substantial concessions to German pride, the Brüning régime might have survived; but instead, the projected customs union between Germany and Austria [1] was frustrated chiefly through French opposition, and the Germans, thus forcibly reminded once again of their ignominious vassalage, listened the more readily to the defiant proposals of the National-Socialists. In 1932, the latter doubled their vote, winning 230 seats in the *Reichstag*, and emerging as the strongest political party of the republic. Hindenburg, who distrusted Hitler as a demagogue, hesitated at first to invest

[1] See above, page 478.

[488]

ADOLF HITLER

The remarkable influence which Hitler gained over the minds and hearts of the German people is largely achieved through his passionate oratory. Opening his speeches on a note of gloomy and concentrated defiance, he can lift his audiences to a pitch of hysterical applause and enthusiasm.

him with the chancellorship; but in January, 1933, he yielded, and a cabinet was formed under Nazi direction.

With their advent to power the National-Socialists undertook a complete reorganization of the republic. A new election, ordered in March, *The* Reichs- 1933, confirmed their supremacy, increasing their parlia- *tag fire* mentary lead to 288, which gave them a clear majority, as they could count upon the support of 52 Nationalist deputies. A fire of incendiary origin which destroyed the *Reichstag* building on the eve of the election was promptly blamed upon the Communists. In retaliation the government suspended civil liberties, suppressed opposition newspapers, and invoked coercive measures against recalcitrant voters. Although the Communist leaders denounced the *Reichstag* conflagration as a Nazi plot, and denied all responsibility for it, they were imprisoned and their party dissolved. The following June, the Social Democratic Party (the Majority Socialists), which had elected 118 representatives, was likewise suppressed and its deputies unseated. Thereupon the Nationalists fused with the Nazis, and the Center Party voluntarily dissolved, leaving but one political organization, the National-Socialists, in control of the government, the *Reichstag*, and the republic.

5. THE TOTALITARIAN STATE

At its first session after the Nazi triumph in the election of March, 1933, the *Reichstag* voted Hitler and his cabinet dictatorial powers for a period of four years. Hitler's avowed purpose, after silencing opposition in the peremptory fashion already described, was to weld Germany into a centralized national state under the domination of one party. The vestiges of particularism which even Bismarck had respected were to be stamped out, the semi-autonomous powers reserved by the leading component states under the federal empire of 1871 and the federal republic of 1919 lapsed, and local diets yielded up their authority to the central government in order that Germany might become a truly unitary state. As a means of increasing the efficiency, economy, and absolutism of the government, this consolidation of federal, state, and local institutions had much to recommend it. But when the leaders of the new régime sought to extend their control over the *Reichswehr* (the small but highly efficient German army), and attempted to reduce youth leagues, labor unions, and even the German Evangelical Church to state control, they awakened apprehension and opposition, and were forced to make some minor compromises. In general, however, the German people supported the Nazi policies with enthusiasm, and accepted Hitler's

[490]

eloquent assurances that loyalty, unity, and discipline would restore the *Reich* to a position of power and dignity among the nations and ease the economic distress through a planned revival of industrial and agricultural activities.

In Germany as in other industrial states the gravest social and economic problem of the post-war era was the necessity of providing relief for the millions of unemployed workers. The National- *Unemploy-* Socialist government attacked this problem aggressively, *ment relief* portioning the *Reich* into thirteen sections under the control of thirteen labor trustees, all supervised by a supreme economic council. Trade unions and strikes were prohibited, for the establishment of wage scales, hours, and conditions of work, and all other regulations governing the relationship between employer and employee, had passed under the supervision of the state. By shortening the working day more jobs were created, and a nation-wide drive raised funds to care for the indigent. Yet the workers were not wholly satisfied with the new system. Like the Italian laborers under the Fascist régime, they found their freedom of action greatly diminished and their welfare relegated to the paternal but bureaucratic care of a committee of experts. Many workers had rallied to the National-Socialist cause in the earlier years because they were attracted by the more radical phrases in the Nazi program, such as "the abolition of all income acquired without work," and "the distribution of the profits of large industries." But the National-Socialist leaders, who had secretly accepted financial aid from the great industrialists in order to achieve their victory, could not afford to alienate such powerful allies by adhering to radical projects which called for an attack upon private and corporate wealth.

By the spring of 1934, the realization that the National-Socialist program was likely to prove more "nationalist" than "socialist" in operation had roused secret discontent among the radical *The "June* members of the Nazi Party. At the same time the "storm *Purge"* troopers," the thousands of uniformed youths who had formed the "shock troops" in the National-Socialist campaigns, were bitterly disillusioned by the report that their leader, Hitler, planned to dissolve them after they had raised him to power by their efforts. Whether a genuine conspiracy had been organized among storm troop officers to precipitate a "second revolution" is not clear, but in June, 1934, Hitler struck a sudden and deadly blow at the suspected malcontents. Over sixty persons who had been marked out for vengeance were shot down in their homes or executed without trial. Following this paralyzing lesson on the dangers of insubordination, Hitler prepared to reduce the number, privileges, and duties of the storm troopers, and transferred his dependence to the *Reichswehr* instead, the officers and soldiers of which had long resented the favors shown the semi-military storm troop detachments.

With Hitler's advent to power, President von Hindenburg, already in failing health, had been forced somewhat into the background of affairs. On August 2, 1934, he died, and a decree of the cabinet invited Hitler to assume the duties of president of the *Reich* in addition to those of chancellor. The German electorate, in a plebiscite held August 19, approved the step by a ninety per cent majority, and *Der Führer* as Hitler was termed, assured in this fashion of the undiminished loyalty of the German people, accepted the presidential office. No previous German leader had been vested with more extraordinary powers.

6. GERMAN FOREIGN POLICY AFTER 1932

In their climb to power the spokesmen of the National-Socialist Movement had insistently proclaimed their determination to free Germany from the stigma of the "War Guilt Clause" in the Treaty of Versailles,[1] to repudiate further reparations payments, and to demand parity in armaments for Germany or an equal degree of disarmament for her neighbors. When the League of Nations refused to countenance the demand for parity in arms, Hitler announced the resignation of Germany from the League (October, 1933), and the German people, on appeal, sustained his act by a plebiscite majority of ninety-five per cent. Thereupon the German government proceeded to ignore the treaty restrictions and took active steps to enlarge the military, naval, and aerial defenses of the *Reich*.

In the matter of reparations the attitude of the new German government proved equally firm, and no further payments were made after the
The economic stalemate adjournment of the Lausanne Conference in 1932.[2] In 1933, German export trade declined sharply, partly as a consequence of the general economic depression and partly as a result of a world-wide boycott of German products which many anti-Fascists supported as a protest against the treatment accorded Jews and Communists under Nazi rule. This fall in trade helped to induce a perilous reduction in the German gold reserve. Payments on all German foreign debts were suspended, and the government declared that Germany could pay neither principal nor interest to foreign bondholders until

---

[1] See above, page 420.   [2] See above, page 475.

more favorable terms could be wrung from their respective governments. The reality of the German dilemma was doubted abroad, and many foreigners suspected the German government of deliberately depressing the export trade and the gold reserve in order to create a pretext for defaulting. For the German people the adverse balance of trade meant a condition of enforced self-sufficiency, and they were urged by their government to find domestic equivalents for the curtailed imports, to the end that Germany might become self-sustaining in peace or war. This ideal of economic self-sufficiency for the nation was extolled under the name of autarchy.

One development which the National-Socialists desired to promote was an Austro-German *Anschluss* or amalgamation. The six and one half million inhabitants of the truncated Austrian State *The fate of* were more than nine tenths German, and many of them *Austria* favored the projected union with their stronger neighbor. Such a step, it was generally agreed, would alleviate the grave economic difficulties to which Austria had fallen heir. As delimited by the Treaty of Saint-Germain,[1] Austria was completely landlocked, with no natural trade outlets. Furthermore, one fourth of the population lived in Vienna, which gave the country a disproportionately large head for a puny body, thus increasing the economic problems and aggravating the political disharmony. The Austrian Socialists, who had organized a democratic republic in 1919, were opposed by a coalition of Catholics and Nationalists, and the form of the government shifted after 1929 toward a Fascist dictatorship. In 1932, Engelbert Dollfuss assumed the chancellorship with the approval of the French, British, and Italian governments, his program based upon the principle that Austrian independence must be maintained and internal order restored. The resistance of the Socialists was broken after severe fighting in February, 1934. Dollfuss then sought to curb and disarm the groups of Nazi agitators in Austria who were clamoring for the *Anschluss*. Believing the moment ripe for a *coup*, desperate Nazis assassinated the chancellor in July, 1934, but the plot to seize control of the government and proclaim a Nazi revolution was frustrated. France and Great Britain authorized Italy to intervene if it were deemed necessary, in order that Austria might be safeguarded from German interference. The German government found it expedient to disown all connection with the Austrian Nazi plots, and the Clerical-Fascist régime at Vienna punished the assassins of Dollfuss and sustained his policies.

The reverse which German policies encountered in Austria was com-

[1] See above, page 424.

pensated six months later by the recovery of the Saar Valley. For-
Germany regains the Saar District tunately, by the opening of 1935 the international tension in Europe had grown easier, and the League of Nations was able to discharge a difficult duty with dignity and success. The Versailles Treaty had provided for a plebiscite in the Saar District after fifteen years to determine whether the inhabitants desired: (1) permanent annexation to France; (2) an independent status under League protection; or (3) reannexation to Germany. An overwhelming majority voted for reunion with their German fatherland, and the French accepted the verdict without opposition. Such a peaceful settlement of a rancorous issue was hailed as an augury of more tranquil and more stable times, and statesmen cast about for a formula which would entice Germany back into the League of Nations and resolve the deadlock concerning German rearmament. With the inequalities created by a one-sided peace treaty largely adjusted, and the economic depression of 1929–33 on the wane, it seemed possible for the people of Europe to look to the future with more hope and confidence than at any time since the World War, although such confidence was tempered by the threats of a second world conflict which already darkened the horizon, and by the specter of unemployment which continued to stalk through the cities.

7. CONCLUSION

Even in relatively tranquil years the tension and the inconsistencies latent in western civilization can hardly fail to provoke grave misgivings in the thoughtful mind. The material achievements of the modern age surpass those of any preceding epoch, and it is perhaps no more than just to pay tribute to these achievements before attention is called to the darker side of the picture. The triumphs of modern science in prolonging and enriching human life have been outlined already in Chapter XXIII. Each year advances the war against disease, introduces new labor-saving devices, marks the attainment of higher speeds, the construction of longer bridges, the erection of taller towers, and the measurement of more distant nebulae. These marvels of science are the chief glory of the contemporary era and it is impossible to overpraise the labor, the devotion, and the inspiration which have made them possible. Nor is there much reason to doubt that the immediate future will prove to be an age of technological development so outstanding that the present will be reduced in comparison to a period of apprenticeship. Machines are destined to become immeasurably more intricate and more powerful, and the marvels and complexities of this machine-dominated civilization cannot fail to increase yearly.

Yet this development imposes a vast responsibility upon the masters of the machines, a responsibility which, it may well prove, they are not prepared for and are not competent to accept. There is a mounting disparity observable between the limitless capacity of the engines and the limited faculties of their human managers. It is easy, for example, to treble the speed of a motor vehicle, but the deliberations and reactions of the driver are limited by his mental and muscular inheritance and cannot be greatly accelerated. This failure of the human machine largely explains why there have been one hundred thousand automobile fatalities in the United States within three years. Similarly, the rotary press and the radio have recently combined to bring the news of the world to the attention of every interested citizen, but the capacity of the average man to select, analyze, and pass judgment upon that news has not expanded in proportion as the information multiplied, and he has found that knowledge spells bewilderment. A third example, perhaps the most ominous, of this growing disparity between the acceleration of mechanized processes and the lag of human adaptation involves the menace of warfare. Few modern diplomats can aspire to reach a decision as quickly as Napoleon was in the habit of doing more than a century ago, yet Napoleon in his swiftest campaign required six weeks to seize the enemy's capital, whereas today any capital in Europe might be bombed from the air *two hours* after the declaration of war. With the danger of war and destruction thus reduced to a matter of hours, deliberation becomes impossible, the human machine breaks down and abandons its rôle of arbiter. The diplomats, as custodians of peace, cannot hope to evolve solutions in such emergencies, and it becomes a matter of the utmost importance to anticipate crises and prepare a channel for the arbitrament of international disputes in advance.

War and poverty remain the most desperate enigmas confronting western civilization, and in democratic countries the solution to them lies in the creation of a more enlightened and more humane citizenry. It seems possible to hope that the patience and ingenuity which have won so many triumphs for European man will not fail him here. Of the four horsemen enumerated in the apocalyptic vision as the four principal scourges of mankind, two, Famine and Pestilence, have been strikingly curbed in their ravages by modern productive methods and medical skill. Even Death, the rider on the pale horse, has been persuaded to allow the average European to live out at least his twenty thousand days. But the rider on the red horse still raises his sword above the nations, and the conquest of war remains the supreme challenge facing modern man. Only the spread of international good-will, transmuting fear to fair-mindedness and national greed to national co-operation, can brighten the hope for peace. The growth of such a spirit will depend upon many factors, but the most important must be the will of anonymous millions in every country who seek to distinguish and to support policies of reason, humanity, and justice.

Appendix A

GENEALOGICAL TABLES

GENEALOGICAL CHART OF THE ENGLISH SOVEREIGNS AFTER 1603

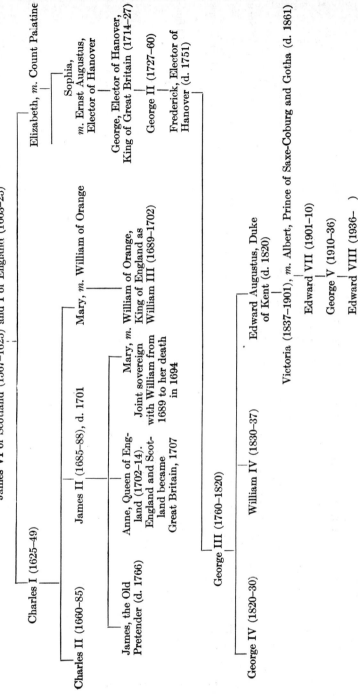

James VI of Scotland (1567–1625) and I of England (1603–25)

Charles I (1625–49)

Elizabeth, *m.* Count Palatine

Charles II (1660–85)

James II (1685–88), d. 1701

Mary, *m.* William of Orange

Sophia,
m. Ernst Augustus,
Elector of Hanover

James, the Old Pretender (d. 1766)

Anne, Queen of England (1702–14). England and Scotland became Great Britain, 1707

Mary, *m.* William of Orange, King of England as William III (1689–1702). Joint sovereign with William from 1689 to her death in 1694

George, Elector of Hanover, King of Great Britain (1714–27)

George II (1727–60)

Frederick, Elector of Hanover (d. 1751)

George III (1760–1820)

George IV (1820–30)

William IV (1830–37)

Edward Augustus, Duke of Kent (d. 1820)

Victoria (1837–1901), *m.* Albert, Prince of Saxe-Coburg and Gotha (d. 1861)

Edward VII (1901–10)

George V (1910–36)

Edward VIII (1936–)

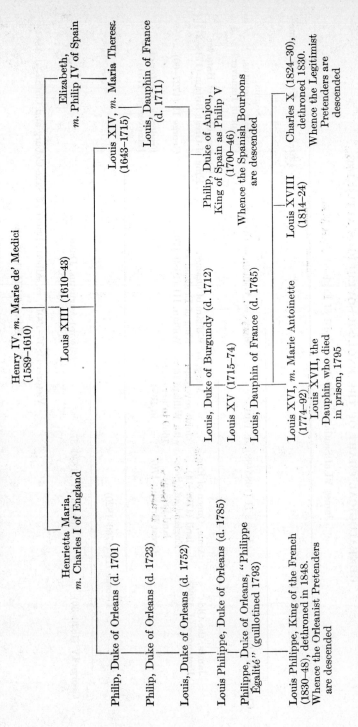

GENEALOGICAL CHART OF THE FRENCH KINGS AFTER 1610

Henry IV, *m.* Marie de' Medici
(1589–1610)

Elizabeth,
m. Philip IV of Spain

Louis XIII (1610–43)

Henrietta Maria,
m. Charles I of England

Louis XIV, *m.* Maria Theresa
(1643–1715)

Louis, Dauphin of France
(d. 1711)

Philip, Duke of Anjou,
King of Spain as Philip V
(1700–46)
Whence the Spanish Bourbons
are descended

Philip, Duke of Orleans (d. 1701)

Philip, Duke of Orleans (d. 1723)

Louis, Duke of Orleans (d. 1752)

Louis Philippe, Duke of Orleans (d. 1785)

Philippe, Duke of Orleans, "Philippe
Égalité" (guillotined 1793)

Louis Philippe, King of the French
(1830–48), dethroned in 1848.
Whence the Orleanist Pretenders
are descended

Louis, Duke of Burgundy (d. 1712)

Louis XV (1715–74)

Louis, Dauphin of France (d. 1765)

Louis XVI, *m.* Marie Antoinette
(1774–92)
Louis XVII, the
Dauphin who died
in prison, 1795

Louis XVIII
(1814–24)

Charles X (1824–30),
dethroned 1830.
Whence the Legitimist
Pretenders are
descended

GENEALOGICAL CHART OF THE BONAPARTE DYNASTY

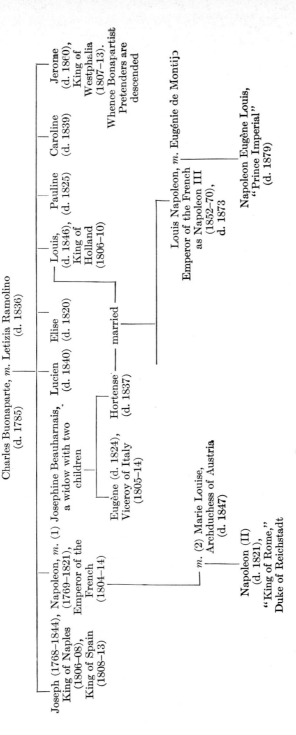

Appendix B

LIST OF RULERS

A LIST OF
EUROPEAN RULERS SINCE THE MIDDLE
OF THE SEVENTEENTH CENTURY

THE PAPACY

Alexander VII, 1655–67
Clement IX, 1667–69
Clement X, 1670–76
Innocent XI, 1676–89
Alexander VIII, 1689–91
Innocent XII, 1691–1700
Clement XI, 1700–21
Innocent XIII, 1721–24
Benedict XIII, 1724–30
Clement XII, 1730–40
Benedict XIV, 1740–58
Clement XIII, 1758–69

Clement XIV, 1769–74
Pius VI, 1775–99
Pius VII, 1800–23
Leo XII, 1823–29
Pius VIII, 1829–30
Gregory XIII, 1831–46
Pius IX, 1846–78
Leo XIII, 1878–1903
Pius X, 1903–14
Benedict XV, 1914–22
Pius XI, 1922 —

AUSTRIA

Leopold I, 1658–1705
Joseph I, 1705–11
Charles II, 1711–40
    (as Holy Roman Emperor he ranked
    as Charles VI)
Maria Theresa, 1740–80
Joseph II, 1780–90
Leopold II, 1790–92

Francis I, 1792–1835
    (as Holy Roman Emperor until he
    abandoned the title in 1806 he
    ranked as Francis II)
Ferdinand I, 1835–48
Francis Joseph, 1848–1916
Charles I, 1916–18
Republic, 1918 —

FRANCE

Louis XIV, 1643–1715
Louis XV, 1715–74
Louis XVI, 1774–92
Republic, 1792–1804
Napoleon I, Emperor of the French,
    1804–14

Louis XVIII, 1814–24
Charles X, 1824–30
Louis Philippe, 1830–48
Second Republic, 1848–52
Napoleon III, Emperor, 1852–70
Third Republic, 1870 —

GREAT BRITAIN (ENGLAND AND SCOTLAND UNTIL 1707)

Charles II, 1660–85
James II, 1685–88
William III, 1689–1702, and Mary II,
    1689–94
Anne, 1702–14
George I, 1714–27
George II, 1727–60

George III, 1760–1820
George IV, 1820–30
William IV, 1830–37
Victoria, 1837–1901
Edward VII, 1901–10
George V, 1910–36
Edward VIII, 1936 —

PRUSSIA

Frederick William, Elector of Brandenburg, 1640–88
Frederick II, Elector of Brandenburg, 1688–1701
   King of Prussia, 1701–13
Frederick William I, 1713–40
Frederick II, 1740–86
Frederick William II, 1786–97

Frederick William III, 1797–1840
Frederick William IV, 1840–61
William I, 1861–88
   German Emperor after 1871
Frederick III, 1888
William II, 1888–1918
Republic, 1918—

RUSSIA

Alexius, 1645–76
Theodore II, 1676–82
Ivan V and Peter I, 1682–89
Peter I "the Great," 1689–1725
Catherine I, 1725–27
Peter II, 1727–30
Anna, 1730–40
Ivan VI, 1740–41
Elizabeth, 1741–62

Peter III, 1762
Catherine II "the Great," 1762–96
Paul, 1796–1801
Alexander I, 1801–25
Nicholas I, 1825–55
Alexander II, 1855–81
Alexander III, 1881–94
Nicholas II, 1894–1917
Union of Socialist Republics, 1917 —

SPAIN

Philip IV, 1621–65
Charles II, 1665–1700
Philip V, 1700–46
Ferdinand VI, 1746–59
Charles III, 1759–88
Charles IV, 1788–1808
Joseph Bonaparte, 1808–13

Ferdinand VII, 1813–33
Isabella II, 1833–68
Amadeo, 1870–73
Republic, 1873–75
Alphonso XII, 1875–85
Alphonso XIII, 1886–1931
Republic, 1931 —

Appendix C

BIBLIOGRAPHY

Bibliography

CHAPTER I

EUROPE IN THE MIDDLE OF
THE SEVENTEENTH CENTURY

SUGGESTIONS FOR FURTHER READING

C. J. H. HAYES, *A Political and Cultural History of Modern Europe* (1932), vol. I, pp. 260–77.
C. P. HIGBY, *History of Europe, 1492–1815* (1927), chap. VI.
D. OGG, *Europe in the Seventeenth Century* (1925), chap. I.
J. BOULENGER, *The Seventeenth Century* (1920), chap. IV.

LONGER STUDIES

H. D. TRAILL and J. S. MANN, *Social England* (1909), vol. IV.
G. RENARD and G. WEULERSSE, *Life and Labor in Europe, XV to XVIII Century* (1926).
C. HUGON, *Social France in the Seventeenth Century* (1911).
H. O. WAKEMAN, *The Ascendancy of France, 1598–1715* (1915).
W. E. SIDNEY, *Social Life in England, 1660–1669* (1892).
E. TROTTER, *Seventeenth Century Life in the Country Parish* (1919).
E. GODFREY, *Home Life under the Stuarts* (1903).

GEOGRAPHICAL REFERENCES

For this and subsequent chapters the student should keep an historical atlas available.
W. R. SHEPHERD, *Historical Atlas* (ed. 1929).
R. MUIR, G. PHILIP, R. M. MCELROY, *Putnam's Historical Atlas, Mediaeval and Modern* (ed. 1927).
J. K. WRIGHT, *The Geographical Basis of European History* (1928), provides a useful short description of the physiography and climate of the European area.

CHAPTER II

LOUIS XIV DOMINATES FRANCE AND
ASPIRES TO DOMINATE EUROPE

SUGGESTIONS FOR FURTHER READING

C. J. H. HAYES, *A Political and Cultural History of Modern Europe* (1932), vol. I, pp. 290–319.

[xiii]

J. E. GILLESPIE, *A History of Europe, 1500–1815* (1928), chap. xv.
T. W. RIKER, *A Short History of Modern Europe* (1935), chap. ii.
D. OGG, *Europe in the Seventeenth Century* (1925), chap. ii.
H. O. WAKEMAN, *The Ascendancy of France, 1598–1715* (1915), chap. ii.
A. GUÉRARD, *The Life and Death of an Ideal* (1928), pp. 150–222.

LONGER STUDIES

J. BOULENGER, *The Seventeenth Century* (1920).
L. B. PACKARD, *The Age of Louis XIV* (1929), and *The Commercial Revolution* (1927).
J. FARMER, *Versailles and the Court under Louis XIV* (1905).
P. J. BLOK, *History of the People of the Netherlands*, 5 vols. (1898–1912), vol. iv.

BIOGRAPHICAL WORKS

A. HASSALL, *Louis XIV* (1901).
L. BERTRAND, *Louis XIV* (English ed. 1928).
E. K. SANDERS, *Bossuet* (1921).
B. MATTHEWS, *Molière, his Life and his Times* (1910).

SOURCES

J. H. ROBINSON, *Readings in European History* (1906), vol. ii, chap. xxxi.
J. H. ROBINSON and C. A. BEARD, *Readings in Modern European History* (1908), vol. i, chaps. i–iii.
H. WEBSTER, *Historical Selections* (1929), nos. 505, 506.

CHAPTER III

THE TRIUMPH OF PARLIAMENTARY GOVERNMENT IN ENGLAND

SUGGESTIONS FOR FURTHER READING

Cambridge Modern History, vol. v, chaps. 5, 6, 8, 9, 10, 11, and 15.
C. J. H. HAYES, *A Political and Cultural History of Modern Europe* (1932), vol. i, chap. x.
T. W. RIKER, *A Short History of Modern Europe* (1935), chap. v.
A. HYMA, *A Short History of Europe, 1500–1815* (1928), chap. vi.
J. E. GILLESPIE, *A History of Europe, 1500–1815* (1928), pp. 344–59.
A. L. CROSS, *A Shorter History of England and Greater Britain* (1921), chaps. xxix–xxxvi.

LONGER STUDIES

A. HASSALL, *The Restoration and the Revolution* (1912).
G. M. TREVELYAN, *England under the Stuarts, 1603–1714* (1910) and *England under Queen Anne*, 3 vols. (1930–34).
D. OGG, *England in the Reign of Charles II*, 2 vols. (1934).

BIOGRAPHICAL WORKS

O. AIRY, *Charles II* (1901).
H. D. TRAILL, *William III* (1911).
C. T. ATKINSON, *Marlborough and the Rise of the British Army* (1921).
M. P.. HOPKINSON, *Anne of England* (1935).

SOURCES

J. H. ROBINSON, *Readings in European History* (1906), vol. II, pp. 259–63.
E. P. CHEYNEY, *Readings in English History* (1908), chaps. XVI, XVII.
H. WEBSTER, *Historical Selections* (1929), nos. 392–95, 511–12.

CHAPTER IV

THE DECLINING EMPIRE OF THE HAPSBURGS

SUGGESTIONS FOR FURTHER READING

Cambridge Modern History, vol. V, chap. XI.
C. J. H. HAYES, *A Political and Cultural History of Modern Europe* (1932), vol. I, chap. VII.
J. E. GILLESPIE, *A History of Europe, 1500–1815* (1928), chaps. XII, XIII.
A. HYMA, *A Short History of Europe, 1500–1815* (1928), chap. VIII.

LONGER STUDIES

W. S. WHITMAN, *Austria* (1906).
L. LEGER, *A History of Austria-Hungary* (1889).
W. COXE, *History of the House of Austria*, 3 vols. (Bohn ed. 1847), vol. III.
J. BRYCE, *The Holy Roman Empire* (1904).
C. E. CHAPMAN, *A History of Spain* (1922).
M. A. S. HUME, *Spain, its Greatness and Decay, 1479–1788* (1898).
K. D. VERNON, *Italy from 1494 to 1790* (1909).
A. VÁMBÉRY, *The Story of Hungary* (1886).
F. SCHEVILL, *The History of the Balkan Peninsula from the Earliest Times to the Present Day* (1922).

SOURCES

J. H. ROBINSON, *Readings in European History* (1906), vol. II, pp. 312–15.

CHAPTER V

THE EMERGENCE OF RUSSIA

SUGGESTIONS FOR FURTHER READING

Cambridge Modern History, vol. v, chaps. XVI–XIX; vol. VI, chaps. X, XIX.
C. J. H. HAYES, *A Political and Cultural History of Modern Europe* (1932), vol. I, chap. VIII.
T. W. RIKER, *A Short History of Modern Europe* (1935), chap. IV.
J. E. GILLESPIE, *A History of Europe, 1500–1815* (1928), chap. XXI.
A. HYMA, *A Short History of Europe, 1500–1815* (1928), chap. IX.
A. HASSALL, *The Balance of Power, 1715–1789* (1925), chaps. V, XI, XIII.
F. NOWAK, *Medieval Slavdom and the Rise of Russia* (1930), chaps. II, III.

LONGER STUDIES

R. N. BAIN, *Slavonic Europe: a Political History of Poland and Russia from 1447 to 1796* (1908).
R. N. BAIN, *The Pupils of Peter the Great: a History of the Russian Court and Empire from 1689 to 1740* (1897).
R. N. BAIN, *The Last King of Poland and his Contemporaries* (1909).
R. N. BAIN, *Charles XII and the Collapse of the Swedish Empire, 1682–1719* (1895).
S. F. PLATONOV, *History of Russia* (1925).
C. HALLENDORFF and A. SCHÜCK, *History of Sweden* (1929).
W. R. MORFILL, *The Story of Poland* (1893).
J. S. ORVIS, *A Brief History of Poland* (1916).

BIOGRAPHICAL WORKS

F. SCHUYLER, *Peter the Great*, 2 vols. (1894).
K. WALISZEWSKI, *Peter the Great*, 2 vols. (1897) and *The Story of a Throne: Catharine II of Russia*, 2 vols. (1895).
K. ANTHONY, *Catharine the Great* (1925).
E. A. B. HODGETTS, *Catharine the Great* (1914).

SOURCES

J. H. ROBINSON, *Readings in European History* (1906), vol. II, chap. XXXII.
J. H. ROBINSON and C. A. BEARD, *Readings in Modern European History* (1908), vol. I, chap. VI.

CHAPTER VI

THE RISE OF PRUSSIA

SUGGESTIONS FOR FURTHER READING

Cambridge Modern History, vol. v, chaps. XX, XXI; vol. VI, chaps. VIII, IX, XX.
C. J. H. HAYES, *A Political and Cultural History of Modern Europe* (1932), vol. I, pp. 329–56.

[xvi]

T. W. RIKER, *A Short History of Modern Europe* (1935), chap. III.
J. E. GILLESPIE, *A History of Europe, 1500–1815* (1928), chap. XX.
A. HYMA, *A Short History of Europe, 1500–1815* (1928), chap. VIII.
A. HASSALL, *The Balance of Power, 1715–1789* (1925), chaps. VI, IX.

LONGER STUDIES

E. F. HENDERSON, *A Short History of Germany*, 2 vols. (1916), vol. II.
G. M. PRIEST, *Germany Since 1740* (1915).
C. T. ATKINSON, *A History of Germany, 1715–1815* (1908).

BIOGRAPHICAL WORKS

N. YOUNG, *Life of Frederick the Great* (1919).
W. F. REDDAWAY, *Frederick the Great and the Rise of Prussia* (1904).
J. F. BRIGHT, *Maria Theresa* (1897).

SOURCES

J. H. ROBINSON, *Readings in European History* (1906), vol. II, pp. 315–28.
J. H. ROBINSON *and* C. A. BEARD, *Readings in Modern European History* (1908), vol. I, chap. V.

CHAPTER VII

OVERSEAS EXPANSION AND THE STRUGGLE FOR COMMERCE AND COLONIES

SUGGESTIONS FOR FURTHER READING

Cambridge Modern History, vol. V, chap. XXII; vol. VI, chaps. II, VI, XV; vol. VII, chaps. I–VIII.
C. J. H. HAYES, *A Political and Cultural History of Modern Europe* (1932), vol. I, chap. IX.
T. W. RIKER, *A Short History of Modern Europe* (1935), chap. VI.
J. E. GILLESPIE, *A History of Europe, 1500–1815* (1928), chap. XVIII.
C. P. HIGBY, *History of Europe, 1492–1815* (1927), chap. X.

LONGER STUDIES

W. C. ABBOTT, *The Expansion of Europe*, 2 vols. (1924).
C. DAY, *A History of Commerce* (1907).
J. E. GILLESPIE, *A History of Geographical Discovery, 1400–1800* (1933).
J. N. L. BAKER, *History of Geographical Discovery and Exploration* (1931).
P. A. MEANS, *The Spanish Main, 1492–1700* (1935).
A. H. BUFFINGTON, *The Second Hundred Years' War, 1689–1815* (1929).
C. BECKER, *The Eve of the Revolution* (1921).
C. M. ANDREWS, *The Colonial Background of the American Revolution* (1924).
C. H. VAN TYNE, *The American Revolution* (1905).

BIBLIOGRAPHY

BIOGRAPHICAL WORKS

I. B. RICHMAN, *Spanish Conquerors; a Chronicle of the Dawn of Empire Overseas* (1919).
H. M. STEPHENS, *Albuquerque and the Portuguese Settlements in India* (1892).
H. W. VAN LOON, *Golden Book of the Dutch Navigators* (1916).
A. KITSON, *Captain James Cook, the Circumnavigator* (1907).
W. T. WAUGH, *James Wolfe, Man and Soldier* (1928).
F. PARKMAN, *Montcalm and Wolfe*, in *Works*, 13 vols. (1922).
B. WILLIAMS, *Life of William Pitt, Earl of Chatham*, 2 vols. (1913).
G. B. MALLESON, *Lord Clive and the Establishment of the English in India* (1895).

SOURCES

J. H. ROBINSON, *Readings in European History* (1906), vol. II, chap. XXXIII.
J. H. ROBINSON and C. A. BEARD, *Readings in Modern European History* (1908), vol. I, chaps. VI, VII.
H. WEBSTER, *Historical Selections* (1929), nos. 424–26, 459–61.

CHAPTER VIII

THE INTELLECTUAL REVOLUTION

SUGGESTIONS FOR FURTHER READING

Cambridge Modern History, vol. V, chap. XXIII.
C. J. H. HAYES, *A Political and Cultural History of Modern Europe* (1932), vol. I, chap. XI.
J. E. GILLESPIE, *A History of Europe, 1500–1815* (1928), chap. XXII.
C. P. HIGBY, *History of Europe, 1492–1815* (1927), chap. XIII.
P. SMITH, *A History of Modern Culture* (1930), vol. I, chap. VI; (1934), vol. II, chap. IV.

LONGER STUDIES

H. S. and E. H. WILLIAMS, *A History of Science*, 5 vols. (1904), vol. II, chaps. IV–VI, XI–XII.
W. T. SEDGWICK and H. TYLER, *A Short History of Science* (1917).
J. H. RANDALL, JR., *The Making of the Modern Mind* (1926).
F. CAJORI, *History of Physics* (1899).
D. E. SMITH, *History of Mathematics* (1925).
A. BERRY, *History of Astronomy* (1898).
J. M. STILLMAN, *The Story of Early Chemistry* (1924).
V. ROBINSON, *The Story of Medicine* (1932).
A. D. WHITE, *History of the Warfare of Science with Theology*, 2 vols. (1910).

BIOGRAPHICAL WORKS

E. S. HALDANE, *Descartes, His Life and Times* (1905).
G. S. BRETT, *Sir Isaac Newton* (1928).

F. MASSON, *Robert Boyle: a Biography* (1914).
H. W. CARR, *Leibniz* (1929).
B. FAŸ, *Benjamin Franklin* (1929).
P. DE KRUIF, *The Microbe Hunters* (1926).

SOURCES

J. H. ROBINSON and C. A. BEARD, *Readings in Modern European History* (1908), vol. I, chap. IX.
H. WEBSTER, *Historical Selections* (1929), nos. 527–34.

CHAPTER IX

GOVERNMENT AND SOCIETY UNDER THE OLD RÉGIME

SUGGESTIONS FOR FURTHER READING

Cambridge Modern History, vol. VIII, chaps. I, II.
C. J. H. HAYES, *A Political and Cultural History of Modern Europe* (1932), vol. I, chap. XII.
T. W. RIKER, *A Short History of Modern Europe* (1935), chap. VII.
A. HYMA, *A Short History of Europe, 1500–1815* (1928), chaps. X, XI.
C. P. HIGBY, *History of Europe, 1492–1815* (1927), chap. XV.
J. E. GILLESPIE, *A History of Europe, 1500–1815* (1928), chaps. XXIV, XXV.
L. GERSHOY, *The French Revolution and Napoleon* (1933), chaps. I–IV.
L. R. GOTTSCHALK, *The Era of the French Revolution* (1929), pp. 1–115.

LONGER STUDIES

E. J. LOWELL, *The Eve of the French Revolution* (1892).
A. H. JOHNSON, *The Age of the Enlightened Despot, 1660–1789* (1925).
H. E. BOURNE, *The Revolutionary Period in Europe* (1914).
G. BRUUN, *The Enlightened Despots* (1929).
D. MORNET, *French Thought in the Eighteenth Century* (1929).
P. SMITH, *A History of Modern Culture* (1934), vol. II; especially chaps. VI and XI.
F. J. C. HEARNSHAW, editor, *The Political and Social Ideas of Some Great French Thinkers of the Age of Reason* (1930).

BIOGRAPHICAL WORKS

J. F. BRIGHT, *Maria Theresa* (1897) and *Joseph II* (1905).
J. ADDISON, *Charles III of Spain* (1900).
A. D. WHITE, *Seven Great Statesmen* (1927), essay on Turgot.
L. SAY, *Turgot* (1888).
J. MORLEY, *Voltaire* (1871) and *Rousseau* (1873).
M. JOSEPHSON, *Rousseau* (1931).
A. SOREL, *Montesquieu* (1888).

SOURCES

J. H. ROBINSON, *Readings in European History* (1906), vol. II, chap. XXXIV.

J. H. ROBINSON and C. A. BEARD, *Readings in Modern European History* (1908), vol. I, chaps. VIII–XI.

J.-J. ROUSSEAU, *The Social Contract* (Everyman's Library ed. 1913), especially Books I and II.

CHAPTER X

THE FRENCH PEOPLE DESTROY THE RELICS OF FEUDALISM AND OVERTURN THE MONARCHY

SUGGESTIONS FOR FURTHER READING

Cambridge Modern History, vol. VIII, chaps. V–VIII.

C. J. H. HAYES, *A Political and Cultural History of Modern Europe* (1932), vol. I, pp. 596–629.

T. W. RIKER, *A Short History of Modern Europe* (1935), chap. VIII.

C. P. HIGBY, *History of Europe, 1492–1815* (1927), chap. XVI.

A. HYMA, *A Short History of Europe, 1500–1815* (1928), chap. XII.

J. E. GILLESPIE, *A History of Europe, 1500–1815* (1928), pp. 494–527.

SHORT HISTORIES OF THE FRENCH REVOLUTION

L. GERSHOY, *The French Revolution, 1789–1799* (1932).

L. GERSHOY, *The French Revolution and Napoleon* (1933).

L. R. GOTTSCHALK, *The Era of the French Revolution* (1929).

C. BRINTON, *A Decade of Revolution, 1789–1799* (1935).

A. MATHIEZ, *The French Revolution* (1928).

L. MADELIN, *The French Revolution* (1928).

R. M. JOHNSTON, *The French Revolution; a Short History* (1909).

S. MATHEWS, *The French Revolution, 1789–1815* (rev. ed. 1923).

E. D. BRADBY, *Short History of the French Revolution, 1789–1795* (1926).

C. D. HAZEN, *The French Revolution*, 2 vols. (1932).

A. J. GRANT and H. TEMPERLEY, *Europe: the Revolutionary and Napoleonic Eras* (1935).

BIOGRAPHICAL WORKS

H. D. SEDGWICK, *La Fayette* (1928).

L. BARTHOU, *Mirabeau* (1913).

H. BELLOC, *Marie Antoinette* (1923).

S. ZWEIG, *Marie Antoinette* (1933).

E. D. BRADBY, *Life of Barnave*, 2 vols. (1915).

For further biographical works see the list at the close of Chapter XI.

DIBLIOGRAPHY

SOURCES

J. H. ROBINSON, *Readings in European History* (1906), vol. II, chap. XXXV.
J. H. ROBINSON and C. A. BEARD, *Readings in Modern European History* (1908), vol. I, chaps. XII and XIII.
F. M. ANDERSON, *Constitutions and Other Select Documents: France, 1789–1901* (1904), pp. 1–253.
H. WEBSTER, *Historical Selections* (1929), nos. 397–403.

CHAPTER XI

THE FIRST FRENCH REPUBLIC AND ITS STRUGGLE TO SURVIVE

SUGGESTIONS FOR FURTHER READING

Cambridge Modern History, vol. VIII, chaps. IX, XII, XV.
C. J. H. HAYES, *A Political and Cultural History of Modern Europe* (1932), vol. I, chap. XII.
T. W. RIKER, *A Short History of Modern Europe* (1935), chap. VIII.
J. E. GILLESPIE, *A History of Europe, 1500–1815* (1928), pp. 527–50.
L. GERSHOY, *The French Revolution and Napoleon* (1933), chaps. XI, XII.
L. R. GOTTSCHALK, *The Era of the French Revolution* (1929), pp. 215–304.

SPECIAL TOPICS

W. B. KERR, *The Reign of Terror, 1793–94* (1927).
C. BRINTON, *The Jacobins; a Study in the New History* (1930).
R. W. PHIPPS, *The Armies of the First French Republic and the Rise of the Marshals of Napoleon,* 3 vols. (1926–31).
M. MINNEGERODE, *The Magnificent Comedy: Days of the Directory* (1931).
W. M. SLOANE, *The French Revolution and Religious Reform* (1901).

BIOGRAPHICAL WORKS

L. MADELIN, *Danton* (1914) and *Figures of the Revolution* (1929).
H. BELLOC, *Danton* (1899) and *Robespierre* (1927).
L. R. GOTTSCHALK, *Jean Paul Marat; a Study in Radicalism* (1927).
C. YOUNG, *A Lady Who Loved Herself: the Life of Madame Roland* (1930).
G. G. VAN DUSEN, *Sieyes: His Life and Nationalism* (1932).
H. BERAUD, *Twelve Portraits of the Revolution* (1928).
J. M. THOMPSON, *Leaders of the French Revolution* (1929).
W. W. STEPHENS, *Women of the French Revolution* (1912).
J. S. SCHAPIRO, *Condorcet and the Rise of Liberalism* (1934).
G. BRUUN, *Saint-Just, Apostle of the Terror* (1932).

SOURCES

J. H. ROBINSON, *Readings in European History* (1906), vol. II, chap. XXXVI.

CHAPTER XII

NAPOLEON AND FRANCE

SUGGESTIONS FOR FURTHER READING

Cambridge Modern History, vol. IX, chaps. I, V–VII.

C. J. H. HAYES, *A Political and Cultural History of Modern Europe* (1932), vol. I, pp. 647–59.

T. W. RIKER, *A Short History of Modern Europe* (1935), chap. X.

J. E. GILLESPIE, *A History of Europe, 1500–1815* (1928), pp. 550–60.

A. HYMA, *A Short History of Europe, 1500–1815* (1928), chap. XIII.

L. GERSHOY, *The French Revolution and Napoleon* (1933), chaps. XIII–XV.

L. R. GOTTSCHALK, *The Era of the French Revolution* (1929), Part II, Book I, chaps. I, II.

BIOGRAPHIES OF NAPOLEON I

J. H. ROSE, *The Life of Napoleon I* (1913).

H. A. L. FISHER, *Napoleon* (1924).

R. M. JOHNSTON, *Napoleon; a Short Biography* (1910).

E. LUDWIG, *Napoleon* (1926).

A. FOURNIER, *Napoleon the First*, 2 vols. (1911).

F. M. KIRCHEISEN, *Napoleon* (1932).

S. WILKINSON, *The Rise of General Bonaparte* (1931).

SOURCES

J. H. ROBINSON, *Readings in European History* (1906), vol. II, chap. XXXVII.

F. M. ANDERSON, *Constitutions and Other Select Documents: France, 1789–1901* (1904), pp. 208–451.

J. H. ROBINSON and C. A. BEARD, *Readings in Modern European History* (1908), vol. I, chaps. XIV, XV.

CHAPTER XIII

NAPOLEON AND EUROPE

SUGGESTIONS FOR FURTHER READING

Cambridge Modern History, vol. IX, chaps. III, IV, IX–XVII.

C. J. H. HAYES, *A Political and Cultural History of Modern Europe* (1932), vol. I, pp. 659–717.

T. W. RIKER, *A Short History of Modern Europe* (1935), chap. X.

A. HYMA, *A History of Europe, 1500–1815* (1928), chap. XIII.

J. E. GILLESPIE, *A History of Europe, 1500–1815* (1928), chap. XXVI.

L. GERSHOY, *The French Revolution and Napoleon* (1933), chaps. XVI–XX.

L. R. GOTTSCHALK, *The Era of the French Revolution* (1929), pp. 356–456.

F. Schevill, *The Making of Modern Germany* (1916), chap. III.
E. F. Henderson, *A Short History of Germany* (1916), vol. II, chaps. VI, VII.
G. M. Priest, *Germany Since 1740* (1915), chaps. IV–VII.

LONGER STUDIES

A. T. Mahan, *The Influence of Sea Power upon the French Revolution and Empire*, 2 vols. (1919), vol. II; especially chaps. XV, XVI, and XVIII.
F. H. Heckscher, *The Continental System* (1922).
H. A. L. Fisher, *Studies in Napoleonic Statesmanship: Germany* (1903).
R. M. Johnston, *The Napoleonic Empire in Southern Italy*, 2 vols. (1904).
G. B. McClellan, *Venice and Bonaparte* (1931).
H. P. George, *Napoleon's Invasion of Russia* (1899).
G. Edmundson, *History of Holland* (1922).

BIOGRAPHICAL WORKS

For biographies of Napoleon see close of Chapter XII.
J. R. Seeley, *Life and Times of Stein, or Germany and Prussia in the Napoleonic Age* (1897).
E. F. Henderson, *Blücher and the Uprising of Prussia Against Napoleon, 1806–1815* (1911).
J. H. Rose, *The Life of William Pitt* (1923).
A. T. Mahan, *Life of Nelson*, 2 vols. (1897).
P. Guedalla, *Wellington* (1932).
G. Lacour-Gayet, *Talleyrand, 1754–1838* (1930), vol. II.
J. McCabe, *Talleyrand* (1906).
N. Forssel, *Fouché, the Man Napoleon Feared* (1928).
A. D. White, *Seven Great Statesmen* (1927), essay on Stein.

SOURCES

J. H. Robinson, *Readings in European History* (1906), vol. II, chap. XXXVIII.

CHAPTER XIV

THE VIENNA CONGRESS

SUGGESTIONS FOR FURTHER READING

Cambridge Modern History, vol. IX, chaps. XIX, XXI.
C. J. H. Hayes, *A Political and Cultural History of Modern Europe* (1932), vol. I, chap. XIV.
T. W. Riker, *A Short History of Modern Europe* (1935), chap. XI.
C. P. Higby, *History of Modern Europe* (1932), chap. II.
J. S. Schapiro, *Modern and Contemporary European History* (1929), chap. IV.
C. D. Hazen, *Europe Since 1815* (1910), chap. I.

LONGER STUDIES

C. K. WEBSTER, *The Congress of Vienna, 1814–1815* (1919).
C. K. WEBSTER, *British Diplomacy, 1813–1815* (1921).
C. K. WEBSTER, *The Foreign Policy of Castlereagh, 1812–1815* (1931).
C. D. HAZEN, W. R. THAYER, and R. H. LORD, *Three Peace Congresses of the Nineteenth Century* (1917).
W. P. CRESSON, *The Holy Alliance* (1922).
W. A. PHILIPS, *The Confederation of Europe* (2d ed. 1919).
Cambridge History of British Foreign Policy (1921), vol. II.
For biographical studies on the leading statesmen at the Congress of Vienna see the close of Chapter XV.

SOURCES

J. H. ROBINSON, *Readings in European History* (1906), vol. II, chap. XXXIX.
J. F. SCOTT and A. BALTZLY, *Readings in European History Since 1814* (1930), chaps. I, II.
J. H. ROBINSON and C. A. BEARD, *Readings in Modern European History* (1908), vol. I, chap. XVI; (1909), vol. II, chap. XVII.
H. WEBSTER, *Historical Selections* (1929), no. 436.

CHAPTER XV

THE ERA OF RESTORATION AND REACTION

SUGGESTIONS FOR FURTHER READING

Cambridge Modern History, vol. X, chaps. I, II, IV–X, XIII.
C. J. H. HAYES, *A Political and Cultural History of Modern Europe* (1932), vol. I, chap. XIV.
T. W. RIKER, *A Short History of Modern Europe* (1935), chap. XI.
C. P. HIGBY, *History of Modern Europe* (1932), chap. V.
E. ACHORN, *European Civilization and Politics Since 1815* (1934), chap. II.
J. S. SCHAPIRO, *Modern and Contemporary European History* (1929), chap. IV.
E. FUETER, *World History, 1815–1920* (1924), chaps. VII–XI.

LONGER STUDIES

F. B. ARTZ, *Reaction and Revolution, 1814–1832* (1934).
A. MAY, *The Age of Metternich, 1814–1848* (1933).
C. K. WEBSTER, *The Foreign Policy of Castlereagh, 1815–1822* (1925).
H. W. V. TEMPERLEY, *The Foreign Policy of Canning* (1925).
D. PERKINS, *The Monroe Doctrine, 1823–1826* (1927).
W. A. PHILIPS, *The War of Greek Independence* (1897).

FOR THE ROMANTIC MOVEMENT

I. BABBITT, *Rousseau and Romanticism* (1917).
C. H. C. WRIGHT, *A History of French Literature* (1925).

[xxiv]

K. Franke, *A History of German Literature* (1909).
O. Elton, *A Survey of English Literature, 1780–1880*, 4 vols. (1912–20).
D. G. Mason, *The Romantic Composers* (1926).

BIOGRAPHICAL WORKS

A. Herman, *Metternich* (1932).
A. Cecil, *Metternich, 1773–1859; a Study of his Period and Personality* (1933).
G. B. Malleson, *Metternich* (1888).
E. L. Woodward, *Three Studies in European Conservatism: Metternich, Guizot and the Catholic Church in the Nineteenth Century* (1929).
W. P. Cresson, *Diplomatic Portraits* (1923).
J. Lucas-Dubreton, *Louis XVIII* (1927).
A. Hassall, *Viscount Castlereagh* (1908).
P. Guedalla, *Wellington* (1932).
H. W. V. Temperley, *Life of Canning* (1905).

SOURCES

J. H. Robinson and C. A. Beard, *Readings in Modern European History* (1909), vol. II, chaps. XIX, XX.
J. F. Scott and A. Baltzly, *Readings in European History Since 1814* (1930), chaps. II, III.
M. Spahr, *Readings in Recent Political Philosophy* (1935), chaps. II, IV.

CHAPTER XVI

THE BOURGEOISIE SECURE CONTROL IN GREAT BRITAIN AND FRANCE

SUGGESTIONS FOR FURTHER READING
Cambridge Modern History, vol. X, chaps. II, III, XV, XVIII–XX.
C. J. H. Hayes, *A Political and Social History of Modern Europe* (1925), vol. II, chaps. XVIII, XIX.
T. W. Riker, *A Short History of Modern Europe* (1935), chap. XI.
C. P. Higby, *History of Modern Europe* (1932), chap. V.
E. Achorn, *European Civilization and Politics Since 1815* (1934), chap. III.
J. S. Schapiro, *Modern and Contemporary European History* (1929), chap. V.

LONGER STUDIES
J. Lucas-Dubreton, *The Restoration and the July Monarchy* (1929).
J. Hall, *The Bourbon Restoration* (1909).
F. B. Artz, *France under the Bourbon Restoration, 1814–1830* (1931).
E. Halevy, *A History of the English People, 1815–1841*, 3 vols. (1924–27).
M. Hovell, *The Chartist Movement* (1918).
F. C. Dietz, *The Industrial Revolution* (1927).

P. Mantoux, *The Industrial Revolution in the Eighteenth Century* (1929).
E. W. Byrn, *The Progress of Invention in the Nineteenth Century* (1900).
J. A. Hobson, *Evolution of Modern Capitalism* (1928).
M. M. Knight, H. E. Barnes, *and* F. Flügel, *Economic History of Europe in Modern Times* (1928).

BIOGRAPHICAL WORKS

G. M. Trevelyan, *Lord Grey and the Reform Bill* (1920) and *John Bright* (1913).
G. D. H. Cole, *Robert Owen* (1925).
P. Guedalla, *Palmerston* (1926).
J. A. Hobson, *Richard Cobden, the International Man* (1919).
J. M. S. Allison, *Thiers and the French Monarchy* (1926).
Dictionary of National Biography for short lives of James Watt, John Kay, Richard Arkwright.

SOURCES

E. P. Cheyney, *Readings in English History* (1908), pp. 679–98.
J. F. Scott *and* A. Baltzly, *Readings in European History Since 1814* (1930), chaps. iii–v.

CHAPTER XVII

THE REVOLUTIONARY MOVEMENT
OF 1848–49 AND ITS COLLAPSE

SUGGESTIONS FOR FURTHER READING

Cambridge Modern History, vol. xi, chaps. ii–vii.
C. J. H. Hayes, *A Political and Social History of Modern Europe* (1925), vol. ii, chap. xix.
T. W. Riker, *A Short History of Modern Europe* (1935), chap. xi.
C. P. Higby, *History of Modern Europe* (1932), chaps. viii, ix.
E. Achorn, *European Civilization and Politics Since 1815* (1934), chap. iv.
J. S. Schapiro, *Modern and Contemporary European History* (1929), chap. xii.
E. Fueter, *World History, 1815–1920* (1924), chaps. xxi, xxiii.

LONGER STUDIES

A. de Lamartine, *History of the French Revolution of 1848* (1875).
F. H. Cheetham, *Louis Napoleon and the Genesis of the Second French Empire* (1908).
F. A. Simpson, *Rise of Louis Napoleon* (1909).
G. M. Priest, *Germany Since 1740* (1915).
E. F. Henderson, *A Short History of Germany* (1916), vol. ii.
J. A. R. Marriott, *The French Revolution of 1848 in its Economic Aspects*, 2 vols. (1913).

C. E. MAURICE, *The Revolutionary Movement of 1848–49 in Italy, Austria-Hungary and Germany* (1887).
C. M. KNATCHBULL-HUGESSEN, *The Political Evolution of the Hungarian Nation* (1908), vol. II.
R. M. JOHNSTON, *The Roman Theocracy and the Republic, 1848–49* (1901).
G. M. TREVELYAN, *Daniel Manin and the Venetian Revolution of 1848* (1923) and *Garibaldi's Defense of the Roman Republic* (1907).

SOURCES

J. H. ROBINSON and C. A. BEARD, *Readings in Modern European History* (1909), vol. II, chap. XX.
J. F. SCOTT and A. BALTZLY, *Readings in European History Since 1814* (1930), chap. V.

CHAPTER XVIII

THE ESTABLISHMENT OF THE SECOND FRENCH EMPIRE: NAPOLEON III

SUGGESTIONS FOR FURTHER READING

Cambridge Modern History, vol. XI, chaps. X, XVII, XXI.
C. J. H. HAYES, *A Political and Social History of Modern Europe* (1925), vol. II, chap. XX.
T. W. RIKER, *A Short History of Modern Europe* (1935), chap. XIII.
C. P. HIGBY, *History of Modern Europe* (1932), chap. XII.
E. ACHORN, *European Civilization and Politics Since 1815* (1934), chap. V.
J. S. SCHAPIRO, *Modern and Contemporary European History* (1929), chap. XIII.

LONGER STUDIES

A. L. GUÉRARD, *Reflections on the Napoleonic Legend* (1924).
G. L. DICKINSON, *Revolution and Reaction in Modern France* (1927).
H. A. L. FISHER, *Bonapartism* (1908).
E. B. HAMLEY, *The War in the Crimea* (1890).
P. F. MARTIN, *Maximilian in Mexico: the Story of the French Intervention, 1861–1867* (1914).
P. GUEDALLA, *The Second Empire* (1922).

BIOGRAPHICAL WORKS

F. A. SIMPSON, *Louis Napoleon and the Recovery of France* (1923).
A. L. GUÉRARD, *French Prophets of Yesterday* (1913).
L. F. MOTT, *Ernest Renan* (1921) and *Sainte Beuve* (1924).
H. GORMAN, *The Incredible Marquis: Alexandre Dumas* (1929).
I. BABBITT, *The Masters of Modern French Prose* (1912).

[xxvii]

SOURCES

J. H. ROBINSON *and* C. A. BEARD, *Readings in Modern European History* (1909), vol. II, chap. XIX, sec. 59.
J. F. SCOTT *and* A. BALTZLY, *Readings in European History Since 1814* (1930), chap. VII, sec. I.

CHAPTER XIX

THE POLITICAL UNIFICATION OF ITALY

SUGGESTIONS FOR FURTHER READING

Cambridge Modern History, vol. XI, chaps. IV, XIV, XIX, XXV.
C. J. H. HAYES, *A Political and Social History of Modern Europe* (1925), vol. II, chap. XX.
T. W. RIKER, *A Short History of Modern Europe* (1935), chap. XIII.
C. P. HIGBY, *History of Modern Europe* (1932), chap. XI.
E. ACHORN, *European Civilization and Politics Since 1815* (1934), chap. V.
J. S. SCHAPIRO, *Modern and Contemporary European History* (1929), chap. XIV.

LONGER STUDIES

B. KING, *A History of Italian Unity*, 2 vols. (1899).
P. ORSI, *Cavour and the Making of Modern Italy* (1923).
R. DE CESARE, *The Last Days of Papal Rome* (1909).
H. R. WHITEHOUSE, *The Collapse of the Kingdom of Naples* (1899).
W. BARRY, *The Papacy and Modern Times* (1911).
J. W. C. WAND, *A History of the Modern Church from 1500 to the Present Day* (1930).

BIOGRAPHICAL WORKS

B. KING, *Mazzini* (1902).
S. BARR, *Mazzini: Portrait of an Exile* (1935).
J. A. R. MARRIOTT, *Makers of Modern Italy* (1901).
G. M. TREVELYAN, *Garibaldi and the Thousand* (1912) and *Garibaldi and the Making of Italy* (1912).
E. L. H. MARTINENGO-CESARESCO, *Cavour* (1898).
W. R. THAYER, *The Life and Times of Cavour*, 2 vols. (1911).
M. PALEOLOGUE, *Cavour* (1927).
A. D. WHITE, *Seven Great Statesmen* (1927), essay on Cavour.

SOURCES

J. H. ROBINSON *and* C. A. BEARD, *Readings in Modern European History* (1909), vol. II, chap. XXI.
J. F. SCOTT *and* A. BALTZLY, *Readings in European History Since 1814* (1930), chap. VII, sec. 3.

CHAPTER XX

THE FORMATION OF THE GERMAN EMPIRE

SUGGESTIONS FOR FURTHER READING

Cambridge Modern History, vol. XI, chaps. XV, XVI.
C. J. H. HAYES, *A Political and Social History of Modern Europe* (1925), vol. II, chap. XX.
T. W. RIKER, *A Short History of Modern Europe* (1935), chap. XIII.
C. P. HIGBY, *History of Modern Europe* (1932), chaps. XIII, XIV.
E. ACHORN, *European Civilization and Politics* (1934), chap. V.
J. S. SCHAPIRO, *Modern and Contemporary European History* (1929), chap. XV.

LONGER STUDIES

A. W. WARD, *Germany, 1815–1870*, 3 vols. (1916–18).
M. SMITH, *Bismarck and German Unity* (1923).
W. ONCKEN, *Napoleon III and the Rhine* (1928).
J. W. HEADLAM, *Bismarck and the Foundation of the German Empire* (1901).
G. B. MALLESON, *The Refounding of the German Empire, 1848–1871* (1904).
R. H. LORD, *The Origins of the War of 1870* (1924).
G. DRAGE, *Austria-Hungary* (1909).

BIOGRAPHICAL WORKS

C. G. ROBERTSON, *Bismarck* (1918).
E. LUDWIG, *Bismarck* (1928).
A. D. WHITE, *Seven Great Statesmen* (1927), essay on Bismarck.
W. MORRIS, *Moltke* (1894).
A. FORBES, *William of Germany* (1888).
J. REDLICH, *Emperor Francis-Joseph of Austria* (1929).

SOURCES

J. H. ROBINSON *and* C. A. BEARD, *Readings in Modern European History* (1909), vol. II, pp. 142–65.
J. F. SCOTT *and* A. BALTZLY, *Readings in European History Since 1814* (1930), chap. VII.

CHAPTER XXI

RUSSIA IN THE NINETEENTH CENTURY

SUGGESTIONS FOR FURTHER READING

Cambridge Modern History, vol. XI, chaps. IX, XXII; vol. XII, chap. XII.
C. J. H. HAYES, *A Political and Social History of Modern Europe* (1925), vol. II, chap. XXV.

BIBLIOGRAPHY

C. P. HIGBY, *History of Modern Europe* (1932), chaps. X, XIX.
E. ACHORN, *European Civilization and Politics Since 1815* (1934), chap. VIII.
J. S. SCHAPIRO, *Modern and Contemporary European History* (1929), chaps. XXIII, XXIV.
P. W. SLOSSON, *Europe Since 1870* (1935), chap. VIII.

LONGER STUDIES

M. KARPOVICH, *Imperial Russia, 1801–1917* (1932).
G. VERNADSKY, *History of Russia* (1930).
F. H. B. SKRINE, *The Expansion of Russia, 1815–1900* (1904).
A. RAMBAUD, *The Expansion of Russia* (1904).
M. BARING, *The Russian People* (1914).
D. M. WALLACE, *Russia* (1912).
B. PARES, *Russia and Reform* (1907).
B. PARES, *A History of Russia* (1928).
W. A. PHILIPS, *Poland* (1915).
W. R. MORFILL, *Poland* (1903).

CHAPTER XXII

THE LESSER STATES OF EUROPE
IN THE NINETEENTH CENTURY

SUGGESTIONS FOR FURTHER READING

Cambridge Modern History, vol. XI, chaps. VIII, XX, XXIII, XXIV; vol. XII, chaps. IX–XI.
C. J. H. HAYES, *A Political and Social History of Modern Europe* (1925), vol. II, chaps. XXIII, XXIV, XXVI.
C. P. HIGBY, *History of Modern Europe* (1932), chap. XX.
J. S. SCHAPIRO, *Modern and Contemporary European History* (1929), chaps. XIX, XXII.

NATIONAL HISTORIES

R. N. BAIN, *Scandinavia: a Political History of Denmark, Norway and Sweden, from 1513 to 1900* (1905).
C. HALLENDORFF *and* A. SCHÜCK, *History of Sweden* (1929).
K. GJERSET, *A History of the Norwegian People,* 2 vols. (1915).
P. J. BLOK, *History of the People of the Netherlands* (1912), vol. V.
G. EDMUNDSON, *History of Holland* (1922).
H. VANDER LINDEN, *Belgium, the Making of a Nation* (1920).
L. VAN DER ESSEN, *A Short History of Belgium* (1916).
W. OECHSLI, *History of Switzerland, 1499–1914* (1922).
M. A. S. HUME, *Modern Spain* (1923).
H. D. SEDGWICK, *Spain: a Short History* (1925).
W. H. KOEBEL, *Portugal, its Land and People* (1909).

H. M. STEPHENS, *Portugal* (1908).
W. MILLER, *The Ottoman Empire and its Successors, 1815–1921* (1921).
W. MILLER, *The Balkans: Rumania, Bulgaria, Serbia and Montenegro* (1908).
W. MILLER, *History of the Greek People, 1821–1923* (1923).
F. SCHEVILL, *The History of the Balkan Peninsula* (1922).
J. BUCHAN, editor, *Bulgaria and Rumania* (1924).

CHAPTER XXIII

THE NEW WORLD WHICH SCIENCE AND INDUSTRY HAVE CREATED

SUGGESTIONS FOR FURTHER READING

Cambridge Modern History, vol. XII, chap. XXIV.
C. J. H. HAYES, *A Political and Social History of Modern Europe* (1925), vol. II, chap. XXI.
T. W. RIKER, *A Short History of Modern Europe* (1935), chap. XIV.
E. ACHORN, *European Civilization and Politics Since 1815* (1934), chap. XII.
J. S. SCHAPIRO, *Modern and Contemporary European History* (1929), chaps. XXVI, XXVII.
F. A. OGG, *The Economic Development of Modern Europe* (1926), XXI–XXIII.
C. HODGES, *The Background of International Relations* (1931), Parts II, VI.

LONGER STUDIES

F. S. MARVIN, *The Century of Hope* (1919).
A. H. BUCK, *The Dawn of Modern Medicine, 1750–1850* (1920).
E. W. BYRN, *The Progress of Invention in the Nineteenth Century* (1900).
J. A. THOMPSON, *An Introduction to Science* (1911).
O. W. CALDWELL and E. E. SLOSSON, *Science Remaking the World* (1927).
E. C. JEFFREY, *Coal and Civilization* (1925).
S. CHASE, *Men and Machines* (1931).
J. A. HOBSON, *The Evolution of Modern Capitalism* (1926).
R. H. TAWNEY, *The British Labor Movement* (1925).
J. R. MACDONALD, *The Socialist Movement* (1911).

BIOGRAPHICAL WORKS

G. T. BETTANY, *Charles Darwin* (1887).
R. VALLERY-RADOT, *Pasteur* (1923).
P. DE KRUIF, *The Microbe Hunters* (1926).
S. P. THOMPSON, *Faraday* (1898).
J. SPARGO, *Karl Marx* (1912).

SOURCES

J. H. ROBINSON, *Readings in European History* (1906), vol. II, chap. XLI.
C. SPAHR, *Readings in Recent Political Philosophy* (1935), chaps. VIII–XI.
H. WEBSTER, *Historical Selections* (1929), nos. 473, 474.

CHAPTER XXIV

THE SOCIAL CONFLICT WITHIN
THREE INDUSTRIAL STATES:
GREAT BRITAIN, FRANCE, AND GERMANY (1871–1914)

SUGGESTIONS FOR FURTHER READING

Cambridge Modern History, vol. XII, chaps. III, V, VI, VII.

C. J. H. HAYES, *A Political and Social History of Modern Europe* (1925), vol. II, chaps. XXI–XXIV.

T. W. RIKER, *A Short History of Modern Europe* (1935), chap. XIV.

C. P. HIGBY, *History of Modern Europe* (1932), chaps. XV, XVI, XXI.

E. ACHORN, *European Civilization and Politics Since 1815* (1934), chaps VI, VII, IX.

J. S. SCHAPIRO, *Modern and Contemporary European History* (1929), chap. XXVIII.

P. W. SLOSSON, *Europe Since 1870* (1935), chaps. III, IV, VI.

J. W. SWAIN, *Beginning the Twentieth Century: a History of the Generation that Made the War* (1933), pp. 1–200.

LONGER STUDIES

L. G. CHIOZZA-MONEY, *Riches and Poverty* (1911).

L. G. CHIOZZA-MONEY, *Insurance Against Poverty* (1912).

C. W. PIPKIN, *The Idea of Social Justice* (1928).

B. G. DE MONTGOMERY, *British and Continental Labor Policy* (1922).

J. C. BRACQ, *France Under the Third Republic* (1916).

C. H. C. WRIGHT, *The History of the Third French Republic* (1916).

P. SABATIER, *Disestablishment in France* (1906).

A. L. GUÉRARD, *French Civilization in the Nineteenth Century* (1914).

C. TOWER, *Germany of Today* (1913).

J. C. CLAPHAM, *Economic Development of France and Germany, 1815–1914* (1921).

W. H. DAWSON, *Bismarck and State Socialism* (1891).

F. C. HOWE, *Socialized Germany* (1915).

P. O. RAY, *Major European Governments* (1931).

F. A. OGG, *The Governments of Europe* (1917).

BIOGRAPHICAL WORKS

O. BURDETT, *W. E. Gladstone* (1928).

SIR E. CLARKE, *Benjamin Disraeli: the Romance of a Great Career* (1926).

A. MAUROIS, *Disraeli* (1927).

L. STRACHEY, *Queen Victoria* (1921).

H. M. HYNDMAN, *Clemenceau* (1919).

SIR F. T. MARZIALS, *Life of Léon Gambetta* (1890).

C. G. ROBERTSON, *Bismarck* (1918).

SOURCES

J. F. Scott and A. Baltzly, *Readings in European History Since 1814* (1930), chap. IX.

CHAPTER XXV

THE COMPETITION AMONG THE INDUSTRIALIZED STATES: THE RACE FOR COLONIES AND MARKETS
(1871–1914)

SUGGESTIONS FOR FURTHER READING

Cambridge Modern History, vol. XII, chaps. XV–XX, XXII, XXV.
C. J. H. Hayes, *A Political and Social History of Modern Europe* (1925), vol. II, chap. XXX.
T. W. Riker, *A Short History of Modern Europe* (1935), chap. XV.
C. P. Higby, *History of Modern Europe* (1932), chaps. XXII, XXIII.
E. Achorn, *European Civilization and Politics Since 1815* (1934), chap. X.
J. S. Schapiro, *Modern and Contemporary European History* (1929), chaps. XXX, XXXI.
P. W. Slosson, *Europe Since 1870* (1935), chaps. V, IX.
P. W. Slosson, *Twentieth Century Europe* (1927), chaps. VI, VII.
C. Hodges, *The Background of International Relations* (1931), Parts VI–VIII.

LONGER STUDIES

J. A. Hobson, *Imperialism* (1902).
P. T. Moon, *Imperialism and World Politics* (1926).
R. Muir, *The Expansion of Modern Europe* (1923).
W. C. Abbott, *The Expansion of Europe* (1924).
H. L. Hoskins, *European Imperialism in Africa* (1930).
C. K. Hobson, *The Export of Capital* (1914).
Sir H. H. Johnston, *A History of the Colonization of Africa by Alien Races* (1913).
N. D. Harris, *Europe and Africa* (1927).
N. D. Harris, *Europe and the East* (1926).
Sir Valentine Chirol, *India* (1922).
V. A. Smith, *The Oxford History of India* (1928).
K. S. Latourette, *The Development of China* (1929).
H. A. Giles, *The Civilization of China* (1911).
H. H. Gowen, *Outline History of Japan* (1927).
J. H. Gubbins, *The Making of Modern Japan* (1922).

BIOGRAPHICAL WORKS

Sir H. H. Johnston, *Livingstone* (1890).
H. W. Little, *Stanley* (1890).
B. Williams, *Cecil Rhodes* (1921).

[xxxiii]

CHAPTER XXVI

THE GROWTH OF ALLIANCES: INTERNATIONAL TENSION AND THE ARMED PEACE (1871–1914)

SUGGESTIONS FOR FURTHER READING

Cambridge Modern History, vol. XII, chaps. I, VI.

C. J. H. HAYES, *A Political and Social History of Modern Europe* (1925), vol. II, chap. XXX.

T. W. RIKER, *A Short History of Modern Europe* (1935), chap. XV.

C. P. HIGBY, *History of Modern Europe* (1932), chaps. XXIV, XXV.

E. ACHORN, *European Civilization and Politics Since 1815* (1934), chaps. XIII, XIV.

J. S. SCHAPIRO, *Modern and Contemporary European History* (1929), chaps. XXXIII, XXXIV.

P. W. SLOSSON, *Europe Since 1870* (1935), chaps. X–XIII.

LONGER STUDIES

H. FEIS, *Europe, the World's Banker* (1930).

J. V. FULLER, *Bismarck's Diplomacy at its Zenith* (1922).

W. L. LANGER, *European Alliances and Alignments* (1931).

A. C. COOLIDGE, *The Origins of the Triple Alliance* (1926).

B. E. SCHMIDT, *Triple Alliance and Triple Entente* (1934).

B. E. SCHMIDT, *The Coming of the War,* 2 vols. (1930).

S. B. FAY, *The Origins of the World War,* 2 vols. (2d ed. 1930).

H. E. BARNES, *The Genesis of the World War* (2d ed. 1927).

R. J. SONTAG, *European Diplomatic History, 1871–1932* (1933).

G. L. DICKINSON, *The International Anarchy, 1904–1914* (1926).

SOURCES

W. H. COOKE *and* E. P. STICKNEY, *Readings in European International Relations Since 1879* (1931), Part I.

CHAPTER XXVII

THE WORLD WAR

SUGGESTIONS FOR FURTHER READING

C. J. H. HAYES, *A Political and Social History of Modern Europe* (1925), vol. II, chap. XXXI.

T. W. RIKER, *A Short History of Modern Europe* (1935), chap. XVI.

C. P. HIGBY, *History of Modern Europe* (1932), chap. XXVI.

E. ACHORN, *European Civilization and Politics Since 1815* (1934), chap. XV.

J. S. SCHAPIRO, *Modern and Contemporary European History* (1929), chap. XXXV.

P. W. SLOSSON, *Europe Since 1870* (1935), chap. XIV.

P. W. SLOSSON, *Twentieth Century Europe* (1927), chaps. X–XII.

[xxxiv]

W. C. LANGSAM, *The World Since 1914* (1934), chaps. I–III.
F. L. BENNS, *Europe Since 1914* (1931), chaps. I, II, IV.

LONGER STUDIES

M. E. DURHAM, *The Sarajevo Crime* (1925).
J. F. SCOTT, *Five Weeks* (1927).
C. J. H. HAYES, *A Brief History of the Great War* (1920).
A. F. POLLARD, *A Short History of the Great War* (1928).
B. H. LIDDELL HART, *The Real War* (1930).
W. S. SEAVER, *Colossal Blunders of the War* (1930).
W. S. CHURCHILL, *The Unknown War* (1931).
H. D. LASSWELL, *Propaganda Technique in the World War* (1927).
SIR H. J. NEWBOLT, *A Naval History of the War, 1914–1918* (1920).
J. E. T. HARPER, *The Truth About Jutland* (1927).
L. GUICHARD, *The Navy Blockade, 1914–1918* (1930).

BIOGRAPHICAL WORKS

R. RECOULY, *Joffre* (1931).
B. H. LIDDELL HART, *Foch, the Man of Orleans* (1932).
C. R. BALLARD, *Kitchener* (1930).
K. TSCHUPPIK, *Ludendorff, the Tragedy of a Military Mind* (1932).
M. GOLDSMITH and F. VEIGT, *Hindenburg, the Man and the Legend* (1930).
C. SEYMOUR, *Woodrow Wilson and the World War* (1922).

CHAPTER XXVIII

THE PEACE SETTLEMENT OF 1919

SUGGESTIONS FOR FURTHER READING

C. J. H. HAYES, *A Political and Social History of Modern Europe* (1925), vol. II, chap. XXXIII.
T. W. RIKER, *A Short History of Modern Europe* (1935), chap. XVII.
C. P. HIGBY, *History of Modern Europe* (1932), chap. XXVII.
E. ACHORN, *European Civilization and Politics Since 1815* (1934), chap. XVI.
J. S. SCHAPIRO, *Modern and Contemporary European History* (1929), chap. XXXVI.
P. W. SLOSSON, *Europe Since 1870* (1935), chaps. XVIII, XIX.
P. W. SLOSSON, *Twentieth Century Europe* (1931), chaps. XV, XVI, XVIII.
F. L. BENNS, *Europe Since 1914* (1931), chaps. VII–IX.
W. C. LANGSAM, *The World Since 1914* (1934), chaps. IV–VI.

LONGER STUDIES

A. C. F. BEALES, *The History of Peace: a Short Account of the Organized Movements for International Peace* (1931).
E. M. HOUSE and C. SEYMOUR, editors, *What Really Happened at Paris* (1921).
C. H. HASKINS and R. H. LORD, *Some Problems of the Peace Conference* (1920).

J. M. Keynes, *The Economic Consequences of the Peace* (1920).
R. Lansing, *The Peace Negotiations: a Personal Narrative* (1921).
E. J. Dillon, *The Inside Story of the Peace Conference* (1920).
J. S. Bassett, *The League of Nations* (1928).
P. J. N. Baker, *The League of Nations at Work* (1926).
C. Eagleton, *International Government* (1932).

BIOGRAPHICAL WORKS

R. Lansing, *The Big Four and Others at the Peace Conference* (1921).
J. H. Edwards, *David Lloyd George* (1929).
Sir C. E. Mallet, *Mr. Lloyd George* (1930).
J. Martet, *Clemenceau* (1930).
R. S. Baker, *What Wilson Did at Paris* (1920).

SOURCES

W. H. Cooke *and* E. P. Stickney, *Readings in European International Relations* (1931), Part IV.

CHAPTER XXIX

RUSSIA UNDER THE RULE OF THE SOVIETS

SUGGESTIONS FOR FURTHER READING

T. W. Riker, *A Short History of Modern Europe* (1935), chap. XIX.
C. P. Higby, *History of Modern Europe* (1932), chap. XXX.
E. Achorn, *European Civilization and Politics Since 1815* (1934), chap. XVII.
J. S. Schapiro, *Modern and Contemporary European History* (1929), chap. XXXVII.
P. W. Slosson, *Europe Since 1870* (1935), chap. XXI.
F. L. Benns, *Europe Since 1914* (1931), chaps. III, XVII.
W. C. Langsam, *The World Since 1914* (1934), chap. XVIII.

LONGER STUDIES

W. H. Chamberlain, *The Russian Revolution, 1917–1921*, 2 vols. (1935).
W. H. Chamberlain, *Soviet Russia* (1930).
G. Vernadsky, *The Russian Revolution, 1917–1931* (1932).
L. Trotsky, *The History of the Russian Revolution*, 3 vols. (1932).
J. Mavor, *The Russian Revolution* (1928).
W. R. Batsell, *Soviet Rule in Russia* (1929).
H. N. Brailsford, *How the Soviets Work* (1927).
C. V. Hoover, *The Economic Life of Soviet Russia* (1931).
M. Doble *and* H. C. Stevens, *Russian Economic Development Since the Revolution* (1928).
M. G. Hindus, *Humanity Uprooted* (1929).
M. G. Hindus, *The Russian Peasant and the Revolution* (1920).
M. G. Hindus, *The Great Offensive* (1933).

BIBLIOGRAPHY

BIOGRAPHICAL WORKS

L. TROTSKY, *My Life: An Attempt at an Autobiography* (1930) and *Lenin* (1935).
D. S. MIRSKY, *Lenin* (1931).
G. VERNADSKY, *Lenin, Red Dictator* (1931).
I. D. LEVINE, *Stalin* (1931).

SOURCES

W. H. COOKE *and* E. P. STICKNEY, *Readings in European International Relations* (1931), nos. 159–62.

CHAPTER XXX

FASCIST ITALY

SUGGESTIONS FOR FURTHER READING

T. W. RIKER, *A Short History of Modern Europe* (1935), chap. XIX.
C. P. HIGBY, *History of Modern Europe* (1932), chap. XXVIII.
E. ACHORN, *European Civilization and Politics Since 1815* (1934), chap. XIX.
J. S. SCHAPIRO, *Modern and Contemporary European History* (1929), chap. XXXIX.
P. W. SLOSSON, *Europe Since 1870* (1935), chap. XXVI.
F. L. BENNS, *Europe Since 1914* (1931), chap. XVI.
W. C. LANGSAM, *The World Since 1914* (1934), chap. XIII.

LONGER STUDIES

J. H. JACKSON, *The Post-War World* (1935).
L. VILLARI, *Italy* (1929).
H. R. SPENCER, *Government and Politics of Italy* (1932).
H. W. SCHNEIDER, *Making the Fascist State* (1928).
H. W. SCHNEIDER *and* S. B. CLOUGH, *Making Fascists* (1929).
B. KING, *Fascism in Italy* (1931).
G. SALVEMINI, *The Fascist Dictatorship in Italy* (1927).
W. PARSONS, *The Pope and Italy* (1932).
F. W. HULLINGER, *The New Fascist State* (1928).
C. E. MAGUIRE, *Italy's International Economic Position* (1929).
A. PENNACHIO, *The Corporative State* (1927).
B. MUSSOLINI, *My Autobiography* (1928).

SOURCES

M. SPAHR, *Readings in Recent Political Philosophy* (1935), chap. XVII.
W. H. COOKE *and* E. P. STICKNEY, *Readings in European International Relations* (1931), nos. 180, 182.

[xxxvii]

CHAPTER XXXI

THE UNITED KINGDOM AND
THE BRITISH EMPIRE COMMONWEALTH

SUGGESTIONS FOR FURTHER READING

E. ACHORN, *European Civilization and Politics Since 1815* (1934), chaps. XVIII, XX.

C. P. HIGBY, *History of Modern Europe* (1932), chap. XXVIII.

J. S. SCHAPIRO, *Modern and Contemporary European History* (1929), chap. XXXII.

P. W. SLOSSON, *Europe Since 1870* (1935), chap. XXIX.

F. L. BENNS, *Europe Since 1914* (1931), chap. XIV.

W. C. LANGSAM, *The World Since 1914* (1934), chaps. X, XI.

LONGER STUDIES

A. SIEGFRIED, *Post-War Britain* (1924).

A. SIEGFRIED, *England's Crisis* (1931).

A. F. PRIBRAM, *England* (1931).

F. PLACHY, *Britain's Economic Plight* (1926).

W. P. HALL, *Empire to Commonwealth* (1928).

A. ZIMMERN, *The Third British Empire* (1926).

R. G. TROTTER, *The British Empire Commonwealth* (1932).

SIR R. L. BORDEN, *Canada in the Commonwealth* (1929).

W. K. HANDCOCK, *Australia* (1931).

A. J. HARROP, *England and New Zealand* (1926).

J. H. HOFMEYR, *South Africa* (1931).

D. GWYNN, *The Irish Free State, 1922–1927* (1928).

SIR V. CHIROL, *India* (1931).

SOURCES

W. H. COOKE *and* E. P. STICKNEY, *Readings in European International Relations* (1931), nos. 164, 179.

CHAPTER XXXII

FRANCE SEEKS SECURITY

SUGGESTIONS FOR FURTHER READING

T. W. RIKER, *A Short History of Modern Europe* (1935), chap. XX.

C. P. HIGBY, *History of Modern Europe* (1932), chap. XXVIII.

E. ACHORN, *European Civilization and Politics Since 1815* (1934), chap. XVIII.

J. S. SCHAPIRO, *Modern and Contemporary European History* (1929), chap. XXXVIII.

P. W. SLOSSON, *Europe Since 1870* (1935), chaps. xxv, xxviii.
F. L. BENNS, *Europe Since 1914* (1931), chap. xiii.
W. C. LANGSAM, *The World Since 1914* (1934), chaps. viii, xii.

LONGER STUDIES

P. VAUCHER, *Post-War France* (1934).
C. J. H. HAYES, *France: a Nation of Patriots* (1930).
R. H. SOLTAU, *French Parties and Politics, 1871–1930* (1930).
C. GIDE, editor, *The Effects of the War upon French Economic Life* (1923).
S. HUDDLESTON, *France* (1927).
W. MACDONALD, *Reconstruction in France* (1922).
W. F. OGBURN and W. JAFFÉ, *The Economic Development of Post-War France* (1929).
F. ALEXANDER, *From Paris to Locarno and After: the League of Nations and the Search for Security* (1928).
P. J. N. BAKER, *Disarmament* (1926).
D. H. MILLER, *The Peace Pact of Paris: a Study of the Briand-Kellogg Treaty* (1928).
J. T. SHOTWELL, *War as an Instrument of National Policy, and its Renunciation in the Pact of Paris* (1929).

SOURCES

W. H. COOKE and E. P. STICKNEY, *Readings in European International Relations* (1931), nos. 166, 170, 173–76, 181.

CHAPTER XXXIII
GERMANY SEEKS EQUALITY

SUGGESTIONS FOR FURTHER READING

T. W. RIKER, *A Short History of Modern Europe* (1935), chap. x.
C. P. HIGBY, *History of Modern Europe* (1932), chap. xxix.
E. ACHORN, *European Civilization and Politics Since 1815* (1934), chap. xviii.
J. S. SCHAPIRO, *Modern and Contemporary European History* (1929), chap. xxxix.
P. W. SLOSSON, *Europe Since 1870* (1935), chap. xxvii.
F. L. BENNS, *Europe Since 1914* (1931), chaps. x, xii.
W. C. LANGSAM, *The World Since 1914* (1934), chap. xv.

LONGER STUDIES

R. H. LUTZ, *The German Revolution of 1918–19* (1922).
R. H. LUTZ, *The Fall of the German Empire*, 2 vols. (1932).
J. F. CARR, *The Old and the New Germany* (1924).
K. KAUTSKY, *The Labour Revolution* (1925).
J. W. ANGELL, *The Recovery of Germany* (1932).

BIBLIOGRAPHY

A. FABRE-LUCE, *Locarno: a Dispassionate View* (1928).
R. MARTEL, *The Eastern Frontiers of Germany* (1930).
C. B. HOOVER, *Germany Enters the Third Reich* (1933).
K. HEIDEN, *A History of National Socialism* (1934).

BIOGRAPHICAL WORKS

H. VON KESSLER, *Walther Rathenau: His Life and Work* (1930).
R. OLDEN, *Stresemann* (1930).
R. WETERSTETTEN and A. M. K. WATSON, *The Biography of President von Hindenburg* (1930).
A. HITLER, *My Battle* (1933).
S. WALLACH, *Hitler* (1933).

SOURCES

W. H. COOKE and E. P. STICKNEY, *Readings in European International Relations Since 1879* (1931), nos. 167, 177, 183.

Index

Index

Abo, treaty of (1743), 74
Abyssinia. *See* Ethiopia
Acadia, ceded to Great Britain, 39
Acre, 172
Act of Settlement, English (1701), 50
Act of Uniformity (1662), 42
Act of Union, England and Scotland (1707), **49-50**
Addison, Joseph, 53
Adowa, battle of (1896), 368
Adrianople, treaty of (1829), 222
Aegean Islands, 61
Afghanistan, 259, 366
Africa, and European powers, **370-74**
Age of Reason. *See* Rationalism
Agriculture, in Great Britain, 335; in Italy, 455; in Russia, 442-45
Aix-la-Chapelle, congress of (1818), 203; treaty of (1668), **36**; treaty of (1748), **86**, 99
Albania, in 20th century, 456
Albuquerque, Affonso de, 94
Alcabala, 58
Alexander VI, Pope, and papal line of demarcation, 94
Alexander I, of Russia, 189-92, **199-202**, 204, 215-16
Alexander II, of Russia, **293-300**
Alexander III, of Russia, **300-02**
Algeciras Conference (1906), 387
Algeria, French occupation of, 367
Almeida, Francisco de, 94
Alphonso XII, of Spain, 310
Alphonso XIII, of Spain, 311
Alsace, acquired by France, 82
America. *See* Colonies
American army, in France, 411-12
Amiens, treaty of (1802), 176
Amsterdam, in 17th century, 62; in 20th century, 308
Anarchism, 299
Andersen, Hans Christian, 307
Anglican Church, in the 17th century, 41, 46
Anglo-Dutch wars, 42-44
Anglo-German rivalry, 384-85
Anglo-Japanese alliance (1902), 385
Anne, Queen of England, 49-50
Anschluss, 478, 493. *See* Austria, after 1918
Aristocracy. *See* Nobles
Aristotle, 118
Armada, Spanish, 95
Armaments, modern, 391-94, 414-15, 478-80, 495
Army, French, 289; German, 283

Artois, Count of (Charles X of France), 144, 145, 147
Asia, and European powers, 374-76
Asiento Treaty (1713), 60, 97-99
Aspern, battle of (1809), 191
Asquith, Herbert, 344
Assignats, 154
Associations Law, France (1901), 350
Auerstädt, battle of (1806), 189
Augsburg, War of the League of, **37-38**
Ausgleich. *See* Austria-Hungary after 1867
Austerlitz, battle of (1805), 188
Australia, 362-63
Austria, in the 17th century, 54-58; in the 18th century, 85; and the French Revolution, 161-75, *passim;* and Napoleon, 185-92, *passim;* in the 19th century, **213-15**, 220, **247-49**; Republic of, after 1918, 424-25, 457, 493. *See also* Austria-Hungary, Holy Roman Empire, Hungary, Bohemia
Austria-Hungary (1867-1918), 282-84
Avignon, annexed to France, 157
Azov, 70, 80

Backward countries. *See* Colonies, Imperialism
Bacon, Sir Francis, 114
Baden, 186; in 19th century, 284-86
Bagdad, 468
Bagdad Railway, 388-89
Bailly, Jean Sylvain, 147
Bakunin, Michael, 299
Balance of power, 7-9, 84-85
Balfour, Arthur, 468
Balfour Declaration, 468
Balkan War (1912), 390; (1913), 390-91
Balzac, Honoré de, 251
Bank of England, 52
Barras, Paul, Vicomte de, 167, **174**
Bastille, capture of the, 147
Battle of the Boyne (1690), 48
Battle of the Nations. *See* Leipzig, battle of
Bavaria, in 18th century, 132, 186-88; in 19th century, 284-86, 354-55
Beachy Head, battle of (1690), 48
Beauharnais, Eugène, 181, 186
Beauharnais, Hortense, 242-43
Beauharnais, Josephine. *See* Josephine, French empress
Beccaria, Cesare, 128-29
Belgium, in the 19th century, 236-37, **308**; in the 20th century, 401-12, 427, 477. *See also* Netherlands, Spanish,

Netherlands, Austrian, Netherlands, Kingdom of 116
Benedetti, Vincent, Count, 288-89
Bentham, Jeremy, 230
Berchtold, Leopold von, 398-402
Berlin, in 17th century, 11; in 19th century, 379
Berlin Decrees, 190
Bernadotte, Jean Baptiste Jules. *See* Charles XIV, of Sweden
Bernhardi, Frederick von, 394
Berry, Duke of, 218
Bessarabia, 201, 478
Beust, Friedrich Ferdinand Freiherr von, 284
Bill of Rights (1689), **47-48**
Bismarck, Otto von, **281-91, 379-80**
Blanc, Louis, 240-42
Blenheim, battle of (1704), 38
Blockade, naval, in World War, 408-15, *passim*
Boer War (1899-1901), 365
Bohemia, in the 17th century, 55; in the 19th century, 247-48. *See also* Austria, Czechoslovakia
Boileau, Nicolas, 32
Bolsheviki, **434-46**
Bombay, acquired by the English, 42
Bonaparte, Jerome, 189
Bonaparte, Joseph, 181, 186
Bonaparte, Louis, 181, 191, 242
Bonaparte, Lucien, 174, 181
Borodino, battle of (1812), 192
Bosnia, annexed by Austria-Hungary, 390
Bossuet, Bishop of Meaux, 22-23
Boulanger, Georges, French general, 349
Boulogne, 188
Bourbon Restoration (France), 193-95, 200, 217-18
Bourgeoisie, in the 18th century, 125-26; in the 19th century, 224-38, *passim*, 330
Boxer Rebellion (China), 375-76
Boyle, Robert, 112
Braddock, Edward, British general, 99
Brandenburg, in the 17th century, 5, 55. *See* Prussia
Brandes, Georg, 307
Brazil, 94
Bremen, city of, in 19th century, 190
Brest-Litovsk, treaty of (1918), 410, 436
Briand, Aristide, 479, 486
Briand-Kellogg Peace Pact (1928), 479-80
Bright, John, 340
British East India Company. *See* East India Company, British
British Empire, 95-106, *passim*, **362-67.** *See* Great Britain
British North America Act (1867), 362
Bruno, Giordano, 108
Brunswick Manifesto (1792), 158

Buffon, George Louis Leclerc, Comte de, 116
Bulgaria, in the 19th century, 314-16; in the 20th century, 390-91, 407-12, 425
Bundesrat, German, 353; of North German Confederation, 286
Bunyan, John, 52
Burgundy, Free County of. *See* Franche Comté
Burke, Edmund, **209-10**
Burma, 366
Burschenschaften, 214
Byron, George Gordon, Lord, 209, 213
Byzantine Empire, influence on Russia, 68-69

Cahiers, 142
Cambodia, 257
Campo Formio, treaty of (1797), 172
Campos, Martínez, 310
Canada, under British rule, 105; Dominion of, 362
Canning, George, 203
Canon law, 458
Cánovas del Castillo, Antonio, 311
Cape Verde Islands, 94
Capital, and the factory system, 226; conflict between labor and, **330-34**; export of, to backward countries, **336-37**
Carbonari, the, 220, 263
Carinthia, duchy, 55
Carlowitz, treaty of (1699), 57, 61
Carlsbad Decrees (1819), 215
Carlyle, Thomas, 340
Carniola, duchy, in 17th century, 55
Carnot, Lazare, 163
Catalonia, 60
Catherine II (the Great), of Russia, **76-81**, 131-32
Catholic Church, in 17th century, 62-63; and the French Revolution, 153-54; and Napoleon, 178; in 19th century, 211, 239-42, 254-55, **274-76**; in 20th century, **459-60**
Catholic Emancipation Bill (1829), 219
Cavour, Camillo di, 261, **267-72**
Center Party, in Germany, 357-60
Central Powers, in World War, **400-12**, *passim*
Cervantes Saavedra, Miguel de, 59
Chamber of Deputies, French, 217-18, 233, 241, 289
Charles, Archduke of Austria, 192
Charles Albert, of Sardinia, 249, 265-67
Charles I, of England, 7
Charles II, of England, 7, 10, **37-45**
Charles X, of France, 218, 233-34. *See also* Artois, Count of
Charles VI, Holy Roman Emperor, 39, 57, 85
Charles II, of Spain, 13, 36-38, 58-60

Charles XII, of Sweden, 72 74
Charles XIII, of Sweden, 305
Charles XIV, of Sweden, 305
Charter of 1814, French, 217–18
Chartist Movement, 231–32
Chateaubriand, François-René de, 211
China, **366-74,** *passim,* 445
Christian IX, of Denmark, 307
Church of England. *See* Anglican Church
Churchill, John, Duke of Marlborough, 38
Cisalpine Republic, 185
Cities, growth of, **327-30**
Civil Constitution of the Clergy, 153–54
Clement XI, Pope, 62
Clergy, 22–23; French, 123–24, 239–40, 256; German, 357
Clericalism, in 19th century, 274–75, 349–52
Clive, Robert, 100
Code Napoléon, 178
Colbert, Jean Baptiste, Marquis de Seignelay, **27-29,** 96
Colonies, British, 102, **362-68;** Dutch, 95–97; French, **367-68;** German, **369-70,** 421; Italian, **368-69;** Portuguese, **93-95;** Spanish, **93-95;** competition for, 93–106, *passim,* 235, **370-78**
Colonization, in 17th and 18th centuries, 93–106; in the 19th century, 335–38, 361, 370–78
Columbus, Christopher, 93
Commerce, in the 18th century, **93-106,** 126–27, 224–25; in the 19th century, **335-38**
Commons, House of, contrast with Third Estate, 40; in the 17th century, 47–48. *See* Parliament
Commutation of peasant services, 134, **148-51**
Concert of Europe (after 1815), **203-05,** 221–23
Concordat (1801), 178, 350
Condé, Louis II, Prince of, 28, 37
Congo, Belgian, 308, 366, 371
Congress of Berlin (1878), 314–16
Congress of Vienna, 196–205
Conservative Party, British, 339–47, *passim,* 463–64. *See* Tories
Constantine, Grand Duke, 216
Constantinople, and Russia, 81, 259–60
Constitutional government in England. *See* Parliament
Consulate, French (1799–1804), 177–80
Continental System (of Napoleon), **190-91**
Conventicle Act, English (1664), 42
Convention of Westminster (1756), 88
Cook, Captain James, 362
Copernicus, Nicolas, 108
Corn Laws, British, 230–31

Corneille, Pierre, 32
Corporation Act, English (1661), 42, 48
Cortez, Hernando, 95
Cosgrave, William Thomas, 466
Cotton, 18. *See also* Spinning
Council of Ancients, France, 167
Council of Five Hundred, France, 167
Crimea, ceded to Russia, 81
Crimean War, 258–61
Cromwell, Oliver, 40
Crucé, Émeric, 8
Custozza, battle of (1848), 249, 267
Cyprus, 315
Czar Liberator. *See* Alexander **II,** of Russia
Czechoslovakia, 425, 477, 479. *See also* Bohemia, Austria

Dalmatia, 61
Danish War (1864), 282
Danton, Jacques, 158–59, 165
Danzig, 421
Dardanelles, in World War, 404
Darwin, Charles, **324-25**
Dawes, Charles Gates, 474
Dawes Plan (1924), 474
Deák, Francis, 284
Declaration of Independence (1776), 103
Declaration of Indulgence (1672), 44; (1687), 46; (1688), 47
Declaration of Paris (1856), 260, 406
Declaration of the Rights of Man (1789), 141, 151
Delcassé, Théophile, 383–84
Democracy, in Great Britain, 339–47; in France, 348–50; in Germany, 353–55. *See also* Reform Bill, British, France in the revolutionary era, Charter of 1814, etc.
Denmark, in the 17th century, 11, 72; in the 18th century, 133; in the 19th century, 306–07
Descartes, René, 113
Desmoulins, Camille, 152
De Valera, Eamon, 466
Diderot, Denis, 77, **128,** 131
Diet of the Holy Roman Empire, 55
Diplomatic Revolution, of the 18th century, 86
Directory, French, **167-68,** 174
Disarmament Conference (1932), 480
Disease, in the 17th century, 16; in the 19th and 20th centuries, **326-27**
Disraeli, Benjamin (Earl of Beaconsfield), 315, 340, 364
Dissenters, English, 41, 47
Divine right of kings, 7–9, 21–22, 121–22
Dollfuss, Englebert, 493
Dover, treaty of (1670), 37, 44
Dresden, treaty of (1745), 86
Dreyfus, Captain Alfred, **349-50**

Dreyfus case, **349-50**
Dryden, John, English poet, 52
Dual Empire. *See* Austria-Hungary
Duma, Russian, 303–04
Dumas, Alexandre, the Younger, 254
Dupleix, Joseph Francis, Marquis, 98–99
Dutch Republic. *See* Netherlands, Dutch
Dutch War (1672–78), **36-37**

East India Company, British, 28, 96, 105, 363; Dutch, 28, 95; French, 98
Ebert, Friedrich, 484
Economic theory, 27–28, 227. *See also* Mercantilism, *Laissez faire*, doctrine of, etc.
Education, in France, 169, 179, 254
Edward VII, of Great Britain, 383, 386
Egypt, British occupation of, 364–65; in 20th century, 468
Elizabeth, Czarina of Russia, 74, 86, 90
Emancipation of the serfs (1861), in Russia, 294
Ems dispatch, 289
Enghien, Duke d', 180
England, 36, **50-53**. For period after 1707, *see* Great Britain
Enlightened despots. *See* Frederick II, of Prussia, Catherine II, of Russia, Joseph II, of Austria, etc.
Entente Powers, and the World War, 400–12
Estates. *See* States General
Ethiopia, Italian influence in, 368, 457
Eugène Beauharnais. *See* Beauharnais, Eugène
Eugène of Savoy, Prince François, 38, 57, 62
Eugénie, French empress, 254
Exclusion Bill (1679), English, 44
Exploration, in 15th and 16th centuries, 93
Eylau, battle of (1806), 189

Factory system, **226-28**. *See also* Industry, modern
Falloux Law (1850), France, 254
Famine, reduction of, in modern period, 321–22
Fascism, Italian, 448–57. *See* Italy, in the 20th century
Fashoda affair, 371
Ferdinand VII, of Spain, 203
Ferdinand I, of the Two Sicilies, 203
Ferdinand II, of the Two Sicilies, 249
Feudalism, destruction of, in France, 149–52. *See also* Nobles
Finland, 201, 301
First Estate. *See* Clergy
Five-Year Plan, Russia, 441–44
Flaubert, Gustave. 254

Florence, in 17th century, 61
Foch, General Ferdinand, 411–12
Fourier, François Marie, 241
"Fourteen Points," in World War, **418-19**, 426–27
France, in the 17th century, 10, **20-39**, 55; in the 18th century, 86, 104, **121-27**; in the revolutionary era, **141-70**; under Napoleon, **171-83**; in the 19th century, 239–44, 258–61, 286–91, 347–52; in the 20th century, 472–82; colonial empire of, **96-100**, 387–88; foreign relations of, after 1871, 382–84; natural frontiers of, 32–33
Franche Comté, in the 17th century, 36–37
Francis I, of Austria, 188, 199
Francis II, Holy Roman Emperor. *See* Francis I, of Austria
Francis II, of the Two Sicilies, 272
Francis Joseph I, of Austria (1848–67), and of Austria-Hungary (1867–1916), 247–48, 283–84
Franco-Prussian War (1870–71), **288-89**
Franco-Russian Convention (1894), 383
Frankfort-on-Main, 245
Frankfort Assembly (1848–49), 245–46
Frankfort, treaty of (1871), 289
Franklin, Benjamin, 116
Franz Ferdinand, Archduke of Austria, assassinated, 398
Frederick III, German Emperor, 359
Frederick I, of Prussia, 83
Frederick II (the Great) of Prussia, 80, **84-92**, 99, 131
Frederick Augustus I, of Saxony, 73
Frederick William, of Brandenburg, 11, 37, 39
Frederick William III, of Prussia, 99–100, 188, 214
Frederick William IV, of Prussia, 245–46
Freedom of the press, in England, 53; in France, 233
French and Indian War. *See* Seven Years' War
French Revolution, the great, **142-74**; of 1830, **233-38**; of 1848, 241–43
Friedland, battle of (1807), 189
Fronde, the, 29

Galileo, Galilei, 107, 109, 115
Gallican Church. *See* Clergy, French
Gama, Vasco da, 93
Gambetta, Léon, 348
Garibaldi, Giuseppe, 266–73, *passim*
General Confederation of Labor, French, 351
Geneva, 430
Genoa, in the 17th century, 61
Gentz, Frederick von, 198
Geography, early knowledge of, 93

George I, of Great Britain, 50
George III, of Great Britain, 103
German Empire. *See* Germany
German government. *See* Germany
German language, 92
Germanic Confederation, in 19th century, 214, 246, 282
Germanies, the, in the 17th century, 11; and the French Revolution, **86-90**, 201; in the 19th century, 236, **244-46, 277-91.** *See also* Germany
Germany, in the 17th century, 11; in the 19th century, **186-90**, 201, 236, **244-46, 277-91;** after 1871, **353-60**, 379–82, 416–28, **482-94.** *See also* Holy Roman Empire, Prussia, Colonies, German, etc.
Ghandi, Mohandas Karamchand, 467
Gibraltar, ceded to Great Britain, 39, 97
Gilbert, William, 109
Gioberti, Vincenzo, 264
Gironde, party of the, 157, 161
Gladstone, William Ewart, 340
"Glorious Revolution" of 1688–89 (England), 37
Goethe, Johann Wolfgang von, 92, 213
Government of National Defense, French (1870), 289
Grand Alliance (1702), 38
Grand Duchy of Tuscany. *See* Italy
Grand Duchy of Warsaw. *See* Poland
Great Britain (for period prior to 1707, *see* England), in the 18th century, 86, **95-106;** and the French Revolution, 161; and Napoleon, 174, **188-95;** in the 19th century, 202, 219–20, 258–61; in the 20th century, 399–400, **460-71;** colonial empire of, **96-106, 364-67,** 370; foreign policy of, 219, 237, 384–86
Great Elector. *See* Frederick William, of Brandenburg
"Great Fear, The," 148
Great Northern War, 72–74
Greece, and Treaty of Carlowitz, 61; and War of Independence, 222; in the 19th century, 313–16
Greek Orthodox Church, in Russia, and Ivan the Great, 68; and Peter the Great, 72
Grenville, George, 102
Grey, Charles, 2d Earl, **230-31**
Grey, Sir Edward, 399–402, *passim*
Grieg, Edvard, 307
Grotius, Hugo, 8
Guild system, survivals of, in 18th century, 134, 150
Guizot, François, 239–41
Gustavus III, of Sweden, 133

Haakon VII, of Norway, 306
Habeas Corpus Act (1679), 45–46; suspended, 219

Hague Conference, 392
Halley, Edmund, 110
Hamburg, 191
Hanover, and Sweden, 73; in Seven Years' War, 88; annexed to Prussia, 283
Hanover, Sophia, Electress of, 50
Hapsburg family, in 17th century, 54–60
Hardenberg, Karl August, Prince, 193
Hardie, Keir, 344
Harvey, William, 110
Heine, Heinrich, 224, 239
Henry Pu-yi, Emperor of Manchukuo, 445
Herzegovina, annexed by Austria-Hungary, 390
Herzen, Alexander, 250, 298
Hesse-Darmstadt, 186; in the 19th century, 284–86
Hindenburg, Paul von, 403, 487, 488, 492
Hitler, Adolf, 484–94
Hobbes, Thomas, 5, 114
Hohenlinden, battle of (1800), 76
Hohenzollerns. *See* Brandenburg, Prussia
Holland. *See* Netherlands, Dutch
Holowczyn, battle of (1708), 73
Holstein, in the 19th century, 245, 283
Holy Alliance, The, **203-04**
Holy Roman Empire, in the 17th century, 82; dissolved, 189. *See also* Germany, Italy, Hapsburgs
Homer, 118
House of Commons. *See* Commons, House of, Parliament, etc.
House of Lords. *See* Lords, House of, and Parliament
Hudson's Bay Company, 42
Hudson Bay Territory, ceded to Great Britain, 39; 96–97
Hugo, Victor, 254
Huguenots, expelled from France, 34–35. *See* Nantes, Edict of
Humanitarianism, 211–12
Hungary, in the 17th century, 55–57; in the 19th century, 247–48; in the 20th century, 424

Ibsen, Henrik, 307
Iceland, 306
Illyrian Provinces, 191
Imperialism, after 1871, **362-78**
India, British acquisitions in, 100; French posts in, 98; in the 19th century, **363-64;** in the 20th century, **466-67**
Indo-China, French, 367
Industrial Revolution, **224-28.** *See also* Industry, modern
Industry, modern, **224-28, 319-22;** in Belgium, 308; in France, 233, 256; in

Germany, 279–80, 355–60; in Great Britain, 224–28, 319–22; in Italy, 455; in Russia, 301
Innocent XI, Pope, 62
Innocent XII, Pope, 23
Inquisition, in Spain, 132
Intellectual Revolution, **107-20.** *See also* Science, modern
Intendants, 26
International, First and Second, 334
Irak, 468
Ireland, in the 17th century, 48–49; in the 19th century, 105; in the 20th century, 346, 464–66
Irish Free State. *See* Ireland
Irish Nationalists, in British Parliament, 344
Irish Nationalist Party, 346
Isabella II, of Spain, 310
Italy, in the 17th century, 12, 60–63; and the French Revolution, 168–71; and Napoleon, 176, 185–86; in the 19th century, 202–03, 236, 247–49, **261-72;** in the 20th century, 406–15, *passim,* **447-57;** colonies, **368-69**
Ivan III (the Great), of Russia, 68
Ivan IV (the Terrible), of Russia, 69

Jacobin Club, 161, 166
Jamaica, 13
James II, of England, 37, **44-49**
James, Duke of York. *See* James II, of England
Jansenists, 33–34
Japan, rise of, **375-78;** and Russia, 377, 445
Jassy, treaty of (1792), 81
Jeffreys, George, Baron, 46
Jellachich, Joseph, Count, 248
Jellicoe, Admiral John Rushworth, 408
Jena, battle of (1806), 189
Jesuits. *See* Society of Jesus
Jews, in Russia, 301; in Palestine, 468–69
John Sobieski, King of Poland, 12; and the siege of Vienna, 55
Joseph II, of Austria, 132
Josephine, French empress, 171, 192
Jugoslavia, 425, 477
July Monarchy, France. *See* Louis Philippe, King of the French
Jutland, battle of (1916), 408

Kapp, Waldemar, 484
Kepler, Johannes, 108, 112
Kerensky, Alexander, 433–34
Kiev, 68
"King of Rome," son of Napoleon I, 181
Kingdom of the Netherlands. *See* Netherlands, Dutch

Kingdom of the Two Sicilies, united to the Italian kingdom, 272
Kiuprili, Mohammed, 57; Achmed, 57
Koch, Robert, 226
Königgrätz, battle of (1866), 273, 283
Kosciusko, Thaddeus, 80
Kossuth, Louis, 248
Krudener, Baroness von, 215
Kuchuk-Kainardji, treaty of (1774), 80
Kulturkampf, 276, 357–58
Kunersdorf, battle of (1759), 90

Labor Movement, British, 343–47
Labor Party, British, 343–46, 463–64
Lafayette, Marie Joseph Motier, Marquis de, 142, 152, 234
La Fontaine, Jean de, 32
Laibach, congress of (1821), 203
Laissez faire, doctrine of, 106, 227, 231
Lamartine, Alphonse, 240
Language, French, elegance of, 32
Lassalle, Ferdinand, 357
Lateran Treaty (1929), 458
Lausanne Settlement (1932), 475
La Vallière, Louise Françoise de, 30
League of Nations, **429-32,** 486
Lebrun, Charles, 33
Leeuwenhoek, Anton van, 110–11
Legion of Honor, 180
Legislation, criminal, 15–16, 126; in Great Britain, 219
Legislative Assembly, French (1791–92), 157–59
Leibnitz, Gottfried Wilhelm von, 113
Leipzig, battle of (1813), 193
Lenin, Nicolai, **234-38**
Le Nôtre, André, 29
Leo XIII, Pope, 276, 352
Leopardi, Giacomo, 263
Leopold of Hohenzollern-Sigmaringen, refuses Spanish throne, 288
Leopold I, of Belgium, 308
Leopold II, of Belgium, 308
Leopold I, Holy Roman Emperor, 12, 37, 54–57
Leuthen, battle of (1757), 90
Liberal Party, British, **339-47**
Liberalism, French, 258; in the 19th century, 220–23
Liberum veto, in Polish Diet, 80
Libya, 369
Ligurian Republic, 186
Linnaeus, Carolus, 116
Lisbon, 190
Literature, English, in the 17th and 18th centuries, 52–53; in the 19th century, 212–13, 250–51
Literature, French, in the Age of Louis XIV, 32–33; in the 18th century, 127–31, *passim,* 134–37; in the 19th century, 251

Literature, German, in the 18th century, 92, 213
Literature, Russian, in the 19th century, 216–17
Literature, Scandinavian, in the 19th and 20th centuries, 307
Lithuania, and Poland, 78; and Russia, 436
Little *Entente*, 477
Lloyd George, David, 344–47
Locarno Pacts (1925), 479, 486
Locke, John, 53, 120, 134–36
Lombardy. *See* Italy
London, in the 17th century, 62
London, treaty of (1832), 312; secret treaty of (1915), 419
Lords, House of, powers curtailed, 340
Lorraine, acquired by France, 85
Louis XIV, of France, 7, 10, **20–39**, 49–52, 122
Louis XIV, of France, 39, 86, 122, 133
Louis XVI, of France, 34, **141–61**, *passim*
Louis XVII, the dauphin, 66, 194
Louis XVIII, of France, 166, 193–94, 209, 217–18
Louis I, of Portugal, 313
Louis Napoleon Bonaparte. *See* Napoleon III
Louis Philippe, King of the French, 234–42, *passim*
Louvois, François Michel le Tellier, Marquis de, 28–29, 35
Louvre, Palace of the, 29
Lübeck, 90, 91
Ludendorff, Erich von, 484
Lunéville, treaty of (1801), 186
Lusitania, torpedoed, 407
Luxemburg, annexed to France, 37
Lyell, Sir Charles, 323

MacMahon, Marshal, Duke of Magenta, 348
Madrid, 60
Magellan, Ferdinand, 93
Magyars, in 19th century, 284. *See also* Hungary
Maintenon, Madame de, 32, 35
Maistre, Joseph de, 211
Malplaquet, battle of (1709), 38
Malthus, Thomas, 227
Manchukuo, 445
Mansart, Jules Hardouin, 29, 33
Manuel II, of Portugal, 312
Manzoni, Alessandro, 263
Marat, Jean Paul, 152
March Revolution (1917), 433. *See* Russia, in 20th century
Maria II, of Portugal, 312
Maria Theresa, of Austria, and Poland, 80
Maria Theresa, Queen of France, 30

Marie Antoinette, Queen of France, **143–44**, 164
Marie Louise, wife of Napoleon I, 181
Marlborough, John Churchill, Duke of, 57
Marne, first battle of the (1914), 402; second battle of the (1918), 411–12
Marx, Karl, **332–34**
Mary, Queen of England with William III, **46–47**
Massacre of Glencoe, 49
Mathematics, modern, **112–13**
Matteotti, Giacomo, 451
Maximilian, Emperor of Mexico, 287
Mazarin, Cardinal, 7
Mazzini, Joseph, 264–66
Medicine, modern, 326
Mendel, Gregor, 276
Mercantilism, **27–28**, 91, 105–06
Mérimée, Prosper, 254
Methodism, 211
Metternich, Klemens Wenzel Nepomuk Lothar, Prince von, **198–201**, 214, 248
Metz, 37; surrender of (1870), 289
Mexico, 287
Milan, in seventeenth century, 39, 61
Milan Decrees (1807), 190
Militarism. *See* Armaments
Military conscription, 391
Milosh I, of Serbia, 312
Milosh Obrenovich III, of Serbia, 314
Milton, John, 52
Minorca, 39, 97
Mirabeau, Honoré Riquetti, Comte de, 145
Moldavia, 259–60
Molière (Jean Baptiste Poquelin), 32
Moltke, Hellmuth von, 283
Money, increase in circulation of, 253
Mongolia, 259, 446
Monmouth, Duke of, 45–46
Monroe, James, 221
Monroe Doctrine, **221**, 287
Montcalm, Louis Joseph, Marquis de, 99
Montenegro, 314
Montespan, Marquise de, 30
Moriscos, in Spain, 58
Morocco, 367, 372, 387–88
Moscow, 70, 193
Mounier, Jean-Joseph, 145
Municipal Corporations Act (1835), 231
Muscovy, **68–69**
Mussolini, Benito, **448–57**
Mutsuhito, 376

Nantes, Edict of (1598), revocation of (1685), 34
Napier, John, 112
Naples. *See* Italy
Napoleon Bonaparte, Emperor of the French, 167, **171–85**

Napoleon III, Emperor of the French, **242-44**, 261, 283
Napoleonic legend, 239–44
Narva, battle of (1700), 72
National Assembly, French (1789–91), **144-56**
National Convention, French (1792–95), **160-67**
National Guard, 152
National Insurance Act, 344
National Liberal Party, German, 357–58
National Socialist Party, German, 488–94
National Workshops. *See* Blanc, Louis
Nationalism, in seventeenth century, 7–8; in nineteenth century, 262–63; German, 277; Italian, 262–73
Nature, modern attitude toward, 118–19
Navigation Acts, British, 42
Navy, British, 385
Near Eastern crises, 389–90
Near Eastern Question. *See* Turkey, Crimean War, Congress of Berlin
Necker, Jacques, 141, 146
Nelson, Horatio, 172, 188
Netherlands, Austrian, 58, 132; Dutch, revolt against Spain, 95; and American War of Independence, 104; and French Revolution, 168; and Napoleon, 191; colonies, 96; Spanish, 36, 38–39
Netherlands, Kingdom of the, 307–08
Neuilly, treaty of (1919), 425
Neuve Chapelle, battle of (1915), 403
New Amsterdam (New York), 42, 96
New Economic Plan, Russia, 437–38
New Zealand, 362–63
Newfoundland, 39, 96–97
Newton, Sir Isaac, 107, **110**, 113–15
Nice, ceded to France (1860), 270–71
Nicholas I, of Russia, 216, 234, 259–60, 292
Nicholas II, of Russia, 302–03, 399, 433, 437
Nihilism, 299–30
Nijmegen, treaty of (1678), **37**
Nile, battle of the (1798), 172
Nobles, French, 23–24, **124**
North German Confederation, **284-87**, 353
Norway, in 18th century, 133; in 19th century, 306
Novara, battle of (1849), 249, 267
November Revolution (1917), Russia, 436
Novi, battle of (1799), 172
Nystad, treaty of (1721), 73

Oates, Titus, 44
October Manifesto (1905), Russia, 303
Old Régime, in France, **121-31**
Oliva, treaty of (1660), 5
Ollivier, Émile, 289
Opium Wars, China, 366

"Orders in Council," British, 190
Orléans, Philip, Duke of, 146, 164
Orsini, Felice, 261
Oscar II, of Sweden, 306
Otto I, of Greece, 223
Oudinarde, battle of (1708), 38
Owen, Robert, 227
Oxford Parliament (1681), 45

Palatinate, Rhenish, 36–37
Palestine, in 20th century, 468–69
Palmerston, Henry John Temple, Viscount, 339
Pan-Slav Movement, 397–99
Papacy, in 17th century, 62; in 19th century, 254, 357–58; in 20th century, 458–59
Papal States, in 19th century, 265, 273; in 20th century, **368-69**
Paris, 253–54; Commune (1871), 347
Paris, treaty of (1763), 100
Paris, treaty of (1783), 104
Paris, treaty of (1856), 260, 313
Parlement of Paris, 24, 134
Parliament, British, 219–23, 228–32, 339–47
Parliament Act, British (1911), 341
Parma. *See* Italy
Pasteur, Louis, 276–326
Peace Societies, 392
Peasants, in 17th century, 16; in 18th century, 124–25; in 19th century, 256
Pershing, General John Joseph, 412
Peter V, of Portugal, 312
Peter I (the Great), of Russia, **69-74**
Philip III, of Spain, 58
Philip IV, of Spain, 36
Philip V, of Spain, **38-39**, 60
Philosophes, the, 127
Physiocrats, 130
Piedmont, 186. *See* Sardinia, Kingdom of
Pietism, 211
Pitt, William, Earl of Chatham, 99
Pitt, William, the younger, **188-89**
Pius VI, Pope, 132
Pius VII, Pope, 180, 203, 211
Pius IX, Pope, 249, 265–73, 458–59
Pizarro, Francisco, 95
Plehve, Venceslas de, 300, 302
Pobiedonostsev, Constantine, 300–02
Poincaré, Raymond, 472–76
Poland, in the 17th century, 5, 11–12, 57, 73; Partition of, **78-81**, 91; and Napoleon, 189, 192; in the 19th century, 201, 297; in the 20th century, 477–79
Pombal, Marquis of, 133
Pomerania, 82–83
Pompadour, Marquise de, 86
Poor Law, English (1834), 231
Popish Plot (1678), 44

Population, in modern times: Austria, 54; England, 10; Europe, 14, 18, 325–27; Denmark, 11; France, 142, 218; Norway, 11; Sweden, 11; Thirteen American Colonies, 103

Portugal, in 17th century, 7, 13; in 18th century, 133, 191; in 19th century, 311–12; colonial empire, 94

Poussin, Nicolas, 33

Prague, treaty of (1866), 273, 283

Pressburg, treaty of (1805), 188

Primogeniture, 217

Proletariat, origins, after Industrial Revolution, **226-32**, 331

Propaganda, in World War, 400–15

Protestantism, in 19th century, 211–12

Proudhon, Pierre Joseph, 298–99

Provence, Count of (Louis XVIII), 144

Prussia, in the 17th century, 83; in the 18th century, **82-92**, 161–68; in the 19th century, 189–90, 201, 213–15, 220, 246. *See* Germany

Prussian System, the, 280–81

Ptolemaeus, Claudius, 108

Pultawa, battle of (1709), 73

Pyrenees, peace of the (1659), 5, 36

Quadrilateral, the (Italian fortresses), 271

Quadruple Alliance. *See* Concert of Europe

Quebec Act (1774), 104–05, 362

Quesnay, François, 130

Racine, Jean, 32

Radetsky, Joseph Wenzel, Count, 247

Radicalism, France, 234–42

Ramilies, battle of (1706), 38

Rapallo, treaty of (1920), 425

Rationalism, rise of, 117; reaction against, 209–13

Realism, in literature, 254

Reform Bill, British (1832), **230-31**

Reform Bill, British (1867), 340

Reform Bill, British (1884), 341

Reichstag, German, **353-60**; of North German Confederation, 286

Reign of Terror, the (1793–94), 164–65

Reinsurance Treaty (1887), 381–82

Religion, in 19th century, 211

Religious toleration, in 17th century, 33, 48

Reparations, German, 421–22, 473–75, 484–85

Republicans, French, in 19th century, 248

Revolution, French (1789–99), **141-70**, *passim*

Revolution of 1688–89, English, **47-49**

Revolution of 1848–49, **239-51**

Rhodes, Cecil, 366

Ricardo, David, 227

Richelieu, Armand de, Cardinal, 7

Risorgimento, the, 263

Rivera, Primo de, 310

Roads, in 17th century, 10

Robespierre, Maximilien, 161, **164-65**

Rochefoucauld, François, Duc de la, 32

Roman Republic (1849), 266

Romantic Movement, **212-13**

Rome, and Revolution of 1848–49, 249; united to Italian Kingdom (1870), 273

Rossbach, battle of (1757), 90

Rousseau, Jean-Jacques, 121, **136-37**, 212

Royalists, French, in 19th century, 349

Rumania, autonomous, 260; in 19th century, 314–16, 390

Russia, in 17th and 18th centuries, **67-81**; and Partition of Poland, 80; and French Revolution, 172; and Napoleon, **192-93**; in 19th century, **215-17**, 220, **258-61**, **292-302**, 314–15; in 20th century, 404, 410, **433-46**; foreign relations (1917–35), 444–45

Russian novel, 216

Russian Revolution (1917), **433-46**

Russo-Japanese War, 302, 377

Russo-Turkish War (1877), 314

Rye House Plot (1683), 65

Saar Valley, 494

Sadowa, battle of. *See* Königgrätz

Saint Gothard, battle of (1663), 57

Saint Petersburg, founding of, 73

Saint-Simon, Henri de, 241

Saint-Simon, Louis de Rouvroy, Duc de, 32

Sainte-Beuve, Charles Augustin, 254

San Stefano, treaty of (1878), 314

Sand, Karl, 215

Sardinia, Kingdom of, in 18th century, 62, 171; in 19th century, 220, 263. *See* Piedmont, Savoy

Savoy, in 17th century, 61, 62; ceded to France (1860), 270–71

Saxony, Electorate of, 73; Kingdom of, 201, 353

Scheer, Admiral Reinhard, 408

Scheldt, river, 39

Schiller, Johann Friedrich, 213

Schleswig, annexed to Prussia (1866), 283

Schleswig-Holstein, 306

Schlieffen Plan, 402–04

Schönbrunn, treaty of (1809), 191

Science, modern, 107–20, **319-27**

Scientific academies, 115

Scott, Sir Walter, 213

Sculpture, modern, 307

Sebastopol, siege of (1854–55), 260

Second Empire, French, 243, **252-61**

Second Estate. *See* Nobles

Second Republic, French, **242-43**

Sedan, battle of (1870), 289

Sepoy Mutiny (1857), 363

INDEX

September Massacres (1792), 159
Serbia, in 19th century, 313–16; and the World War, 397–400; and Austria-Hungary, 397–99
Serfdom, in France, 125; in Russia, 293–94
Seven Weeks' War (1866), 273
Seven Years' War (1756–63), 74–75, **88-90**, 100–01
Sévigné, Marie de Rabutin-Chantal, Marquise de, 32
Shaw, George Bernard, 299
Shelley, Percy Bysshe, 213
Shimonoseki, treaty of (1895), 377
Sicily, in 18th century, 62; ceded to Duke of Savoy, 39
Sieyès, Emmanuel Joseph, 174
Silesia, acquired by Prussia, 85, 90
Sino-Japanese War, 375
Six Acts, England, 219
"Six Points" of Chartism. *See* Chartist Movement
Slave trade, 39
Slavery, abolition of, in British dominions, 231
Slavophiles, Russia, 297
Slavs, characteristics of, 68; in Austro-Hungarian Empire, 247–48, 284
Smith, Adam, 106, 227
Social conditions, in 17th century, **14-19**; France, in 19th century, 256.
Social Democratic Party. *See* Socialist Party, German
Social insurance, German, **358-59**
Social legislation, British, **344-47**
Socialist Party, British. *See* Labor Party
Socialist Party, France, 239–44, **350-52**
Socialist Party, German, **355-60**
Socialist Revolutionaries, Russia, 301
Society of Jesus, 133, 211
South Africa, 365
South German States, 188, 283–87
Soviet régime. *See* Russia, after World War
Soviets, 434–35
Spain, in the 17th and 18th centuries, 7, 19, **58-60**, 86, 132; and the French Revolution, 168; and Napoleon, 191; in the 19th century, **221**, 309–11; and the American War of Independence, 104; colonial empire of, 94–95, 221
Spanish-American War (1898), 311
Spanish Guelderland, ceded to Prussia, 39
Spanish Revolution (1931), 311
Spinning, machines for, 225
Stanislaus Leszcznyski, of Poland, 73
States, system of centralized territorial, **6-9**
States General, in France, in 18th century, **141-44**. *See* National Assembly

Statute of Westminster (1931), 469–70
Steam engine, 225
Stein, Heinrich Friedrich Karl, Baron vom, 193
Stolypin, Peter, 302
Storthing (Norwegian Parliament), 306
Strasbourg, 37
Streltzi, revolt of the, 70
Stresemann, Gustav, 486–87
Strindberg, August, 307
Struensee, Johann Friedrich, Count, 133
Students, German, in 19th century, **215**
Styria, duchy of, 55
Submarine boats, in World War, 407–10
Suffrage, extension of, in Great Britain, 229–32
Supernatural, in medieval thought, 116–20, *passim*
Sweden, in 17th and 18th centuries, 5, 11, 36, 69, 133; in 19th century, 202, 305–06
Swift, Jonathan, 53
Switzerland, in 17th century, 7, **308-09**
Sybel, Heinrich von, 278
Syllabus of Errors (1864), 75
Syndicats, French, **350-52**

Talleyrand-Périgord, Charles Maurice de, 194, 200
Tangiers, 42
Tannenberg, battle of (1914), 403
Tennis Court Oath (1789), 144–45
Tennyson, Alfred, Lord, 339
Terrorists, Russian, 300
Test Act, English (1673), 46, 48
Thiers, Louis Adolphe, 239–40, 289–90, 348
Third Estate, French, in 17th century, 24; in 18th century, 125–26, 143. *See* States General, Bourgeoisie, Peasants
Third Republic, French, 289, 348
"Third Section," Russia, 216, 296
Thorwaldsen, Albert Bertel, 307
Tilsit, Peace of (1807), **188-90**
Tolerance, growth of, 117
Toleration Act, English (1689), 48
Tolstoy, Count Leo, 297
Tories, 44, 219, 229. *See* Conservatives
Toul, annexed by Louis XIV, 37
Townshend Acts (1767), 103
Trade. *See* Commerce
Trade Boards Act (1909), 344
Trade Union Act (1871), 343
Trade unions, 331
Trafalgar, battle of (1805), 188
Transportation, in 17th century, 10, 14; in 19th century, 320
Transylvania, 57
Triple Alliance, **381-94**
Triple *Entente*, **385-94**
Troppau, Congress of (1820), 203
Troppau Protocol (1820), 220

Tunis, French occupation of, 367
Turenne, Henri de la Tour d'Auvergne, Vicomte de, 28, 37
Turgot, Anne Robert Jacques, 134
Turin, treaty of (1860), 271
Turkestan, 259
Turkey, in 17th century, **55-57**, 70, 132; in 18th century, 222, **259-61**; in 19th century, 312, 389-90; and World War, **404-15**, 426
Turks. *See* Turkey
Tuscany, in 17th century, 61

Ukraine, 57
Ulm, battle of (1805), 188
Ulster. *See* Ireland
Ultramontanism, 211
Ultra-royalists, France, 218
Union of South Africa. *See* South Africa
Union of Soviet Socialist Republics. *See* Russia
United Provinces. *See* Netherlands, Dutch
United States, established, 104; and the Monroe Doctrine, 221; and the World War, 407-15.
Utilitarians, 230.
Utrecht, Peace of (1713-14), **39**, 57, 97-98

Vatican Council (1869-70), 275
Vauban, Sébastien 'e Prestre de, 28
Vendée, insurrection in, 162
Venetia, united to Italian Kingdom, 273
Venice, 12-13, 61. *See* Italy
Verdun, 37; attack on (1916), 403
Verona, Congress of (1822), 221
Versailles, 152; palace of, 29-30
Versailles, treaty of (1919), 416-28
Victor Amadeus II, of Savoy, 62
Victor Emmanuel I, of Sardinia, 220
Victor Emmanuel II, of Sardinia and, after 1860, of Italy, **267-73**
Victor Emmanuel III, of Italy, 450
Vienna, 11-12; siege of (1683), 57
Vienna, treaty of (1864), 282
Villafranca, truce of (1859), 271
Vladivostok, 259, 445
Voltaire (François Marie Arouet), 77, 92, 99, **127-38**

War debts, 475
War of the Austrian Succession, 98-99
War of Devolution, 36
War of Jenkins's Ear. *See* War of the Austrian Succession

War of Liberation, against Napoleon, 193
War of the Polish Succession, 85
War of the Spanish Succession, **38-39**
Wartburg Festival (1817), 214-15
Washington Naval Conference (1922), 462
Waterloo, battle of (1815), 195
Watt, James, 225
Webb, Sidney and Beatrice, 344
Weimar Assembly (1919), 424
Wellesley, Sir Arthur. *See* Wellington, Duke of
Wellington, Arthur Wellesley, Duke of, 191, 195, 230
Wells, Herbert George, 344
Wesley, Charles, 211
Wesley, John, 211
West Indies, 102
"Westernizers," Russia, 298
Westphalia, Kingdom of, 189
Westphalia, peace of (1648), 5
Whigs, 38, 229. *See* Liberals
William of Orange, King of England as William III, **37-38**, 96
William I, of Prussia, German Emperor after 1871, 278-91, *passim*, 358
William II, German Emperor, 359-60
William I, of United Netherlands, 237, 308
Wilson, Woodrow, and the World War, **409-13, 416-28**
Witt, John de, 37
Witte, Sergei de, 302
Wolfe, James, General, 99
Woman Suffrage, in Great Britain, 342
Wordsworth, William, 212
Working class, France, 256. *See also* Proletariat
Workingmen's Compensation Act (1906), 344
World Court, 431
World War, **397-412**; losses in, 413-15
Wren, Christopher, 53
Württemberg, in 19th century, 186-88, 284-86, 354-55

"Young Italy," 264. *See* Mazzini, Joseph
Young, Owen D., 474
Young Plan (1929), 474
Ypres, 403

Zemstvos, 294-95
Zola, Émile, 349
Zollverein, 244-45, 279-80, 287
Zorndorf, battle of (1758), 90

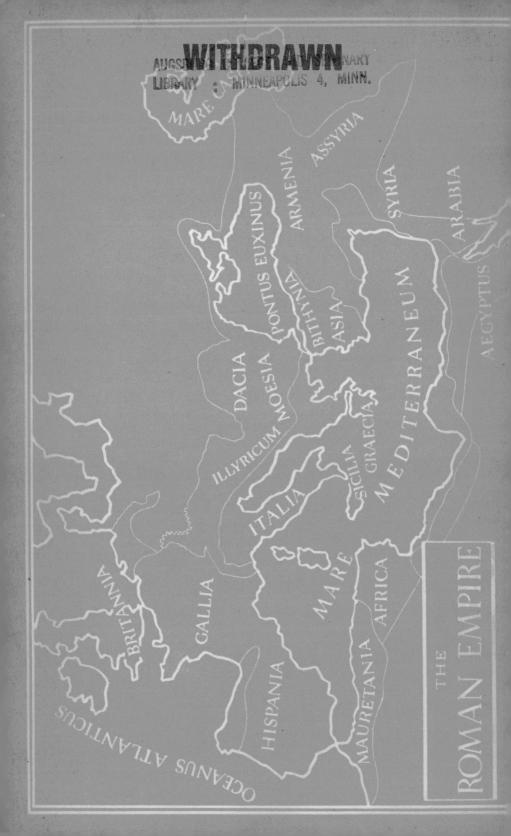

MARE

MARE

MEDITERRANEUM

MARE

OCEANUS ATLANTICUS

PONTUS EUXINUS

ARMENIA

ASSYRIA

SYRIA

ARABIA

AEGYPTUS

BITHYNIA

ASIA

DACIA

MOESIA

ILLYRICUM

GRAECIA

SICILIA

ITALIA

GALLIA

BRITANNIA

HISPANIA

MAURETANIA

AFRICA

THE ROMAN EMPIRE